Street by Street

BRISTOL, [illegible]

BRADFORD-ON-AVON, CLEVEDON, PORTISHEAD, TROWBRIDGE, WESTON-SUPER-MARE, YATE

Avonmouth, Bradley Stoke, Chipping Sodbury, Congresbury, Keynsham, Kingswood, Mangotsfield, Midsomer Norton, Nailsea, Radstock, Severn Beach, Thornbury, Yatton

2nd edition April 2005

Original edition printed May 2001

Published by AA Publishing (a trading name of Automobile Association Developments Limited, whose registered office is Southwood East, Apollo Rise, Farnborough, Hampshire, GU14 0JW. Registered number 1878835).

Mapping produced by the Cartography Department of The Automobile Association. (A02255)

A CIP Catalogue record for this book is available from the British Library.

Printed by Oriental Press in Dubai

Ref: ML060z

Key to map pages ii-iii
Key to map symbols iv–1
Enlarged map pages 2-7
Main map pages 8-141
Index – towns & villages 142
Index – streets 143-166
Index – featured places 166-170
Acknowledgements 170

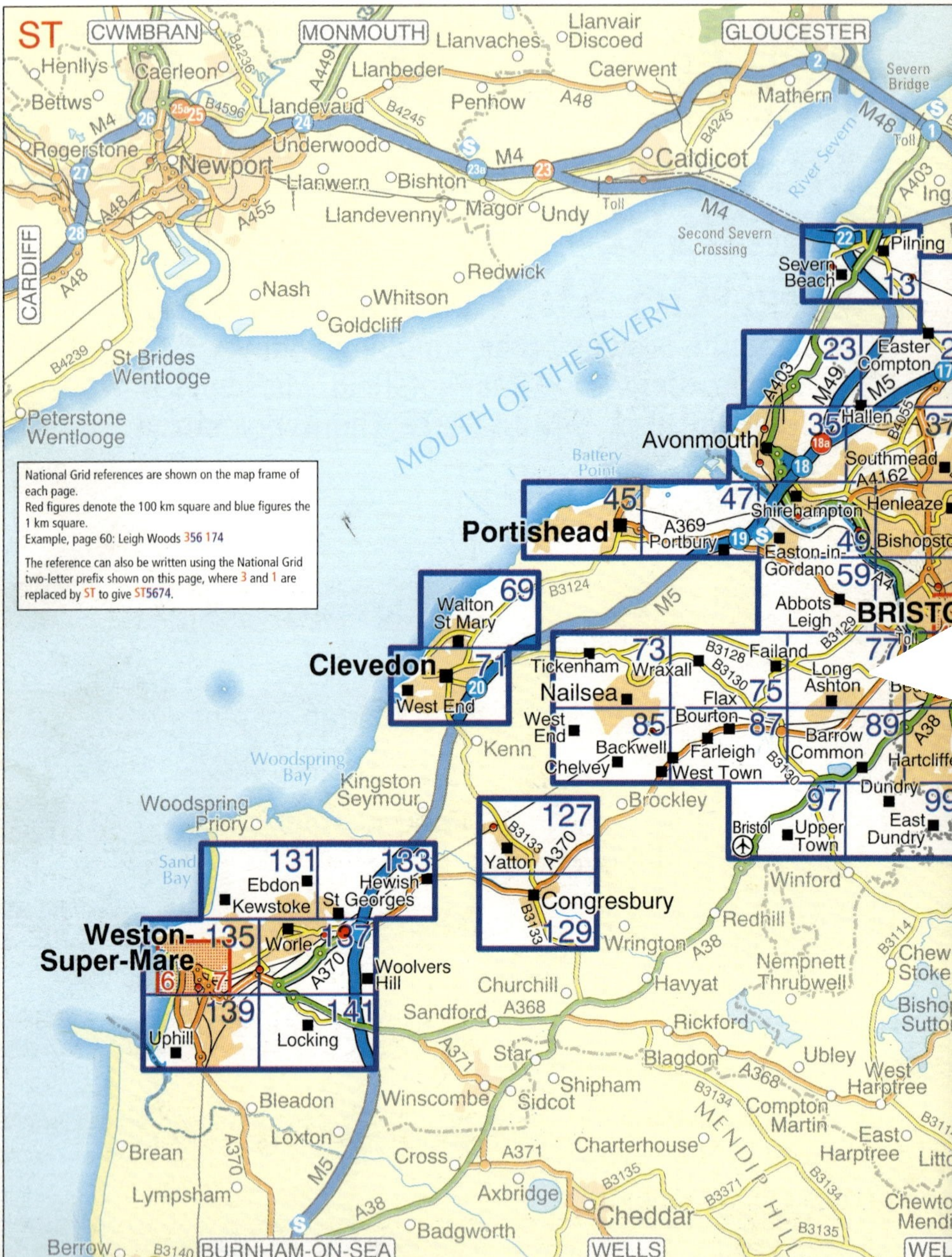

Scale of enlarged map pages 1:10,000 6.3 inches to 1 mile

0 1/4 miles 1/2

0 1/4 1/2 kilometres 3/4 1

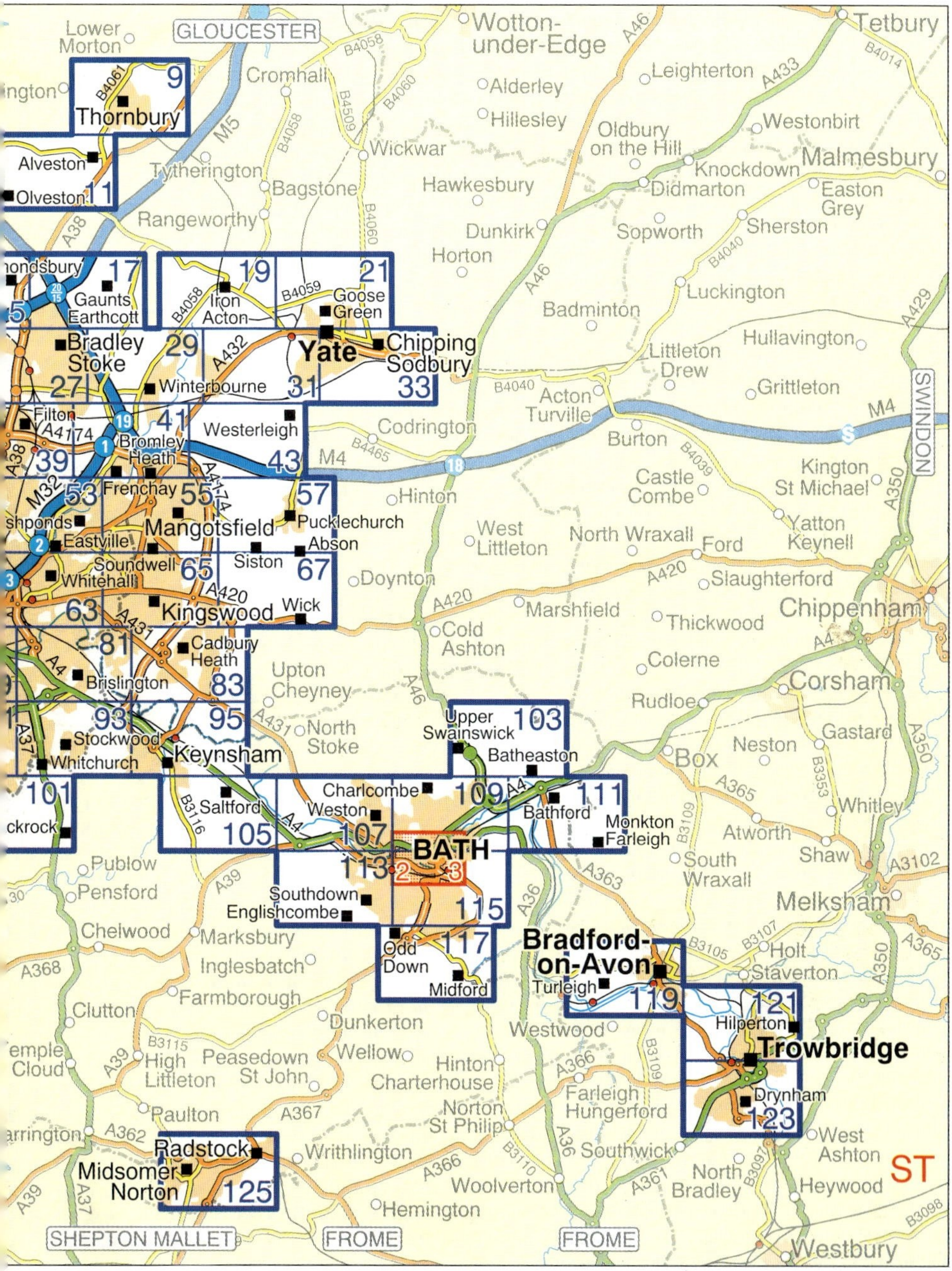

4.2 inches to 1 mile

Scale of main map pages 1:15,000

0	1/4	miles	1/2	3/4	1

0	1/4	1/2	kilometres 3/4	1	1 1/4	1 1/2

- Junction 9 — Motorway & junction
- Services — Motorway service area
- Primary road single/dual carriageway
- Services — Primary road service area
- A road single/dual carriageway
- B road single/dual carriageway
- Other road single/dual carriageway
- Minor/private road, access may be restricted
- One-way street
- Pedestrian area
- Track or footpath
- Road under construction
- Road tunnel
- P — Parking
- P+ — Park & Ride
- Bus/coach station
- Railway & main railway station
- Railway & minor railway station
- Underground station
- Light railway & station
- Preserved private railway
- LC — Level crossing
- Tramway
- Ferry route
- Airport runway
- County, administrative boundary
- Mounds
- 17 — Page continuation 1:15,000
- 3 — Page continuation to enlarged scale 1:10,000
- River/canal, lake, pier
- Aqueduct, lock, weir
- 465 Winter Hill — Peak (with height in metres)
- Beach
- Woodland
- Park
- Cemetery
- Built-up area
- Featured building

- City wall
- Hospital with 24-hour A&E department
- Post Office
- Public library
- Tourist Information Centre
- Seasonal Tourist Information Centre
- Petrol station, 24 hour
  Major suppliers only
- Church/chapel
- Public toilets
- Toilet with disabled facilities
- Public house
  AA recommended
- Restaurant
  AA inspected
- Madeira Hotel — Hotel
  AA inspected
- Theatre or performing arts centre
- Cinema
- Golf course
- Camping
  AA inspected
- Caravan site
  AA inspected
- Camping & caravan site
  AA inspected
- Theme park
- Abbey, cathedral or priory
- Castle

- Historic house or building
- Wakehurst Place NT — National Trust property
- Museum or art gallery
- Roman antiquity
- Ancient site, battlefield or monument
- Industrial interest
- Garden
- Garden Centre
  Garden Centre Association Member
- Garden Centre
  Wyevale Garden Centre
- Arboretum
- Farm or animal centre
- Zoological or wildlife collection
- Bird collection
- Nature reserve
- Aquarium
- Visitor or heritage centre
- Country park
- Cave
- Windmill
- Distillery, brewery or vineyard
- IKEA store

2
Sion Hill
A
B
C
D
E
108
107
113
114
1
2
3
4
5
6
7
374
65
64
Weston Lane
King Edward Pre Prep School
The Bath Priory Hotel
Gainsborough Gardens
Linden Gardens
Cranwells Pk
Cranwells Park
Cranhill Road
Cotswold Way
Cavendish Crs
Cavendish Road
All Saints Rd
Lansdown East
The Royal Sch for Dept
St James's Park
Park Street
Park St Ms
Portland Pl
Portland Terrace
Northampton St
Harley St
Surgery
Approach Golf Course
Weston Road
Park Lane
Park Gardens
Oakfield Close
Badminton Gdns
Audley Close
Audley Park Road
Audley Grove
Edward Street
Hungerford Rd
Audley Av
Westhall Rd
Royal Victoria Park
Victoria Monument
Cotswold Way
St Michael's Cemetery
St Michael's Rd
Cork Terrace
Tennyson Rd
Cork St
Lark Place
St John's Rd
Augusta Place
Locksbrook Place
Marlborough Buildings
Marlborough Lane
The Royal Crescent Hotel
Royal Crescent
St Andrews CE Primary School
Julian Rd
Rivers St
Circus
Georgian House No.1
Brock Street
Gravel Walk
Royal Avenue
BA1
Museum of Costume & Fashion Research Cen
Bandstand
Pavilion
Parkside Infant School
Register Office
Charlotte St
A4
Upper Bristol Road
Victoria Park Business Cen
River Avon
Avon Walkway
Comfortable Place
Onega Terrace
Albion Terrace
Albion Place
Georges Buildings
St Georges Place
Crescent Gardens
Nelson Vls
Nelson Pl West
Stanhope St
St Anns Place
Monmouth Pl
New King Street
Bath Natural Hlth Clinic
Norfolk Crs
James St West
Herschel House Mus
Green Park Station Market
Superstore
Midland Br Rd
Ashley Terrace
Shaftesbury Av
Council Building
Windsor Villas
Windsor Bridge Rd
A3604
Midland Road
Victoria Br Rd
Victoria Bridge Rd
Roseberry Place
Morley Terrace
Bristol Road
A36
Vernon Terrace
Vernon Pk
Inverness Rd
Victoria Buildings
Dorset Cl
St Peters Terrace
Ivo Peters Rd
Pines Way Ind Est
B3118
Green Park Mews
Green Park
Salvation Army
A367
Charles St
Brook Road
South Vw Road
Denmark Rd
Caledonian Road
Oldfield Park Infant School
Express by Holiday Inn
Broughham Hayes
Bellotts Rd
Twerton Cemetery
Highland Terrace
Ayr St
Stuart Pl
Dorset St
Victoria Ter
Hayesfield School (Lower)
Cemetery
Sydenham Buildings
Westmoreland St
Sydenham Rd
Bath Riverside Business Park
Riverside Rd
Riverside Court
Riverside Business Park
Lower Bristol Rd
Oldfield Park Station
Lyndhurst Road
Ringwood Rd
Millmead Road
Triangle N
Triangle W
Triangle Villas
Triangle East
Stanley Rd W
Crandale Rd
Livingstone Road
Moorland Road
Cheltenham St
Works
Oldfield Old Boys RFC
Westmoreland Station Road
The Square
Oldfield Park
Lower Oldfield Park
Cedar Wy
Thornbank Pl
South Av
Maybrick Rd
Mayfield Rd
Herbert Road
Shaftesbury Rd
Winchester Rd
Canterbury Road
Livingstone Terrace
Upper Oldfield Park
Hayesfield School Technology College
Surgery
Hayden Cl
Wells Road
Crescent View
Park Av
Hayesfield Pk
Beechen Cliff
Hayes Place
West Av
Dartmouth Avenue
Claude Terrace
Cynthia Road
St Kilda's Road
Faulkland Rd
Beckhampton Rd
Third Avenue
King Edward Road
Junction Road
Oldfield Rd
Oldfield Road
Lymore Gardens
Lymore Avenue
Claude Av
Melcombe Rd
Second Av
Wansdyke Business Centre
Oldfield Park Junior School
Catholic Primary School
Oldfield Lane
Maple Gardens
Durley Park
Bloomfield Avenue
1 grid square represents 250 metres

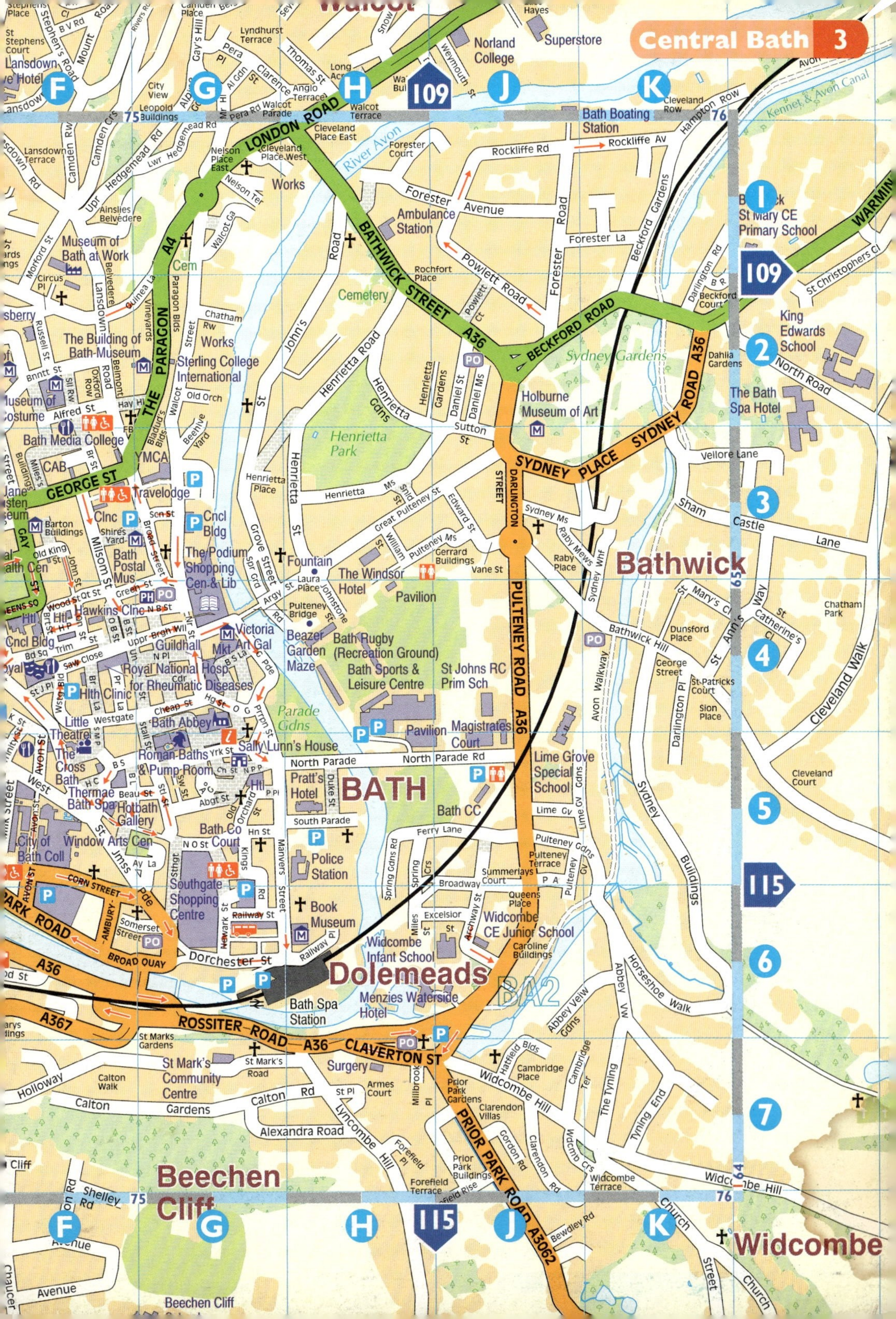
Walcot
Lansdown
Lyndhurst Terrace
Norland College
Superstore
Hayes
F
G
H
J
K
109
Walcot Terrace
Camden Crs
Lansdown Terrace
Upr Hedgemead Rd
Lwr Hedgemead Rd
London Road
Cleveland Place East
Cleveland Place West
Nelson Place East
Nelson Ter
Works
River Avon
Forester Court
Bath Boating Station
Cleveland Row
Hampton Row
Kennet & Avon Canal
Rockliffe Rd
Rockliffe Av
Forester Avenue
Forester Rd
Forester La
Ambulance Station
Beckford Gardens
St Mary CE Primary School
Darlington Rd
St Christophers Cl
Warminster
Ainslies Belvedere
Museum of Bath at Work
Morford St
Circus Pl
A4
Cem
Walcot Ga
John's Rd
Bathwick Street
A36
Rochfort Place
Powlett Road
Powlett Ct
Cemetery
Beckford Road
Beckford Court
King Edwards School
North Road
Dahlia Gardens
Sydney Gardens
Sydney Road
The Paragon
Vineyards
Guinea La
Paragon Blds
Chatham Rw
Works
Sterling College International
Old Orch
The Building of Bath Museum
Belmont
Russell St
Bath Media College
Museum of Costume
Alfred St
Hay Hl
Bladud's Blds
Beehive Yard
Henrietta Road
Henrietta Gdns
Henrietta Park
Henrietta Gardens
Daniel St
Daniel Ms
PO
Sutton St
Holburne Museum of Art
The Bath Spa Hotel
Vellore Lane
CAB
YMCA
George St
Travelodge
Gay St
Barton Buildings
Clnc
Shires Yard
Milsom St
Broad Street
Cncl Bldg
The Podium Shopping Cen & Lib
Henrietta Place
Henrietta Ms
Henrietta St
Great Pulteney St
Edward St
Darlington Street
Sydney Place
Sydney Ms
Raby Mews
Raby Place
Sham Castle Lane
Bathwick
Bath Postal Mus
Hawkins Clnc
Green St
Grove Street
Fountain
Laura Place
Johnstone St
The Windsor Hotel
William St
Pulteney Ms
Gerrard Buildings
Vane St
Pavilion
Pulteney Bridge
Pulteney Road
Sydney Whf
Bathwick Hill
St Mary's Cl
Ann's Way
St Catherine's Cl
Chatham Park
Dunsford Place
George Street
St Patricks Court
Sion Place
Darlington Pl
Cleveland Walk
Cncl Bldg
Upr Brgh Wll
Guildhall
Victoria Art Gal
Mkt
Beazer Garden Maze
Bath Rugby (Recreation Ground)
Bath Sports & Leisure Centre
St Johns RC Prim Sch
Royal National Hosp for Rheumatic Diseases
Hlth Clinic
Westgate
Cheap St
Bath Abbey
Parade Gdns
Pavilion
Magistrates Court
Lime Grove Special School
Avon Walkway
Cleveland Court
Little Theatre
Sally Lunn's House
North Parade
North Parade Rd
The Cross Bath
Roman Baths & Pump Room
Thermae Bath Spa
Beau St
Hotbath Gallery
Pratt's Hotel
Duke St
BATH
Bath CC
Lime Gv
Sydney Buildings
Abgt St
Orchard St
South Parade
Ferry Lane
Pulteney Gdns
Pulteney Terrace
City of Bath Coll
Window Arts Cen
Bath Co Court
Hn St
Kings
Manvers Street
Police Station
Spring Gdns Rd
Spring Crs
Broadway
Summerlays Court
Queens Place
Corn Street
Ambury
Southgate Shopping Centre
Railway St
Book Museum
Excelsior St
Widcombe CE Junior School
Caroline Buildings
Horseshoe Walk
Abbey Vw
115
Park Road
Somerset Street
Broad Quay
Newark St
Dorchester St
Railway Pl
Widcombe Infant School
Dolemeads
BA2
Menzies Waterside Hotel
Abbey View Gdns
A36
Bath Spa Station
A367
Rossiter Road
Claverton St
Cambridge Place
Hatfield Blds
Cambridge Ter
The Tyning
Tyning End
St Marks Gardens
St Mark's Community Centre
St Mark's Road
Surgery
Armes Court
Millbrook Pl
Prior Park Gardens
Widcombe Hill
Clarendon Villas
Holloway
Calton Walk
Calton Gardens
Calton Rd
St Pl
Lyncombe Hill
Alexandra Road
Forefield Pl
Prior Park Road
Gordon Rd
Clarendon Rd
Wdcmb Crs
Widcombe Terrace
Prior Park Buildings
Forefield Terrace
Beechen Cliff
Shelley Rd
Church Street
Widcombe
A3062
Bewdley Rd
Avenue
Beechen Cliff
1
2
3
4
5
6
7
75
76
64
65

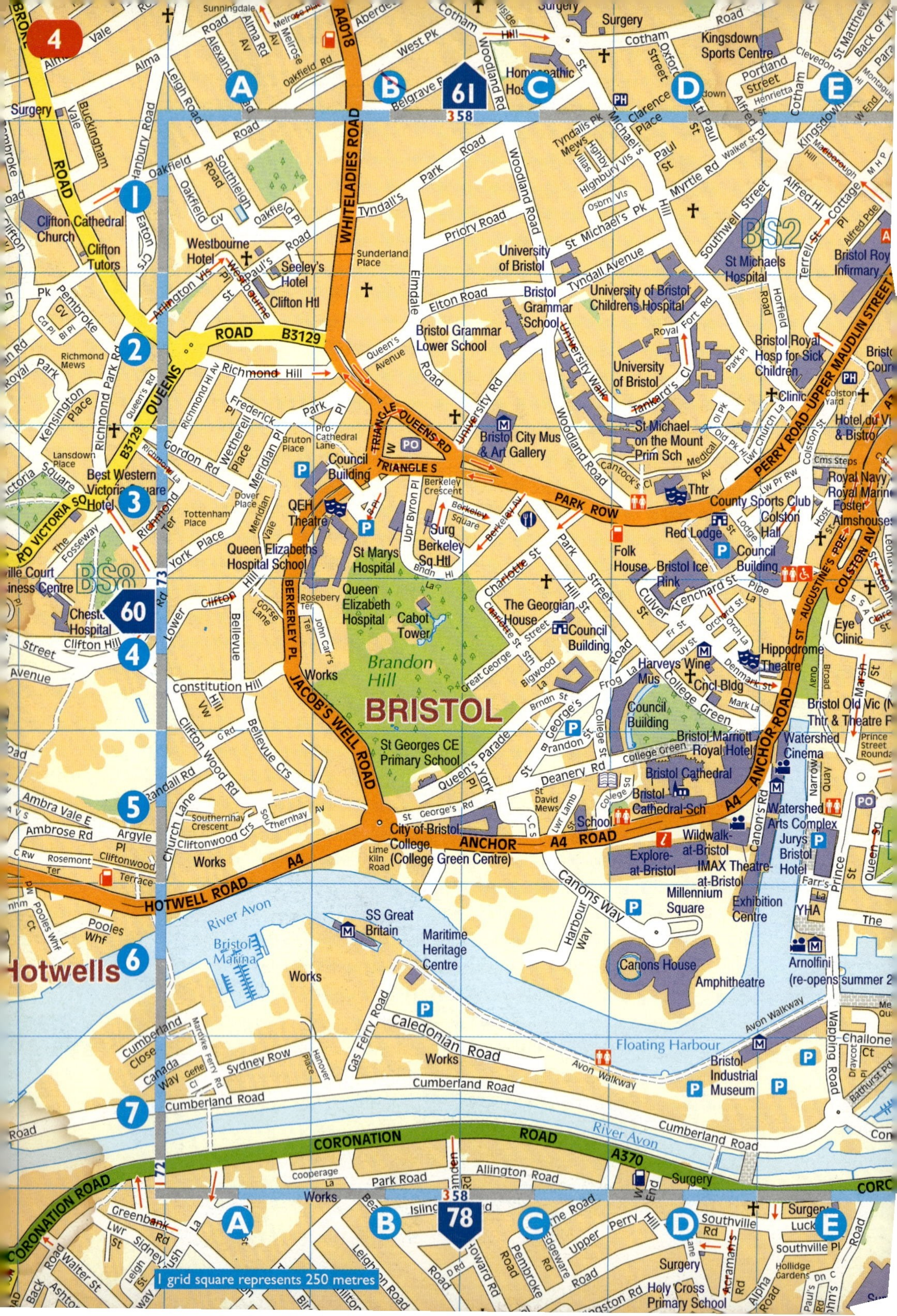
BRISTOL
BS8
BS2
A
B
C
D
E
1
2
3
4
5
6
7
61
60
78
3 58
Hotwells
Clifton Cathedral Church
Clifton Tutors
Westbourne Hotel
Seeley's Hotel
Clifton Htl
Best Western Victoria Square Hotel
Chesterfield Hospital
Queens Road
B3129
Whiteladies Road
A4018
Tyndall's Park Road
Priory Road
Woodland Road
University of Bristol
Bristol Grammar School
Bristol Grammar Lower School
University of Bristol Childrens Hospital
St Michaels Hospital
Bristol Royal Infirmary
Bristol Royal Hosp for Sick Children
St Michael on the Mount Prim Sch
Bristol City Mus & Art Gallery
Council Building
QEH Theatre
Queen Elizabeths Hospital School
St Marys Hospital
Queen Elizabeth Hospital
Cabot Tower
Brandon Hill
St Georges CE Primary School
Berkeley Square
Surg Berkeley Sq Htl
The Georgian House
Park Row
Perry Road
Upper Maudlin Street
Colston Hall
Colston Av
Red Lodge
Folk House
Bristol Ice Rink
Hippodrome Theatre
Harveys Wine Mus
Cncl Bldg
College Green
Bristol Marriott Royal Hotel
Bristol Cathedral
Bristol Cathedral Sch
Watershed Cinema
Watershed Arts Complex
Jurys Bristol Hotel
Bristol Old Vic (N) Thtr & Theatre R
Anchor Road
A4
City of Bristol College (College Green Centre)
Explore-at-Bristol
Wildwalk-at-Bristol
IMAX Theatre-at-Bristol
Millennium Square
Exhibition Centre
YHA
Canons Way
Canons House
Amphitheatre
Arnolfini (re-opens summer 2
Jacob's Well Road
Berkeley Pl
Hotwell Road
River Avon
Bristol Marina
SS Great Britain
Maritime Heritage Centre
Works
Caledonian Road
Cumberland Road
Floating Harbour
Avon Walkway
Bristol Industrial Museum
Wapping Road
Coronation Road
A370
Sydney Row
Gas Ferry Road
Holy Cross Primary School
Surgery
1 grid square represents 250 metres

Stokes Croft
North Street
Coroners Court
The Picture House
Council Building
Cncl Bldg
Travel Inn
Haymarket Walk
The Haymarket
Bond Street
Newfoundland St A4032
Newfoundland
Riverside Leisure Centre
John Wesley's Chapel (The New Room)
Horsefair
Broadmead
The Arcade
The Eye Clinic
Register Office
Quakers Friars
Penn Street
The Mall Galleries
Odeon Cinema
Fairfax St
Newgate
Broad Weir
Castle Park
Police Crown Court
City Business Park
Lord Chancellors Department
All Saints Exhibition Centre
Wine St
Avon Walkway
Bristol Marriott
Castle Street
A4044
A420 Old Market
BS2
Lawfords Gate
Lamb St
Trinity Rd
Clarence Rd
Police Stn
West St
Kingsland Trading Est
St Phillips Road
St Nicholas of Tolentine RC Prim Sch
Stapleton
City Business Park
Redcross Street
Jacob Street
Unity Street
Waterloo Rd
Midland Road
Health Clinic
Narrow Pln
Passage St
Broad Pln
Bristol Bridge
Georges Square
St Nicholas Mkt
The Brigstow Hotel
Victoria St
Counterslip
Fire Station
Temple Back
City Inn Hotel
Temple Way
A4044 Temple Way
Old Bread St
Police Station
Hannah More Primary School
Kilkenny Street
Avon St
Works
Temple Back East
Travel Inn
Custom Ho
Welsh Back
Redcliff Backs
Three Queens' La
Thomas Lane
Mitchell La
Church La
Tower La
Oxford Street
Freestone Rd
Silverthorne Lane
The Square
Friary
Pipe Lane
Open University
Portwall Lane
Redcliffe Way
Chatterton Ho
British Empire & Commonwealth Museum
Bristol Temple Meads Station
Council Building
Cattle Market Road
Feeder Road
Avon Trading Estate
Victoria Rd
Stanhope Street
St Mary's Redcliffe
Colston Pde
Redcliffe Parade
Barossa Pl
Express by Holiday Inn
Templegate
Somerset Street
Bath Bridge
Bristol Arena (area under development)
Guinea St
Bristol General Hospital
Prewett Street
St Mary Redcliffe & Temple Sch
A370
Clarence Road
A4 Bath Road
Burton Cl
Bedminster Bridge
York Road
Spring St
Whitehouse Place
William Street
RSPCA & Dogs Home
Wincombe Trading Estate
Albert Rd
Avon Walkway
F G H J K I
1 2 3 4 5 6 7
59 60 62 72 73 79

6
WESTON-SUPER-MARE
Weston Bay
134
138
A
B
C
D
E
1
2
3
4
5
6
7
Weston College of Further Education
Birkett Rd
Camp Rd
Trinity Road
South Road
Atlantic Road
Hamilton Road
T Pl
Highbury Road
Shrubbery Avenue
Tower Wk
St Matthew's Close
Grove Park Road
Queen's Road
All Saints' Road
Tichborne Road
Cecil Rd
Madeira Rd
Paragon Rd
Atlantic Road South
Madeira Cove Hotel
Atlantic Business Park
Shrubbery Ter
Shrubbery Road
Shrubbery Walk
St Peter's Av
St John's Close
Victoria Park
Timbertop Aparthotel
Birnbeck Road
Anchor Head Hotel
New Ocean Hotel
Marine Lake
Upper Church Road
Greenfield Pl
Park Place
Royal Crs
Lower Church Rd
Grove La
Edinburgh Place
Bristol Road
Coombe Rd
Old Knightstone Theatre
Knightstone Cswy
Knightstone Road
Vctr Pl
South Ter
Weston College
High St
Connaught Place
Victoria Quadrant
Grove Rd
Playhouse Thtr
Surgery
Lauriston Hotel
Heritage Cen
West Street
Worthy Pl
Worthy La
Royal Hotel
South Pde
Waterloo St
Model Yacht Pond
Winter Gardens & Pavilion
Royal Parade
High Street
North Street
Palmer St
Palmer Rw
Hopkins St
Burlington St
Cambridge Place
St M Ter
Salisbury Terrace
Sovereign Shopping Centre
V Sq
Meadow St
Orchard St
Back St
Alma Street
Grand Pier
Leisure Pavilion
Alexandra Pde
Weston-Super-Mare Co Court
York St
Richmond St
Gloucester St
St James St
Works
Regent Street
Odeon Cinema
Wallscote Rd
Hildesheim Court
Superstore
Oxford St
Dolphin Square Shopping Centre
Union St
Town Hall
MARINE PDE
Indoor Market
AMF Bowling
Cncl Bldg
CAB
Carlton St
Walliscote Primary School
Magistrates Court
Police Station
Salvation Army
Beaconsfield Rd
Surgery
Ashbrook House School
Walliscote Road
Neva Rd
Sea Life Aquarium
A370
Ellenborough Park North
Ellenborough Park
Ellenborough Park Road
Ellenborough Crs
Ellenborough Park South
Marine Parade
Tropicana Leisure Complex
Corpus Christi RC Primary School
Albert Road
Clevedon Road
BEACH ROAD
Walliscote Road
Whitecross Road
Severn Road
Model Yacht Pond
Parade
PO
P
1 grid square represents 250 metres

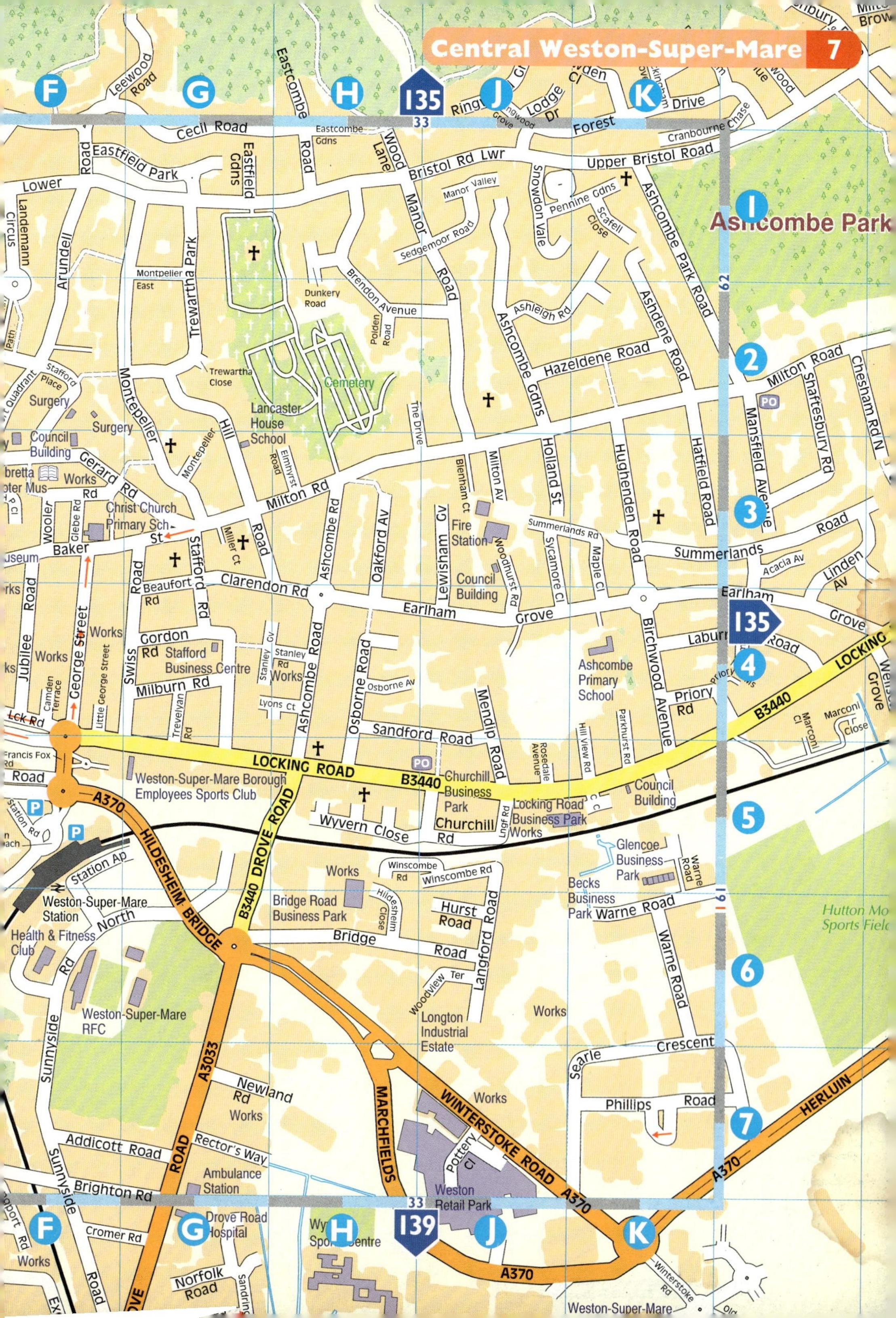
F
G
H
J
K
135
33
Leewood Road
Eastcombe Road
Cecil Road
Eastcombe Gdns
Wood Lane
Lodge Dr
Forest
Drive
Cranbourne Chase
Eastfield Park
Eastfield Gdns
Lower
Bristol Rd Lwr
Upper Bristol Road
Landemann Circus
Arundell Road
Manor Valley
Manor Road
Snowdon Vale
Pennine Gdns
Scafell Close
I
Ashcombe Park
Montpelier East
Trewartha Park
Sedgemoor Road
Dunkery Road
Brendon Avenue
Polden Road
Ashleigh Rd
Ashcombe Park Road
Ashdene Road
62
Ashcombe Gdns
Hazeldene Road
2
Milton Road
Shaftesbury Rd
Chesham Rd N
PO
Stafford Place
Surgery
Trewartha Close
Cemetery
Lancaster House School
The Drive
Montepelier
Hill
Council Building
Gerard Rd
Works
Elmhyrst Road
Milton Rd
Blenheim Ct
Milton Av
Holland St
Hughenden Road
Hatfield Road
Mansfield Avenue
3
Christ Church Primary Sch
Glebe Rd
Wooler Rd
Baker St
Miller Ct
Stafford Rd
Road
Ashcombe Rd
Oakford Av
Lewisham Gv
Fire Station
Woodhurst Rd
Summerlands Rd
Sycamore Cl
Maple Cl
Summerlands Road
Acacia Av
Linden Av
Jubilee Road
George Street
Beaufort Rd
Clarendon Rd
Council Building
Earlham Grove
Earlham Grove
135
Gordon Rd
Stafford Business Centre
Stanley Gv
Stanley Rd
Works
Swiss Road
Little George Street
Camden Terrace
Milburn Rd
Ashcombe Road
Osborne Road
Osborne Av
Lyons Ct
Trevelyan Rd
Ashcombe Primary School
Birchwood Avenue
Laburnum Road
4
Priory Rd
Locking
B3440
Marconi Close
Marconi Cl
Sandford Road
Mendip Road
Rosedale Avenue
Hill View Rd
Parkhurst Rd
Locking Rd
Francis Fox Rd
Locking Road
B3440
Weston-Super-Mare Borough Employees Sports Club
Churchill Business Park
Council Building
A370
Drove Road
Wyvern Close
Churchill Rd
Locking Road Business Park
Works
5
Station Rd
P
Station Ap
Hildesheim Bridge
B3440 Drove Road
Winscombe Rd
Winscombe Rd
Works
Glencoe Business Park
Warne Road
Weston-Super-Mare Station
North
Bridge Road Business Park
Hildesheim Close
Hurst Road
Langford Road
Becks Business Park
Warne Road
Health & Fitness Club
Rd
Bridge Road
Hutton Moor Sports Field
6
Woodview Ter
Warne Road
Weston-Super-Mare RFC
Longton Industrial Estate
Works
Sunnyside
A3033
Searle Crescent
Newland Rd
Works
Marchfields
Winterstoke Road
Works
Phillips Road
7
Herluin
Addicott Road
Rector's Way
Road
Pottery Cl
A370
Sunnyside
Brighton Rd
Ambulance Station
Weston Retail Park
A370
33
Cromer Rd
Drove Road Hospital
H
139
J
K
Works
Norfolk Road
A370
Winterstoke Rd
Weston-Super-Mare

1 grid square represents 500 metres

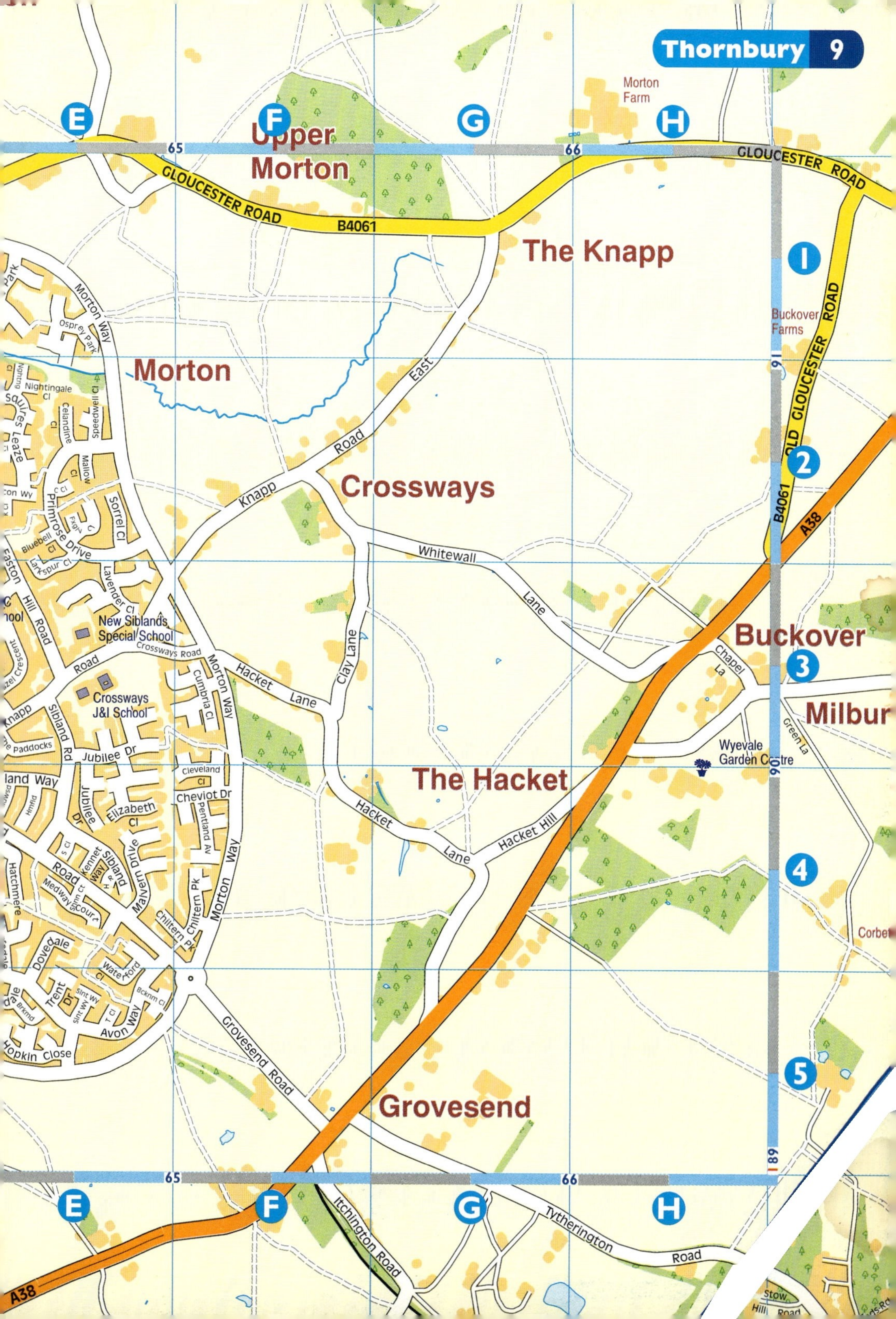
Upper Morton
Morton Farm
Gloucester Road
B4061
The Knapp
Buckover Farms
Old Gloucester Road
Morton
Morton Way
Osprey Park
Nightingale Cl
Speedwell Cl
Celandine
Mallow Cl
Squires Leaze
Primrose Drive
Sorrel Cl
Bluebell Cl
Larkspur Cl
Lavender Cl
Easton Hill Road
New Siblands Special School
Crossways Road
Crossways J&I School
Knapp Road East
Crossways
Whitewall Lane
Clay Lane
Hacket Lane
Cumbria Cl
Sibland Rd
Jubilee Dr
The Paddocks
Cleveland Cl
Cheviot Dr
Pentland Av
Elizabeth Cl
Jubilee Dr
Sibland Way
Kennet Way
Malvern Drive
Sibland Road
Medway Court
Hatchmere
Dovedale
Chiltern Pk
Waterford Cl
Trent Dr
Avon Way
Hopkin Close
The Hacket
Hacket Hill
Buckover
Chapel La
Milbur
Green La
Wyevale Garden Centre
A38
Corbet
Grovesend Road
Grovesend
Itchington Road
Tytherington Road
Stow Hill Road
E
F
G
H
I
65
66
91
90
89
2
3
4
5

BS35
A
B
C
D
1
2
3
4
5
360
61
89
88
87
B4461
Lane
Marshacre La
Elberton
Elberton Road
Aust Road
New Leaze
Hazel Farm
Oldown Country Park
Foxholes Lane
Old Down
Vicarage Lane
Olveston CE Primary School
Olveston
The Street
Ley La
Common
Denys Ct
Denys Ct
PO
Bramley Cl
Laxton Cl
Russet Cl
Orchard Rise
Haw Lane
Green Ct
New Road
The Gn
The Green
Surgery
Upper Tockington Road
Catherine Hill
Pool Cnr
Old Down Hill
Tockington Manor School
Washingpool Hill Road
Manor Pk
Manor Cl
Alveston Road
Pump Lane
The Down
The Inner Down
Sheepcome Farm
Tockington
Mill Lane
Lane
ction 21
1 grid square represents 500 metres

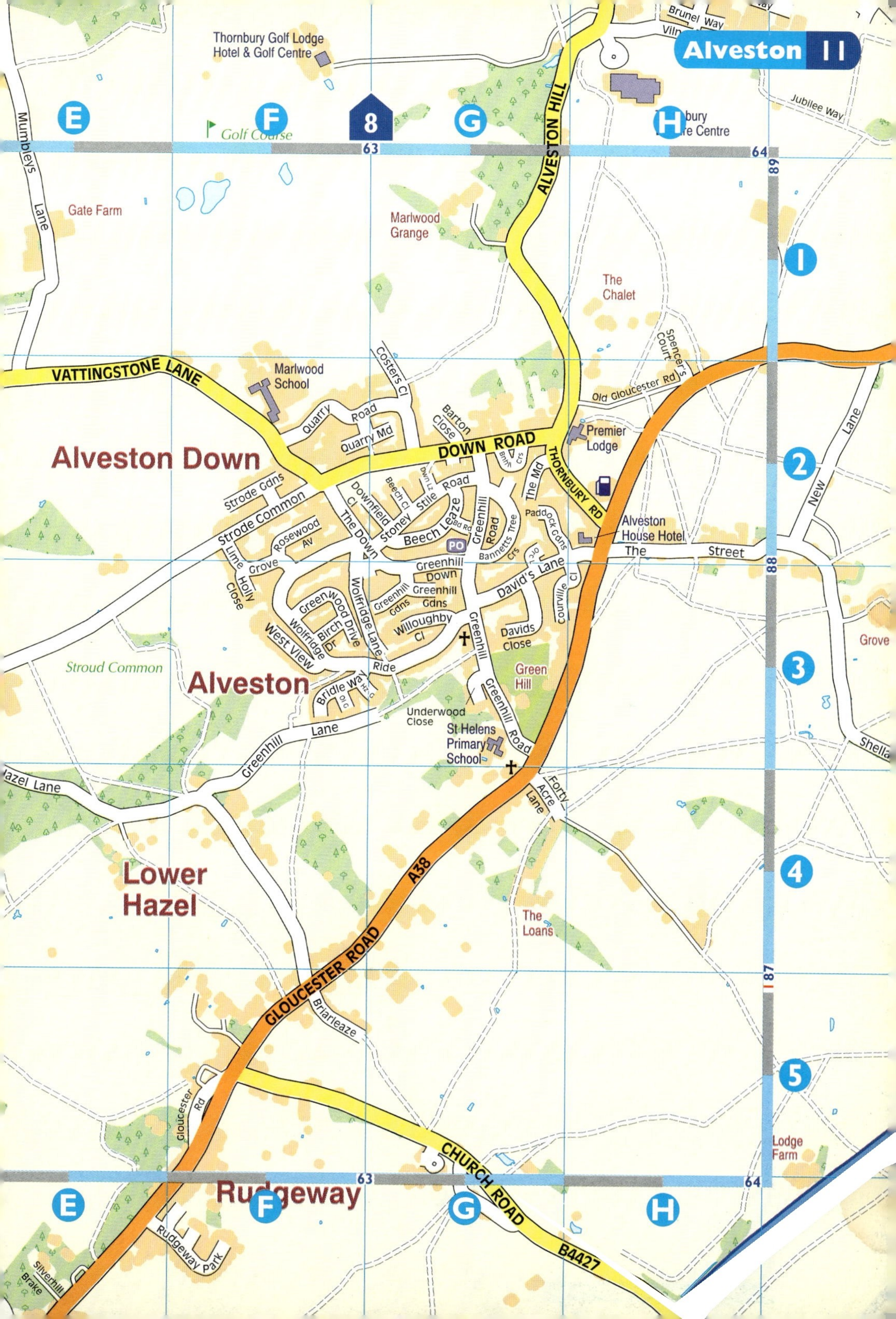
Thornbury Golf Lodge
Hotel & Golf Centre
Brunel Way
Jubilee Way
bury
re Centre
Golf Course
E
F
8
G
H
63
64
89
88
87
I
2
3
4
5
Mumbleys Lane
Gate Farm
Marlwood
Grange
ALVESTON HILL
The
Chalet
Spencer's
Court
VATTINGSTONE LANE
Marlwood
School
Costers Cl
Quarry
Road
Quarry Md
Barton
Close
DOWN ROAD
Old Gloucester Rd
Premier
Lodge
THORNBURY RD
Alveston Down
Strode Gdns
Strode Common
The Down
Downfield
Beech Cl
Stoney Stile Road
Beech Leaze
Greenhill Road
Bannetts Tree
The Md
Paddock Gdns
Alveston
House Hotel
The Street
New Lane
Rosewood
Av
Lime Close
Holly Close
Grove
Greenhill
Down
Greenhill
Gdns
David's Lane
Courville Cl
Green Wood Drive
Wolfridge Lane
Birch Dr
Wolfridge
West View
Willoughby
Cl
Greenhill
Davids
Close
Green
Hill
Grove
Ride
Stroud Common
Alveston
Bridle Way
Underwood
Close
St Helens
Primary
School
Greenhill Road
Greenhill Lane
Hazel Lane
Forty
Acre
Lane
Shella
Lower
Hazel
The
Loans
A38
GLOUCESTER ROAD
Briarleaze
Gloucester Rd
CHURCH ROAD
Lodge
Farm
Rudgeway
Rudgeway Park
Silverhill
Brake
B4427

New Passage
Severn Way
REDWICK ROAD
M4
Junction 22
Shaft Road
B4064
GREEN LANE
BEACH AVENUE
Beach Road
Osborne Rd
Gorse Cover Rd
Little Green Lane
Church Rd
Church Road
Severn Wy
PO
Salmon Cl
Station Road
St Cl
Severn Beach Stn
Severn Beach CP School
Severn Beach
M49
Riverside Park
Albert Rd
Victoria Crs
Ableton Lane
Sc Wy
Denny Isle Dr
Prospect Rd
Abbott Rd
A403
ROAD
Central
Avlon Works
A
B
C
D
1
2
3
4
5
353
54
84
85
86
1 grid square represents 500 metres

Severn Beach
Worthy Farms
wick
E
F
G
H
SEVERN ROAD
NORTHWICK ROAD
56
57
Walning Farm
86
M4
1
ROAD
B4055
REDWICK RD
Wick Rd
SEVERN
Ch Av
Keen's Cl
Vicarage Rd
Whitehouse Rd
The Glebe
The Glebe
R Gdns
PO
Pilning
2
Bank Road
CROSS HANDS ROAD
Wainbridge Crs
Jcksn Cl
Cranmoor Gn
Torrs Farm
85
Rookery Lane
Pilning CP School
3
Bank Road
14
MARSH COMMON
Council Building
Pilning Station
Ellinghurst Farm
Rednend Farm
4
B4055
84
Gilslake
Shaymoor Lane
5
Marsh Common
Station Road
Brynleaze Farm
Covier Way
Holloway Road
Collins
Dyer's Common
BLACKHOR
Washingpool

1 grid square represents 500 metres

The Niatts
Lane
E
F
G
H
M4
Fernhill Farm
60
61
85
84
83
Tockington Lane
Cemetery
Marshwall Lane
Almondsbury
Lower Court Farm
Lower Court Road
Court Vw
Cl
Church Road
The Pound
The Bowl Inn Hotel
Glebe Fld
The
Scop
Forest Hills
The Quarries
Old Aust Road
Bishop's Wead
GLOUCESTER ROAD
A38
Flore
Crantock Dr
Crantock Dr
Park
Surgery
Almondsbury CE Primary School
Hollow Road
The Hill
Red House Lane
BS32
Townsend
Hill
Knole Cl
Church Vw
Sundays Hill
Over Lane
Oaklands Dr
Junction 16
16
Almondsbury Town FC
North Bristol RFC
M5
Knole Pk
Knole Pk
Over Lane
PO
New Leaze
Ash Ridge Road
Woodlands
The Park
Lane
Grange Cl
Bradley Stoke Way
Park Avenue
Aztec West
Aztec Hotel
Woodlands La
Oaktree Crescent
Stanshaws Close
Avenue
Park
Hempton Lane
The Av
The Close
The Common
Coniston Primary School
Council Building
Blakeney Road
Epney Cl
Elmore Road
Road
PO
26
Waterside Dr
Patchway High School
Rudford Cl
Shellmor
Highnam Cl
Standish Av
Cranham Dr
Patchway CE Primary School
PATCHWAY
1
2
3
4
5

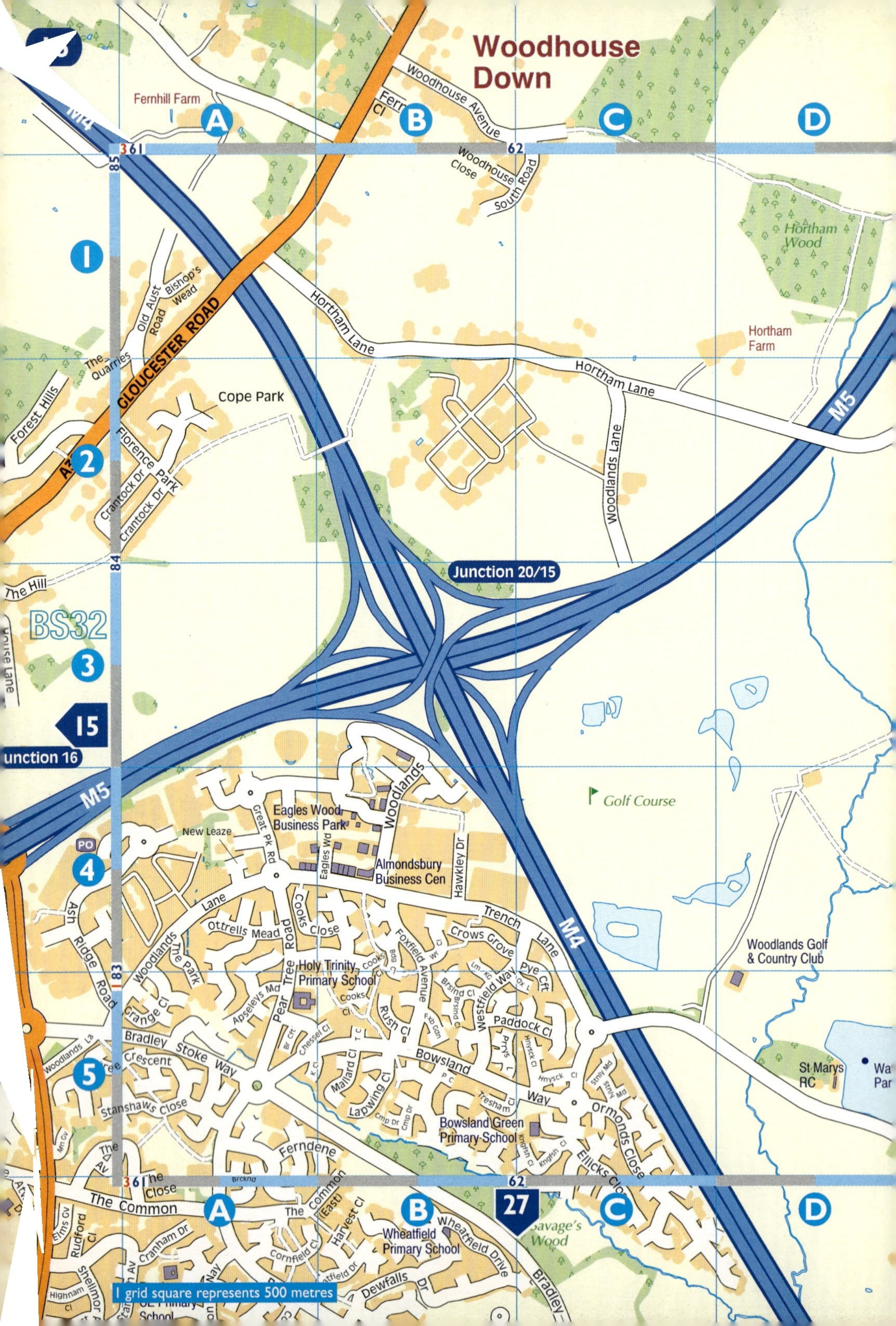

Woodhouse Down
Fernhill Farm
A
B
C
D
M4
Woodhouse Avenue
Fern Cl
361
62
Woodhouse Close
South Road
85
1
Hortham Wood
Hortham Lane
Hortham Farm
Bishop's Wead
Old Aust Road
GLOUCESTER ROAD
The Quarries
Forest Hills
Cope Park
Florence Park
Crantock Dr
2
M5
Woodlands Lane
Junction 20/15
84
The Hill
BS32
3
15
Junction 16
Golf Course
Eagles Wood Business Park
Woodlands
New Leaze
Great Pk Rd
Eagles Wd
Almondsbury Business Cen
Hawkley Dr
PO
4
Ash Ridge Road
Trench Lane
Ottrells Mead
Cooks Close
Crows Grove
Foxfield Avenue
Woodlands Golf & Country Club
Woodlands
The Park
Pear Tree Road
Holy Trinity Primary School
Westfield Way
Pye Cft
83
Grange Cl
Apseleys Md
Rush Cl
Paddock Cl
Bradley Stoke Way
Chessel Cl
Woodlands La
Crescent
5
Bowsland Way
Mallard Cl
Lapwing Cl
St Marys RC
Stanshaws Close
Ormonds Close
Bowsland Green Primary School
Ferndene
The Av
The Close
Ellicks Close
27
The Common
The Common (East)
Harvest Cl
Wheatfield Primary School
Wheatfield Drive
Savage's Wood
Rudford Cl
Elms Gv
Cranham Dr
Cornfield Cl
Dewfalls Dr
Highnam Cl
Shellmor Cl
Bradley
1 grid square represents 500 metres

Oldfields Lane
Earth
Green
E
F
G
H
64
65
85
84
83
B4427
Oldfield Farm
Ringhurst Farm
1
2
3
4
5
Gaunt's Earthcott
Gaunt's Earthcott Lane
OLD GLOUCESTER ROAD
Frogland Cross
Perrinpit Road
Gloucester Road Farm
North Woods
28

B4059
A
B
C
D
66
67
85
84
83
1
2
3
4
5
Latteridge
Folly Road
Sheephouse Farm
Ladden Brook
Laddenside Farm
Elm Farm
B4058
Hoover's Lane
BRISTOL ROAD
Frome Valley Walkway
Cog Mill Farm
Perrinpit Farm
Perrinpit Road
29
Frampton

Patch Elm Lane
Manor
Road
Mudgedown Farm
E
F
G
H
68
69
85
84
83
Lane
Chaingate Lane
WOTTON ROAD
B4058
North Road
1
2
3
4
5
Dyer's Lane
Acton Court
Acton Lodge
Engine Common
Iron Acton
Hill House
YATE ROAD
Mission Road
Latteridge Rd
Park St
High Street
Police Station
Wotton Road
Iron Acton CE Primary School
Holly Hill
20
Station Road
Cem
Chillwood Cl
Yate Town FC
Lodge
IRON ACTON WAY
The Oaklands Business Park
Pool Farm
Wade Rd
Algars Manor
Nibley Lane
Great Western Business Park
Yate Rd
Lodge Road
Lavenham Rd
Beeches Trading Estate
Waverley Road
Bridge Road
Hope Road
Frome Valley Walkway
River Frome
30
Nibley
BADMINTON
Goodrich Cl
Turner Dr
Woodward Av
ROAD

20
19
31
A
B
C
D
1
2
3
4
5
70
71
85
84
83
Engine Common
Goose Green
YATE
Nibley
BS37
Tan House Farm
Tanhouse Lane
Manor Road
Lane
North Road
Engine Common Lane
Dyer's Lane
Mission Road
North Road Primary School
PO
Council Building
Yate Outdoor Sports Complex
Brimsham Green School
Broad Lane
Broad La
GOOSE GREEN WAY
B4059
IRON ACTON WAY
Lodge Road
Yate Town FC
The Oaklands Business Park
Wade Rd
Chrch Rd
Armstrong Way
Great Western Business Park
Dean Rd
Collett Wy
Frome Va Walkway
Northavon Business Cen
Northridge Business Centre
Stover Trading Estate
Lavenham Rd
Beeches Trading Estate
Waverley Road
Lawrence Drive
Frome Valley Walkway
Millbrook Rd
Wellington Dr
YATE ROAD
Yate Station
BADMINTON ROAD
BADMINTON RD
STATION ROAD
South Av
Badminton Road Trading Estate
Goodr
Turner Dr
Sunnyside La
Moorland
Chatterton Road
Moordell Close
Wellstead Av
Thorn Close
Lyndale Rd
Cranleigh Road
Priors Lea
North Avon Magistrates Court
Stanshawe Crs
Cleeve Rd
Nailsworth Avenue
Dursley Close
Surgery
Surg
KENNEDY
Yate Leisure Centre
Long Croft
Randolph Avenue
Hay Leaze
Long Mead
Eastfield Drive
Dryleaze
Leechpool Way
The Brake
Summers Mead
Eastfield Dr
Clayfield
Meadow Mead
Lower Moor Road
Sthrind Av
Hampden Cl
Halifax Road
York Cl
Wellington Road
Sturmer Close
Homefield
Oak Cl
Bader Cl
Ash Cl
Wavell Cl
Greenways Road
Celestine Road
Blenheim Drive
Mountbatten Cl
Lancaster Road
Cambrian Drive
Ullswater Cl
Frome Bank Junior School
Cranleigh Court Infant School
Cheshire Cl
Greenways
Crowthers Av
Church Road
Whitley Close
Parnall Crescent
Windsor Dr
Cranleigh Court Road
Tyndale Avenue
Templar Road
Madison Close
Spar Rd
Beaufort Rd
Windsor Drive
Birch Road
Longs Dr
Longs Drive
Plover Cl
Fox Av
Cranleigh Ct Rd
Gathorne Rd
Milton Rd
Milton Cl
The Leaze
Home Orch
Poole Court Drive
Council Building
The Glen
Tyning Close
School Walk
1 grid square represents 500 metres

nhouse Lane
Yate Rocks
Bury Hill
Jubilee Way
E
F
G
H
72
73
85
84
83
1
2
3
4
5
Yate Rocks
Brinsham Lane
GRAVEL HILL ROAD (NORTH)
The Rocks
Coopers Dr
Barkers Mead
Eastfield
PEG HILL
LOVE LANE
Love Lane
SOUTHFIELD WY
B4060
Mead Riding
Jubilee Way
Lime Croft
The Dingle
Tylers Farm
Gravel Hl Rd
Hester Wd
Greenways Road
Crmr Cl
Corbett Cl
Lark Rl
Cornwall Crs
Wiltshire Avenue
Kent Av
Golf Course
Chipping Sodbury Golf Club
Stub Riding
GOOSE GREEN WAY
Churchfarm Close
Somerset Avenue
Dorset Way
WICKWAR ROAD
Horton Road
Jubilee Way
Walnut Avenue
Elm Gdn
Melrose Avenue
St Mary's Wy
Mercier Cl
Firgrove Crs
Ridge Junior School
B4059
Portway Lane
St Johns Way
Broadway Infant School
Melrose Cl
Newlyn Wy
Highway
Ridgeway
Couzens Cl
Couzens Close
Ross Close
Closes
Horton Rd
Brookfield Cl
Manor Way
Vayre Close
STATION ROAD
Cemetery
LINK ROAD
cil Building
Bowling Hill Business Park
Quarry Rd
32
Barnhill Road
Chipping Edge Est
Grace Close
Brook Street
Hatters' Lane
Batten Court
Bennett's Court
BOWLING HILL
Town Hall
Rogers Ct
Frome Rd
Walshe Av
HIGH ST
BROAD ST
TT Trading Estate
Brandash Rd
Police
Estoril
Ridings
CHIPP

1 grid square represents 500 metres

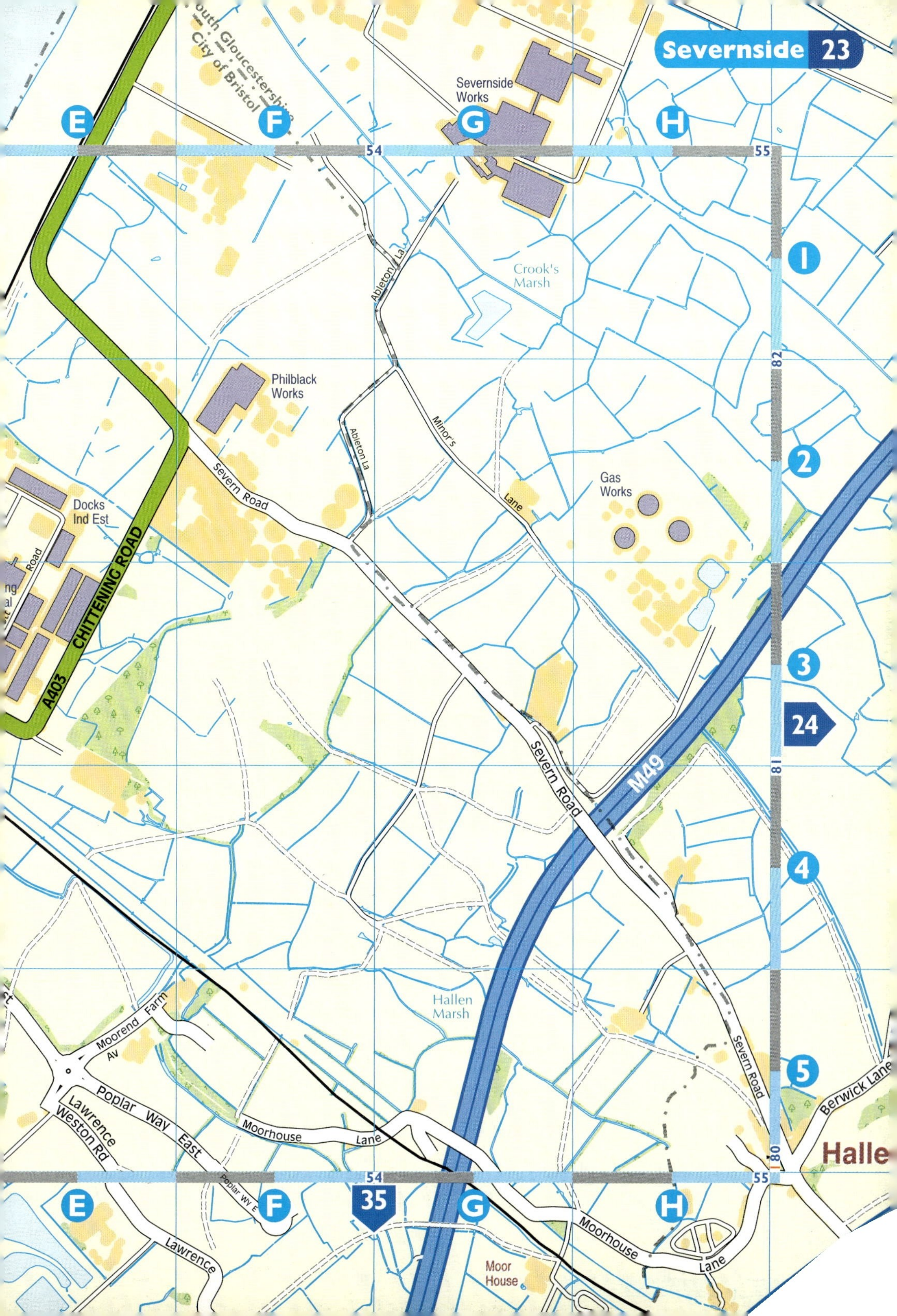

Severnside Works
South Gloucestershire
City of Bristol
Crook's Marsh
Ableton La
Philblack Works
Minor's Lane
Gas Works
Docks Ind Est
Road
Severn Road
CHITTENING ROAD
A403
M49
24
Hallen Marsh
Moorend Farm Av
Poplar Way East
Lawrence Weston Rd
Moorhouse Lane
Berwick Lane
Halle
Poplar Wy E
Lawrence
35
Moor House
E
F
G
H
1
2
3
4
5
54
55
82
81
80

24
23
36
A
B
C
D
1
2
3
4
5
355
56
82
81
180
Spaniorum View
The La
Farm Lane
Green Lane
Vimpennys Lane
Brook Farm
Berwick Lane
Compton Greenfield
Berwick Cl
Spaniorum Farm
Elmington Manor Farm
Sampson House Business Park
Berwick Lodge
Berwick Lane
Berwick
M5
BS10
Berwick Lane
Hallen
Saracens RC
Clifton RC
B4055
ST RD
Haw Wood
Sun Life Sports Club
B4055
STATION RD
Oakhill
Lane
1 grid square represents 500 metres

E
F
14
G
Over
H
58
59
PO
HILL
B4055
Home Farm Way
Cooke's Dr
Church Road
pton
Over Lane
Lane
I
M5
82
Falcon Cl
Falcon Dr
Falcon Drive
Falcon Wk
Beving Close
2
Linn Close
Kestrel Cl
Martin Close
Patchway Trading Estate
B4055 BLACKHORSE HILL
Bristol Golf Club
Golf Course
Hollywood Tower
CRIBBS CSWY
Junction 17
Superstore
Olympus Road
Britannia Road
Coniston
Concorde Road
Highwood Lane
Highwood Lane
3
Lysander Rd
Centaurus Road
Pegasus Road
Jupiter Road
26
Highwood La
Merlin Road
Lysander Road
Cribbs Causeway Retail Park
Cribbs Causeway Regional Shopping Cen
81
Travelodge
CRIBBS CAUSEWAY
Lysander Road
Merlin Road
4
Highwood Road
Premier Lodge (Bristol North West)
Catbrain La
Catbrain Hill
VUE Cinema
Catbrain
way
The Laurels
CRIBBS CAUSEWAY
5
Filton Airfield
80
58
59
E
F
37
G
H
South Gloucestershire
City of Bristol
Fishpool
Charlton
Charlton

Aztec West
Aztec Hotel
Park Ave
Avenue
Park
Woodlands La
Hempton Lane
Atwell Dr
Patchway High School
Coniston Primary School
Council Building
PO
Park Leaze
Pk
Leaze
C Ct
Blakeney Road
Epney Cl
Elmore Road
Waterside Dr
PATCHWAY
Highnam Cl
Sandhurst Cl
Maisemore A
Elms Gv
Rudford Cl
A38
Road
Tidenham Wy
Severn Wy
Bevington Wk
Bevington Cl
Bevington Close
Coniston Road
Arlingham Way
Bradley
Road
N Pl
Longney Place
Coniston Road
Falcon Wk
Falcon Cl
Falcon Dr
Falcon Drive
M5
Pretoria Road
Durban Road
Worthing Road
Stroud Road
Cavendish Road
Windermere Road
Road
Derwent Cl
Thirlmere Rd
Rodway
Swallow Dr
Linnet Close
Martin Close
Eagle Dr
Kestrel Cl
Patchway Trading Estate
Brighton Rd
Callicroft Infant Sch
Lee Close
Council Building
Callicroft Junior Sch
Patchway Health Clinic
Hawthorn Close
Rodway Road
Cranbourne Rd
Southsea Road
Ashford Rd
Hazeldene Rd
Callicroft Road
Willow Close
Bay Tree Close
Cedar Close
Larch Wy
Sycamore Dr
Fir Tree Cl
Birch Close
Highwood Road
Coniston Road
Olympus Road
Britannia Road
Concorde Road
Lane
Jupiter Road
Pegasus Road
Highwood La
Highwood Road
Grove Industrial Estate
Redfield Road
Brookfield Rd
Amberley
Holy Fam RC Prim
Pains
Galli
Are RF
B4057
GIPS
Works
GLOUCESTER ROAD NORTH
Airfield
South Gloucestershire
City of Bristol
Charlton Gd
Works
Northway
Cleve Rd
Filton Hill Primary School
Filton College
Blenheim Drive
House
Canberra
ROAD NORTH
A B C D
1 2 3 4 5
359 60 82 81 80
15 25 38
1 grid square represents 500 metres

BRADLEY STOKE
Little Stoke
Stoke Gifford
Great Stoke
Savage's Wood
Wheatfield Primary School
Patchway CE Primary School
Bowsland Green Primary School
Stoke Lodge J&I School
Meadowbrook Primary School
Stokes Medical Centre
Little Stoke Primary School
St Marys Catholic School
Baileys Court Prim Sch
St Marys Catholic Prim Sch
St Michaels CE Prim Sch
Stoke Gifford Local Centre
Bradley Stoke Way
Baileys Court Road
Great Meadow Road
Webbs Wd Rd
Brook Way
Hatchet Road
Station Rd
Gipsy Patch La
GIPSY PATCH LA
B4057
WINTERBOURNE ROAD
Trench Lane
Bowsland Way
Ferndene
The Common
Savages Wood Rd
Hawkins Crescent
Juniper Way
Little Stoke Lane
Rossall Avenue
Kingsway
Queensway
Bush Avenue
Brookcote Dr
Orion Dr
Orpheus Av
Mead Road
Oxbarton
Ratcliffe Drive
Dumaine Av
Touchstone Av
Rock Lane
Sandringham Rd
North Road
Brins Close
Field Farm Close
Hunts Gnd Rd
Parkway
Trevelyan Wk
Bakers Gnd
Gt Stoke Wy
Manor Farm Crs
Winsbury Way
Merryweather Close
Bourton Av
Dyrham Pde
Clay Lane
Farley Close
Braydon Av
Kemperleye Way
Linden Dr
Diana Gardens
Sherbourne Av
The Bluebells
Pursey Dr
Robbins Cl
Berkeleys Md
Ellan Hay Road
The Green
Bristol
E
F
G
H
I
2
3
4
5
16
28
34
39
62
63
80
81
82

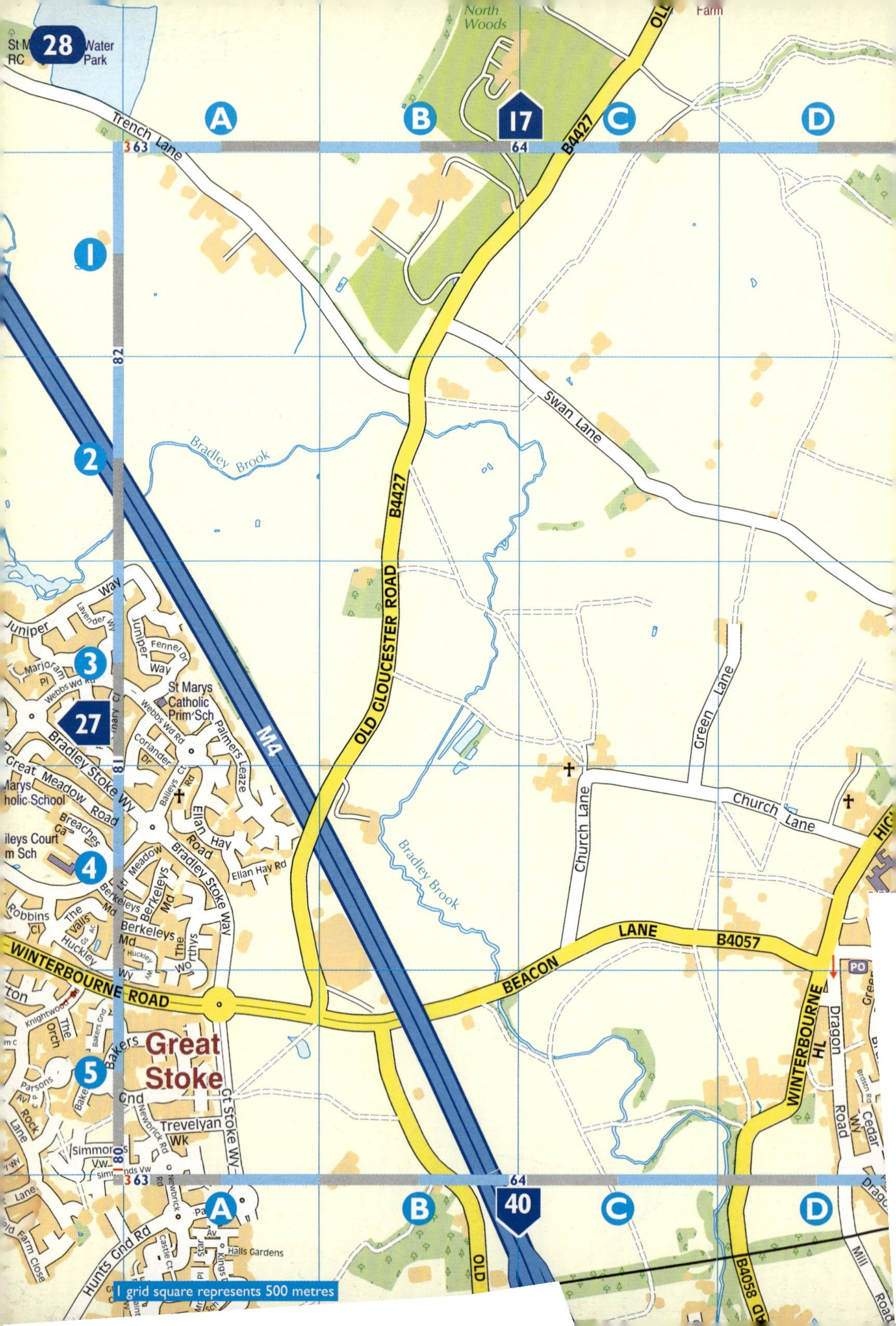
28
17
27
40
A
B
C
D
1
2
3
4
5
North Woods
Water Park
St M RC
Farm
Trench Lane
B4427
OLD GLOUCESTER ROAD
Swan Lane
Bradley Brook
M4
Juniper Way
Lavender Wy
Fennel Dr
Marjoram Pl
Webbs Wd Rd
St Marys Catholic Prim Sch
Bradley Stoke Wy
Great Meadow Road
Coriander Dr
Palmers Leaze
Baileys Ct Rd
Ellan Hay Road
Ellan Hay Rd
Breaches Ga
Bradley Stoke Way
Robbins Cl
The Vails
Berkeleys Md
Huckley Wy
The Worthys
WINTERBOURNE ROAD
BEACON LANE B4057
Green Lane
Church Lane
Great Stoke
Bakers Gnd
Knightwood Rd
The Orch
Parsons Av
Rock Lane
Trevelyan Wk
Newbrick Rd
Simmonds Vw
Gt Stoke Wy
Hunts Gnd Rd
Castle Ct
Halls Gardens
Winterbourne Hl
Dragon Road
Cedar Wy
PO
B4058
Mill Road
1 grid square represents 500 metres

Perrinpit Farm
E
F
18
G
H
66
67
Perrinpit Road
North Corner
Frampton Cotterell
BRISTOL ROAD
Conifer Cl
Church Road
Western Av
Robel Av
School Road
Mill Lane
Rectory Rd
Beaufort Rd
Foxe Rd
Brookside Dr
Church Cl
Church Road
Frampton Cotterell CE Primary School
Rectory Road
Meadow Md
Bridge Wy
Stanford Close
Camberley Dr
Court Road
Mount Cl
Rylestone Close
Park Row
Surgery
Rectory Rd
Clyde Rd
Goosegreen
Rockside Gardens
York Gdns
Park Lane
St Peter's Crs
Sunnyside
South View
Brockridge La
Ryecroft Road
I
2
3
4
5
82
81
80
Bourne Cl
Watley's End
Cannans
Manor La
Beaver Cl
Woodend
Footes La
West Rdg
Road
Chapel La
B4058
Gazzard Cl
Star Barn Rd
Lewton
England's Crs
Factory Rd
The Gully
Harris Barton
Park La
Wayside Cl
Frome Vw
St Michael's Cl
Nicholls
Park Avenue
Sallys Wy
Masons Vw
North Road
Salem Rd
Saint Francis Drive
Watley's End
Park Av
Medway Dr
Langt
30
Bell
Newland Av
BS36
Heather Av
Beesmoor
Ridings Rd
The Cl
Elm Park Primary School
Friary Grange Park
Branksome Dr
Abbeydale
St Francis Dr
Nightingale Close
Park Lane
Kelbra Crs
St Saviours Rise
The Ridings
Manor Cl
Crofton Fields
Cloisters Road
Lane
Hither Mead
Butterfield Cl
Blackberry Dr
Road
Vicarage Rd
River Frome
Frome Valley Walkway
Heath Cl
Burrough Wy
Linden Cl
Orchard Cl
Hicks Common Road
Lane
BADMINTON
Station Road
The Brake
Hicks Common
Rathbone Close
Deacon Cl
Frome Wy
Barton Cl
Pendock Rd
Huckford Rd
Crossman Av
Bradley Av
Matford Cl
Avenue
Surgery
Park Lane
E
F
41
G
H
Station Road
Rose Cl
Quarry La
Harcombe Hill
Frome Valley
Huckford La
Park La
A432
Winterbourne Down
The Kendleshire Golf Club

Frome Valley Walkway
River Frome
19
A
B
C
D
367
68
Tubb's Bottom
1
2
3
4
5
82
81
80
Frampton End Rd
Mayshill
BADMINTON ROAD
A432
Cemetery
Mill Lane
Church Cl
Church Road
Bridge Wy
PO
Frampton End
Surgery
Clyde Rd
Park Lane
Goosegreen
Rockside Gardens
Lwr Stone Cl
Highcroft Junior School
Watermore Cl
St Peter's Crs
Sunnyside
South View
Brockridge La
Ryecroft Road
Upr Stone Cl
Meadow View
Gledemoor Dr
Alexandra Road
Millennium Cl
Frog Lane
Oakwood Gdns
Homestead Cl
Woodend
Brockeridge Infant School
The Cswy
Rushton Dr
Wayleaze
Footshill
West Rdg
Road
Upr Chapel La
Hillside
Lrkfld
Wayside Cl
29
Langthorn
Chapel La
Lower Chapel
The Land
Ridgeway
Boundary Rd
Main Vw
Woodside Rd
Coalville Road
Woodside Road
Medway Dr
Mill Cl
Bell
Newlands Av
The Rdg
Heathcote Dr
Rose Lane
Rose Oak La
Burcombe Cl
Heather Av
Beesmoor
Oldlands Av
Ridings Rd
The Cl
PO
Kelbra Crs
Rise
Fernleaze
Ch La
Surgery
Watters
St Saviours
The Ridings
Manor Cl
Bell Rd
South Vw
Crs Cl
Dormer
Coalpit Heath
Hither
Blackberry Dr
Road
Vicarage Rd
South Vw Rl
The Manor CE Primary School
Roundways
Station Road
Heath Gardens
Road
St Anne's Dr
The Brake
Rathbone Close
Ram Hill
Broad La
Henfield
42
Ram Hill
The Kendleshire
1 grid square represents 500 metres
Serridge

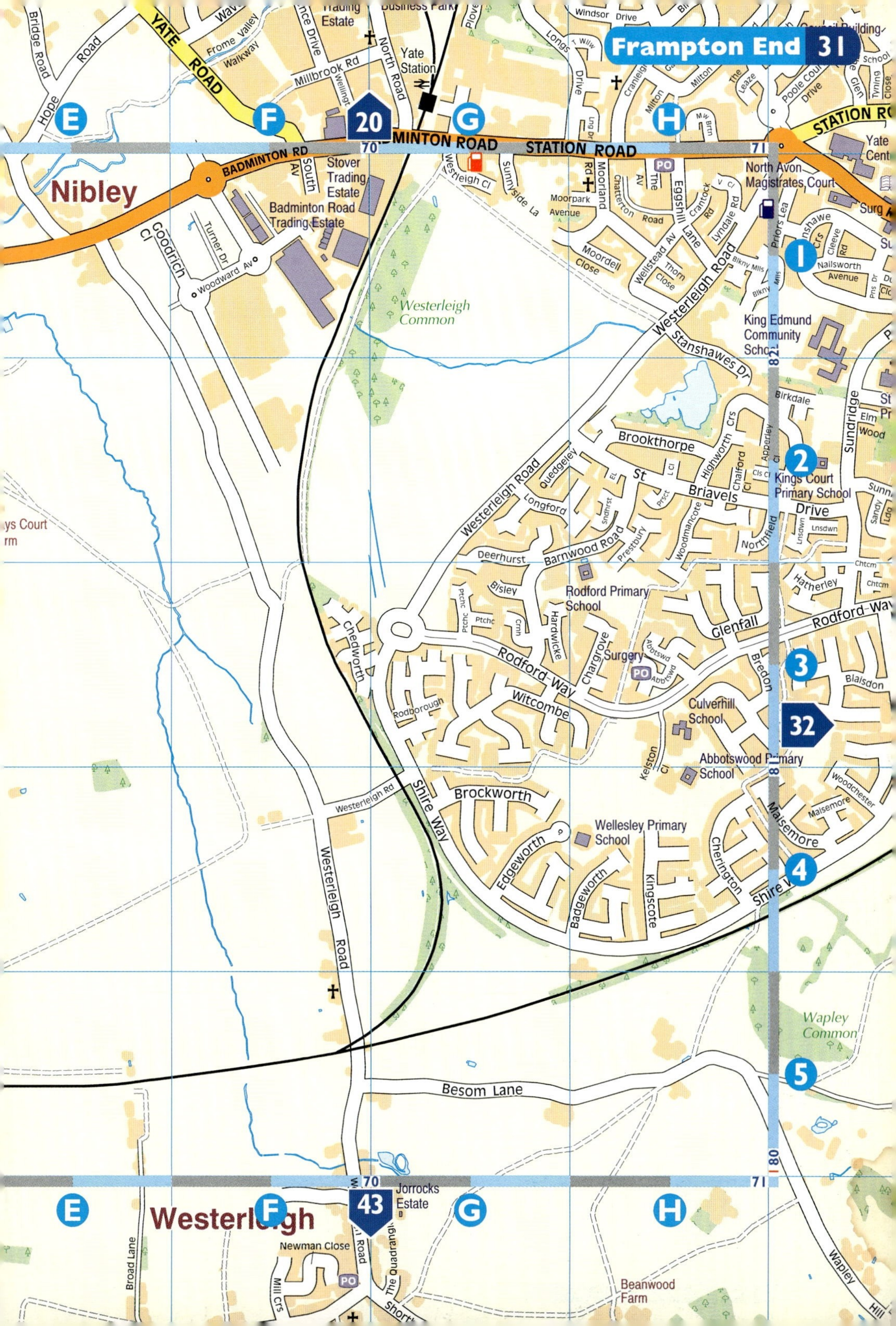

Frampton End 31
Yate Station
North Road
Millbrook Rd
Trading Estate
Business Park
Frome Valley Walkway
YATE ROAD
Bridge Road
Hope Road
BADMINTON RD
BADMINTON ROAD
STATION ROAD
Nibley
South Av
Stover Trading Estate
Badminton Road Trading Estate
Turner Dr
Woodward Av
Goodrich Cl
Westleigh Cl
Sunnyside La
Windsor Drive
Longs Drive
Moorland Rd
Moorpark Avenue
Moordell Close
Chatterton Road
The Av
Eggshill Lane
Wellstead Av
Thorn Close
Crantock Rd
Lyndale Rd
Milton
Cranleigh
The Leaze
Poole Court Drive
North Avon Magistrates Court
Priors Lea
Nailsworth Avenue
Cleeve Rd
Yate Cent
Surg
School
STATION RO
Westerleigh Road
Westerleigh Common
Stanshawes Dr
King Edmund Community School
Birkdale
Sundridge
Elm Wood
Brookthorpe
Highworth Crs
Chalford Cl
Apperley Cl
Kings Court Primary School
St Briavels Drive
Quedgeley
Longford
Prestbury
Woodmancote
Northfield
Deerhurst
Barnwood Road
Rodford Primary School
Hatherley
Bisley
Hardwicke
Chargrove
Surgery
PO
Glenfall
Rodford Way
Bredon
Blaisdon
Chedworth
Rodborough
Witcombe
Culverhill School
Abbotswood Primary School
Kelston Cl
32
Woodchester
Maisemore
Brockworth
Shire Way
Wellesley Primary School
Edgeworth
Badgeworth
Kingscote
Cherington
Westerleigh Rd
Westerleigh Road
Wapley Common
Besom Lane
Jorrocks Estate
43
Westerleigh
Newman Close
Broad Lane
Mill Crs
The Quadrangle
Beanwood Farm
Wapley Hill
E F G H I
1 2 3 4 5
70 71 80 81

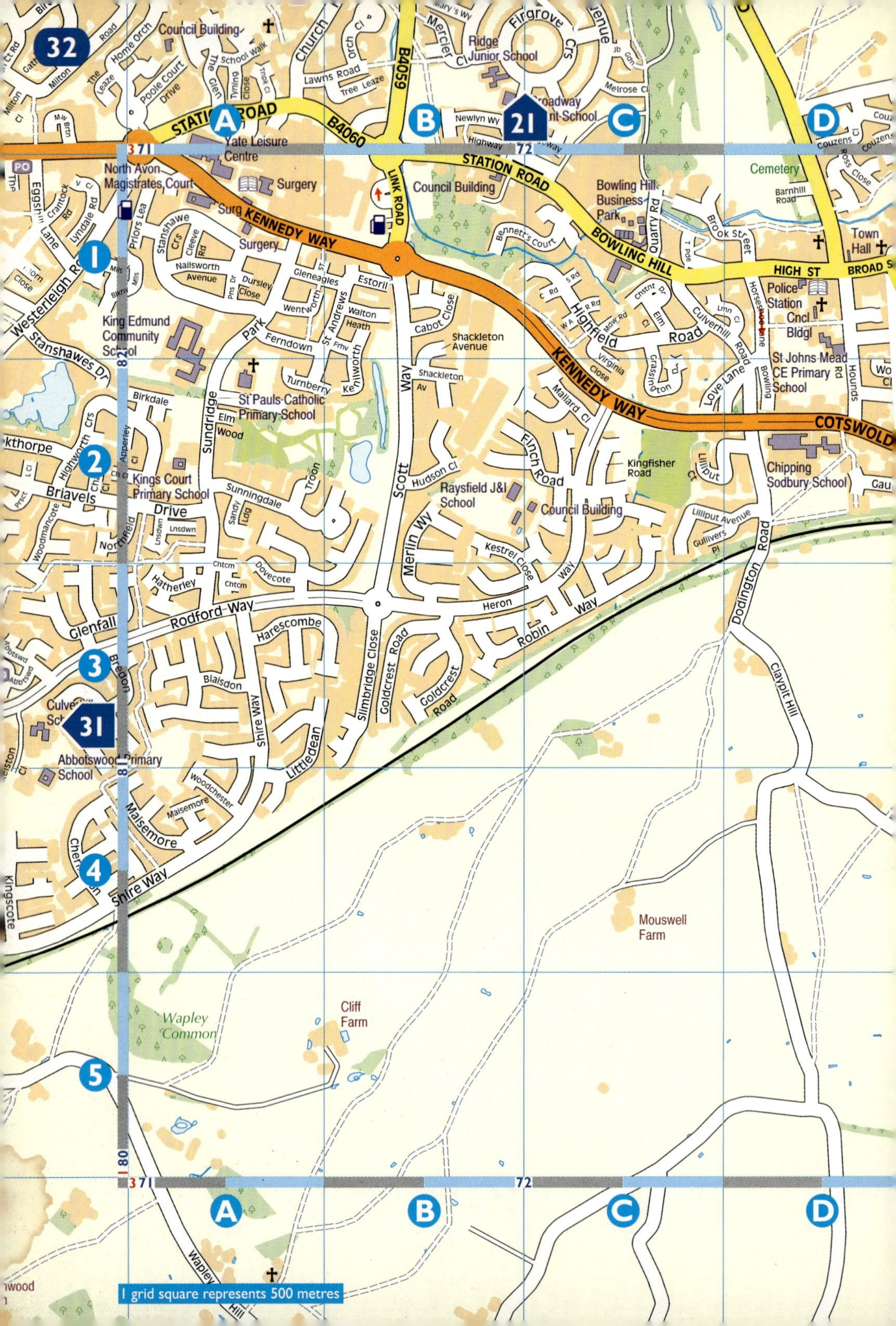
32
21
31
A
B
C
D
1
2
3
4
5
371
72
82
81
80
STATION ROAD
B4060
B4059
LINK ROAD
KENNEDY WAY
BOWLING HILL
HIGH ST
BROAD ST
COTSWOLD
Council Building
Ridge Junior School
Broadway Infant School
Firgrove Crs
Yate Leisure Centre
North Avon Magistrates Court
Surgery
Council Building
Bowling Hill Business Park
Cemetery
Town Hall
Police Station
Cncl Bldgl
St Johns Mead CE Primary School
Chipping Sodbury School
King Edmund Community School
St Pauls Catholic Primary School
Kings Court Primary School
Raysfield J&I School
Council Building
Abbotswood Primary School
Westerleigh Rd
Stanshawes Dr
Eggshill Lane
Lyndale Rd
Crantock Rd
Priors Lea
Stanshawe Crs
Cleeve Rd
Nailsworth Avenue
Dursley Close
Gleneagles
Wentworth
St Andrews
Walton Heath
Estoril
Ferndown
Turnberry
Kenilworth
Park
Sundridge
Elm Wood
Birkdale
Highworth Crs
Apperley Cl
Briavels
Drive
Northfield
Woodmancote
Sunningdale
Troon
Sandy Ldg
Hatherley
Dovecote
Glenfall
Rodford Way
Harescombe
Blaisdon
Shire Way
Littledean
Woodchester
Maisemore
Breadon
Shire Way
Kingscote
Scott Way
Cabot Close
Shackleton Avenue
Shackleton Av
Hudson Cl
Merlin Wy
Slimbridge Close
Goldcrest Road
Heron Way
Robin Way
Kestrel Close
Finch Road
Mallard Cl
Kingfisher Road
Highfield Road
Virginia Close
Bennett's Court
Quarry Rd
Brook Street
Culverhill Road
Love Lane
Horseshoe Lane
Bowling Rd
Lilliput Ct
Lilliput Avenue
Gullivers Pl
Dodington Road
Claypit Hill
Mouswell Farm
Cliff Farm
Wapley Common
Wapley Hill
1 grid square represents 500 metres

Portway Lane
Portway Lane
Johns
Horton Rd
Brookfield Cl
Way
Close
Vayre Close
Grace Close
Batten Court
Rogers Ct
Frome Rd
Walshe Av
Brandash Rd
Wnt
Ridings Cl
Trading
Gorlands Road
Hartley Cl
Cesson Close
St Johns Way
Jenner Cl
HORSE STREET
B4060
Mead Rd
Kingrove Crs
dmans Road
Wdmns V
Horse St
Wickham Cl
Smarts Green
Green Hayes
Blanchards
Station Cl
A432
BADMINTON ROAD
BADMINTON ROAD
Colts Gn
Monarch's Way
Harwoodgate Farm
Park's Farm
Commonmead
Jubilee Lane
CHIPPING SODBURY
Frome Valley Way
Colt's Green
Hayes Farm
A432
PO
Chapel Lane
Chapel Lane
rove Lane
Kingrove Common
Mill Lane
gton Lane
Dodington Lane
Coomb's End
Dodington Manor
Dodington
Lydes
E
F
G
H
I
2
3
4
5
74
75
82
81
80

22
47
A
B
C
D
1
2
3
4
5
351
52
80
79
78
St Andrew's Road
Ironchurch Road
Severnside Trading Estate
Severnside Trading Estate
Fuel Depot
Kings Weston Lane
St Andrews Road Station
Works
St Georges Industrial Estate
Hydro Estate
AVON
Haslemere Industrial Estate
Jubilee Wy
Haslemere Industrial Estate
Third
Way
A403
Docks
St Brendans Trading Estate
LC
King Rd Av
Avonmouth Wy W
CROWLEY WAY
Avonmo
First Way
Severnside Trading Estate
M5
Jutland Rd
McLaren Rd
Richmond Ter
King St
Napier St
Clayton St
Meadow St
Gloucester Road
St Andrew's Rd
St Brendan's Wy
BRISTOW BROADWAY
Police Stn
LC
Avonmouth Station
Council Building
Napier Rd
Green Lane
Avonmouth Rd
PO
Collins St
Avonmouth Medical Cen
Portview Road
Farr St
Davis St
Poole St
Cook Street
Marsh St
Avonbridge Trading Estate
Atlantic
AVONMOU ROAD
Akeman Wy
Leeming Wy
Robin Cousin Sports Centre
PORTWAY
Pages Md
Catherine St
Primary School
River Road
Surgery
Portview Trading Estate
Victoria Road
Avon Riverside Estate
Avon G Industrial
Portway Trading
West
Ermine Way
Road
George's
Marsh La
1 grid square represents 500 metres

35
23
E
F
G
H
I
53
54
80
79
78
Humber Wy
Moorend Av
Poplar Way
Lawrence Weston Rd
Moorhouse Lane
Poplar Wy E
Lawrence Weston Road
Moorhouse
Moor House
Poplar Farm
Boundary Rd
M49
M5
2
UTH
Kings Weston Lane
Junction 18a
Ballast Lane
BS11
Avonmouth Way
Fifth Wy
Willment Way
Second Way
Lescren Way
Fourth Way
Atwood Dr
Lyminton Wal
3
St Bedes RC School
36
City of Bristol College (Lawrence Weston Centre)
Lawrence Weston
Stile Acres
Drive
Saltmarsh Drive
Ridingleaze
Ottery Cl
Broadlands
Capel Rd
Surgery
4
Commonfield Rd
Awdelett Cl
Little Md
Oakhanger Drive
Meere Bank
Cncl Bldg
Kirkby Rd
Med Cen
Astry Cl
Brookthorpe Av
Goodring Hl
Elm Cl
Campbell Farm Dr
Long Cross
Our Lady of the Rosary RC Prim Sch
Kings Weston Lane
Tide Gv
Deans Md
Banfield Cl
The Gastons
Moor Grove
Junction 18
KINGS
B4057
5
Napier Miles Road
Kingsweston Special School
Avon Primary School
Barrack's La
Weston Park Primary School
Sadlier Cl
Henacre Rd
Long Cross
Badenham Gv
Weston Drive
Tufton Av
Playford Gdns
Middleton Rd
Hallards Cl
Windcliff Crs
Merrimans Rd
Shire Gdns
The Bean Acre
Kings Weston Avenue
Council Building
Old Quarry Road
Nigel Pk
Barrowmead Drive
Hopewell Gdns
Mancroft Avenue
49
Lane
Council Building
Old Park Rd
LOWER HIGH STREET
Meadow Grove
Home Gnd
Westbury
Twyford House

BS10
Hallen
24
Severn Road
Berwick Lane
Haw Wood
Moorhouse Lane
Moor House
Oakhill
Windsor Crs
Hallen Road
M5
South Gloucestershire
City of Bristol
Treverdowe Wk
Silverhill Road
Birdale Cl
Meadowland
Greenl
Cotrith Gv
Marissal Rd
Marissal Cl
PO
Henbury School
B4055
Darley Cl
Hill End Dr
Springwood Dr
Windmill Lane
Woodside Gv
Royal Cl
Convent Cl
Hallen Rd
Hallen Cl
Battersby Wy
Gray Close
Henbury Lodge Hotel
HENBURY ROAD
Church La
Blaise Hamlet
Blaise Hamlet (NT)
Woodgrove Rd
Castle Cl
Blaise Castle House Museum
Henbu
Bank Leaze Primary School
Weston Road
Atwood Drive
Aylminton Walk
Corbet Cl
Musgrove Cl
Long Cross
Cemetery
Sedes RC School
35
Orlebar Gdns
Chapel Lane
Stradling Rd
Redwick Cl
Vincent Cl
De Clifford Rd
Courtney Cl
Mauncell Rd
Lawrence Weston
Knovill Cl
Caldicot Cl
Stowick Crs
City of Bristol College (Lawrence Weston Centre)
Stile Acres
Drive
Deering Cl
Quarry La
Commonfield Rd
Awdelett Cl
Fernhill Lane
Surgery
Rockwell Av
Ridingleaze
Kirkby Rd
Broadlands
Capel Road
Oakhanger Drive
Little Md
Cncl Bldg
Med Cen
Astry Cl
Brookthorpe Av
Meere Bank
WESTON ROAD
KINGS
Kings Weston Hill
Goodring Hl
Deans Md
Banfield Cl
The Gastons
Southwood Drive East
Benville Avenue
Chardstock Avenue
Golf Course
B4057
Napier Miles Road
Coombe Dingle
Southwood Av
Ardern Cl
Southwood Drive
Aldercombe Road
Arbutus Drive
Grove Road
Pitchcombe Gdns
Kingsweston Special School
Bowden Cl
Council Building
Lane
Southside Cl
49
Grove Av
Long Acres Cl
Sea Mills Infant School
Westbury La
The Dingle
A4162
CANFORD
Hutton Cl
Churchill Dr
Beverley Gdns
Sandyleaze
Canford Crematorium
Cemetery
Hallen Dr
Dingle
1 grid square represents 500 metres
A
B
C
D
1
2
3
4
5
355
56
80
79
78

Saracens RC
Clifton RC
Sun Life Sports Club
Filton Airfield
STATION RD
B4055
A4018
WYCK BECK ROAD
PASSAGE ROAD
BRENTRY HILL
B4057 CROW LANE
FALCONDALE ROAD
HENBURY HILL
HENBURY ROAD
CANFORD ROAD
Brentry
Southmead
Brentry Primary School
Brentry Hospital
Council Building
Magistrates Court
The John Milton Health Clinic
Surgery
Henbury Swimming Pool
Blaise Prim Sch
Henbury Old Boys AFC
Golf Club
Dunmail Primary School
Southmead Hlth Centre
Council Bldg
Embleton Primary School
Badocks Wood Primary School
Elmfield Special School
Westbury on Trym CE Primary School
Police Station
Swanmoor Crs
Tranmere Av
Fishpool Hill
Okebourne Road
Knole Lane
Charlton Road
Twenty Acres Road
Concorde Drive
Ambleside Avenue
Gosforth Road
Greystoke Avenue
Doncaster Road
Embleton Rd
Crescent
Dragonswell Rd
Sheepwood Rd
Monsdale Drive
Machin Rd
Peverell Drive
Arnall Drive
The Ridgeway
Ridgeway Ct
Northover Road
Westover Road
Falcondale Wk
Grasmere Cl
Shipley Rd
Holmwood Gdns
Lakewood Road
Tuffley Rd
Kelston Road
Cherington Road
Farington Rd
Kendon Drive
Home Gnd
Eastfield Rd
Wellington
Westbury Ct Rd
Canford La
Merlin Cl
Hyland Grove
Southover Cl
Eastover Cl
Westacre Close
Chapel Gdns
Burghill Rd
Lorton Rd
Ullswater
Trowbridge Road
Ashburton Rd
Westleigh Rd
Charfield Road
Coleford
Lydney Road
Bradwell Gv
Delvin Rd
Pen Park Road
Charlton Rd
Briarside Road
Chakeshill Drive
Brewerton Cl
Okebourne Close
Dorester Cl
Elderberry Wk
Robin Cl
Strathearn Dr
Pine Rd
Bidwell Cl
Nursery Gdns
Marlwood Dr
Epworth Rd
Crow Lane
Grayle Rd
Ellsworth Rd
Richeson Walk
Challender Av
Satchfield Crs
Trymwood Cl
Didsbury Cl
Blaisdon Cl
Staveley Crs
Lanercost Rd
Ravenglass Crs
Dunmail Road
Wigton Crs
Glencoyne Sq
Westbury on Trym
SOUTHMEAD ROAD
B4056
E
F
G
H
I
2
3
4
5
25
38
50
51
57
58
78
79
80

Filton Airfield
A
B
26
C
D
359
60
80
79
78
1
2
3
4
5
37
51
South Gloucestershire
City of Bristol
Works
Filton Golf Club
Fairway Industrial Centre
Golf Course
Golf Course Lane
New Road
Link Road
Homestead Road
GLOUCESTER ROAD NORTH
A38
Filton College
Station Road
Church Rd
The Shield Retail Cen
Premier Lodge
LINK ROAD
Filton Recreat Centre
Council Building
Springfields
Elm Park
Police Stn
Charborough Road
Charborough Road Primary School
Dunkeld Avenue
Clyde Grove
Rannoch Road
SOUTHMEAD ROAD
B4056
Ascot Road
Fonthill Primary School
Fonthill Road
Stanton Road
Knighton Rd
Felstead Road
Home Cl
Pen Park Road
Kenmore Crs
Kenmore Dr
Braemar Avenue
Braemar Crs
Pitlochry Cl
Bronckseа Rd
Lomond Rd
Elgin Av
The Wickets
Gayner Road
Pine Gv
Shield Road Primary School
Northville
Eden Grove
Park Rd
St Teresa's Catholic Primary School
Biddestone Rd
Luckington Road
Lyddington Rd
Council Building
Monks Park School
Monk's Park Avenue
Surgery
Latton Rd
Northwick Rd
Prim Sch
St Gregory's Road
Sheridan Rd
Shelley Wy
Macauley Road
Shakespeare Avenue
Montreal Avenue
Toronto Road
Hazel Grove
Filton Avenue
Beverley Road
Boston Road
Doone Rd
Manx Rd
Ramsey Rd
Jocelyn Rd
Norley Rd
Douglas Rd
Reynold's Wk
Bridge Wk
Melton
Horfield Sports Centre
FILTON ROAD
Grittleton Road
Alderton Road
Priory Gdns
Early Wy
Tyndalls Way
Dorian Wy
Dorian Road
St Lucia Cl
Inkerman Cl
Tilling Road
Southmead Hospital
Bell Cl
Bishop Mnr Road
Horfield Primary School
Kendon Dr
Cherington Road
Wellington Wk
Kelston Road
A&E
Kingsholm Road
Longford Av
Charlton Road
Charlton Gdns
Charlton Mead Drive
Tereslake Gn
Pensfield Park
Stream Cl
Parkers Cl
Bindon Dr
Dorester Cl
Drive
Chakeshill
Bracewell Gdns
Turnbridge Rd
Redshelf Wk
Briarside Road
Rockstowes Wy
Wye Croft Cl
Chetwode Cl
Homeleaze Rd
Park Road
Maggs Cl
Dunmail Primary School
Dunmail Road
Ennerdale Road
Lanercost Road
Greystoke Avenue
Council Bldg
Royston Wk
Avn Cl
Eastleigh Rd
Westleigh Rd
Cranmore Crs
Ringwood Crs
Berry Hl Cl
Charfield Road
Coleford Road
Lydney Road
Shetland Rd
Wilton Cl
Ashburton Rd
Danbury Crs
Sarum Crs
Bradwell Gv
Delvin Rd
Tuffley Rd
Cranham Rd
SOUTHMEAD ROAD
Waterdale Gdns
1 grid square represents 500 metres

Stoke Gifford
Filton
Harry Stoke
E
F
G
H
I
27
40
52
53
61
62
80
79
78
2
3
4
5
Northway
Filton Hill Primary School
Blenheim Drive
Lower House Crescent
Canberra Grove
Filton Avenue
Meadowsweet Av
Bude Road
Conygre Grove
Bridgman Grove
Council Building
Charles Rd
Warren Road
Holmdale Road
Hunter's Way
Ventnor Rd
A4174
Station Road
Mackie Road
Mackie Grove
Mackie Avenue
Roycroft Rd
Stanley Av
Stanley Crs
Nutfield Gv
Abbey Wood Business Park
Emma-Chris Way
The Sidings
Pilkington Cl
STATION ROAD
Abbey Wood Business Park
Superstore
Filton Abbey Wood Station
Wallscourt Rd
Mortimer Road
Ninth Av
Kipling Rd
Eighth Avenue
Ashley Down Old Boys RC
Lockleaze School
Bonnington Walk
Hogarth Walk
Eastlake Close
Stothard Road
Landseer Avenue
Thorncroft Cl
Highmore Gdns
South Gloucestershire
Hatchet Road
Constantine Av
Samian Wy
Ratcliffe Dr
Gatesby Md
Albany
Dumaine Av
Hawthorn Wy
Touchstone Av
Fabian Dr
Travers Wk
St Michaels CE Prim Sch
Rock Lane
Barn Owl Wy
Field Farm Close
Stoke Gifford Medical Centre
Beaufort Crs
North Road
The Green
Britannia Crs
Buckingham Dr
Gloucester Cl
Kent Cl
Sandringham Road
York Close
Gatcombe Dr
Elizabeth Crs
Hatchet La
Bristol Parkway Station
Church Rd
Church Road
Highfields Cl
Swallows Ct
New Road
Brierly Furlong
Filton High School
City of Bristol College
Whitley Md
Railton Jones Cl
Westfield Lane
Harry Stoke Road
Fox Den Road
Express by Holiday Inn
Great Stoke Way
Lime Kiln Cl
Fox Den Rd
Superstore
Filton La
FILTON ROAD
The Avenue
The Gardens
Crescent
Bristol Business Park
Coldharbour Lane
University of the West of England (Frenchay Campus)
Cemetery
Casson Dr
Hawksmoor La
Wright Wy
Lancelot Rd
Paxton
Lutyens Cl
Trellick Wk
Jellicoe Av
Parnell Rd
Wren Cl
Thomas
Stoke Lane
PO

40
28
39
53
64
63
Great Stoke
Harry Stoke
Hambrook
Frenchay
Whites
Brom Heath
Junction 19
Junction 1
M4
M32
A4174
B4058
B4427
OLD GLOUCESTER ROAD
BRISTOL RD
BRISTOL ROAD
Old Gloucester Road
Bristol Parkway Station
Stoke Gifford Medical Centre
St Michaels CE Prim Sch
Holiday Inn
Bristol Business Park
Cemetery
Frenchay Hospital
A&E
Frenchay Village Museum
Frenchay CE Primary School
Hambrook Lane
Curtis Lane
Church Road
Hunts Gnd Rd
Rock Lane
Field Farm Close
Brins Close
Halls Gardens
Kings Dr
Adelante Cl
Parkway
Simmonds Vw
Trevelyan Wk
Touchstone Av
Dorcas Av
Dumaine Av
Ratcliffe Drive
Fabian Dr
Beaufort Crs
Highfields Cl
Whitley Md
Railton Jones Cl
Westfield Lane
Harry Stoke Road
Players Close
Mapstone Close
Sturden Lane
Sunnyside Lane
The Stream
Maules La
Filton Road
Common Mead Lane
Coldharbour Lane
The Avenue
The Crescent
The Gardens
Fernbrook Cl
Filton Rd
Lynton Way
Harford Dr
Penn Drive
Beckspool Road
Manor Place
Park Crescent
Elliott Av
Riverwood Rd
Grove Bank
Marlborough Dr
The Pk
Wadham Dr
Malmains Drive
Homestead Gdns
Grange Pk
Cleeve Road
Valley Walkway
Beckspool Rd
Begbrook Park
Froomshaw Road
Follot Close
Stanshaw Road
Oaklands Drive
Sterncourt Rd
Bradeston Grove
The Newlands
Cliff Ct Dr
Church Road
The Common
Frenchay Hill
Chapel La
River Frome
Lancelot Rd
Paxton
Parnell Road
Wren Cl
Stoke Lane
PO
A
B
C
D
1
2
3
4
5
80
79
78

Hicks Common
Winterbourne Down
Kendleshire
Pye Corner
Moorend
Downend
Blackhorse
Vinney
Hambrook Sports Club
Hambrook Primary School
Bromley Heath J&I School
Blackhorse Primary School
St Augustine of Canterbury RC Prim
Downend School
Travel Inn
Surgery
Frome Valley Walkway
River Frome
Down Road
Station Road
Church Road
Mill Road
Moorend Road
Worrel's Lane
Bury Hill
Cuckoo Lane
Church Lane
Coalsack Lane
Badminton Road
Bromley Heath Road
Quaker's Road
Four Acre Road
Blackhorse Lane
Westbourne Road
Park Road
A432
A4174
A4058
M4
Folly Brook
The Brooms
29
42
55
54
65
66
78
79
80

42
Rathbone Close
Ram
Hill
Broad La
Henfield
30
A
B
C
D
67
68
80
79
78
Ram Hill
Park La
Huckford La
A432
1
2
3
4
5
The Kendleshire Golf Club
Serridge House
Henfield Road
Ruffet
Road
Kendleshire
Bitterwell Close
Henfield
Golf Course
Coalsack Lane
ROAD
Boxhedge
Farm
Lane
The
Hollows
Cooks Lane
Henfield Business Park
M4
41
The Brooms
Westons
Brake
A4174
Folly Brook
Westerleigh Road
Farendell Rd
Longmead Rd
Westons Hill Drive
Patch
Howsmoor
Lane
Salmons Way
Bye Mead
Travel Inn
Cousins Way
Hicks Av
Thomas Avenue
Hill Close
Lyde Green
Emerson
55
Meadgate
Mendip Crs
Dibden Lane
Adderly Gate
PO
1 grid square represents 500 metres

Besom Lane
E
F
31
G
H
69
70
80
Westerleigh
Jorrocks Estate
Westerleigh Road
Newman Close
Broad Lane
Mill Crs
PO
The Quadrangle
Shorthill Road
Old Mill Close
1
Beanwood Farm
2
B4465
Westerleigh Road
Westerle Hill
79
B4465
3
Cliff Farm
Westerleigh Crematorium
Leigh Lane
Leigh Lane
4
Leigh Farm
WESTERLEIGH ROAD
78
Batchfield Lan
M4
5
69
70
56
E
F
G
57
H
Parkfield
Road
St Aldam's Ash Farm

1 grid square represents 500 metres

E
F
G
H
Battery Point
Swimming Pool
Woodlands Road
46
47
Woodhill
Woodhill Bay
Kilkenny Bay
Esplanade Road
Lake Road
Beach Road West
Rodmoor Rd
Battery Lane
Woodhill Road
The Knoll
Pier Road
Pier Cl
East Wd Pl
Leigh View Road
Sally Hl
Burlington Road
Fircliff Pk
South Vw
Woodhill Av
South Av
Seville Rd
Seville Ct
Gardner Road
Beach Rd E
Lower Burlington Rd
A369 STATION ROAD
Portishead Primary Sch
Parish Wharf Leisure Centre
Police Station
Cabstand
Harbour Road
Harbour Rd
Harbour Road Trading Estate
Portbury Wharf
Portishead Business Park
Old Mill Road
WYNDHAM WAY A369
Raleigh Rise
Springfield Rd
West Hill
Kilkenney Pl
Nr Gdn
White Pk Ldg
Combe Av
Combe Fields
Way
Ferndale Rd
Combe Rd
Stoke Rd
Orchrd Cl
West Hl Gdns
Friary Rd
Avon Way
est Hill
PO
Hghlnds Rd
Chnnl Vw Rd
Ch Vw Crs
Severn Road
Queen's Av
Ripleside
Briary Road
Leeside
Downside Road
Slade Road
B3124 HIGH STREET
Victoria Sq
Portishead Health Centre
Albert Rd
Travel Inn
Serbert Wy
Serbert Rd
Quays Av
Conference Av
Peartree Fld
Galingale Wy
3
46
Tydeman Rd
Lambourn
Roath Road
Church Cl
Vc Cl
Cncl Bldg
Halletts Wy
Rc Cl
Brampton Way
Lower Down Road
The Deans
The Rowans
Oak Dr
Downs
Cedar Wy
Newlands Hill
Will Cl
Birch Gv
Elm Wk
Church Rd North
Church Rd South
St Peters CE Primary School
Bnhm Wy
B Cl
Burford Cl
Clvt Cl
Forester Rd
Tdr Rd
Norfolk Road
Exeter Rd
Winford Cl
Ly Cl
Stff Rd
Denston Dr
Mendip Leisure Cen
Greystoke Business Cen
The Garstons
St Peters Road
ORTISHEAD
St Mary's Road
The Paddock
Court Cl
T Cl
Falcon Cl
Cadbury Rd
Glebe Av
Glebe Rd
Portland Dr
Heron Gdns
Jacobs Meadow
The Bramleys
4
BRISTOL ROAD
B3124 PORTBURY COMMON
Middle Bridge
Capenor Close
Wetlands Lane
Spring Ri
Weston Wd Rd
Greenfield Park
Gordano School
St Joseph's Catholic Primary School
Maysfield Cl
5
Weston Wood
Underwood Road
Honeylands
CLEVEDON ROAD
Cemetery
Clapton Lane
Hollis Av
Mead Rd
North Weston
75
76
77
1
2

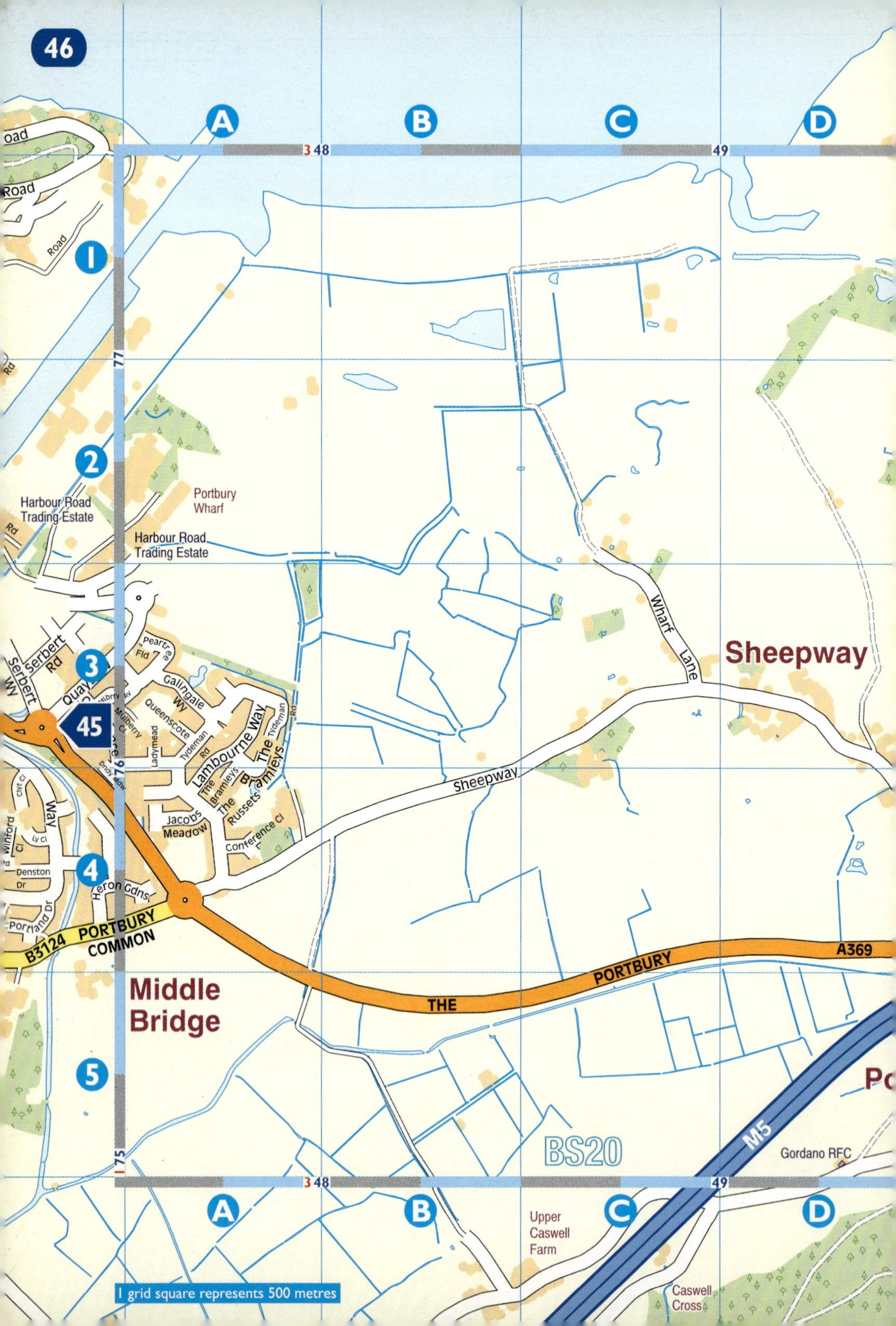
A
B
C
D
348
49
1
2
3
4
5
77
76
175
Road
Road
Road
Rd
Portbury Wharf
Harbour Road Trading Estate
Harbour Road Trading Estate
Rd
Serbert Rd
Serbert
Quay
Peartree Fld
Galingale Wy
Queenscote
Mulberry Cl
Ladymead
Tydeman Rd
Lambourne Way
The Tydeman Rd
The Bramleys
The Bramleys
The Russets
Jacobs Meadow
Conference Cl
Dndy Mdw
Way
Wilford
Denston Dr
Portland Dr
Heron Gdns
45
B3124 PORTBURY COMMON
Middle Bridge
Sheepway
Sheepway
Wharf Lane
THE PORTBURY
A369
M5
BS20
Gordano RFC
Upper Caswell Farm
Caswell Cross
Po
1 grid square represents 500 metres

The Royal Portbury Dock
E
F
G
34
H
50
51
Road
Marsh La
St George's
Gordano Road
Portbury Sawmills Industrial Estate
Royal
Portbury
Dock
Road
Marsh Lane
Redland Rd
City of Bristol
North Somerset
77
1
2
3
4
5
First Avenue
Portbury Way
Garonor Way
Gordano Way
Bradley Road
Royal Portbury Dock Road
Lodw
48
76
Marsh Lane
M5
Junction 19
A369 THE PORTBURY HUNDRED
Beechwood Rd
Church Rd
The
Debecca's La
Gordano Rd
Priory
Ol P Rd
Priory Gdns
Wyndham Crs
Mnr Cl
Church Rd
Hay Ct
Walnut Cl
Days Inn Hotel
Gordano Service Area
Priory Rd
Church La
St Marys CE VA Primary School
High Street
Priory Farm Trading Estate
High St
ury
St George's Hill
A369
EAST GORD
Rectory
MARTCOMBE
Forge End
Brittan Place
Hillside
75
Mill Close
Mill Lane
Portbu

Shirehampton
Lodway
Pill
EASTON-IN-GORDANO
Ham Green
River Avon
City of Bristol
North Somerset
M5
A4
PORTWAY
AVONMOUTH ROAD
LOWER HIGH STREET
HIGH STREET
B4054
MARTCOMBE ROAD
Surgery
Avon Riverside Estate
Avonbank Industrial Centre
Avon Gorge Industrial Est
Portway Trading Estate
Robin Cousins Sports Centre
Avonbridge Trading Estate
Avon Primary School
Council Building
Shirehampton Prim Sch
Health Cen
Prim Sch
Cem
Shirehampton Stn
City & Port of Bristol Social & Sports Club
Orchard View (Ham Green Hospital)
Heywood Health Centre
Crockerne CE Primary School
St Katherines School
Markham Farm
Sunnyside Farm Trading Estate
Kings Weston Avenue
Old Quarry Road
Meadow Grove
Old Park Rd
West Town
Watling Wy
Barrow Hill Rd
Barrow Hill Crs
Fairford Rd
Springfield Av
Priory Road
Walton Rd
Church Leaze
Bradley Crs
Station Road
Station Rd
St Bernard's Rd
Pembroke Rd
Penpole Av
Oaktree Ct
Home Gnd
Dursley Road
Nibley Rd
Coaley Rd
Myrtle Dr
Avon Rd
Marine Pde
Severn Rd
Mariner's Wy
Hardwick Rd
Monmouth Rd
Lodway Gdns
Lodway Cl
Oak Gv
Stoneyfields
Breaches
Trinder Rd
Beechwood Rd
Church Rd
Debecca's La
Gordano Gdns
Gordano Rd
Lodway
Newsome Av
Easton Rd
Churchpath Rd
Heywood Rd
Watchhouse Rd
Underbanks
Mt Pleasant Ter
Eirene Ter
Rudgleigh Rd
Bramley Cl
The Moorings
Westward Drive
Cross Lanes
Crockerne Drive
Davin Crs
Overhill
Anchor Wy
Brookside
Orchard Lea
Ham Green
The Green
Macrae Rd
Hart Cl
Fitzharding Road
Sturmey Wy
Cabot Way
Lime Tree Gv
Pill Road
Avon Walkway
Priory Rd
Priory Gdns
Wyndham Crs
Rectory Road
Hay Ct
Church Rd
Walnut Cl
George's Hill
Victoria Road
Catherine St
Barrack's La
Merrimans Rd
I
2
3
4
5
A
B
C
D
34
47
58
35
3 52
53
77
76
1 75
1 grid square represents 500 metres

Coombe Dingle
Sea Mills
Shirehampton Park
Golf Course
Weston Park Primary School
Kingsweston Special School
Council Building
Twyford House CC
Shirehampton CC
Shirehampton Park Golf Club
Sea Mills Infant School
Sea Mills Junior Sch
Surg
Manor Farm AFC
Sea Mills Station
Stoke Bishop CE Primary School
Chapel Pill Farm
Leigh Court Business Centre
City of Bristol
North Somerset
Avon Walkway
River Avon
SHIREHAMPTON ROAD B4054
B4054
B4057
SYLVAN WAY
A4162
DINGLE ROAD
A4 PORTWAY
A4
Southwood Drive East
Moor Grove
Napier Miles Road
Barrowmead
Avenue
Westbury Lane
Brookleaze
Woodleaze
Riverleaze
Roman Way
Glenavon Park
Mariners Dr
Old Sneed Park
Church
Stoke Paddock Rd
Cheyne Road
Newlyn Av
Lyndale Av
Cedar Pk
Trym Side
Meadway
Sea Mills Lane
Avon Way
Branscombe Rd
Horseshoe Dr
Cavendish Gdns
Bishops Knoll
Bramble Dr
Bramble La
Chancel Cl
Knoll Hill
Valerian Cl
Riverside Cl
Northleach Wk
Burford Gv
Sunny Hill
West Pde
The Crs
Blaise Wk
Wood End Wk
Coombe Dale
St Edyth's Rd
Weston Cl
Ashcroft Rd
Dingle Vw
Hallen Dr
Aldercombe Road
Southwood Drive
Arbutus Drive
Bowden Grove Av
Long Acres Cl
Pitchcombe Gdns
Briercliffe Road
Haytor Pk
Coombe Br Av
Wyedale Av
Elberton Road
Lux Furlong
Alveston Grove
Falland Cresent
Bowerleaze
Clapton Wk
Trym Cross Rd
Druid
St Hilary Cl
Stoke
Avon V
Ardern Cl
Benville
Badenham
Middleton Rd
Moorend Gdns
Sadlier Cl
Tufton Av
Weston Drive
Cross
Lane
E F G H I
1 2 3 4 5
54 55
75 76 77
36 50 59
PO
Sne

50
Coombe Dingle
36
37
A
B
C
D
1
2
3
4
5
49
60
Westbury on Trym
Stoke Bishop
Sneyd Park
BS9
A4162 CANFORD LANE
CANFORD ROAD
DINGLE ROAD
FALCONDALE ROAD
WESTBURY ROAD
WESTBURY HILL
HENBURY HILL
HENBURY ROAD
HIGH ST
A4018
B4054
STOKE LANE
PARRY'S LANE
CROSS ELMS LANE
A4 PORTWAY
River Avon
Cemetery
Canford Crematorium
Surgery
Works
Badminton Junior School
Elmlea J&I School
Stoke Bishop CE Primary School
The Red Maids School
St Ursulas High School
University Hall
Trinity Theological College
Durdham Down
Coombe Lane
Stoke Grove
Great Brockeridge
Druid Hill
Old Sneyd Av
Old Sneyd Road
Mariners Drive
Church Road
Stoke Hill
Pitch and Pay Lane
Downleaze
Hollybush Lane
Saville Road
Stoke Paddock Rd
Woodland Grove
Rayleigh Rd
Sandyleaze
Briercliffe Road
Reedley Road
Shaplands
Eastmead Lane
Hazelwood Road
Seawalls Road
Ivywell Road
Rockleaze
Ladies Mile
Julian Rd
Knoll Hill
Glenavon Pk
1 grid square represents 500 metres

Elmfield Special School
E
F
G
H
38
58
59
SOUTHMEAD ROAD
Kelston Road
Wellington Wk
Southmead Hospital
Horfield Primary School
Horfield Sports Centre
FILTON ROAD
A38
Police Station
Surgery
SOUTHMEAD ROAD
Home Gnd
Eastfield Rd
Cherington Road
Farington Rd
Kendon Drive
Bishop Mnr Road
Maskelyne Av
Tilling Road
Dorian Road
St Lucia Crs
Inkerman Cl
Wellington Road
Bishopthorpe Road
Horfield Common
Council Building
GLOUCESTER ROAD
Wessex Avenue
Bayswater Road
Highbury Rd
I
Eastfield
Henleaze
West Broadway
Abbots Way
Francombe Gv
B4056
B4468
Grange Park
Dorset Rd
Oakwood Rd
Rockside Dr
Hill Grove
The Crescent
Laurie Crs
Kellaway Crs
Wellington Hill
B4469
Horf
2
Bristol Rovers FC & Bristol RFC (Memorial Stadium)
Golden Hill
Henleaze Pk Dr
Ridgehill
Wanscow Walk
Knights Close
The Dr
Henleaze Pk
Woodhouse Gv
Church Road
Strathmore Rd
Quarrington Rd
Lawrence Gv
Henley Grove
Holmes Grove
Owen Gv
Springfield Grove
Henleaze J&I School
Claremont Special Sch
KELLAWAY AVENUE
Longmead
Maple Road
Ashley Down J&I School
3
Springfield Av
Falcondale Way
Brean Down Av
Russell Gv
Radnor Road
Avenue Road
Radnor Bus Cen
HM Prison
ASHLEY DOWN Rd
52
Merton Rd
Works
Queen's Drive
Kings Drive
Bishop Road
Cambridge Rd
Dongola Av
Seymour Rd
Muller Av
Queen's Rd
Ralph Rd
LINDEN ROAD
King's Avenue
Bishop Road Primary School
Monmouth Rd
Bishopston House Clinic
Nevil Road
Kennington Av
4
City of Bristol College (Brunel Centre)
Westbury Park
Paulton Drive
St Bonaventures RC Primary Sch
Melbourne Rd
Cricklade Rd
Ashley
Gloucestershire CCC (County Ground)
COLDHARBOUR ROAD
Harcourt Rd
Cranbrook Road
B4054
Bishopston
Egerton Rd
City of Bristol College (Brunel Centre)
Berkeley Road
Metford Road
Logan Road
Bristol North Baths
Sommerville Road
Ashton Park Rd
5
Redland
Claremont
CRANBROOK ROAD
Hazelton Rd
Shadwell Rd
Wolseley Rd
Raglan Rd
GLOUCESTER ROAD
Belmont Rd
St Andrew's Park
Works
Williamson Rd
61
Redland High School for Girls
Clarendon Rd
Police Stn
Surg
BS6
Montpelier
Windsor Road
Burghley Road
ASHLEY HILL

52
38
51
62
A
B
C
D
1
2
3
4
5
Horfield
Ashley Down
Montpelier
Lockleaze
BS7
Horfield Sports Centre
Ashley Down Old Boys RC
Filton Avenue J&I School
Horfield Health Centre
Bristol Civil Service Sports Club
Bristol Rovers FC & Bristol RFC (Memorial Stadium)
Romney Avenue J&I School
Police Station
Superstore
Heath House Priory Hospital
Glenfrome Prim Sch
City of Bristol College (Brunel Centre)
Gloucestershire CCC (County Ground)
Sefton Park J&I School
St Thomas More Catholic School
Wallis Estate
Works
Pur Down
St Andrew's Park
Council Building
Ashley Down J&I School
IKEA
Retail Park
St Werburgh's Prim School
Eastville Health Centre
Sikh Temple
Parkway Trading Estate
Junction
GLOUCESTER ROAD A38
FILTON ROAD
MULLER ROAD
B4469
B4052
ASHLEY DOWN ROAD
ASHLEY HILL
STAPLETON ROAD
M32
BELL HILL
Sir John's Lane
Lockleaze Road
Constable Road
Romney Avenue
Filton Avenue
Wessex Avenue
Highbury Rd
Dorchester Road
Camborne Road
Wordsworth
Shaldon Road
Stottbury Road
Rousham Road
Glenfrome Road
Eastgate Road
Narroways Rd
Kennington Avenue
Seymour Rd
Nevil Road
Sefton Park Rd
Montreal Avenue
Shakespeare Avenue
Toronto Road
Doone Rd
Dorian Road
Landseer Avenue
Brangwyn Grove
Hogarth Walk
Bonnington Walk
Dovercourt Road
Downend Road
Springfield Av
Bromley Rd
Queen's Rd
Ralph Road
Muller Av
Ashley Down
Melita Road
Leopold Road
Windsor Road
Maurice Rd
Walsingham Road
Cotswold Road
Heath House Lane
Heath House La
Lindsay Rd
Crowther Park
Elmcroft Crs
Allfoxton Rd
Dormer Road
Ingmire Rd
Heyford Av
Glenfrome
Woburn Road
Heath Road
Cottrell Road
Welsford Rd
Averay Road
Colston's Collegiate School
1 grid square represents 500 metres

A&E
Frenchay Village Museum
40
62
63
Casson Dr
Hawksmoor
Wright
Lancelot Rd
Paxton
Lutyens Cl
Trellick Wk
Admiral Cl
Jellicoe Av
Parnell
Wren Cl Road
Thomas Wy
Stoke Lane
Harbour
Oaklands Drive
Follot Close
Froomshaw Road
Begbrook Park
The Newlands
Pearces
Cliff Ct Dr
Sterncourt Rd
Bradeston Grove
Stanshaw Road
Kynges Mill Cl
South Gloucestershire
City of Bristol
River Frome
FRENCHAY PARK ROAD
Five Acre Drive
Clark Dr
Broomhill
M32
Nuthatch Drive
Wren Drive
Wytherlies Drive
Nuthatch Gardens
Begbrook Lane
Dryleaze Road
Brockworth Crs
Frome Valley Road
Alberton Road
Begbrook Dr
Stonechat Gdns
Ham La
Sheldrake Drive
Begbrook Primary School
Brook La
Willow Bed Close
Perrymans Close
Duchess Way
Long Meadow
Bryn Cl
Brinkworthy Rd
River View
Broom Hill
The Chippings
B4458 PARK ROAD
Hedgemead Vw
University of the West of England (Glenside Campus)
Fromeside Clinic
Blackberry Hill Hospital
Fishponds
University of the West of England (St Matthias Campus)
College Road
College Ct
Glaisdale Rd
College House
Elfin Rd
Oldbury Court Road
Victoria Park
Symington
54
The Chine
Estcourt Gardens
Wickham Hill
Wickham Court
Wickham Gln
Blackberry Hill
Blackberry Avenue
Small La
Small Lane
Manor Road
Snowdon Road
Pound Dr
Pound La
Eastbury Rd
N Devon Rd
Lambrook Road
Colston Hill
Stapleton
Timber Dene
Trendlewood Park
Earlsmead
Colston Dale
Grove Road
Whitefield Fishponds Community School
New Buildings
Snowdon Close
Channon's Hill
Station Av
Courtfield Gv
CE Prim Sch
Guinea La
Beechwood Rd
Radley Road
Coronation Av
Brook Road
Fishponds Health Cen
Station Road
New Station Rd
Graeme Cl
New Station Wy
Superstore
Everest Road
Everest Av
Grove Road
Grove Park Terrace
Alexandra Pk
Stoke View Business Park
ROAD
Station Way
Hockeys La
Parnall Rd
Parnall Road Industrial Estate
Goodneston Road
Filwood Road
FOREST ROAD
Lodge Causeway
Works
Lodge Causeway Trading Estate
Avon Business Park
Mendip View Avenue
Enfield Road
Bexley
Chewton
Tredegar Rd
B4465
Redhill Drive
Redhill Cl
Thingwall
Hawkesbury Road
Elmgrove Rd
Brentry Road
Ernestville Rd
Dunkirk Rd
Star La
Alcove Rd
FISHPONDS
A432
Ridgeway
Ridgeway Park Cemetery
Ashdene Avenue
Elmhurst Av
Oakdene Av
Park Av
Marina Gardens
Balaclava Industrial Estate
Chester Park J&I School
Honiton Rd
Abingdon Road
Dominion Road
Balaclava Road
Park Pl
Ridgeway
Road
Vera Road
Tiverton Wk
Rowan Close
Mayfield Av
Chatsworth
RC Primary School
Charminster Rd
PO
Works
School Cl
Park
Stonebridge
Hill
Gloucester St
Edwr St
Rivers Lane
63
Clay Hill
Moorlands Rd
Mayfield Park North
Mayfield Park South
BERKELEY RD
B4048
LODGE
Elgin Rd
Fitzroy Rd
Chester Pk Road
Argyle
Linden
Russell
Greenbank Cemetery
ROSE GREEN
Wainbrook Dr
The Glades
Clay Bottom
Ridgeway Industrial Centre
Superstore
Fishponds Trading Estate
Maggs La
Anthea Rd
Oak Lane
Holly Lodge Cl
Holly Lodge Road
Atlas Close
Holly Cl
ROAD
E
F
G
H
I
2
3
4
5

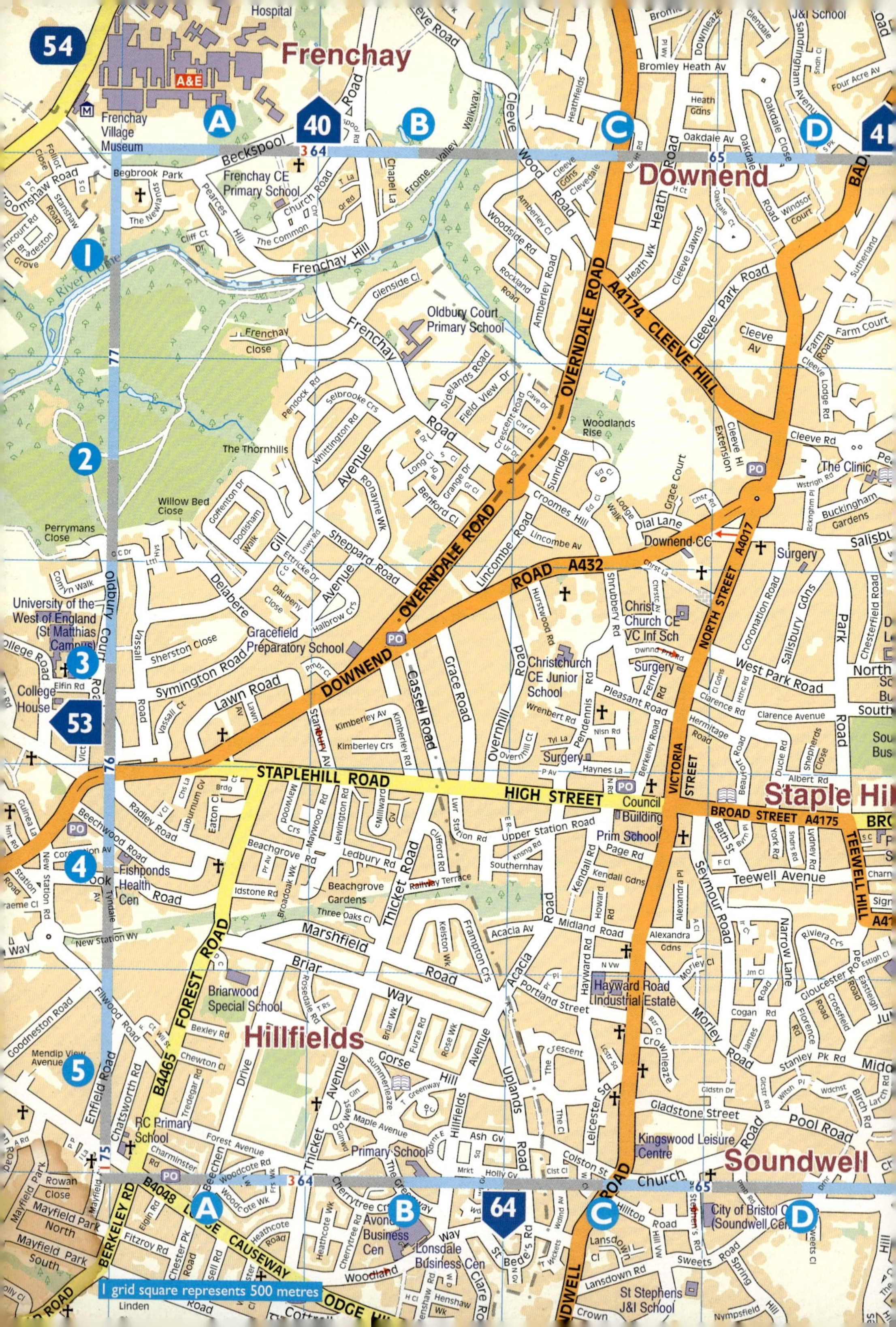

54
Hospital
Frenchay
A&E
Frenchay Village Museum
A
40
B
C
D
41
Beckspool
3 64
65
Downend
Bromley Heath Av
Heath Gdns
Oakdale Av
Oakdale Close
Four Acre Av
Sandringham Avenue
J&I School
Begbrook Park
Frenchay CE Primary School
The Newlands
Pearces Hill
Church Road
The Common
Chapel La
Frome Valley Walkway
Cleeve Wood Road
Frenchay Hill
Cliff Ct Dr
Roman Road
Stanshaw Road
Bradeston Grove
River Frome
Glenside Cl
Oldbury Court Primary School
Woodside Rd
Rockland Road
Amberley Road
Amberley Cl
Heath Wk
Cleeve Lawns
Cleeve Park Road
Cleeve Av
Farm Court
Sutherland
Frenchay Close
Frenchay Road
Sidelands Road
Field View Dr
Crescent Road
Selbrooke Crs
Pendock Rd
Whittington Rd
Avenue
Ronayne Wk
Long Cl
Benford Cl
Grange Dr
OVERNDALE ROAD
A4174 CLEEVE HILL
Woodlands Rise
Cleeve Hill Extension
Cleeve Lodge Rd
Cleeve Rd
The Clinic
Buckingham Gardens
Salisbury
The Thornhills
Willow Bed Close
Perrymans Close
Goffenton Dr
Dodisham Walk
Gill Avenue
Sheppard Road
Etticke Dr
Daubeny Close
Halbrow Crs
Croomes Hill
Lincombe Road
Lincombe Av
Sunridge
Lodge Walk
Grace Court
Dial Lane
Downend CC
A4017
NORTH STREET
Surgery
Comyn Walk
University of the West of England (St Matthias Campus)
Oldbury Court Road
Delabere
Vassall
Sherston Close
Symington Road
Gracefield Preparatory School
DOWNEND ROAD A432
PO
Cassell Road
Grace Road
Hurstwood Rd
Shrubbery Rd
Christ Church CE VC Inf Sch
Christchurch CE Junior School
Coronation Road
Salisbury Gdns
Park Road
Chesterfield Road
West Park Road
North
College Road
Elfin Rd
College House
53
Vassall Ct
Lawn Road
Stanbury Av
Kimberley Av
Kimberley Crs
Kimberley Rd
Overnhill Road
Overnhill Ct
Wrenbert Rd
Pendennis Rd
Pleasant Road
Berkeley Road
Clarence Rd
Clarence Avenue
Hermitage Road
Beaufort Road
Ducie Rd
Shepherds Close
Albert Rd
Haynes La
STAPLEHILL ROAD
HIGH STREET
Council Building
VICTORIA STREET
Staple Hill
BROAD STREET A4175
TEEWELL HILL
Teewell Avenue
Radley Road
Laburnum Gv
Eaton Cl
Beechwood Road
Coronation Av
Fishponds Health Cen
Station Road
New Station Rd
Tyndale Av
New Station Wy
Beachgrove Rd
Maywood Rd
Lewington Rd
Millward Gv
Ledbury Rd
Idstone Rd
Broadoak Wk
Beachgrove Gardens
Three Oaks Cl
Thicket Road
Clifford Rd
Station Rd
Railway Terrace
Upper Station Road
Southernhay
Prim School
Page Rd
Kendall Gdns
Kendall Rd
Howard Rd
Seymour Road
Alexandra Pl
Narrow Lane
Riviera Crs
Marshfield Road
Briar Way
Kelston Wk
Frampton Crs
Acacia Av
Acacia Road
Midland Road
Alexandra Gdns
Morley Cl
Gloucester Rd
Crossfield
Eastleigh
FOREST ROAD
B4465
Briarwood Special School
Rosedale Rd
Portland Street
Hayward Rd
Hayward Road Industrial Estate
Morley Road
Cogan Rd
Florence Rd
Stanley Pk Rd
Hillfields
Bexley Rd
Chewton Cl
Tredegar Rd
Drive
Goodneston Road
Mendip View Avenue
Fitwood Road
Enfield Road
Chatsworth Rd
Gorse Hill
Summerleaze
Furze Rd
Rose Wk
Avenue
Uplands Road
The Crescent
Crownleaze
Gladstone Street
Pool Road
Birch Rd
RC Primary School
Maple Avenue
Hillfields Avenue
Ash Gv
Leicester Sq
Kingswood Leisure Centre
Soundwell
Forest Avenue
Charminster Rd
Beechen Drive
Woodcote Rd
Primary School
Colston St
Holly Gv
Church Road
1 75
B4048
Cherrytree Cr
The Greenway
Avon Business Cen
Lonsdale Business Cen
64
Bede's Rd
Hilltop Road
Lansdown Cl
Stephen's Rd
City of Bristol College (Soundwell Cen)
Sweets Road
Spring Hill
Mayfield Park North
Mayfield Park South
Rowan Close
BERKELEY ROAD
Fitzroy Rd
Chester Pk Road
Elgin Rd
Sell Rd
LODGE CAUSEWAY
Heathcote Road
Heathcote Wk
Woodland Way
Clare Rd
Lansdown Rd
St Stephens J&I School
Crown
Nympsfield
Linden
1 grid square represents 500 metres

Blackhorse
Vinney Green
Emerson's Green
Mangotsfield
BS16
Blackhorse Primary School
Downend School
Cemetery
Stanbridge Primary School
Barley Close Prim Sch
Council Building
Mangotsfield CE Primary School
Police Station
Mangotsfield United FC
Mangotsfield School
Mangotsfield Golf Club
Deers Wood Primary Sch
Travel Inn
Golf Course
A4174
A4175
B4465
MANGOTSFIELD ROAD
COSSHAM STREET
POMPHREY HILL
STATION ROAD
STATION RD LINK
Westerleigh Road
Dibden Lane
Elm Tree Av
Springfield Road
Stockwell Drive
Springleaze
Jubilee Crescent
Blackhorse Road
Emersons Green Lane
Church Farm Road
Richmond Road
St James's St
Northcote Road
Burley Grove
Gerrish Avenue
Rodway Hill
Manor Road
Bridge Road
Charnhill Drive
Hot Water La
Carsons Rd
Shaw Cl
Hill House Road
Fairlyn Drive
Bridge Rd
42
56
65
E
F
G
H
1
2
3
4
5
66
67
76
77
75

56
42
43
55
66
A
B
C
D
1
2
3
4
5
368
69
77
76
75
Lyde Green
Parkfiel
Pucklechur
Shortwood
Siston
Shortwood Lodge
Dennisworth Farm
Northmea Farm
Lodge Farm
Golf Course
A4174
B4465
MAIN ROAD B4465
SHORTWOOD HILL
SHORTWOOD
HILL
Cattybrook Road North
Cattybrook Rd
Parkfield Road
The Vale
Park
Siston Lane
Bridge Rd
Emrs Wy
Bampton Cl
Bishop Rd
Corinum Cl
Pinkers Md
Applin Gn
1 grid square represents 500 metres

Pucklechurch
M4
Lane
WESTERLEIGH ROAD
E
F
G
H
70
71
St Aldam's
Ash Farm
I
77
Lower Fie
Farm
2
Pucklechurch CE
Primary School
Surgery
Cranford
Farm
Road
Farlands
Edmund
Court
Lansdown
Rd
Castle Road
Feltham
Road
Hill Vw Rd
Homefield Rd
Queen's
Rd
PO
Abson
Rd
Marsh
Farm
Orchard Rd
Poplar Dr
B4465
Dnnswrt
Maple
Wk
Birch Dr
Cedar
Wy
Holly
Cl
3
Becket Court
St
Aldams
Drive
Chrr Ct
Hawkridge Dr
Hoddon Lane
Hoddon
Lane
Hawthorne
Cl
Oak Tree Av
Kestrel Dr
Crs
Eagle
Partridge Rd
Gl Wy
M Rdg
Wd Crs
76
Pucklechurch
Trading Estate
Becket Court
Oak
Tree
Av
Cossham
Rd
Back Lane
Dyrham
Close
Redford
Lane
4
5
Rookery Lane
75
70
71
E
F
67
G
H
Abson

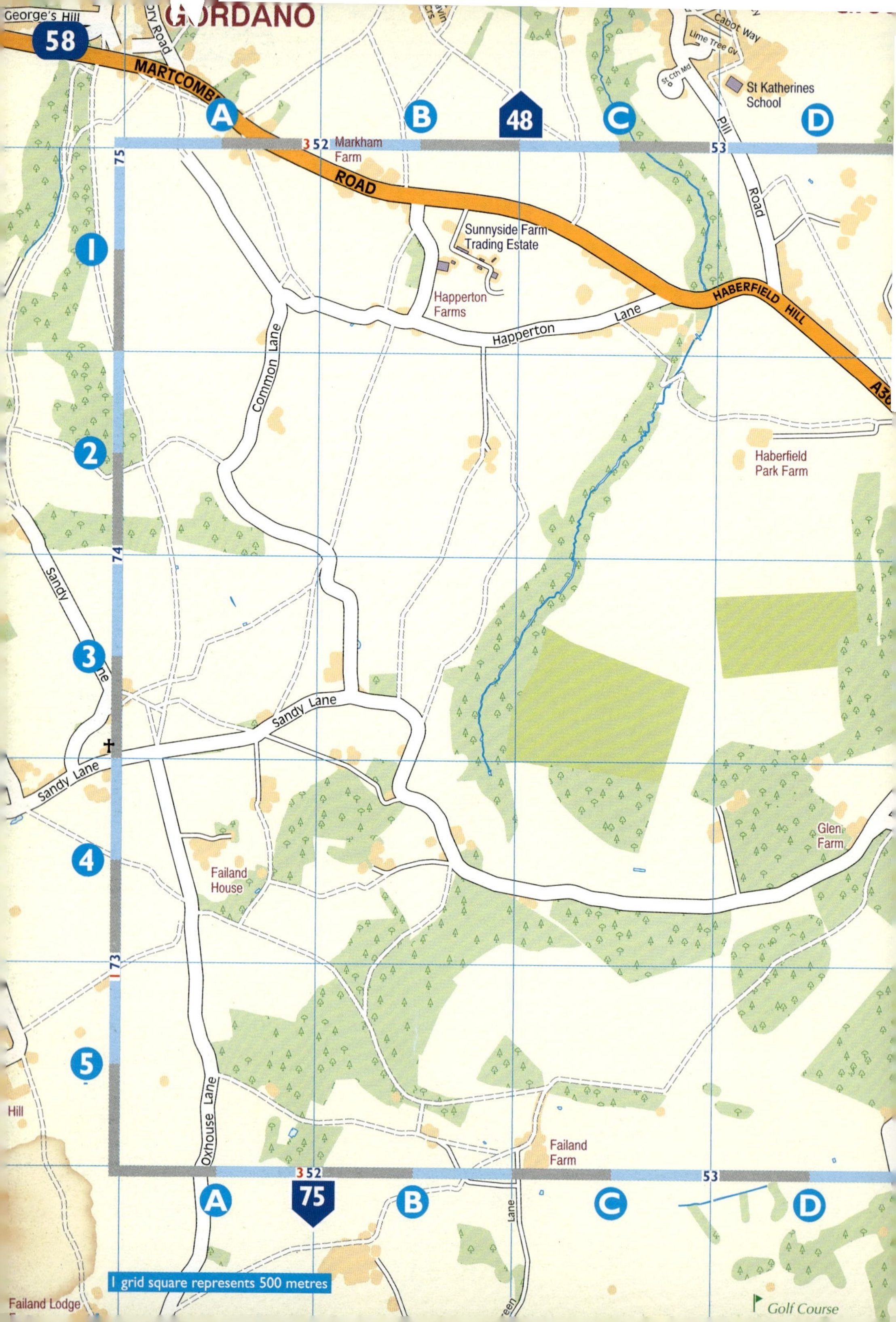

GORDANO
George's Hill
58
MARTCOMBE ROAD
A
B
48
C
D
Cabot Way
Lime Tree Gv
St Cth Md
St Katherines School
Pill Road
Markham Farm
Sunnyside Farm Trading Estate
Happerton Farms
Happerton Lane
HABERFIELD HILL
A36
Common Lane
Haberfield Park Farm
Sandy Lane
Glen Farm
Failand House
Oxhouse Lane
Failand Farm
Hill
Lane
75
1 grid square represents 500 metres
Failand Lodge
Golf Course

Abbots Leigh
Leigh Woods
Leigh Court Business Centre
Church Rd
Church Road
Monarch's Way
Home Farm Road
Harris Lane
Knight Cott Rd
Sandy Lane
Glen Av
Manor Lane
Manor Road
The Mnr Cl
Manor House
A369
ABBOTS LEIGH ROAD
Ashgrove Av
Clifton College Sports Club
Valley Rd
North
BS8
B3129
BEGGAR BUSH LANE
Upper Farm
Cotham Park Rugby Club
A4 PORTWAY
River Avon
Avon Walkway
Bishops Knoll
Bramble La
Chancel Cl
Knoll Hill
Ck Fl Rd
St Mry Rd
E
F
G
H
I
2
3
4
5
54
55
73
74
75
49
60
76
77

60
Sneyd Park
Church
Julian Cl
Pitch And Pay Park
Pitch and Pay Lane
Stoke Hill
Stoke Park Road
South
Downleaze
Bramble Dr
Bramble La
Bishops Knoll
Chancel Cl
Hazelwood Road
Goodeve Rd
Seawalls Road
Avon Gv
Tfr Avenue
Ivywell Road
Julian
Rockleaze
Well House Cl
50
Stoke Road
Clay Pit Rd
Durdham
Torwood Hse Sch
A4 PORTWAY
River Avon
Avon Walkway
Circular Road
Ladies Mile
Council Building
Grove Day
UPPER BELGRAVE ROAD
Westbury Rd
Worrall Mews
Worrall Rd
Downfield Rd
Highland Place
Rd Prim Sch
Wellington Park
Surg
Downfield Rd
Bristol Old Vic Theatre School
Apsley Road
Beaufort Road
Osborne
Duchess Rd
Miles Rd
Clifton Down
Clifton College Preparatory School
Surgery
Butcombe Pre-Prep Sch
Bristol Zoo Gardens
Northcote Rd
Guthrie Rd Sch
All Saints' Rd
Thorndale Mews
Alma V Rd
Alma
PEMBROKE ROAD
B4467
Surgery
A4176 CLIFTON DOWN
College Road
Clifton College
Clifton
Leigh Woods
A4 PORTWAY
BRIDGE VALLEY ROAD
Clifton Down
Cecil Rd
Canynge Road
College Flds
Redgrave Theatre
Clifton Pk Rd
Pembroke Rd
Clifton Cathedral Church
59
Worcester Ter
Cobblestone Ms
Litfield Rd
Percival Road
Clifton Close
Camp Rd
Clifton High Sch & Lower Sch
Park
Avon Gorge Nature Reserve
Surg
Vyvyan Ter
Richmond Mews
The Sisters of the Temple
Down
Clifton
Christchurch Rd
Lansdown Rd
Royal Pk
Kensington Pl
Avon Gorge
Gloucester Row
B3129
Manilla Rd
PO
Lord Chancellors Department
Rodney Htl
CLIFTON DOWN RD
Mortimer Rd
Toll
Clnc
Victoria Sq
Lansdown Place
Htl
Monarch's Way
Nightingale Valley
Suspension Bridge
Sion Hl
Sion Pl
Portland St
Valley Rd
North Road
B3129
Sion La
West Mall
Caledonia Place
Princess Victoria St
Bus Cen
MERCHANTS RD
VICTORIA SQ
The Fosseway
Chester Hosp
ROAD
Vicarage Road
Bannerleigh Rd
Church Road
St Mary Rd
Avon Walkway
A4 HOTWELL ROAD
Princes
Royal York Crescent
Cornwallis Grove
Hensman's Hl
Regents St
Clifton Hl
Wellington Terrace
York Gdns
Leigh Woods
BRIDGE ROAD
Cypress Gdns
The Avon Gorge Hotel
Princes Buildings
Cornwallis Crs
Goldney Av
Polygon Rd
Hotwells
The Polygon
ROWNHAM HILL
Burwalls Road
North Somerset
City of Bristol
Windsor Ter
Granby Hl
Hotwells Prim Sch
Clifton Vale
Goldney Rd
Ambra Vale E
Ambrose Rd
Crosby Rw
Albermarle Terrace
HOTWELL RD
PO
CABOT WY
Charles Pl
Oldfield Pl
MERCHANTS RD
Dowry Place
A369
77
BASIN RD
CUMB
BRUNEL LOCK RD
Cumberland Basin
Council Building
Pooles Whf
1 grid square represents 500 metres

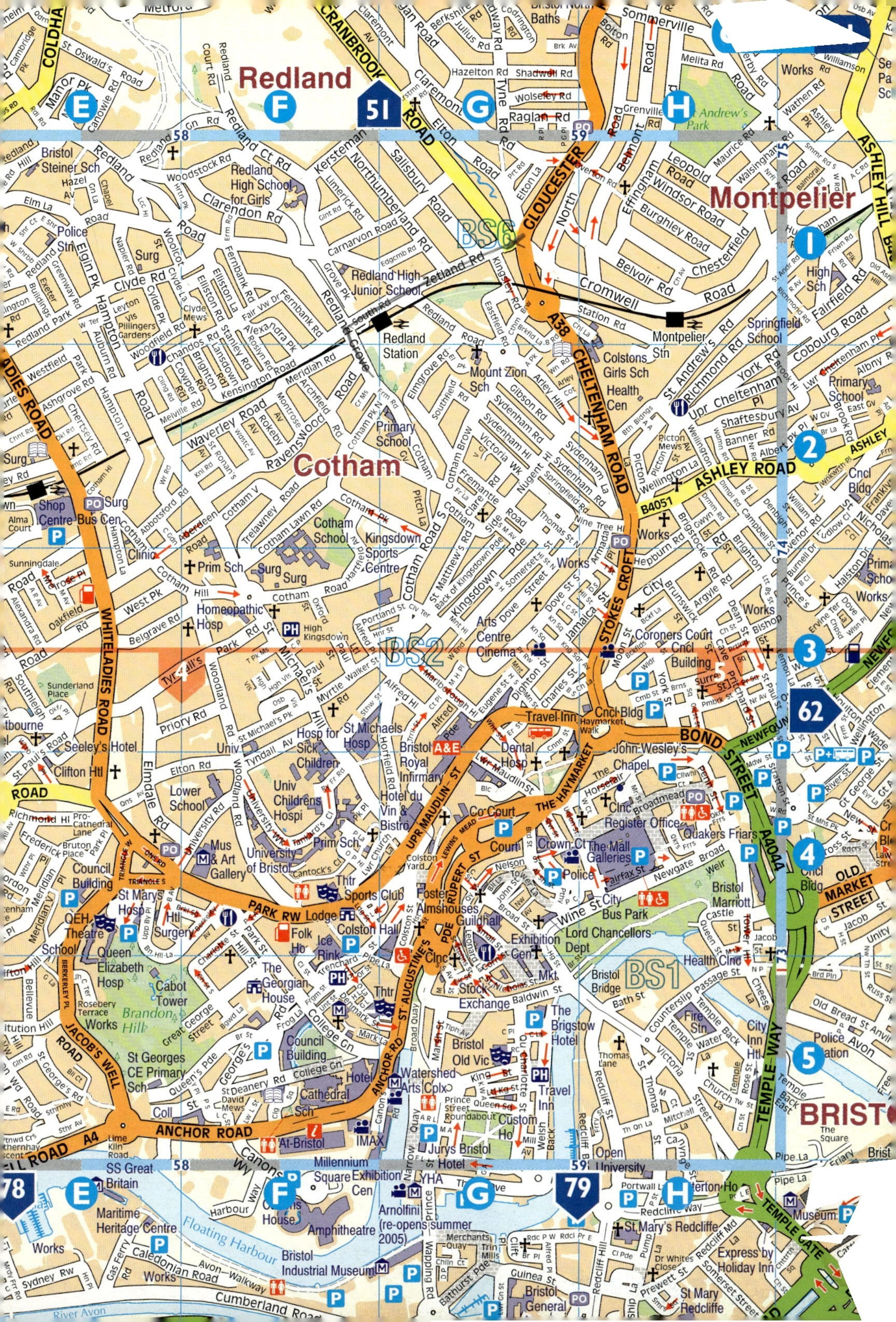

Redland
Cotham
Montpelier
BRIST
BS6
BS2
BS1
E
F
G
H
51
62
78
79
58
59
1
2
3
4
5
Redland Station
Montpelier Stn
Redland High School for Girls
Redland High Junior School
Bristol Steiner Sch
Colstons Girls Sch
Mount Zion Sch
Primary School
Cotham School
Kingsdown Sports Centre
Homeopathic Hosp
High Kingsdown
Arts Centre Cinema
Coroners Court
Cncl Bldg
Travel Inn
Haymarket Walk
John Wesley's Chapel
Bristol Royal Infirmary
Hosp for Sick Children
St Michaels Hosp
Univ Childrens Hospi
University of Bristol
Mus & Art Gallery
Lower School
Seeley's Hotel
Clifton Htl
Council Building
St Marys Hosp
QEH Theatre
Queen Elizabeth Hosp
Cabot Tower
Brandon Hill
The Georgian House
St Georges CE Primary Sch
Council Building
Cathedral
Colston Hall
Foster Almshouses
Guildhall
Exhibition Cen
Stock Exchange
Lord Chancellors Dept
City Bus Park
Police
The Mall Galleries
Register Office
Quakers Friars
Bristol Marriott
Old Vic
The Brigstow Hotel
Watershed Arts Cplx
Jurys Bristol Hotel
Custom Ho
Travel Inn
Health Clnc
City Inn Htl
Police Station
IMAX
At-Bristol
Millennium Square
Exhibition Cen
YHA
SS Great Britain
Maritime Heritage Centre
Amphitheatre
Arnolfini (re-opens summer 2005)
Bristol Industrial Museum
Floating Harbour
River Avon
Express by Holiday Inn
Museum
St Mary Redcliffe
Bristol General
Open University
WHITELADIES ROAD
CHELTENHAM ROAD
GLOUCESTER ROAD
STOKES CROFT
BOND STREET
THE HAYMARKET
UPR MAUDLIN ST
PARK RW
ANCHOR ROAD
JACOB'S WELL ROAD
TEMPLE WAY
TEMPLE GATE
OLD MARKET STREET
ASHLEY ROAD
ASHLEY HILL
CRANBROOK ROAD
A38
A4044
B4051
A4
Cotham Hill
Cotham Road
Cotham Brow
St Michael's Hill
Park Row
Woodland Rd
Elmdale Rd
Tyndall Av
Hampton Rd
Kingsdown Pde
Dove St
Nine Tree Hl
Picton St
Richmond Rd
York Rd
Cromwell Road
Belvoir Rd
Zetland Rd
Waverley Road
Clyde Rd
Westfield
Elton Rd
Clarendon Rd
Redland Ct Rd
Redland Grove
Baldwin St
Broad Quay
Marsh St
King St
Queen Sq
Prince St
Redcliffe Way
Redcliff Hill
Victoria St
Bath St
Cumberland Road
Sommerville Road
Grenville Rd
Sydenham Rd
St Andrew's Rd
Upr Cheltenham Pl
Springfield School

62
52
61
79
Junction
Junction 3
Montpelier
Easton
Barton Hill
BRISTOL
BS2
St Andrew's Park
Ashley Hill B4052
Ashley Road
Stapleton Road
Fishponds Road
M32
Easton Way
A432
Easton Road
B4465
Lawrence Hill
A420
Barrow Road
A4320
St Philips Causeway
Temple Way
A4044
Newfoundland Way A4032
Newfoundland St
Bond Street
Old Market Street
West St
Lamb St
Trinity Rd
Clarence Rd
Temple Gate
Feeder Road
Silverthorne Lane
Gas Lane
Cole Road
Sefton Park J&I School
Parkway Trading Estate
Ashley Trading Est
Wallis Estate
IKEA
Superstore
Retail Park
Council Building
St Werburgh's Prim School
Stapleton Road Station
Millpond Prim Sch
Clinic
Riverside Leisure Cen
St Gabriel's Business Park
Easton Business Centre
Lawnwood Road Industrial Estate
Lawrence Hill Industrial Park
Lawrence Hill Station
Lawrence Hill Health Centre
Easton CE Primary Sch
City Business Park
Wadehurst Industrial Park
Kingsland Trading Est
City of Bristol College (Folly Lane Centre)
Carlyle Business Centre
Barton Hill Prim Sch
Barton Hill Infant School
Barton Hill Trading Estate
Corbett Ho Clinic
Russell Town Industrial Park
Whitehall Trading Est
The City Academy Bristol
Eastville Health Centre
Sikh Temple
Bristol Marriott
Quakers Friars
Police Station
Bristol Temple Meads Station
Temple Trading Estate
Kings Bus Park
Showcase Cinema
Hollywood Bowl
Eldonwall Trading Estate
Unicorn Business Park
Chandos Trading Estate
Industrial Camwal
St Mary Redcliffe
1 grid square represents 500 metres
(area under development)

Ridgeway
Clay Hill
Speedwell
Whitehall
St George
Crew's Hole
St Anne's Park
Conham
BS5
Cemetery
Greenbank Cemetery
Avon View Cemetery
St George's Park
Lodge Causeway Trading Estate
Avon Business Park
Balaclava Industrial Estate
Chester Park J&I School
RC Primary School
Superstore
Fishponds Trading Estate
Ridgeway Industrial Centre
Works
Eastpark Trading Estate
Crofts End Industrial Estate
Speedwell Swimming Baths
Speedwell Technology College
Whitehall Primary School
Soaphouse Industrial Estate
Bush Industrial Est
Summerhill J&I School
St George Health Centre
Council Building
St Patricks RC Primary School
Springwater Park Trading Estate
Beehive Trading Estate
Air Balloon Hill J&I School
Netham Industrial Est
Satellite Business Park
Netham Park Ind Estate
Netham Industrial Estate
Riverside Business Park
Trading Estate
Business Park
St Annes J&I School
St Annes Park Prim Sch
Humphrys Barton
A432
A431
A420
B4465
B4469
B4048
Stonebridge Park
Royate Hill
Rose Green Road
Gordon Road
Lyppiatt Rd
Church Road
Summerhill Road
Clouds Hill Road
Bell Hill Road
Air Balloon Road
Brook Road
Whitefield Road
Berkeley Rd
Speedwell Road
Deep Pit Rd
Green Road
Chapel La
Holly Lodge Road
Mayfield Park North
Mayfield Park South
Whitehall Av
Crown Hill
Plummer's Hill
Park Crescent
Cossham Rd
Beaufort Road
Crew's Hole Road
Netham Road
Blackswarth Rd
St Anne's Road
Wootton Crs
Guildford Road
Robertson Road
Troopers' Hill
Fir Tree Lane
Niblett's Hill
Nicholas Lane
Dundridge Lane
St Aldan's Road
Headford Avenue
Hillside
Ventnor Road
Selby Road
Cecil Avenue
Meadow Vale
Whiteway
Newbridge Rd
Highworth Rd
St Anne's Pk Rd
First Avenue
Rochester Rd
Conham Rd
Church Road
Hillburn Rd
Bourne La
Memorial Rd
80
81
64
53
62
63
E
F
G
H
I
2
3
4
5

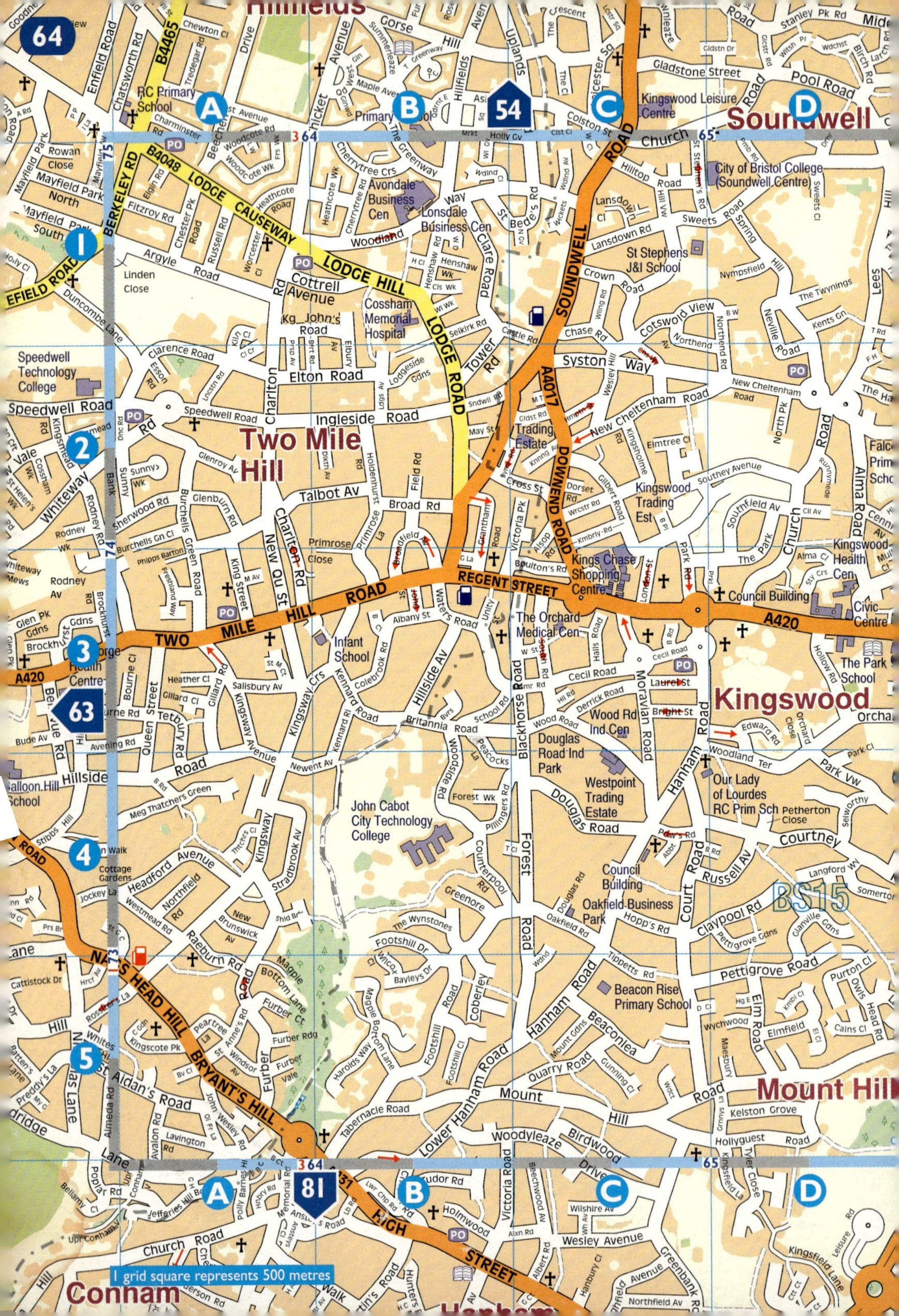

64
54
63
81
A
B
C
D
1
2
3
4
5
Soundwell
Two Mile Hill
Kingswood
Mount Hill
Conham
BS15
Hillfields
Berkeley Rd
B4465
B4048 Lodge Causeway
Lodge Hill
Lodge Road
Soundwell Road
A4017
Downend Road
Regent Street
Two Mile Hill Road
A420
Nags Head Hill
Bryant's Hill
High Street
RC Primary School
Kingswood Leisure Centre
City of Bristol College (Soundwell Centre)
Avondale Business Cen
Lonsdale Business Cen
Cossham Memorial Hospital
St Stephens J&I School
Speedwell Technology College
Kingswood Trading Est
Kings Chase Shopping Centre
The Orchard Medical Cen
Infant School
Council Building
Civic Centre
Kingswood Health Cen
The Park School
Douglas Road Ind Park
Wood Rd Ind Cen
Westpoint Trading Estate
Our Lady of Lourdes RC Prim Sch
John Cabot City Technology College
Council Building
Oakfield Business Park
Beacon Rise Primary School
Balloon Hill School
Health Centre
Linden Close
Speedwell Road
Ingleside Road
Elton Road
Charlton Rd
Argyle Road
Cottrell Avenue
Clarence Road
Syston Way
New Cheltenham Road
Cotswold View
Crown Road
Gladstone Street
Pool Road
Church Rd
Hanham Road
Forest Road
Blackhorse Road
Moravian Road
Douglas Road
Britannia Road
Kingsway Avenue
Headford Avenue
Raeburn Rd
Magpie Bottom Lane
Lower Hanham Road
Mount Hill Road
Tabernacle Road
Woodyleaze Drive
Wesley Avenue
Holmwood
Courtney Road
Pettigrove Road
Claypool Rd
Russell Av
Kelston Grove
Hollyguest Road
Church Road
1 grid square represents 500 metres

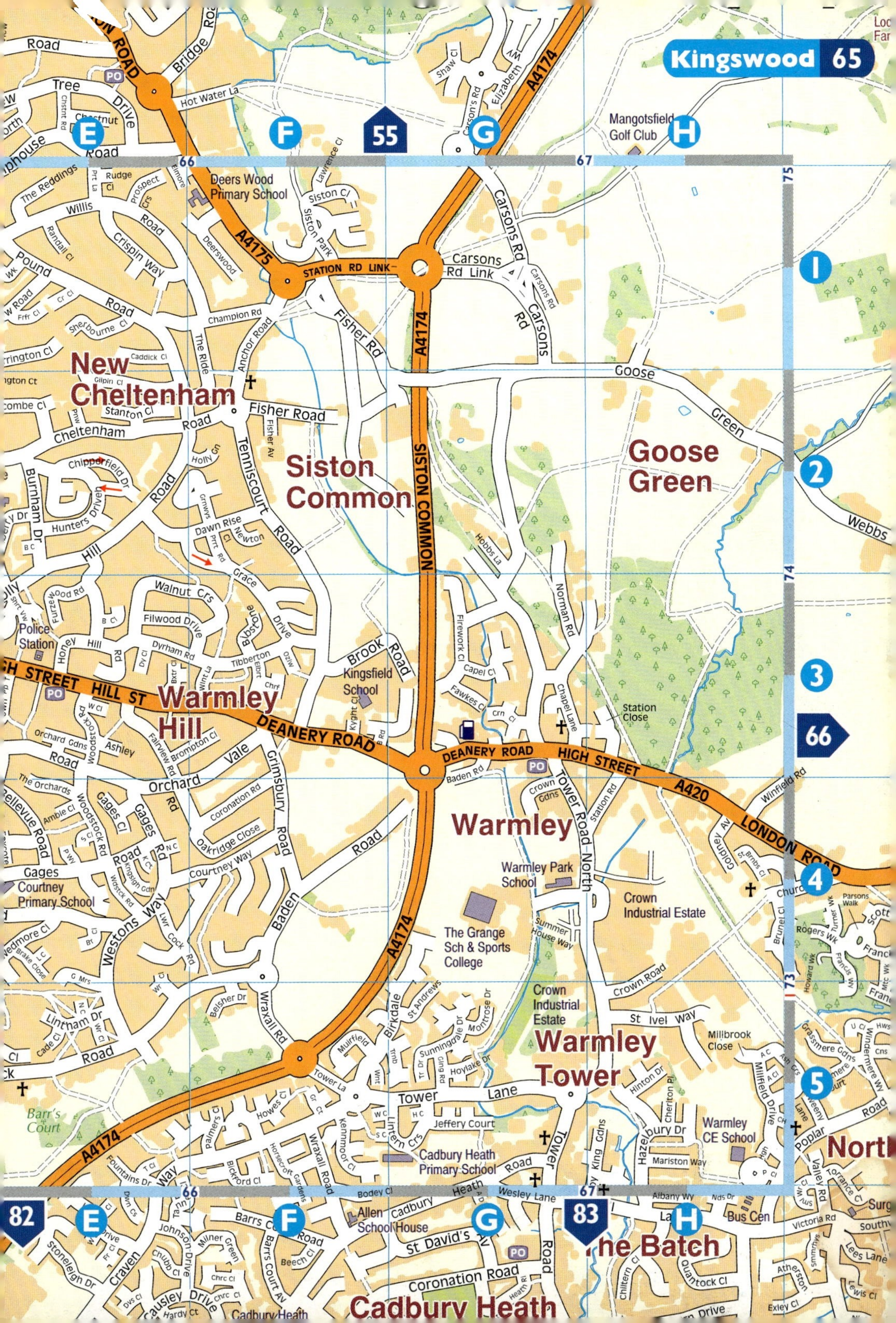
New Cheltenham
Siston Common
Goose Green
Warmley Hill
Warmley
Warmley Tower
The Batch
Cadbury Heath
Mangotsfield Golf Club
Deers Wood Primary School
Kingsfield School
Police Station
Courtney Primary School
Warmley Park School
The Grange Sch & Sports College
Crown Industrial Estate
Cadbury Heath Primary School
Warmley CE School
Allen School House
Station Close
Barr's Court
STATION RD LINK
SISTON COMMON
DEANERY ROAD
HIGH STREET
HILL ST
LONDON ROAD
A4174
A4175
A420
Hot Water La
Carsons Rd Link
Fisher Road
Goose Green
Webbs
Tenniscourt Road
Cheltenham Road
Orchard Road
Grimsbury Road
Baden Road
Tower Road North
Tower Lane
Tower Road
Wraxall Rd
Weston's Way
Courtney Way
Crown Road
St Ivel Way
Poplar Road
Coronation Road
St David's Av
Wesley Lane
Bodey Cl
Victoria Rd
Jeffery Court
55
66
82
83
E
F
G
H
1
2
3
4
5
67
73
74
75

66
Lodge Farm
Siston
Northmea Farm
A
B
56
C
D
368
69
75
1
Green
2
Webbs Heath
Siston Lane
Blue Lodge
74
Webb's Heath
3
65
Heath
Lodge Road
Holbrook
A420
Winfield Rd
Webbs
Hill
Holbrook
LONDON ROAD
Chesley
4
Church Av
Parsons Walk
Say Walk
Scott Wk
Rogers Wk
Turner Wk
Francis Wy
Howard Wk
Francis Way
A4175
Bridge Yate
HOMEAPPLE HILL
73
Millbrook Close
Grassmere Gdns
Windermere Wy
Thirlmere Court
5
Road
Willow Cl
Lane
RIDING BARN HILL
A420
Warmley CE School
Poplar
North Common
Cann
Valley Rd
Torrance Cl
Nds Dr
Surgery
Bus Cen
Victoria Rd
BATH ROAD
83
The Green
Lees Lane
Atherston
Victoria Rd
Quantock Cl
Drive
1 grid square represents 500 metres

Rookery Lane
57
E
F
G
H
70
71
75
74
73
I
2
3
4
5
Abson
Bottoms Farm
Lodge Road
Abson Road
Cleeve Lane
Gatherham Farm
Ham Lane
Doynto
Road
Rock
Rock Road
Monarch's Way
Common
Lane
Holbrook Lane
Wick Rocks
Parkers Avenue
Hill
St Anne's Dr
Milford Av
Mendip Vw
St Helens Dr
Mendip Vw
St Francis Dr
The Crs
Boyd Cl
Vw
Mendip
Naishcombe
View Ct
PO
Willow Cl
Church Rd
Wick CE Primary School
CHURCH ROAD
HIGH STREET
Police Station
Surgery
London Road
LONDON ROAD
A420
Monarch's Way
Court Lane
Wick
Barrow
Hill
Road
Lane
Greenway Farm
BS30

A
B
C
D
1
2
3
4
5
3 40
41
74
73
1 72
Margaret's Bay
Golf Course
Clevedon Golf Club
Ladye Bay
Ladye Point
Linkside
Bay Road
Edgehill Rd
CASTLE ROAD
B3124
HOLLY LANE
Clynder Gv
Ladye Bay
Walton Park Hotel
Walton St Mary
Channel Road
Edward Rd W
Brackenwood Rd
Clevedon Community School
Conygar
Argyle Rd
Cambridge Gv
Cambridge Road
The Av
Edward Road
Wayside Dr
Edward Road S
WELLINGTON TERRACE
Robin Lane
Orme Dr
Durbin Park Rd
Kings La
Woodside Rd
Rippleside Road
Woodland Glade
Castle Vw Rd
King's Road
Old Park Road
Bennetts Way
Clevedon Pier
Friary Cl
MARINE PARADE
Marine Hl
Dial Hill Road
Castle Wood Cl
Valley Road
Strawberry Hl
The Croft
Clevedon Bay
Gv Rd
Road
Community Mental Health Cen.
70
Zig Zag
Road
Esmond Grove
Road
Chestnut Gv
ROAD
All Saints East Clevedon CE Primary School
Alexandra
Gdns Rd
Thackeray Av
Ash Gv
BEACH
Bellevue Rd
Hill
WALTON
All Saints
1 grid square represents 500 metres

Down
Walton Bay
Pigeon House Bay
E
F
G
H
43
44
Farley
I
Walton Down
74
Hack's Wood
B3124
2
3
Walton-in-Gordano
Walton
Walton Moor
73
Drove
4
Norton's Wood
Harley Lane
Clevedon Lane
Nortons Wood Lane
5
M5
Norton's Wood
Cadbury Camp Lane West
72
Orchard Av
43
44
E
F
G
H
Hill Lane
CLEVEDON ROAD
B3130
Court Wood

CLEVEDON
Clevedon Pier
Clevedon Bay
Salthouse Bay
Hangstone Hill
West End
68
A
B
C
D
1
2
3
4
5
339
40
72
71
170
WELLINGTON TER
MARINE PARADE
THE BEACH
ELTON ROAD
Robin Lane
Durbin Park Rd
Friary Cl
Marine Hill
Community Mental Health Cen
Lea Gv
Copse Road
Alexandra Road
Hill Road
Zig Zag
Dial Hill Road
Bellevue Rd
Herbert Rd
Hill Road
Seavale Rd
Army Training Corps
Linden Rd
Hallam Road
Victoria Rd
Prince's Road
Linden Rd
Surgery
Sunnyside Rd
Chapel Hill
Police Stn
St John's Road
Marson Rd
Council Building
Pyne Point
St Brandons School
West Way
The Homestead
OLD CHURCH ROAD
B3130
Clevedon Fruit Mkt
Curzon Cinema
KENN RD
CT WESTERN RD
Oldville Av
B3133
Salthouse Rd
Pizey Avenue Industrial Estate
Long Av
Pizey Close
Pizey Avenue
West Croft
Church Rd
Old Church Rd
Beach Av
Knowles Rd
Speedwell Industrial Est
Fernville Est
Glebe Rd
Coleridge Vale Road N
Coleridge Vale Road S
Avenue
Southey Road
Coleridge Rd
Cemetery
Church Cl
Westbourne Avenue
Westbourne Crs
Pill Way
Yeo Way
Southern Way
Tennyson Avenue
Saltings Cl
Drive
St Andrew's
Keene's Way
Strode Road
Churchill
Windsor Cl
Kimberley Rd
Ruddymead
Westerleigh Road
Ashton Cl
Farleigh Road
Ashley Rd
Wedmore Road
Sunnyvale
Lavington Close
The Leys
Saxby Cl
Strode Wy
Five C Business Centre
St John the Evangelist CE Prim Sch
Tweed Rd
Hayward Cl
Cherry Hay
St Michael's Av
Kenn Road
Halswell Rd
Butterfield Pk
Fosseway
Blackthorn Sq
Jubilee Pl
Blackmoor
Holland Rd
Mary Elton Primary School
Southern Way
The Tynings
Rushmoor
Yeolands Dr
Netherways
Turner Way
Ransford
Eastlea
Deer Mead
Tuckmill
Strode Rd
Brknrdg Cl
Wdngtn Rd
Cavell Ct
Millcross
Chipping Cross
Cobley Cft
Cannons Gate
Stonebridge
Tutton Wy
Banks Cl
Westfield
River Md
Longacre
Oakley
Bkr Cl
Millcross
Catemead
The Hyde
Patch Cft
Freelands
Byfields
Strode Road
Colehouse Lane
Lane
Colehouse Lane
B3133
Dowlais Farm
Road
Strode
1 grid square represents 500 metres

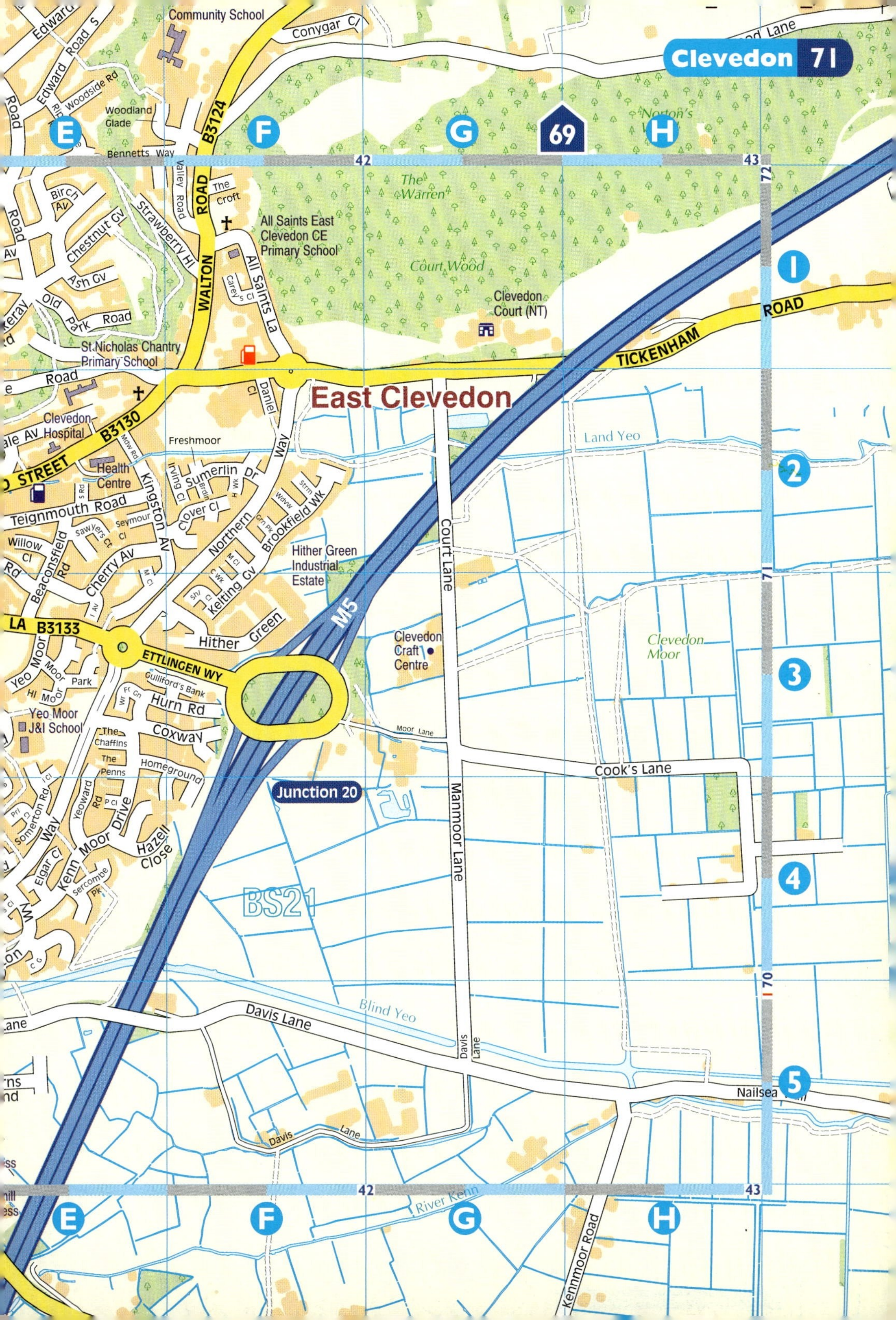

Clevedon 71
69
East Clevedon
Community School
Conygar Cl
Edward Road S
Woodside Rd
Woodland Glade
Bennetts Way
B3124
WALTON ROAD
Valley Road
The Croft
Strawberry Hl
All Saints East Clevedon CE Primary School
All Saints La
Carey's Cl
The Warren
Court Wood
Norton's
Clevedon Court (NT)
TICKENHAM ROAD
Birch Av
Chestnut Gv
Ash Gv
Old Park Road
St.Nicholas Chantry Primary School
Road
Daniel Cl
Clevedon Hospital
B3130
STREET
Health Centre
Freshmoor
Sumerlin Dr
Irving Cl
Kingston Av
Teignmouth Road
Seymour Cl
Sawyers Ct
Clover Cl
Northern Way
Brookfield Wk
Willow Cl
Beaconsfield Rd
Cherry Av
Kelting Gv
Hither Green Industrial Estate
Hither Green
Court Lane
Land Yeo
M5
B3133
ETTLINGEN WY
Yeo Moor
Moor Park
Hl Moor
Yeo Moor J&I School
Gulliford's Bank
Hurn Rd
Coxway
The Chaffins
The Penns
Homeground
Clevedon Craft Centre
Moor Lane
Cook's Lane
Clevedon Moor
Junction 20
Manmoor Lane
Somerton Rd
Way
Yeoward Rd
Moor Drive
Hazell Close
Kenn Moor
Elgar Cl
Sercombe Pk
BS21
Blind Yeo
Davis Lane
Nailsea Wall
Davis Lane
River Kenn
Kenmoor Road
E
F
G
H
1
2
3
4
5
42
43
72
71
70

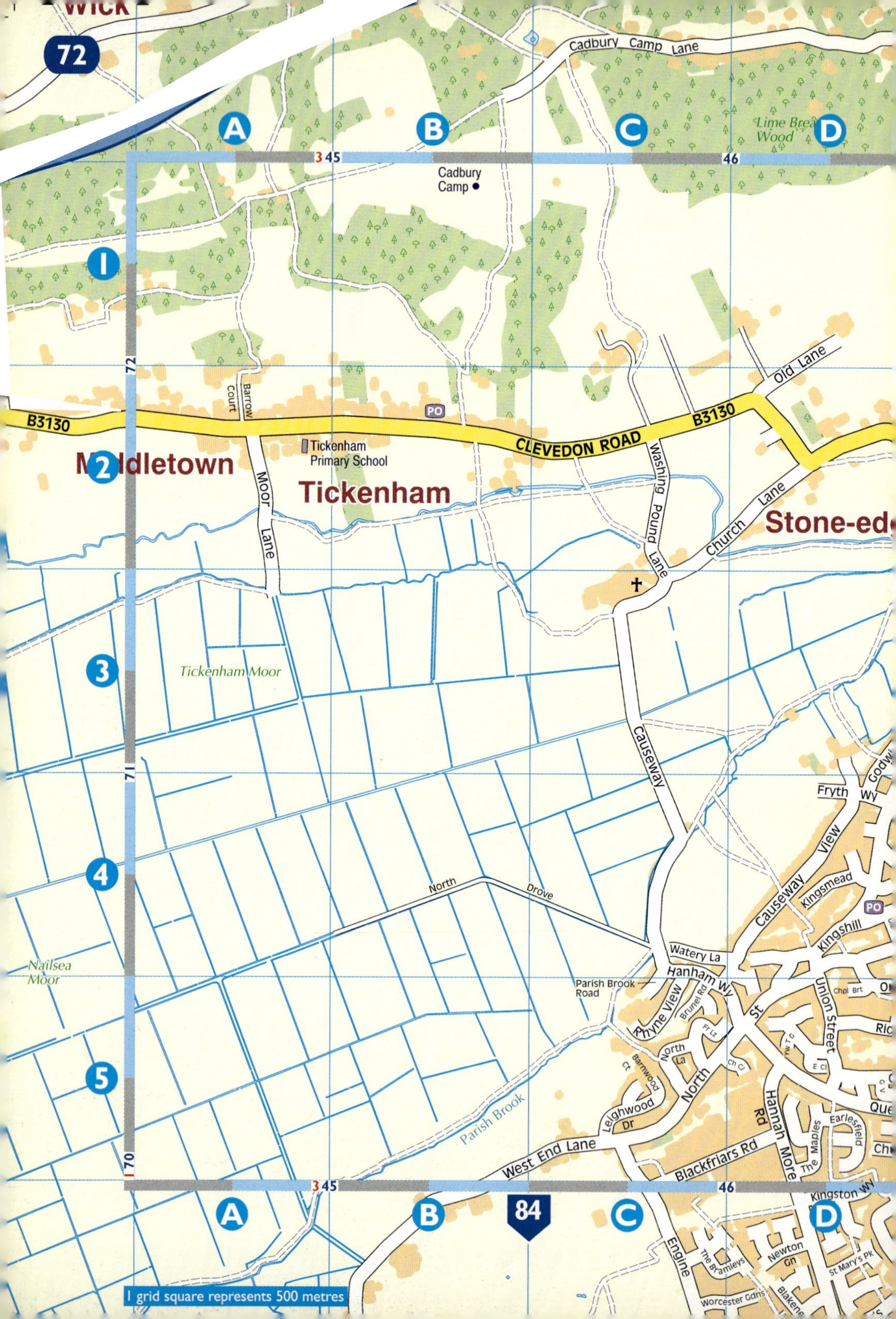

72
Cadbury Camp Lane
Lime Breach Wood
Cadbury Camp
A
B
C
D
345
46
1
2
3
4
5
72
71
70
Old Lane
Barrow Court
B3130
PO
Tickenham Primary School
CLEVEDON ROAD
Middletown
Tickenham
Stone-edge
Moor Lane
Washing Pound Lane
Church Lane
Tickenham Moor
Causeway
Fryth Wy
Godwin
Causeway View
Kingsmead
Kingshill
North Drove
Watery La
Nailsea Moor
Hanham Wy
Parish Brook Road
Rhyne View
Brunel Rd
Union Street
North La
Barnwood Ct
North St
Ch Cl
E Cl
Hannah More Rd
Leighwood Dr
Parish Brook
West End Lane
Blackfriars Rd
The Maples
Earlesfield
84
Kingston Wy
Engine
The Bramleys
Newton Gn
St Mary's Pk
Worcester Gdns
Blakeney
1 grid square represents 500 metres

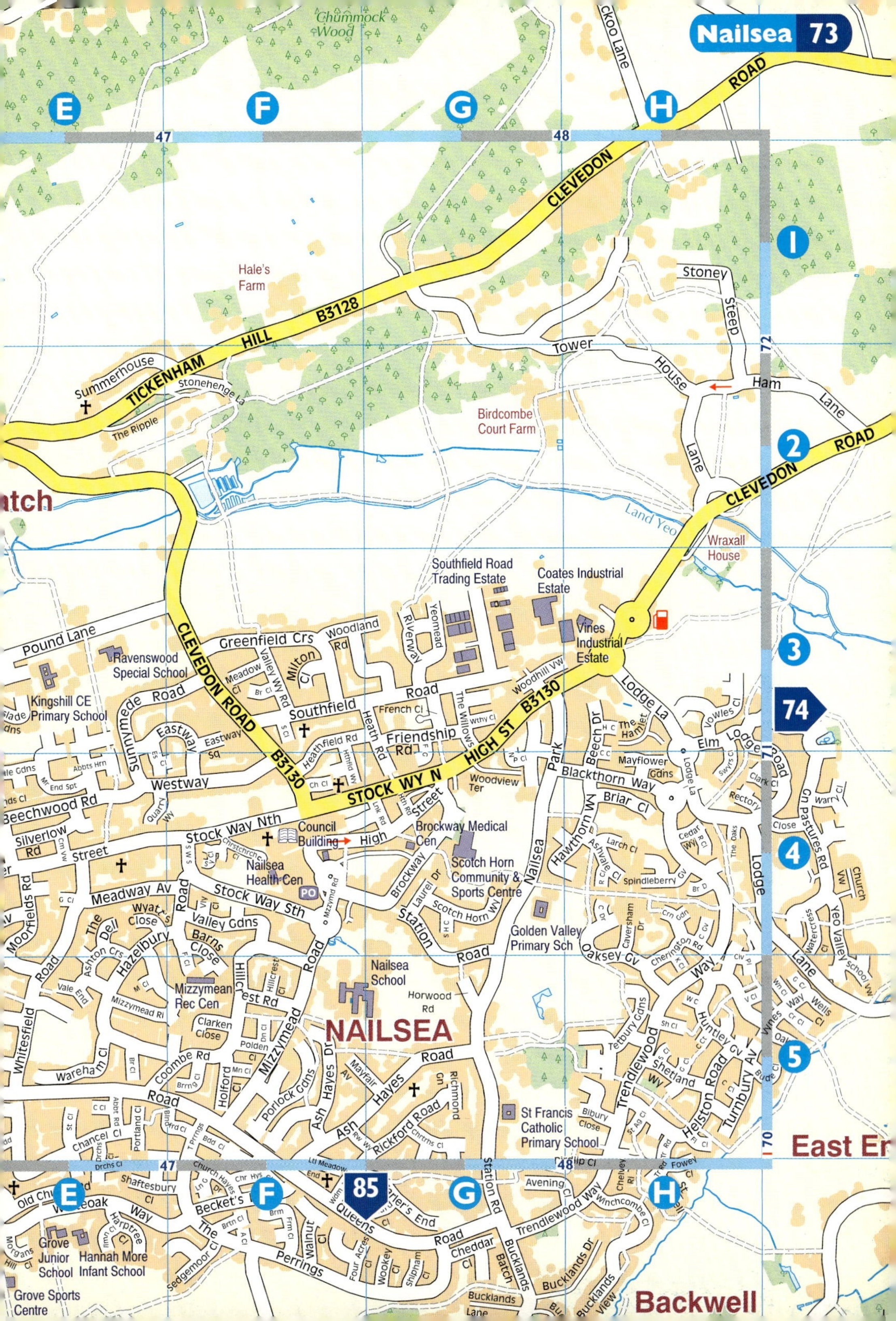

Chummock Wood
E
F
G
H
47
48
CLEVEDON ROAD
Hale's Farm
TICKENHAM HILL B3128
Summerhouse
Stonehenge La
The Ripple
Stoney Steep
Tower House Lane
Ham Lane
Birdcombe Court Farm
I
2
3
4
5
72
71
70
74
85
Land Yeo
Wraxall House
CLEVEDON ROAD
Southfield Road Trading Estate
Coates Industrial Estate
Vines Industrial Estate
Pound Lane
Ravenswood Special School
Kingshill CE Primary School
Greenfield Crs
Woodland Rd
Milton Cl
Riverway
Yeomead
CLEVEDON ROAD B3130
Southfield Road
French Cl
Friendship Rd
The Willows
Woodhill Vw
HIGH ST B3130
STOCK WY N
Heath Rd
Heathfield Rd
Sunnymede Road
Eastway
Eastway Sq
Westway
Beechwood Rd
Silverlow Rd
Street
Stock Way Nth
Council Building
High Street
Brockway Medical Cen
Scotch Horn Community & Sports Centre
Nailsea Health Cen
PO
Woodview Ter
Park
Beech Dr
The Hamlet
Lodge La
Elm Lodge Road
Vowles Cl
Mayflower Gdns
Blackthorn Way
Briar Cl
Hawthorn Wy
Larch Cl
Spindleberry Gv
Rectory Close
Gn Pastures Rd
Church
Yeo Valley
Lodge Lane
Meadway Av
Wyatt's Close
Stock Way Sth
Valley Gdns
Barns Close
The Dell
Hazelbury Road
Ashton Crs
Moorfields Rd
Whitesfield Road
Vale End
Mizzymead Ri
Mizzymead Road
Mizzymean Rec Cen
Hillcrest Rd
Clarken Close
Polden Cl
Brockway
Laurel Dr
Scotch Horn Wy
Station Road
Nailsea School
Horwood Rd
Golden Valley Primary Sch
Oaksey Gv
Caversham Dr
Cherington Rd
Way
Watercress
Wells Cl
NAILSEA
Wareham Cl
Coombe Rd
Holford Cl
Porlock Gdns
Ash Hayes Dr
Hayes Road
Mayfair Av
Richmond Gn
Rickford Road
Ash
Tetbury Gdns
Trendlewood Way
Shetland Wy
Huntley Gv
Helston Road
Turnbury Av
St Francis Catholic Primary School
Bibury Close
Road
Chancel Cl
Portland Cl
Shaftesbury Cl
Church Hayes Dr
Queens Road
Station Rd
Avening Cl
Winchcombe Cl
Fowey
East Er
Old Church Rd
Weetoak Way
Harptree Cl
Becket's
The Perrings
Walnut Cl
Four Acres Cl
Wookey Cl
Shipham Cl
Cheddar Cl
Bucklands Batch
Trendlewood Way
Bucklands Dr
Bucklands View
Bucklands Lane
Grove Junior School
Hannah More Infant School
Grove Sports Centre
Sedgemoor Cl
Backwell

ROAD
B3128
Portbury Lane
A
B
C
D
3 49
50
1
Stoney
Steep
Wraxall Court
Wraxall
Hill
72
House
Ham
Lane
2
Lane
CLEVEDON
ROAD
B3130
Wraxall CE
Primary School
BRISTOL
ROAD
Tyntes
Wraxall
Wraxall House
The Grove
B3130
3
Hazel
Farm
73
Elm
Lodge
Road
Lodge La
Rectory
Close
Gn Pastures Rd
Clark Cl
Warry Cl
B3130
Cedar
4
Lodge
Church
Yeo Valley
Watercress
Gable
Farm
Cherington Rd
Way
Lane
School
Brook
Farm
Backwell
Bow
Wells
Oakhill
5
Huntley
Shetland
Turnbury Av
Helston Rd
Backwell Common
East End
70
Fowey
St Austell
86
1 grid square represents 500 metres
Backwell
Backwell

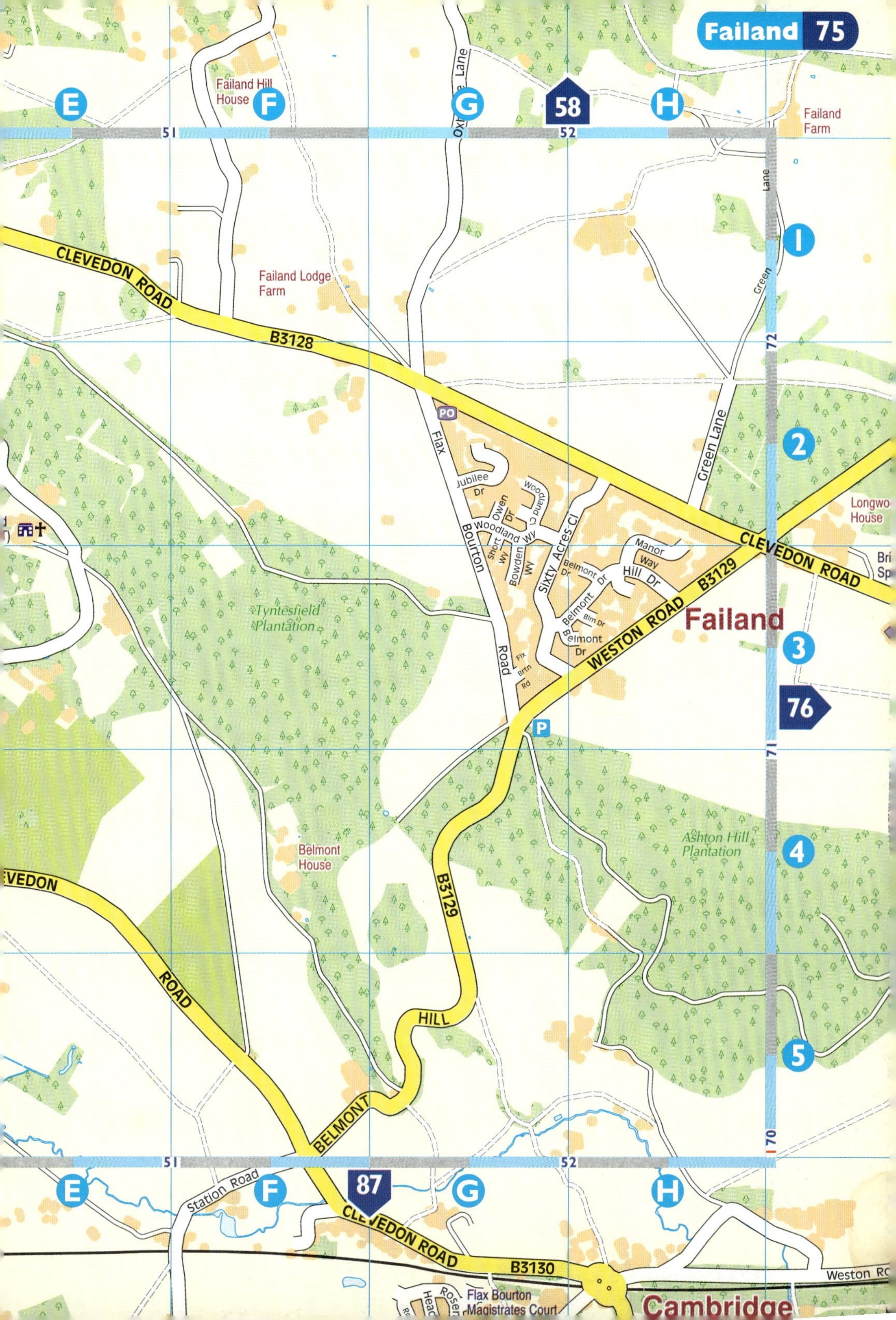
Failand Hill House
Oxhouse Lane
58
Failand Farm
E
F
G
H
51
52
Lane
I
Green
CLEVEDON ROAD
Failand Lodge Farm
B3128
72
PO
Flax
Bourton
Road
Jubilee Dr
Owen Dr
Woodland Cl
Woodland Wy
Short Wy
Bowden Wy
Sixty Acres Cl
Green Lane
2
Longwood House
Manor Way
Hill Dr
Belmont Dr
Blm Dr
Flx Brtn Rd
CLEVEDON ROAD
B3129
WESTON ROAD
Failand
3
Tyntesfield Plantation
76
P
71
Ashton Hill Plantation
4
Belmont House
CLEVEDON
ROAD
B3129
HILL
BELMONT
5
70
87
Station Road
CLEVEDON ROAD
B3130
Weston Road
Flax Bourton Magistrates Court
Cambridge

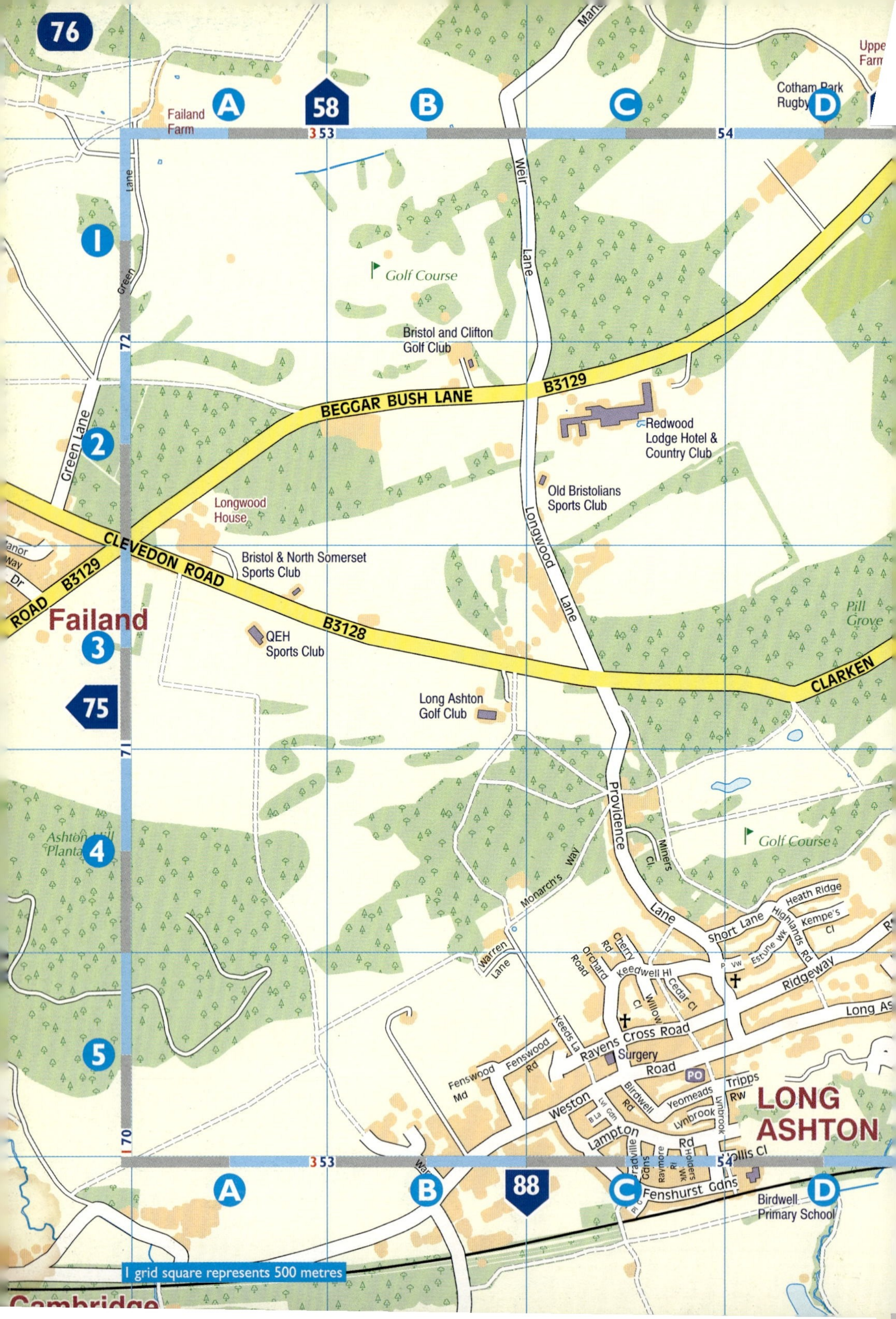
58
A
B
C
D
Failand Farm
Cotham Park Rugby
Upper Farm
353
54
Weir Lane
Lane
Green Lane
Green Lane
Golf Course
Bristol and Clifton Golf Club
BEGGAR BUSH LANE
B3129
Redwood Lodge Hotel & Country Club
Old Bristolians Sports Club
Longwood House
Longwood Lane
Manor Way
Dr
CLEVEDON ROAD
ROAD
B3129
Bristol & North Somerset Sports Club
Failand
QEH Sports Club
B3128
CLARKEN
Pill Grove
75
Long Ashton Golf Club
72
71
70
Providence Lane
Miners Cl
Golf Course
Ashton Hill Plantation
Monarch's Way
Heath Ridge
Short Lane
Highlands Rd
Kempe's Cl
Estune Wk
Warren Lane
Cherry Rd
Orchard Road
Keedwell Hl
Willow Cl
Cedar Cl
Ridgeway
Long Ashton Rd
Keeds La
Ravens Cross Road
Surgery
Road
PO
Fenswood Md
Fenswood Rd
Weston
Birdwell Rd
Yeomeads
Tripps Rw
Lynbrook
LONG ASHTON
Lampton Rd
Gradville Gdns
Raymore Ri
Holders Wk
Hollis Cl
Fenshurst Gdns
88
Birdwell Primary School
1 2 3 4 5
1 grid square represents 500 metres
Cambridge

Leigh Woods
BRIDGE ROAD
ROWNHAM HILL
The Avon
E
F
G
60
H
55
56
A369
I
BRUNEL WAY
Ashton Court Estate
Kennel Ldg Rd
Bower Ashton
Ashton Court
University of the West of England
CLANAGE ROAD
72
2
Courtlands La
Parklands Road
Rwn Cl
Blackmoors La
BRUNEL WAY
Ashton Park School
COOMBE
Ashton Gate Trading Estate
Ashton Vale Road
3
Longbrook Trading Estate
Carla Trading Estate
78
B3128
ASHTON ROAD
A370
B3128
P+
Church Lane
71
Ashton
Long Ashton Road
Glebe Cl
Folleigh Cl
Folleigh Dr
Lodge Dr
Westward Gdns
North Leaze
Folleigh Lane
Northleaze Prim Sch
Hillside Rd
Parsonage Rd
Glebe Rd
Yanley Lane
Catley Gv
Ryecroft Ri
Brook Cl
Theynes Croft
Lyvedon Wy
Copford La
Long Ashton Business Park
North Somerset
City of Bristol
4
Silbury
Ashton Vale Primary School
Avebury Rd
Ashton Drive
Works
Road
Langley Crs
Atyeo Cl
Risdale Rd
Tregarth Rd
Trevanna Rd
Tregarth Rd
5
Brook Gate
South Liberty Lane
South
70
A370
Yanley La
Yanley
89
South Bristol Crematorium
Cemetery

78
60
6
77
90
Hotwells
Ashton Gate
Ashton Vale
Bedminster
Bedminster Down
BS3
A
B
C
D
1
2
3
4
5
357
58
71
70
The Avon Gorge Hotel
Princes Buildings
Hotwells Sch
Cornwallis Crs
Goldney Av
Polygon
Goldney Rd
Clifton Vale
Ambra Vale E
Constitution Hill
Jacob's Well Road
Works
St Georges CE Primary Sch
Council Building
Cathedral
Queen's Pde
Deanery Rd
College Gn
Anchor Road
Coll
Sch
At-Bristol
Millennium Square
Canons Wy
Canons House
Harbour Wy
Amphitheatre
Hotwell Road
Cabot Wy
Cumberland Basin
Basin Rd
Brunel Lock Rd
Merchants Rd
Pooles Whf
Bristol Marina
SS Great Britain
Maritime Heritage Centre
Floating Harbour
Council Building
Cumberland Cl
Sydney Rw
Gas Ferry Rd
Caledonian Road
Avon Walkway
Bristol Industrial Museum
Cumberland Road
River Avon
Coronation Road
A370
Cooperage La
Park Rd
Allington Rd
Islington Rd
Brunel Way
A369
Clanage Road
University of the West of England
Parklands Road
Courtlands
Blackmoors La
Clift House Road
Jessop U/P
Frayne Rd
Works
Greenbank Rd
Coronation Rd
Back Rd
Walter St
Greenway
Bush La
Upton Road
Hamilton Road
Birch Road
Leighton Rd
Beauley Rd
Howard Rd
Stackpool Rd
Osborne Rd
Surgery
Kings Rd
Lydstep Ter
Prim Sch
Swimming Pool
Dean Lane
Salvation Army
A3029
Primary School
Raleigh Rd
Lime Road
Cathorne Rd
Exeter Rd
North Street
Greville Road
Vicarage Rd
Surgery
Works
B3120
Street
Bower Ashton Terrace
Ashton Road
Duckmoor Rd Ind Est
Durnford St
Ashville Rd
Friezewood Rd
Carrington Rd
Truro Rd
Balfour Rd
Marsh Rd
Bristol City FC (Ashton Gate)
Ashton Gate Trading Estate
Ashton Vale Road
Longbrook Trading Estate
Carla Trading Estate
Raynes Rd
Gerald Rd
Banwell Rd
Duckmoor Road
Frobisher Rd
Dampier Rd
Drake Rd
Foxcote Rd
Sturdon Rd
Breach Rd
Luckwell Road
Ashfield Rd
Beryl Rd
Chessel St
Pearl St
Ruby St
Primary School
Sheene Lane
Sheene Court Ind Est
Sheene Road
Sheene Wy
British Rd
Works
Prospect Terrace
South Bristol Retail Park
Smyth Rd
Irby Road
Core Rd
Bower Road
School
Road
Aubrey Rd
West Vw Rd
Garnet St
Palmyra Rd
Elmdale Rd
Avonleigh Rd
West St
Argus Rd
Cripps Rd
Argus Hope Ct Rd
Clinton Rd
Works
Winterstoke Road
Hendre Rd
Stella Grove
Greenhill Gv
Gore's Marsh Rd
Longmoor Court
Longmoor Rd
Collister Crs
Luckwell Rd
Thanet Rd
A38
Brighton Crs
Honeywick Close
Shepton Wk
Bedminster Road
Works
Ashton Vale Primary School
Avebury Rd
Ashton Dr
Superstore
Phoenix Business Park
Avon Works
Works
Marsh Lane
Winterstoke Rd
Hall Street
Mansfield St
Primary School
Highbury Rd
Matlock Rd
Somermead
Ashton Drive
Works
Swiss Road
Liberty Industrial Park
South Liberty Lane
Parson Street Station
Bedminster Road
Bedminster Down Rd
Parson Street
Aylesbury Crs
Parson St
Hastings Rd
Barnack Trading Centre
Risdale Road
Tregarth Rd
Trevanna Rd
Langley Crs
Liberty Lane
South Liberty Lane
Hartcliffe Way
Ilchester Crs
Bristol Vale Trading Estate
Novers Hill Trading Estate
Hills Barton
Ilchester Rd
South Bristol Crematorium
Cemetery
Luisgate Rd
Banwell Cl
Cheddar Grove Primary School
Surgery
Eastlyn Road
Brooklyn Road
Valley Rd
Vale Lane
Novers Hill
Bridgwater Road
1 grid square represents 500 metres

BRISTOL
Bristol Old Vic
Brigstow Hotel
Watershed Arts Cplx
Travel Inn
Custom Ho
Jurys Bristol Hotel
YHA
The Grove
Redcliffe Way
Open University
Chatterton Ho
Pipe La
Friary
Bristol Temple Meads Station
Council Building
Museum
Market
Feeder Rd
Police Station
Avon Street
Works
Oxford St
Gas Lane
Silverthorne Lane
St Mary's Redcliffe
Express by Holiday Inn
Temple Gate
Bath Road
Cattle Mkt Rd
Bath Bridge
Bristol Arena (area under development)
Merchants Quay
Bristol General Hospital
Commercial Rd
Guinea St
St Mary Redcliffe & Temple Sch
Clarence Road
A370
Burton Cl
Bedminster Bridge
York Road
Mead Street
Mead Rise
Surgery
Nelson Parade
New Charlotte St
Bedminster Pde
East St
Superstore
Business Cen
Council Building
Windmill Hill City Farm
Windmill Farm Bus Centre
Dalby Av
Bedminster Stn
St Catherines Industrial Estate
St Mary Redcliffe CE VC Primary School
Victoria Park
Windmill Hill
Princess St
William St
Whitehouse St
Spring St
Clifton View
Richmond St
Hill Street
William St
St Luke's Rd
St Luke's Crs
Windsor Ter
Stevens Crs
Wells Rd
A4
YMCA
St John's La
Bushy Pk
Knowle Rd
Bayham Rd
Haverstock Road
Brecknock Rd
Crowndale Rd
Perret's Park
Avon Walkway
Avon St
Albert Road
Avon Trading Estate
Chandos Trading Estate
Industrial Camwal Estate
Chapel Street
Feeder Road
Albert Crescent
Victoria Terrace
Victoria Road
RSPCA & Dogs Home
Wincombe Trad Est
Fy Steps Ind Estate
Totterdown Bridge Industrial Estate
Albert Road
Bath Road
Works
Arno's Vale
Arno's Cemetery
Hillcrest Primary School
School Rd
Park Street
Somerset Rd
Clyde Rd
A37
Wells
Clev School
Fraser St
Gwilliam St
Windmill Hl
Somerset Terrace
Cotswold Road
Mendip Rd
Quantock Rd
Dunkerry Rd
Brendon Rd
Mascot Rd
Paultow Rd
Kensal Rd
Victoria Park J&I School
Nutgrove Av
Fitzgerald Road
Sylvia Avenue
Tyning Rd
Ketch Rd
Ravenhill Road
Rookery Road
Belluton Rd
Calcott Rd
Norton Road
Woodbridge Rd
St John's Lane
B3122
Redcatch Road
Lower Knowle
Weymouth Rd
St Johns Lane Health Centre
Sidmouth Rd
Council Building
Wingfield Road
Beckington Rd
Andover Road
Axbridge Road
Stoneleigh Rd
Stoneleigh Crs
Melbury Rd
Friendship Rd
Council Building
Broadwalk Shopping Centre
City of Bristol College (Bedminster Centre)
Torpoint Rd
Kingswear Road
Wedmore Vale
Glyn Vale
Daventry Road
Newquay Rd
Exmouth Rd
Minehead Road
Teignmouth Road
Broad Wk
Knowle Park J&I School
Queenshill Rd
Queensdale Crescent
Knowle
Crossways Road
Greenleaze
Kingshill Rd
Broadfield Road
Springleaze
Hill Crest
Cavan Wk
Kildare Rd
Donegal Rd
Kenmare Rd
Lisburn Road
Galway Rd
Kerry Rd
Tavistock Rd
Ilminster Av
Crediton Crs
Bodmin Wk
Downton Rd
Headford Rd
Tralee Wk
Novers Pk
Novers Park
Downton Road
William Budd Health Cen
Florence Brown Community
Police Stn
Bantry Rd
Barnstaple Rd
Connaught Rd
Connaught Primary School
Ilminster Avenue
Filwood Park
Ilminster Avenue Prim Sch
Salcombe Rd
Council Building
Airport Road
Westleigh Park
Hengrove
Poyntz Rd
59
60
62
70
71
72
80
91

80
62
79
92
A
B
C
D
1
2
3
4
5
St Philips Causeway
A4320
Feeder Road
Monarch's Way
Barton Hill Trading Estate
St Vincents Trading Estate
Riverside Business Park
Kings Bus Park
Works Trading Estate
Unicorn Business Park
Showcase Cinema
Hollywood Bowl
Temple Trading Estate
Eldonwall Trading Estate
Industrial Camwal Estate
Victoria Terrace
Albert Crescent
Albert Road
Silverthorne Lane
Central Trading Estate
Totterdown Bridge Industrial Estate
St Annes Park Primary Sch
St Anne's Pk Rd
First Avenue
St Annes J&I School
Brooklea Clinic
Hardenhuish Road
Savoy Road
Hillsborough Road
Bloomfield Road
Wick Road
Sunnydene
Woodcroft Rd
Allison Road
Arno's Vale
A4
Arno's Vale Cemetery
Arno's Court Park
Arno's Manor Hotel
Superstore
Council Building
Sandy Park Road
Bath Road
Repton Road
Harrow Road
Winchester Road
Junior School
Manworthy Road
Hillcrest Primary School
Somerset Road
Cleve House School
Wells Road
B3122
Broadwalk Shopping Centre
Jubilee Public Baths
Talbot Road
BS4
Eagle Road
Bristol Hill
Brislington Trading Estate
Bath Road
Brislington Hill
Callington Road
A4174
B3119
West Town Lane
West Town Lane J&I School
Brislington Retail Park
Carmel Christian Centre & School
Knowle
Crossways Road
Greenleaze
Queensdale Crescent
Broadfield Road
Springleaze
A37
Airport Road
Wootton Park
Knowle Golf Club
Hungerford Road
Westbrook Road
Council Building
Cemetery
St Luke's Gardens
1 grid square represents 500 metres

Brislington 81
64
82
93
E
F
G
H
E
F
G
H
1
2
3
4
5
63
64
70
71
Conham
Broom Hill
Hanham
Hanham Green
Hicks Gate
River Avon
BRYANT'S HILL
HIGH STREET
A431
A4174
A4
BATH ROAD
Church Road
Conham Hill
Conham Road
Lwr Conham Vale
Memorial Road
Samuel White Road
Gover Road
Common Road
Castle Farm Road
Abbots Road
Central Avenue
Whittucks Road
Eastwood Road
Jersey Avenue
Broomhill Road
Wyndham Crescent
Capgrave Crs
Ironmould Lane
Dixon Road
Emery Road
St Aidan's Road
Nicholas Lane
Niblett's Hill
Dundridge Lane
Hanham Bus Park
Samuel Whites Inf Sch
Hanham Abbots Jun Sch
Hanham High School
Christchurch CE Primary School
Brislington Trading Estate
Bonville Business Centre
Bonville Trading Est
Dixon Business Centre
Hotspots Indoor Sports Centre
Industrial Estate
Bristol Harlequins RFC
Bristol Rovers FC
St Brendans RC Sixth Form College
Brislington House
Wyevale Garden Centre
Brislington School
Monarch's Way
South Gloucestershire
City of Bristol
Bath & North East Somerset
Surgery
PO
Works Humphrys Barton
Cncl Bldg
Ferry Road

82
64
65
81
94
Mount Hill
Hanham
Stone Hill
Longwell Green
Oldland
Keynsham Hams
Primary School
Beaconlea
Hanham Road
Lower Hanham Road
Mount Road
Quarry Road
Gunning Cl
Mount Gdns
Elm Road
Elmfield
Cains Cl
Cade Cl
Cock Road
Wychwood
Maesbury
Kelston Grove
Barr's Court
Woodyleaze
Birdwood
Drive
Victoria Road
Tudor Rd
Holmwood
Chapel Rd
Beechwood Av
Wilshire Av
Wesley Avenue
Albert Rd
Alxn Rd
Hanbury Cl
Highfield Avenue
Greenbank Road
Northfield Av
Westfield Cl
Colthurst Drive
De Verose Ct
Kingsfield La
Tyler Close
Kingsfield Lane
Leisure Rd
Hunters Road
Central Avenue
Grange Av
Hunters Rd E
Abbots Av
Whittucks Cl
The Meadows
Iles Close
Forest Edge
Rangers Wk
Surgery
Hanham Abbots Jun Sch
White Road
Whittucks Road
Gover Road
Crosslea
Abbots Road
STONEHILL
A4174
Hillcroft Cl
Aldermoor Way
Kingsfield La
Stone Hill Business Centre
MARSHAM WAY
A4174
Craven Way
Craven Cl
Barrs Court Primary School
Fountains Dr
Way
LaCock Drive
Stoneleigh Dr
Craven
Johnson Drive
Milner Green
Causley Drive
Hardy Ct
Chubb Cl
Stephens Drive
Barrs Court Road
Barrs Court Av
Beech Cl
Cadbury Heath Health Centre
Newton
Hampton Close
Parkwall Primary School
Wraxall Road
Bickford Cl
Howes Cl
Palmers Cl
Tower La
Muirfield
Stourton Dr
Swash Drive
Oram Ct
Allington Dr
Cox Ct
Woodward Drive
Parkwall Crs
Parkwall Road
Earlstone Cl
The Gv
Earlstone Crescent
Home Md
Far Handstones
Long Handstones
Gt Dowles
Princes Ct
Francis Pl
Moor Croft Dr
Fox Ct
Archer Ct
Brayne Ct
Steel Ct
Shellards Road
Field La
A431
Watson's Rd
Bgwr Dr
California
Edgewood Cl
Long Beach Road
Elderwood Dr
Burbank Cl
Ferndale Av
Orland Wy
Cloverdale Dr
Cottonwood Dr
Burney Way
Beach
Williams Cl
Longwell Green CP School
BATH ROAD
Pearsall Road
Larksleaze Rd
Ellacombe Road
Stanhope Road
Balmoral Rd
Ceres Close
Wnd Rd
Court Farm Road
Sallybarn Close
Kilnhurst Cl
Greenview
Roseville Av
Sheridan Wy
Rutland Av
Oldbury Chase
WILLSBRIDGE
Ferry Road
Monarch's Way
A4175
Gloucestershire
Somerset
1 grid square represents 500 metres

Warmley Tower
Millbrook Close
Warmley CE School
North Common
66
The Batch
Cadbury Heath
Cowhorn Hill
Oldland Common
Willsbridge
Park Way
Bus Cen
Surgery
Redfield Edge Primary School
West Court Farm
Simplex Trading Estate
The Sir Bernard Lovell School
Avon Valley Railway
St Annes CE Prim Sch
Cherry Garden Primary School
Willsbridge Mill Museum & Nature Reserve
Bitton Station
Golden Valley
Boyd Farm
Meadow School
BATH ROAD
A4175
HIGH STREET
BARRY ROAD
CHERRY GARDEN ROAD
A431 BATH ROAD
Redfield Hill
Beach
Newpit Lane
Golden Valley Lane
Ryedown Lane
Clay Lane
Pines Road
School Road
North Street
West Street
Westcourt Drive
Henfield Crs
Malvern Drive
Coronation Road
Park Road
Brereton Way
Mill Lane
Wesley Lane
Tower Road
South Road
Victoria Rd
Southway Dr
Lees Lane
Poplar Road
Millers Drive
Fallowfield
Noble Av
Coombes Way
Westland Avenue
Glenwood Dr
Stanley Gdns
Maple Cl
Berenda Dr
Gilroy Close
Grangeville Cl
Sunnyvale Dr
St Annes Drive
St Helens Dr
The Beeches
Oakleigh Gdns
Kenilworth Drive
Ludlow Close
Caldicot Close
Corfe Pl
Stanway
Cherry Gdns
Monarch's Way
Kings
PO
67
68
72
71
70
95
E
F
G
H
1
2
3
4
5

72
West End
Kenn Moor Gate
Nursebatch Farm
Netherton Wood
Nailsea Court
Midgell Farm
Parish Brook
Blind Yeo
Breach Lane
Breach La
Nailsea Moor Lane
Nailsea Wall Lane
West End La
Netherton Wood Lane
Chelvey Road
Engine Lane
Blackfriars Rd
Hannah More Rd
Leighwood Dr
Barnwood Ct
North La
Kingston Wy
The Bramleys
Newton Gn
St Mary's Pk
Worcester Gdns
Blakeney Gv
Allington Gdns
Fern Gv
R Gv
St Mary's
The Uplands
Earlesfield
Drove
A
B
C
D
1
2
3
4
5
3 45
46
70
69
1 68
1 grid square represents 500 metres

NAILSEA
Backwell Common
Backwell
West Town
Chelvey
Chelvey Batch
East E
St Francis Catholic Primary School
Grove Junior School
Hannah More Infant School
Grove Sports Centre
Nailsea & Backwell Station
West Leigh Infant School
Backwell RFC
Backwell School
Police Station
Brockley Elm Farm
Backwell Hill House
Whiteoak Way
Old Church Rd
Becket's Lane
Queens Road
Perrings
Station Rd
Trendlewood Way
Bucklands Batch
Bucklands Lane
Bucklands Dr
Bucklands View
Station Close
Station Road
Waverley Road
The Av
Moorfield Rd
Moor Lane
Westfield Rd
Rodney Road
Orchard Rd
Bramley Dr
Rushmoor Lane
WEST TOWN ROAD
A370
MAIN ROAD
Church Lane
Hilldale Road
Oakleigh Cl
Hillside Road
Karen Cl
Chelvey Road
Chelvey Lane
Brockley Lane
Kellways
Backwell Common
Coombe Rd
Hayes Road
Mizzymead
Whitesfield
Trendlewood
Shetland Wy
Helston Rd
Turnbury
Austell Cl
Winchcombe Cl
Avening Cl
Cheddar Cl
Wookey Cl
Shipham Cl
Four Acres Cl
Walnut Cl
Farler's End
Shaftesbury Cl
Harptree Cl
Sedgemoor Cl
73
86
47
48
70
69
68
E
F
G
H
I
2
3
4
5

86
74
85
A
B
C
D
1
2
3
4
5
349
50
70
69
68
East End
Backwell Common
Backwell Green
Farleigh
BS48
Backwell Bow
Backwell Common
Chapel Hill
A370
FARLEIGH ROAD
WEST TOWN ROAD
Backwell Hill Road
Backwell Hl Rd
Stancombe La
Backwell House
George Close
Fairfield Md
Fairfield Wy
Fairfield PNEU School
Uncombe Cl
Church Lane
Court Cl
Church La
Church Town
Backwell Junior School
Backwell School
Backwell Leisure Centre
Backwell Medical Cen
PO
Police Station
Station Road
Meadow Close
Dark Lane
St Andrews Rd
St John's Rd
Summer lands
Church Lane
Hilldale Road
Oakleigh Cl
Karen Dr
Karen Cl
Hillside Road
St Margaret's La
Bramley Dr
Westfield Rd
Westfield Cl
Mariners Dr
Orchard Rd
The Av
Helston Road
Turnbury Av
Shetland Wy
Huntley Gv
Oakhill
Vynes
Wells Cl
Bude Cl
Fowey Cl
St Austell Cl
Russett Cl
Long Lane
1 grid square represents 500 metres

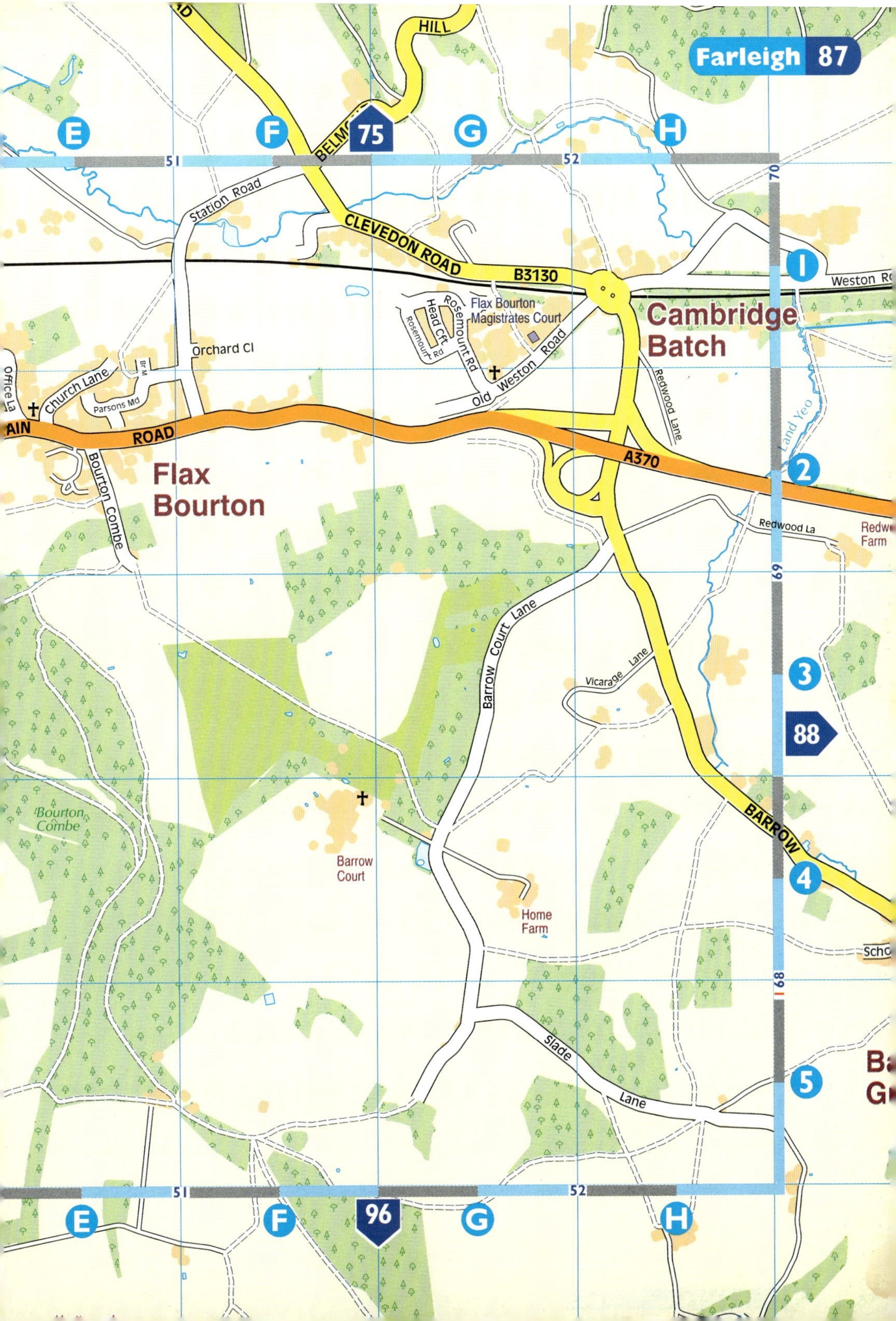
Farleigh 87
75
88
96
E
F
G
H
1
2
3
4
5
51
52
70
69
68
HILL
BELMO
Station Road
CLEVEDON ROAD
B3130
Weston Ro
Flax Bourton Magistrates Court
Cambridge Batch
Head Cft
Rosemount Rd
Rosemount Rd
Orchard Cl
Old Weston Road
Redwood Lane
Office La
Church Lane
Br M
Parsons Md
AIN
ROAD
A370
Land Yeo
Flax Bourton
Bourton Combe
Redwood La
Redw Farm
Barrow Court Lane
Vicarage Lane
BARROW
Bourton Combe
Barrow Court
Home Farm
Scho
Slade Lane
Ba Gr

LONG ASHTON
Long As
Ravens Cross Road
Surgery
Road
PO
Keeds La
Fenswood Rd
Fenswood Md
Weston
Birdwell
Yeomeads
Tripps Rw
Lynbrook
Lamb
Rd
Bradville Gdns
Raymore Ri
Holders Wk
Hollis Cl
Fenshurst Gdns
Birdwell Primary School
Warren La
Weston Road
Cambridge Batch
Redwood Lane
Land Yeo
A370
Redwood La
Redwood Farm
Wildcountry Lane
Monarch's Way
Barrow Hospital
Barrow Wood
BARROW STREET
School La
PO
Barns Close
Barrow Gurney
Hern Lane
B3130
Hobbs Lane
Reservoir
Reservoir
Reservoir
A38
A B C D
1 2 3 4 5
3 53
54
70
69
1 68
76
87
97
1 grid square represents 500 metres

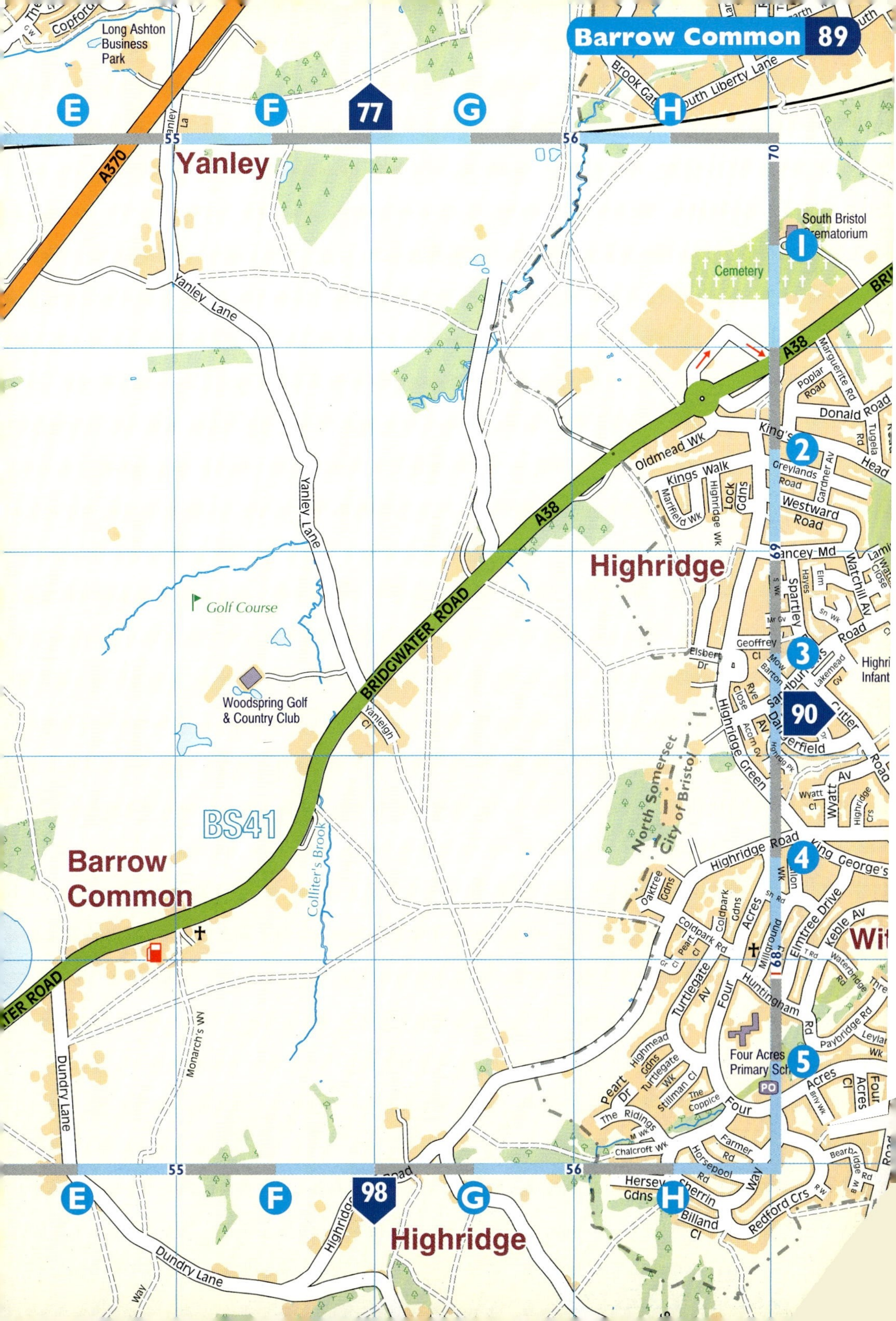
Long Ashton
Business
Park
Copford
A370
Yanley La
E
F
77
G
H
55
56
70
69
68
Yanley
Brook Gate
South Liberty Lane
South Bristol
Crematorium
I
Cemetery
Yanley Lane
A38
Marguerite Rd
Poplar Road
Donald Road
King's Head
Tugela Rd
2
Oldmead Wk
Kings Walk
Marifield Wk
Highridge Wk
Lock Gdns
Greylands Road
Gardner Av
Westward Road
Highridge
Spartley
Elm
Watchill Av
Road
Golf Course
Geoffrey Cl
3
Elsbert Dr
Rye Close
Lakemead Gv
Highridge Infant
Woodspring Golf
& Country Club
BRIDGWATER ROAD
Yanleigh Cl
Highridge Green
90
Cutler
Dangerfield
Road
Acorn Gv
Wyatt Av
Wyatt Cl
Highridge Crs
North Somerset
City of Bristol
BS41
Highridge Road
4
King George's
Barrow
Common
Colliter's Brook
Oaktree Gdns
Coldpark Gdns
Coldpark Rd
Acres
Millground
Elmtree Drive
Keble Av
Waterbridge Rd
Turtlegate Av
Four
Huntingham Rd
Paybridge Rd
Monarch's Wy
Dundry Lane
Highmead Gdns
Turtlegate Wk
Stillman Cl
The Coppice
Four Acres
Primary Sch
5
Acres Cl
Four Acres
Peart Dr
The Ridings
Chalcroft Wk
Farmer Rd
Horsepool Rd
Way
Bearbridge Rd
Hersey Gdns
Sherrin
Billand Cl
Redford Crs
E
F
98
G
H
Highridge Road
Highridge
Dundry Lane

90
78
89
99
A
B
C
D
1
2
3
4
5
357
58
70
69
68
South Liberty Lane
Tregarth
South
Liberty
Bristol Vale Trading Estate
Barnack Trading Centre
Novers Hill Trading Estate
Hastings
Barton
Ilchester
A38
BEDMIN
BRIDGWATER ROAD
HARTCLIFFE WAY
South Bristol Crematorium
Cemetery
Bedminster Down
Cardill Cl
Luisgate Rd
Lewis Rd
Eastlyn Road
Ilchester Road
Brooklyn Rd
Banwell Cl
Cheddar Grove Primary School
Surgery
Valley Rd
Brunel
Winford Gv
Langford Road
Felton Gv
Cheddar Gv
Farleigh Wk
Wraxall Gv
Tyntesfield Rd
Wrington Crs
Bishopsworth Road
Hill Vw Rd
Ellis Av
Garth Rd
Crantock Av
Headley Lane
Vale Lane
Novers Hill
Belstone
Novers Lane J&I School
Farnaby Close
Marguerite Rd
Poplar Road
Donald Road
Alexandra Road
Tugela Rd
Bedminster Down School
Nailsea Cl
Denston Wk
The Malago
Brookview Wk
Rise
Maytree Cl
Bampton Cl
Peter's
Headley Park
Broadleas
Pennlea
Headley Wk
Maytree Av
Willoughby Close
Giffords Pl
Police Station
King's Head Lane
Kings Walk
Greylands Road
Gardner Av
Westward Road
Highridge Wk
Lock Gdns
Dancey Md
Lamington Cl
Watchill Av
Watchill Close
Headley Pk Rd
Durleigh Cl
Pentire Av
Ltl Headley Cl
Headley Park Primary Sch
Hillyfield Road
Headley Lane
Headley Ct
Vicarage Rd
Manor Rd
Walnut Wk
Chestnut Wk
Headley Road
Brookdale Rd
Durville Rd
PO
Spartley Dr
Ilex Cl
Elmfield Cl
Bishopsworth CE Junior School
Highridge Infant School
Peter Cole Dr
Bishopsworth Swimming Pool
Chapel Rd
Cater Road
Sandburrows
Lakemead Gv
Cutler Road
Fernsteed Rd
Church Road
Perrycroft Av
Perrycroft Rd
Derham Road
Whitchurch Lane
Whitland
Hengrove Way
Dangerfield
Bishopsworth
Coleshill Drive
Colemead
Acresbush Cl
Goulston Rd
Selley Wk
Gatehouse Wy
BS13
Wyatt Av
Wyatt Cl
Highridge Crs
East Rdg Dr
Surgery
Grange Road
Gatcombe Road
Chaundey Gv
Stillingfleet Road
Maynard Cl
Greenditch Av
Highridge Road
King George's Road
Cullon Wk
Brwry Rd
Riverland Dr
St Pius X RC Primary School
Withywood Community School
Smithmead
Collinson Rd
Randolph Av
Fulford Rd
Fulford Road
Wymbush Crs
Coldpark Gdns
Acres
Elmtree Drive
Keble Av
Withywood
Gatehouse Wk
Hosey Wk
Elvard Rd
Sheeps Crft
Arundel Cl
Murford Av
Hareclive Road
Fulford Centre
Pavey Rd
Pavey Cl
Woodmead Gdns
Coldpark Rd
Turtlegate Av
Four Acres
Huntingham Rd
Waterbridge Rd
Three Wls Rd
Queen's Rd
Withywood Rd
Gay Elms Rd
Ashland Rd
Molesworth Dr
Heyron Walk
Kilmersdon Rd
Halswell Gdns
Cncl Bldg
Grinfield Av
Hartcliffe Health Cen
Clinic
Gay Elms Primary Sch
Molesworth Close
Fair Furlong Primary School
Fair Furlong
Murford Wk
Meriet Av
Borver Gv
Moxham Drive
Paybridge Rd
Leyland Wk
Broad Oak Rd
Whiting Rd
Arthurswood Rd
Vowell Cl
Lynde Cl
Herridge Cl
Herridge Rd
Honey Garston Rd
Four Acres Primary School
Acres Cl
Four Acres
Pigott Av
Culverwell Road
Hareclive Primary School
Bellamy Av
Greatwood Cl
Stillman Cl
The Coppice
Farmer Rd
Horsepool Rd
Sherrin Way
Cobhorn Dr
Pesley Cl
Clarence Rd
Bishport Avenue
Bishport
Newland Road
Newland Wk
Kencot Wk
Hartgill Cl
Bourchier Gdns
Pawlett Road
Crosscombe Drive
Blagrove Crs
Gibbsfold Rd
Brocks Rd
Bishport
Queen's Rd
1 grid square represents 500 metres
City of Bristol
Somerset

Novers Park
Filwood Park
Hengrove Park
Hartcliffe
Hengrove
E
F
G
H
79
92
100
59
60
70
69
68
1
2
3
4
5
Airport Road
A4174
Hengrove Way
Connaught Primary School
Police Stn
William Budd Health Cen
Florence Brown Community School
Filwood Swimming Baths
School of Christ The King RC
Ilminster Avenue Prim.Sch
Council Building
Petherton Road Infant School
Tyning Hengrove Junior School
South Bristol Business Park
Travel Inn
Hengrove Leisure Park
Cineworld
Recreation Ground
Perry Court Junior School
St Bernadette RC Primary
Whitchurch Health Centre
Hawkfield Business Park
Whitchurch Sports Centre
City of Bristol College (Hartcliffe Centre)
Teyfant Community School
Hartcliffe School
Wansdyke Primary Sch
Bridge Farm J&I School
The Business Park
Hill Farm
Whitchurch Lane
Bamfield
Western Drive
Hawkfield Road
Hawkfield Way
Hawkfield Close
Bishport Av
Teyfant Road
Totshill Dr
Shortwood Rd
Witch Hazel Road
Longway Avenue
Goodwin Dr
Court Road
Tanorth Road
Edgefield Road
Edgefield Close
Maplestone Rd
Birnie Road
Fortfield Road
Evercreech Road
Allerton Road
Heathfield
Chiltern Cl
Wharnecliffe
Oatlands Avenue
Armada Rd
Quickthorn Cl
Briery Leaze Road
Paddock Gdns
Moreton Close
Cranwell Gv
Throgmorton Road
Willinton Road
Alard Rd
Padstow Rd
Torrington Avenue
Ilminster Avenue
Springleaze
Broadfield Road
Hengrove Avenue
Petherton Road
Cadogan Rd
Westleigh Park
Fanshawe Road
Walsh Avenue
Leda Avenue
Clatworthy Drive
Tarnock Avenue
Hayles Road
Great Walk
Wardour Rd
Wallingford Road
Creswicke Road
Hartcliffe Road
Filwood Broadway
Broadbury Road
Barnstaple Road
Chepstow Rd
St Whytes Road
Leinster Av
Lisburn Road
Kenmare Rd
Kerry Rd
Daventry Road
Teignmouth Rd
Crediton Crs
Gerrard Close
Inns Ct Av
Inns Ct Dr
Tallis Gv
Farrant Cl
Lambert Cl
Whitchurch
Hengrove Leisure Park

92
Knowle
Greenleaze
Crescent
Kingshill Rd
Broadfield Road
Springleaze
Dundry View
Hill Crest
Ponsford Rd
Imperial Wk
Wootton Park
WOOTTON PARK CALLINGTON ROAD
Hither Bath Br
West Town Lane J&I School
80
WEST TOWN LANE B3119
W Town La
Grace Pk Rd
Hungerford Road
Hungerford Crs
Brislington Retail Park
A
B
C
D
361
62
70
AIRPORT ROAD
A37
Kew Walk
West Town Pk
Westwood Rd
Westbrook Road
Knowle Golf Club
Hungerford
Hungerford Cl
Hungerford Gdns
Cadogan Rd
Oakdale Rd
Birchdale Road
Westleigh Park
Beechmount Gv
Hengrove Av
Whitwell Rd
Hengrove Lane
Imber Ct
Ravenhead Dr
Appledore Cl
Petherton
Long Eaton Drive
WEST TOWN LANE B3119
Council Building
Beryl Gv
Imperial Rd
Warmington Road
Hazelbury Road
Mowbray Road
Clive Rd
WELLS A37 ROAD
Beechwood Close
Golf Course
Hemplow Close
Newnham Close
Manston Close
Kinsale Road
Petherton Road Infant School
Dennor Park
Petherton Gdns
Road
Fanshawe Road
Leda Avenue
Walsh Avenue
Hengrove Community College/ Post 16 Centre
Tyning Hengrove Junior School
Sturminster Road
Amercombe Wk
Lyons Ct Rd
Ilsyn Gv
Lanesborough Ri
Longreach Grove
Henciffe Rd
New Fosseway Special School
David's Road
Whittock Square
Hengrove
Havyat Road
Cornhill Dr
Tyning Cl
Cross Walk
Archer Wk
The Coots
Ashwell Cl
Burnbush Cl
Sideland Close
New Fosseway Road
Loxton Sq
Stavordale Grove
Gladstone Road
Fossedale Avenue
Counterslip Gardens
Woodleigh Gardens
Whitecross Av
Sturminster Cl
Harrington Av
Harrington Road
Atkins Cl
Cornish Rd
Cornish Wk
Stockwood
St Bernadettes RC Primary School
St Bernadettes Catholic Sec Sch
Badgers Holt
Whitecross Av
Aylmer Crs
91
Armada Rd
Whitchurch Health Centre
Chessington Avenue
Kylross Av
Gilda Crescent
Valentine Cl
Gilda Sq W
Gilda Cl
The Drive
Tibbott Wk
Tibbott Rd
Dutton Road
Whittock Road
Burnbush Primary School
Ladman Grove
Ladman Rd
Marne Close
Waycroft Primary School
Eaton Cl
Selden Rd
Harden Rd
Dental Health Centre
Yeomanside Cl
Wharnecliffe Gardens
Fortfield Road
Copthorne Cl
Priddy Dr
Priddy Ct
Allerton Gdns
Shipham Cl
Holford Ct
Ridgeway Gardens
Wells Close
Cowling Drive
Cowling Rd
Hooper Rd
Showering Road
Maple Close
Hollway Road
Bagnell Rd
Exton Close
Butcombe Walk
Pennard Ct
Addiscombe Road
Lane
Binley Gv
Stockwood Road
Materman Road
Goslet Rd
Battson Rd
Cranwell Gv
Bracton Drive
Doulton Wy
Minton Close
Eastcote Park
Saltwell Avenue
Sturminster Rd
Craydon Road
Craydon Grove
Burfoot Road
Burfoot Gdns
168
Moreton Close
Evercreech Road
Allerton Crs
Ridgeway
BS14
Dene Road
Whitchurch Primary School
Stockwood Green Primary School
Denleigh Close
Allerton
Chiltern Cl
Maggs Lane
Cncl Bldg
The Witheys
Churchways
St Nicholas Road
Washing Pound La
PO
Whitchurch
Bridge Farm J&I School
Grass Meers Dr
Hazel Cote Road
Highdale Cl
Church Road
Church Mdw
Blackacre
Staunton Lane
Staunton Flds
Oldbridge
Halfacre La
Halfacre Close
Charnwood Road
101
BRISTOL
Sleep Lane
grid square represents 500 metres

Bristol Rovers FC
St Brendans RC Sixth Form College
Brislington House
81
A4
BATH ROAD
Stockwood Rd
E
F
G
H
63
64
70
Hicks Gate
A4174
Bath & North East Somerset
Ferry Road
Wyevale Garden Centre
Brislington School
City of Bristol
Bath and North East Somerset
A4
Durley Hill
I
La
A4175
Durley
2
DURLEY HILL
Stockwood Road
Stockwood Hill
69
Stockwood Vale
Stockwood Vale Golf Club
Golf Course
Broadlands School
3
Francis
94
Warman Cl
Warman Rd
Road
Derricke Road
Matthews Close
Lane
Townsend Close
Townsend Road
Road
Coape Rd
Wheathill Close
Mendip Close
Selworthy Close
St George
Lockingwell
Heathfield Close
Staple Grove
Holcombe
4
Westfield Close
Charlton Road
Keynsham Primary School
Monmouth Rd
Ludlow Close
Lays Drive
Barnard Walk
68
Queens
Lays Farm
Lincoln Close
Caernarvon
Caroline Cl
Durham Grove
PO
Warwick
5
Norfolk Grove
Walton Close
Farleigh Road
Longmeadow Road
Birch Ct
Maple Walk
Cedar Dr
Holmoak Road
Walnut Close
Oak Tree Wk
Holly Wk
The Brambles
E
F
63
G
64
H

94
82
93
104
A
B
C
D
1
2
3
4
5
365
66
70
69
68
Somerset
A4174
A4175
Ferry Road
Ferry Rd
Monarch's Way
Somerdale
Keynsham Hams
Somerdale Road North
Hams Rd
Cross St
Somerdale Road
Durley
Durley Hill
Cemetery
Lockwood Hill
KEYNSHAM BY-PASS
Keynsham RFC
Keynsham Town FC
A4175 BRISTOL ROAD
STATION ROAD
Keynsham Station
Dryleaze
Chandos Road
Priory Rd
The Avenue
Abbey Pk
Surgery
The Park
Avon Walkway
KEYNSHAM ROAD
River Avon
Avon Mill Lane
Avon Cl
Tennyson Cl
Vandyck Av
Unity Road
A4
Broadlands School
B6 Sixth Form Centre
Broadlands Avenue
Francis Road
St Ladoc Road
Culvers Road
Milward Road
St Johns Ct
Cranmore Av
Surg
HIGH ST
Ashton Way
Back La
Temple Primary School
St Anne's Avenue
St George's Rd
Winscombe Cl
Wheathill Close
Lockingwell Road
Mendip Close
Park Close
West View Road
Mayfields
B3116
Avon Road
Dragons Hl
Gaston Av
Heathfield
Westfield Close
Cleeve Gv
Staple Grove
Charlton Road
Keynsham Primary School
Handel Rd
The Clinic
Rock Road
The Labbott
Hawthorns Lane
Carpenters La
Temple St
Keynsham Leisure Centre
BATH HL
Dragons Hill Ct
Police Station
Gainsborough Road
Reynolds Close
Turner Cl
Lytton Gv
B3116 BATH ROAD
KEYNSHA
Charlton Park
St Johns Primary School
Sherwood Road
Sherwood Close
Courtlands
Albert Road
Dapps Hl
Monmouth Close
Ludlow Close
Barnard Walk
Kelston Road
Queens Road
Caernarvon Road
Lays Drive
Faireacres Cl
St Clements Road
Keynsham Hospital
Steel Mills
WELLSWAY B3116
Limekilns Cl
Surg
Severn Wy
Welland Rd
Kennet Rd
Tamar Rd
Derwent Grove
Hillis Close
Wellsway School
Chandag J&I School
PO
Tevio Road
Cherwell Rd
Lincoln Close
Kenilworth Cl
Durham Grove
Tenby Rd
Berkeley Gdns
Cameroons Cl
Princess Cl
Park Road
Balmoral Rd
Edinburgh Rd
Compton Gn
Warwick Road
Richmond Cl
Avenue
Amberley Close
Lulworth Road
Dudley Close
Farleigh Road
Walton Close
Coronation
River Chew
Orwell Drive
Lambourn Rd
Clyde Av
Chelmer Grove
Chandag Road
Windrush Road
Torridge Road
Walden Rd
Calder Close
Longmeadow Road
Maple Walk
Willow Walk
Birch Ct
Holmoak Road
Cedar Dr
Newlands Rd
Dunster Road
Tmwrth Rd
Hurn Lane
Minsmere Road
Walnut Close
Oak Tree Wk
Holly Wk
The Brambles
Castle Primary School
St Clements Ct
Rivers' Way
Dene Cl
Medway
Conway Gn
Evenlode Way
Waveney Road
Lyndhurst Road
Sunnymead
1 grid square represents 500 metres

Station
A431 BATH ROAD
The Park
Cherry Gdns
Brr Cl
CHERRY
Golden
E
F
83
G
H
67
68
70
A431 BATH ROAD
Avon Valley Railway
Clay
Clay Lane
Meadow School
Croft Cl
Kings Sq
Tayman Rdg
Mill La
PO
Monarch's Way
Harrington Close
A431 HIGH STREET
Aubrey Meads
Edwin Short Cl
Church Lane
Church Road
Bitton
1
Field Grove Farm
Monarch's Way
2
South Gloucestershire
Bath and North East Somerset
Avon Walkway
3
Avon Valley Country Park
Avon Walkway
Avon Farm
Ashmead
Ashmead Ind Est
Road
Business Centre
Pixash Lane
World's End Lane
Ellsbridge Close
BATH ROAD
A4
4
Lane
Avon
Avon Walkway
69
68
5
Copse Road
Kelston Cl
Wedmore Rd
Chelwood Rd
Wick House Cl
Brockley Road
Stratton Rd
C Cl
Norman Road
Hinton Cl
High Street
Homefield Rd
Homefield Cl
Homefield
Jena Ct
Ilford Close
Lansdown
Beech Road
Claverton Rd
Boyd Road
Roundmoor
Road
105
BS31

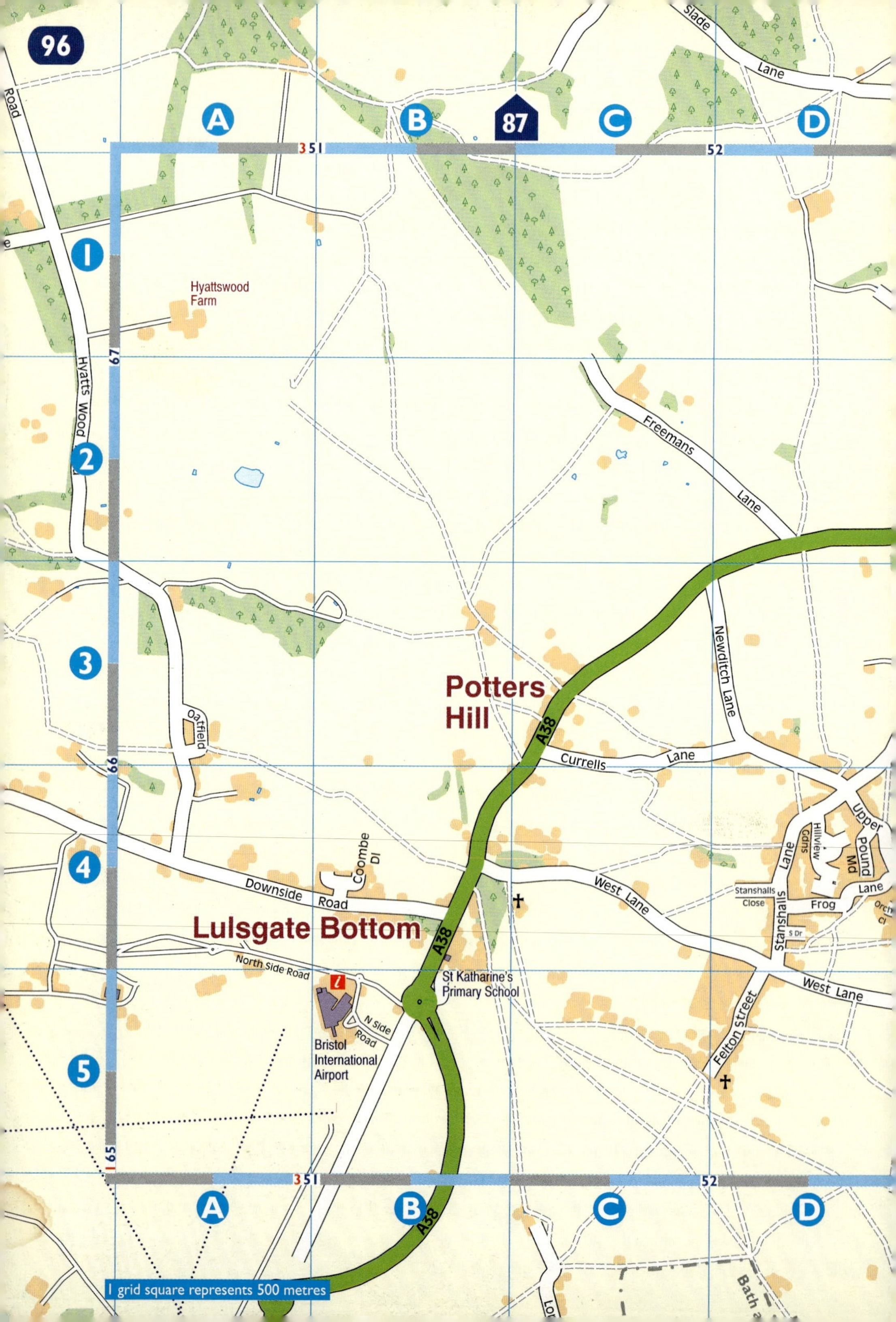

87
A
B
C
D
351
52
1
2
3
4
5
67
66
165
Slade Lane
Road
Hyattswood Farm
Hyatts Wood Road
Freemans Lane
Newditch Lane
Potters Hill
A38
Oatfield
Currells Lane
Upper Pound Lane
Hillview Gdns
Md
Coombe Dl
Downside Road
West Lane
Stanshalls Close
Frog Lane
Stanshalls Lane
S Dr
Lulsgate Bottom
North Side Road
St Katharine's Primary School
N Side Road
Bristol International Airport
Felton Street
1 grid square represents 500 metres

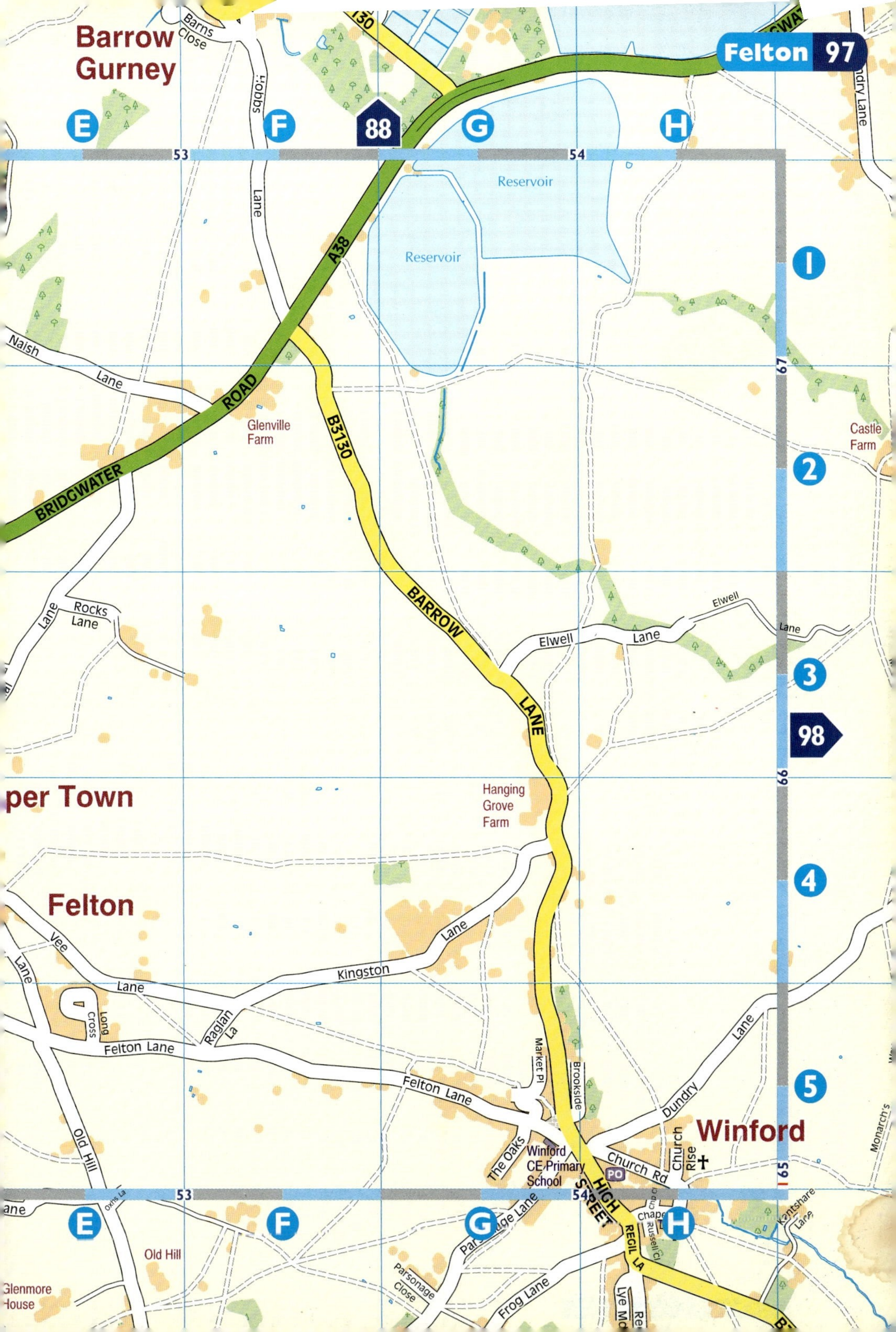

Barrow Gurney
Barns Close
Hobbs Lane
88
E
F
G
H
53
54
Reservoir
Reservoir
A38
Naish Lane
ROAD
BRIDGWATER
Glenville Farm
B3130
BARROW
LANE
Rocks Lane
Lane
Elwell Lane
Elwell Lane
Castle Farm
1
2
3
4
5
67
66
65
98
per Town
Hanging Grove Farm
Felton
Vee Lane
Kingston Lane
Long Cross
Raglan La
Felton Lane
Felton Lane
Old Hill
Market Pl
Brookside
Dundry Lane
Winford
The Oaks
Winford CE Primary School
Church Rd
Church Rise
PO
HIGH STREET
Oxhs La
Old Hill
Glenmore House
Parsonage Lane
Parsonage Close
Frog Lane
REGIL LA
Chapel
Russell Cl
Lye Mo
Kentshare Lane
Monarch's

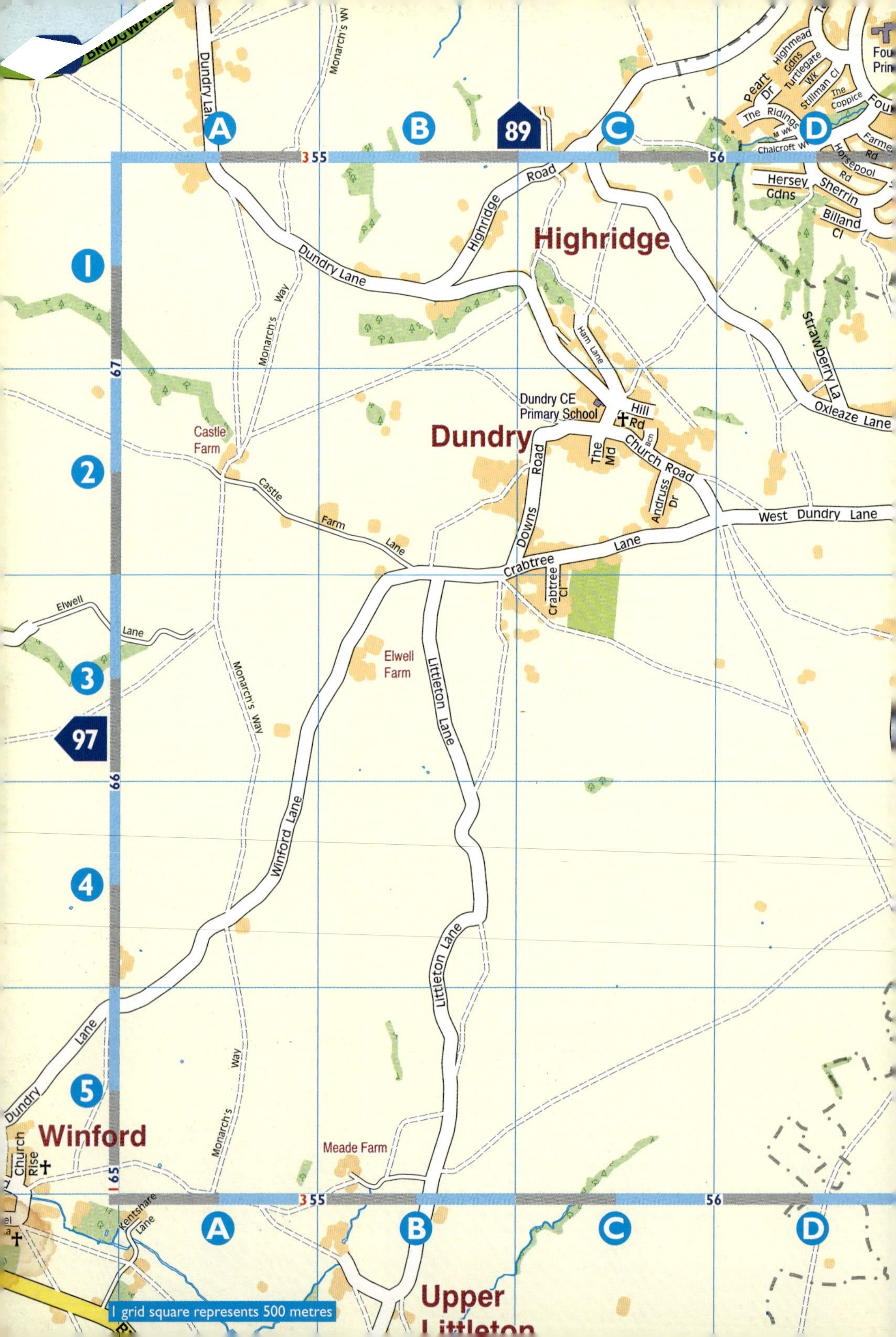

BRIDGWATER
Dundry Lane
Monarch's Way
A
B
89
C
D
355
56
Road
Highridge
Highridge
Dundry Lane
Four
Prin
Highmead Gdns
Peart Dr
Turtlegate Wk
Stillman Cl
The Coppice
The Ridings
M Wk
Chalcroft Wk
Farmer Rd
Horsepool Rd
Hersey Gdns
Sherrin
Billand Cl
Strawberry La
Oxleaze Lane
1
2
3
4
5
67
66
65
Castle Farm
Castle Farm Lane
Ham Lane
Dundry CE Primary School
Hill Rd
Dundry
Downs Road
The Md
Church Road
Bch
Andruss Dr
West Dundry Lane
Crabtree Lane
Crabtree Cl
Elwell Lane
Elwell Farm
Littleton Lane
97
Winford Lane
Dundry Lane
Winford
Church Rise
Meade Farm
Kentshare Lane
Upper Littleton
1 grid square represents 500 metres

Maiden Head
East Dundry
North Wick
City of Bristol
North Somerset
Bath and North East Somerset
East Dundry Lane
Whitchurch Lane
Upton Lane
Wells Road
Broadoak Hill
Queen's Road
Spring La
Three Peaks Walk
Elton Farm
Bishport Avenue
Newland Road
Culverwell Road
Hareclive Road
Hareclive Primary School
Hartcliffe Health Cen
Moxham Drive
Pawlett Road
Crosscombe Drive
Blagrove Crs
Aldwick Av
Tewther Road
Englishcombe Rd
Fair Furlong Primary School
Fair Furlong
Pigott Av
Vowell Cl
Murford Av
Meriet Av
Herridge Cl
Honey Garston Rd
Borver Gv
Bellamy Av
Brocks Rd
Gibbsfold Rd
Greatwood Cl
Symes Av
Sampsons Rd
Oxleaze
Miltons Cl
Holbrook Crs
Branche Gv
Hollister's Dr
Dowling Rd
Chelvy Cl
St John Crs
Cncl Building
Cncl Bldg
Hartgill Cl
Bourchier Gdns
Kencot Wk
Bishport Cl
Newland Wk
Clayplece Rd
Cobhorn Dr
Pesley Cl
Four Acres
Acres Cl
Broad Oak Rd
Leyland Wk
Paybridge Rd
Molesworth Close
Primary Sch
Clinic
Whiting Rd
Arthurswood Rd
Bowring Cl
Mellent Av
Northway
Mc Rd
Halswell Gdns
Lynde Cl
Grinfield
E
F
G
H
I
2
3
4
5
57
58
65
66
67
90
100

100
91
99
Hareclive Road
City of Bristol College (Hartcliffe Centre)
Teyfant Community School
Hartcliffe School
Knightsbridge Pk
Bishport Av
Sampsons Rd
Greatwood Cl
Gibbsfold Rd
Brocks Rd
Symes Av
Holbrook Crs
Miltons Cl
Hollister's Dr
Dowling Rd
Branche Gv
Bishport Avenue
Road
Cncl Building
Chelvy Cl
Upjohn Crs
Crewther Road
Aldwick Av
Englishcombe Rd
Mellent Av
Barbour Rd
Barbour Gdns
Maidenhead Rd
Tynte Av
Lampton Road
Lampton Grove
Lampton Av
Teyfant Road
Shortwood Rd
Witch Hazel Road
The Business Park
Longway Avenue
Rookery Way
Wansdyke Primary
School Cl
Goodwin Dr
Belland Dr
Park Wd Cl
Denleigh Close
Woodmarsh Cl
Yewcroft Cl
Grass Meers Dr
Court Farm Road
Coulson's Rd
Meadowside Dr
Leaholme Gdns
Halfacre Close
Hennessy Cl
Tanorth Road
Coldrick Cl
Edgefield Close
Edgefield Rd
Tanorth Cl
Hill Farm
Maplestone Rd
Bordesley Rd
Kilbirnie Road
Longacre Road
Greenacre Rd
Oldacre Road
Abbots Close
Holbeach
Arrowfield Cl
City of Bristol
Bath and North East Somerset
East Dundry Road
Three Peaks Walk
Maes Knoll Fort
North Wick
Northwick Road
Model Farm
Norton Lane
Norton Court
Church Road
Chalk Farm Cl
Three Walk
Norton Hawkfield
Norton Malreward
A
B
C
D
1
2
3
4
5
3 59
60
67
66
1 65
1 grid square represents 500 metres

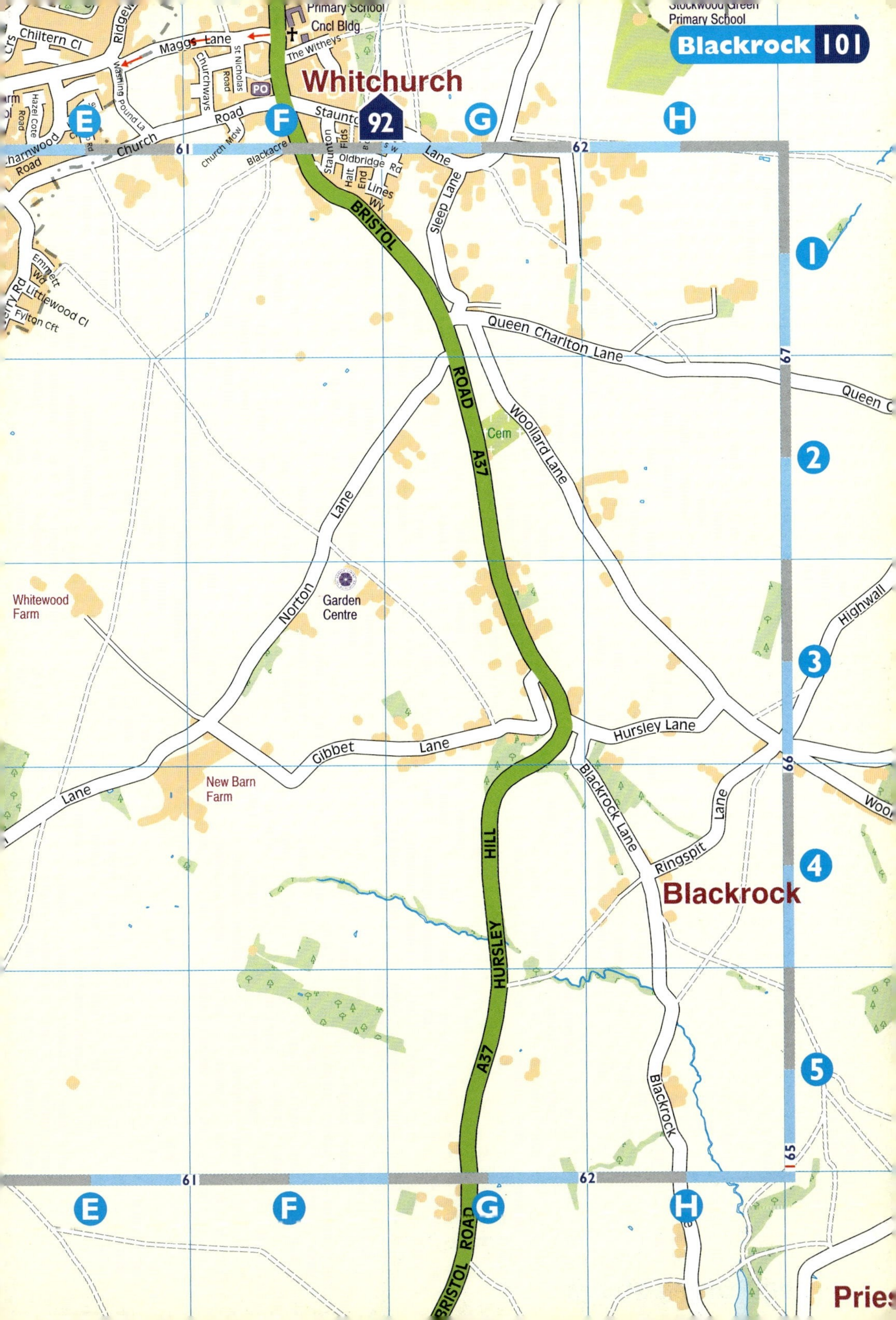
Whitchurch
Blackrock
Pries
Primary School
Stockwood Green Primary School
Cncl Bldg
PO
92
Chiltern Cl
Maggs Lane
The Witheys
St Nicholas Road
Churchways
Washing Pound La
Hazel Cote Road
Charnwood Road
Church Road
Church Mdw
Blackacre
Staunton Flds
Oldbridge Rd
Halt End
Lines Wy
Lane
Sleep Lane
BRISTOL ROAD
A37
Queen Charlton Lane
Queen C
Cem
Woollard Lane
Emmett Wd
Littlewood Cl
Fylton Cft
Norton Lane
Garden Centre
Whitewood Farm
New Barn Farm
Gibbet Lane
Lane
Hursley Lane
Blackrock Lane
Ringspit Lane
Highwall
Woo
HURSLEY HILL
Blackrock
BRISTOL ROAD
E
F
G
H
1
2
3
4
5
61
62
65
66
67

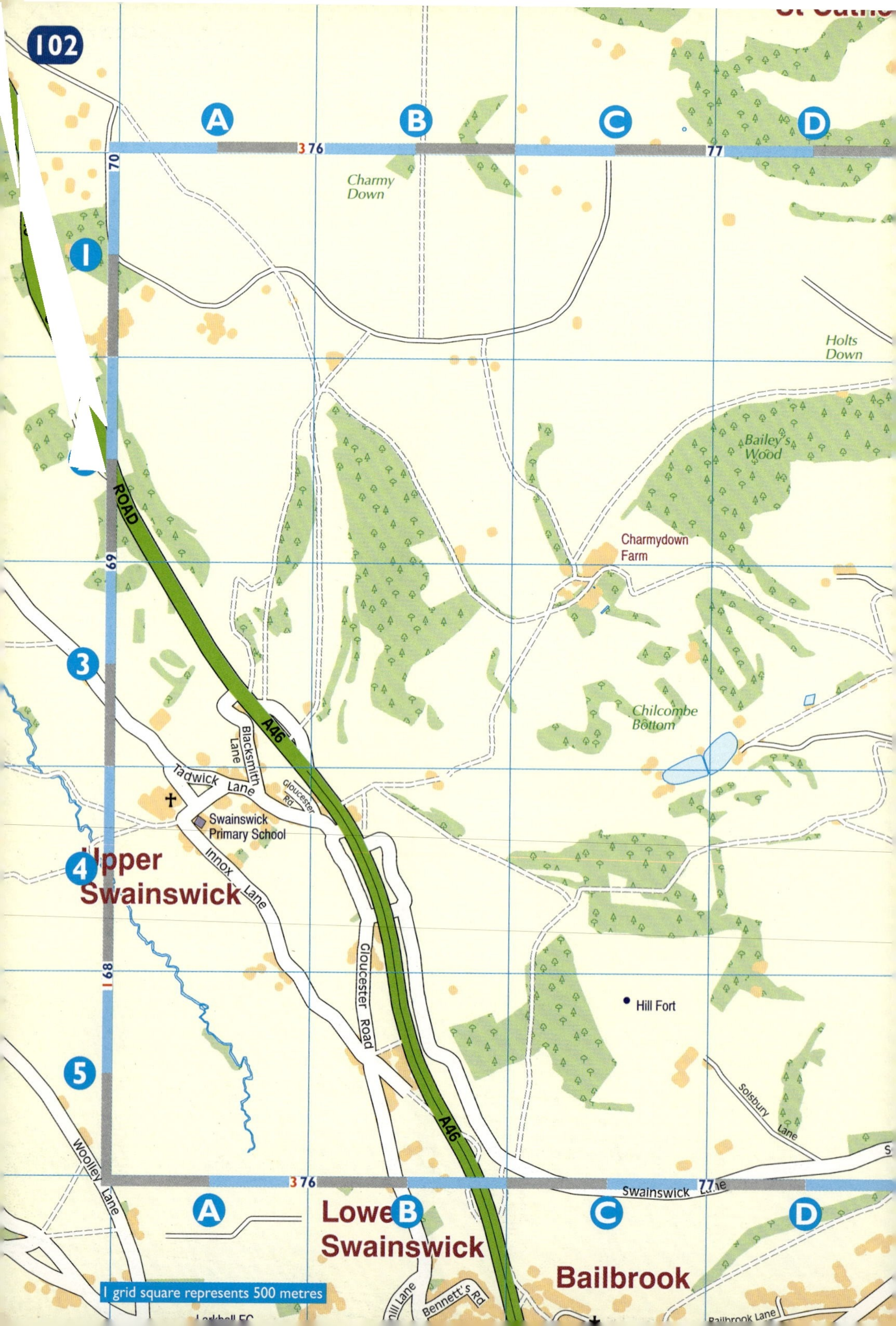

A
B
C
D
376
77
70
69
68
1
3
4
5
Charmy Down
Holts Down
Bailey's Wood
Charmydown Farm
Chilcombe Bottom
ROAD
A46
Blacksmith Lane
Tadwick Lane
Gloucester Rd
Swainswick Primary School
Upper Swainswick
Innox Lane
Gloucester Road
Hill Fort
Solsbury Lane
Woolley Lane
Swainswick Lane
Lower Swainswick
Bailbrook
Bennett's Rd
Bailbrook Lane
1 grid square represents 500 metres

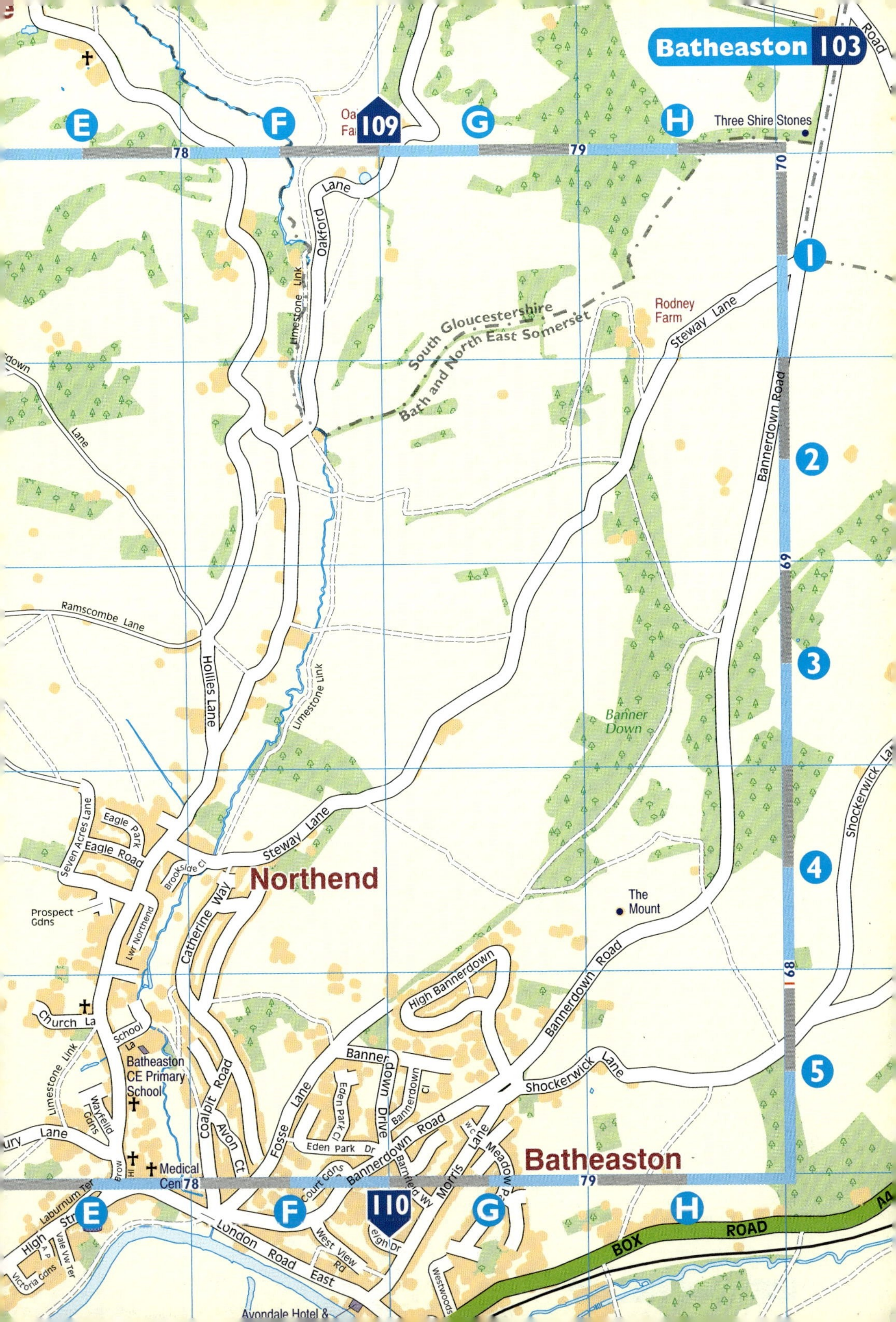
E
F
109
G
H
Three Shire Stones
Road
78
79
70
Lane
Oakford
Limestone Link
South Gloucestershire
Bath and North East Somerset
Rodney Farm
Steway Lane
1
Bannerdown Road
2
Lane
69
Ramscombe Lane
3
Hollies Lane
Limestone Link
Banner Down
Shockerwick Lane
Seven Acres Lane
Eagle Park
Eagle Road
Brookside Cl
Steway Lane
Catherine Way
Northend
4
Prospect Gdns
Lwr Northend
The Mount
Bannerdown Road
68
High Bannerdown
Church La
School La
Batheaston CE Primary School
Limestone Link
Wayfeild Gdns
Banner down Drive
Eden Park Cl
Bannerdown Cl
Shockerwick Lane
5
Coalpit Road
Avon Ct
Fosse Lane
Eden Park Dr
Bannerdown Road
Lane
Brow
Medical Cen
Court Gdns
Barnfield Wy
Morris Lane
Meadow
Batheaston
78
79
110
Laburnum Ter
High Str
E
F
G
H
Vale Vw Ter
Victoria Gdns
London Road East
West View Rd
Westwoods
BOX ROAD
A4
Avondale Hotel &

104
94
95
Hospital
Edinburgh Rd
Compton Gn
Road
Tmwrth Rd
St Clements Ct
River
B3116
Orwell Drive
Clyde Av
Chelmer
Trent
Lambourn Rd
Cherwell Rd
Windrush Road
Torridge Road
Marden Rd
Walden Rd
Calder Close
Minsmere Road
Lane
Dene Cl
Medway Cl
Conway Gn
Medway Dr
Evenlode Way
Witham Road
Waveney Road
Lyndhurst Road
BS31
Sunnymead
Oakfield Road
Cary Road
Martock Rd
Rhode Cl
Manor Road
Two Rivers Way
Chewton Place
Hghf Rd
Nunney Close
Hutton Cl
Lytes Cary
Mells Cl
Tilley Cl
Banwell Cl
Grange
Manse Cl
Lawson Close
Keynsham Manor
Courtenay Road
Cadbury Rd
Chalfield Cl
Hardington Dr
The Homestead
Maesbury Rd
Sunhill Rise
Chewton
Road
Uplands
Depot
Burnett Business Park
Gypsy Lane
B3116 BURNETT HILL
Two Rivers Way
Burnett
Middlepiece Lane
River Chew
ROAD
A4
A
B
C
D
1
2
3
4
5
366
67
66
65
1 grid square represents 500 metres
Stantonbu

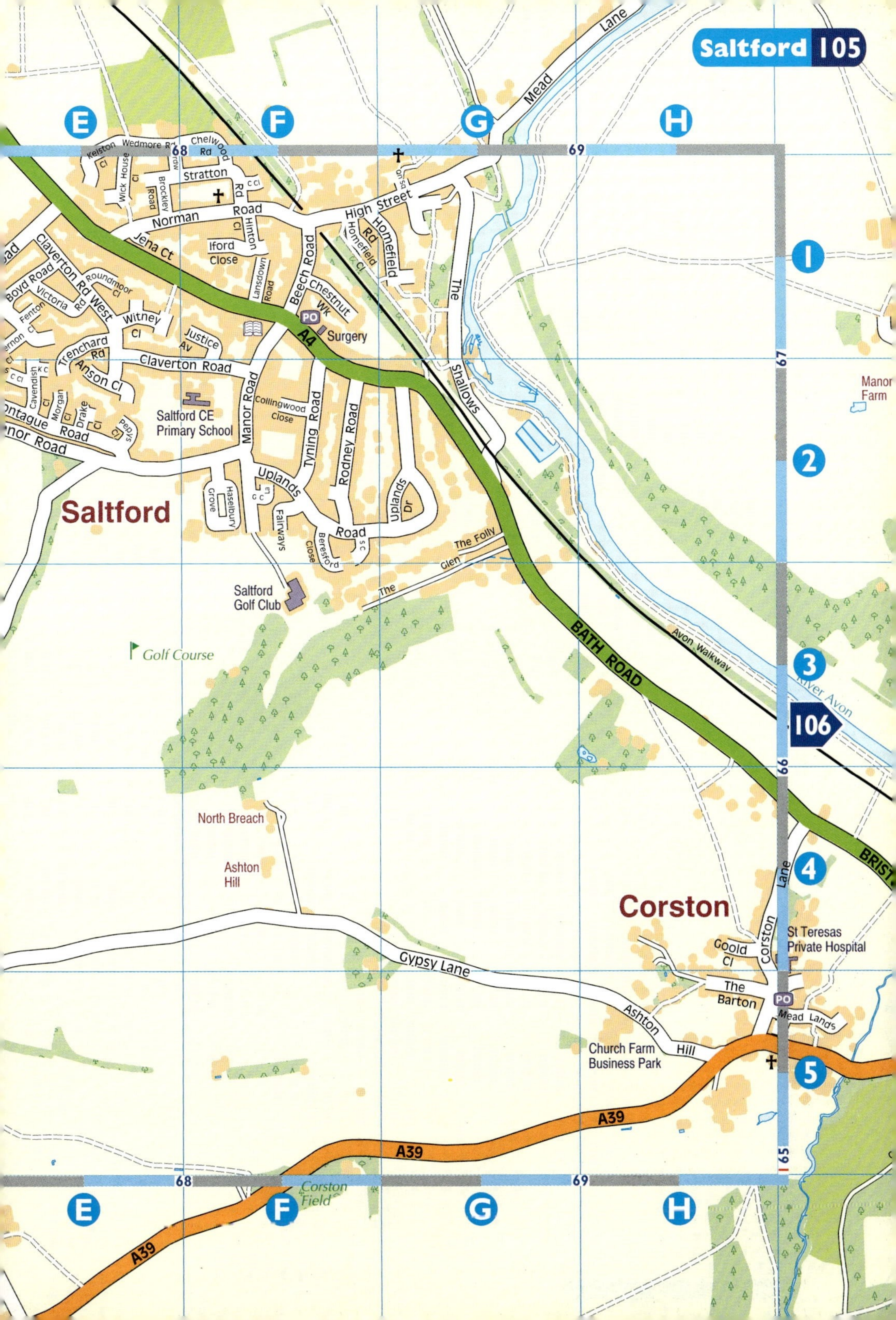
E
F
G
H
1
2
3
4
5
68
69
67
66
65
106
Saltford
Corston
Mead Lane
Kelston
Wedmore Rd
Chelwood Rd
Stratton Rd
Wick House Cl
Brockley Road
Norman Road
Hinton Cl
Iford Close
Jena Ct
High Street
Homefield Rd
Homefield Cl
The Shallows
Claverton Rd West
Boyd Road
Victoria Rd
Roundmoor Cl
Fenton
Witney Cl
Justice Av
Lansdown Road
Beech Road
Chestnut Wk
PO
Surgery
A4
Trenchard Rd
Anson Cl
Claverton Road
Cavendish
Morgan Cl
Drake Cl
Pepys Cl
Montague Road
Manor Road
Saltford CE Primary School
Manor Road
Collingwood Close
Tyning Road
Rodney Road
Uplands Road
Uplands Dr
Haselbury Grove
Fairways
Beresford Close
The Folly
The Glen
Saltford Golf Club
Golf Course
BATH ROAD
Avon Walkway
River Avon
Manor Farm
North Breach
Ashton Hill
Gypsy Lane
Ashton Hill
Corston Lane
Goold Cl
St Teresas Private Hospital
The Barton
Mead Lands
Church Farm Business Park
A39
Corston Field
BRIST

A
B
C
D
370
71
1
2
3
4
5
67
66
165
Kelston
Manor Farm
A431
Kelston Park
Cotswold Way
Dean Hill House
KELSTON
Avon Walkway
River Avon
105
River Avon
Avon Walkway
BRISTOL ROAD A4
Corston Lane
St Teresas Private Hospital
Goold Cl
The Barton
PO
Mead Lands
Hill
PH
A4 BRISTOL ROAD
Corston Drive
Pennyquic
112
PO
Newton St Loe
1 grid square represents 500 metres

Sulians RFC
Heather Farm
Beckford's Tower Museum
E
F
G
H
72
73
Upper Weston
Napier Road
Falconer Rd
Duncan Gdns
Kinber Cl
Leighton Road
Greenacres
Broadmoor Lane
Broadmoor Vale
Heathfield Cl
Lansdown Lane
The Macies
Haviland Grove
Weston Farm Lane
Mortimer Cl
The Weal
Brd Pk
Hvl Pk
Weston All Saints Primary School
Westbrook Pk
Symes Pk
Vernslade
Eastfield Avenue
Holcombe Green
Podgers Dr
Blind Lane
Deanhill Lane
Wstmd Gdn
Brookfield Park
I
67
2
Primros
High Street
Wellington Blds
Trafalgar Rd
Lynfield Park
Church St
Southlands
Purplewent Drive
Weston
Cotswold Way
Anchor Rd
Church Road
Lucklands Rd
Crown Road
Crown Hill
3
Penn Hill Road
Chandler Cl
Greenbank Gardens
St Marys RC Primary School
Manor Rd
Manor Villas
The Grove
Weston Park
Weston Park West
108
East
ROAD
Oldfield School
Frankland Close
Penn Lea Road
Meadow Gdns
West Lea Rd
East Lea Rd
Penn Gdns
S L Rd
Weston Lane
66
Royal United Hospital
A&E
Manor Park
Penn Lea Road
Newbridge
Burleigh Gdns
Partis Way
King Edward Pre-Prep School
Gainsborough Gdns
Cranwells Park
Linden Gdns
4
The Bath Priory Hotel
New Bridge
P+
A4
Old Newbridge Hill
The Mews
Newbridge Gdns
NEWBRIDGE HILL
A431
Evelyn Rd
Lansdown CC
Combe Park
Cedric Road
Badminton Gdns
Oakfield Cl
Park Gdns
Park Lane
Bath Marina & Caravan Park
Sldn Cl
Westfield Pk
Combe Gv
Audley Park Road
Audley Cl
Westhall Rd
Surg
Newbridge St Johns CE Inf Sch
Apsley Road
A36
LOWER BRISTOL ROAD
Brassmill Lane
Homelea Pk East
NEWBRIDGE
Newbridge Junior School
Lyme Rd
Charmouth Rd
Cedric Cl
Lower Weston
Audley Gv
Edward Street
Audley Av
Tennyson Rd
Brassmill Lane Trading Estate
Rudmore Park
Rossiyn Rd
Horstmann Cl
Foxcombe Rd
Kennington Rd
Chelsea Rd
Locksbrook Cemetery
Hungerford Rd
Cemetery
St John's Rd
5
UPPER
Victoria Park Business C
Avon Walkway
Avon Park
The Maltings Industrial Est
ROAD
Park Rd
Council Building
A4
Sh Av
Windsor Villas
WINDSOR BRIDGE RD
A3604
65
Station Rd
Ashley Avenue
Surg
Kaynton Mead
Clarence Pl
Avondale Rd
Redland Park
ewton Mill Ca nd Camping Pa
St Michaels CE Junior School
Woodhouse Rd
Walwyn Cl
113
Locksbrook Road
Ashmans Yd
Locksbrook Trading Est
Rsbrry Rd
Lockbrook
A36
Day Crescent
Road
Cleeve Green
How Hill
Clyde Gdns
Ferry Rd
Fl Rd
Vernon Pk
Bellotts Road
South View Rd
D Rd

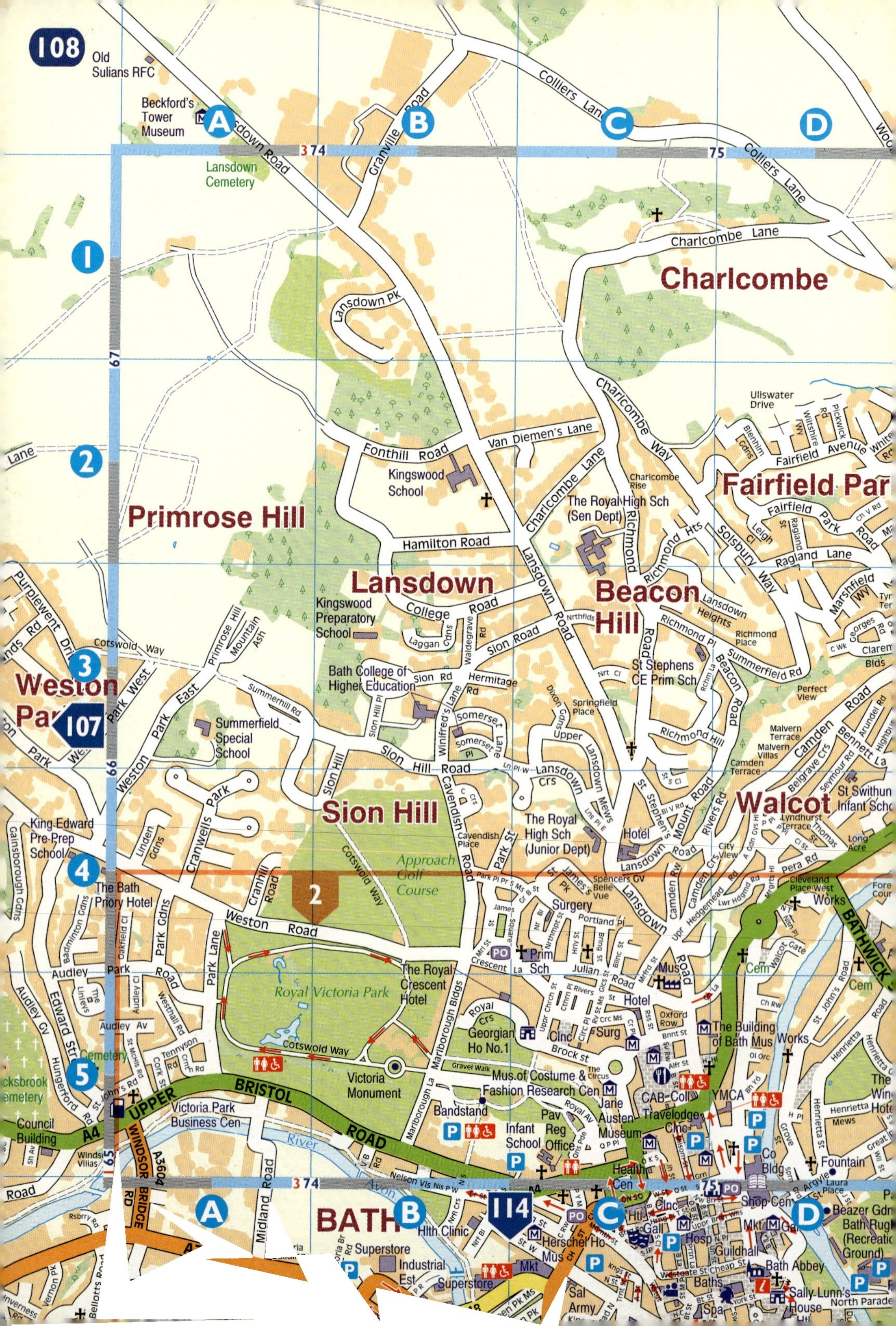
108
Old Sulians RFC
Beckford's Tower Museum
Lansdown Road
Lansdown Cemetery
Granville Road
Colliers Lane
Charlcombe Lane
Charlcombe
Lansdown Pk
Fonthill Road
Van Diemen's Lane
Kingswood School
Hamilton Road
Charlcombe Way
Charlcombe Rise
The Royal High Sch (Sen Dept)
Richmond Hts
Ullswater Drive
Fairfield Avenue
Fairfield Park
Solsbury Way
Ragland Lane
Marshfield Wy
Primrose Hill
Lansdown
Beacon Hill
Kingswood Preparatory School
College Road
Laggan Gdns
Waldegrave Rd
Sion Road
Lansdown Heights
Richmond Place
Richmond Pl
Summerfield Rd
Purplewent Dr
Cotswold Way
Weston Park
107
Mountain Ash
Summerhill Rd
Bath College of Higher Education
Hermitage Rd
Somerset Lane
St Stephens CE Prim Sch
Springfield Place
Richmond Hill
Perfect View
Camden Road
Malvern Terrace
Malvern Villas
Camden Terrace
Summerfield Special School
Weston Park East
Weston Park West
Sion Hill Road
Lansdown Crs
Upper Lansdown Mews
Walcot
St Swithun Infant Sch
Sion Hill
Cavendish Road
Cavendish Place
The Royal High Sch (Junior Dept)
Hotel
Lansdown Road
Mount Road
Rivers Rd
City View
Lyndhurst Terrace
Long Acre
King Edward Pre-Prep School
Cranwells Park
Linden Gdns
Cranhill Road
Approach Golf Course
Park St
Spencers Gv
Belle Vue
Pera Rd
Cleveland Place West
Works
Bathwick
Gainsborough Gdns
The Bath Priory Hotel
Weston Road
Park Gdns
Park Lane
Oakfield Cl
Surgery
Portland Pl
Camden Rw
Camden Crs
Upr Hedgemead Rd
Lwr Hedgemead Rd
Badminton Gdns
Audley Park Road
Audley Gv
Edward St
Royal Victoria Park
The Royal Crescent Hotel
Marlborough Bldgs
Crescent
Prim Sch
Julian Road
Mus
Cem
Walcot Gate
St John's Road
Westhall Rd
Audley Av
Royal Crs
Georgian Ho No.1
Clnc
Surg
Brock St
Oxford Row
The Building of Bath Mus
Henrietta Road
Hungerford Rd
Cemetery
Locksbrook Cemetery
Tennyson Rd
Cork St
St John's Rd
Cotswold Way
Victoria Monument
Gravel Walk
The Circus
Mus. of Costume & Fashion Research Cen
Jane Austen Museum
CAB-Colls
Travelodge
YMCA
Henrietta St
Henrietta Mews
Grove St
Council Building
A4
Upper Bristol Road
Victoria Park Business Cen
Windsor Bridge Rd
A3604
River Avon
Bandstand
Infant School
Reg Office
Pav
Royal Av
Health Cen
Clnc
Co Bldg
Fountain
Laura Place
Winds Villas
Road
Rsbrry Rd
Midland Road
Nelson Vis
BATH
114
Hlth Clinic
Superstore
Industrial Est
Mkt
Herschel Ho
Mus
Shop Cen
Gall
Hosp
Guildhall
Bath Abbey
Beazer Gdns
Bath Rugby (Recreation Ground)
Baths
Spa
Sally Lunn's House
North Parade
Sal Army
Vernon Pk
Belloits Road
A B C D
1 2 3 4 5
374 75 67 66 165
Charlcombe Lane

Lower Swainswick
Bailbrook
Larkhall
Lambridge
Bathampton
Bathwick
Swainswick Lane
Solsbury Lane
Bailbrook Lane
London Road West
A4 London Road West
A4 London Road
A46
A4
A36
Warminster Road
Beckford Road
Sydney Road
River Avon
Kennet & Avon Canal
Avon Walkway
Alice Park
Larkhall FC
Gloucester Road
Deadmill Lane
Bennett's Rd
Charlcombe Lane
Valley View Close
Hill View Rd
Rose Hill
Valley View Rd
Ferndale Rd
Swainswick Gdns
Oriel Gdns
Elm Grove
Fuller Road
Woodlands Pk
Uph Dr
Coxley Drive
Spring La
Spring Vale
Junior School
Eldon Place
Dafford St
Dafford's Blds
Brooklyn Rd
St Saviour's Road
Brougham Place
Pitman Court
Larkhall Pl
Brookleaze Buildings
Larkhall Terrace
Upper Lamb St
Lambridge St
Salisbury Rd
Worcester Park
Havory
Beaufort Pl
Beaufort Mews
Beaufort West
St Saviours Infant Sch
St Saviours Terrace
Bay Tree Road
Hawarden Ter
Vale View Place
Eastville
Dowding Rd
Wallace Rd
Holland Rd
Claremont Road
Belgrave Road
Health Centre
Chilton Rd
Upper East Hayes
Middle Lane
Worcester Terrace
Percy Place
Grosvenor Pl
Grosvenor Gardens
Grosvenor Bridge Rd
Ringswell Gardens
Surg
Superstore
Norland College
Bath Boating Station
Hampton Row
Rockliffe Av
Rockliffe Rd
Forester Av
Forester Road
Forester La
Beckford Gdns
Darlington Rd
Powlett Road
Bathwick St Mary CE Primary School
Minster Way
Trossachs Drive
St George's Hill
St Christophers Cl
King Edwards Junior School
King Edwards School
North Road
Holburne Museum of Art
Vellore La
The Bath Spa Hotel
Sham Castle Lane
Sydney Mews
Raby Mews
Raby Place
Sydney Whf
St Mary's Cl
St Ann's Way
Chatham Park
Cleveland Walk
Bathwick Hill
Darlington Pl
Cleveland Court
Lime Grove Special Sch
Golf Course
Bath Golf Club
Golf Course Road
Sham Castle
Toll
Toll Br Rd
Kennet Park
Meadow La
Bathampton Lane
Devonshire Road
Miller Wk
Down Lane
High Street
Holcombe
The Normans
Laburnum Ter
Vale Vw Ter
Wayfield Gdns
PO
PH
E
F
G
H
1
2
3
4
5
76
77
67
66
65
102
110
115

Batheaston
Bathford
Batheaston CE Primary School
Medical Centre
Solsbury Lane
Limestone Link
Wayfield Gdns
Coalpit Road
Avon Ct
Eden Park Cl
Eden Park Dr
Bannerdown Dr
Bannerdown Cl
Bannerdown Road
Shockerwick Lane
Court Gdns
Farmfield Wy
Morris La
Meadow Park
Warleigh Dr
West View Rd
Westwoods
Laburnum Ter
High Street
Vale Vw Ter
Victoria Gdns
London Road East
Avondale Hotel & Waterside Restaurant
BOX ROAD
A4
Toll Br Rd
Toll
Avon
Mill Lane
Bathampton Primary School
Church Cl
Tyning Road
LC
Limestone Link
Avon Walkway
PH
PO
Harbutts
Kennet Park
The Normans
Down Lane
Holcombe Vale
Holcombe Lane
Devonshire Road
Holcombe Close
Downside Cl
Holcombe Farm
Hantone Hill
Bathford Hill
Ostlings Lane
Church Street
Manor Dr
Bathford Prim Sch
Dovers Lane
Mountain Wood
Dovers Park
Chrch Cl
Court La
Pump Lane
A363
BRADFORD ROAD
Warleigh Lane
Warleigh Lodge Farm
Nature Reserve
Bathampton Wood
WARMINSTER ROAD
A36
Avon Walkway
River Avon
Warleigh Manor
Kennet & Avon
103
109
1 grid square represents 500 metres

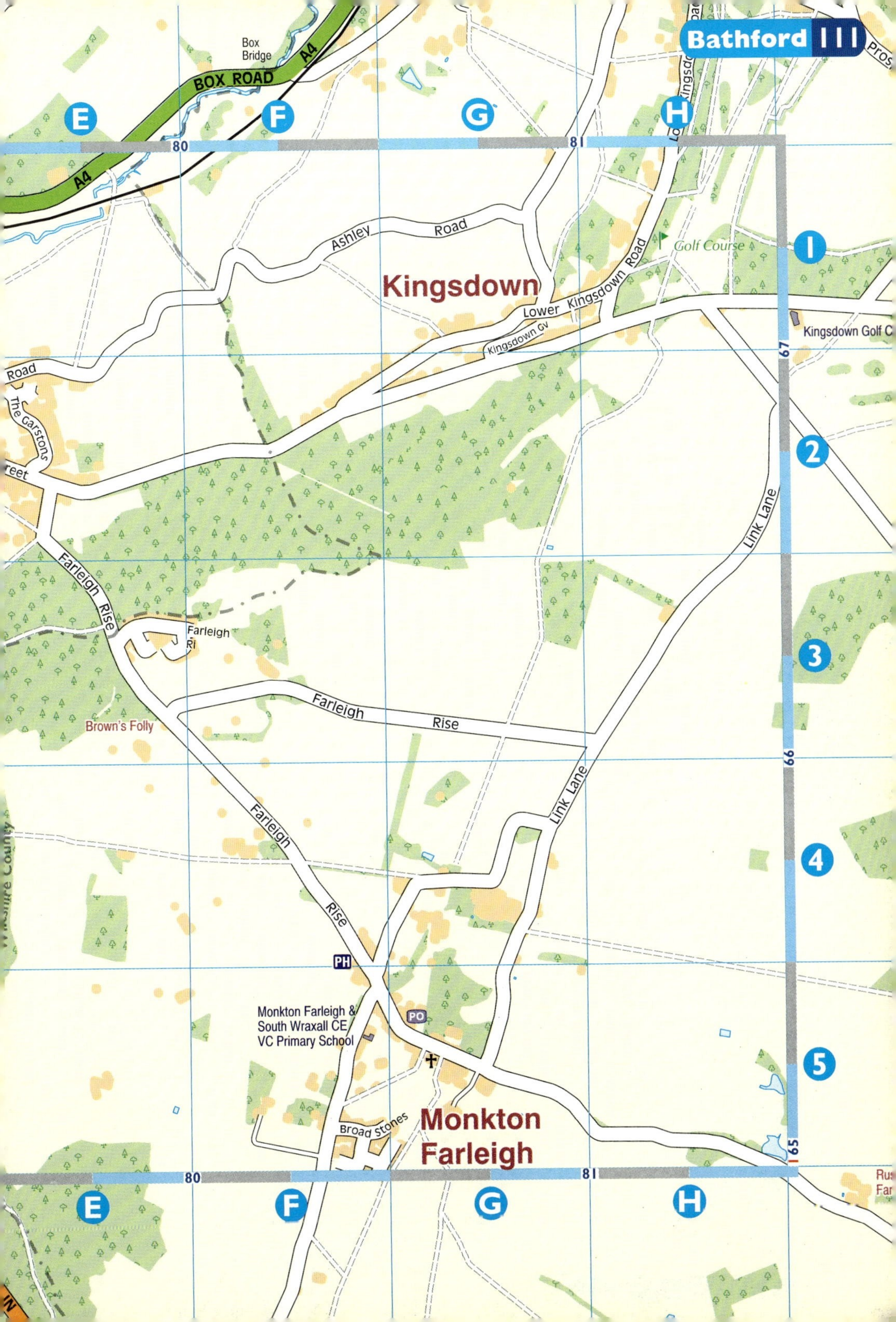
Box Bridge
BOX ROAD
A4
E
F
G
H
80
81
Ashley Road
Golf Course
I
Kingsdown
Lower Kingsdown Road
Kingsdown Gv
Kingsdown Golf C
67
Road
The Carstons
reet
2
Link Lane
Farleigh Rise
Farleigh Ri
3
Brown's Folly
Farleigh Rise
66
Link Lane
Farleigh Rise
4
PH
PO
Monkton Farleigh & South Wraxall CE VC Primary School
5
Broad Stones
Monkton Farleigh
65
80
81
E
F
G
H

112
106
PH
A
B
C
D
370
71
65
64
63
1
2
3
4
5
Corston Drive
Pennyquick
PO
Newton St Loe
Pennyquick
Clays End
Bath Spa University College
Newton Park College
Newton Brook
Pennsylvania Farm
1 grid square represents 500 metres

Lower Weston
Newbridge Junior School
Brassmill Lane Trading Estate
Lower Bristol Road
Newbridge Road
Upper Bristol Road
A4
A431
A3604
A36
Windsor Bridge Rd
Victoria Park Business Centre
Cemetery
Council Building
107
Locksbrook Road
Locksbrook Road Trading Est
Locksbrook
Ashmans Yd
Kaynton Mead
Redland Park
Newton Mill Caravan and Camping Park
St Michaels CE Junior School
Day Crescent
Newton Road
Cleeve Green
Pennard Green
Cameley Green
Shaws Way
Twerton Infant Sch
Twerton
Watery Lane
How Hill
Dominion Road
Freeview Road
High St
Albany Road
Loxton Dr
Landseer Rd
Bath City FC
Highland Rd
Twerton Cemetery
King George's Rd
Lansdown View
Shophouse Road
South Twerton
Millmead Road
West Avenue
Oldfield Park Station
Triangle North
Moorland Rd
Herbert Road
Cynthia Road
Dartmouth Av
Claude Terrace
Victoria Cl
Lymore Avenue
Lymore Gdns
Claude Av
St Kilda's Rd
Faulkland Rd
Melcombe Rd
Wansdyke Business Centre
Oldfield Park Junior School
Lymore Ter
Sheridan Road
Garrick Road
Poolemead Road
Whiteway Road
Wedgwood Rd
Eleanor Close
Linley Close
Cncl Bldg
Kelston View
St Michaels Road
Haycombe Dr
West Cl
Whiteway
Rosewarn Cl
Haycombe Drive
Blagdon Park
The Hollow
Cotswold Vw
The Brow
Innox Road
Parry Close
Elliston Drive
Langdon Rd
Sladebrook Road
Southdown Road
Teddington Cl
Ivy Grove
Ivy Avenue
Coronation Avenue
Hillcrest Drive
Elm Grove
Chestnut Gv
Ash Gv
Beech Gv
The Oval
Moorfields
Oak Av
Cedar Gv
Englishcombe Lane
Kingsway
Stirtingale Road
Stirtingale Av
Hycombe Farm
Haycombe Cemetery
Crematorium
Garden Centre
Southdown
Roundhill Park
Lytton Gdns
Alderley Rd
Wedmore Park
Mount Road
Glebe Road
Oriel Grove
Burford Cl
Southdown Av
Roundhill Gv
Melrose Gv
Southdown J&I School
Mount Gv
Belmore Gdns
Haycombe La
Whiteway Av
Marsden Road
Georgian View
Kingsfield
Ambleside Road
Edgeworth Road
Rowacres
Canons Cl
Padleigh Hill
Culverhay Sports Centre
Culverhay School
Rush Hill
Somerdale View
Corston View
Somerdale Av
Bloomfield Drive
Hampset CC
Weatherly Av
St Philips CE Primary School
Frome Road
Wansdyke Road
Washpool Lane
Innox Gv
Breach Wood
Old Culverhaysians RFC
Fosse
Vernham Grove
Barrow Road
Kingsway
114
E
F
G
H
1
2
3
4
5
72
73
65
64
63

114
108
113
116
A
B
C
D
1
2
3
4
5
74
75
65
64
63
BATH
Oldfield Park
Beechen Cliff
Kingsway
Bloomfield
Odd Down
Fox Hill
The Oval
A4
A36
A367
A3604
B3111
B3118
UPPER BRISTOL ROAD
WINDSOR BRIDGE RD
LOWER BRISTOL RD
GREEN PARK ROAD
WELLS ROAD
ROSSITER RD
JUNCTION RD
OLDFIELD ROAD
BRADFORD ROAD
CORN ST
River Avon
Cotswold Way
Victoria Monument
Victoria Park Business Cen
Georgian Ho No.1
Mus of Costume & Fashion Research Cen
Bandstand
Jane Austen
Travelodge
YMCA
CAB
Coll
Health Cen
Royal Av
Brock St
Circus
Gravel Walk
Marlborough La
Council Building
Windsor Villas
Midland Road
Victoria Buildings
Superstore
Industrial Est
Hlth Clinic
Herschel Ho
Mus
Mkt
Sal Army
Guildhall
Bath Abbey
Baths
Spa
Sally Lunn's House
Arts Cen
Bath Coll
Southgate Shop Cen
Police Stn
Book Mus
Bath Spa Stn
Bath Rugby (Recreation Ground)
Beazer Gdn
Fountain
Henrietta Mews
Express by Holiday Inn
Cemetery
Hayesfield Sch (Lower)
Bus Park
Oldfield Old Boys RC
Works
Green Park
Twerton Cemetery
Oldfield Park Inf Sch
Oldfield Park Station
South View Rd
Caledonian Rd
Brook Road
Lorne Rd
Millmead Road
Ringwood Rd
West Avenue
Triangle North
Moorland Rd
Shaftesbury Road
Winchester Road
Canterbury
Lower Oldfield Pk
College
Upper Oldfield Park
Surg
Thornbank Pl
Crescent View
Holloway
St Mark's Community Cen
Calton Gdns
Alexandra Rd
Lyncombe
Claude Terrace
Cynthia Road
Herbert Road
Beckhampton Road
Third Avenue
Second Avenue
First Av
King Edward Rd
Walnut Dr
Maple Gdns
Durley Pk
Bloomfield Avenue
Maple Gv
Wansdyke Business Cen
St Johns Cath Prim Sch
Oldfield Park Junior School
Lymore Gdns
Monksdale Road
Hillside Road
Cotswold Road
Poplar Cl
Hazel Gv
Elm Grove
Chestnut Gv
Ash Gv
Beech Gv
Moorfields Road
Moorlands J&I School
Willow Green
Egerton Rd
Hensley Road
Hensley Gdns
Chantry Mead Road
Wentworth House Hotel
Shakespeare Avenue
Chaucer Road
Kipling Avenue
Milton Avenue
Longfellow Avenue
Devonshire Buildings
Greenway Court
Greenway Lane
Beechen Cliff School
Lyncombe Vale
Paragon School
Bruton Av
Byron Rd
Shelley Rd
Englishcombe Lane
Bloomfield Park
Bloomfield Road
Hatfield Rd
St Luke's Rd
Castle Gdns
Entry Hill Gdns
Entry Hill
Entry Hill Dr
Lynbrook La
Stirling Av
Cedar Gv
Acacia Gv
Oak Av
Englishcombe Way
Westfield Cl
Bloomfield Drive
Hampset CC
Somerdale Av
Somerdale View
Weatherly Av
St Philips CE Primary School
Frome Road
Wansdyke Road
Barrow Road
Old Fosse Rd
Vernham Grove
Chelwood Dr
Entry Rise
Hawthorn Grove
Down Av
Ivy Bank Park
Entry Hill Park
Drake Av
Sedgemoor Road
Queen's Drive
Kewstoke Rd
Meare Road
Axbridge Rd
Quantocks
Porlock Road
Fox Hill
Horsecombe Brow
Clevedale Rd
St Martins Hospital
1 grid square represents 500 metres

Holburne Museum of Art
School
North Road
Sydney Road
A36
Vellore La
The Bath Spa Hotel
Bathwick
Sham Castle Lane
109
Golf Course
E
F
G
H
76
78
65
64
63
Raby Place
Sydney Whf
St Mary's Cl
St Ann's Way
Chatham Park
Bath Golf Club
Golf Course Road
Sham Castle
Lime Grove Special Sch
Bathwick Hill
Darlington Pl
Cleveland Walk
Cleveland Court
Sydney Buildings
Pulteney
Quarry Road
Convocation Avenue
University of Bath
University of Bath Sports Training Village
North Road
Bathwick Hill
Woodland Place
Queens Place
Caroline Buildings
Widcombe
Widcombe Hill
Horseshoe Walk
Abbey Vw Gdns
The Tyning
Tyning End
Cambridge Ter
Bathwick Cemetery
The Avenue
Copseland
Oakley
Woodland Gv
Beech Av
Norwood Av
Clarendon Villas
Clarendon Rd
Church St
Clarence Terrace
Claverton Court
Quarry Rock Gardens
Claverton Down Road
Prospect Rd
Macaulay Bldgs
Daisy Bank
A3062 Ralph Allen Drive
Church Lane
Pope's Walk
Cem
Perrymead
Claverton Down
Prior Park (NT)
Flatwoods Rd
Chedworth Cl
Hazleton
Priory Close
Prior Park College
The Bath Clinic
Claverton Down Road
Civil Service Sports Club
Ralph Allen School
Trinity Road
Hadley Rd
Farrs Lane
Stonehouse Lane
North Road
Paddock Woods
Tyning Road
Gladstone Rd
St. Winifreds
Shaft Road
North Road
Surgery
The Avenue
The Firs
117
Combe Grove Hotel & Country Club
Combe Road
Church
Primary School
Belmont Rd
Road
Monkton Combe Junior School
Shaft Road
The Croft
PO
Bramble Way

Rush Hill
Edgeworth
Somerdale View
Corston View
Bloomfield Drive
Bloomfield Rise
Quarry
Old
Bloomfield
Hampset CC
Somerdale Av
Weatherly
Frome Road
St Philips Primary School
Odd Down
114
A
B
C
D
373
74
Barrow Road
Wansdyke Road
PO
Chelwood Dr
Old Fosse Road
Vernham Grove
Odins Road
Shickle Grove
Upper Bloomfield Road
Stanway Cl
Oolite Road
Beeches
Old Culverhaysians RFC
1
2
3
4
5
62
61
60
Eastover Gv
Clare Gdns
Colbourne Rd
WELLSWAY
A367
Oolite Gv
Lympsham Green
St Martins Hospital
A3062 FROME ROAD
St Martins Garden Prim Sch
Cranmore Pl
Abingdon Gdns
Banwell Road
Fosse Gdns
Mendip Gardens
Fullers Wy
Wansdyke School
Margaret Coates Special School
Old Frome Rd
Hansford Square
Entry Rise
Entry Hill
Hansford Cl
Hill Av
Quarry Cl
BRADFORD
Southstoke Road
MIDFORD
Ivy Bank Park
Entry Hill Park
Drake Av
Oakhill Rd
Vernham Wood
St Gregorys Catholic College
Rideg Green Cl
Willow Cl
Kilkenny Lane
Sulis Manor Road
Holly Dr
Hazel Way
Alder Wy
Burnt House Road
Poplar Rd
P+
Odd Down FC
Sulis Manor
Combe Hay Lane
Southstoke Lane
Pack
PH
Rowley Wood
Hodshill
Week Farm
Avon Walkway
Rowley House
Brook Cam
Cemetery
Combe Hay
1 grid square represents 500 metres

Odd Down 117
115
Fox Hill
Combe Down RC
Combe Down
Monkton Combe
Tucking Mill
Midford
Midford Castle
Midford Brook
Horsecombe Vale
Wiltshire County
Bath and North East Somerset
North Road
A3062
NORTH ROAD
B3110
MIDFORD HILL
Summer Lane
Beechwood Road
Belmont Rd
Church Road
Shaft Road
St. Winifreds Dr
Midford Road
Midford Lane
Old Midford Road
Lane
Avon Walkway
Avon Walk way
Queen's Drive
Kewstoke Rd
Fox Hill
Quantocks
Porlock Road
Grove
Horsecombe Brow
Cleevedale Rd
Horsecombe Gv
Horsecombe Vale
Greendown Pl
Bramble Way
Stonehouse Cl
Stonehouse Lane
Trinity Road
Hadley Rd
Farrs
The Firs
The Avenue
Westerleigh Rd
Combe Road
Rock La
Byfield
The Paddocks
Surgery
Primary School
PO
PH
Monkton Combe Pre-Prep School
Monkton Combe Junior School
Ralph Allen School
Prior Park College
Paddock Woods
Bumper's Batch
Tyning Road
Gladstone Rd
E
F
G
H
I
2
3
4
5
76
77
62
61
60
hstoke
Pipeh

Great Ashley
A
B
C
D
380
81
62
61
60
1
2
3
4
5
B3108
Hollybush Cl
The Mead
Broomground
Fieldins
Northfield
Saxon Wy
Ashley La
White Horse Rd
PO
Tyning Road
Winsley Rd
Dane Rise
Winsley
Alfred Way
Poston Wy
St Nicholas Cl
Dn Cl
Winsley CE Primary School
Bradford Road
Late Broads
Limpley Stoke Road
Bradford Rd
Quarry Close
Cottles Lane
Turleigh
Green Lane
River Avon
Macmillan Way
Kennet and Avon Canal
Avoncliff Station
PH
Macmillan Way
Avoncliff
Lye Green
Woodside
Bobbin La
Friary Cl
Staples Hill
Westwood
Westwood With Iford Primary School
Leslie Rise
The Pastures
Tynings Way
Boswell
1 grid square represents 500 metres

BRADFORD-ON-AVON
Ashley
Leigh
Woolley Green
Woolley
Widbrook
Maplecroft
Northleigh
Leigh Park Hotel
Woolley Grange Hotel
Bradford-on-Avon Community Hospital
St Laurence School
Christ Church CE Primary Sch
Surgery
Bradford on Avon Swimming Pool
Health Centre
Bradford-on-Avon Station
Tithe Barn
Fitzmaurice Primary Sch
Treenwood Industrial Estate
Elmcross Business Park
B3105
BATH ROAD
A363
B3109
SLADESBROOK
WINSLEY ROAD
MASONS LA
MARKET ST
SILVER ST
HOLT ROAD
NEW ROAD
SPRINGFIELD
FROME RD
FROME ROAD
ST MARGARET'S ST
TROWBRIDGE RD
MT PLEASANT
Ashley Road
Leigh Park Road
Berryfield Rd
Christchurch Rd
Palmer Dr
Huntingdon Ri
Huntingdon St
Church Acre
Priory Cl
Priory Pk
Conigre Hill
Bear Cl
Magnon Rd
Churches
Elmfield
Westfield
Downs View
Downs Cl
Budbury Tyning
Budbury Rdg
Budbury Pl
The Wilderness
Newtown
Church St
Wine St
Sandy Leaze
Hare Knapp
Rickfield
Meadowfield
Grove Leaze
Belcombe Road
Barton Orch
Bridge St
Woolley Street
Woolley Drive
Woolley St
Woolley Ter
Cemetery Lane
Kingsfield
Whitehill
Whiteheads La
Highfield Rd
Bancroft
Bainton Cl
Grange Vw
Upr Regents Pk
Regents Pl
Greenland View
Avon Cl
Downavon
Laurence Rd
Kingston Av
Avonfield Av
Culver Rd
Loddon Wy
Southville Rd
St Aldhelm Rd
Mythern Meadow
Widbrook View
Pound Lane
Kennet Gdns
Macmillan Way
Poulton
Jones Hill
Southleigh
Elms Cross Dr
Spencers Orch
Chanterelle
Baileys Barn
Palairet Cl
Road
Piplar Ground
Southway
Barn Piece
Follyfield
Bassetts Pasture
Methuen Cl
Deverell Cl
Fitzmaurice Cl
Poulton La
Hobhouse Cl
Moulton Drive
John Rennie Cl
Rowden Lane
Frome Road
82
83
62
61
60
E
F
G
H
1
2
3
4
5
120

120
Cemetery
Stavert
A
B
C
D
3 84
85
Great Bradford Wood
River Avon
Mythern Meadow
Avonfield Av
Rd
Loddon Wy
119
60
John Rennie Cl
1
2
River Avon
Kennet & Avon Canal
idbrook
3
A363
Lady Down Farm
59
TROWLE
4
Langford Road
Melton Rd
Francis Street
Jenkins St
Charles Street
Westcroft Street
PO
Shails Lane Industrial Estate
B3106
River Way
Hill St
Trowle Common
Westwood Road
Westwood Road
Ketton Cl
Clipsham Ri
COCK HILL
A363
Charnwood Rd
Helmdon Rd
Broadmead
Cloford Cl
Oak Tree Close
Leafield Pl
Chepston Pl
Sherborne
Shore Pl
Chilmark Rd
Barnack Cl
Ancaster Cl
Cranmore Cl
Lynwood Rd
Elliott Pl
Walwayne Court Primary School
Innox Mill Cl
Innox Road
Linden Place
Bryer Ash Business Park
5
158
3 84
85
BRADFORD ROAD
A
B
C
D
122
Woburn Cl
Chalfont Cl
Road
Meadway
Brook Meadow
Brook
Crawley Crs
Rossett Gdns
Avenue
St Augustines Cath Sch & Tech Coll
Warbler Cl
Surgery
Trowbridge Station
St Johns RC Prim Sch
Westbourne Gdns
STALLARD ST
RD
1 grid square represents 500 metres

Hilperton Marsh
Hilperton
TROWBRIDGE
BA14
E
F
G
H
86
87
1
2
3
4
5
60
59
58
123
New Terrace
Marsh Road
B3105
Hill Street
B3106
Canal Road
Hammond Way
Elm Cl
Staverton CE Primary School
School Lane
Smallbrook Gardens
Marina Dr
Swan Dr
The Slipway
Thestfield Dr
Towpath Road
Tudor Dr
Saxon Dr
Navigator Cl
Kings Gdns
Hanover Cl
Wyke Rd
Wyke Road
Carisbrooke Crs
Compton Cl
Princess Gdns
Queens Gardens
St Mary's Gardens
Saxon Drive
St Mary's Cl
Foxglove Dr
Horse Road
Canal Rd
Marshmead
Newleaze
Greenhill Gdns
Hilperton CE Primary School
Dymott Sq
Whaddon Lane
Whaddon Lane
Cherry Gardens
The Knap
St Michaels Cl
Church St
Nr Cl
Devizes
Hayes Cl
Avon Way
Kennet Way
Ivy Cl
Brick Lane
Greenway Gdns
The Down
Cemetery
The Downside Pk
Trowbridge Parochial Junior School
Osborne Rd
Victoria Road
Albert Road
Victoria Gardens
Fulney Cl
Middle Lane
Raglethorpe Road
Raglethorpe Gv
Fieldways Hotel & Health Club
Albany Cl
Trowbridge Rd
Ashton Rise
Ashton Road
Ashton Rd
Apsley Close
A361
Castley Road
Newhurst Pk
Woodhouse Gdns
Hilperton Drive
The Mead Primary School
Avonvale Road
Murray Road
Palmer Road
Islington
Windermere Rd
Coniston Road
The Mount
Fulford Rd
Rodwell Park
Cleveland Gdns
Royce Clnc
Victoria Rd
Halfway Cl
The Beeches
Kenton Dr
Grasmere
Pepperacre Lane
Hilperton Road
Faverole Way
Painters Mead
Gibbs Leaze
Hackett Pl
Leap Ga
Corbin Road
Cusance Way
Walmesley Chase
Montague Court
Paxcroft Brook
Prospect Place
Downhayes Rd
Lower Ct
Surgery
York Buildings
Delamere Road
Lowmead
Thomas St
Springfield Park
Stancomb Av
Ravenscroft Gdns
Timbrell St
Cross St
George Street
Bellefield Crs
The Halve
Taylors Vw
Union St
Duke Street
Church Street
Larkrise Sch
Paxcroft Primary Sch
Quarterway La
Eastbourne Road
Furlong Gdns
Lark Down
Barn Glebe
Yerbury Street
Polebarn Road
County Way
Harford St
Clark's Pl
Ashton Street
Heather Sh
Paxcroft Way
Lyneham Wy
Cornbrash Rd
Stokehill
Green Lane
Green Lane Farm
Parsonage Road
Moyle Pk
Orpington Wy
Castle Place Shopping Centre
Town Hall
Roundstone Prep School
Castle Place Leisure Centre
Castle St
Market St
Silver St
St Stephen's Pl
Surgery
West Ashton Road
Clarendon Road
Green Lane
Kenwood Cl
Honeymans Cl
Slowgrove Cl
Cadby Cl
Clarence Rd
Amouracre
Trowbridge RFC
PO
P

122
120
A
B
C
D
1
2
3
4
5
58
57
56
3 84
85
Westwood Road
Chepston Pl
Sherborne
Shore Pl
Leafield Pl
Charnwood
Helmdon Rd
Broadmead
Chilmark Rd
Barnack Cl
Ancaster Cl
Cranmore Cl
Cloford Cl
Lynwood Rd
Walwayne Ct Primary School
Oak Tree Close
A363
Innox Mill Cl
Innox Road
Linden Place
Bradford Road
Shails Lane Industrial Estate
B3106
River Way
Bryer Ash Business Park
Station Way
Hill St
Shires Shopping Centre
Trowbridge Station
Stallard St
Bythesea Rd
Surgery
St Johns RC Prim Sch
Westbourne Gdns
Westbourne Rd
West St
Newtown Com Prim School
Wiltshire Council Offices
Newtown
Woburn Cl
Halfront Cl
Meadway
Widbrook Meadow
Brook Rd
Crawley Crs
Rossett Gdns
Acacia Cl
Christin Court
Bridge Avenue
Berkeley Rd
Farleigh Avenue
St Augustines Cath Sch & Tech Coll
Warbler Cl
Nightingale Rd
Wren Ct
Swallow Dr
Surgery
WINGFIELD ROAD
A366
Millington Drive
Hungerford Av
Tower Cl
Barnes Cl
The John of Gaunt School
Avenue Road
Gloucester Road
Park Street
Bond Street
Waterworks Rd
Wesley Road
Frome Road
COUNTY WAY
Studley Green
Azalea Dr
Road
Glebe Road
Elmdale Rd
Eastview Road
Talbot Road
Westfield Road
Blair Road
North Way
Kensington Flds
Lambrok Road
Rodsleigh
Summerleaze
Studley Green Primary School
Manor Close
Manor Road
Pitman Avenue
Allen Road
Rock Road
Gladstone Road
FROME ROAD
A361
Yeoman Way
BRADLEY ROAD
A363
Trowbridge Sports Centre
The Clarendon School
St Johns Hospital
Rutland
Field Way
Lambrok Cl
Frampton Ct
Gainsborough Rise
PO
Wiltshire College Trowbridge
Arc Theatre
Beech Grove
Walnut Grove
Cedar Gv
Larch Gv
Laurel Gv
Maple Gv
College Road
Sycamore Gv
Whiterow Park
Webbers Court
St John's Crs
Upper Studley
Church Flds
Church Lane
Silver Meadow
FROME RD
Lilac Gv
Willow Gv
Almond Gv
Silver Rd
Birch Close
Alder Close
Hazel Grove
Grove Primary School
Hawthorn Gv
Silver St Lane
Baydon Cl
Surgery
Silver Street Lane
Sandringham Road
Holyrood Cl
Balmoral Road
Kingsdown Road
Heddington Cl
Spring Mdw
WHITE ROW HILL
Wintersloe Rd
Bewley Rd
Broughton Rd
Westmead Crs
Marston Road
P
Southwick Country Park
Southwick Court
FROME ROAD
Fleur De Lys Drive
Chantry Gdns
Brook
Lane
Cleaver
North Bradley
Southwick
Fairfield Meadows
Church St
Arnold Road
Chantry Gdns
1 grid square represents 500 metres
Southwick CE

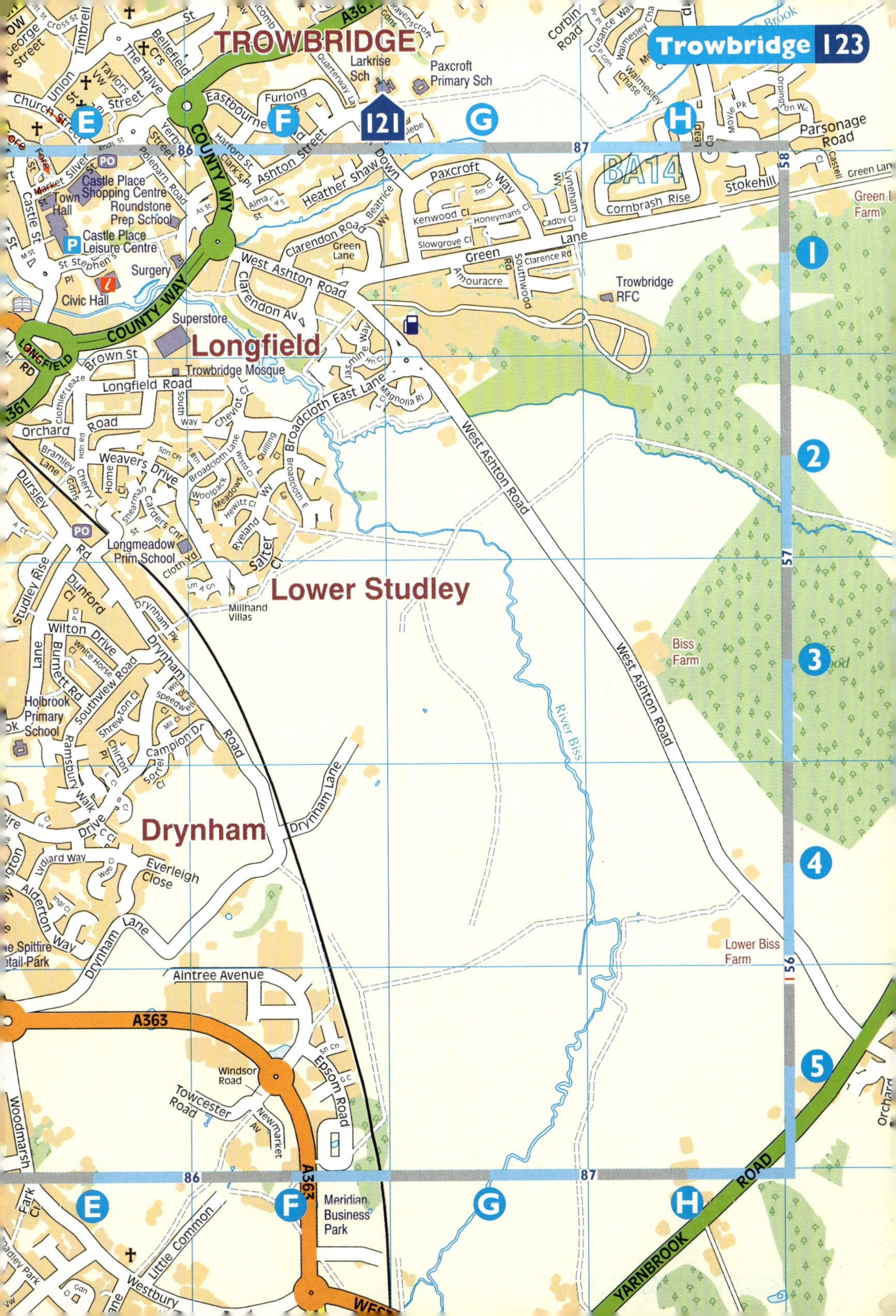
TROWBRIDGE
Longfield
Lower Studley
Drynham
Larkrise Sch
Paxcroft Primary Sch
121
E
F
G
H
1
2
3
4
5
86
87
58
57
56
BA14
Cross St
George Street
Timbrell
Bellefield Crs
The Halve
Taylors Vw
Union St
Church Street
Eastbourne
Furlong
Quarterway La
Ravenscroft Gdns
Corbin Road
Cusance Way
Walmesley Chase
Parsonage Road
Green Lane
Green Lane Farm
Castle Place Shopping Centre
Town Hall
Roundstone Prep School
Castle Place Leisure Centre
St Stephen's Pl
Surgery
Civic Hall
COUNTY WAY
LONGFIELD RD
A361
Superstore
Trowbridge Mosque
Yerbury Street
Polebarn Road
Harford St
Clark's Pl
Ashton Street
Heather Shaw
Down
Alma St
Paxcroft Way
Kenwood Cl
Honeymans Cl
Slowgrove Cl
Cadby Cl
Lyneham Wy
Cornbrash Rise
Stokehill
Clarendon Road
Beatrice Wy
Green Lane
West Ashton Road
Clarendon Av
Southwood Rd
Clarence Rd
Amouracre
Trowbridge RFC
Brown St
Longfield Road
Clothier Leaze
Orchard Road
South Way
Cheviot Cl
Broadcloth East Lane
Magnolia Ri
Jasmine Way
Broadcloth Lane
Quilling Cl
Weavers Drive
Bramley Lane
Cherry Gdns
Home Cl
Shearman St
Carders Cnr
Woolpack Meadows
Hewitt Cl
Ryeland Wy
Salter Cl
Cloth Yd
Dursley Rd
PO
Longmeadow Prim School
Millhand Villas
Studley Rise
Dunford Cl
Wilton Drive
White Horse Cl
Burnett Rd
Southview Road
Drynham Pk
Drynham Road
Speedwell Cl
Campion Dr
Shrewton Cl
Chirton Pl
Sorrel Cl
Holbrook Primary School
Ramsbury Walk
Drynham Lane
Lydiard Way
Alderton Way
Everleigh Close
The Spitfire Retail Park
River Biss
Biss Farm
Lower Biss Farm
Aintree Avenue
A363
Windsor Road
Towcester Road
Newmarket Av
Epsom Road
Woodmarsh
Meridian Business Park
Little Common
Westbury
YARNBROOK ROAD
Orchard

Thicket Mead
Welton
Westfield
MIDSOMER NORTON
Norton Hill
Kitley Hill
Wilton Hill
A362 WEST ROAD
A362
RADSTOCK
NORTHMEAD ROAD
B3355
PHILLIS HILL B3355
SALISBURY RD
NORTH RD
CHURCH LANE
HIGH ST
STATION RD
SILVER STREET
FOSSEWAY
A367
Clover Cl
Clandown
Firtree Av
Meadow Rd
Memorial Hospital
Monger Lane
Harts Paddock
Boxbury Hill
Bowlditch Lane
Bince's Lodge Lane
Old Millard's Hl
Millard's Hill
Green Tree Rd
Gladstone St
Welton Grove
Greenhill Pl
Greenhill Rd
Sunnymead
Spencer Dr
Beaufort Av
Long Barnaby
East Wd
Wellow Brook Meadow
Valley Wk
Welton Vale
Rock Road
Welton Primary School
Burlington Rd
Somer Avenue
Hayes Park Road
Vivien Avenue
St John's Crs
St Mark's Rd
Clevedon Rd
Berkeley Av
Welton Rovers FC
Surgery
Underhill Av
Underhill Lane
Hayes Road
High Meadows
North Road
Elm Vw
Railway Vw
Lilac Ter
Orchard Avenue
Greenacres
Pinewood Road
Pinewood Gv
Longvernal Primary School
Mandy Mdw
Dymboro Av
Dymboro Cl
The Dymboro
Midsomer Norton Primary School
Council Building
Church Ct
The Island
Town Hall
South Road
Rackvernal Rd
Gullock Tyning
South Wansdyke Sports Centre
Pit Road
Shelley Rd
Wesley
Shakespeare Rd
Avenue
Ruskin Road
Longfellow Road
Kingsley Road
Kipling Rd
Chaucer Rd
Keats Rd
Fosse Way Special Sch
Westfield Primary School
Paulton Road
Redfield Gv
Redfield
Park House Clinic
Somervale School
St Chad's Av
St Chad's Gn
Fern Cl
Ivy Walk
Nightingale Wy
Woodpecker Av
Linnet Wy
Kingfisher Dr
Robin Cl
Old Pit Rd
Hawthorne Industrial Estate
St Peter's Rd
Laburnum Gv
Millfield
Sunridge Pk
Steam Mills
River Somer
Park Way
Charlton Rd
Norton Hill School
Lynwood Cl
The Timbers
Lynton Rd
Hazel Terrace
Hazel Gv
First Avenue
Hillside Crs
Hillside Road
Avenue
Chilcompton Road
Withies
Withies Pk
Cautletts Cl
Riverside Rd
Riverside Cl
Riverside Gdns
Riverside Wk
Staddlestones
Furlong Close
Withies Lane
Grange End
Boundary Cl
Charlton Park
Westfield Industrial & Trading Estate
Charlton Lane
St Benedicts RC Primary School
Centurion Hotel
Fosseway Golf Course
Golf Course
Fossfield Rd
White
1 grid square represents 500 metres

Clandown
Chapel Rd
PO
Clandown CE Primary School
Springfield Pl
Chapel Lawn
Round Hill
E
F
G
H
I
68
69
Coomb End
A367
Bristol Road
BATH NEW ROAD
Mendip Wy
Springfield Crs
Springfield Cl
Springfield Buildings
Tamblyn Cl
Woodborough La
Woodborough Road
Tyning
Radstock Infant School
Morley Ter
Stoneable Rd
Plovers Ri
Daneacre Rd
Tyning Hill
Fosse Lane
Radstock Museum
Waldegrave Ter
Wellow Brook
Waterloo Road
Pines Wy
Pine Ct
Mill Road
55
SOMERVALE ROAD
Council Building
Frts Rd
The St
Surgery
A362
FROME ROAD
2
Council Building
Frome Old Rd
Carlingford Ter
Vale Vw
Road
Welton Road
Five Arches Cl
Kilmersdon Magistrates Court
T Drng
Norton Radstock College
St Nicholas CE Infant Sch
Church St
St Nicholas CE Junior Sch
Queen's Rd
Hawthorn Rd
Lillington Road
Lillington Cl
Huish Ct
Sycamore Rd
Mells
Radstock Town FC
Highfields
WELLS ROAD
Alder Ter
Wl Cl
Pn Wk
Acacia Rd
Maple Drive
Birch Road
Meadow Vw
Cedar Ter
Beech Terrace
Oak Terrace
C Ter
L Ter
Holly Wk
Jubilee Rd
Bryant Av
West Hill
May Tree Rd
RADSTOCK
Kilmersdon Road
3
Elm Tree Av
Park Road
Cherry Tree Cl
Rowan Ct
Ash Ct
Tree Ct
Chestnut Cl
Surgery
Waterside Crs
Waterside Road
Glebelands
Magnolia Rd
Waterford Park
Redwood Cl
Grove Wood Road
54
Haydon Ga
Haydon Industrial Est
Larch Ct
The Leaze
Waterside Wy
Lincombe Rd
Briar Cl
Linden Cl
Haydon
Haydon Hill
4
Huish Hou
Fourth Av
First Av
Third Av
5
Le Fa
Bath & North East Somerset
Somerset County
Waterside Farm
53
Waterside Lane
Kilmersdon CE Primary School
Lane

126
Ham Lane
NORTH END ROAD
North End
B3133
Moor Road
Hillsea
Laurel Farm
Way
Meadowland
Hawthorn Crs
Gregory Md
Briar Md
Grange Farm Rd
NORTH END
Arnolds Way
Horsecastle Farm Rd
Jones Cl
Wakedean Gdns
The Wd Kilns
Wemberham La
Horsecastle Close
Wemberham Crs
Station Rd
Kenn Moor Road
Moorside
Bramblewood
Mkt Ind Est
South Vw
The PK
Park Av
Laurel Ter
Barberry Farm
Durban Wy
Stowey Road
Horsecastle
Arnolds Wy
Yatton Station
LC
Ashleigh Crs
Ashleigh Rd
Grassmere Rd
The Av
The Rdg
HIGH STREET
Cherry Gv
Cherry Cl
Myrtle Gdns
Shiners Elms
Grace Cl
Heathgate
Elborough Av
Lodge Cl
Mendip Road
Derham PK
Yatton J&I School
Stowey Road
Well Lane
YATTON
Beech Rd
Barnard's Cl
Westaway
Claverham Cl
Council Building
Marsh Rd
The Batch
West Rd
Elm Wk
Elm Cl
Church Rd
Church La
Church Cl
Surgery
Mendip Gdns
Court Av
Rectory Dr
Rectory Way
Rock Rd
Henley Park
Claverham CC
Henley
Biddle St
Chescombe
Binhay Road
Mendip Road
Bramley Cl
Cadbury Farm Road
B3133
FROST HILL
Hill Frost
Frost Hill
Wood
SMALLWAY
128
Garden Centre
BRISTOL ROAD
WESTON
A
B
C
D
1
2
3
4
5
42
43
65
66
67
1 grid square represents 500 metres

Claverham
Cleeve
Lower Claverham
Brockley Way
Littlewood Lane
Jasmine Lane
Streamcross
High Street
Franklin's Wy
Dunsters Rd
Chestnut Dr
Orchard Ct
PO
Broadcroft
Broadcroft Av
Broadcroft Cl
Claverham Rd
Claverham Pk
Court De Wyck Primary School
Hunt's Lane
Chapel Lane
Wht Hs Rd
Hollowmead Cl
Claverham Road
Bishops Road
Meetinghouse Lane
Bishops Md
Graitney Cl
Cleeve Drive
Wdvw Dr
Millier Road
Storybox Theatre
MAIN ROAD
A370
Cleeve Court
Warner Cl
Plunder St
Chapel La
Cleeve Road
Rhodyate La
HILL
RHODYATE
Blind La
BS49
King's Wood
Woolmers
Hill
The Woodlands
Ball Wood
Wrington Md
Wrington Lane
Hill Pk
Weetwood Rd
E
F
G
H
I
2
3
4
5
45
46
65
66
67
129

126
A
B
C
D
1
2
3
4
5
342
43
64
63
162
Congresbury Moor
Garden Centre
SMALLWAY
B3133
BRIST
KENT RO
Smllw
S Ml
WESTON ROAD
River Yeo
Old Weston Rd
Stepstones Farm
Lane
Dolemoor
A370 STATION ROAD
Station Close
The Glebe Infant.Sch
Surgery
St Andrews Junior School
Chrc Dr
Bridge Farm Sq
Broad St
HIGH STREET
Paul's Cswy
Orc Cl
Cl
Dolemoor Lane
The Cswy
Dolemoor Lane
Stonewell Drive
Stonewell Gv
Stonewell Pk Rd
PO
Stonewell La
Silverstone Wy
Yew Tree Pk
Silver Stre
Cardi
Mendip Spring
1 grid square represents 500 metres

127
E
F
G
H
45
46
A370
Hill
The Woodlands
Ball Wood
Wrington Lane
Weetwood Rd
Verlands
Cobthorn Way
S Side
CONGRESBURY
Montreux Farm
Urchinwood Manor
Urchinwood Lane
Wrington Road
Two Rivers Way
Iwood
Iwood Lane
Udley
West Hay
Weir Rd
Park
Road
Mulberry Rd
River Yeo
Venus Street
Nomis Park
BRINSEA ROAD
Poplar Farm
Stoney Croft House
B3133
STOCK LANE
Brinsea
Brinsea Lane
Lane
Stock
I
2
3
4
5
64
63
62

Sand Rhyne
Beach Road
A
B
C
D
333
34
Sandbay Farm
1
2
3
4
5
65
64
63
Sand Farm Lane
Sand Farm
St Bridges Close
Myrtle Tree Crescent
Sand Bay
Beach Road
Court Road
Elmsley Lane
Sand Road
Lower Norton Lane
Norton La
PO
Kewstoke
Sth Crs
Crookes Lane
Kewside
Kewside
Manor Gardens
Orchard Close
Kewstoke Road
Kewstoke Primary School
Commodore Hotel
P
Beach Road
Monks Hill
Woodspring Crescent
Golf Course
Woodspring Av
Toll
Worlebury Golf Club
Worlebury
Worlebury Park Road
Furze Road
W Lnk Cl
Greenacre
Cliff Road
135
Furze Cl
Worlebury CE VA First School
Milton
Milbury Gardens
The Crs
The Crs
The Gln
Penrice Close
Road

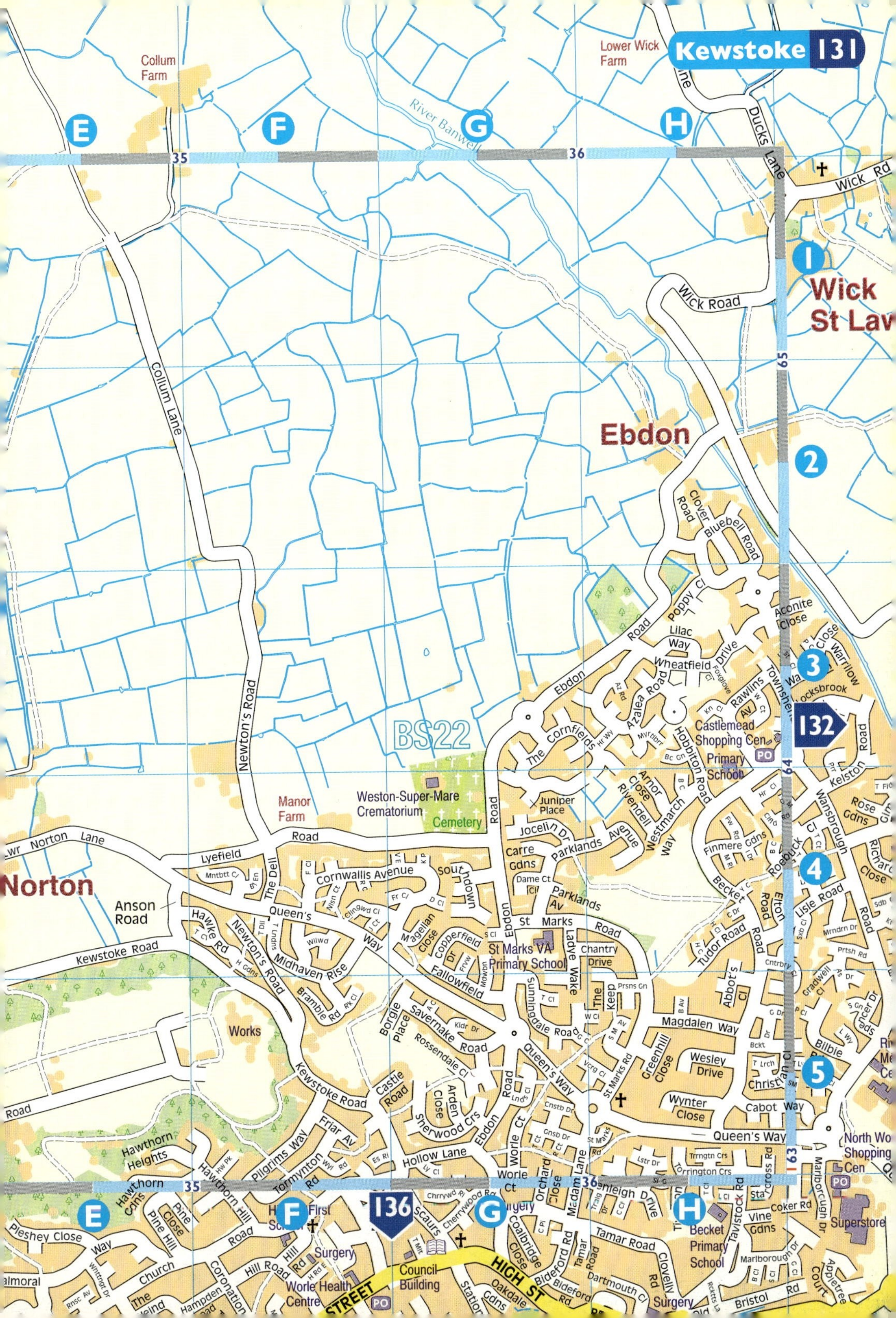

Kewstoke 131
132
136
Collum Farm
Lower Wick Farm
River Banwell
Ducks Lane
Wick Rd
Wick Road
Wick St Lav
Collum Lane
Ebdon
Clover Road
Bluebell Road
Poppy Cl
Aconite Close
Lilac Way
Wheatfield Drive
Warrilow Close
Locksbrook
Townshend
Ebdon Road
Azalea Road
Rawlins Av
Castlemead Shopping Cen
Primary School
Hobbiton Road
The Cornfields
BS22
Newton's Road
Juniper Place
Arnor Close
Rivendell
Westmarch Way
Kelston Road
Rose Gdns
Wansbrough
Finmere Gdns
Roebuck Cl
Richards Close
Manor Farm
Weston-Super-Mare Crematorium
Cemetery
Lwr Norton Lane
Road
Lyefield Road
Norton
Anson Road
The Dell
Cornwallis Avenue
Southdown
Jocelin Dr
Carre Gdns
Parklands Avenue
Dame Ct
Parklands Av
Becket Road
Elton Road
Lisle Road
Queen's Way
Hawke Rd
Newton's Road
Midhaven Rise
Magellan Close
Copperfield Dr
St Marks Road
St Marks VA Primary School
Ladye Wake
Chantry Drive
Tudor Road
Kewstoke Road
Brambie Rd
Fallowfield
Sunningdale Road
The Keep
Abbot's Cl
Gradwell Cl
Works
Borgie Place
Savernake Road
Rossendale Cl
Magdalen Way
Bilbie
Greenhill Close
Wesley Drive
Christian Cl
Castle Road
Arden Close
Sherwood Crs
St Marks Rd
Wynter Close
Cabot Way
Queen's Way
North Worle Shopping Cen
Friar Av
Hawthorn Heights
Pilgrims Way
Tormynton Rd
Hollow Lane
Worle Ct
Orchard Close
Madam Lane
Denleigh Drive
Torrington Crs
Tavistock Rd
Cross Rd
Coker Rd
Marlborough Dr
Superstore
Hawthorn Gdns
Pine Close
Pine Hill
Hawthorn Hill
First School
Scaurs
Cherrywood Rd
Surgery
Coalbridge Close
Bideford Rd
Tamar Road
Tamar Road
Dartmouth Cl
Clovelly Rd
Becket Primary School
Vine Gdns
Appletree Court
Pleshey Close
Way
Church Road
Coronation Road
Hill Road
Worle Health Centre
Council Building
High St
Street
Station
Oakdale Gdns
Bristol Rd
Hampden Road
Almoral
Road
E
F
G
H
I
2
3
4
5
35
36
65
64
63

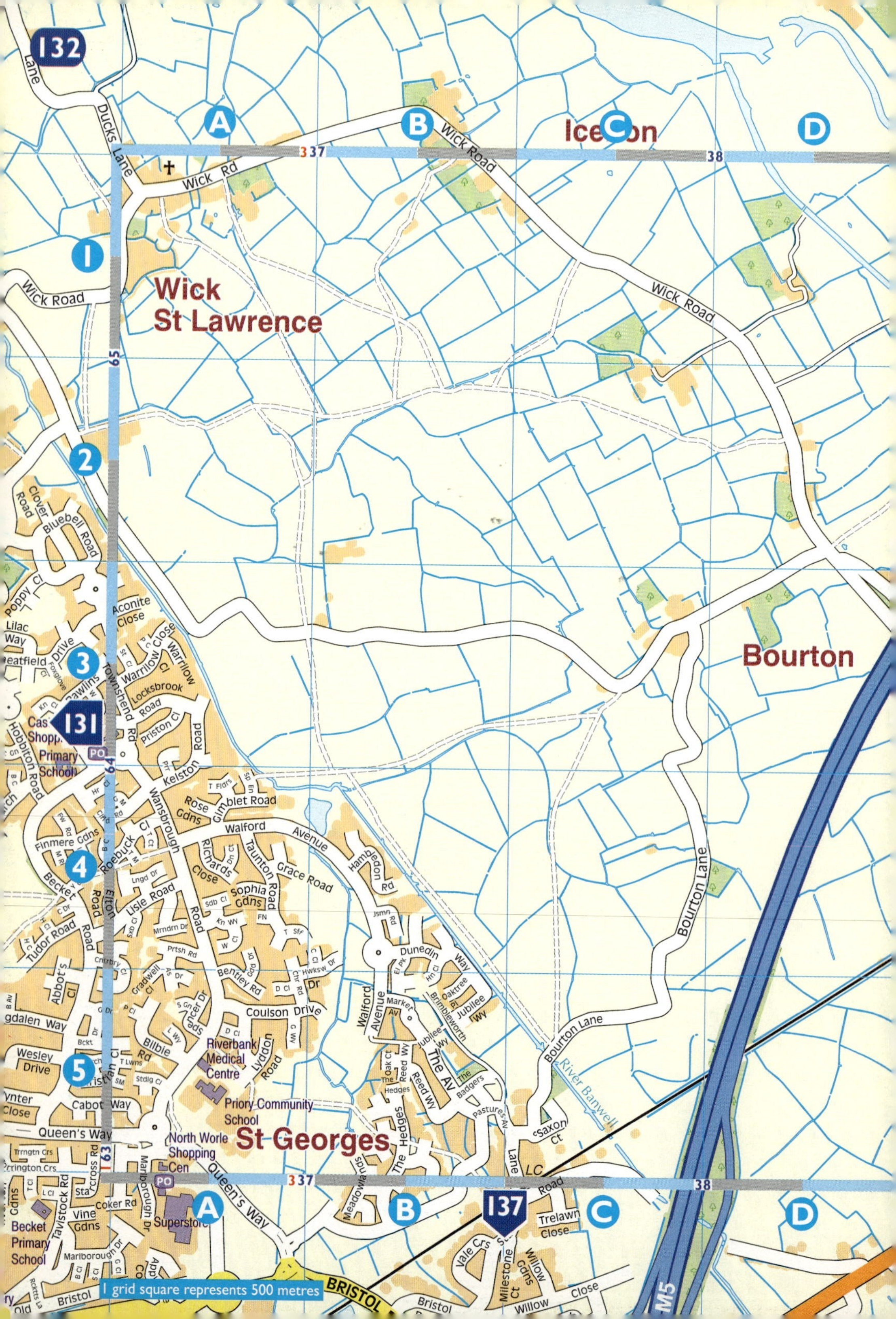

132
131
137
A
B
C
D
1
2
3
4
5
337
38
65
64
63
Wick St Lawrence
Iceton
Bourton
St Georges
Ducks Lane
Lane
Wick Rd
Wick Road
Bourton Lane
River Banwell
M5
BRISTOL
Clover Road
Bluebell Road
Poppy Cl
Lilac Way
Aconite Close
Warrilow Close
Townshend Rd
Locksbrook Road
Priston Cl
Kelston Road
Hobbiton Road
Primary School
PO
Wansbrough
Gimblet Road
Rose Gdns
Walford Avenue
Finmere Gdns
Roebuck Cl
Richards Close
Taunton Road
Grace Road
Hambledon Rd
Sophia Gdns
Lisle Road
Becket Road
Tudor Road
Elton Road
Abbot's Cl
Gradwell Cl
Bentley Rd
Coulson Drive
Dunedin Way
Walford Avenue
Market Av
Brimblewworth
Oaktree Pl
Jubilee Wy
The Av
Reed Wy
The Hedges
Badgers
Pastures Av
Saxon Ct
Riverbank Medical Centre
Lyddon Road
Bilbie Rd
Wesley Drive
Cabot Way
Queen's Way
Priory Community School
North Worle Shopping Cen
Marlborough Dr
Superstore
Tavistock Rd
Vine Gdns
Coker Rd
Becket Primary School
Meadowlands
Trelawn Close
Vale Crs
Milestone Ct
Willow Gdns
Willow Close
Bristol
1 grid square represents 500 metres

E
F
G
H
39
40
M5
Little River
River Yeo
I
65
2
LC
A370
Oldbridge River
Hewish
West Hewish
St Annes CE Primary School
3
ick Rd
64
Works
A370
Puxton
4
Maysgreen Lane
May's Lane
May's Green
5
Puxton Road
63
39
40
A370
E
F
G
H
Doubleton Farm
Road
Barn Lane

A
B
C
D
1
2
3
4
5
WESTON-SUPER-MARE
Weston Bay
Worlebury Hill
Kewstoke Road
Life Boat Station
Pier
Anchor Head
Birkett Road
Westcliff College of Further Education
South Road
Atlantic Road
Shrubbery Avenue
Cecil Road
Madeira Cove Hotel
Atlantic Bus Pk
Shrubbery Road
Peter's Av
Grove Pk Rd
Queen's Road
All Saints' Rd
Tichborne Road
Kew Road
Anchor Head Hotel
New Ocean Hotel
Marine Lake
Upper Church Road
St John's Road
Close Timbertop Aparthotel
Lower Road
Coombe Rd
Arundell Road
Old Knightstone Theatre
Knightstone Causeway
Knightstone Road
Park Pl
Royal Crs
Southside
Bristol Road
Weston College
Lauriston Hotel
Playhouse Theatre
Surgery
Lambretta Scooter Mus
Waterloo St
Model Yacht Pond
Royal Parade
Royal Hotel
High Street
North St
Palmer St
Winter Gardens & Pavilion
Sovereign Shop Cen
Orchard Street
Time Machine Mus
Baker Street
Meadow St
Leisure Pavilion
Grand Pier
MARINE PDE
A370
Alexandra Parade
Regent St
Co Court
Works
Oxford St
Cinema
Superstore
Dolphin Square Shopping Centre
Town Hall
CAB
Mag Cts
Station Road
Carlton St
Salvation Army
Prim Sch
Police Stn
Graham Road
Surgery
Neva Road
Weston-super-Mare Stn
Sea Life Aquarium
Ashbrook House Sch
Ellenborough Pk N
Ellenborough Park
Ellenborough Park S
Ellenborough Crs
Albert Avenue
Ridgeway Av
Sunnyside Rd
Corpus Christi RC Primary School
Tropicana Leisure Complex
Albert Rd
Clevedon Road
Clifton Road
ROAD
Dickenson Rd
138
Model Yacht Pond
Parade
BEACH
Wallscote
Whitecross Rd
Severn Road
Clarence Road North
Clarence Park
331
32
63
62
61
1 grid square represents 500 metres

Commodore Hotel
Beach Road
Kewstoke Road
Kewstoke Primary School
Monks Hill
Woodspring Crescent
Spring Av
Golf Course
Worlebury Hill Road
Toll
Worlebury
130
Worlebury Golf Club
E
F
G
H
33
34
63
Furze Road
Worlebury Park Road
Cliff Road
Hillcroft Close
Greenacre
St David's Cl
Furze Cl
Worlebury CE VA First School
Milton Gardens
The Crs
The Gln
Pleshey Close
Worlebury Hill Road
Naunton Wy
Tirley Wy
Drive
Penrice Close
Windsor Road
Powis Cl
Wigmore Gardens
Spring
Ashbury
Rendcomb Cl
Prescot Close
Milton Brow
Furland Road
Hill
Edgecombe Avenue
Priests Way
I
Weston Woods
Eastcombe Road
Ringwood Gv
Lodge Drive
Pendlesham Gdns
Underwood Avenue
Hillside Gdns
Upper Bristol Road
Bristol Road
Upper
The Crs
Roslyn Av
Baytree Road
Woodcliff Road
Westbrook Road
Seabrook Rd
Milton Junior School
Milton CP Infant School
Caveners Ct
Forest Drive
Cranbourne Cha
Eastcombe Gardens
Wood La
7
Lower Bristol Rd
Manor Va
Ashcombe Park Road
Ashcombe Park
Fairfield Cl
Farm Rd
Milton Pk
Clarkson Av
Grove Road
Cedar Av
Belvedere Crs
Drysdale Close
Milton
Tree Vw
Bay Vw
2
Dunkery Road
Brendon Av
Manor Road
Snowdon V
Ashleigh Road
Ashdene Road
Milton Road
Bathurst Road
Salisbury Road
Milton Gn
Chelswood Av
62
Baytree School
Lancaster House School
Cemetery
Polden Road
Ashcombe Gardens
Hazeldene Road
Surgery
Belgrave Road
Woodstock Road
Chesham Road N
Shaftesbury Road
Grove
Florence
Somerdale Avenue
Somerdale Cl
Chalfont Road
Cardigan Crs
Ewart Rd
Warwick Close
Carsdale Close
Carsdale Road
Farndale Rd
3
Hill
The Dr
Milton Road
Mansfield Av
Hughenden Road
Hatfield Road
Capell Close
St Austell Rd
Rutland Close
B3440
Saville Crs
Saville Rd
Locking Moor Rd
136
Oakford Av
Grove
Lewisham Grove
Milton Av
Holland St
Fire Station
Council Building
Summerlands Road
Chesham Rd S
Linden Av
Linden Av
Charter Road
Newbourne Rd
Fernlea Road
Fullens Cl
Maitlands
Stafford Rd
Clarendon Rd
Earlham Grove
Earlham Gv
Works
Stafford Business Cen
Gordon Road
Stanley Gv
Works
Osborne Avenue
Mendip Rd
Ashcombe Primary School
Laburnum Road
Birchwood Av
Priory Rd
Locking Road
Brookland Road
Southmead Road
Wellsea Grove
Hutton Moor Road
West Milton Station
Clover
4
Milburn Rd
Lyons Ct
Ashcombe Road
Osborne Road
Sandford Rd
Churchill Business Park
Rosedale Av
Hill View Road
Parkhurst Road
Council Building
B3440 Locking
Marconi Cl
Puttingthorpe Dr
Selwood Close
Hornets RFC
Weston-Super-Mare Borough Employees Sports Club
Drove Rd
Wyvern Cl
Locking Road Business Park
Churchill Rd
Glencoe Business Park
Warne Rd
Hutton Moor Leisure Centre
Aisecombe Wy
Works
Bridge Road Business Park
Winscombe Rd
Hurst Rd
Becks Business Park
Warne Road
Warne Road
Travel Inn
Hutton Moor Sports Fields
Way
Weston Express Business Park
Aisecombe Way
Hutton Moor La
61
Bridge Road
Langford Road
Longton Ind Est
Works
5
Crescent
Herluin
Newland Road
Works
Rector's Way
Ambulance Station
Winterstoke Road
A370 Marchfields
Works
Pottery Cl
Searle
Phillips Road
A370
A3033
Drove Road
Weston Retail Park
33
34
Hutton Moor Lane
Drove Road Hospital
Wyvern Sports Centre
Marchfields Way
139
Norfolk Rd
Amberey Road
Wyvern Community School
Weston-Super-Mare AFC
Winters
Old Jct Rd
Works
Kensington Rd
Airfield

136
131
135
140
A
B
C
D
1
2
3
4
5
335
36
63
62
61
Worle
Milton
Works
Worlebury Hill Road
Hawthorn Heights
Kewstoke Road
Castle Road
Friar Av
Rossendale Cl
Sherwood Crs
Queen's Way
Magdalen Way
Wesley Drive
Greenhill Close
Wynter Close
St Marks Rd
Pilgrims Wy
Tormynton Rd
Hawthorn Hill
Hawthorn Gdns
Pine Close
Pine Hill
Pleshey Close
Balmoral Way
Church Road
Hillside First School
Surgery
Hill Road
Worle Health Centre
Coronation Road
The Rows
Hampden Road
The Weind
Wayside
Priests Way
St Martins CE Junior School
Windsor Road
Spring Terrace
Wigmore Gardens
Edgecombe Avenue
Westbrook Road
Seabrook Rd
Springfield Av
Woodcliff Road
Drysdale Close
Baytree Road
Rosslyn Av
Milton Road
Tree Vw
Bay Tree Vw
Locking Road
Cranford Cl
High Street
Nutwell Rd
Greenwood Rd
Mendip Av
Council Building
Station Road
High St
Oakdale Gdns
Coalbridge Close
Bideford Rd
Tamar Road
Dartmouth Cl
Clovelly Rd
Becket Primary School
Prean Gn
Westwood Cl
Bristol Road
Old Bristol Road
New Bristol Road
B3440
Mendip Green First School
Copley Gdns
Cygnet Crescent
Sandpiper Drive
Osprey Gdns
Fulmar Road
Coralberry Dr
Blackberry Drive
Silverberry Road
Lime Cl
Larchgrove Crs
The Poplars
Verbena Way
Holly Cl
Blackthorn
Magnolia Av
Moor Lane
Lapwing Gardens
Redwing Dr
Gannet Rd
Plover Cl
Mead Vale
Worle Community School
Mead Vale Primary School
Raven Cl
Kestrel Drive
Heron Cl
Robin Cl
Starling Cl
Woodpecker Drive
Flamingo Crescent
Pelican Cl
Kingfisher Close
Partridge Close
Peregrine Road
Puffin Cl
Eagle Close
Falcon Crescent
Wren Cl
Swallow Gdns
Mead Vale
Baytree School
Martindale Court
Martindale Rd
Garsdale Road
Farndale Rd
Teesdale Close
Eskdale Cl
Corondale Road
Cardigan Crs
Chelswood Av
Ewart Rd
Bathurst Road
Salisbury Road
West Milton Station
Locking Moor Rd
Clover Ct
Fullens Cl
Maitlands
Teasel Walk
Sloe Cl
Damson Rd
Plumtree Rd
Aspen Park Rd
Camberley Wk
Spruce Wy
Old Mill Wy
Badgers Wy
Pollard Rd
Shrewsbury Bow
Bransby Way
Sefton Sq
Jasmine Wy
Moor La
Moor Lane
Vale Mill Wy
Castle Wy
Longridge Wy
Griffen Road
Stroud Wy
Moor Lane
The Swallows
Charlock Rd
A370
Somerset Avenue
Aisecombe Wy
Weston Express Business Park
Locking Head Drove
Drove Farm
The Helicopter Museum
Weston Business Park
Laneys Drove
A371
Locking Farm Industrial Est
Airfield
1 grid square represents 500 metres

Bilbie Rd
Riverbank Medical Centre
Lyddon Road
Jubilee Wy
Oak Ct
The Hedges
Reed Wy
Reed Wy
The Av
The Badgers
Pastures
Bourton
River Banwell
Saxon Ct
Priory Community School
St Georges
North Shopping Cen
E
F
132
G
H
37
38
LC
63
PO
Superstore
Queen's Way
Meadowlands
Station Road
Trelawn Close
A370
Doubleton Farm
Rols
Marlborough Dr
Appletree Court
B3440
BRISTOL ROAD
Vale Crs
Milestone Ct
Willow Gdns
Bristol Road
Willow Close
Ash Cl
M5
Apple Farm
Park Way
Worle Station
B3440
Junction 21
BRISTOL RD
Warleys La
West Rols
A370
Diamond Batch
Yarbury Way
Summer Lane
Darmead
SOMERSET AVENUE
West Wick
Scot Elm Dr
Way Wick
2
Sunnybank Ct
Weston Gateway Caravan Site
Bank Wy
Rowan Pl
Elmham Wy
Primary
West Wick
Summer Lane
Hedge Cl
Harvest Lane
Yew Tree Dr
Churchland Wy
Wolvers Hill Road
62
store
3
Silver Moor Lane
Summer Lane
Cannaway's Farm
Eton Lane
Wolvers Hill Road
4
Wolvershill Manor
Woolvers Hill
61
Varsity Way
Woolvers Way
Rd
Oxford Square
Road
Anson Road
Larkhill
Russell
5
M5
Road
Leedham
Road
141
Woolvers Hl Rd
Mc Crae Road
Lower Pde Gnd Rd
Parkes Road
Summer
Park Farm

Weston Bay
A
B
C
D
134
1
2
3
4
5
60
59
58
331
32
Ellenborough Pk N
Ellenborough Park
Ellenborough Park S
Corpus Christi RC Primary School
Tropicana
Albert Avenue
Ridgeway
Sunnyside Rd
Albert Rd
Clevedon Road
Clifton Road
Model Yacht Pond
Marine Parade
BEACH
A370
Walliscote
Whitecross Road
Clifton Av
Langport Rd
Works
Severn Road
PO
Clarence Road North
Exeter Rd
St Paul's Rd
Clarence Park
Clarence Rd E
Clarence Gv Rd
Severn Avenue
Malvern Road
Clarence Road South
Surgery
Quantock Road
Wl Rd S
Moorland Road
Marine Parade
Wyncroft School
Ctn Ave
Clinic
Lst Rd
Ts Ms
Works
Southend Road
Weston-Super-Mare Golf Club
Charlton Road
Nithsdale Road
Health Cen
Woodland Rd
UPHILL ROAD NORTH
Beachlands Hotel
Elmsleigh Road
Frenchay Road
DEVONSHIRE ROAD
Selbourne Rd
Addiscombe Road
Brean Down Avenue
Delapre Road
Stanhope
Golf Course
Broadoak Road
A3033
Broadoak Community School
Weston-Super-Mare CC
WINDWHISTLE ROAD
Windwhistle Lane
Coldharbour La
Uphill Manor
Uphill
Brean Down Farm
Wingard Cl
St A Av
Uphill Road
Moseley Grove
West Haven Special School
New Church Road
T Ps
PO
Berkeley Crs
Thornbury Rd
Ellsmr Rd
Uphill Prim Sch
St Nicholas Rd
Links Road
Council Building
Church
Westfield Close
B Ed Rd
Thornbury Drive
Rhyne Terr
Laurel Drive
Gv
Ash
Close
Willow
Sandcroft Av
Southfield Close
Old
Underhill Dr
South
Weston-Super-Mare General Hospital
A&E
Ltl Orch
Uphill Way
Grange Road
Folly Lane
Uphill Road South
Grange Close
The Gran
North Somerset
Somerset County
West Mendip Way
1 grid square represents 500 metres

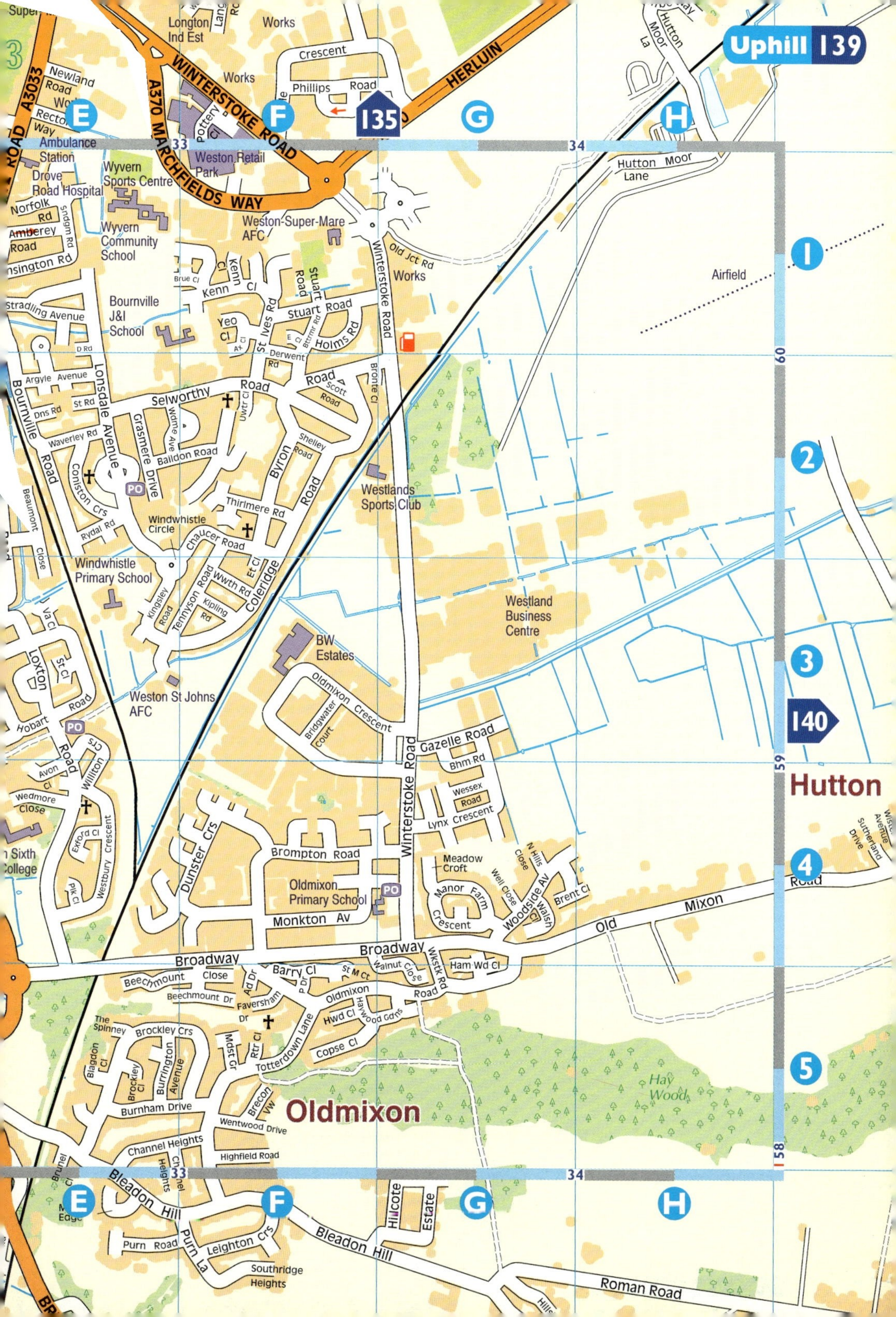
E
F
G
H
135
140
33
34
60
59
58
I
2
3
4
5
Longton Ind Est
Works
Crescent
Phillips Road
WINTERSTOKE ROAD
HERLUIN
A3033
A370 MARCHFIELDS WAY
Newland Road
Rectory Way
Ambulance Station
Drove Road Hospital
Wyvern Sports Centre
Weston Retail Park
Pottery Cl
Norfolk Rd
Amberey Road
Wyvern Community School
Weston-Super-Mare AFC
Hutton Moor Lane
Hutton Moor La
Airfield
Old Jct Rd
Works
Winterstoke Road
Stuart Road
Kenn Cl
Brue Cl
Bournville J&I School
Stradling Avenue
Yeo Cl
St Ives Rd
Holms Rd
Derwent Rd
Argyle Avenue
Bournville Road
Lonsdale Avenue
Selworthy Road
Scott Road
Bronte Cl
Grasmere Drive
Baildon Road
Shelley Road
Byron Road
Waverley Rd
Coniston Crs
Beaumont Close
Rydal Rd
Windwhistle Circle
Thirlmere Rd
Chaucer Road
Westlands Sports Club
Windwhistle Primary School
Kingsley Road
Tennyson Road
Kipling Rd
Coleridge
Westland Business Centre
Loxton Road
BW Estates
Oldmixon Crescent
Bridgwater Court
Weston St Johns AFC
Hobart Road
Gazelle Road
Bhm Rd
Wessex Road
Lynx Crescent
Winterstoke Road
Hutton
Wedmore Close
Avon Cl
Williton Crs
Westbury Crescent
Sixth College
Dunster Crs
Brompton Road
Oldmixon Primary School
Meadow Croft
Manor Farm Crescent
Well Close
N Hills Close
Woodside Av
Walsh Cl
Brent Cl
Sutherland Drive
Road
Old Mixon
Monkton Av
Broadway
Broadway
Beechmount Close
Beechmount Dr
Barry Cl
Faversham Dr
Walnut Close
Ham Wd Cl
Oldmixon Road
Hwd Cl
Haywood Gdns
Copse Cl
Totterdown Lane
The Spinney
Brockley Crs
Blagdon Cl
Brockley Cl
Burrington Avenue
Burnham Drive
Brecon Vw
Wentwood Drive
Oldmixon
Hay Wood
Channel Heights
Highfield Road
Bleadon Hill
Purn Road
Purn La
Leighton Crs
Southridge Heights
Hilcote Estate
Bleadon Hill
Roman Road
PO

140
136
139
A
B
C
D
1
2
3
4
5
335
36
60
59
58
The Helicopter Museum
Weston Business Park
Laneys Drove
Drove Farm
Locking Head Drove
Locking Head
A371
Locking Farm Industrial Estate
Homefield Industrial Estate
Homefield
The Orchard
Bramley Cl
Bchwd Av
Beechwood Av
Manor Gdns
ELM TREE ROAD B3368
Elm Grove
Rydal Av
Grenville Avenue
Bn Rd
Byron Cl
South Lawn
S Lawn Close
T Gn
Lychgate Pk
PO
Locking
The Bury
Conifer Way
Willow
Poplar Wk
Dr.
Conifer Wy
West End Farm
Airfield
Moor
Hutton
BS24
The Croft
L Md Cl
Hg Wy
Briar Road
Elizabeth Close
Moor Lane
Moor Croft Road
Spring Wd Gdns
L Gdns
Hillside West
Elmvale Drive
Vereland Road
S Rd
O Dr
Holm Rd
Bisdee Rd
St Mary's Rd
Payne Rd
Farm Rd
Elmhurst Rd
Sw Cl
Willow Drive
Eastfield Rd
Barrow Rd
Weston Way
Hutton Hill
Wistreria Avenue
Sutherland Drive
Wn Cl
Main Road
Mixon Road
Church Lane
Gsn Cl
Orchard Rd
Robin Drive
Hutton Primary School
Lower Canada
Canada Coombe
Hay Wood
West Way
1 grid square represents 500 metres

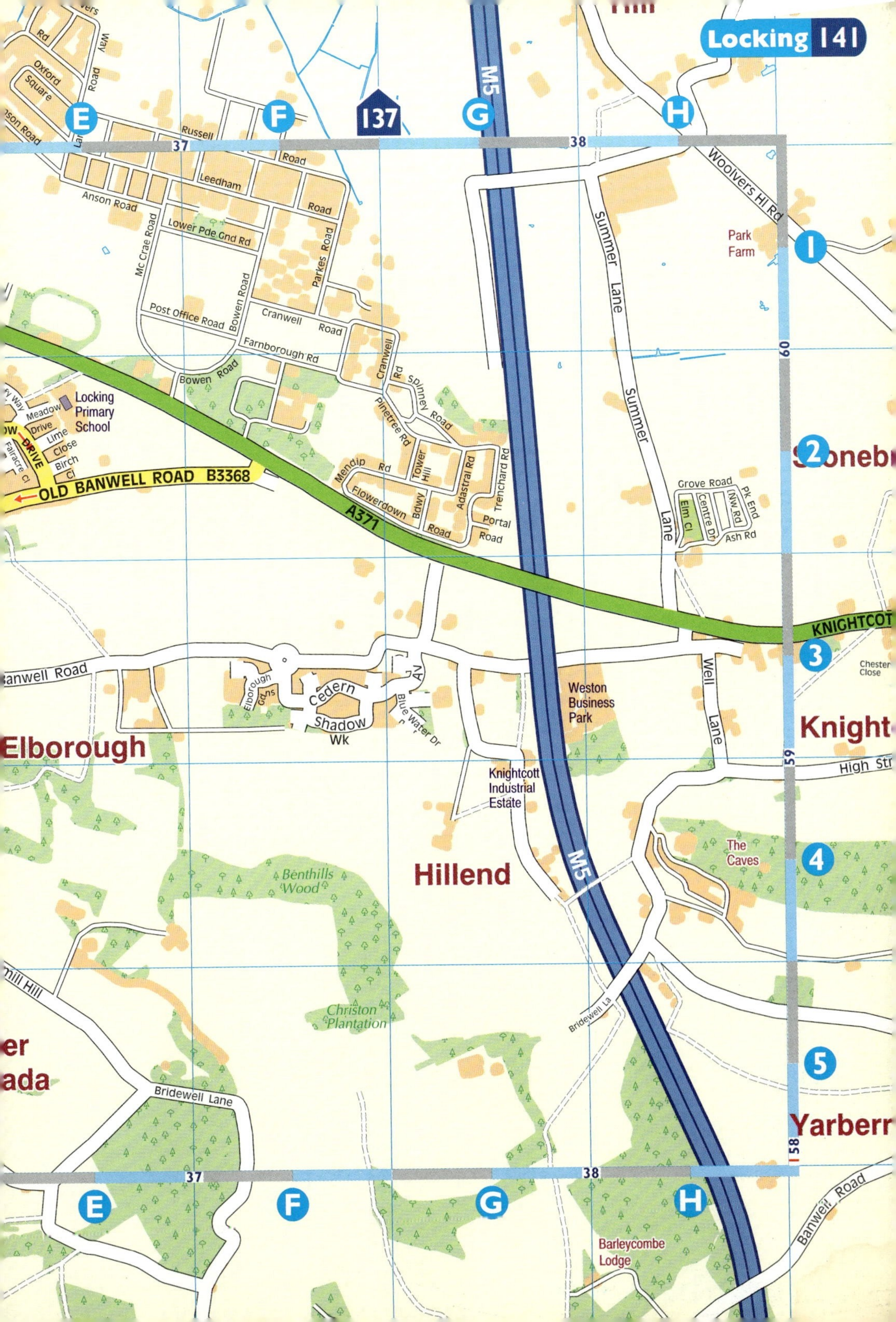

137
M5
Russell Road
Leedham Road
Anson Road
Oxford Square
Lower Pde Gnd Rd
Mc Crae Road
Parkes Road
Post Office Road
Bowen Road
Cranwell Road
Farnborough Rd
Cranwell Rd
Spinney Road
Pinetree Rd
Tower Hill
Mendip Rd
Flowerdown Road
Bdwy
Adastral Rd
Trenchard Rd
Portal Road
Locking Primary School
Meadow Drive
Lime Close
Birch Cl
Fairacre Cl
OLD BANWELL ROAD B3368
A371
Woolvers Hl Rd
Park Farm
Summer Lane
Grove Road
Elm Cl
Centre Dr
Nw Rd
Pk End
Ash Rd
Stonebr
KNIGHTCOT
Chester Close
Knight
Banwell Road
Elborough Gdns
Cedern Av
Shadow Wk
Blue Water Dr
Elborough
Weston Business Park
Well Lane
High Str
Knightcott Industrial Estate
Hillend
Benthills Wood
The Caves
Christon Plantation
Bridewell La
Bridewell Lane
Yarberr
Barleycombe Lodge
Banwell Road
E
F
G
H
I
2
3
4
5
37
38
58
59
60

Abbots Leigh 59 G3
Abson 67 G1
Almondsbury 15 G2
Alveston 11 F3
Alveston Down 11 E2
Arno's Vale 80 A2
Ashcombe Park 7 K1
Ashley Down 52 A4
Ashton Gate 78 A2
Ashton Vale 78 A4
Avoncliff 118 B5
Avonmouth 34 D2
Aztec West 15 G5
Backwell 85 G3
Backwell Common 85 H1
Backwell Green 86 C1
Bailbrook 109 G1
Barrow Common 89 E4
Barrow Gurney 88 A5
Barton Hill 62 D5
The Batch 83 E1
Bath 3 H5
Bathampton 109 H4
Batheaston 103 G5
Bathford 110 D2
Bathwick 3 K3
Beacon Hill 108 C3
Bedminster 78 C3
Bedminster Down 90 C1
Beechen Cliff 3 G7
Berwick 24 B4
Bishopston 51 G4
Bishopsworth 90 A4
Blackhorse 55 E1
Blackrock 101 H4
Blaise Hamlet 36 C3
Bloomfield 114 B4
Bourton 132 D3
Bower Ashton 77 G2
Bradford-on-Avon 119 G3
Bradley Stoke 27 G2
Brentry 37 G2
Bridge Yate 66 B4
Brislington 80 D4
Bristol 4 B5
Bromley Heath 40 D3
Broomhill 53 F2
Broom Hill 81 F2
Buckover 9 H3
Burnett 104 C5
Cadbury Heath 82 D1
Cambridge Batch 87 H1
Catbrain 25 F4
Charlcombe 108 C1
Chelvey 85 E4
Chipping Sodbury 33 F1
Clarence Park 138 C1
Claverham 127 F2
Claverton Down 115 H4
Clay Hill 63 G1
Clays End 112 C1
Cleeve 127 H3
Clevedon 70 B1
Clifton 60 C3
Coalpit Heath 30 B4
Colt's Green 33 G2
Combe Down 117 E1
Compton Greenfield 24 C2
Congresbury 128 D2
Conham 81 F1
Coombe Dingle 36 B5
Corston 105 H4
Cotham 61 F2
Cowhorn Hill 83 F2
Crew's Hole 63 G4
Cribbs Causeway 24 D4
Crossways 9 F2
Dodington 33 G5
Dolemeads 3 H6
Downend 54 C1
Drynham 123 E4
Dundry 98 B2
East Clevedon 71 F2
East Dundry 99 G3
East End 74 A5
Easter Compton 24 D1
Eastfield 51 E1
Easton 62 D2
Easton-in-Gordano 48 A5
Eastville 52 D5
Ebdon 131 H2
Elberton 10 A1
Elborough 141 E3
Emerson's Green 55 G2
Engine Common 20 A2
Englishcombe 112 D5
Failand 75 H3
Fairfield Park 108 D2
Farleigh 86 B2
Farley 69 F1
Felton 97 E4
Filton 39 E2
Filwood Park 91 G1
Fishponds 53 G3
Flax Bourton 87 E2
Fox Hill 114 D5
Frampton Cotterell 29 G1
Frampton End 30 A2
Frenchay 40 C5
Frogland Cross 17 G3
Frost Hill 126 C5
Gaunt's Earthcott 17 F2
Golden Hill 51 F2
Goose Green 20 C4
Goose Green 65 H2
Great Stoke 28 A5
Grovesend 9 G5
The Hacket 9 G4
Hallen 24 A5
Hambrook 40 D3
Ham Green 48 D5
Hangstone Hill 70 C2
Hanham 81 H1
Hanham Green 81 H3
Harry Stoke 39 H3
Hartcliffe 91 E5
Haydon 125 F4
Headley Park 90 C2
Henbury 36 D3
Henfield 42 C2
Hengrove 91 H3
Hengrove Park 91 F3
Henleaze 51 F2
Hewish 133 H3
Hicks Common 29 F5
Hicks Gate 93 G1
Highridge 89 H3
Highridge 98 C1
Hillend 141 G4
Hillfields 54 A5
Hilperton 121 H3
Hilperton Marsh 121 G1
Holbrook Common 66 D3
Horfield 52 A2
Horsecastle 126 B2
Hotwells 60 D5
Hutton 140 A4
Iron Acton 19 E3
Iwood 129 G3
Kelston 106 B1
Kendleshire 41 H2
Kenn Moor Gate 84 A5
Kewstoke 130 B4
Keynsham 94 D4
Kingsdown 111 G1
Kingsway 114 A4
Kingswood 64 D3
The Knapp 9 G1
Knowle 79 H5
Lambridge 109 F2
Lansdown 108 B3
Larkhall 109 E2
Latteridge 18 C1
Lawrence Weston 35 G4
Leigh Woods 59 H5
Little Stoke 27 E3
Locking 140 D2
Lockleaze 52 D1
Locksbrook 113 H1
Lodway 48 A3
Long Ashton 76 D5
Longfield 123 E1
Longwell Green 82 B3
Lower Canada 140 D4
Lower Hazel 11 E4
Lower Knowle 79 E4
Lower Studley 123 F3
Lower Swainswick 109 F1
Lower Weston 107 H5
Lulsgate Bottom 96 A4
Lyde Green 42 D5
Lye Green 118 D5
Maiden Head 99 E3
Mangotsfield 55 E3
Marsh Common 13 G5
May's Green 133 G5
Mayshill 30 C1
Mead Riding 21 F3
Middle Bridge 46 A5
Midford 117 F4
Midsomer Norton 124 B4
Milton 136 A2
Monkton Combe 117 H1
Monkton Farleigh 111 G5
Montpelier 61 H1
Moorend 41 F3
Morton 9 E2
Mount Hill 64 D5
Nailsea 73 F5
Netham 62 D5
Newbridge 107 F4
New Cheltenham 65 E2
Newton St Loe 112 C1
Nibley 31 E1
North Common 66 A5
North Corner 29 F1
Northend 103 F4
North Weston 45 G5
North Wick 99 H4
Norton 131 E4
Norton Hill 124 C5
Norton's Wood 69 F4
Novers Park 91 E1
Odd Down 116 B1
Old Down 10 C4
Oldfield Park 2 B6
Oldland 82 D3
Oldland Common 83 G3
Oldmixon 139 F5
Olveston 10 A4
The Oval 113 H3
Over 14 D5
Parkfield 56 D1
Patchway 26 C1
Perrymead 115 E4
Pill 48 B4
Pilning 13 F2
Portbury 46 D5
Portishead 45 E4
Potters Hill 96 B3
Primrose Hill 108 A2
Pucklechurch 56 D3
Pye Corner 41 E2
Radstock 125 F3
Ram Hill 42 C1
Redland 51 F5
Ridgeway 53 G5
The Rocks 21 E2
Rush Hill 113 G5
St Anne's Park 63 F5
St George 63 H4
St Georges 132 A5
Saltford 105 E2
Sea Mills 49 G2
Severn Beach 12 D3
Sheepway 46 D3
Shirehampton 48 B1
Shortwood 56 A4
Sion Hill 108 B4
Siston 56 C5
Siston Common 65 F2
Sneyd Park 50 A5
Somerdale 94 B2
Soundwell 54 D5
Southdown 113 F4
Southmead 37 G4
Southstoke 116 D3
South Twerton 113 H2
Speedwell 63 H1
Staple Hill 54 D4
Stapleton 53 E4
Stockwood 92 C3
Stockwood Vale 93 G3
Stoke Bishop 50 B4
Stoke Gifford 27 F5
Stone-edge Batch 72 D2
Stone Hill 82 B2
Stub Riding 21 G4
Studley Green 122 B2
Thicket Mead 124 A1
Thornbury 8 C3
Tickenham 72 A2
Trowbridge 121 F5
Trowle Common 120 A4
Tucking Mill 117 H2
Turleigh 118 C3
Twerton 113 F2
Two Mile Hill 64 A2
Tyning 125 H1
Tyntesfield 74 D2
Uphill 138 B4
Uphill Manor 138 D3
Upper Canada 140 D5
Upper Studley 122 A4
Upper Town 96 D4
Upper Weston 107 G1
Vinney Green 55 F1
Walcot 108 D4
Walton-in-Gordano 69 E3
Walton St Mary 68 C4
Warmley 65 G4
Warmley Hill 65 E3
Warmley Tower 65 G5
Watley's End 29 G3
Way Wick 137 H2
Webb's Heath 66 B3
Welton 124 C2
Westbury on Trym 50 B1
Westbury Park 51 E4
West End 70 A3
West End 84 B2
Westerleigh 43 F1
Westfield 124 D3
West Hewish 133 F3
West Hill 44 D3
Weston 107 F3
Weston Park 107 H3
Weston-Super-Mare 6 A3
West Town 85 G4
West Wick 137 F2
Whitchurch 92 B5
Whitehall 62 D2
Whiteshill 40 D2
Whiteway 113 F3
Wick 67 G5
Wick St Lawrence 132 A1
Widcombe 115 F3
Willsbridge 83 E4
Windmill Hill 79 F3
Winford 97 H5
Winsley 118 A2
Winterbourne 28 D4
Winterbourne Down 41 G1
Withywood 90 A4
Woodhill 45 F1
Woolley 119 H2
Woolvers Hill 137 H5
Worle 136 B2
Worlebury 130 A5
Wraxall 74 B2
Yanley 89 F1
Yate 20 D5
Yate Rocks 21 E1
Yatton 126 C3

USING THE STREET INDEX

Street names are listed alphabetically. Each street name is followed by its postal town or area locality, the Postcode District, the page number, and the reference to the square in which the name is found.

Standard index entries are shown as follows:

Abbeydale *FRCTL/WBN* BS36 ....**29** E4

Street names and selected addresses not shown on the map due to scale restrictions are shown in the index with an asterisk:

Abbey Churchyard
CBATH/BATHN BA1 * **3** F4

GENERAL ABBREVIATIONS

ACC	ACCESS
ALY	ALLEY
AP	APPROACH
AR	ARCADE
ASS	ASSOCIATION
AV	AVENUE
BCH	BEACH
BLDS	BUILDINGS
BND	BEND
BNK	BANK
BR	BRIDGE
BRK	BROOK
BTM	BOTTOM
BUS	BUSINESS
BVD	BOULEVARD
BY	BYPASS
CATH	CATHEDRAL
CEM	CEMETERY
CEN	CENTRE
CFT	CROFT
CH	CHURCH
CHA	CHASE
CHYD	CHURCHYARD
CIR	CIRCLE
CIRC	CIRCUS
CL	CLOSE
CLFS	CLIFFS
CMP	CAMP
CNR	CORNER
CO	COUNTY
COLL	COLLEGE
COM	COMMON
COMM	COMMISSION
CON	CONVENT
COT	COTTAGE
COTS	COTTAGES
CP	CAPE
CPS	COPSE
CR	CREEK
CREM	CREMATORIUM
CRS	CRESCENT
CSWY	CAUSEWAY
CT	COURT
CTRL	CENTRAL
CTS	COURTS
CTYD	COURTYARD
CUTT	CUTTINGS
CV	COVE
CYN	CANYON
DEPT	DEPARTMENT
DL	DALE
DM	DAM
DR	DRIVE
DRO	DROVE
DRY	DRIVEWAY
DWGS	DWELLINGS
E	EAST
EMB	EMBANKMENT
EMBY	EMBASSY
ESP	ESPLANADE
EST	ESTATE
EX	EXCHANGE
EXPY	EXPRESSWAY
EXT	EXTENSION
F/O	FLYOVER
FC	FOOTBALL CLUB
FK	FORK
FLD	FIELD
FLDS	FIELDS
FLS	FALLS
FLS	FLATS
FM	FARM
FT	FORT
FWY	FREEWAY
FY	FERRY
GA	GATE
GAL	GALLERY
GDN	GARDEN
GDNS	GARDENS
GLD	GLADE
GLN	GLEN
GN	GREEN
GND	GROUND
GRA	GRANGE
GRG	GARAGE
GT	GREAT
GTWY	GATEWAY
GV	GROVE
HGR	HIGHER
HL	HILL
HLS	HILLS
HO	HOUSE
HOL	HOLLOW
HOSP	HOSPITAL
HRB	HARBOUR
HTH	HEATH
HTS	HEIGHTS
HVN	HAVEN
HWY	HIGHWAY
IMP	IMPERIAL
IN	INLET
IND EST	INDUSTRIAL ESTATE
INF	INFIRMARY
INFO	INFORMATION
INT	INTERCHANGE
IS	ISLAND
JCT	JUNCTION
JTY	JETTY
KG	KING
KNL	KNOLL
L	LAKE
LA	LANE
LDG	LODGE
LGT	LIGHT
LK	LOCK
LKS	LAKES
LNDG	LANDING
LTL	LITTLE
LWR	LOWER
MAG	MAGISTRATE
MAN	MANSIONS
MD	MEAD
MDW	MEADOWS
MEM	MEMORIAL
MKT	MARKET
MKTS	MARKETS
ML	MALL
ML	MILL
MNR	MANOR
MS	MEWS
MSN	MISSION
MT	MOUNT
MTN	MOUNTAIN
MTS	MOUNTAINS
MUS	MUSEUM
MWY	MOTORWAY
N	NORTH
NE	NORTH EAST
NW	NORTH WEST
O/P	OVERPASS
OFF	OFFICE
ORCH	ORCHARD
OV	OVAL
PAL	PALACE
PAS	PASSAGE
PAV	PAVILION
PDE	PARADE
PH	PUBLIC HOUSE
PK	PARK
PKWY	PARKWAY
PL	PLACE
PLN	PLAIN
PLNS	PLAINS
PLZ	PLAZA
POL	POLICE STATION
PR	PRINCE
PREC	PRECINCT
PREP	PREPARATORY
PRIM	PRIMARY
PROM	PROMENADE
PRS	PRINCESS
PRT	PORT
PT	POINT
PTH	PATH
PZ	PIAZZA
QD	QUADRANT
QU	QUEEN
QY	QUAY
R	RIVER
RBT	ROUNDABOUT
RD	ROAD
RDG	RIDGE
REP	REPUBLIC
RES	RESERVOIR
RFC	RUGBY FOOTBALL CLUB

RI....RISE
RP....RAMP
RW....ROW
S....SOUTH
SCH....SCHOOL
SE....SOUTH EAST
SER....SERVICE AREA
SH....SHORE
SHOP....SHOPPING
SKWY....SKYWAY
SMT....SUMMIT
SOC....SOCIETY
SP....SPUR
SPR....SPRING
SQ....SQUARE
ST....STREET
STN....STATION
STR....STREAM
STRD....STRAND
SW....SOUTH WEST
TDG....TRADING
TER....TERRACE
THWY....THROUGHWAY
TNL....TUNNEL
TOLL....TOLLWAY
TPK....TURNPIKE
TR....TRACK
TRL....TRAIL
TWR....TOWER
U/P....UNDERPASS
UNI....UNIVERSITY
UPR....UPPER
V....VALE
VA....VALLEY
VIAD....VIADUCT
VIL....VILLA
VIS....VISTA
VLG....VILLAGE
VLS....VILLAS
VW....VIEW
W....WEST
WD....WOOD
WHF....WHARF
WK....WALK
WKS....WALKS
WLS....WELLS
WY....WAY
YD....YARD
YHA....YOUTH HOSTEL

POSTCODE TOWNS AND AREA ABBREVIATIONS

ALMDB....Almondsbury
AVONM....Avonmouth
BATHSE....Bath south & east
BLAG/CWMG/WR....Blagdon/Chew.Magna/Wrington
BMSTR....Bedminster
BMSTRD/HC/WWD....Bedminster Down/Hartcliffe/Withywood
BNWL....Banwell
BOAV....Bradford-on-Avon
BOS....Burnham-on-Sea
BRSG/KWL/STAPK....Brislington/Knowle/St Anne's Park
BRSTK/PCHW....Bradley Stoke/Patchway
CBATH/BATHN....Central Bath/Bath north
CBRIS/FH....Central Bristol/Floating Harbour
CBRISNE....Central Bristol north & east
CFTN/FAIL....Clifton/Failand
CHPMW/MSHF....Chippenham west/Marshfield
CLVDN....Clevedon
COR/BOX....Corsham/Box
EVILLE/WHL....Eastville/Whitehall
FRCTL/WBN....Frampton Cotterell/Winterbourne
HGRV/WHIT....Hengrove/Whitchurch
HNBRY/STHM....Henbury/Southmead
HNLZ/SM/SNYPK/WT....Henleaze/Sea Mills/Sneyd Park/Westbury on Trym
HORF/LLZ....Horfield/Lockleaze
KEYN....Keynsham
KGWD/HNM....Kingswood/Hanham
LGASH....Long Ashton
MANG/FISH....Mangotsfield/Fishponds
MTN/WRL....Milton/Worle
NAIL....Nailsea
OLD/WMLY/WICK....Oldland/Warmley/Wick
OMX/HUT/LCK....Oldmixon/Hutton/Locking
PLTN/PENS....Paulton/Pensford
PTSHD/EG....Portishead/Easton-in-Gordano
RDLND/MONT....Redland/Montpelier
RDSTK/MIDN....Radstock/Midsomer Norton
THNB/SVB....Thornbury/Severn Beach
TRWBR....Trowbridge
WSM....Weston-Super -Mare
WUE....Wotton-under-Edge
YATE/CS....Yate/Chipping Sodbury
YTN/CONG....Yatton/Congresbury

A

Abbey Churchyard
CBATH/BATHN BA1 * 3 F4
Abbey Ct *BRSG/KWL/STAPK* BS4 ..81 E1
Abbeydale *FRCTL/WBN* BS36 ....29 E4
Abbeygate St *CBATH/BATHN* BA1 ..3 G5
Abbey Gn *CBATH/BATHN* BA1 ....3 G5
Abbey Pk *KEYN* BS31 ....94 C3
Abbey Rd
HNLZ/SM/SNYPK/WT BS9 ....50 C2
Abbey St *CBATH/BATHN* BA1 * 3 G4
Abbey Vw *BATHSE* BA2 ....3 K6
Abbey View Gdns *BATHSE* BA2 ....3 J6
Abbeywood Dr
HNLZ/SM/SNYPK/WT BS9 ....49 H3
Abbots Av *KGWD/HNM* BS15 ....81 H2
Abbotsbury Rd *NAIL* BS48 ....73 E5
Abbots Cl *HGRV/WHIT* BS14 ....100 D1
MTN/WRL BS22 ....131 H5
Abbotsford Rd
RDLND/MONT BS6 ....61 E2
Abbots Horn *NAIL* BS48 ....73 E4
Abbots Leigh Rd *CFTN/FAIL* BS8 ..59 G4
Abbots Rd *KGWD/HNM* BS15 ....81 H4
Abbots Wy
HNLZ/SM/SNYPK/WT BS9 ....51 G2
Abbotswood
KGWD/HNM BS15 ....64 C4
YATE/CS BS37 ....31 H3
Abbott Rd *THNB/SVB* BS35 ....12 C4
Aberdeen Rd *RDLND/MONT* BS6 ..61 E2
Abingdon Gdns *BATHSE* BA2 ....116 B2
Abingdon Rd *MANG/FISH* BS16 ....53 H5
Ableton La *HNBRY/STHM* BS10 ....23 G1
THNB/SVB BS35 ....12 C3
Ableton Wk
HNLZ/SM/SNYPK/WT BS9 ....49 G3
Abraham Cl *EVILLE/WHL* BS5 ....62 C3
Abson Rd *MANG/FISH* BS16 ....57 E3
OLD/WMLY/WICK BS30 ....67 F2
Acacia Av *MANG/FISH* BS16 ....54 B4
WSM BS23 ....135 G3
Acacia Cl *MANG/FISH* BS16 ....54 B5
Acacia Ct *KEYN* BS31 ....93 H5
Acacia Crs *TRWBR* BA14 ....122 B1
Acacia Gv *BATHSE* BA2 ....113 H4
Acacia Ms *MANG/FISH* BS16 * 54 C4
Acacia Rd *MANG/FISH* BS16 ....54 C5
RDSTK/MIDN BA3 ....125 F3
Aconite Cl *MTN/WRL* BS22 ....131 H3
Acorn Gv
BMSTRD/HC/WWD BS13 ....89 H3
Acraman's Rd *BMSTR* BS3 ....78 D2
Acresbush Cl
BMSTRD/HC/WWD BS13 ....90 B4
Acton Rd *MANG/FISH* BS16 ....53 H5
Adams Hay
BRSG/KWL/STAPK BS4 ....80 C5
Adastral Rd
OMX/HUT/LCK BS24 ....141 G2
Adcroft Dr *TRWBR* BA14 ....121 E5
Adcroft St *TRWBR* BA14 ....121 E5
Adderly Ga *MANG/FISH* BS16 ....55 G1
Addicott Rd *WSM* BS23 ....7 F7
Addiscombe Rd
HGRV/WHIT BS14 ....92 A4
WSM BS23 ....138 D2
Addison Rd *BMSTR* BS3 ....79 F3
Adelaide Pl *EVILLE/WHL* BS5 ....62 C3
MANG/FISH BS16 ....53 G4
Adelaide Ter *MANG/FISH* BS16 * ..53 H4
Adelante Cl *BRSTK/PCHW* BS34 ....40 B1
Admiral Cl *BRSTK/PCHW* BS34 ....53 E1
Agate St *BMSTR* BS3 ....78 C3
Aiken St *EVILLE/WHL* BS5 ....62 C5
Ainslies Belvedere
CBATH/BATHN BA1 ....3 F1
Aintree Av *TRWBR* BA14 ....123 E5
Aintree Dr *MANG/FISH* BS16 ....41 G4
Air Balloon Rd *EVILLE/WHL* BS5 ..63 H4
Airport Rd *HGRV/WHIT* BS14 ....91 H1
Aisecombe Wy *WSM* BS23 ....135 H5
Akeman Wy *AVONM* BS11 ....34 D5
Alanscourt
OLD/WMLY/WICK BS30 * 83 E1
Alard Rd *BRSG/KWL/STAPK* BS4 ....91 G2
Albany Cl *TRWBR* BA14 ....121 G4
Albany Ga *BRSTK/PCHW* BS34 ....27 G5
Albany Rd *BATHSE* BA2 ....113 G1
RDLND/MONT BS6 ....62 A2
Albany St *KGWD/HNM* BS15 ....64 B3
Albany Wy
OLD/WMLY/WICK BS30 ....83 F1
Albermarle Rw *CFTN/FAIL* BS8 ....60 C5
Albermarle Ter *CFTN/FAIL* BS8 ....60 C5
Albert Av *WSM* BS23 ....6 E7
Albert Crs *CBRISNE* BS2 ....79 H1
Albert Gv South
EVILLE/WHL BS5 ....63 G3
Alberton Rd *MANG/FISH* BS16 ....53 G2
Albert Pde *EVILLE/WHL* BS5 ....62 D3
Albert Pk *RDLND/MONT* BS6 ....62 A2
Albert Park Pl
RDLND/MONT BS6 ....61 H2
Albert Pl *BMSTR* BS3 ....78 D2
HNLZ/SM/SNYPK/WT BS9 ....50 D1
Albert Qd *WSM* BS23 ....7 G3
Albert Rd *CBRISNE* BS2 ....79 H2
CLVDN BS21 ....70 C2
KEYN BS31 ....94 B4
KGWD/HNM BS15 ....82 A1
MANG/FISH BS16 ....54 D4
PTSHD/EG BS20 ....45 G3
THNB/SVB BS35 ....12 C3
TRWBR BA14 ....121 G3
WSM BS23 ....6 E7
Albert Ter *BATHSE* BA2 * 113 H1
MANG/FISH BS16 ....53 G4
Albion Cl *MANG/FISH* BS16 ....55 E3
Albion Dr *TRWBR* BA14 ....122 C1
Albion Pl *CBATH/BATHN* BA1 ....2 C3
Albion Rd *EVILLE/WHL* BS5 ....62 C2
Albion St *EVILLE/WHL* BS5 ....62 D3
Albion Ter *CBATH/BATHN* BA1 ....2 C3
Alcove Rd *MANG/FISH* BS16 ....53 F5
Aldeburgh Pl *TRWBR* BA14 ....122 A3
Alder Cl *TRWBR* BA14 ....122 C4
Aldercombe Rd
HNLZ/SM/SNYPK/WT BS9 ....36 B5
Alderdown Cl *AVONM* BS11 ....35 H5
Alder Dr *EVILLE/WHL* BS5 ....63 F2
Alderley Rd *BATHSE* BA2 ....113 F3
Aldermoor Wy
OLD/WMLY/WICK BS30 ....82 B2
Alderney Av
BRSG/KWL/STAPK BS4 ....81 E2
Alder Ter *RDSTK/MIDN* BA3 ....125 F2
Alderton Rd *HORF/LLZ* BS7 ....38 B5
Alderton Wy *TRWBR* BA14 ....123 E4
Alder Wy *BATHSE* BA2 ....116 B2
Aldwick Av
BMSTRD/HC/WWD BS13 ....99 H1
Alec Ricketts Cl *BATHSE* BA2 ....113 E2
Alexander Buildings
CBATH/BATHN BA1 * 109 E3
Alexander Wy *YTN/CONG* BS49 ..126 B4
Alexandra Cl *MANG/FISH* BS16 ....54 C4
Alexandra Gdns
MANG/FISH BS16 ....54 C4
Alexandra Pde *WSM* BS23 ....6 E4
Alexandra Pk *MANG/FISH* BS16 ....53 G4
RDLND/MONT BS6 ....61 F1
Alexandra Pl *MANG/FISH* BS16 ....54 C4
Alexandra Rd *BATHSE* BA2 ....3 G7
BMSTRD/HC/WWD BS13 ....90 A2
CFTN/FAIL BS8 ....61 E3
CLVDN BS21 ....70 C1
FRCTL/WBN BS36 ....30 B3
HNBRY/STHM BS10 ....37 H5
KGWD/HNM BS15 ....81 H1
Alexandra Wy *THNB/SVB* BS35 ....8 C1
Alford Rd *BRSG/KWL/STAPK* BS4 ..80 B4
Alfred Ct *WSM* BS23 ....6 E4
Alfred Hl *CBRISNE* BS2 ....4 E1
Alfred Pde *CBRISNE* BS2 ....4 E1
Alfred Pl *CBRIS/FH* BS1 ....5 F6
CBRISNE BS2 ....61 F3
Alfred Rd *BMSTR* BS3 ....79 E3
RDLND/MONT BS6 ....50 D4
Alfred St *CBATH/BATHN* BA1 ....3 F2
CBRISNE BS2 ....62 B5
EVILLE/WHL BS5 ....62 D3
WSM BS23 ....7 F4
Algiers St *BMSTR* BS3 ....79 E3
Alison Gdns *NAIL* BS48 ....85 H2
Allanmead Rd *HGRV/WHIT* BS14 ..92 A1
Allen Rd *TRWBR* BA14 ....122 C2
Allerton Crs *HGRV/WHIT* BS14 ....92 A5
Allerton Gdns *HGRV/WHIT* BS14 ..92 A4
Allerton Rd *HGRV/WHIT* BS14 ....91 H5
Allfoxton Rd *HORF/LLZ* BS7 ....52 B5
All Hallows Rd *EVILLE/WHL* BS5 ..62 C3
Allington Dr
OLD/WMLY/WICK BS30 ....82 C2
Allington Gdns *NAIL* BS48 ....84 D1
Allington Rd *BMSTR* BS3 ....4 C7
Allison Av
BRSG/KWL/STAPK BS4 ....80 D2
Allison Rd
BRSG/KWL/STAPK BS4 ....80 D3
All Saints Gdns *CFTN/FAIL* BS8 * ..60 D3
All Saints' La *CBRIS/FH* BS1 ....5 F4
CLVDN BS21 ....71 F1
All Saints Rd
CBATH/BATHN BA1 * 108 C4
CFTN/FAIL BS8 ....60 D3
WSM BS23 ....6 E1
All Saints' St *CBRIS/FH* BS1 ....5 F3
Alma Cl *KGWD/HNM* BS15 ....64 D3
Alma Ct *CFTN/FAIL* BS8 ....61 E2
Alma Rd *CFTN/FAIL* BS8 ....60 D3
KGWD/HNM BS15 ....64 D2
Alma Road Av *CFTN/FAIL* BS8 ....61 E3
Alma St *TRWBR* BA14 ....123 F1
WSM BS23 ....6 E4
Alma Vale Rd *CFTN/FAIL* BS8 ....60 D3
Almeda Rd *EVILLE/WHL* BS5 ....63 H5
Almond Cl *MTN/WRL* BS22 ....136 D2
Almond Gv *TRWBR* BA14 ....122 C4
Almond Wy *MANG/FISH* BS16 ....55 E3
Almorah Rd *BMSTR* BS3 ....79 F3
Alpha Rd *BMSTR* BS3 ....79 E2
Alpine Gdns
CBATH/BATHN BA1 ....108 D4
Alpine Rd *EVILLE/WHL* BS5 ....62 D2
Alsop Rd *KGWD/HNM* BS15 ....64 C3
Alton Rd *HORF/LLZ* BS7 ....52 A2
Altringham Rd *EVILLE/WHL* BS5 ..63 E2
Alverstoke *HGRV/WHIT* BS14 ....91 G2
Alveston Hl *THNB/SVB* BS35 ....11 G1
Alveston Rd *ALMDB* BS32 ....10 C4
Alveston Wk
HNLZ/SM/SNYPK/WT BS9 ....49 G1
Alwins Ct
OLD/WMLY/WICK BS30 ....82 C2
Amberey Rd *WSM* BS23 ....139 E1
Amberlands Cl *NAIL* BS48 ....85 H2
Amberley Cl *KEYN* BS31 ....94 B5
MANG/FISH BS16 ....54 C1
Amberley Rd
BRSTK/PCHW BS34 ....26 D2
MANG/FISH BS16 ....54 C1
Amble Cl *KGWD/HNM* BS15 ....65 E4
Ambleside Av
HNBRY/STHM BS10 ....37 G4
Ambleside Rd *BATHSE* BA2 ....113 G5
Ambra Ter *CFTN/FAIL* BS8 * 60 D5
Ambra V *CFTN/FAIL* BS8 ....60 D5
Ambra V East *CFTN/FAIL* BS8 ....60 D5
Ambra V West *CFTN/FAIL* BS8 ....60 D5
Ambrose Rd *CFTN/FAIL* BS8 ....60 D5
Ambury *BATHSE* BA2 ....3 F6
Amercombe Wk
HGRV/WHIT BS14 ....92 C2
Amery La *CBATH/BATHN* BA1 ....3 F5
Amouracre *TRWBR* BA14 ....123 G1
Ancaster Cl *TRWBR* BA14 ....120 B5
Anchor Cl
BRSG/KWL/STAPK BS4 ....63 G5
Anchor Rd *CBATH/BATHN* BA1 ....107 G3
CBRIS/FH BS1 ....4 C5
KGWD/HNM BS15 ....65 F2
Anchor Wy *PTSHD/EG* BS20 ....48 C4
Andereach Cl *HGRV/WHIT* BS14 ....92 A1
Andover Rd
BRSG/KWL/STAPK BS4 ....79 G4
Andruss Dr *LGASH* BS41 ....98 C2
Angers Rd
BRSG/KWL/STAPK BS4 ....79 G2
Anglesea Pl *CFTN/FAIL* BS8 ....60 D1
Anglo Ter *CBATH/BATHN* BA1 * ..108 D4
Annandale Av *MTN/WRL* BS22 ..136 B2
Anson Cl *KEYN* BS31 ....105 E2
Anson Rd *MTN/WRL* BS22 ....131 E4
OMX/HUT/LCK BS24 ....137 E5
Ansteys Cl *KGWD/HNM* BS15 ....81 G1
Anstey's Rd *KGWD/HNM* BS15 ....81 G1
Anstey St *EVILLE/WHL* BS5 ....62 C2
Anthea Rd *EVILLE/WHL* BS5 ....63 F1
Antona Ct *AVONM* BS11 ....48 B1
Antona Dr *AVONM* BS11 ....48 C1
Antrim Rd
HNLZ/SM/SNYPK/WT BS9 ....51 E2
Anvil Rd *YTN/CONG* BS49 * 127 F2
Anvil St *CBRISNE* BS2 ....5 K4
Apperley Cl *YATE/CS* BS37 ....31 H2
Appleby Wk
BRSG/KWL/STAPK BS4 ....91 E2
Appledore Cl *HGRV/WHIT* BS14 ....92 A1
Applegate *HNBRY/STHM* BS10 ....37 G2
Appletree Ct *MTN/WRL* BS22 ....137 E1
Applin Gn *MANG/FISH* BS16 ....55 H2
Approach Rd *CBRIS/FH* BS1 * 5 K6
Appsley Cl *MTN/WRL* BS22 ....135 H2
Apseleys Md *ALMDB* BS32 ....16 A5
Apsley Ms *CFTN/FAIL* BS8 * 60 D2
Apsley Rd *CBATH/BATHN* BA1 ....107 F5
CFTN/FAIL BS8 ....60 D2
Apsley St *EVILLE/WHL* BS5 ....62 D1
Arbutus Dr
HNLZ/SM/SNYPK/WT BS9 ....49 H1
The Arcade *CBRIS/FH* BS1 ....5 G2
Archer Ct
OLD/WMLY/WICK BS30 ....82 C3
Archer Wk *HGRV/WHIT* BS14 ....92 D3
The Arches *TRWBR* BA14 * 121 E5
Archfield Rd
RDLND/MONT BS6 ....61 F2
Archway St *BATHSE* BA2 ....3 J6
Ardagh Ct *HORF/LLZ* BS7 * 52 A1
Arden Cl *ALMDB* BS32 ....27 G4
MTN/WRL BS22 ....131 G5
Ardenton Wk
HNBRY/STHM BS10 ....37 F2
Ardern Cl
HNLZ/SM/SNYPK/WT BS9 ....36 A5
Argus Ct *BMSTR* BS3 ....78 D4
Argus Rd *BMSTR* BS3 ....78 D3
Argyle Av *WSM* BS23 ....139 E2
Argyle Dr *YATE/CS* BS37 ....20 D3
Argyle Pl *CFTN/FAIL* BS8 ....60 D5
Argyle Rd *CBRISNE* BS2 ....61 H3
CLVDN BS21 ....68 B5
MANG/FISH BS16 ....64 A1
Argyle St *BMSTR* BS3 ....78 D2
CBATH/BATHN BA1 ....3 G4
EVILLE/WHL BS5 ....62 D1
Argyle Ter *BATHSE* BA2 * 113 H1
Arley Cottages
RDLND/MONT BS6 ....61 G2
Arley Hl *RDLND/MONT* BS6 ....61 G2
Arley Pk *RDLND/MONT* BS6 ....61 G2
Arley Ter *EVILLE/WHL* BS5 ....63 F2
Arlingham Wy
BRSTK/PCHW BS34 ....26 A2
Arlington Rd
BRSG/KWL/STAPK BS4 ....63 E5
Arlington Vls *CFTN/FAIL* BS8 ....60 D4
Armada Pl *CBRIS/FH* BS1 ....61 H3
Armada Rd *HGRV/WHIT* BS14 ....91 H3
Armes Ct *BATHSE* BA2 ....3 H7
Armidale Av *RDLND/MONT* BS6 ....61 H2
Armoury Sq *EVILLE/WHL* BS5 ....62 B3
Armstrong Dr
OLD/WMLY/WICK BS30 ....83 E1
Armstrong Wy *YATE/CS* BS37 ....20 B4
Arnall Dr *HNBRY/STHM* BS10 ....37 E4
Arneside Rd *HNBRY/STHM* BS10 ..37 H4
Arnor Cl *MTN/WRL* BS22 ....131 H4
Arno's St *BRSG/KWL/STAPK* BS4 ..79 H2
Arras Cl *TRWBR* BA14 ....122 D3
Arrowfield Cl *HGRV/WHIT* BS14 ..100 D2
Artemesia Av *MTN/WRL* BS22 ....136 B3
Arthurs Cl *MANG/FISH* BS16 ....55 H2
Arthur Skemp Cl
EVILLE/WHL BS5 * 62 C4
Arthur St *CBRISNE* BS2 ....79 H1
EVILLE/WHL BS5 ....62 D3
Arthurswood Rd
BMSTRD/HC/WWD BS13 ....90 B5
Arundel Cl
BMSTRD/HC/WWD BS13 ....90 C5
Arundell Rd *WSM* BS23 ....7 F2
Arundel Rd *CBATH/BATHN* BA1 ..108 D3
HORF/LLZ BS7 ....51 G5
Ascot Cl *MANG/FISH* BS16 ....41 G4
Ascot Rd *HNBRY/STHM* BS10 ....38 A3
Ashbourne Cl
OLD/WMLY/WICK BS30 ....65 H5
Ashburton Rd
HNBRY/STHM BS10 ....37 H4
Ashbury Dr *MTN/WRL* BS22 ....135 G2
Ash Cl *BRSTK/PCHW* BS34 ....27 F3
MTN/WRL BS22 ....137 G1
YATE/CS BS37 ....20 C4
Ashcombe Cl
OLD/WMLY/WICK BS30 ....65 H5
Ashcombe Crs
OLD/WMLY/WICK BS30 ....65 H5
Ashcombe Gdns *WSM* BS23 ....7 J2
Ashcombe Park Rd *WSM* BS23 ....7 K1
Ashcombe Rd *WSM* BS23 ....7 H4
Ashcott *HGRV/WHIT* BS14 ....91 G3
Ashcroft Av *KEYN* BS31 ....94 A4
Ashcroft Rd
HNLZ/SM/SNYPK/WT BS9 ....49 H1
Ashdene Av *EVILLE/WHL* BS5 ....53 E5
Ashdene Rd *WSM* BS23 ....7 K2
Ashdown Rd *PTSHD/EG* BS20 ....44 D2
Asher La *CBRISNE* BS2 ....5 J2
Ashfield Pl *RDLND/MONT* BS6 ....62 A2
Ashfield Rd *BMSTR* BS3 ....78 C3
Ashfield Ter *BMSTR* BS3 * 78 C3
Ashford Dr
OMX/HUT/LCK BS24 ....139 F5
Ashford Rd *BATHSE* BA2 ....114 A3
BRSTK/PCHW BS34 ....26 C3
Ash Gv *BATHSE* BA2 ....113 H3
CLVDN BS21 ....71 E1
MANG/FISH BS16 ....54 B5
WSM BS23 ....138 D4
Ashgrove *THNB/SVB* BS35 ....8 D3
Ashgrove Av *CFTN/FAIL* BS8 ....59 G4
HORF/LLZ BS7 ....52 A4
Ashgrove Cl *HORF/LLZ* BS7 ....52 A4
Ashgrove Pl *HORF/LLZ* BS7 ....52 A3
Ashgrove Rd *BMSTR* BS3 ....78 C3
HORF/LLZ BS7 ....52 A4
RDLND/MONT BS6 ....61 E2
Ash Hayes Dr *NAIL* BS48 ....73 F5
Ash Hayes Rd *NAIL* BS48 ....73 F5
Ashland Rd
BMSTRD/HC/WWD BS13 ....90 B5
Ash La *ALMDB* BS32 ....14 D4
Ashleigh Crs *YTN/CONG* BS49 ....126 B3
Ashleigh Gv *TRWBR* BA14 ....122 D2
Ashleigh Rd *WSM* BS23 ....7 J2
YTN/CONG BS49 ....126 B3
Ashley *KGWD/HNM* BS15 ....65 E3
Ashley Av *CBATH/BATHN* BA1 ....107 H5
Ashley Cl *BOAV* BA15 ....119 E1
HORF/LLZ BS7 ....52 A4
Ashley Court Rd
RDLND/MONT BS6 ....62 A1
Ashley Down Rd *HORF/LLZ* BS7 ..51 H3
Ashley Grove Rd *CBRISNE* BS2 ....62 B2
Ashley Hl *RDLND/MONT* BS6 ....52 A5

Ashley La BOAV BA15 ....118 C2
Ashley Pde CBRISNE BS2 ....62 A1
Ashley Pk RDLND/MONT BS6 ....52 A5
Ashley Rd CBATH/BATHN BA1 ....110 D2
CLVDN BS21 ....70 B4
RDLND/MONT BS6 ....61 H2
Ashley St CBRISNE BS2 ....62 B2
Ashley Ter
CBATH/BATHN BA1 * 107 H5
Ashman Cl EVILLE/WHL BS5 ....62 B3
Ashmans Yd
CBATH/BATHN BA1 ....113 G1
Ashmead TRWBR BA14 ....122 D3
Ashmead Ct TRWBR BA14 ....123 E2
Ashmead Pk KEYN BS31 * 95 E4
Ashmead Rd KEYN BS31 ....95 E4
Ashmead Wy CBRIS/FH BS1 ....78 A1
Ash Ridge Rd ALMDB BS32 ....15 H4
Ash Rd BNWL BS29 ....141 H2
HORF/LLZ BS7 ....51 H3
Ashton Av CBRIS/FH BS1 ....78 B1
Ashton Cl CLVDN BS21 ....70 B4
Ashton Crs NAIL BS48 ....73 E5
Ashton Dr BMSTR BS3 ....77 H5
Ashton Gate Rd BMSTR BS3 ....78 B2
Ashton Gate Ter BMSTR BS3 ....78 B2
Ashton Hl BATHSE BA2 ....105 H5
Ashton Ri TRWBR BA14 ....121 H4
Ashton Rd BMSTR BS3 ....78 A3
LGASH BS41 ....77 F3
TRWBR BA14 ....121 H4
Ashton St TRWBR BA14 ....123 F1
Ashton Vale Rd BMSTR BS3 ....77 H3
Ashton Wy KEYN BS31 ....94 B3
Ash Tree Ct RDSTK/MIDN BA3 ....125 F3
Ashvale Cl NAIL BS48 ....73 H4
Ashville Rd BMSTR BS3 ....78 B2
Ash Wk HNBRY/STHM BS10 ....37 G2
Ashwell Cl HGRV/WHIT BS14 ....92 D3
Ashwicke HGRV/WHIT BS14 ....91 G3
Aspen Park Rd
MTN/WRL BS22 ....136 B3
Aspley Cl CBATH/BATHN BA1 ....107 G5
Assembly Rooms La
CBRIS/FH BS1 * 4 E5
Astry Cl AVONM BS11 ....35 H4
Atchley St EVILLE/WHL BS5 ....62 C4
Atherston
OLD/WMLY/WICK BS30 ....83 F1
Athlone Wk
BRSG/KWL/STAPK BS4 ....79 F5
Atholl Cl MTN/WRL BS22 ....131 G5
Atkins Cl HGRV/WHIT BS14 ....92 D3
Atlantic Rd AVONM BS11 ....34 D5
Atlantic Rd South WSM BS23 ....6 A1
Atlas Cl EVILLE/WHL BS5 ....63 H1
Atlas Rd BMSTR BS3 ....79 F3
Atlas St CBRISNE BS2 ....80 A1
Atwell Dr ALMDB BS32 ....26 D1
Atwood Dr AVONM BS11 ....36 A3
Atyeo Cl BMSTR BS3 ....77 H5
Aubrey Meads
OLD/WMLY/WICK BS30 ....95 H1
Aubrey Rd BMSTR BS3 ....78 C3
Auburn Av
OLD/WMLY/WICK BS30 ....83 E3
Auburn Rd RDLND/MONT BS6 ....61 E1
Auckland Cl WSM BS23 ....139 E4
Audley Av CBATH/BATHN BA1 ....107 H5
Audley Cl CBATH/BATHN BA1 ....2 A2
Audley Gv CBATH/BATHN BA1 ....107 H5
Audley Park Rd
CBATH/BATHN BA1 * 2 B2
Audrey Wk
HNLZ/SM/SNYPK/WT BS9 ....51 G2
Augusta Pl CBATH/BATHN BA1 ....2 A3
Augustine's Cl PTSHD/EG BS20 ....44 B4
Austen Dr MTN/WRL BS22 ....132 A4
Austen Gv HORF/LLZ BS7 ....38 D5
Autumn Ms
OMX/HUT/LCK BS24 ....136 D3
Avalon Cl YTN/CONG BS49 ....126 A2
Avalon Rd EVILLE/WHL BS5 ....64 A5
Avebury Rd BMSTR BS3 ....77 H4
Avening Cl NAIL BS48 ....85 G1
Avening Rd KGWD/HNM BS15 ....63 H3
Avenue Rd TRWBR BA14 ....122 C1
The Avenue BATHSE BA2 ....115 H2
BATHSE BA2 ....117 F1
BRSTK/PCHW BS34 ....15 H5
BRSTK/PCHW BS34 ....27 E4
CFTN/FAIL BS8 ....60 D2
CLVDN BS21 ....68 B5
EVILLE/WHL BS5 ....63 G4
HNLZ/SM/SNYPK/WT BS9 ....60 A1
HORF/LLZ BS7 ....51 H5
KEYN BS31 ....94 B2
MANG/FISH BS16 ....39 H4
MTN/WRL BS22 ....132 B5
NAIL BS48 ....85 H2
YATE/CS BS37 ....31 H1
YTN/CONG BS49 ....126 B3
Averay Rd MANG/FISH BS16 ....52 D4
Avon Cl BOAV BA15 ....119 H4
BRSG/KWL/STAPK BS4 ....63 G5
KEYN BS31 ....94 C3
WSM BS23 ....139 E4
Avon Ct CBATH/BATHN BA1 ....103 F5
Avon Crs CBRIS/FH BS1 ....78 B1
Avondale Buildings
CBATH/BATHN BA1 ....109 E2
Avondale Ct
OLD/WMLY/WICK BS30 * 82 C4
Avondale Pl
CBATH/BATHN BA1 ....110 A1
Avondale Rd
CBATH/BATHN BA1 ....107 G5
Avondown Cl
HNBRY/STHM BS10 ....38 A3
Avondown Ct BMSTR BS3 * 78 D4
Avonfield Av BOAV BA15 ....119 H4
Avon Gv
HNLZ/SM/SNYPK/WT BS9 ....60 A1
Avonlea KGWD/HNM BS15 ....81 H1
Avonleaze
HNLZ/SM/SNYPK/WT BS9 ....49 G3
Avonleigh Rd BMSTR BS3 ....78 C4
Avon Meads CBRISNE BS2 * 80 B1
Avon Mill La KEYN BS31 ....94 C3
Avonmouth Rd AVONM BS11 ....34 D5
Avonmouth Wy AVONM BS11 ....34 D4
Avonmouth Wy West
AVONM BS11 ....34 C3
Avon Pk CBATH/BATHN BA1 ....107 F5
EVILLE/WHL BS5 ....63 E4
Avon Rd
BMSTRD/HC/WWD BS13 ....90 B3
KEYN BS31 ....94 C4
PTSHD/EG BS20 ....48 B3
Avonside Rd CBRISNE BS2 ....62 D5
Avonside Wy
BRSG/KWL/STAPK BS4 ....63 G5
Avon St BATHSE BA2 ....3 F6
CBRISNE BS2 ....5 J4
Avon V
HNLZ/SM/SNYPK/WT BS9 ....50 A4
Avonvale Rd EVILLE/WHL BS5 ....62 D4
TRWBR BA14 ....121 E4
Avon Vw KGWD/HNM BS15 ....81 G3
Avon Walkway BATHSE BA2 ....116 C5
CBATH/BATHN BA1 ....2 D4
CBRISNE BS2 ....79 H1
OLD/WMLY/WICK BS30 ....95 F3
PTSHD/EG BS20 ....48 C4
Avon Wy HNBRY/STHM BS10 ....38 A5
HNLZ/SM/SNYPK/WT BS9 ....49 H3
PTSHD/EG BS20 ....45 F3
THNB/SVB BS35 ....8 D4
TRWBR BA14 ....121 E3
Avonwood Cl AVONM BS11 ....48 D2
Awdelett Cl AVONM BS11 ....36 A4
Axbridge Cl NAIL BS48 ....85 F1
Axbridge Rd BATHSE BA2 ....114 D5
BRSG/KWL/STAPK BS4 ....79 G4
Axe & Cleaver La
TRWBR BA14 * 123 E5
Axe Cl WSM BS23 ....139 F1
Aycote Cl MTN/WRL BS22 ....135 H1
Aylesbury Crs BMSTR BS3 ....78 C5
Aylesbury Rd BMSTR BS3 ....78 C5
Aylmer Crs HGRV/WHIT BS14 ....92 A3
Aylminton Wk AVONM BS11 ....36 A3
Ayr St BATHSE BA2 ....2 A5
Azalea Dr TRWBR BA14 ....122 B2
Azalea Rd MTN/WRL BS22 ....131 H3

B

Backfields CBRISNE BS2 ....5 G1
Backfields La CBRISNE BS2 ....61 H3
Back La KEYN BS31 ....94 B3
MANG/FISH BS16 ....57 F4
PTSHD/EG BS20 ....48 B4
Back of Kingsdown Pde
RDLND/MONT BS6 ....61 G3
Back Rd BMSTR BS3 ....78 B2
Back Stoke La
HNLZ/SM/SNYPK/WT BS9 ....50 C2
Back St TRWBR BA14 ....120 D5
WSM BS23 ....6 E4
Backwell Bow NAIL BS48 ....74 A5
Backwell Common NAIL BS48 ....85 H2
Backwell Hill Rd NAIL BS48 ....86 C2
Backwell Vw NAIL BS48 * 74 B2
Backwell Wk
BMSTRD/HC/WWD BS13 ....90 A1
Badenham Gv AVONM BS11 ....35 G5
Baden Rd EVILLE/WHL BS5 ....62 D4
KGWD/HNM BS15 ....65 G4
Bader Cl YATE/CS BS37 ....20 C4
Badger Ri PTSHD/EG BS20 ....44 B5
Badgers Cl ALMDB BS32 ....16 B4
Badgers Holt HGRV/WHIT BS14 ....92 B3
Badger's La ALMDB BS32 ....14 C5
The Badgers MTN/WRL BS22 ....132 B5
Badgers Wk
BRSG/KWL/STAPK BS4 ....80 C4
Badgers Wy
OMX/HUT/LCK BS24 ....136 C3
Badgeworth YATE/CS BS37 ....31 H4
Badmington Rd
MANG/FISH BS16 ....41 G5
Badminton Ct YATE/CS BS37 * 20 B5
Badminton Gdns
CBATH/BATHN BA1 ....107 H4
Badminton Rd CBRISNE BS2 ....62 A2
FRCTL/WBN BS36 ....41 H2
MANG/FISH BS16 ....54 D1
YATE/CS BS37 ....31 F1
YATE/CS BS37 ....33 E2
Baglyn Av KGWD/HNM BS15 ....55 E5
Bagnell Cl HGRV/WHIT BS14 ....92 D4
Bagnell Rd HGRV/WHIT BS14 ....92 D4
Bagworth Dr
OLD/WMLY/WICK BS30 ....82 C3
Bailbrook Gv
CBATH/BATHN BA1 ....109 F1
Bailbrook La
CBATH/BATHN BA1 ....109 H1
Baildon Rd WSM BS23 ....139 E2
Bailey Cl MTN/WRL BS22 ....136 B3
Baileys Barn BOAV BA15 ....119 G5
Baileys Court Rd ALMDB BS32 ....27 G4
Baileys Mead Rd
MANG/FISH BS16 ....52 D3
Bainton Cl BOAV BA15 ....119 H2
Baker Cl CLVDN BS21 ....70 B5
Bakersfield
OLD/WMLY/WICK BS30 ....82 D3
Bakers Gnd BRSTK/PCHW BS34 ....27 H5
Baker St WSM BS23 ....7 F3
Balaclava Rd MANG/FISH BS16 ....53 G5
Baldwin St CBRIS/FH BS1 ....5 F4
Balfour Rd BMSTR BS3 ....78 C3
Ballance St CBATH/BATHN BA1 ....3 F1
Ballast La AVONM BS11 ....35 E3
Balmain St
BRSG/KWL/STAPK BS4 ....79 H2
Balmoral Cl BRSTK/PCHW BS34 ....39 G1
Balmoral Ct MANG/FISH BS16 ....55 F3
Balmoral Rd KEYN BS31 ....94 B5
OLD/WMLY/WICK BS30 ....82 C4
RDLND/MONT BS6 ....62 A1
TRWBR BA14 ....122 C4
Balmoral Wy MTN/WRL BS22 ....135 H1
Baltic Pl PTSHD/EG BS20 ....48 C4
Bamfield HGRV/WHIT BS14 ....91 G2
Bampton Cl
BMSTRD/HC/WWD BS13 ....90 C2
MANG/FISH BS16 ....55 H2
Bampton Cft MANG/FISH BS16 ....55 H2
Bampton Dr MANG/FISH BS16 ....41 E5
Bancroft BOAV BA15 ....119 G1
Banfield Cl AVONM BS11 ....35 H5
Bangor Gv
BRSG/KWL/STAPK BS4 ....81 E1
Bangrove Wk AVONM BS11 ....35 F5
Banister Gv
BRSG/KWL/STAPK BS4 ....91 E2
Bank Pl PTSHD/EG BS20 ....48 C4
Bank Rd AVONM BS11 ....22 D3
KGWD/HNM BS15 ....64 C3
THNB/SVB BS35 ....13 F2
Banks Cl CLVDN BS21 ....70 D5
Bankside MANG/FISH BS16 ....55 E4
Bankside Rd
BRSG/KWL/STAPK BS4 ....80 C3
Bannerdown Cl
CBATH/BATHN BA1 ....103 G5
Bannerdown Dr
CBATH/BATHN BA1 ....103 F5
Bannerdown Rd
CBATH/BATHN BA1 ....110 B1
Bannerleigh La CFTN/FAIL BS8 ....60 B5
Bannerleigh Rd CFTN/FAIL BS8 ....60 B4
Bannerman Rd EVILLE/WHL BS5 ....62 C3
Banner Rd RDLND/MONT BS6 ....61 H2
Bannetts Tree Crs
THNB/SVB BS35 ....11 G2
Bantock Cl
BRSG/KWL/STAPK BS4 ....91 E3
Bantry Rd
BRSG/KWL/STAPK BS4 ....91 F1
Banwell Cl
BMSTRD/HC/WWD BS13 ....90 B1
KEYN BS31 ....104 B2
Banwell Rd BATHSE BA2 ....116 B2
BMSTR BS3 ....78 B3
OMX/HUT/LCK BS24 ....141 E3
Baptist St EVILLE/WHL BS5 ....62 B2
Barberry Farm Rd
YTN/CONG BS49 ....126 B2
Barbour Gdns
BMSTRD/HC/WWD BS13 ....100 A1
Barbour Rd
BMSTRD/HC/WWD BS13 ....100 A1
Barcroft Cl KGWD/HNM BS15 ....64 B3
Barkers Md YATE/CS BS37 ....21 E3
Barker Wk EVILLE/WHL BS5 ....62 B2
Barkleys Hl MANG/FISH BS16 ....52 D3
Barley Cl FRCTL/WBN BS36 ....29 H2
MANG/FISH BS16 ....55 F2
Barley Cft
HNLZ/SM/SNYPK/WT BS9 ....50 C3
Barley Cross MTN/WRL BS22 * 131 H3
Barnabas St CBRISNE BS2 ....61 H2
Barnaby Cl RDSTK/MIDN BA3 ....124 B2
Barnack Cl TRWBR BA14 ....120 B5
Barnard's Cl YTN/CONG BS49 ....126 C4
Barnard Wk KEYN BS31 ....94 A5
Barnes Cl TRWBR BA14 ....122 B2
Barnes St EVILLE/WHL BS5 ....63 E3
Barnfield Wy
CBATH/BATHN BA1 ....103 G5
Barn Glebe TRWBR BA14 ....121 G5
Barnhill Rd YATE/CS BS37 ....32 D1
Barn Owl Wy
BRSTK/PCHW BS34 ....27 H5
Barn Piece BOAV BA15 ....119 G5
Barns Cl NAIL BS48 ....73 F4
NAIL BS48 ....88 B5
Barns Gnd CLVDN BS21 ....71 E5
Barnstaple Rd
BRSG/KWL/STAPK BS4 ....91 F1
Barnstaple Wk
BRSG/KWL/STAPK BS4 ....91 G1
Barnwood Ct NAIL BS48 ....72 C5
Barnwood Rd YATE/CS BS37 ....31 G3
Barossa Pl CBRIS/FH BS1 ....5 F7
Barrack's La AVONM BS11 ....35 E5
Barratt St EVILLE/WHL BS5 ....62 C2
Barrington Cl KGWD/HNM BS15 ....65 E1
Barrington Ct KGWD/HNM BS15 ....64 D2
Barrow Ct CLVDN BS21 ....72 A2
Barrow Court La NAIL BS48 ....87 G3
Barrow Hl
OLD/WMLY/WICK BS30 ....67 E5
Barrow Hill Crs AVONM BS11 ....48 B1
Barrow Hill Rd AVONM BS11 ....48 B2
Barrow La
BLAG/CWMG/WR BS40 ....97 G3
Barrowmead Dr AVONM BS11 ....35 G5
Barrow Rd BATHSE BA2 ....116 A1
CBRISNE BS2 ....62 B4
OMX/HUT/LCK BS24 ....140 B4
The Barrows MTN/WRL BS22 ....135 H4
Barrow St NAIL BS48 ....87 H4
Barrs Court Av
OLD/WMLY/WICK BS30 ....82 D1
Barrs Court Rd
OLD/WMLY/WICK BS30 ....82 D1
Barry Cl OLD/WMLY/WICK BS30 ....83 F5
OMX/HUT/LCK BS24 ....139 F5
Barry Rd OLD/WMLY/WICK BS30 ....83 F4
Bartlett's Rd BMSTR BS3 ....78 D4
Bartlett St CBATH/BATHN BA1 ....3 F3
Bartley St BMSTR BS3 ....79 E2
Barton Buildings
CBATH/BATHN BA1 ....3 F3
Barton Cl BRSG/KWL/STAPK BS4 ....63 G5
FRCTL/WBN BS36 ....29 E5
THNB/SVB BS35 ....11 G2
Barton Ct EVILLE/WHL BS5 ....62 D5
Barton Gn EVILLE/WHL BS5 * 62 C4
Barton Hill Rd EVILLE/WHL BS5 ....62 C5
Bartonia Gv
BRSG/KWL/STAPK BS4 ....80 C5
Barton Mnr CBRISNE BS2 ....62 B5
Barton Orch BOAV BA15 ....119 F3
Barton Rd CBRISNE BS2 ....5 K4
Barton St CBATH/BATHN BA1 ....3 F4
CBRIS/FH BS1 * 5 F1
EVILLE/WHL BS5 * 62 D5
The Barton BATHSE BA2 ....105 H5
KGWD/HNM BS15 ....81 G2
Barton V CBRISNE BS2 ....5 K4
Barwick AVONM BS11 * 48 D1
Barwood Cl KGWD/HNM BS15 ....65 E3
Bassetts Pasture BOAV BA15 ....119 G5
Batchfield La YATE/CS BS37 ....43 H5
The Batch YTN/CONG BS49 ....126 B4
Bates Cl EVILLE/WHL BS5 ....62 B3
Bathampton La BATHSE BA2 ....109 H3
Bath Br BRSG/KWL/STAPK BS4 ....5 J7
Bath Buildings
RDLND/MONT BS6 ....61 H2
Bathford Hl
CBATH/BATHN BA1 ....110 C2
Bath Hl KEYN BS31 ....94 C4
Bath New Rd
RDSTK/MIDN BA3 ....125 G1
Bath Rd BRSG/KWL/STAPK BS4 ....5 K7
KEYN BS31 ....94 D4
OLD/WMLY/WICK BS30 ....66 A5
OLD/WMLY/WICK BS30 ....82 C3
OLD/WMLY/WICK BS30 ....83 E5
THNB/SVB BS35 ....8 C4
Bath Road Brislington Hl
BRSG/KWL/STAPK BS4 ....80 D4
Bath St BMSTR BS3 ....78 B2
CBATH/BATHN BA1 ....3 F5
CBRIS/FH BS1 ....5 G4
MANG/FISH BS16 ....54 D4
Bathurst Pde CBRIS/FH BS1 ....4 E7
Bathurst Rd MTN/WRL BS22 ....135 H2
Bathwell Rd
BRSG/KWL/STAPK BS4 ....79 H3
Bathwick Hl BATHSE BA2 ....3 K4
Bathwick Ri BATHSE BA2 ....3 K2
Bathwick St BATHSE BA2 ....3 H1
Batley Ct
OLD/WMLY/WICK BS30 ....83 G2
Batstone Cl
CBATH/BATHN BA1 ....108 D2
Battenburg Rd
EVILLE/WHL BS5 ....63 H3
Batten Ct YATE/CS BS37 ....33 E1
Batten's La EVILLE/WHL BS5 ....63 H5
Battens Rd EVILLE/WHL BS5 ....64 A4
Battersby Wy
HNBRY/STHM BS10 ....36 D3
Battersea Rd EVILLE/WHL BS5 ....62 D3
Battery La PTSHD/EG BS20 ....45 G2
Battson Rd HGRV/WHIT BS14 ....92 D5
Baugh Gdns MANG/FISH BS16 ....41 F4
Baxter Cl KGWD/HNM BS15 ....65 E3
Baydon Cl TRWBR BA14 ....122 D4
Bay Gdns EVILLE/WHL BS5 ....62 D1
Bayham Rd
BRSG/KWL/STAPK BS4 ....79 H3
Bayleys Dr KGWD/HNM BS15 ....64 B5
Baynton Meadow
MANG/FISH BS16 ....55 H2
Baynton Rd BMSTR BS3 ....78 B2
Bay Rd CLVDN BS21 ....68 B4
Bayswater Av
RDLND/MONT BS6 ....51 E4
Bayswater Rd HORF/LLZ BS7 ....52 A1
Bay Tree Cl BRSTK/PCHW BS34 ....26 B3
Bay Tree Rd
CBATH/BATHN BA1 ....109 E2
CLVDN BS21 ....71 E3
Baytree Rd MTN/WRL BS22 ....135 H2
Bay Tree Vw MTN/WRL BS22 ....136 A2
Baytree Vw MTN/WRL BS22 ....136 A2
Beach Av CLVDN BS21 ....70 C3
THNB/SVB BS35 ....12 C2
Beach End Rd WSM BS23 ....138 B4
Beachgrove Gdns
MANG/FISH BS16 ....54 B4
Beachgrove Rd
MANG/FISH BS16 ....54 A4
Beach Hl PTSHD/EG BS20 ....45 F2
Beachley Wk AVONM BS11 ....48 C1
Beach Rd THNB/SVB BS35 ....12 B3
WSM BS23 ....138 C1
Beach Rd East
PTSHD/EG BS20 ....45 G2
Beach Rd West PTSHD/EG BS20 ....45 F2
The Beach CLVDN BS21 ....70 C1
Beacon La MANG/FISH BS16 ....28 B5
Beaconlea KGWD/HNM BS15 ....64 C5
Beacon Rd CBATH/BATHN BA1 ....108 D3
Beaconsfield Cl
EVILLE/WHL BS5 ....62 C5
Beaconsfield Rd
BRSG/KWL/STAPK BS4 ....80 A3
CFTN/FAIL BS8 ....60 D1
CLVDN BS21 ....71 E3
EVILLE/WHL BS5 ....63 F3
WSM BS23 ....6 E5
Beaconsfield St
EVILLE/WHL BS5 ....62 C5
Beale Cl HGRV/WHIT BS14 * 92 D3
Beam St EVILLE/WHL BS5 ....62 D4
The Bean Acre AVONM BS11 ....35 E5
Beanhill Crs THNB/SVB BS35 ....11 G2
Bean St EVILLE/WHL BS5 * 62 B2
Bearbridge Rd
BMSTRD/HC/WWD BS13 ....90 A5
Bear Cl BOAV BA15 ....119 E2
Bearfield Buildings BOAV BA15 ....119 F1
Beatrice Wy TRWBR BA14 ....123 F1
Beauchamp Rd HORF/LLZ BS7 ....51 G4
Beauford Sq CBATH/BATHN BA1 ....3 F4
Beaufort Av
RDSTK/MIDN BA3 ....124 B2
Beaufort Cl EVILLE/WHL BS5 ....63 E4
Beaufort Crs BRSTK/PCHW BS34 ....39 H1
Beaufort East
CBATH/BATHN BA1 ....109 F3
Beaufort Ms
CBATH/BATHN BA1 ....109 E3
Beaufort Pl
CBATH/BATHN BA1 ....109 F3
MANG/FISH BS16 ....40 C4
Beaufort Rd CFTN/FAIL BS8 ....60 D2
EVILLE/WHL BS5 ....63 E4
FRCTL/WBN BS36 ....29 G2
HORF/LLZ BS7 ....52 A2
KGWD/HNM BS15 ....64 A1
MANG/FISH BS16 ....54 D4
MANG/FISH BS16 ....55 F1
WSM BS23 ....7 G4
YATE/CS BS37 ....20 C5
Beaufort St BMSTR BS3 ....78 D4
EVILLE/WHL BS5 ....62 B3
Beaufort Vls
CBATH/BATHN BA1 * 109 E3
Beaufort Wy
HNBRY/STHM BS10 ....38 A5
Beaufort West
CBATH/BATHN BA1 ....109 E3
Beauley Rd BMSTR BS3 ....78 C2
Beaumont Cl
OLD/WMLY/WICK BS30 ....82 D3
WSM BS23 ....139 E2
Beaumont St EVILLE/WHL BS5 ....62 B3
Beaumont Ter EVILLE/WHL BS5 ....62 B3
Beau St CBATH/BATHN BA1 ....3 F5
Beaver Cl FRCTL/WBN BS36 ....29 F3
Beazer Cl MANG/FISH BS16 ....54 C5
Beck Cl MANG/FISH BS16 ....55 H2
Becket Ct MANG/FISH BS16 ....57 E4
Becket Dr MTN/WRL BS22 ....131 H5
Becket Rd MTN/WRL BS22 ....131 H4
Becket's La NAIL BS48 ....85 F1
Beckford Ct BATHSE BA2 ....3 K2
Beckford Gdns BATHSE BA2 ....3 K1
HGRV/WHIT BS14 ....100 D1
Beckford Rd BATHSE BA2 ....3 J2
Beckhampton Rd BATHSE BA2 ....2 B7
Beckington Rd BMSTR BS3 ....79 G4
Beckington Wk BMSTR BS3 ....79 G4
Beckspool Rd MANG/FISH BS16 ....40 D5
Beddoe Cl BOAV BA15 * 119 H5
Bedford Crs HORF/LLZ BS7 ....52 A3
Bedford Rd WSM BS23 ....138 D2
Bedford St CBATH/BATHN BA1 ....108 D4
Bedminster Br BMSTR BS3 ....79 F2
Bedminster Down Rd
BMSTR BS3 ....78 C4
Bedminster Pde BMSTR BS3 ....79 E2
Bedminster Pl BMSTR BS3 ....79 E2
Bedminster Rd BMSTR BS3 ....78 D4
Bedwin Cl PTSHD/EG BS20 ....44 C4
Beech Av BATHSE BA2 ....115 H3
Beech Cl
OLD/WMLY/WICK BS30 ....82 D1
THNB/SVB BS35 ....11 G2
Beechcroft LGASH BS41 ....98 C2
Beechcroft Wk HORF/LLZ BS7 ....38 D5
Beech Dr NAIL BS48 ....73 H4
Beechen Cliff BATHSE BA2 ....2 E7
Beechen Cliff Rd BATHSE BA2 ....2 E7
Beechen Dr MANG/FISH BS16 ....64 A1
Beeches Gv
BRSG/KWL/STAPK BS4 ....80 C4
The Beeches ALMDB BS32 ....27 F2
BATHSE BA2 ....116 B1
BRSG/KWL/STAPK BS4 ....80 D1
OLD/WMLY/WICK BS30 ....83 F4
TRWBR BA14 ....121 G4
Beechfield Cl LGASH BS41 ....77 F4
Beech Gv BATHSE BA2 ....113 H3
TRWBR BA14 ....122 C3
Beech Leaze THNB/SVB BS35 ....11 G2
Beechmont Dr
OMX/HUT/LCK BS24 ....139 F5
Beechmount Cl
OMX/HUT/LCK BS24 ....139 E5
Beechmount Dr
OMX/HUT/LCK BS24 ....139 E5
Beechmount Gv
HGRV/WHIT BS14 ....92 A1
Beech Rd HORF/LLZ BS7 ....51 H3
KEYN BS31 ....105 F1
YTN/CONG BS49 ....126 C3
Beech Ter RDSTK/MIDN BA3 ....125 E3
Beechwood Av
KGWD/HNM BS15 ....82 A1
OMX/HUT/LCK BS24 ....140 D2
Beechwood Cl
HGRV/WHIT BS14 ....92 B1
Beechwood Rd BATHSE BA2 ....117 F1
MANG/FISH BS16 ....53 H4
NAIL BS48 ....73 E4
PTSHD/EG BS20 ....44 B4
PTSHD/EG BS20 ....47 H4
Beehive Yd CBATH/BATHN BA1 ....3 G3
Beesmoor Rd FRCTL/WBN BS36 ....29 H3
Begbrook Dr MANG/FISH BS16 ....53 G2
Begbrook La MANG/FISH BS16 ....53 G2
Begbrook Pk MANG/FISH BS16 ....53 H1
Beggar Bush La CFTN/FAIL BS8 ....76 A2
Beggarswell Cl CBRISNE BS2 ....62 A3
Belcombe Rd BOAV BA15 ....119 E3
Belfast Wk
BRSG/KWL/STAPK BS4 ....91 F1
Belgrave Crs
CBATH/BATHN BA1 ....108 D4
Belgrave Hl CFTN/FAIL BS8 ....60 D1
Belgrave Pl
CBATH/BATHN BA1 * 108 D4
CFTN/FAIL BS8 ....60 D4

Belgrave Rd
CBATH/BATHN BA1 ....109 E3
CFTN/FAIL BS8 ....4 B1
MTN/WRL BS22 ....135 G3
Bellamy Av
BMSTRD/HC/WWD BS13 ....90 D5
Bellamy Cl KGWD/HNM BS15 ....81 F1
Belland Dr HGRV/WHIT BS14 ....91 G5
Bella Vista Rd
CBATH/BATHN BA1 ....108 C4
Bell Barn Rd
HNLZ/SM/SNYPK/WT BS9 ....50 A2
Bell Cl HNBRY/STHM BS10 ....51 H1
Bellefield Crs TRWBR BA14 ....121 E5
Bellevue CFTN/FAIL BS8 ....4 A4
Bellevue Cl KGWD/HNM BS15 ....64 D4
Bellevue Crs CFTN/FAIL BS8 ....4 A5
Bellevue Pk
BRSG/KWL/STAPK BS4 ....80 C4
Belle Vue Rd EVILLE/WHL BS5 ....62 D2
Bellevue Rd
BRSG/KWL/STAPK BS4 ....79 G2
CLVDN BS21 ....70 D1
EVILLE/WHL BS5 ....63 H3
KGWD/HNM BS15 ....65 E4
Bellevue Ter
BRSG/KWL/STAPK BS4 ....79 G2
BRSG/KWL/STAPK BS4 ....80 C4
Bell Hl MANG/FISH BS16 ....52 D4
Bell Hill Rd EVILLE/WHL BS5 ....63 H3
Bellhouse Wk AVONM BS11 ....36 A4
Bell La CBRIS/FH BS1 ....5 F3
Bellotts Rd BATHSE BA2 ....113 H1
Bell Rd FRCTL/WBN BS36 ....30 A4
Belluton Rd
BRSG/KWL/STAPK BS4 ....79 H3
Belmont CBATH/BATHN BA1 ....3 F2
Belmont Dr BRSTK/PCHW BS34 ....27 G5
CFTN/FAIL BS8 ....75 H3
Belmont Hl NAIL BS48 ....75 G4
Belmont Rd BATHSE BA2 ....117 G1
BRSG/KWL/STAPK BS4 ....80 B2
RDLND/MONT BS6 ....61 H1
Belmont St EVILLE/WHL BS5 ....62 C2
Belmore Gdns BATHSE BA2 ....113 G4
Beloe Rd HORF/LLZ BS7 ....51 G3
Belroyal Av
BRSG/KWL/STAPK BS4 ....81 E3
Belsher Dr KGWD/HNM BS15 ....65 F5
Belstone Wk
BRSG/KWL/STAPK BS4 ....90 D2
Belton Rd EVILLE/WHL BS5 ....62 C2
PTSHD/EG BS20 ....44 D2
Belvedere CBATH/BATHN BA1 ....3 F1
Belvedere Crs MTN/WRL BS22 ....135 H2
Belvedere Rd
RDLND/MONT BS6 ....50 D5
Belvoir Rd BATHSE BA2 * 2 A7
RDLND/MONT BS6 ....61 H1
Bence Ct KGWD/HNM BS15 ....64 A5
Benford Cl MANG/FISH BS16 ....54 B2
Bennett La CBATH/BATHN BA1 ....108 D3
Bennett Rd EVILLE/WHL BS5 ....63 F4
Bennett's Ct YATE/CS BS37 ....32 B1
Bennett's Rd
CBATH/BATHN BA1 ....109 F1
Bennett St CBATH/BATHN BA1 ....3 F2
Bennetts Wy CLVDN BS21 ....68 C5
Bensaunt Gv
HNBRY/STHM BS10 ....38 A1
Bentley Cl HGRV/WHIT BS14 ....100 C1
Bentley Rd MTN/WRL BS22 ....132 A5
Benville Av
HNLZ/SM/SNYPK/WT BS9 ....36 B5
Berenda Dr
OLD/WMLY/WICK BS30 ....83 E3
Beresford Cl KEYN BS31 ....105 F2
Beresford Gdns
CBATH/BATHN BA1 ....107 F1
Berkeley Av CFTN/FAIL BS8 ....4 C3
HORF/LLZ BS7 ....51 G5
RDSTK/MIDN BA3 ....124 B2
Berkeley Cl MANG/FISH BS16 ....41 G5
Berkeley Crs CFTN/FAIL BS8 ....4 B3
WSM BS23 ....138 B4
Berkeley Gdns KEYN BS31 ....94 A5
Berkeley Gn EVILLE/WHL BS5 ....62 D1
MANG/FISH BS16 ....40 C4
Berkeley Gv EVILLE/WHL BS5 ....62 D1
Berkeley Md ALMDB BS32 ....28 A4
Berkeley Pl
CBATH/BATHN BA1 * 108 D4
CFTN/FAIL BS8 ....4 A4
Berkeley Rd HORF/LLZ BS7 ....51 G5
KGWD/HNM BS15 ....64 C4
MANG/FISH BS16 ....63 H1
RDLND/MONT BS6 ....50 D4
TRWBR BA14 ....122 B1
Berkeleys Md ALMDB BS32 ....27 H4
Berkeley Sq CFTN/FAIL BS8 ....4 B3
Berkeley St EVILLE/WHL BS5 ....52 D5
Berkeley Wy MANG/FISH BS16 ....55 G1
Berkshire Rd HORF/LLZ BS7 ....51 G5
Berners Cl
BRSG/KWL/STAPK BS4 * 91 E2
Berrow Wk BMSTR BS3 ....79 F4
Berryfield Rd BOAV BA15 ....119 G1
Berry Hill Cl
HNBRY/STHM BS10 ....38 A4
Berry La HORF/LLZ BS7 ....52 B2
Berwick Cl THNB/SVB BS35 ....24 B2
Berwick La HNBRY/STHM BS10 ....24 A5
Berwick Rd EVILLE/WHL BS5 ....62 C1
Beryl Gv HGRV/WHIT BS14 ....92 B1
Beryl Rd BMSTR BS3 ....78 C3
Besom La YATE/CS BS37 ....31 G5
Bethel Rd EVILLE/WHL BS5 ....63 G3
Betjeman Ct
OLD/WMLY/WICK BS30 ....82 D1
Bevan Ct BRSTK/PCHW BS34 ....38 C3
Beverley Av MANG/FISH BS16 ....41 G4
Beverley Cl EVILLE/WHL BS5 ....64 A5
Beverley Gdns
HNLZ/SM/SNYPK/WT BS9 ....50 A1
Beverley Rd HORF/LLZ BS7 ....38 C5
Beverstone KGWD/HNM BS15 ....64 B3
Beverston Gdns AVONM BS11 ....36 A3
Bevington Cl
BRSTK/PCHW BS34 ....26 A1
Bevington Wk
BRSTK/PCHW BS34 ....26 A1
Bewdley Rd BATHSE BA2 ....115 E3
Bewley Rd TRWBR BA14 ....122 D4
Bexley Rd MANG/FISH BS16 ....54 A5
Bibstone KGWD/HNM BS15 ....65 F3
Bibury Av BRSTK/PCHW BS34 ....26 D2
Bibury Cl
HNLZ/SM/SNYPK/WT BS9 ....51 G1
NAIL BS48 ....73 H5
Bibury Crs
HNLZ/SM/SNYPK/WT BS9 ....51 G1
KGWD/HNM BS15 ....81 H1
Bickerton Cl HNBRY/STHM BS10 ....37 E2
Bickford Cl
OLD/WMLY/WICK BS30 ....65 F5
Bickley Cl KGWD/HNM BS15 ....81 G4
Biddestone Rd HORF/LLZ BS7 ....38 B4
Biddisham Cl NAIL BS48 ....73 F5
Biddle St YTN/CONG BS49 ....126 A4
Bideford Crs
BRSG/KWL/STAPK BS4 ....91 G1
Bideford Rd MTN/WRL BS22 ....136 C1
Bidwell Cl HNBRY/STHM BS10 ....37 G2
Bifield Cl HGRV/WHIT BS14 ....93 E4
Bifield Gdns HGRV/WHIT BS14 ....92 D4
Bifield Rd HGRV/WHIT BS14 ....93 E4
Bigwood La CBRIS/FH BS1 ....4 C4
Bilberry Cl
HNLZ/SM/SNYPK/WT BS9 ....36 B5
Bilbie Cl HNBRY/STHM BS10 ....51 G2
Bilbie Rd MTN/WRL BS22 ....132 A5
Bilbury La CBATH/BATHN BA1 ....3 F5
Billand Cl
BMSTRD/HC/WWD BS13 ....98 D1
Bince's Lodge La
RDSTK/MIDN BA3 ....124 C1
Bindon Dr HNBRY/STHM BS10 ....38 A1
Binhay Rd YTN/CONG BS49 ....126 C4
Binley Gv HGRV/WHIT BS14 ....92 C4
Binmead Gdns
BMSTRD/HC/WWD BS13 ....90 C5
Birbeck Rd
HNLZ/SM/SNYPK/WT BS9 ....50 B3
Birchall Rd RDLND/MONT BS6 ....51 F4
Birch Av CLVDN BS21 ....71 E1
Birch Cl BRSTK/PCHW BS34 ....26 A3
OMX/HUT/LCK BS24 ....141 E2
Birch Ct KEYN BS31 ....93 H5
Birch Cft HGRV/WHIT BS14 ....100 D1
Birchdale Rd
HGRV/WHIT BS14 ....91 H1
Birch Dene NAIL BS48 ....73 H4
Birch Dr MANG/FISH BS16 ....57 E3
THNB/SVB BS35 ....11 F3
The Birches NAIL BS48 * 73 H4
Birch Gv PTSHD/EG BS20 ....45 F4
Birch Rd BMSTR BS3 ....78 C2
KGWD/HNM BS15 ....54 D5
RDSTK/MIDN BA3 ....125 F3
YATE/CS BS37 ....20 C5
Birchwood Av WSM BS23 ....7 K4
Birchwood Ct
BRSG/KWL/STAPK BS4 * 63 G5
Birchwood Rd
BRSG/KWL/STAPK BS4 ....80 D2
Birdale Cl HNBRY/STHM BS10 ....36 D2
Birdcombe Cl NAIL BS48 ....73 F3
Birdlip Cl NAIL BS48 ....85 G1
Birdwell La LGASH BS41 ....76 C5
Birdwell Rd LGASH BS41 ....76 C5
Birdwood KGWD/HNM BS15 ....64 C5
Birkbeck Ct WSM BS23 * 6 D5
Birkdale OLD/WMLY/WICK BS30 ....65 G5
YATE/CS BS37 ....32 A2
Birkett Rd WSM BS23 ....134 A2
Birkin St CBRISNE BS2 ....62 A5
Birnbeck Rd WSM BS23 ....6 A1
Bisdee Rd OMX/HUT/LCK BS24 ....140 A3
Bishop Av MTN/WRL BS22 ....131 H5
Bishop Manor Rd
HNBRY/STHM BS10 ....51 G1
Bishop Ms CBRISNE BS2 * 61 H3
Bishop Rd HORF/LLZ BS7 ....51 F4
MANG/FISH BS16 ....55 H2
Bishops Cl
HNLZ/SM/SNYPK/WT BS9 ....50 B5
Bishops Cove
BMSTRD/HC/WWD BS13 ....90 A4
Bishops Knoll
HNLZ/SM/SNYPK/WT BS9 ....49 H5
Bishops Md YTN/CONG BS49 ....127 G3
Bishops Rd YTN/CONG BS49 ....127 F3
Bishop St CBRISNE BS2 ....61 H3
Bishop's Wd ALMDB BS32 ....16 A1
Bishopsworth Rd
BMSTRD/HC/WWD BS13 ....78 B5
Bishop Ter CBRISNE BS2 * 61 H3
Bishopthorpe Rd
HNBRY/STHM BS10 ....51 G1
Bishport Av
BMSTRD/HC/WWD BS13 ....90 B5
BMSTRD/HC/WWD BS13 ....91 E5
BMSTRD/HC/WWD BS13 ....99 H1
Bishport Cl
BMSTRD/HC/WWD BS13 ....90 C5
Bisley YATE/CS BS37 ....31 G3
Bissex Md MANG/FISH BS16 ....55 G3
Biss Meadow TRWBR BA14 ....122 B1
Bittern Cl MTN/WRL BS22 ....136 C2
Bitterwell Cl FRCTL/WBN BS36 ....42 C2
Blackacre HGRV/WHIT BS14 ....101 E1
Blackberry Av MANG/FISH BS16 ....53 F3
Blackberry Dr FRCTL/WBN BS36 ....29 H4
MTN/WRL BS22 ....136 D2
Blackberry Hl MANG/FISH BS16 ....53 F3
Blackbird Cl RDSTK/MIDN BA3 ....124 C4
Blackdown Ct HGRV/WHIT BS14 ....92 A4
Blackdown Rd PTSHD/EG BS20 ....44 D3
Blackfriars CBRIS/FH BS1 ....5 F2
Blackfriars Rd NAIL BS48 ....84 C1
Blackhorse Hl THNB/SVB BS35 ....25 F2
Blackhorse La MANG/FISH BS16 ....41 H5
Blackhorse Pl MANG/FISH BS16 ....55 F2
Blackhorse Rd
KGWD/HNM BS15 ....64 C4
MANG/FISH BS16 ....55 F2
Blackmoor CLVDN BS21 ....70 C4
Blackmoor Rd CFTN/FAIL BS8 ....58 D1
Blackmoors La BMSTR BS3 ....77 H3
Blackmore Dr BATHSE BA2 ....113 G2
Blackrock La
HGRV/WHIT BS14 ....101 G4
Blacksmith La
CBATH/BATHN BA1 ....102 A3
Blackswarth Rd
EVILLE/WHL BS5 ....63 E4
Blackthorn Cl
BMSTRD/HC/WWD BS13 ....91 E4
Blackthorn Dr ALMDB BS32 ....27 F3
Blackthorn Gdns
MTN/WRL BS22 ....136 D2
Blackthorn Rd
BMSTRD/HC/WWD BS13 ....91 E4
Blackthorn Sq CLVDN BS21 ....70 D4
Blackthorn Wk
KGWD/HNM BS15 ....64 D1
Blackthorn Wy NAIL BS48 ....73 G4
Bladen Cl PTSHD/EG BS20 ....45 H4
Bladud's Buildings
CBATH/BATHN BA1 ....3 G3
Blagdon Cl BMSTR BS3 ....79 F4
OMX/HUT/LCK BS24 ....139 E5
Blagdon Pk BATHSE BA2 ....113 F3
Blagrove Cl
BMSTRD/HC/WWD BS13 ....99 H1
Blagrove Crs
BMSTRD/HC/WWD BS13 ....99 H1
Blair Rd TRWBR BA14 ....122 B2
Blaisdon MTN/WRL BS22 ....136 A4
YATE/CS BS37 ....32 A3
Blaisdon Cl HNBRY/STHM BS10 ....37 E4
Blaise Hamlet
HNBRY/STHM BS10 * 36 D3
Blaise Wk
HNLZ/SM/SNYPK/WT BS9 ....49 H2
Blake End MTN/WRL BS22 ....131 F4
Blakeney Gv NAIL BS48 ....84 D1
Blakeney Mills YATE/CS BS37 ....31 H1
Blakeney Rd BRSTK/PCHW BS34 ....26 A1
HORF/LLZ BS7 ....52 B1
Blake Rd HORF/LLZ BS7 ....52 C2
Blakes Rd THNB/SVB BS35 ....8 C3
Blanchards YATE/CS BS37 ....33 E2
Blandford Cl
HNLZ/SM/SNYPK/WT BS9 ....51 E2
NAIL BS48 ....73 E5
Blenham Ct WSM BS23 ....7 J3
Blenheim Cl MTN/WRL BS22 ....136 D1
Blenheim Dr BRSTK/PCHW BS34 ....39 E1
YATE/CS BS37 ....20 B4
Blenheim Gdns
CBATH/BATHN BA1 ....108 D2
Blenheim Rd RDLND/MONT BS6 ....51 E5
Blenheim St EVILLE/WHL BS5 ....62 B2
Blenheim Wy PTSHD/EG BS20 ....45 H4
Blenman Cl MANG/FISH BS16 ....53 H1
Blethwin Cl HNBRY/STHM BS10 ....37 E4
Blind La CBATH/BATHN BA1 ....107 H2
YTN/CONG BS49 ....127 F4
Bloomfield Av BATHSE BA2 ....114 B3
Bloomfield Dr BATHSE BA2 ....114 A5
Bloomfield Gv BATHSE BA2 ....114 B4
Bloomfield Pk BATHSE BA2 ....114 B4
Bloomfield Ri BATHSE BA2 ....114 A5
Bloomfield Ri North
BATHSE BA2 * 114 A5
Bloomfield Rd BATHSE BA2 ....114 A5
BRSG/KWL/STAPK BS4 ....80 B2
Bloomfield Road Link
BRSG/KWL/STAPK BS4 ....80 B2
Bloy St EVILLE/WHL BS5 ....62 D2
Bluebell Cl THNB/SVB BS35 ....9 E2
Bluebell Rd MTN/WRL BS22 ....131 H2
The Bluebells ALMDB BS32 ....27 H3
Blueberry Wy MTN/WRL BS22 ....136 C2
Blue Water Dr
OMX/HUT/LCK BS24 ....141 G3
Blythe Gdns MTN/WRL BS22 * 131 H5
Boat Stall La CBATH/BATHN BA1 ....3 G4
Bobbin La BOAV BA15 ....118 C5
Bockenem Cl THNB/SVB BS35 ....9 E5
Bodey Cl OLD/WMLY/WICK BS30 ....82 D1
Bodmin Wk
BRSG/KWL/STAPK BS4 ....91 G1
Bodyce Rd THNB/SVB BS35 ....11 G2
Bolton Rd HORF/LLZ BS7 ....51 H5
Bond St CBRIS/FH BS1 ....5 H1
TRWBR BA14 ....122 D2
Bonnington Wk HORF/LLZ BS7 ....52 C1
Bonville Rd
BRSG/KWL/STAPK BS4 ....80 D5
Booth Rd BMSTR BS3 ....78 D2
Boot La BMSTR BS3 ....79 E2
Bordesley Rd HGRV/WHIT BS14 ....100 D1
Boreal Wy OMX/HUT/LCK BS24 ....136 C3
Borgie Pl MTN/WRL BS22 ....131 F5
Borleyton Wk
BMSTRD/HC/WWD BS13 ....90 A5
Borver Gv
BMSTRD/HC/WWD BS13 ....90 C5
Boscombe Crs MANG/FISH BS16 ....55 E1
Boston Rd HORF/LLZ BS7 ....38 C5
Boswell St EVILLE/WHL BS5 ....62 D1
Botham Cl MTN/WRL BS22 ....131 H4
Botham Dr
BRSG/KWL/STAPK BS4 ....80 D5
Bottom Cl HGRV/WHIT BS14 ....91 H3
Boucher Pl CBRISNE BS2 * 62 B1
Boulevard WSM BS23 ....6 E3
Boulters Rd
BMSTRD/HC/WWD BS13 ....90 D5
Boulton's Rd KGWD/HNM BS15 ....64 C3
Boundary Cl RDSTK/MIDN BA3 ....124 C5
WSM BS23 ....138 D3
Boundary Rd AVONM BS11 ....35 E1
FRCTL/WBN BS36 ....30 B3
OMX/HUT/LCK BS24 ....136 C4
Bourchier Gdns
BMSTRD/HC/WWD BS13 ....99 G1
Bourne Cl FRCTL/WBN BS36 ....29 E3
KGWD/HNM BS15 ....64 A3
Bourne Rd KGWD/HNM BS15 ....63 H3
Bourneville Rd EVILLE/WHL BS5 ....63 E3
Bournmil Cl BOAV BA15 ....118 A2
Bournville Rd WSM BS23 ....139 E2
Boursland Cl ALMDB BS32 ....16 B5
Bourton Av BRSTK/PCHW BS34 ....27 E2
Bourton Cl BRSTK/PCHW BS34 ....27 E2
Bourton Combe NAIL BS48 ....87 E2
Bourton La MTN/WRL BS22 ....132 C5
Bourton Md LGASH BS41 * 76 D5
NAIL BS48 ....87 E1
Bourton Wk
BMSTRD/HC/WWD BS13 ....90 B1
Boverton Rd BRSTK/PCHW BS34 ....39 E2
Bowden Cl
HNLZ/SM/SNYPK/WT BS9 ....36 B5
Bowden Pl MANG/FISH BS16 ....55 E1
Bowden Rd EVILLE/WHL BS5 ....63 F2
Bowden Wy CFTN/FAIL BS8 ....75 G3
Bowen Rd OMX/HUT/LCK BS24 ....141 F1
Bower Ashton Ter BMSTR BS3 ....78 A2
Bowerleaze
HNLZ/SM/SNYPK/WT BS9 ....49 G3
Bower Rd BMSTR BS3 ....78 B3
Bower Wk BMSTR BS3 ....79 F3
Bowling Hl YATE/CS BS37 ....32 C1
Bowling Rd YATE/CS BS37 ....32 D2
Bow Md
BRSG/KWL/STAPK BS4 * 80 C5
Bowring Cl
BMSTRD/HC/WWD BS13 ....99 H1
Bowsland Wy ALMDB BS32 ....16 B5
Bowstreet La THNB/SVB BS35 ....25 E2
Boxhedge Farm La
FRCTL/WBN BS36 ....42 D2
Box Rd CBATH/BATHN BA1 ....110 D1
Boyce Cl BATHSE BA2 ....113 E2
Boyce Dr CBRISNE BS2 ....62 B1
Boyce's Av CFTN/FAIL BS8 ....60 D4
Boyd Cl OLD/WMLY/WICK BS30 ....67 E4
Boyd Rd KEYN BS31 ....105 E1
Brabazon Rd
BRSTK/PCHW BS34 ....39 E3
Bracewell Gdns
HNBRY/STHM BS10 ....37 H1
Bracey Dr MANG/FISH BS16 ....54 B2
Brackenbury Dr
BRSTK/PCHW BS34 ....27 G5
Brackendene ALMDB BS32 ....27 E1
Brackenwood Rd CLVDN BS21 ....68 C4
Bracton Dr HGRV/WHIT BS14 ....91 H5
Bradeston Gv MANG/FISH BS16 ....53 H1
Bradford Cl CLVDN BS21 ....70 C4
Bradford Rd BATHSE BA2 ....116 D1
BOAV BA15 ....118 B2
CBATH/BATHN BA1 ....110 C3
TRWBR BA14 ....120 C5
Bradhurst St EVILLE/WHL BS5 ....62 C5
Bradley Av AVONM BS11 ....48 D2
FRCTL/WBN BS36 ....29 E5
Bradley Crs AVONM BS11 ....48 D2
Bradley Rd BRSTK/PCHW BS34 ....26 B2
PTSHD/EG BS20 ....47 F3
TRWBR BA14 ....122 D2
Bradley Stoke Wy ALMDB BS32 ....16 A5
ALMDB BS32 ....27 H3
Bradstone Rd FRCTL/WBN BS36 ....28 D5
Bradville Gdns LGASH BS41 ....88 C1
Bradwell Gv HNBRY/STHM BS10 ....37 H5
Braemar Av HORF/LLZ BS7 ....38 C4
Braemar Crs HORF/LLZ BS7 ....38 C4
Bragg's La CBRISNE BS2 ....5 K2
Braikenridge Cl CLVDN BS21 ....70 C4
Braikenridge Rd
BRSG/KWL/STAPK BS4 ....80 C2
Brainsfield
HNLZ/SM/SNYPK/WT BS9 ....50 C2
Brake Cl ALMDB BS32 ....27 G4
KGWD/HNM BS15 ....65 E4
The Brake FRCTL/WBN BS36 ....30 A5
YATE/CS BS37 ....20 D2
Bramble Dr
HNLZ/SM/SNYPK/WT BS9 ....49 H5
Bramble La
HNLZ/SM/SNYPK/WT BS9 ....49 H5
Bramble Rd MTN/WRL BS22 ....131 F5
Bramble Wy BATHSE BA2 ....115 E5
Bramblewood YTN/CONG BS49 ....126 B2
Brambling Wk MANG/FISH BS16 ....53 G2
Bramley Cl
OMX/HUT/LCK BS24 ....140 D2
PTSHD/EG BS20 ....48 B4
THNB/SVB BS35 ....10 A4
YTN/CONG BS49 ....126 B4
Bramley Ct
OLD/WMLY/WICK BS30 ....82 C2
Bramley Dr NAIL BS48 ....85 H4
Bramley La TRWBR BA14 ....123 E2
Bramley Sq YTN/CONG BS49 * 129 E3
The Bramleys NAIL BS48 ....84 C1
PTSHD/EG BS20 ....46 A4
Brampton Wy PTSHD/EG BS20 ....45 H3
Branche Gv
BMSTRD/HC/WWD BS13 ....100 A1
Brandash Rd YATE/CS BS37 ....33 E1
Brandon Hill La CFTN/FAIL BS8 ....4 B4
Brandon Steep CBRIS/FH BS1 ....4 C4
Brandon St CBRIS/FH BS1 ....4 C5
Brangwyn Gv HORF/LLZ BS7 ....52 C2
Brangwyn Sq MTN/WRL BS22 ....136 C1
Branksome Crs
BRSTK/PCHW BS34 ....39 E2
Branksome Dr
BRSTK/PCHW BS34 ....39 E2
FRCTL/WBN BS36 ....29 E4
Branksome Rd
RDLND/MONT BS6 ....51 E5
Bransby Wy
OMX/HUT/LCK BS24 ....136 D3
Branscombe Rd
HNLZ/SM/SNYPK/WT BS9 ....49 H4
Branscombe Wk
PTSHD/EG BS20 ....44 C5
Branwhite Cl HORF/LLZ BS7 ....52 C1
Brassmill La
CBATH/BATHN BA1 ....107 F5
Bratton Rd
BRSG/KWL/STAPK BS4 ....91 E2
Braunton Rd BMSTR BS3 ....78 D3
Braydon Av BRSTK/PCHW BS34 ....27 F2
Brayne Ct
OLD/WMLY/WICK BS30 ....82 C3
Breaches Ga ALMDB BS32 ....27 H4
The Breaches PTSHD/EG BS20 ....48 A4
Breach La NAIL BS48 ....84 A2
Breach Rd BMSTR BS3 ....78 B3
Brean Down Av
HNLZ/SM/SNYPK/WT BS9 ....51 E3
WSM BS23 ....138 C2
Brecknock Rd
BRSG/KWL/STAPK BS4 ....79 H3
Brecon Rd
HNLZ/SM/SNYPK/WT BS9 ....50 D2
Brecon Vw
OMX/HUT/LCK BS24 ....139 F5
Bredon YATE/CS BS37 ....31 H3
Bredon Cl KGWD/HNM BS15 ....65 E4
Bredon Nook Rd
HNBRY/STHM BS10 ....51 F1
Bree Cl MTN/WRL BS22 ....131 H4
Brendon Av WSM BS23 ....7 H1
Brendon Cl
OLD/WMLY/WICK BS30 ....83 F2
Brendon Rd BMSTR BS3 ....79 E3
PTSHD/EG BS20 ....44 D3
Brenner St EVILLE/WHL BS5 ....62 C1
Brent Cl OMX/HUT/LCK BS24 ....139 G4
Brent Rd HORF/LLZ BS7 ....52 A3
Brentry Av EVILLE/WHL BS5 ....62 C4
Brentry La HNBRY/STHM BS10 ....37 G4
Brentry Rd MANG/FISH BS16 ....53 F4
Brereton Wy
OLD/WMLY/WICK BS30 ....83 E2
Brewerton Cl
HNBRY/STHM BS10 ....37 H2
Brewhouse CBRIS/FH BS1 * 5 G4
Briar Cl NAIL BS48 ....73 H4
RDSTK/MIDN BA3 ....125 E4
Briar Ct PTSHD/EG BS20 ....48 B4
Briarfield Av KGWD/HNM BS15 ....81 H1
Briarleaze THNB/SVB BS35 ....11 F5
Briar Md YTN/CONG BS49 ....126 A2
Briar Rd OMX/HUT/LCK BS24 ....140 B3
Briars Ct BATHSE BA2 * 113 F3
Briarside Rd HNBRY/STHM BS10 ....37 H2
The Briars NAIL BS48 ....85 G2
Briar Wk MANG/FISH BS16 ....54 B5
Briar Wy MANG/FISH BS16 ....54 A4
Briarwood
HNLZ/SM/SNYPK/WT BS9 ....50 C2
Briary Rd PTSHD/EG BS20 ....45 F3
Briavels Gv RDLND/MONT BS6 ....62 A1
Brick La TRWBR BA14 ....121 E3
Brick St CBRISNE BS2 ....5 K2
Bridewell La CBATH/BATHN BA1 ....3 F4
OMX/HUT/LCK BS24 ....141 E5
Bridewell St CBRIS/FH BS1 ....5 F2
Bridge Av TRWBR BA14 ....122 B1
Bridge Cl HGRV/WHIT BS14 ....92 B5
Bridge Farm Cl
HGRV/WHIT BS14 * 100 D1
Bridge Farm Sq
YTN/CONG BS49 ....128 D2
Bridgeleap Rd MANG/FISH BS16 ....41 G5
Bridge Rd BATHSE BA2 ....113 H2
CFTN/FAIL BS8 ....60 A5
EVILLE/WHL BS5 ....52 C5
KGWD/HNM BS15 ....55 E5
WSM BS23 ....7 H6
YATE/CS BS37 ....19 H5
Bridges Ct MANG/FISH BS16 ....54 A4
Bridges Dr MANG/FISH BS16 ....54 B2
Bridge St BOAV BA15 ....119 G3
CBRIS/FH BS1 ....5 F4
EVILLE/WHL BS5 ....63 E1
Bridge Valley Rd CFTN/FAIL BS8 ....60 B3
Bridge Wk HORF/LLZ BS7 ....38 D5
Bridge Wy FRCTL/WBN BS36 ....29 H2
Bridgman Gv
BRSTK/PCHW BS34 ....39 E2
Bridgwater Ct
OMX/HUT/LCK BS24 ....139 F3
Bridgwater Rd
BMSTRD/HC/WWD BS13 ....90 A1
NAIL BS48 ....88 D5
WSM BS23 ....138 D4
Bridle Wy THNB/SVB BS35 ....11 F3
Briercliffe Rd
HNLZ/SM/SNYPK/WT BS9 ....50 A1
Brierly Furlong
BRSTK/PCHW BS34 ....39 G2
Briery Leaze Rd
HGRV/WHIT BS14 ....91 H4
Brighton Crs BMSTR BS3 ....78 C4
Brighton Pk EVILLE/WHL BS5 ....62 C3
Brighton Pl KGWD/HNM BS15 ....64 C2
Brighton Rd BRSTK/PCHW BS34 ....26 B2
RDLND/MONT BS6 ....61 F2
WSM BS23 ....7 F7
Brighton St CBRISNE BS2 ....61 H2
Brighton Ter BMSTR BS3 ....78 C4
Bright St EVILLE/WHL BS5 ....62 C4
KGWD/HNM BS15 ....64 C3
Brigstocke Rd CBRISNE BS2 ....61 H2
Brimbles HORF/LLZ BS7 ....39 E3
Brimbleworth La
MTN/WRL BS22 ....132 B5
Brinkworthy Rd
MANG/FISH BS16 ....53 E2

Brinmead Wk
BMSTRD/HC/WWD BS13 ....99 E1
Brins Cl BRSTK/PCHW BS34 ....40 A1
Brinsea Rd YTN/CONG BS49 ....129 E4
Brinsham La YATE/CS BS37 ....21 F1
Briscoes Av
BMSTRD/HC/WWD BS13 ....90 D5
Bristol Br CBRIS/FH BS1 ....5 G4
Bristol Hl BRSG/KWL/STAPK BS4 ..80 C4
Bristol Pkwy North
BRSTK/PCHW BS34 * 40 B1
Bristol Rd BATHSE BA2 ....106 A4
FRCTL/WBN BS36 ....29 F2
HGRV/WHIT BS14 ....101 F1
KEYN BS31 ....94 A3
MANG/FISH BS16 ....40 C5
MTN/WRL BS22 ....137 E1
NAIL BS48 ....74 B2
PTSHD/EG BS20 ....45 G4
RDSTK/MIDN BA3 ....125 G1
THNB/SVB BS35 ....8 C5
YTN/CONG BS49 ....128 D1
Bristol Rd Lower WSM BS23 ....7 H1
Bristow Broadway
AVONM BS11 ....34 D4
Britannia Crs
BRSTK/PCHW BS34 ....27 F5
Britannia Rd
BRSTK/PCHW BS34 ....25 H3
EVILLE/WHL BS5 ....62 C2
KGWD/HNM BS15 ....64 B3
Britannia Wy CLVDN BS21 ....70 C4
British Rd BMSTR BS3 ....78 D3
British Rw TRWBR BA14 ....120 D5
Brittan Pl PTSHD/EG BS20 ....47 F5
Britten Ct
OLD/WMLY/WICK BS30 ....82 C2
Brixham Rd BMSTR BS3 ....78 D4
Brixton Rd EVILLE/WHL BS5 ....62 C3
Brixton Road Ms
EVILLE/WHL BS5 ....62 C3
Broadbury Rd
BRSG/KWL/STAPK BS4 ....91 F1
Broadcloth East La
TRWBR BA14 ....123 F2
Broadcloth La TRWBR BA14 ....123 F2
Broad Cft ALMDB BS32 ....16 A5
Broadcroft Av YTN/CONG BS49 ..127 F2
Broadcroft Cl
YTN/CONG BS49 ....127 F2
Broadfield Av
KGWD/HNM BS15 ....64 B3
Broadfield Rd
BRSG/KWL/STAPK BS4 ....79 H5
Broadlands CLVDN BS21 ....71 F2
Broadlands Av KEYN BS31 ....94 A3
Broadlands Dr AVONM BS11 ....35 H4
Broad La FRCTL/WBN BS36 ....30 B5
YATE/CS BS37 ....20 C3
YATE/CS BS37 ....43 F1
Broadleas
BMSTRD/HC/WWD BS13 ....90 C2
Broadleaze AVONM BS11 ....48 C1
Broadleys Av
HNLZ/SM/SNYPK/WT BS9 ....51 E1
Broadmead CBRIS/FH BS1 ....5 G2
TRWBR BA14 ....120 B5
Broadmead La KEYN BS31 ....94 D3
Broadmoor La
CBATH/BATHN BA1 ....107 F1
Broadmoor Pk
CBATH/BATHN BA1 ....107 G2
Broadmoor V
CBATH/BATHN BA1 ....107 F1
Broadoak Hl LGASH BS41 ....99 E2
Broad Oak Rd
BMSTRD/HC/WWD BS13 ....90 A5
Broadoak Rd WSM BS23 ....138 C3
Broad Oaks CFTN/FAIL BS8 ....60 B5
Broadoak Wk
MANG/FISH BS16 ....54 A4
Broad Pln CBRISNE BS2 ....5 J4
Broad Quay BATHSE BA2 ....3 F6
CBRIS/FH BS1 ....4 E4
Broad Rd KGWD/HNM BS15 ....64 B2
Broad Stones BOAV BA15 ....111 F5
Broadstone Wk
BMSTRD/HC/WWD BS13 ....91 E4
Broad St CBATH/BATHN BA1 ....3 G3
CBRIS/FH BS1 ....5 F3
MANG/FISH BS16 ....54 D4
TRWBR BA14 ....120 D5
YATE/CS BS37 ....32 D1
YTN/CONG BS49 ....128 D2
Broad Wk
BRSG/KWL/STAPK BS4 ....79 G4
Broadway BATHSE BA2 ....3 J6
KEYN BS31 ....95 G5
OMX/HUT/LCK BS24 ....139 E5
OMX/HUT/LCK BS24 ....141 G2
YATE/CS BS37 ....21 E5
Broadway Av
HNLZ/SM/SNYPK/WT BS9 ....51 G2
Broadway Ct
CBATH/BATHN BA1 * 3 H6
Broadway Rd
BMSTRD/HC/WWD BS13 ....90 A4
HORF/LLZ BS7 ....51 G5
Broadways Dr MANG/FISH BS16 ..53 G1
Broad Weir CBRIS/FH BS1 ....5 H3
Brock End PTSHD/EG BS20 ....44 B5
Brockhurst Gdns
KGWD/HNM BS15 ....63 H3
Brockhurst Rd
KGWD/HNM BS15 ....63 H3
Brockley Cl BRSTK/PCHW BS34 ....27 E3
NAIL BS48 ....73 E5
OMX/HUT/LCK BS24 ....139 E5
Brockley Crs
OMX/HUT/LCK BS24 ....139 E5
Brockley La NAIL BS48 ....85 E5
Brockley Rd KEYN BS31 ....105 E1
Brockley Wk
BMSTRD/HC/WWD BS13 ....90 B1
Brockley Wy YTN/CONG BS49 ....127 G1
Brockridge La
FRCTL/WBN BS36 ....30 A3
Brocks Rd
BMSTRD/HC/WWD BS13 ....99 H1
Brock St CBATH/BATHN BA1 ....2 E2
Brockway NAIL BS48 ....73 G4
Brockwood BOAV BA15 * 118 C2
Brockworth YATE/CS BS37 ....31 G4
Brockworth Crs
MANG/FISH BS16 ....53 G2
Bromfield Wk
MANG/FISH BS16 ....55 G1
Bromley Dr
MANG/FISH BS16 ....41 E5
Bromley Heath Av
MANG/FISH BS16 ....41 E5
Bromley Heath Rd
MANG/FISH BS16 ....41 E3
Bromley Rd HORF/LLZ BS7 ....52 A3
Brompton Cl KGWD/HNM BS15 ....65 E3
Brompton Rd
OMX/HUT/LCK BS24 ....139 F4
Broncksea Rd HORF/LLZ BS7 ....38 C4
Bronte Cl WSM BS23 ....139 F2
Brook Cl LGASH BS41 ....77 E5
Brookcote Dr
BRSTK/PCHW BS34 ....27 F4
Brookdale Rd
BMSTRD/HC/WWD BS13 ....90 C3
Brookfield Av HORF/LLZ BS7 ....51 G5
Brookfield Cl YATE/CS BS37 ....33 E1
Brookfield La
RDLND/MONT BS6 ....61 G1
Brookfield Pk
CBATH/BATHN BA1 ....107 G2
Brookfield Rd B
RSTK/PCHW BS34 ....26 D2
RDLND/MONT BS6 ....61 G2
Brookfield Wk CLVDN BS21 ....71 F2
OLD/WMLY/WICK BS30 ....83 F3
Brook Ga BMSTR BS3 ....77 H5
Brook Hl RDLND/MONT BS6 ....61 H2
Brookland Rd MTN/WRL BS22 ....135 G4
RDLND/MONT BS6 ....51 G3
Brook La MANG/FISH BS16 ....53 F2
RDLND/MONT BS6 ....62 A2
Brooklea
OLD/WMLY/WICK BS30 ....83 E2
Brookleaze
HNLZ/SM/SNYPK/WT BS9 ....49 H3
Brookleaze Buildings
CBATH/BATHN BA1 ....109 E2
Brook Lintons
BRSG/KWL/STAPK BS4 ....80 C3
Brooklyn Rd
BMSTRD/HC/WWD BS13 ....90 C1
CBATH/BATHN BA1 ....109 F2
Brookmead THNB/SVB BS35 ....9 E5
Brook Rd BATHSE BA2 ....2 A5
BMSTR BS3 ....79 E2
EVILLE/WHL BS5 ....63 G2
KGWD/HNM BS15 ....65 F3
MANG/FISH BS16 ....53 H4
MANG/FISH BS16 ....55 E2
RDLND/MONT BS6 ....62 A2
TRWBR BA14 ....122 B1
Brookside
BLAG/CWMG/WR BS40 ....97 G5
PTSHD/EG BS20 ....48 C5
Brookside Cl ....
CBATH/BATHN BA1 ....103 E4
Brookside Dr FRCTL/WBN BS36 ....29 H2
Brookside Rd
BRSG/KWL/STAPK BS4 ....80 D4
Brook St EVILLE/WHL BS5 ....62 D4
YATE/CS BS37 ....32 C1
Brookthorpe YATE/CS BS37 ....31 H2
Brookthorpe Av AVONM BS11 ....35 H5
Brookview Wk
BMSTRD/HC/WWD BS13 ....90 C2
Brook Wy ALMDB BS32 ....27 F2
Broom Farm Cl NAIL BS48 ....85 F1
Broomground BOAV BA15 ....118 B2
Broom Hl MANG/FISH BS16 ....53 F3
Broomhill Rd
BRSG/KWL/STAPK BS4 ....81 E3
The Brooms MANG/FISH BS16 ....41 H3
Brougham Hayes BATHSE BA2 ....2 B5
Brougham Pl
CBATH/BATHN BA1 ....109 F2
Broughton Rd TRWBR BA14 ....122 C4
Brow Hl CBATH/BATHN BA1 ....110 A1
Browning Ct HORF/LLZ BS7 ....39 E5
Brownlow Rd WSM BS23 ....138 D2
Brown St TRWBR BA14 ....123 E2
The Brow BATHSE BA2 ....113 G2
Broxholme Wk AVONM BS11 ....35 G5
Bruce Av EVILLE/WHL BS5 ....62 D2
Bruce Rd EVILLE/WHL BS5 ....62 D2
Brue Cl WSM BS23 ....139 E1
Brunel Cl
OLD/WMLY/WICK BS30 ....65 H4
Brunel Lock Rd CBRIS/FH BS1 ....78 A1
Brunel Rd
BMSTRD/HC/WWD BS13 ....90 A1
NAIL BS48 ....72 C5
Brunel Wy BMSTR BS3 ....77 H3
THNB/SVB BS35 ....8 C5
Brunswick Pl
CBATH/BATHN BA1 * 3 F2
CBRIS/FH BS1 * 78 B1
Brunswick Sq CBRISNE BS2 ....5 G1
Brunswick St
CBATH/BATHN BA1 ....109 E3
CBRISNE BS2 ....61 H3
EVILLE/WHL BS5 ....62 D4
Bruton Av BATHSE BA2 ....114 C3
PTSHD/EG BS20 ....44 D3
Bruton Cl EVILLE/WHL BS5 ....63 G3
NAIL BS48 ....85 F1
Bruton Pl CFTN/FAIL BS8 ....4 A3
Bryansons Cl MANG/FISH BS16 ....53 E2
Bryant Av RDSTK/MIDN BA3 ....125 E3
Bryant Gdns CLVDN BS21 ....70 C4
Bryants Cl MANG/FISH BS16 ....40 D4
Bryant's Hl EVILLE/WHL BS5 ....64 A5
Bryniand Av HORF/LLZ BS7 ....51 H4
Buchanans Whf North
CBRIS/FH BS1 * 5 G5
Buchanans Whf South
CBRIS/FH BS1 * 5 G5
Buckingham Dr
BRSTK/PCHW BS34 ....39 G1
Buckingham Gdns
MANG/FISH BS16 ....54 D2
Buckingham Pl
MANG/FISH BS16 ....54 D2
Buckingham Rd
BRSG/KWL/STAPK BS4 ....80 C1
OMX/HUT/LCK BS24 ....139 G4
Buckingham St BMSTR BS3 ....78 D4
Buckingham V
CFTN/FAIL BS8 ....60 D3
Buckland Gn MTN/WRL BS22 ....131 H3
Bucklands Batch NAIL BS48 ....85 G1
Bucklands Dr NAIL BS48 ....85 G1
Bucklands Gv NAIL BS48 ....85 G1
Bucklands La NAIL BS48 ....85 G1
Bucklands Vw NAIL BS48 ....85 H1
Buckleaze Cl TRWBR BA14 ....123 E4
Budbury Pl BOAV BA15 ....119 F2
Budbury Rdg BOAV BA15 ....119 F2
Budbury Tyning BOAV BA15 ....119 E2
Bude Av EVILLE/WHL BS5 ....63 H3
Bude Cl NAIL BS48 ....73 H5
Bude Rd BRSTK/PCHW BS34 ....39 E2
Buller Rd
BRSG/KWL/STAPK BS4 ....80 B4
Bull La EVILLE/WHL BS5 ....63 G5
PTSHD/EG BS20 ....48 B4
Bull Pit BOAV BA15 ....119 G3
Bumper's Batch BATHSE BA2 ....117 E2
Bunting Ct MTN/WRL BS22 ....136 B2
Burbank Cl
OLD/WMLY/WICK BS30 ....82 D3
Burchells Green Cl
KGWD/HNM BS15 ....64 A3
Burchells Green Rd
KGWD/HNM BS15 ....64 A2
Burcombe Cl FRCTL/WBN BS36 ....30 B3
Burcott Rd AVONM BS11 ....22 C5
Burden Cl ALMDB BS32 ....27 G4
Burderop Cl TRWBR BA14 * 123 E4
Burfoote Gdns
HGRV/WHIT BS14 ....92 D5
Burfoot Rd HGRV/WHIT BS14 ....92 D5
Burford Cl BATHSE BA2 ....113 G4
PTSHD/EG BS20 ....45 H4
Burford Gv AVONM BS11 ....49 E3
Burgage Cl YATE/CS BS37 ....32 D2
Burghill Rd HNBRY/STHM BS10 ....37 F4
Burghley Ct FRCTL/WBN BS36 ....29 E5
Burghley Rd RDLND/MONT BS6 ..61 H1
Burgis Rd HGRV/WHIT BS14 ....92 C3
Burleigh Gdns
CBATH/BATHN BA1 ....107 F4
Burley Av MANG/FISH BS16 ....55 E3
Burley Crest MANG/FISH BS16 ....55 E2
Burley Gv MANG/FISH BS16 ....55 E2
Burlington Rd PTSHD/EG BS20 ....45 H1
RDLND/MONT BS6 ....61 E1
RDSTK/MIDN BA3 ....124 D2
Burlington St
CBATH/BATHN BA1 ....2 E1
WSM BS23 ....6 E3
Burnbush Cl HGRV/WHIT BS14 ....92 D3
Burnell Dr CBRISNE BS2 ....62 A3
Burneside Cl
HNBRY/STHM BS10 ....37 H3
Burnett Hl KEYN BS31 ....104 B4
Burnett Rd TRWBR BA14 ....123 E3
Burney Wy
OLD/WMLY/WICK BS30 ....82 D3
Burnham Cl KGWD/HNM BS15 ....65 E2
Burnham Dr KGWD/HNM BS15 ....65 E2
OMX/HUT/LCK BS24 ....139 E5
Burnham Rd AVONM BS11 ....48 C2
BATHSE BA2 ....113 H1
Burnt House Rd BATHSE BA2 ....116 B2
Burrington Av
OMX/HUT/LCK BS24 ....139 E5
Burrington Cl NAIL BS48 ....73 F5
Burrington Wk
BMSTRD/HC/WWD BS13 ....90 B1
Burrough Wy
FRCTL/WBN BS36 ....29 E5
Burton Cl CBRIS/FH BS1 ....5 G7
Burton Ct CFTN/FAIL BS8 * 4 A3
Burton St CBATH/BATHN BA1 ....3 F4
Burwalls Rd CFTN/FAIL BS8 ....60 B5
Burycourt Cl AVONM BS11 ....35 H4
Bury Hl MANG/FISH BS16 ....41 F2
Bury Hill Vw MANG/FISH BS16 ....41 H4
The Bury OMX/HUT/LCK BS24 ....140 D3
Bush Av BRSTK/PCHW BS34 ....27 E5
Bushy Pk BMSTR BS3 ....79 G2
Butcombe Wk HGRV/WHIT BS14 ..92 A4
Butlers Cl EVILLE/WHL BS5 ....63 G4
Butlers Wk EVILLE/WHL BS5 ....63 G5
Buttercliffe Ri LGASH BS41 * 77 F3
Butterfield Cl
HNBRY/STHM BS10 ....51 H1
Butterfield Pk CLVDN BS21 ....70 C4
Butterfield Rd
HNBRY/STHM BS10 ....51 H1
Butterfield Cl FRCTL/WBN BS36 ..29 H4
Buttermere Rd WSM BS23 ....139 F1
Butterworth Ct
BRSG/KWL/STAPK BS4 ....91 E2
Butt La THNB/SVB BS35 ....8 D1
Buxton Wk HORF/LLZ BS7 ....38 D5
Bye Md MANG/FISH BS16 ....41 H5
Byfield BATHSE BA2 ....117 F1
Byfields CLVDN BS21 ....70 C5
Byron Cl OMX/HUT/LCK BS24 ....140 C2
Byron Pl CFTN/FAIL BS8 ....4 B3
MANG/FISH BS16 ....54 D4
Byron Rd BATHSE BA2 ....114 C3
OMX/HUT/LCK BS24 ....140 D2
WSM BS23 ....139 F2
Byron St CBRISNE BS2 ....62 A2
EVILLE/WHL BS5 ....62 D4
Bythesea Rd TRWBR BA14 ....122 D1

C

Cabot Cl KEYN BS31 ....105 E2
YATE/CS BS37 ....32 B1
Cabot Ri PTSHD/EG BS20 ....44 D3
Cabot Wy CFTN/FAIL BS8 ....60 C5
MTN/WRL BS22 ....131 H5
PTSHD/EG BS20 ....48 C5
Cabstand PTSHD/EG BS20 ....45 G2
Cadbury Farm Rd
YTN/CONG BS49 ....126 C4
Cadbury Heath Rd
OLD/WMLY/WICK BS30 ....83 E1
Cadbury Rd KEYN BS31 ....104 B2
PTSHD/EG BS20 ....45 G4
Cadbury Sq YTN/CONG BS49 * 129 E3
Cadby Cl TRWBR BA14 ....123 G1
Caddick Cl KGWD/HNM BS15 ....65 E1
Cade Cl BRSTK/PCHW BS34 ....27 G5
KGWD/HNM BS15 ....65 E5
Cadogan Rd HGRV/WHIT BS14 ....91 H1
Caen Rd BMSTR BS3 ....79 E3
Caernarvon Rd KEYN BS31 ....93 H5
Caine Rd HORF/LLZ BS7 ....52 A1
Cains Cl KGWD/HNM BS15 ....64 D5
Cairn Cl NAIL BS48 ....73 H5
Cairn Gdns FRCTL/WBN BS36 ....41 F1
Cairns' Crs CBRISNE BS2 ....62 A2
Cairns Rd RDLND/MONT BS6 ....51 E3
Calcott Rd
BRSG/KWL/STAPK BS4 ....79 H3
Caldbeck Cl HNBRY/STHM BS10 ..38 A3
Calder Cl KEYN BS31 ....94 D5
Caldicot Cl AVONM BS11 ....36 B3
OLD/WMLY/WICK BS30 ....83 E4
Caledonian Rd BATHSE BA2 ....2 A5
CBRIS/FH BS1 ....4 B6
Caledonia Pl CFTN/FAIL BS8 ....60 C5
California Rd
OLD/WMLY/WICK BS30 ....82 D3
Callicroft Rd
BRSTK/PCHW BS34 ....26 C3
Callington Rd
BRSG/KWL/STAPK BS4 ....80 C5
Callowhill Ct CBRIS/FH BS1 ....5 G2
Calton Gdns BATHSE BA2 ....3 F7
Calton Rd BATHSE BA2 ....3 G7
Calton Wk BATHSE BA2 ....3 F7
Camberley Dr FRCTL/WBN BS36 ..29 F2
Camberley Rd
BRSG/KWL/STAPK BS4 ....90 D1
Camberley Wk MTN/WRL BS22 ..136 B4
Camborne Rd HORF/LLZ BS7 ....52 B1
Cambrian Dr YATE/CS BS37 ....20 D4
Cambridge Crs
HNLZ/SM/SNYPK/WT BS9 ....50 D1
Cambridge Gv CLVDN BS21 ....68 B5
Cambridge Pk
RDLND/MONT BS6 ....51 E5
Cambridge Pl BATHSE BA2 ....3 J7
WSM BS23 ....6 D3
Cambridge Rd CLVDN BS21 ....68 B5
HORF/LLZ BS7 ....51 G4
Cambridge St BMSTR BS3 ....79 G2
EVILLE/WHL BS5 ....62 D4
Cambridge Ter BATHSE BA2 ....3 J7
Camden Crs CBATH/BATHN BA1 ....3 F1
Camden Rd CBATH/BATHN BA1 ..108 D3
Camden Rw CBATH/BATHN BA1 ....3 F1
Camden Ter
CBATH/BATHN BA1 ....108 D3
CFTN/FAIL BS8 ....60 D5
WSM BS23 ....7 F4
Cameley Gn BATHSE BA2 ....113 E1
Camelford Rd EVILLE/WHL BS5 ....63 E2
Cameron Wk HORF/LLZ BS7 ....52 D2
Cameroons Cl KEYN BS31 ....94 B4
Camerton Cl KEYN BS31 ....105 F1
Camerton Rd EVILLE/WHL BS5 ....63 E2
Campbell Farm Dr AVONM BS11 ..35 G4
Campbell St CBRISNE BS2 ....61 H2
Campian Wk
BRSG/KWL/STAPK BS4 ....91 E3
Campion Cl MTN/WRL BS22 ....136 A4
THNB/SVB BS35 ....9 E2
Campion Dr ALMDB BS32 ....16 B5
TRWBR BA14 ....123 E3
Camp Rd CFTN/FAIL BS8 ....60 C4
Camp Rd North WSM BS23 ....134 A2
Camp Vw FRCTL/WBN BS36 ....41 F1
NAIL BS48 ....73 E4
Camwal Rd CBRISNE BS2 ....79 H1
Canada Coombe
OMX/HUT/LCK BS24 ....140 C4
Canada Wy CBRIS/FH BS1 ....78 B1
Canal Br BATHSE BA2 * 3 J7
Canal Rd TRWBR BA14 ....121 E4
Canberra Crs
OMX/HUT/LCK BS24 ....136 D5
Canberra Gv BRSTK/PCHW BS34 ..39 E1
Canford La
HNLZ/SM/SNYPK/WT BS9 ....37 E5
Canford Rd
HNLZ/SM/SNYPK/WT BS9 ....50 C1
Cannans Cl FRCTL/WBN BS36 ....29 E3
Cann La OLD/WMLY/WICK BS30 ....66 B5
Cannons Ga CLVDN BS21 ....70 C5
Cannon St CBRIS/FH BS1 ....5 F2
Canons Cl BATHSE BA2 ....113 G5
Canon's Rd CBRIS/FH BS1 ....4 E5
Canon's Wk KGWD/HNM BS15 ....64 D1
Canons Wy CBRIS/FH BS1 ....4 C6
Canowie Rd RDLND/MONT BS6 ....51 E5
Cantell Gv HGRV/WHIT BS14 ....93 E4
Canterbury Cl MTN/WRL BS22 ....131 H4
YATE/CS BS37 ....20 D4
Canterbury Rd BATHSE BA2 ....2 B6
Canterbury St EVILLE/WHL BS5 ....62 C5
Cantock's Cl CFTN/FAIL BS8 ....4 C3
Canvey Cl HNBRY/STHM BS10 ....51 H1
Canynge Rd CFTN/FAIL BS8 ....60 C3
Canynge Sq CFTN/FAIL BS8 ....60 C3
Canynge St CBRIS/FH BS1 ....5 G5
Capel Cl KGWD/HNM BS15 ....65 G3
Capell Cl MTN/WRL BS22 ....135 G3
Capel Rd AVONM BS11 ....36 A4
Capenor Cl PTSHD/EG BS20 ....45 F4
Capgrave Cl
BRSG/KWL/STAPK BS4 ....81 F3
Capgrave Crs
BRSG/KWL/STAPK BS4 ....81 F3
Caraway Gdns
EVILLE/WHL BS5 ....62 D1
Carberry Vw
OMX/HUT/LCK BS24 ....136 D3
Carders Cnr TRWBR BA14 ....123 E2
Cardigan Crs MTN/WRL BS22 ....135 H3
Cardigan Rd
HNLZ/SM/SNYPK/WT BS9 ....51 E2
Cardill Cl
BMSTRD/HC/WWD BS13 ....90 B1
Cardinal Cl BATHSE BA2 ....116 B2
Carey's Cl CLVDN BS21 ....71 F1
Carice Gdns CLVDN BS21 ....70 D5
Carisbrooke Crs TRWBR BA14 ....121 F1
Carisbrooke Rd
BRSG/KWL/STAPK BS4 ....91 E1
Carlingford Terrace Rd
RDSTK/MIDN BA3 ....125 H2
Carlow Rd
BRSG/KWL/STAPK BS4 ....91 F1
Carlton Ct
HNLZ/SM/SNYPK/WT BS9 * 50 D1
Carlton Man North WSM BS23 * 6 D5
Carlton Man South WSM BS23 * 6 D5
Carlton Pk EVILLE/WHL BS5 ....62 D3
Carlton Rw TRWBR BA14 ....122 D3
Carlton St WSM BS23 ....6 D5
Carlyle Rd EVILLE/WHL BS5 ....62 D2
Carmarthen Cl YATE/CS BS37 ....21 E3
Carmarthen Gv
OLD/WMLY/WICK BS30 ....83 E5
Carmarthen Rd
HNLZ/SM/SNYPK/WT BS9 ....50 D2
Carnarvon Rd
RDLND/MONT BS6 ....61 F1
Caroline Buildings BATHSE BA2 ....3 J6
Caroline Cl KEYN BS31 ....93 H5
YATE/CS BS37 ....21 G5
Caroline Pl CBATH/BATHN BA1 * 3 F1
Carpenter Cl WSM BS23 ....7 K5
Carpenters La KEYN BS31 ....94 B4
Carre Gdns MTN/WRL BS22 ....131 G4
Carrington Rd BMSTR BS3 ....78 B2
Carson's Rd MANG/FISH BS16 ....55 G5
Carsons Road Link
MANG/FISH BS16 ....65 G1
Carter Wk ALMDB BS32 ....27 F2
Cartledge Rd EVILLE/WHL BS5 ....62 D2
Cassell Rd MANG/FISH BS16 ....54 B3
Cassey Bottom La
EVILLE/WHL BS5 ....63 H4
Casson Dr MANG/FISH BS16 ....39 H5
Castle Cl HNBRY/STHM BS10 ....36 D3
NAIL BS48 ....86 D2
Castle Coombe THNB/SVB BS35 ....8 D2
Castle Ct BRSG/KWL/STAPK BS4 ..80 B2
BRSTK/PCHW BS34 ....40 B1
THNB/SVB BS35 ....8 C3
Castle Farm La LGASH BS41 ....98 A2
Castle Farm Rd
KGWD/HNM BS15 ....81 H4
Castle Gdns BATHSE BA2 ....114 B4
Castle Rd CLVDN BS21 ....68 B4
KGWD/HNM BS15 ....64 B1
MANG/FISH BS16 ....57 F2
MTN/WRL BS22 ....131 F5
OLD/WMLY/WICK BS30 ....83 F3
Castle St CBRISNE BS2 ....5 H3
THNB/SVB BS35 ....8 B2
TRWBR BA14 ....123 E1
Castle Vw
OMX/HUT/LCK BS24 ....136 C3
Castle View Rd CLVDN BS21 ....68 B5
Castlewood Cl CLVDN BS21 ....70 D1
Castley Rd TRWBR BA14 ....121 H4
Catbrain Hl HNBRY/STHM BS10 ....25 F4
Catbrain La HNBRY/STHM BS10 ..25 F4
Catemead CLVDN BS21 ....70 C5
Cater Rd
BMSTRD/HC/WWD BS13 ....90 C3
Catharine Pl CBATH/BATHN BA1 ....2 E2
Catherine Mead St BMSTR BS3 ....78 D2
Catherine St AVONM BS11 ....48 B1
Catherine Wy
CBATH/BATHN BA1 ....103 F4
Catley Gv LGASH BS41 ....77 E5
Cattistock Dr EVILLE/WHL BS5 ....63 H5
Cattle Market Rd CBRIS/FH BS1 ....5 J7
Cattybrook Rd
MANG/FISH BS16 ....56 A3
Cattybrook Rd North
MANG/FISH BS16 ....56 A3
Cattybrook St EVILLE/WHL BS5 ....62 C3
Caulfield Rd MTN/WRL BS22 ....131 H4
Causeway CLVDN BS21 ....72 C3
The Causeway
FRCTL/WBN BS36 ....30 A3
YTN/CONG BS49 ....128 D2
Causeway Vw NAIL BS48 ....72 D4
Causley Dr
OLD/WMLY/WICK BS30 ....82 C1
Cautletts Cl RDSTK/MIDN BA3 ....124 A4
Cavan Wk
BRSG/KWL/STAPK BS4 ....79 E5
Cave Dr MANG/FISH BS16 ....54 C2

Cave Gv MANG/FISH BS16..........55 G1
Cavell Ct CLVDN BS21..........70 C4
Cavendish Cl KEYN BS31..........105 E2
Cavendish Crs
CBATH/BATHN BA1..........108 B4
Cavendish Gdns
HNLZ/SM/SNYPK/WT BS9..........49 H4
Cavendish Pl
CBATH/BATHN BA1..........108 B4
Cavendish Rd
BRSTK/PCHW BS34..........26 B2
CBATH/BATHN BA1..........108 B4
HNLZ/SM/SNYPK/WT BS9..........50 D3
Caveners Ct MTN/WRL BS22..........135 G2
Caversham Dr NAIL BS48..........73 H4
Cave St CBRISNE BS2..........61 H3
Cecil Av EVILLE/WHL BS5..........63 G2
Cecil Rd CFTN/FAIL BS8..........60 C3
KGWD/HNM BS15..........64 C3
WSM BS23..........134 D2
Cedar Av MTN/WRL BS22..........135 H2
Cedar Cl BRSTK/PCHW BS34..........26 B3
LGASH BS41..........76 C5
OLD/WMLY/WICK BS30..........83 E2
Cedar Dr KEYN BS31..........94 A5
Cedar Gv BATHSE BA2..........114 A4
HNLZ/SM/SNYPK/WT BS9..........50 A3
TRWBR BA14..........122 C3
Cedarhurst Rd
PTSHD/EG BS20..........44 B5
Cedar Pk
HNLZ/SM/SNYPK/WT BS9..........50 A3
Cedar Rw AVONM BS11 *..........49 E2
Cedar Ter RDSTK/MIDN BA3..........125 E3
Cedar Wy BATHSE BA2..........2 D6
FRCTL/WBN BS36..........28 D5
MANG/FISH BS16..........57 E3
NAIL BS48..........73 H4
PTSHD/EG BS20..........45 E4
Cedern Av
OMX/HUT/LCK BS24..........141 F3
Cedric Cl CBATH/BATHN BA1..........107 H5
Cedric Rd CBATH/BATHN BA1..........107 H4
Celandine Cl THNB/SVB BS35..........9 E2
Celestine Rd YATE/CS BS37..........20 B4
Celia Ter
BRSG/KWL/STAPK BS4..........63 G5
Cemetery La BOAV BA15..........119 H2
Cemetery Rd
BRSG/KWL/STAPK BS4..........79 H3
Cennick Av KGWD/HNM BS15..........64 D2
Centaurus Rd
BRSTK/PCHW BS34..........25 G3
Central Av KGWD/HNM BS15..........81 H1
Central Wy CLVDN BS21..........70 D4
Centre Dr BNWL BS29..........141 H2
Ceres Cl OLD/WMLY/WICK BS30..........82 C4
Cerimon Ga BRSTK/PCHW BS34..........27 G5
Cerney Gdns NAIL BS48..........73 H4
Cerney La AVONM BS11..........48 D3
Cesson Cl YATE/CS BS37..........33 E1
Chadleigh Gv
BRSG/KWL/STAPK BS4..........90 D2
Chaffinch Dr RDSTK/MIDN BA3..........124 C4
TRWBR BA14..........122 B1
The Chaffins CLVDN BS21..........71 E3
Chaingate La YATE/CS BS37..........19 G1
Chakeshill Cl
HNBRY/STHM BS10..........37 H2
Chakeshill Dr
HNBRY/STHM BS10..........37 H2
Chalcombe Cl
BRSTK/PCHW BS34..........27 E2
Chalcroft Wk
BMSTRD/HC/WWD BS13..........89 H5
Chalfield Cl KEYN BS31..........104 B2
Chalfont Cl TRWBR BA14..........120 B5
Chalfont Rd MTN/WRL BS22..........135 H3
Chalford Cl YATE/CS BS37..........31 H2
Chalk Farm Cl
PLTN/PENS BS39..........100 D5
Chalks Rd EVILLE/WHL BS5..........63 E3
Challender Av
HNBRY/STHM BS10..........37 E3
Challoner Ct CBRIS/FH BS1..........4 E7
Challow Dr MTN/WRL BS22..........135 G1
Champion Rd KGWD/HNM BS15..........65 F1
Champneys Av
HNBRY/STHM BS10..........37 E2
Chancel Cl
HNLZ/SM/SNYPK/WT BS9..........50 A5
NAIL BS48..........73 E5
Chancery St EVILLE/WHL BS5..........62 C4
Chandag Rd KEYN BS31..........94 D5
Chandler Cl CBATH/BATHN BA1..........107 G3
Chandos Rd KEYN BS31..........94 B2
RDLND/MONT BS6..........61 E2
Channel Hts
OMX/HUT/LCK BS24..........139 E5
Channell's Hl
HNLZ/SM/SNYPK/WT BS9..........37 F5
Channel Rd CLVDN BS21..........68 B4
Channel View Crs
PTSHD/EG BS20..........45 E3
Channel View Rd
PTSHD/EG BS20..........45 E3
Channon's Hl MANG/FISH BS16..........53 G4
Chanterelle Pk BOAV BA15..........119 F5
Chantry Cl NAIL BS48..........72 C5
Chantry Dr MTN/WRL BS22..........131 G4
Chantry Gv AVONM BS11..........36 B3
Chantry La MANG/FISH BS16..........41 G4
Chantry Mead Rd BATHSE BA2..........114 B4
Chantry Rd CFTN/FAIL BS8..........61 E2
THNB/SVB BS35..........8 C2
Chapel Barton BMSTR BS3..........78 D4
NAIL BS48..........72 D5
Chapel Cl NAIL BS48..........73 F4
Chapel Ct CBATH/BATHN BA1 *..........3 F5
Chapel Gdns HNBRY/STHM BS10..........37 F4
Chapel Green La
RDLND/MONT BS6..........61 E1
Chapel Hl CLVDN BS21..........70 D2
NAIL BS48..........86 C1
Chapel La AVONM BS11..........36 A3
EVILLE/WHL BS5..........63 F1
KGWD/HNM BS15..........65 G3
MANG/FISH BS16..........54 B1
WUE GL12..........9 H3
YTN/CONG BS49..........127 F3
Chapel Rd
BMSTRD/HC/WWD BS13..........90 B3
EVILLE/WHL BS5..........62 C2
KGWD/HNM BS15..........81 H1
Chapel Rw CBATH/BATHN BA1..........2 E4
PTSHD/EG BS20..........48 B4
Chapel St CBRISNE BS2..........79 H1
THNB/SVB BS35..........8 C4
Chapel Wy
BRSG/KWL/STAPK BS4..........63 F5
Chaplin Rd EVILLE/WHL BS5..........62 C2
Chapter St CBRISNE BS2..........61 H3
Charborough Rd
BRSTK/PCHW BS34..........38 C3
Chard Cl NAIL BS48..........85 G1
Chard Rd CLVDN BS21..........70 D4
Chardstock Av
HNLZ/SM/SNYPK/WT BS9..........36 B5
Charfield KGWD/HNM BS15..........65 F3
Charfield Rd
HNBRY/STHM BS10..........37 H4
Chargrove
OLD/WMLY/WICK BS30..........65 H5
YATE/CS BS37..........31 H3
Charis Av HNBRY/STHM BS10..........51 F1
Charlcombe La
CBATH/BATHN BA1..........108 C2
Charlcombe Ri
CBATH/BATHN BA1..........108 C2
Charlcombe View Rd
CBATH/BATHN BA1..........108 D2
Charlcombe Wy
CBATH/BATHN BA1..........108 C2
Charlecombe Ct
HNLZ/SM/SNYPK/WT BS9 *..........50 C2
Charlecombe Rd
HNLZ/SM/SNYPK/WT BS9..........50 C2
Charles Av BRSTK/PCHW BS34..........39 H1
Charles Cl THNB/SVB BS35..........8 D1
Charles Pl CFTN/FAIL BS8..........60 D5
Charles Rd BRSTK/PCHW BS34..........39 E2
Charles St CBATH/BATHN BA1..........2 E4
CBRIS/FH BS1..........5 F1
TRWBR BA14..........120 D5
Charlock Rd
MTN/WRL BS22..........136 A4
Charlotte St CBATH/BATHN BA1..........2 E4
CBRIS/FH BS1..........4 C4
CBRISNE BS2..........5 J1
TRWBR BA14..........121 E5
Charlotte St South CBRIS/FH BS1..4 C4
Charlton Av BRSTK/PCHW BS34..........38 C3
WSM BS23..........138 C2
Charlton Gdns
HNBRY/STHM BS10..........38 A1
Charlton La HNBRY/STHM BS10..........37 F2
RDSTK/MIDN BA3..........124 D5
Charlton Mead Dr
HNBRY/STHM BS10..........38 A1
Charlton Pk KEYN BS31..........94 A4
RDSTK/MIDN BA3..........124 C5
Charlton Pl HNBRY/STHM BS10..........38 A2
Charlton Rd HNBRY/STHM BS10..........37 G4
KGWD/HNM BS15..........64 A2
RDSTK/MIDN BA3..........124 C4
WSM BS23..........138 C2
Charlton St EVILLE/WHL BS5..........62 C4
Charlton Vw PTSHD/EG BS20..........45 F3
Charminster Rd
MANG/FISH BS16..........54 A5
Charmouth Rd
CBATH/BATHN BA1..........107 G5
Charnell Rd MANG/FISH BS16..........54 D4
Charnhill Brow
MANG/FISH BS16..........55 F4
Charnhill Crs MANG/FISH BS16..........55 E4
Charnhill Dr MANG/FISH BS16..........55 E4
Charnhill Rdg MANG/FISH BS16..........55 F4
Charnhill V MANG/FISH BS16..........55 E4
Charnwood MANG/FISH BS16..........55 F4
Charnwood Rd
HGRV/WHIT BS14..........101 E1
TRWBR BA14..........120 A5
Charterhouse Cl NAIL BS48..........73 G5
Charterhouse Rd
EVILLE/WHL BS5..........63 E3
Charter Rd MTN/WRL BS22..........135 G3
Charter Wk HGRV/WHIT BS14..........91 H3
Chasefield La MANG/FISH BS16..........54 A4
Chase Rd KGWD/HNM BS15..........64 C1
The Chase MANG/FISH BS16..........54 B5
Chatcombe YATE/CS BS37..........32 A3
Chatham Pk BATHSE BA2..........115 F1
Chatham Rw CBATH/BATHN BA1..........3 G2
Chatsworth Pk THNB/SVB BS35..........8 D2
Chatsworth Rd
BRSG/KWL/STAPK BS4..........80 B2
MANG/FISH BS16..........54 A5
Chatterton Gn HGRV/WHIT BS14..........91 G5
Chatterton Rd YATE/CS BS37..........31 H1
Chatterton Sq CBRIS/FH BS1..........5 H7
Chaucer Rd BATHSE BA2..........114 C3
RDSTK/MIDN BA3..........124 C4
WSM BS23..........139 F2
Chaundey Gv
BMSTRD/HC/WWD BS13..........90 C4
Cheapside CBRISNE BS2..........62 A3
Cheapside St BMSTR BS3..........79 G2
Cheap St CBATH/BATHN BA1..........3 G4
Cheddar Cl NAIL BS48..........85 G1
Cheddar Gv
BMSTRD/HC/WWD BS13..........90 B1
Chedworth KGWD/HNM BS15..........54 D5
YATE/CS BS37..........31 F3
Chedworth Rd HORF/LLZ BS7..........52 B2
Cheese La CBRISNE BS2..........5 H4
Chelford Gv BRSTK/PCHW BS34..........26 D2
Chelmer Gv KEYN BS31..........94 C5
Chelmsford Wk
BRSG/KWL/STAPK BS4..........81 E1
Chelsea Cl KEYN BS31..........94 D4
Chelsea Pk EVILLE/WHL BS5..........62 D3
Chelsea Rd CBATH/BATHN BA1..........107 H5
EVILLE/WHL BS5..........62 C2
Chelston Rd
BRSG/KWL/STAPK BS4..........91 E2
Chelswood Av MTN/WRL BS22..........135 H3
Cheltenham Crs
RDLND/MONT BS6 *..........61 G2
Cheltenham La
RDLND/MONT BS6..........61 G1
Cheltenham Rd
RDLND/MONT BS6..........61 G2
Cheltenham St BATHSE BA2..........2 D6
Chelvey Est NAIL BS48 *..........85 F5
Chelvey La NAIL BS48..........85 F5
Chelvey Ri NAIL BS48..........85 H1
Chelvey Rd NAIL BS48..........84 D3
Chelvy Cl
BMSTRD/HC/WWD BS13..........100 A1
Chelwood Dr BATHSE BA2..........116 B1
Chelwood Rd AVONM BS11..........48 C1
KEYN BS31..........95 H5
Chepstow Pl TRWBR BA14..........120 A5
Chepstow Pk MANG/FISH BS16..........41 G4
Chepstow Rd
BRSG/KWL/STAPK BS4..........91 E1
Chequers Cl
OLD/WMLY/WICK BS30..........83 F3
Cherington KGWD/HNM BS15..........81 G1
YATE/CS BS37..........31 H4
Cherington Rd
HNBRY/STHM BS10..........51 F1
NAIL BS48..........73 H5
Cheriton Pl
HNLZ/SM/SNYPK/WT BS9..........51 E1
OLD/WMLY/WICK BS30..........65 H5
Cherry Av CLVDN BS21..........71 E3
Cherry Cl YTN/CONG BS49..........126 B3
Cherry Garden La
OLD/WMLY/WICK BS30..........83 E4
Cherry Garden Rd
OLD/WMLY/WICK BS30..........83 F5
Cherry Gdns
OLD/WMLY/WICK BS30..........83 F5
TRWBR BA14..........121 H3
TRWBR BA14..........123 E2
Cherry Gv MANG/FISH BS16..........55 F2
YTN/CONG BS49..........126 B3
Cherry Hay CLVDN BS21..........70 D4
Cherry La CBRIS/FH BS1..........5 F1
Cherry Rd LGASH BS41..........76 C4
NAIL BS48..........73 E5
YATE/CS BS37..........32 C1
Cherry Tree Cl KEYN BS31..........93 H5
RDSTK/MIDN BA3..........125 F3
Cherrytree Ct MANG/FISH BS16..........57 F3
Cherrytree Crs
MANG/FISH BS16..........64 B1
Cherrytree Rd
KGWD/HNM BS15..........64 B1
Cherry Wd
OLD/WMLY/WICK BS30..........83 E4
Cherrywood Ri
MTN/WRL BS22..........136 C1
Cherrywood Rd
MTN/WRL BS22..........136 C1
Chertsey Rd RDLND/MONT BS6..........61 E2
Cherwell Cl THNB/SVB BS35..........8 D5
Cherwell Rd KEYN BS31..........94 D5
Chescombe Rd
YTN/CONG BS49..........126 B4
Chesham Rd North
MTN/WRL BS22..........135 G3
Chesham Rd South
MTN/WRL BS22..........135 G3
Chesham Wy
KGWD/HNM BS15..........64 C2
Cheshire Cl YATE/CS BS37..........20 D4
Chesle Cl PTSHD/EG BS20..........44 B5
Cheslefield PTSHD/EG BS20..........44 A5
Chesle Wy PTSHD/EG BS20..........44 B5
Chesley Hl
OLD/WMLY/WICK BS30..........66 C4
Chessel Cl ALMDB BS32..........16 A5
Chessel Ct BMSTR BS3 *..........78 C4
Chessell Av THNB/SVB BS35..........13 E2
Chessel St BMSTR BS3..........78 C3
Chessington Av
HGRV/WHIT BS14..........92 A4
Chesterfield Av
RDLND/MONT BS6..........61 H1
Chesterfield Rd
MANG/FISH BS16..........54 D3
RDLND/MONT BS6..........61 H1
Chestermaster Cl ALMDB BS32..........15 G2
Chester Park Rd
MANG/FISH BS16..........64 A1
Chester Rd EVILLE/WHL BS5..........63 F2
Chesters OLD/WMLY/WICK BS30..........82 D2
Chester St EVILLE/WHL BS5..........62 C1
Chesterton Dr NAIL BS48..........73 H4
The Chestertons BATHSE BA2..........110 A4
Chestnut Av MTN/WRL BS22..........136 D2
Chestnut Cha NAIL BS48..........73 H4
Chestnut Cl HGRV/WHIT BS14..........92 D4
RDSTK/MIDN BA3..........125 F3
YTN/CONG BS49..........128 D2
Chestnut Ct MANG/FISH BS16..........55 F3
Chestnut Dr THNB/SVB BS35..........8 D3
YATE/CS BS37..........32 C1
YTN/CONG BS49..........127 E2
Chestnut Gv BATHSE BA2..........113 H3
BOAV BA15..........118 C5
CLVDN BS21..........71 F1
TRWBR BA14..........122 C4
Chestnut Rd KGWD/HNM BS15..........55 E5
LGASH BS41..........77 E4
MANG/FISH BS16..........54 C2
Chestnut Wk
BMSTRD/HC/WWD BS13..........90 B3
KEYN BS31..........105 F1
Chestnut Wy KGWD/HNM BS15..........55 E5
Chetwode Cl
HNBRY/STHM BS10..........38 A2
Chevening Cl
BRSTK/PCHW BS34..........39 G1
Cheverell Cl TRWBR BA14..........123 E4
Cheviot Cl TRWBR BA14..........123 F2
Cheviot Dr THNB/SVB BS35..........9 F4
Cheviot Wy
OLD/WMLY/WICK BS30..........83 F1
Chewton Cl MANG/FISH BS16..........54 A5
Cheyne Rd
HNLZ/SM/SNYPK/WT BS9..........50 A2
Chichester Wy
OMX/HUT/LCK BS24..........136 D3
YATE/CS BS37..........20 C4
Chillington Ct
BRSTK/PCHW BS34..........26 A1
Chillwood Cl YATE/CS BS37..........19 F4
Chilmark Rd TRWBR BA14..........120 B5
Chiltern Cl HGRV/WHIT BS14..........92 A5
OLD/WMLY/WICK BS30..........83 F1
Chiltern Pk THNB/SVB BS35..........9 F4
Chilton Rd
BRSG/KWL/STAPK BS4..........91 H1
CBATH/BATHN BA1..........109 E3
The Chimes NAIL BS48..........84 D1
The Chine MANG/FISH BS16..........53 E3
Chine Vw MANG/FISH BS16..........41 G5
Chiphouse Rd KGWD/HNM BS15..........64 D1
Chipperfield Dr
KGWD/HNM BS15..........65 E2
Chipping Cross CLVDN BS21..........70 C5
The Chippings MANG/FISH BS16..........53 E3
Chirton Pl TRWBR BA14..........123 E3
Chisbury St EVILLE/WHL BS5..........52 D5
Chittening Rd AVONM BS11..........23 E3
Chock La
HNLZ/SM/SNYPK/WT BS9..........50 D1
Christchurch Av
MANG/FISH BS16..........54 C3
Christchurch Cl NAIL BS48..........73 F4
Christchurch La
MANG/FISH BS16..........54 C2
Christchurch Pth South
WSM BS23 *..........7 F3
Christchurch Rd BOAV BA15..........119 G1
CFTN/FAIL BS8..........60 D4
Christian Cl MTN/WRL BS22..........131 H5
Christina Ter CFTN/FAIL BS8 *..........78 B1
Christin Ct TRWBR BA14..........122 B1
Christmas Steps CBRIS/FH BS1..........4 E3
Christmas St CBRIS/FH BS1..........4 E3
Chubb Cl OLD/WMLY/WICK BS30..........82 C1
Church Acre BOAV BA15..........119 F2
Church Av EVILLE/WHL BS5..........62 C2
HNLZ/SM/SNYPK/WT BS9..........50 B4
OLD/WMLY/WICK BS30..........65 H4
Church Cl BATHSE BA2..........110 A2
CBATH/BATHN BA1..........110 C2
CLVDN BS21..........70 A3
FRCTL/WBN BS36..........29 H2
PTSHD/EG BS20..........45 G3
YTN/CONG BS49..........126 C4
Church Ct RDSTK/MIDN BA3..........124 B3
Church Dr YTN/CONG BS49..........128 D2
Churches BOAV BA15..........119 F2
Churchfarm Cl YATE/CS BS37..........21 E4
Church Farm Rd
MANG/FISH BS16..........55 G2
Church Flds TRWBR BA14..........122 B4
Church Hayes Cl NAIL BS48..........85 F1
Church Hayes Dr NAIL BS48..........85 F1
Church Hl
BRSG/KWL/STAPK BS4..........80 D4
Churchill Av CLVDN BS21..........70 C3
Churchill Cl CLVDN BS21..........70 C3
OLD/WMLY/WICK BS30..........82 D1
Churchill Dr
HNLZ/SM/SNYPK/WT BS9..........50 A1
Churchill Rd
BRSG/KWL/STAPK BS4..........80 B2
WSM BS23..........7 J5
Churchland Wy
OMX/HUT/LCK BS24..........137 E3
Church La BATHSE BA2..........115 F3
BMSTR BS3..........79 E3
CBATH/BATHN BA1..........103 E5
CBRIS/FH BS1..........5 H5
CFTN/FAIL BS8..........4 A5
CLVDN BS21..........72 C2
EVILLE/WHL BS5..........63 E3
FRCTL/WBN BS36..........28 C4
FRCTL/WBN BS36..........30 A4
HNBRY/STHM BS10..........36 D3
LGASH BS41..........77 F4
MANG/FISH BS16..........41 G4
NAIL BS48..........72 D5
NAIL BS48..........86 A4
NAIL BS48..........87 E2
OLD/WMLY/WICK BS30..........95 H2
OMX/HUT/LCK BS24..........140 A4
PTSHD/EG BS20..........47 F5
RDSTK/MIDN BA3..........124 B3
TRWBR BA14..........122 B4
YTN/CONG BS49..........126 C4
Church Leaze AVONM BS11..........48 C2
Church Mdw HGRV/WHIT BS14..........101 F1
Church Pde
BRSG/KWL/STAPK BS4..........80 D4
Churchpath Rd PTSHD/EG BS20..........48 A4
Church Pl PTSHD/EG BS20..........48 B4
Church Ri
BLAG/CWMG/WR BS40..........97 H5
Church Rd ALMDB BS32..........15 G2
BATHSE BA2..........117 G1
BLAG/CWMG/WR BS40..........97 H5
BMSTR BS3..........78 D3
BMSTRD/HC/WWD BS13..........90 B4
BRSTK/PCHW BS34..........38 D2
BRSTK/PCHW BS34..........39 H2
CBATH/BATHN BA1..........107 H3
CFTN/FAIL BS8..........59 G2
CFTN/FAIL BS8..........60 A5
EVILLE/WHL BS5..........63 E3
FRCTL/WBN BS36..........29 G1
FRCTL/WBN BS36..........41 F1
HGRV/WHIT BS14..........101 E1
HNLZ/SM/SNYPK/WT BS9..........50 A5
HNLZ/SM/SNYPK/WT BS9..........50 D1
HORF/LLZ BS7..........51 H2
KGWD/HNM BS15..........64 D3
KGWD/HNM BS15..........81 G1
LGASH BS41..........98 C2
MANG/FISH BS16..........54 A1
MANG/FISH BS16..........64 C1
MTN/WRL BS22..........136 A1
OLD/WMLY/WICK BS30..........67 E5
OLD/WMLY/WICK BS30..........95 H1
PLTN/PENS BS39..........100 D5
PTSHD/EG BS20..........47 H4
THNB/SVB BS35..........8 C2
THNB/SVB BS35..........11 G5
THNB/SVB BS35..........12 D2
THNB/SVB BS35..........25 E1
YATE/CS BS37..........20 D5
YTN/CONG BS49..........126 C4
Church Rd North
PTSHD/EG BS20..........45 G3
Church Rd South
PTSHD/EG BS20..........45 G4
Churchside MANG/FISH BS16..........54 A1
Church Sq RDSTK/MIDN BA3..........124 B3
Church St BOAV BA15..........119 F3
CBATH/BATHN BA1..........3 G5
CBATH/BATHN BA1..........107 G3
CBATH/BATHN BA1..........110 C2
CBRIS/FH BS1..........5 H5
EVILLE/WHL BS5..........62 C2
EVILLE/WHL BS5..........62 C5
RDSTK/MIDN BA3..........125 G2
TRWBR BA14..........121 E5
TRWBR BA14..........121 H3
Church Town NAIL BS48..........86 B4
Church Vw ALMDB BS32..........15 F3
NAIL BS48..........74 A4
Church Wk PTSHD/EG BS20..........48 B4
Churchward Cl
KGWD/HNM BS15..........81 F1
Churchward Rd
MTN/WRL BS22..........132 A5
YATE/CS BS37..........20 A4
Churchways HGRV/WHIT BS14..........92 B5
Churchways Av HORF/LLZ BS7..........51 H2
Churchways Crs HORF/LLZ BS7..........51 H2
Churchlands Rd BMSTR BS3..........78 C4
Churston Cl HGRV/WHIT BS14..........100 D1
The Circle BATHSE BA2..........113 G4
Circular Rd
HNLZ/SM/SNYPK/WT BS9..........60 B1
Circus Ms CBATH/BATHN BA1..........2 E2
Circus Pl CBATH/BATHN BA1..........2 E2
The Circus CBATH/BATHN BA1..........2 E2
City Rd CBRISNE BS2..........61 H3
City Vw CBATH/BATHN BA1..........108 D4
The Clamp
OLD/WMLY/WICK BS30..........83 F3
Clanage Rd BMSTR BS3..........77 H2
Clapton La PTSHD/EG BS20..........45 G5
Clapton Wk
HNLZ/SM/SNYPK/WT BS9..........49 G3
Clare Av HORF/LLZ BS7..........51 F5
Clare Gdns BATHSE BA2..........116 B1
Claremont Av HORF/LLZ BS7..........51 F5
Claremont Buildings
CBATH/BATHN BA1..........108 D3
Claremont Gdns CLVDN BS21..........71 E4
Claremont Rd
CBATH/BATHN BA1..........109 E3
HORF/LLZ BS7..........51 G5
Claremont St EVILLE/WHL BS5..........62 B2
Claremont Ter
CBATH/BATHN BA1 *..........108 D3
Claremont Wk
CBATH/BATHN BA1..........108 D3
Clarence Av MANG/FISH BS16..........54 D3
Clarence Gdns MANG/FISH BS16..........54 D3
Clarence Grove Rd WSM BS23..........138 D1
Clarence Pl CBATH/BATHN BA1..........107 G5
CBRISNE BS2..........4 D1
Clarence Rd CBRIS/FH BS1..........79 F2
CBRISNE BS2..........62 B4
KGWD/HNM BS15..........64 A2
MANG/FISH BS16..........54 C3
TRWBR BA14..........123 G1
Clarence Rd East WSM BS23..........138 D1
Clarence Rd North WSM BS23..........138 C1
Clarence Rd South WSM BS23..........138 C1
Clarence St
CBATH/BATHN BA1..........108 D4
Clarence Ter BATHSE BA2..........115 G3
Clarendon Av TRWBR BA14..........123 F1
Clarendon Rd BATHSE BA2..........3 J7
RDLND/MONT BS6..........61 F1
TRWBR BA14..........123 F1
WSM BS23..........7 G3
Clarendon Vls BATHSE BA2..........3 J7
Clare Rd EVILLE/WHL BS5..........62 C1
KGWD/HNM BS15..........64 B1
RDLND/MONT BS6..........61 G2
Clare St CBRIS/FH BS1..........4 E4
EVILLE/WHL BS5..........62 D3
Clare Wk THNB/SVB BS35..........8 C2
Clark Cl NAIL BS48..........73 H4
Clark Dr MANG/FISH BS16..........53 G2
Clarken Cl NAIL BS48..........73 F5
Clarken Coombe LGASH BS41..........76 D3
Clarke St BMSTR BS3..........79 E2
Clarkson Av MTN/WRL BS22..........135 H2
Clark's Pl TRWBR BA14..........125 F1
Clark St EVILLE/WHL BS5..........62 B5
Clatworthy Dr
HGRV/WHIT BS14..........91 H2
Claude Av BATHSE BA2..........113 H3
Claude Ter BATHSE BA2..........113 H2
Clavell Rd HNBRY/STHM BS10..........37 E3
Claverham Cl YTN/CONG BS49..........126 D3
Claverham Pk YTN/CONG BS49..........127 F2

Claverham Rd
MANG/FISH BS16 ....53 H3
YTN/CONG BS49 ....127 F3
Claverton Buildings
BATHSE BA2 * 3 H7
Claverton Ct BATHSE BA2 ....115 H3
Claverton Down Rd
BATHSE BA2 ....115 G5
Claverton Rd KEYN BS31 ....105 E2
Claverton Rd West KEYN BS31 ..105 E1
Claverton St BATHSE BA2 ....3 H7
Clay Bottom EVILLE/WHL BS5 ....63 E1
Clayfield YATE/CS BS37 ....20 D2
Clayfield Rd
BRSG/KWL/STAPK BS4 ....80 D3
Clay Hl EVILLE/WHL BS5 ....63 F1
Clay La BRSTK/PCHW BS34 ....27 E3
OLD/WMLY/WICK BS30 ....83 G5
THNB/SVB BS35 ....9 F3
Claymore Crs KGWD/HNM BS15 ..64 A2
Claypiece Rd
BMSTRD/HC/WWD BS13 ....90 A5
Claypit Hl YATE/CS BS37 ....32 D3
Clay Pit Rd
HNLZ/SM/SNYPK/WT BS9 ....50 D5
Claypool Rd KGWD/HNM BS15 ....64 C4
Clayton Cl PTSHD/EG BS20 ....45 H4
Clayton St AVONM BS11 ....34 B4
EVILLE/WHL BS5 ....62 C3
Cleave St CBRISNE BS2 ....62 B1
Cleeve Av MANG/FISH BS16 ....54 D1
Cleevedale Rd BATHSE BA2 ....117 E1
Cleeve Dr YTN/CONG BS49 ....127 G3
Cleeve Gdns MANG/FISH BS16 ....54 C1
Cleeve Gn BATHSE BA2 ....113 E1
Cleeve Gv KEYN BS31 ....94 A4
Cleeve Hl MANG/FISH BS16 ....54 C1
Cleeve Hill Extension
MANG/FISH BS16 ....54 D2
Cleeve Hill Rd YTN/CONG BS49 ..127 H4
Cleeve La
OLD/WMLY/WICK BS30 ....67 G2
Cleeve Lawns MANG/FISH BS16 ..54 C1
Cleeve Lodge Rd
MANG/FISH BS16 ....54 D1
Cleeve Park Rd
MANG/FISH BS16 ....54 C1
Cleeve Pl NAIL BS48 ....73 H5
Cleeve Rd
BRSG/KWL/STAPK BS4 ....80 A3
MANG/FISH BS16 ....40 D5
YATE/CS BS37 ....32 A1
Cleevewood Pk
MANG/FISH BS16 * 41 E5
Cleeve Wood Rd
MANG/FISH BS16 ....40 D5
Clement St CBRISNE BS2 ....5 J1
Clevedale MANG/FISH BS16 ....54 C1
Clevedon La CLVDN BS21 ....69 H5
Clevedon Rd CFTN/FAIL BS8 ....75 E1
HORF/LLZ BS7 ....51 G4
NAIL BS48 ....73 H2
NAIL BS48 ....74 D4
NAIL BS48 ....87 F1
PTSHD/EG BS20 ....45 F5
RDSTK/MIDN BA3 ....124 B2
WSM BS23 ....6 D7
Clevedon Ter RDLND/MONT BS6 ..61 G3
Cleveland Cl THNB/SVB BS35 ....9 F4
Cleveland Ct BATHSE BA2 ....115 F1
Cleveland Gdns TRWBR BA14 ....121 F4
Cleveland Pl East
CBATH/BATHN BA1 ....3 H1
Cleveland Pl West
CBATH/BATHN BA1 ....3 G1
Cleveland Rw BATHSE BA2 * 109 E4
Cleveland Wk BATHSE BA2 ....115 F1
Cleve Rd BRSTK/PCHW BS34 ....38 D1
Clewson Ri HGRV/WHIT BS14 ....100 C1
Cliff Court Dr MANG/FISH BS16 ....54 A1
Clifford Gdns AVONM BS11 ....48 D2
Clifford Rd MANG/FISH BS16 ....54 B4
Cliff Rd MTN/WRL BS22 ....135 F1
Clift House Rd BMSTR BS3 ....78 B2
Clifton Av WSM BS23 ....138 D1
Clifton Cl CFTN/FAIL BS8 ....60 C4
Clifton Down CFTN/FAIL BS8 ....60 C3
Clifton Down Rd CFTN/FAIL BS8 ..60 D4
Clifton Gv
HNLZ/SM/SNYPK/WT BS9 ....50 B3
Clifton High Gv
HNLZ/SM/SNYPK/WT BS9 * 50 B3
Clifton Hl CFTN/FAIL BS8 ....60 D5
Clifton Pk CFTN/FAIL BS8 ....60 D3
Clifton Park Rd CFTN/FAIL BS8 ....60 C3
Clifton Pl EVILLE/WHL BS5 ....62 B3
Clifton Rd CFTN/FAIL BS8 ....60 D5
Clifton St BMSTR BS3 ....78 D3
Clifton V CFTN/FAIL BS8 ....60 D5
Clifton Vale Cl CFTN/FAIL BS8 ....60 D5
Clifton Vw BMSTR BS3 ....79 G2
Cliftonwood Crs CFTN/FAIL BS8 ....4 A5
Clifton Wood Rd CFTN/FAIL BS8 ....4 A5
Cliftonwood Ter CFTN/FAIL BS8 ..60 D5
Clift Pl CBRIS/FH BS1 ....5 F6
Clift Rd BMSTR BS3 ....78 B2
Clinton Rd BMSTR BS3 ....78 D4
Clipsham Ri TRWBR BA14 ....120 B5
Clive Rd HGRV/WHIT BS14 ....92 B2
Cloford Cl TRWBR BA14 ....120 B5
Cloisters Rd FRCTL/WBN BS36 ....29 E4
Clonmel Rd
BRSG/KWL/STAPK BS4 ....79 E5
Closemead CLVDN BS21 ....70 D4
The Close BRSTK/PCHW BS34 ....27 E1
FRCTL/WBN BS36 ....30 A4
HNBRY/STHM BS10 ....24 D5
MANG/FISH BS16 ....54 C5
THNB/SVB BS35 ....8 C4
Clothier Leaze TRWBR BA14 ....123 E2
Cloth Yd TRWBR BA14 ....123 E3
Clouds Hill Av EVILLE/WHL BS5 ....63 F3
Clouds Hill Rd EVILLE/WHL BS5 ....63 G3
Clovelly Cl EVILLE/WHL BS5 ....63 G3
Clovelly Rd EVILLE/WHL BS5 ....63 G3
MTN/WRL BS22 ....136 D1
Clover Cl CLVDN BS21 ....71 F2
Clover Ct MTN/WRL BS22 ....136 A4
Cloverdale Dr
OLD/WMLY/WICK BS30 ....82 D3
Clover Gnd
HNLZ/SM/SNYPK/WT BS9 ....37 G5
Cloverlea Rd
OLD/WMLY/WICK BS30 ....83 F1
Clover Leaze
BRSTK/PCHW BS34 ....27 F4
Clover Rd MTN/WRL BS22 ....131 H2
Clyde Av KEYN BS31 ....94 C5
Clyde Gdns BATHSE BA2 ....113 G1
EVILLE/WHL BS5 ....64 A5
Clyde Gv BRSTK/PCHW BS34 ....38 C3
Clyde La RDLND/MONT BS6 ....61 E1
Clyde Ms RDLND/MONT BS6 ....61 F1
Clyde Rd BRSG/KWL/STAPK BS4 ..79 H3
FRCTL/WBN BS36 ....29 H2
RDLND/MONT BS6 ....61 E1
Clydesdale Cl TRWBR BA14 ....122 D4
Clyde Ter BMSTR BS3 ....78 D3
BRSG/KWL/STAPK BS4 ....79 H3
Clynder Gv CLVDN BS21 ....68 C4
Coach Rd BOAV BA15 ....119 F3
Coalbridge Cl MTN/WRL BS22 ....136 C1
Coaley Rd AVONM BS11 ....48 C3
Coalpit Rd CBATH/BATHN BA1 ....103 F5
Coalsack La FRCTL/WBN BS36 ....42 A2
Coalville Rd FRCTL/WBN BS36 ....30 B3
Coape Rd HGRV/WHIT BS14 ....93 E4
Coates Gv NAIL BS48 ....73 H4
Coates Wk
BRSG/KWL/STAPK BS4 ....91 E3
Cobblestone Ms CFTN/FAIL BS8 ..60 D4
Cobden St EVILLE/WHL BS5 ....62 D4
Coberley KGWD/HNM BS15 ....64 B5
Cobhorn Dr
BMSTRD/HC/WWD BS13 ....90 A5
Cobley Cft CLVDN BS21 ....70 C5
Cobourg Rd RDLND/MONT BS6 ....62 A2
Cobthorn Wy YTN/CONG BS49 ..129 E1
Cock Hl TRWBR BA14 ....120 B5
Cock Rd KGWD/HNM BS15 ....64 D5
Codrington Pl CFTN/FAIL BS8 ....60 D4
Codrington Rd HORF/LLZ BS7 ....51 G5
Cogan Rd MANG/FISH BS16 ....54 D5
Cogsall Rd HGRV/WHIT BS14 ....93 E3
Coker Rd MTN/WRL BS22 ....136 D1
Colbourne Rd BATHSE BA2 ....116 B1
Colchester Crs
§BRSG/KWL/STAPK BS4 ....91 E2
Coldharbour La
MANG/FISH BS16 ....39 H5
WSM BS23 ....138 C3
Coldharbour Rd
RDLND/MONT BS6 ....51 E5
Coldpark Gdns
BMSTRD/HC/WWD BS13 ....89 H4
Coldpark Rd
BMSTRD/HC/WWD BS13 ....89 H4
Coldrick Cl HGRV/WHIT BS14 ....100 C1
Colebrook Rd KGWD/HNM BS15 ..64 B3
Coleford Rd HNBRY/STHM BS10 ..38 A5
Colehouse La CLVDN BS21 ....70 D5
Colemead
BMSTRD/HC/WWD BS13 ....90 C4
Coleridge Rd CLVDN BS21 ....70 C2
EVILLE/WHL BS5 ....52 D5
WSM BS23 ....139 F3
Coleridge Vale Rd East
CLVDN BS21 ....70 D2
Coleridge Vale Rd North
CLVDN BS21 ....70 C3
Coleridge Vale Rd South
CLVDN BS21 ....70 C3
Coleridge Vale Rd West
CLVDN BS21 ....70 C3
Cole Rd CBRISNE BS2 ....62 C5
Colesborne Cl YATE/CS BS37 ....31 H2
Coleshill Dr
BMSTRD/HC/WWD BS13 ....90 C4
Colin Cl THNB/SVB BS35 ....8 C3
College Av MANG/FISH BS16 ....53 H3
College Ct MANG/FISH BS16 ....53 H3
College Flds CFTN/FAIL BS8 ....60 C3
College Gn CBRIS/FH BS1 ....4 D5
College Park Dr
HNBRY/STHM BS10 ....37 E4
College Rd CBATH/BATHN BA1 ..108 B3
CFTN/FAIL BS8 ....60 C3
HNLZ/SM/SNYPK/WT BS9 ....50 D1
MANG/FISH BS16 ....53 H3
TRWBR BA14 ....122 C3
College Sq CBRIS/FH BS1 ....4 C5
College St CBRIS/FH BS1 ....4 C4
College Vw
CBATH/BATHN BA1 * 108 D3
Collet Cl MTN/WRL BS22 ....132 B4
Collett Cl KGWD/HNM BS15 ....81 G1
Collett Wy YATE/CS BS37 ....20 B4
Colliers Break
MANG/FISH BS16 ....55 G3
Collingbourne Cl
TRWBR BA14 * 123 E4
Collingwood Av
KGWD/HNM BS15 ....64 D2
Collingwood Cl KEYN BS31 ....105 F2
MTN/WRL BS22 ....131 F4
Collingwood Rd
RDLND/MONT BS6 ....61 E2
Collin Rd
BRSG/KWL/STAPK BS4 ....80 C2
Collins Av BRSTK/PCHW BS34 ....27 E4
Collinson Rd
BMSTRD/HC/WWD BS13 ....90 C4
Collins St AVONM BS11 ....34 C5
Collier Crs BMSTR BS3 ....78 B4
Collum La MTN/WRL BS22 ....131 E1
Coln Sq THNB/SVB BS35 ....8 D4
Colombo Crs WSM BS23 ....138 D3
Colston Av CBRIS/FH BS1 ....4 E4
Colston Cl FRCTL/WBN BS36 ....41 F1
MANG/FISH BS16 ....54 C5
Colston Dl MANG/FISH BS16 ....53 F4
Colston Fort CBRISNE BS2 * 61 G3
Colston Hl MANG/FISH BS16 ....53 E4
Colston Pde CBRIS/FH BS1 ....5 G6
Colston Rd EVILLE/WHL BS5 ....62 D2
Colston St CBRIS/FH BS1 ....4 E3
MANG/FISH BS16 ....54 C5
Colston Yd CBRISNE BS2 ....4 E2
Colthurst Dr KGWD/HNM BS15 ....82 A1
Colts Gn YATE/CS BS37 ....33 G2
Colwyn Rd EVILLE/WHL BS5 ....62 D2
Combe Av PTSHD/EG BS20 ....45 F2
Combe Cross Wk
BMSTRD/HC/WWD BS13 ....99 G1
Combe Flds PTSHD/EG BS20 ....45 F2
Combe Gv CBATH/BATHN BA1 ....107 G5
Combe Pk CBATH/BATHN BA1 ....107 H4
Combermere THNB/SVB BS35 ....9 E4
Combe Rd BATHSE BA2 ....117 F1
PTSHD/EG BS20 ....45 G3
Combe Road Cl BATHSE BA2 ....117 F1
Combeside BATHSE BA2 * 114 D3
Combe Side NAIL BS48 ....85 H2
Combfactory La
EVILLE/WHL BS5 ....62 C3
Comb Paddock
HNLZ/SM/SNYPK/WT BS9 ....51 E1
Comfortable Pl BATHSE BA2 ....2 B3
Commercial Rd CBRIS/FH BS1 ....4 E7
The Common East ALMDB BS32 ..27 E1
Commonfield Rd
AVONM BS11 ....36 A4
Common La PTSHD/EG BS20 ....58 A2
Common Mead La
MANG/FISH BS16 ....40 B4
Commonmead La
YATE/CS BS37 ....33 H1
Common Rd FRCTL/WBN BS36 ....29 F3
KGWD/HNM BS15 ....81 G3
The Common
BRSTK/PCHW BS34 ....26 D1
MANG/FISH BS16 ....54 A1
Compton Cl TRWBR BA14 ....121 F2
Compton Dr
OMX/HUT/LCK BS24 ....136 B4
Compton Gn KEYN BS31 ....94 B5
Compton Md NAIL BS48 * 88 A5
Compton St EVILLE/WHL BS5 ....62 D4
Comyn Wk MANG/FISH BS16 ....53 H3
Concorde Dr
HNBRY/STHM BS10 ....37 G4
Concorde Rd
BRSTK/PCHW BS34 ....26 A3
The Concourse
BRSG/KWL/STAPK BS4 ....80 C4
Condor Cl MTN/WRL BS22 ....136 A3
Condover Rd
BRSG/KWL/STAPK BS4 ....81 E3
Conduit Pl CBRISNE BS2 ....62 B2
Conduit Rd CBRISNE BS2 ....62 B2
Conference Av PTSHD/EG BS20 ..45 H3
Conference Cl PTSHD/EG BS20 ....46 A4
Congleton Rd EVILLE/WHL BS5 ....63 E3
Conham Hl KGWD/HNM BS15 ....81 F1
Conham Rd KGWD/HNM BS15 ....81 E1
Conifer Cl FRCTL/WBN BS36 ....29 G1
MANG/FISH BS16 ....54 C2
Conifer Wy
OMX/HUT/LCK BS24 ....140 B1
Conigre Hl BOAV BA15 ....119 F2
Coniston Av
HNLZ/SM/SNYPK/WT BS9 ....50 B2
Coniston Cl
OLD/WMLY/WICK BS30 ....66 A5
Coniston Crs WSM BS23 ....139 E2
Coniston Rd BRSTK/PCHW BS34 ..26 A2
TRWBR BA14 ....121 F4
Connaught Pl WSM BS23 ....6 D2
Connaught Rd
BRSG/KWL/STAPK BS4 ....91 F1
Connection Rd BATHSE BA2 ....113 F1
Constable Cl KEYN BS31 ....94 C3
Constable Dr MTN/WRL BS22 ....131 G5
Constable Rd HORF/LLZ BS7 ....52 B2
Constantine Av
BRSTK/PCHW BS34 ....27 G5
Constitution Hl CFTN/FAIL BS8 ....4 A4
Convent Cl HNBRY/STHM BS10 ....36 C2
Convocation Av BATHSE BA2 ....115 H1
Conway Gn KEYN BS31 ....104 B1
Conway Rd
BRSG/KWL/STAPK BS4 ....80 B2
Conygar Cl CLVDN BS21 ....68 D5
Conygre Gv BRSTK/PCHW BS34 ....39 F2
Conygre Rd BRSTK/PCHW BS34 ....39 E2
Cook Cl OLD/WMLY/WICK BS30 ....83 F2
Cooke's Dr THNB/SVB BS35 ....25 E1
Cooks Cl ALMDB BS32 ....16 B5
Cook's Folly Rd
HNLZ/SM/SNYPK/WT BS9 ....60 A1
Cook's La CLVDN BS21 ....71 H3
FRCTL/WBN BS36 ....42 C2
Cooksley Rd EVILLE/WHL BS5 ....62 D3
Cook St AVONM BS11 ....34 C5
Cookworthy Cl EVILLE/WHL BS5 ..62 C5
Coombe Av THNB/SVB BS35 ....8 C2
Coombe Bridge Av
HNLZ/SM/SNYPK/WT BS9 ....50 A2
Coombe Cl HNBRY/STHM BS10 ....36 C2
Coombe Dl
HNLZ/SM/SNYPK/WT BS9 ....49 H2
NAIL BS48 ....96 B4
Coombe Gdns
HNLZ/SM/SNYPK/WT BS9 ....50 B2
Coombe Hay La BATHSE BA2 ....116 A2
Coombe La
HNLZ/SM/SNYPK/WT BS9 ....50 A2
Coombe Orch
RDSTK/MIDN BA3 * 125 G1
Coombe Rd EVILLE/WHL BS5 ....62 D1
NAIL BS48 ....73 E5
WSM BS23 ....6 E2
Coombe Rocke
HNLZ/SM/SNYPK/WT BS9 * 50 A2
Coombes Wy
OLD/WMLY/WICK BS30 ....83 G2
Coombe Wy HNBRY/STHM BS10 ..37 E4
Cooperage Rd EVILLE/WHL BS5 ..62 D4
Co-operation Rd
EVILLE/WHL BS5 ....62 D2
Cooper Rd
HNLZ/SM/SNYPK/WT BS9 ....50 C1
THNB/SVB BS35 ....8 C5
Coopers Dr YATE/CS BS37 ....21 E2
The Coots HGRV/WHIT BS14 ....92 D3
Copeland Dr HGRV/WHIT BS14 ....92 A4
Cope Pk ALMDB BS32 ....16 A2
Copford La LGASH BS41 ....77 E5
Copley Ct KGWD/HNM BS15 ....82 B1
Copley Gdns HORF/LLZ BS7 ....52 C2
MTN/WRL BS22 ....136 C1
Copperfield Dr MTN/WRL BS22 ..131 G4
Coppice Hl BOAV BA15 ....119 G2
The Coppice ALMDB BS32 ....27 G3
BMSTRD/HC/WWD BS13 ....89 H5
Copse Cl OMX/HUT/LCK BS24 ....139 F5
Copseland BATHSE BA2 ....115 G2
Copse Rd
BRSG/KWL/STAPK BS4 ....80 A3
CLVDN BS21 ....70 C1
KEYN BS31 ....95 F5
Copthorne Cl HGRV/WHIT BS14 ....92 A4
Coralberry Dr MTN/WRL BS22 ....136 C2
Corbet Cl AVONM BS11 ....36 A3
Corbett Cl YATE/CS BS37 ....21 E3
Corbin Rd TRWBR BA14 ....121 G5
Cordwell Wk
HNBRY/STHM BS10 ....51 G1
Corey Cl CBRISNE BS2 ....62 A2
Corfe Cl NAIL BS48 ....73 E5
Corfe Crs KEYN BS31 ....94 B4
Corfe Pl OLD/WMLY/WICK BS30 ..83 E5
Corfe Rd BRSG/KWL/STAPK BS4 ..91 E2
Coriander Dr ALMDB BS32 ....28 A3
Coriander Wk EVILLE/WHL BS5 ....62 D1
Corinum Cl MANG/FISH BS16 ....55 H2
Cork Pl CBATH/BATHN BA1 * 2 A3
Cork St CBATH/BATHN BA1 ....2 A2
Cork Ter CBATH/BATHN BA1 ....2 A2
Cormorant Cl MTN/WRL BS22 ....136 C2
Cornbrash Ri TRWBR BA14 ....123 H1
Corner Cft CLVDN BS21 ....70 D4
Cornfield Cl ALMDB BS32 ....27 E1
The Cornfields MTN/WRL BS22 ..131 G3
Cornhill Dr HGRV/WHIT BS14 ....91 H2
Cornish Gv HGRV/WHIT BS14 ....92 D3
Cornish Rd HGRV/WHIT BS14 ....92 D3
Cornish Wk HGRV/WHIT BS14 ....92 D3
Cornleaze
BMSTRD/HC/WWD BS13 ....90 B4
Corn St CBATH/BATHN BA1 ....3 F5
CBRIS/FH BS1 ....5 F4
Cornwall Crs YATE/CS BS37 ....21 E4
Cornwallis Av CFTN/FAIL BS8 ....60 C5
MTN/WRL BS22 ....131 F4
Cornwallis Crs CFTN/FAIL BS8 ....60 C5
Cornwallis Gv CFTN/FAIL BS8 ....60 C5
Cornwall Rd HORF/LLZ BS7 ....51 G4
Coronation Av BATHSE BA2 ....113 H4
KEYN BS31 ....94 A5
MANG/FISH BS16 ....53 H4
Coronation Cl
OLD/WMLY/WICK BS30 ....82 D1
Coronation Pl CBRIS/FH BS1 * 5 F4
Coronation Rd BMSTR BS3 ....78 B2
CBATH/BATHN BA1 ....2 A2
KGWD/HNM BS15 ....65 F4
MANG/FISH BS16 ....54 D3
MTN/WRL BS22 ....136 B1
OLD/WMLY/WICK BS30 ....83 E1
Corondale Rd MTN/WRL BS22 ....136 A3
Corridor CBATH/BATHN BA1 ....3 G4
Corsley Wk
BRSG/KWL/STAPK BS4 ....91 G1
Corston Dr BATHSE BA2 ....112 A1
Corston La BATHSE BA2 ....105 H4
Corston Vw BATHSE BA2 ....113 H5
Corston Wk AVONM BS11 ....48 B1
Cossham Cl THNB/SVB BS35 ....8 D2
Cossham Rd EVILLE/WHL BS5 ....63 E3
MANG/FISH BS16 ....57 F4
Cossham St MANG/FISH BS16 ....55 G3
Cossham Wk EVILLE/WHL BS5 ....63 H2
Cossington Rd
BRSG/KWL/STAPK BS4 ....91 G1
Cossins Rd RDLND/MONT BS6 ....51 E5
Costers Cl THNB/SVB BS35 ....11 G1
Costiland Dr
BMSTRD/HC/WWD BS13 ....90 A3
Cote Dr
HNLZ/SM/SNYPK/WT BS9 ....50 D4
Cote House La
HNLZ/SM/SNYPK/WT BS9 ....50 D3
Cote La
HNLZ/SM/SNYPK/WT BS9 ....50 D3
Cote Lea Pk
HNLZ/SM/SNYPK/WT BS9 ....51 E1
Cote Paddock
HNLZ/SM/SNYPK/WT BS9 ....50 C4
Cote Pk
HNLZ/SM/SNYPK/WT BS9 ....50 B2
Cote Rd
HNLZ/SM/SNYPK/WT BS9 ....50 D4
Cotham Brow
RDLND/MONT BS6 ....61 G2
Cotham Gdns
RDLND/MONT BS6 ....61 E2
Cotham Gv
RDLND/MONT BS6 ....61 G2
Cotham Hl
RDLND/MONT BS6 ....61 E3
Cotham Lawn Rd
RDLND/MONT BS6 ....61 F3
Cotham Pk RDLND/MONT BS6 ....61 F2
Cotham Park Man
RDLND/MONT BS6 * 61 F2
Cotham Pk North
RDLND/MONT BS6 ....61 F2
Cotham Pl RDLND/MONT BS6 * 61 F3
Cotham Rd RDLND/MONT BS6 ....61 F3
Cotham Rd South
RDLND/MONT BS6 ....4 E1
Cotham Side RDLND/MONT BS6 ..61 G2
Cotham V RDLND/MONT BS6 ....61 F2
Cotman Wk HORF/LLZ BS7 ....52 C2
MTN/WRL BS22 ....136 C1
Cotrith Gv HNBRY/STHM BS10 ....36 D2
Cotswold Cl PTSHD/EG BS20 ....45 G4
Cotswold Rd BATHSE BA2 ....114 A3
BMSTR BS3 ....79 E3
YATE/CS BS37 ....32 D2
Cotswold Vw BATHSE BA2 ....113 G2
KGWD/HNM BS15 ....64 C1
Cotswold Wy CBATH/BATHN BA1 ..2 C2
Cottage Gdns EVILLE/WHL BS5 ....63 H4
Cottage Pl CBRISNE BS2 ....4 E1
Cottington Ct KGWD/HNM BS15 ..82 B1
Cottisford Rd EVILLE/WHL BS5 ....52 C4
Cottle Gdns HGRV/WHIT BS14 ....93 E3
Cottle Rd HGRV/WHIT BS14 ....93 E3
Cottles La BOAV BA15 ....118 C3
Cottonwood Dr
OLD/WMLY/WICK BS30 ....82 D3
Cottrell Av KGWD/HNM BS15 ....64 A1
Cottrell Rd EVILLE/WHL BS5 ....52 D5
Coulson Dr MTN/WRL BS22 ....132 A5
Coulson's Cl HGRV/WHIT BS14 ....100 D1
Coulson's Rd HGRV/WHIT BS14 ..100 D1
Coulson Wk KGWD/HNM BS15 ....64 B1
Counterpool Rd
KGWD/HNM BS15 ....64 B4
Counterslip CBRIS/FH BS1 ....5 G4
Counterslip Gdns
HGRV/WHIT BS14 ....92 B3
Countess Wk MANG/FISH BS16 ....53 E2
County St
BRSG/KWL/STAPK BS4 ....79 H2
County Wy TRWBR BA14 ....121 F5
TRWBR BA14 ....122 D2
Court Av BRSTK/PCHW BS34 ....27 H5
YTN/CONG BS49 ....126 B4
Court Cl HORF/LLZ BS7 ....51 H1
NAIL BS48 ....86 B4
PTSHD/EG BS20 ....45 G4
Courtenay Crs
BRSG/KWL/STAPK BS4 ....91 E2
Courtenay Rd KEYN BS31 ....104 B2
Courteney Crs
BRSG/KWL/STAPK BS4 ....91 E2
Court Farm Rd
HGRV/WHIT BS14 ....100 C1
OLD/WMLY/WICK BS30 ....82 A5
Courtfield Gv MANG/FISH BS16 ....53 H4
Court Gdns CBATH/BATHN BA1 ....110 B1
YATE/CS BS37 * 32 A2
Courtlands ALMDB BS32 ....27 E1
KEYN BS31 ....94 B4
Courtlands La BMSTR BS3 ....77 H2
Court La CBATH/BATHN BA1 ....110 C2
CLVDN BS21 ....71 G2
Courtney Rd KGWD/HNM BS15 ....64 D4
Courtney Wy KGWD/HNM BS15 ..65 F4
Court Pl MTN/WRL BS22 ....136 C1
Court Rd FRCTL/WBN BS36 ....29 F2
HORF/LLZ BS7 ....52 A2
KGWD/HNM BS15 ....64 C4
MTN/WRL BS22 ....130 B3
OLD/WMLY/WICK BS30 ....83 E3
Courtside Ms RDLND/MONT BS6 ..61 F2
Court St TRWBR BA14 ....122 D1
Court View Cl AVONM BS11 ....15 G2
Courville Cl THNB/SVB BS35 ....11 G3
Cousins Cl HNBRY/STHM BS10 ....36 C2
Cousins Ms
BRSG/KWL/STAPK BS4 ....63 G5
Cousins Wy MANG/FISH BS16 ....41 H5
Couzens Cl YATE/CS BS37 ....21 H5
Couzens Pl BRSTK/PCHW BS34 ....27 H5
Coventry Wk
BRSG/KWL/STAPK BS4 ....63 G5
Cowdray Rd
BRSG/KWL/STAPK BS4 ....91 E2
Cowhorn Hl
OLD/WMLY/WICK BS30 ....83 F2
Cowler Wk
BMSTRD/HC/WWD BS13 ....90 A5
Cowling Dr HGRV/WHIT BS14 ....92 B4
Cowling Rd HGRV/WHIT BS14 ....92 B4
Cowper Rd RDLND/MONT BS6 ....61 E2
Cowper St EVILLE/WHL BS5 ....62 D4
Cox Ct OLD/WMLY/WICK BS30 ....82 C2
Coxley Dr CBATH/BATHN BA1 ....109 E2
Coxway CLVDN BS21 ....71 E3
Crabtree Cl LGASH BS41 ....98 C3
Crabtree La LGASH BS41 ....98 B3
Crabtree Pk CLVDN BS21 * 70 C4
Crabtree Wk EVILLE/WHL BS5 ....63 E1
Cradock Cl
OLD/WMLY/WICK BS30 ....82 D2
Cranberry Wk
HNLZ/SM/SNYPK/WT BS9 ....36 B5
Cranbourne Cha WSM BS23 ....7 K1
Cranbourne Rd
BRSTK/PCHW BS34 ....26 B3
Cranbrook Rd
RDLND/MONT BS6 ....51 F5
Crandale Rd BATHSE BA2 ....2 A6
Crandell Cl HNBRY/STHM BS10 ....37 E1
Crane Cl KGWD/HNM BS15 ....65 G3
Cranford Cl MTN/WRL BS22 ....136 A2
Cranham YATE/CS BS37 ....31 G3
Cranham Cl KGWD/HNM BS15 ....65 E1
Cranham Dr
BRSTK/PCHW BS34 ....27 E1
Cranham Rd
HNBRY/STHM BS10 ....37 H5
Cranhill Rd CBATH/BATHN BA1 ....2 B1
Cranleigh BATHSE BA2 ....116 D2
Cranleigh Court Rd
YATE/CS BS37 ....20 C5

Cranleigh Gdns
HNLZ/SM/SNYPK/WT BS9 ....50 B4
Cranleigh Rd HGRV/WHIT BS14 ....92 A4
Cranmoor Gn THNB/SVB BS35......13 F2
Cranmore Av KEYN BS31 ....94 B3
Cranmore Cl TRWBR BA14 ....120 B5
Cranmore Crs
HNBRY/STHM BS10.....................38 A4
Cranmore Pl BATHSE BA2............116 B2
Cranside Av
RDLND/MONT BS6.......................51 F5
Cransley Crs
HNLZ/SM/SNYPK/WT BS9 ....51 F1
Crantock Av
BMSTRD/HC/WWD BS13 ....90 C1
Crantock Dr ALMDB BS32..............15 H2
Crantock Rd YATE/CS BS37 ....31 H1
Cranwell Gv HGRV/WHIT BS14......91 H4
Cranwell Rd
OMX/HUT/LCK BS24 ....141 F2
Craven Cl
OLD/WMLY/WICK BS30..............82 C1
Craven Wy
OLD/WMLY/WICK BS30..............82 C1
Crawford Cl CLVDN BS21 ....70 B4
Crawley Crs TRWBR BA14............122 B1
Craydon Gv HGRV/WHIT BS14 ......92 C5
Craydon Rd HGRV/WHIT BS14 ......92 C4
Craydon Wk HGRV/WHIT BS14 ....92 C4
Crediton Crs
BRSG/KWL/STAPK BS4 ....79 G5
Crescent Gdns
CBATH/BATHN BA1 ....2 D3
Crescent La CBATH/BATHN BA1......2 D1
Crescent Rd MANG/FISH BS16......54 B2
The Crescent
HNLZ/SM/SNYPK/WT BS9 ....49 H2
HNLZ/SM/SNYPK/WT BS9 ....51 F2
MANG/FISH BS16.........................40 A4
MANG/FISH BS16.........................54 C5
MTN/WRL BS22 ....135 G2
NAIL BS48 ....85 H3
OLD/WMLY/WICK BS30..............67 E4
Crescent Vw BATHSE BA2 ....2 E7
Cresswell Cl MTN/WRL BS22 ......136 D1
The Crest BRSG/KWL/STAPK BS4..80 B4
Creswicke Av KGWD/HNM BS15 ..81 H1
Creswicke Rd
BRSG/KWL/STAPK BS4 ....91 F2
Crewkerne Cl NAIL BS48.................74 A5
Crew's Hole Rd
EVILLE/WHL BS5 ....63 E4
Cribbs Cswy HNBRY/STHM BS10..25 E5
Cricket Field Gn NAIL BS48 * 73 E4
Cricklade Ct NAIL BS48 ....73 H5
Cricklade Rd HORF/LLZ BS7 ....51 H4
Cripps Rd BMSTR BS3 ....78 D3
Crispin La THNB/SVB BS35 ....8 C3
Crispin Wy KGWD/HNM BS15........65 E1
Crockerne Dr PTSHD/EG BS20......48 B5
Croft Av MANG/FISH BS16 ....52 D4
Croft Cl OLD/WMLY/WICK BS30....95 G1
Crofters Wk ALMDB BS32..............27 F2
Crofton Av HORF/LLZ BS7 ....51 H2
Crofton Flds FRCTL/WBN BS36 ....29 E4
Croft Rd CBATH/BATHN BA1 ......109 E3
Crofts End Rd EVILLE/WHL BS5....63 F2
The Croft CLVDN BS21.....................71 F1
MANG/FISH BS16.........................55 E3
NAIL BS48 ....85 H2
OLD/WMLY/WICK BS30 * 83 F3
OMX/HUT/LCK BS24 ....140 B3
TRWBR BA14 ....122 D3
Croft Vw
HNLZ/SM/SNYPK/WT BS9 ....51 F1
Crokeswood Wk AVONM BS11 ....35 H4
Crome Rd HORF/LLZ BS7 ....52 C1
Cromer Rd EVILLE/WHL BS5..........62 D1
WSM BS23 ....138 D1
Cromwell Ct KGWD/HNM BS15 ....82 B1
Cromwell Dr MTN/WRL BS22......131 H4
Cromwell Rd EVILLE/WHL BS5......63 H3
RDLND/MONT BS6......................61 G1
Cromwells Hide
MANG/FISH BS16.........................53 F3
Crookes La MTN/WRL BS22 ....130 B4
Croomes Hl MANG/FISH BS16 ......54 C2
Cropthorne Rd HORF/LLZ BS7......38 D4
Cropthorne Rd South
HORF/LLZ BS7 ....38 D5
Crosby Rw CFTN/FAIL BS8 ....60 D5
Crosscombe Dr
BMSTRD/HC/WWD BS13 ....99 G1
Cross Elms La
HNLZ/SM/SNYPK/WT BS9 ....50 B3
Crossfield Rd MANG/FISH BS16....54 D5
Cross Hands Rd THNB/SVB BS35..13 F2
Cross Lanes PTSHD/EG BS20 ....48 A4
Crossleaze Rd KGWD/HNM BS15..81 H3
Crossley Cl FRCTL/WBN BS36........29 F3
Crossman Av FRCTL/WBN BS36....29 E5
Crossman Wk CLVDN BS21............71 F2
Cross St KEYN BS31 ....94 C2
KGWD/HNM BS15 ....64 B2
TRWBR BA14 ....121 E5
WSM BS23 ....6 E4
Cross Tree Gv ALMDB BS32 ....27 F2
Cross Wk HGRV/WHIT BS14 ....91 H3
Crossways Rd THNB/SVB BS35 ......9 E3
Crow La CBRIS/FH BS1 ....5 F4
HNBRY/STHM BS10.....................37 E3
Crowley Wy AVONM BS11 ....34 C4
Crowndale Rd
BRSG/KWL/STAPK BS4 ....79 H3
Crown Gdns
OLD/WMLY/WICK BS30..............65 G4
Crown Hl CBATH/BATHN BA1......107 H3
EVILLE/WHL BS5 ....63 C3
Crown Hill Wk EVILLE/WHL BS5....63 G3
Crownleaze MANG/FISH BS16 ......54 C5
Crown Rd CBATH/BATHN BA1 ....107 G3
KGWD/HNM BS15 ....64 C1
OLD/WMLY/WICK BS30..............65 H5
Crows Gv ALMDB BS32 ....16 B4
Crowther Pk HORF/LLZ BS7..........52 B4
Crowther Rd HORF/LLZ BS7..........52 B4
Crowthers Av YATE/CS BS37 ....20 D4
Crowther St BMSTR BS3................78 C3
Croydon St EVILLE/WHL BS5 ....62 C3
The Crunnis ALMDB BS32 ....27 G4
Crusty La PTSHD/EG BS20 ....48 B3
Crystal Wy ALMDB BS32 ....27 G2
Cuckoo La FRCTL/WBN BS36 ....41 G2
Cuffington Av
BRSG/KWL/STAPK BS4 ....80 C2
Culverhill Rd YATE/CS BS37 ....32 C1
Culver Rd BOAV BA15 ....119 H4
Culvers Cl KEYN BS31 ....94 B3
Culvers Rd KEYN BS31.....................94 B3
Culver St CBRIS/FH BS1 ....4 D4
The Culvert ALMDB BS32 ....27 F2
Culverwell Rd
BMSTRD/HC/WWD BS13 ....90 B5
Cumberland Basin
CFTN/FAIL BS8 ....78 B1
Cumberland Basin Rd
CFTN/FAIL BS8 ....78 A1
Cumberland Cl CBRIS/FH BS1 ......78 B1
Cumberland Gv
RDLND/MONT BS6.......................62 A1
Cumberland Pl CFTN/FAIL BS8......60 C5
Cumberland Rd CBRIS/FH BS1 ....78 B1
Cumberland Rw
CBATH/BATHN BA1 ....2 E4
Cumberland St CBRISNE BS2..........5 G1
Cumbria Cl THNB/SVB BS35 ....9 F3
Cunningham Gdns
MANG/FISH BS16.........................54 A3
Curland Gv HGRV/WHIT BS14........92 A4
Curlew Cl MANG/FISH BS16 * 53 G2
Curlew Gdns MTN/WRL BS22......136 C2
Currells La
BLAG/CWMG/WR BS40 ....96 C3
Curtis La BRSTK/PCHW BS34 ....40 B2
Cusance Wy TRWBR BA14 ....121 H5
Custom Cl HGRV/WHIT BS14 ....91 H2
Cutler Rd
BMSTRD/HC/WWD BS13 ....90 A3
Cygnet Crs MTN/WRL BS22 ....136 C2
Cylde Pk RDLND/MONT BS6..........61 E1
Cynder Wy MANG/FISH BS16........41 H4
Cynthia Rd BATHSE BA2 ....113 H2
Cypress Gdns CFTN/FAIL BS8........60 B5
Cypress Gv
HNLZ/SM/SNYPK/WT BS9 ....51 F2
Cypress Ter RDSTK/MIDN BA3....125 E3
Cyrus Ct MANG/FISH BS16 ....55 G1

D

Dafford's Buildings
CBATH/BATHN BA1 ....109 E2
Dafford St CBATH/BATHN BA1....109 F2
Dahlia Gdns BATHSE BA2 ....3 K2
Daisy Bank BATHSE BA2 ....115 E3
Daisy Rd EVILLE/WHL BS5..............62 D1
Dakin Cl BRSG/KWL/STAPK BS4 ....79 G5
Dakota Dr HGRV/WHIT BS14 ....91 H5
Dalby Av BMSTR BS3......................79 E3
Daldry Gdns THNB/SVB BS35........10 A4
Dale St CBRISNE BS2 ....5 J1
EVILLE/WHL BS5 ....63 G3
Daley Cl MTN/WRL BS22..............132 A5
Dalkeith Av KGWD/HNM BS15......64 B2
Dalrymple Rd
RDLND/MONT BS6.......................61 H2
Dalston Rd BMSTR BS3...................78 C2
Dalton Sq CBRISNE BS2..................61 H3
Dame Court Cl
MTN/WRL BS22 ....131 G4
Dampier Rd BMSTR BS3 ....78 B3
Damson Rd MTN/WRL BS22........136 B4
Danbury Crs HNBRY/STHM BS10..37 H4
Danbury Wk
HNBRY/STHM BS10.....................37 H4
Dandy's Meadow
PTSHD/EG BS20...........................45 H3
Daneacre Rd RDSTK/MIDN BA3..125 H1
Dane Cl BOAV BA15 ....118 B2
Dane Ri BOAV BA15 ....118 B2
Dangerfield Av
BMSTRD/HC/WWD BS13 ....89 H3
Daniel Cl CLVDN BS21 ....71 F2
Daniel Ms BATHSE BA2 ....3 J2
Daniel St BATHSE BA2 ....3 J2
Dano View Gdns
PTSHD/EG BS20...........................45 F3
Dapps Hl KEYN BS31 ....94 C4
Dark La NAIL BS48 ....86 A4
Darley Cl HNBRY/STHM BS10........36 C2
Darlington Pl BATHSE BA2 ....3 K5
Darlington Rd BATHSE BA2 ....3 K2
Darlington St BATHSE BA2..............3 J3
Darmead OMX/HUT/LCK BS24....137 E2
Darnley Av HORF/LLZ BS7 ....52 A2
Dart Cl THNB/SVB BS35....................8 C4
Dartmoor St BMSTR BS3 ....78 C2
Dartmouth Av BATHSE BA2 ....113 H2
Dartmouth Cl MTN/WRL BS22....136 C1
Dart Rd CLVDN BS21 ....70 D4
Daubeny Cl MANG/FISH BS16 ......54 A3
Daventry Rd
BRSG/KWL/STAPK BS4 ....79 G5
Davey St CBRISNE BS2 ....62 A2
Davey Ter CBRISNE BS2 * 62 A2
Davids Cl THNB/SVB BS35..............11 G3
David's La THNB/SVB BS35............11 G3
David's Rd HGRV/WHIT BS14 ....92 B3
David St CBRISNE BS2.....................5 J3
Davies Dr BRSG/KWL/STAPK BS4..81 E1
Davin Crs PTSHD/EG BS20 ....48 B5
Davis Cl OLD/WMLY/WICK BS30....82 C1
Davis Ct THNB/SVB BS35 ....8 D2
Davis La CLVDN BS21......................70 D5
Davis St AVONM BS11 ....34 C5
Dawes Cl CLVDN BS21 ....70 D4
Dawley Cl FRCTL/WBN BS36..........29 E3
Dawlish Rd BMSTR BS3...................79 E4
Dawn Ri KGWD/HNM BS15............65 F2
Daws Ct MANG/FISH BS16 ....54 A4
Day Crs BATHSE BA2 ....113 E1
Day's Rd CBRISNE BS2...................62 B5
Deacon Cl FRCTL/WBN BS36 ....29 E5
Deacons Cl MTN/WRL BS22 ....136 B1
Deadmill La CBATH/BATHN BA1..109 F1
Dean Av THNB/SVB BS35 ....8 D2
Dean Cl KGWD/HNM BS15 ....81 F2
MTN/WRL BS22 ....132 A5
Dean Crs BMSTR BS3......................78 D2
Deanery Rd CBRIS/FH BS1 ....4 C5
KGWD/HNM BS15 ....65 G3
Deanhill La CBATH/BATHN BA1 ..107 F2
Dean La BMSTR BS3 ....78 D2
Dean Rd AVONM BS11.....................22 C5
YATE/CS BS37 ....20 B4
Dean's Dr EVILLE/WHL BS5............63 H1
Deans Md AVONM BS11 ....35 H5
The Deans PTSHD/EG BS20 ....45 E4
Dean St BMSTR BS3.......................78 D2
CBRISNE BS2 ....61 H3
Debecca's La PTSHD/EG BS20 ......48 A4
De Clifford Rd AVONM BS11 ....36 B3
Deep Coombe Rd BMSTR BS3 ......78 B4
Deep Pit Rd EVILLE/WHL BS5........63 G2
Deerhurst KGWD/HNM BS15 ....64 D1
YATE/CS BS37 ....31 G2
Deering Cl AVONM BS11 ....36 A4
Deer Md CLVDN BS21 ....70 B4
Deerswood KGWD/HNM BS15......65 F1
Delabere Av MANG/FISH BS16......54 A3
Delamere Rd TRWBR BA14..........121 E4
Delapre Rd WSM BS23 ....138 D3
De La Warre Ct
BRSG/KWL/STAPK BS4 * 63 G5
Delius Gv BRSG/KWL/STAPK BS4 ..91 E2
The Dell ALMDB BS32 ....27 G3
HNLZ/SM/SNYPK/WT BS9 ....50 C3
MTN/WRL BS22 ....131 F4
NAIL BS48 ....73 E4
OLD/WMLY/WICK BS30..............83 F1
Delvin Rd HNBRY/STHM BS10 ......37 H5
Denbigh St CBRISNE BS2 ....61 H2
Dene Cl KEYN BS31 ....104 A1
Dene Rd HGRV/WHIT BS14 ....92 B5
Denleigh Cl HGRV/WHIT BS14 ......91 H5
Denmark Pl HORF/LLZ BS7............51 H5
Denmark Rd BATHSE BA2................2 A5
Denmark St CBRIS/FH BS1 ....4 D4
Denning Ct MTN/WRL BS22 ....132 A4
Dennisworth MANG/FISH BS16 ....57 E3
Dennor Pk HGRV/WHIT BS14 ....92 A2
Denny Cl PTSHD/EG BS20..............44 D3
Denny Isle Dr THNB/SVB BS35......12 C4
Denny Vw PTSHD/EG BS20 ....44 C3
Dennyview Rd CFTN/FAIL BS8......59 E3
Denston Dr PTSHD/EG BS20 ....45 H4
Denston Wk
BMSTRD/HC/WWD BS13 ....90 B2
Denton Patch MANG/FISH BS16 ..55 G1
Dentwood Gv
HNLZ/SM/SNYPK/WT BS9 ....49 G1
Denys Ct THNB/SVB BS35..............10 A4
Derby Rd HORF/LLZ BS7 ....51 H5
Derby St EVILLE/WHL BS5..............63 E4
Derham Cl YTN/CONG BS49 ....126 B3
Derham Pk YTN/CONG BS49 ......126 C4
Derham Rd
BMSTRD/HC/WWD BS13 ....90 B4
Dermot St CBRISNE BS2 *..............62 B2
Derricke Rd HGRV/WHIT BS14 ......93 E3
Derrick Rd KGWD/HNM BS15........64 C3
Derry Rd BMSTR BS3......................78 C4
Derwent Cl BRSTK/PCHW BS34 ....26 C2
Derwent Gv KEYN BS31 ....94 D4
Derwent Rd EVILLE/WHL BS5 ......63 G2
WSM BS23 ....139 F2
Devaney Cl
BRSG/KWL/STAPK BS4 ....81 E1
Deverell Cl BOAV BA15 ....119 H5
De Verose Ct KGWD/HNM BS15....82 B2
Devon Gv EVILLE/WHL BS5............62 D3
Devon Rd EVILLE/WHL BS5............62 D2
Devonshire Buildings
BATHSE BA2 ....114 C3
Devonshire Dr PTSHD/EG BS20....44 C3
Devonshire Pl BATHSE BA2 ....114 C3
Devonshire Rd BATHSE BA2........109 H3
RDLND/MONT BS6......................51 E4
WSM BS23 ....138 D3
Dewfalls Dr ALMDB BS32 ....27 F1
Dial Hill Rd CLVDN BS21 ....68 B5
Dial La BLAG/CWMG/WR BS40 ......97 E3
MANG/FISH BS16.........................54 C2
Diamond Batch
OMX/HUT/LCK BS24 ....137 E2
Diamond Rd EVILLE/WHL BS5 ......63 G4
Diamond St BMSTR BS3 ....78 D3
Diana Gdns ALMDB BS32 ....27 G3
Dibden Cl MANG/FISH BS16 ....41 H5
Dibden La MANG/FISH BS16..........55 F1
Dibden Rd MANG/FISH BS16 ....41 H5
Dickens Cl HORF/LLZ BS7 ....38 D5
Dickenson Rd WSM BS23 ....6 E7
Dickenson's Gv
YTN/CONG BS49........................129 E3
Didsbury Cl HNBRY/STHM BS10 ..37 E4
Dighton Ga BRSTK/PCHW BS34 ....27 G5
Dighton St CBRISNE BS2..................5 F1
Dingle Cl
HNLZ/SM/SNYPK/WT BS9 ....49 H2
Dingle Rd
HNLZ/SM/SNYPK/WT BS9 ....49 H1
The Dingle FRCTL/WBN BS36 ....41 F2
HNLZ/SM/SNYPK/WT BS9 ....49 H1
YATE/CS BS37 ....21 E3
Dingle Vw
HNLZ/SM/SNYPK/WT BS9 ....49 H1
Dinglewood Cl
HNLZ/SM/SNYPK/WT BS9 ....50 A1
Dings Wk CBRISNE BS2 ....62 B5
Dixon Gdns CBATH/BATHN BA1 ..108 C3
Dixon Rd BRSG/KWL/STAPK BS4 ..81 E4
Dock Gate La CFTN/FAIL BS8 *......78 B1
Dodington La YATE/CS BS37 ....32 D4
Dodington Rd YATE/CS BS37........32 D3
Dodisham Wk MANG/FISH BS16 ..54 A2
Dolemoor La YTN/CONG BS49 ....128 A2
Dolman Cl HNBRY/STHM BS10......36 D2
Dominion Rd BATHSE BA2 ....113 F1
MANG/FISH BS16.........................53 G5
Donald Rd
BMSTRD/HC/WWD BS13 ....90 A2
Doncaster Rd
HNBRY/STHM BS10.....................37 G4
Donegal Rd
BRSG/KWL/STAPK BS4 ....79 E5
Dongola Av HORF/LLZ BS7............51 H4
Dongola Rd HORF/LLZ BS7............51 H4
Doone Rd HORF/LLZ BS7 ....38 C5
Dorcas Av BRSTK/PCHW BS34 ......27 H5
Dorchester Cl NAIL BS48.................85 E1
Dorchester Rd HORF/LLZ BS7 ......52 B1
Dorchester St CBATH/BATHN BA1..3 G6
Dorester Cl HNBRY/STHM BS10....37 H1
Dorian Cl HORF/LLZ BS7 ....51 H1
Dorian Rd HORF/LLZ BS7 ....51 H1
Dorian Wy HNBRY/STHM BS10 ....38 B5
Dormer Cl FRCTL/WBN BS36 ....30 B4
Dormer Rd EVILLE/WHL BS5 ....52 B5
Dorset Cl BATHSE BA2......................2 B5
Dorset Gv CBRISNE BS2 ....62 B1
Dorset Rd
HNLZ/SM/SNYPK/WT BS9 ....51 E2
KGWD/HNM BS15 ....64 C2
Dorset St BATHSE BA2 ....2 A5
BMSTR BS3..................................78 C3
Dorset Wy YATE/CS BS37 ....21 F4
Douglas Rd HORF/LLZ BS7 ....52 A1
KGWD/HNM BS15 ....64 C4
WSM BS23 ....139 E1
Doulton Wy HGRV/WHIT BS14......91 H4
Dovecote YATE/CS BS37.................32 A3
Dovecote Cl TRWBR BA14 ....122 B1
Dovedale THNB/SVB BS35 ....9 E5
Dove La CBRISNE BS2 ....62 A3
Dovercourt Rd HORF/LLZ BS7 ......52 B3
Dover Pl CBATH/BATHN BA1 * 108 D3
CFTN/FAIL BS8 ....4 A3
Dovers La CBATH/BATHN BA1 ....110 D2
Dovers Pk CBATH/BATHN BA1 ....110 D2
Dove St CBRISNE BS2 ....61 G3
Dove St South CBRISNE BS2 ....5 F1
Dovey Ct
OLD/WMLY/WICK BS30..............83 F1
Dowdeswell Cl
HNBRY/STHM BS10.....................37 E2
Dowding Cl YATE/CS BS37 ....21 H5
Dowding Rd
CBATH/BATHN BA1 ....109 E3
Dowland Gv
BRSG/KWL/STAPK BS4 ....91 E3
Dowling Rd
BMSTRD/HC/WWD BS13 ....100 A1
Down Av BATHSE BA2..................117 E1
Downavon BOAV BA15................119 G4
Down Cl PTSHD/EG BS20 ....44 C3
Downend Pk HORF/LLZ BS7..........52 A3
Downend Park Rd
MANG/FISH BS16.........................54 C3
Downend Rd HORF/LLZ BS7 ....52 A3
KGWD/HNM BS15 ....64 C2
MANG/FISH BS16.........................54 C3
Downfield KEYN BS31 * 94 A4
Downfield Cl THNB/SVB BS35 ......11 F2
Downfield Dr FRCTL/WBN BS36 ..29 H2
Downfield Rd CFTN/FAIL BS8........60 D2
Downhayes Rd TRWBR BA14......121 E4
Down La BATHSE BA2 ....110 A3
Downleaze
HNLZ/SM/SNYPK/WT BS9 ....50 C5
MANG/FISH BS16.........................41 E5
PTSHD/EG BS20...........................44 D3
Down Leaze THNB/SVB BS35........11 G2
Downman Rd HORF/LLZ BS7 ....52 B3
Down Rd FRCTL/WBN BS36 ....41 F1
PTSHD/EG BS20...........................44 B5
THNB/SVB BS35...........................11 G2
Downs Cl BOAV BA15 ....119 E2
MTN/WRL BS22 ....136 C2
Downs Cote Av
HNLZ/SM/SNYPK/WT BS9 ....50 C2
Downs Cote Dr
HNLZ/SM/SNYPK/WT BS9 ....50 C2
Downs Cote Gdns
HNLZ/SM/SNYPK/WT BS9 ....50 C2
Downs Cote Pk
HNLZ/SM/SNYPK/WT BS9 ....50 D2
Downs Cote Vw
HNLZ/SM/SNYPK/WT BS9 ....50 D2
Downside PTSHD/EG BS20............45 F3
Downside Close
OLD/WMLY/WICK BS30..............82 C1
Downside Cl BATHSE BA2............110 A3
Downside Pk NAIL BS48 *..............96 A3
TRWBR BA14 ....121 F4
Downside Rd
CFTN/FAIL BS8 ....60 D2
NAIL BS48 ....96 A4
WSM BS23 ....139 E2
Downs Pk East
HNLZ/SM/SNYPK/WT BS9 ....50 D3
Downs Pk West
HNLZ/SM/SNYPK/WT BS9 ....50 D3
Downs Rd
HNLZ/SM/SNYPK/WT BS9 ....50 D2
LGASH BS41 ....98 C2
The Downs PTSHD/EG BS20..........44 D4
Downs Vw BOAV BA15 ....119 E2
The Down ALMDB BS32 ....10 D4
THNB/SVB BS35...........................11 F2
TRWBR BA14 ....121 F4
Downton Rd
BRSG/KWL/STAPK BS4 ....79 E5
Dowry Pl CFTN/FAIL BS8................78 A1
Dowry Rd CFTN/FAIL BS8 ....60 D5
Dowry Sq CFTN/FAIL BS8 ....60 C5
Dragon Ct EVILLE/WHL BS5 *........63 F2
Dragon Rd FRCTL/WBN BS36........28 D5
Dragons Hill Cl KEYN BS31 ....94 C4
Dragons Hill Ct KEYN BS31............94 C4
Dragons Hill Gdns KEYN BS31 ......94 C4
Dragonswell Rd
HNBRY/STHM BS10.....................37 F3
Dragon Wk EVILLE/WHL BS5 ....63 G2
Drake Av BATHSE BA2..................114 C5
Drake Cl KEYN BS31.....................105 E2
MTN/WRL BS22 ....131 G4
Drake Rd BMSTR BS3 ....78 B3
Drakes Wy PTSHD/EG BS20 ....44 D3
Draycot Pl CBRIS/FH BS1 ....4 E7
Draycott Rd HORF/LLZ BS7 ....52 A3
Draydon Rd
BRSG/KWL/STAPK BS4 ....90 D2
Drayton Cl HGRV/WHIT BS14 ....92 A1
Drayton Rd
HNLZ/SM/SNYPK/WT BS9 ....36 B5
The Dring RDSTK/MIDN BA3 ......125 F2
The Drive HGRV/WHIT BS14 ....92 B4
HNLZ/SM/SNYPK/WT BS9 ....51 E3
WSM BS23 ....7 H2
Drove Rd WSM BS23 ....7 G5
Druetts Cl HNBRY/STHM BS10......51 H2
Druid Cl
HNLZ/SM/SNYPK/WT BS9 ....50 B3
Druid Hl
HNLZ/SM/SNYPK/WT BS9 ....50 B3
Druid Rd
HNLZ/SM/SNYPK/WT BS9 ....50 A4
Druid Stoke Av
HNLZ/SM/SNYPK/WT BS9 ....49 H3
Druid Woods
HNLZ/SM/SNYPK/WT BS9 ....49 H3
Drummond Ct
OLD/WMLY/WICK BS30..............82 C2
Drummond Rd CBRISNE BS2 ....61 H2
MANG/FISH BS16.........................53 G5
Dr Whites Cl CBRIS/FH BS1 ....5 G7
Dryleaze KEYN BS31 ....94 B2
YATE/CS BS37 ....20 D2
Dryleaze Rd MANG/FISH BS16......53 G2
Drynham La TRWBR BA14 ....123 E5
Drynham Pk TRWBR BA14 ....123 E3
Drynham Rd TRWBR BA14..........123 E3
Drysdale Cl MTN/WRL BS22 ....135 H2
Dubbers La EVILLE/WHL BS5 ....63 F1
Dublin Crs
HNLZ/SM/SNYPK/WT BS9 ....51 E2
Duchess Rd CFTN/FAIL BS8 ....60 D2
Duchess Wy MANG/FISH BS16......53 E3
Ducie Rd EVILLE/WHL BS5 ....62 C4
MANG/FISH BS16.........................54 D4
Duckmoor Rd BMSTR BS3 ....78 B3
Dudley Cl KEYN BS31.....................94 B5
Dudley Ct
OLD/WMLY/WICK BS30..............82 C2
Dudley Gv HORF/LLZ BS7 ....38 C5
Dugar Wk RDLND/MONT BS6........51 F5
Duke St BATHSE BA2 ....3 H5
TRWBR BA14 ....121 E5
Dulverton Rd HORF/LLZ BS7 ....51 G4
Dumaine Av BRSTK/PCHW BS34 ..27 G5
Dumfries Pl WSM BS23................138 D1
Duncan Gdns
CBATH/BATHN BA1 ....107 F1
Duncombe La KGWD/HNM BS15..63 H1
Duncombe Rd KGWD/HNM BS15 64 A2
Dundas Cl HNBRY/STHM BS10......36 D3
Dundonald Rd
RDLND/MONT BS6.......................51 E5
Dundridge Gdns
EVILLE/WHL BS5 ....63 H5
Dundridge La EVILLE/WHL BS5 ....63 H5
Dundry Cl KGWD/HNM BS15 ....64 C5
Dundry La
BLAG/CWMG/WR BS40 ....97 H5
LGASH BS41 ....89 E5
Dundry Vw
BRSG/KWL/STAPK BS4 ....79 H5
Dunedin Wy MTN/WRL BS22 ......132 B4
Dunford Cl TRWBR BA14 ....123 E3
Dunford Rd BMSTR BS3 ....79 E3
Dunkeld Av BRSTK/PCHW BS34....38 C3
Dunkerry Rd BMSTR BS3 ....79 E3
Dunkery Cl NAIL BS48 ....73 F5
Dunkery Rd WSM BS23....................7 H2
Dunkirk Rd MANG/FISH BS16........53 G5
Dunmail Rd HNBRY/STHM BS10 ..37 H3
Dunmore St BMSTR BS3 * 79 G2
Dunsford Pl BATHSE BA2 ....3 K4
Dunster Crs
OMX/HUT/LCK BS24 ....139 F4
Dunster Gdns
OLD/WMLY/WICK BS30..............83 E4
Dunster Rd
BRSG/KWL/STAPK BS4 ....91 G1
KEYN BS31 ....94 B5
Dunsters Rd YTN/CONG BS49 ....127 F2
Durban Rd BRSTK/PCHW BS34 ....26 B2
Durban Wy YTN/CONG BS49 ......126 B2
Durbin Park Rd CLVDN BS21 ....68 A5
Durbin Wk EVILLE/WHL BS5..........62 B3
Durdham Pk
RDLND/MONT BS6.......................50 D5
Durham Gv KEYN BS31 ....94 A5
Durham Rd CBRISNE BS2 ....62 B1
Durleigh Cl
BMSTRD/HC/WWD BS13 ....90 B3
Durley Hl KEYN BS31......................93 H2
Durley La KEYN BS31......................94 A2
Durley Pk BATHSE BA2 ....114 B3
Durnford Av BMSTR BS3 ....78 B2
Durnford St BMSTR BS3................78 B2
Dursley Cl YATE/CS BS37 ....32 A1
Dursley Rd AVONM BS11 ....48 D3
TRWBR BA14 ....123 E2

Durville Rd BMSTRD/HC/WWD BS13 90 C3
Durweston Wk HGRV/WHIT BS14 92 B1
Dutton Cl HGRV/WHIT BS14 92 C3
Dutton Rd HGRV/WHIT BS14 92 C4
Dutton Wk HGRV/WHIT BS14 92 C3
Dyers Cl BMSTRD/HC/WWD BS13 91 E5
Dyer's La YATE/CS BS37 19 H1
Dylan Thomas Ct OLD/WMLY/WICK BS30 * 82 D1
Dymboro Av RDSTK/MIDN BA3 124 A3
Dymboro Cl RDSTK/MIDN BA3 124 A3
Dymboro Gdns RDSTK/MIDN BA3 124 A3
The Dymboro RDSTK/MIDN BA3 124 A3
Dymott Sq TRWBR BA14 121 H3
Dyrham Cl HNLZ/SM/SNYPK/WT BS9 51 G2
KGWD/HNM BS15 65 E3
MANG/FISH BS16 57 F4
THNB/SVB BS35 8 D1
Dyrham Pde BRSTK/PCHW BS34 27 E2
Dyrham Rd KGWD/HNM BS15 65 E3
Dyson Cl YTN/CONG BS49 126 B3

E

Eagle Cl MTN/WRL BS22 136 A3
Eagle Crs MANG/FISH BS16 57 F4
Eagle Dr BRSTK/PCHW BS34 26 A2
Eagle Pk CBATH/BATHN BA1 103 E4
Eagle Rd BRSG/KWL/STAPK BS4 80 C4
CBATH/BATHN BA1 103 E4
The Eagles YTN/CONG BS49 126 B3
Eagles Wd ALMDB BS32 16 B4
Earlesfield NAIL BS48 72 D5
Earl Russell Wy EVILLE/WHL BS5 62 C4
Earlsmead MANG/FISH BS16 53 E4
Earlstone Cl OLD/WMLY/WICK BS30 82 D2
Earlstone Crs OLD/WMLY/WICK BS30 82 D2
Earl St CBRIS/FH BS1 5 F1
Early Wy HNBRY/STHM BS10 38 B5
Easedale Cl HNBRY/STHM BS10 38 A3
Eastbourne Av CBATH/BATHN BA1 * 109 E3
Eastbourne Rd EVILLE/WHL BS5 62 C3
TRWBR BA14 121 F5
Eastbury Cl THNB/SVB BS35 8 D3
Eastbury Rd MANG/FISH BS16 53 H4
East Cl BATHSE BA2 113 F2
Eastcombe Gdns WSM BS23 7 H1
Eastcombe Rd WSM BS23 135 E2
Eastcote Pk HGRV/WHIT BS14 92 A4
East Cft HNLZ/SM/SNYPK/WT BS9 51 F1
East Dundry La LGASH BS41 99 E2
East Dundry Rd H
GRV/WHIT BS14 100 C2
Eastfield HNLZ/SM/SNYPK/WT BS9 51 E1
Eastfield Av CBATH/BATHN BA1 107 G2
Eastfield Dr YATE/CS BS37 20 D3
Eastfield Gdns WSM BS23 7 G1
Eastfield Pk WSM BS23 7 F1
Eastfield Rd HNLZ/SM/SNYPK/WT BS9 50 D1
OMX/HUT/LCK BS24 140 B4
RDLND/MONT BS6 61 G1
Eastfield Ter HNLZ/SM/SNYPK/WT BS9 51 E2
Eastgate Rd EVILLE/WHL BS5 52 C5
East Gv RDLND/MONT BS6 62 A2
East Hill Eastfield Rd HNLZ/SM/SNYPK/WT BS9 * 50 D1
Eastlake Cl HORF/LLZ BS7 52 C1
Eastland Av THNB/SVB BS35 8 D2
Eastland Rd THNB/SVB BS35 8 D2
Eastlea CLVDN BS21 70 B4
East Lea Rd CBATH/BATHN BA1 107 F4
Eastleigh Cl MANG/FISH BS16 54 D4
Eastleigh Rd HNBRY/STHM BS10 38 A4
MANG/FISH BS16 54 D4
Eastlyn Rd BMSTRD/HC/WWD BS13 90 C1
East Md RDSTK/MIDN BA3 124 C2
Eastmead La HNLZ/SM/SNYPK/WT BS9 50 B4
Eastnor Rd HGRV/WHIT BS14 100 D1
Easton Hill Rd THNB/SVB BS35 9 E2
Easton Rd CBRISNE BS2 62 B4
PTSHD/EG BS20 48 B4
Easton Wy EVILLE/WHL BS5 62 B2
Eastover Cl HNLZ/SM/SNYPK/WT BS9 37 F5
Eastover Gv BATHSE BA2 116 A1
East Pde HNLZ/SM/SNYPK/WT BS9 49 H2
East Pk EVILLE/WHL BS5 62 D1
East Park Dr EVILLE/WHL BS5 62 D1
East Priory Cl HNLZ/SM/SNYPK/WT BS9 50 D1
East Ridge Dr BMSTRD/HC/WWD BS13 90 A4
East Shrubbery RDLND/MONT BS6 61 E1
East St AVONM BS11 34 B4
BMSTR BS3 78 D2
CBRISNE BS2 5 J1
East Vw MANG/FISH BS16 55 E2
Eastview Rd TRWBR BA14 122 B2
Eastville CBATH/BATHN BA1 109 E3
East Wy BATHSE BA2 113 F2
Eastway NAIL BS48 73 E3
Eastway Cl NAIL BS48 73 E3
Eastway Sq NAIL BS48 73 F3
Eastwood Crs BRSG/KWL/STAPK BS4 81 E2
East Wood Pl PTSHD/EG BS20 45 G1
Eastwood Rd BRSG/KWL/STAPK BS4 81 E2
Eastwoods CBATH/BATHN BA1 * 110 C1
Eaton Cl HGRV/WHIT BS14 92 D4
MANG/FISH BS16 54 A4
Eaton Crs CFTN/FAIL BS8 60 D3
Eaton St BMSTR BS3 78 D3
Ebdon Rd MTN/WRL BS22 131 G3
Ebenezer La HNLZ/SM/SNYPK/WT BS9 50 B2
Ebenezer St EVILLE/WHL BS5 63 E4
Eden Gv HORF/LLZ BS7 38 D4
Eden Park Cl CBATH/BATHN BA1 103 F5
Eden Park Dr CBATH/BATHN BA1 103 F5
Eden Ter CBATH/BATHN BA1 * 109 E2
Eden Vls CBATH/BATHN BA1 * 109 F2
Edgar Buildings CBATH/BATHN BA1 * 3 F3
Edgecombe Av MTN/WRL BS22 136 A1
Edgecumbe Rd RDLND/MONT BS6 61 G1
Edgefield Cl HGRV/WHIT BS14 100 C1
Edgefield Rd HGRV/WHIT BS14 100 C1
Edgehill Rd CLVDN BS21 68 B4
Edgeware Rd BMSTR BS3 78 D2
MANG/FISH BS16 54 B4
Edgewood Cl HGRV/WHIT BS14 92 A1
OLD/WMLY/WICK BS30 82 D3
Edgeworth YATE/CS BS37 31 G4
Edgeworth Rd BATHSE BA2 113 H5
Edinburgh Pl WSM BS23 6 D2
Edinburgh Rd KEYN BS31 94 B5
Edington Gv HNBRY/STHM BS10 37 F3
Edmund Cl MANG/FISH BS16 54 C2
Edmund Ct MANG/FISH BS16 57 E2
Edna Av BRSG/KWL/STAPK BS4 80 D3
Edward Rd BRSG/KWL/STAPK BS4 80 A2
CLVDN BS21 68 C5
KGWD/HNM BS15 64 D3
Edward Rd South CLVDN BS21 68 C5
Edward Rd West CLVDN BS21 68 C4
Edward St BATHSE BA2 3 J3
CBATH/BATHN BA1 107 H5
EVILLE/WHL BS5 62 D3
Edwin Short Cl OLD/WMLY/WICK BS30 95 H1
Effingham Rd RDLND/MONT BS6 61 H1
Egerton Brow HORF/LLZ BS7 51 G4
Egerton Rd BATHSE BA2 114 B3
HORF/LLZ BS7 51 G5
Eggshill La YATE/CS BS37 31 H1
Eighth Av HORF/LLZ BS7 39 E5
Eirene Ter PTSHD/EG BS20 48 C4
Elberton KGWD/HNM BS15 65 F3
Elberton Rd HNLZ/SM/SNYPK/WT BS9 49 G1
THNB/SVB BS35 10 A4
Elborough Av YTN/CONG BS49 126 B3
Elborough Gdns OMX/HUT/LCK BS24 141 F3
Elbury Av KGWD/HNM BS15 64 B1
Elcombe Cl TRWBR BA14 122 D4
Elderberry Wk HNBRY/STHM BS10 37 H3
Elderwood Dr OLD/WMLY/WICK BS30 82 D3
Elderwood Rd HGRV/WHIT BS14 92 A2
Eldon Pl CBATH/BATHN BA1 109 E2
Eldon Ter BMSTR BS3 79 E3
Eldon Wy BRSG/KWL/STAPK BS4 80 B1
Eldred Cl HNLZ/SM/SNYPK/WT BS9 49 H3
Eleanor Cl BATHSE BA2 113 F2
Eleventh Av HORF/LLZ BS7 39 E4
Elfin Rd MANG/FISH BS16 53 H3
Elgar Cl BRSG/KWL/STAPK BS4 91 E3
CLVDN BS21 71 E4
Elgin Av HORF/LLZ BS7 38 C4
Elgin Pk RDLND/MONT BS6 61 E1
Elgin Rd MANG/FISH BS16 64 A1
Eliot Cl HORF/LLZ BS7 38 D5
WSM BS23 139 F3
Elizabeth Cl OMX/HUT/LCK BS24 140 A3
THNB/SVB BS35 9 E4
Elizabeth Crs BRSTK/PCHW BS34 39 H1
Elizabeths Ms BRSG/KWL/STAPK BS4 63 G5
Elizabeth Wy MANG/FISH BS16 55 G5
Ellacombe Rd OLD/WMLY/WICK BS30 82 B4
Ellan Hay Rd ALMDB BS32 28 A4
Ellbridge Cl HNLZ/SM/SNYPK/WT BS9 50 A3
Ellenborough Crs WSM BS23 6 E7
Ellenborough Gdns WSM BS23 * 6 E7
Ellenborough Pk North WSM BS23 6 D6
Ellenborough Park Rd WSM BS23 6 E6
Ellenborough Pk South WSM BS23 6 D6
Ellesmere THNB/SVB BS35 8 D4
Ellesmere Rd BRSG/KWL/STAPK BS4 80 C5
KGWD/HNM BS15 64 B2
WSM BS23 138 C4
Ellfield Cl BMSTRD/HC/WWD BS13 90 A3
Ellicks Cl ALMDB BS32 16 C5
Ellicott Rd HORF/LLZ BS7 52 A2
Ellinghurst Cl HNBRY/STHM BS10 37 F3
Elliott Av MANG/FISH BS16 40 D4
Elliott Pl TRWBR BA14 120 B5
Ellis Av BMSTRD/HC/WWD BS13 90 B1
Ellis Pk MTN/WRL BS22 132 B5
Elliston Dr BATHSE BA2 113 G3
Elliston La RDLND/MONT BS6 61 F1
Elliston Rd RDLND/MONT BS6 61 F1
Ellsbridge Cl KEYN BS31 95 E4
Ellsworth Rd HNBRY/STHM BS10 37 E3
Elm Cl AVONM BS11 35 G4
BNWL BS29 141 H2
BRSTK/PCHW BS34 27 F3
NAIL BS48 72 D5
YATE/CS BS37 32 C1
YTN/CONG BS49 126 B4
Elmcroft Crs HORF/LLZ BS7 52 B4
Elmdale Crs THNB/SVB BS35 8 D3
Elmdale Gdns MANG/FISH BS16 * 53 H4
Elmdale Rd BMSTR BS3 78 C4
CFTN/FAIL BS8 4 B2
TRWBR BA14 122 B2
Elmfield BOAV BA15 119 F2
KGWD/HNM BS15 64 D5
Elmfield Cl KGWD/HNM BS15 64 D5
Elmfield Rd HNLZ/SM/SNYPK/WT BS9 37 F5
Elm Gv BATHSE BA2 113 H3
CBATH/BATHN BA1 109 F2
OMX/HUT/LCK BS24 140 C2
Elmgrove Av EVILLE/WHL BS5 62 C3
Elmgrove Dr YATE/CS BS37 21 E5
Elmgrove Pk RDLND/MONT BS6 61 G2
Elmgrove Rd MANG/FISH BS16 53 F5
RDLND/MONT BS6 61 G2
Elmham Wy OMX/HUT/LCK BS24 137 E2
Elm Hayes BMSTRD/HC/WWD BS13 90 A3
Elmhirst Gdns YATE/CS BS37 21 F5
Elmhurst Av EVILLE/WHL BS5 53 E5
Elmhurst Rd OMX/HUT/LCK BS24 140 B4
Elmhyrst Rd WSM BS23 7 H3
Elming Down Cl BRSTK/PCHW BS34 27 F4
Elm La RDLND/MONT BS6 61 E1
Elmlea Av HNLZ/SM/SNYPK/WT BS9 50 C3
Elmleigh Av MANG/FISH BS16 55 G3
Elmleigh Cl MANG/FISH BS16 55 F3
Elmleigh Rd MANG/FISH BS16 55 F3
Elm Lodge Rd NAIL BS48 73 H3
Elmore KGWD/HNM BS15 55 E5
YATE/CS BS37 31 H2
Elmore Rd BRSTK/PCHW BS34 26 B1
HORF/LLZ BS7 52 B2
Elm Pk BRSTK/PCHW BS34 38 D3
Elm Rd HORF/LLZ BS7 51 H3
KGWD/HNM BS15 64 D5
Elms Cross Dr BOAV BA15 119 F4
Elms Gv BRSTK/PCHW BS34 26 D1
Elmsleigh Rd WSM BS23 138 C2
Elmsley La MTN/WRL BS22 130 D3
The Elms BOAV BA15 119 F1
Elm Tree Av MANG/FISH BS16 55 F1
RDSTK/MIDN BA3 125 E3
Elmtree Cl KGWD/HNM BS15 64 C2
Elmtree Dr BMSTRD/HC/WWD BS13 90 A4
Elm Tree Pk PTSHD/EG BS20 * 47 E4
Elm Tree Rd CLVDN BS21 70 D3
OMX/HUT/LCK BS24 140 C2
Elmvale Dr OMX/HUT/LCK BS24 140 C4
Elm Vw RDSTK/MIDN BA3 124 C2
Elm Wk PTSHD/EG BS20 45 F4
YTN/CONG BS49 126 B4
Elm Wd YATE/CS BS37 32 A2
Elsbert Dr BMSTRD/HC/WWD BS13 89 H3
Elstree Rd EVILLE/WHL BS5 63 F2
Elton La HORF/LLZ BS7 61 G1
Elton Rd CFTN/FAIL BS8 4 B2
CLVDN BS21 70 C2
HORF/LLZ BS7 51 G5
KGWD/HNM BS15 64 A2
MTN/WRL BS22 131 H4
Elton St CBRISNE BS2 5 K1
Elvard Cl BMSTRD/HC/WWD BS13 90 B5
Elvard Rd BMSTRD/HC/WWD BS13 90 B4
Elvaston Rd BMSTR BS3 79 F3
Elwell La LGASH BS41 97 H3
Ely Gv HNLZ/SM/SNYPK/WT BS9 49 G1
Embassy Rd EVILLE/WHL BS5 63 F2
Embassy Wk EVILLE/WHL BS5 63 F2
Embercourt Dr NAIL BS48 85 H3
Embleton Rd HNBRY/STHM BS10 37 G3
Emersons Green La MANG/FISH BS16 55 G2
Emerson Sq HORF/LLZ BS7 38 D5
Emersons Wy MANG/FISH BS16 55 H1
Emery Rd BRSG/KWL/STAPK BS4 81 E5
Emet Gv MANG/FISH BS16 55 G2
Emet La MANG/FISH BS16 55 G2
Emily Pl CFTN/FAIL BS8 * 60 C4
Emlyn Rd EVILLE/WHL BS5 62 D1
Emma-Chris Wy BRSTK/PCHW BS34 39 F3
Emmett Wd HGRV/WHIT BS14 101 E1
Emra Cl EVILLE/WHL BS5 63 G2
Enfield Rd MANG/FISH BS16 53 H5
Engine Common La YATE/CS BS37 20 B1
Engine La NAIL BS48 84 C1
England's Crs FRCTL/WBN BS36 29 E3
Englishcombe La BATHSE BA2 113 H4
Englishcombe Pk BATHSE BA2 * 113 H3
Englishcombe Rd BMSTRD/HC/WWD BS13 99 H1
Englishcombe Wy BATHSE BA2 114 A4
Ennerdale Cl WSM BS23 139 F1
Ennerdale Rd HNBRY/STHM BS10 38 A3
Entry Hl BATHSE BA2 114 C4
Entry Hill Dr BATHSE BA2 114 C5
Entry Hill Gdns BATHSE BA2 114 C4
Entry Hill Pk BATHSE BA2 114 C5
Entry Ri BATHSE BA2 116 D1
Epney Cl BRSTK/PCHW BS34 26 B1
Epsom Cl MANG/FISH BS16 41 G4
Epsom Rd TRWBR BA14 123 F5
Epworth Rd HNBRY/STHM BS10 37 F3
Erin Wk BRSG/KWL/STAPK BS4 91 E1
Ermine Wy AVONM BS11 48 B1
Ermleet Rd RDLND/MONT BS6 61 F1
Ernest Barker Cl EVILLE/WHL BS5 * 62 C4
Ernestville Rd MANG/FISH BS16 53 G5
Ervine Ter CBRISNE BS2 62 A3
Esgar Ri MTN/WRL BS22 131 F5
Eskdale THNB/SVB BS35 9 E5
Eskdale Cl MTN/WRL BS22 136 A3
Esmond Gv CLVDN BS21 70 D1
Esplanade Rd PTSHD/EG BS20 45 F1
Essery Rd EVILLE/WHL BS5 62 D1
Esson Rd KGWD/HNM BS15 64 A2
Estcourt Gdns MANG/FISH BS16 53 E3
Estelle Pk EVILLE/WHL BS5 * 62 D1
Estoril YATE/CS BS37 32 B1
Estune Wk LGASH BS41 76 D5
Etloe Rd RDLND/MONT BS6 50 D4
Eton La BNWL BS29 137 G4
Eton Rd BRSG/KWL/STAPK BS4 80 C3
Ettlingen Wy CLVDN BS21 71 E3
Ettricke Dr MANG/FISH BS16 54 A2
Eugene St CBRISNE BS2 5 F1
EVILLE/WHL BS5 5 K1
Evans Cl BRSG/KWL/STAPK BS4 81 E1
Evans Rd RDLND/MONT BS6 61 E1
Evelyn Rd CBATH/BATHN BA1 107 G4
HNBRY/STHM BS10 37 H5
Evelyn Ter CBATH/BATHN BA1 * 108 D3
Evenlode Gdns AVONM BS11 49 E3
Evenlode Wy KEYN BS31 104 B1
Evercreech Rd HGRV/WHIT BS14 91 H5
Everest Av MANG/FISH BS16 53 F4
Everest Rd MANG/FISH BS16 53 F4
Everleigh Cl TRWBR BA14 123 E4
Eve Rd EVILLE/WHL BS5 62 C2
Ewart Rd MTN/WRL BS22 135 H3
Ewell Rd HGRV/WHIT BS14 92 A3
Excelsior St BATHSE BA2 3 H6
Excelsior Ter RDSTK/MIDN BA3 124 C3
Exeter Buildings RDLND/MONT BS6 61 E1
Exeter Rd BMSTR BS3 78 C2
PTSHD/EG BS20 45 H4
WSM BS23 138 D1
Exford Cl WSM BS23 139 E4
Exley Cl OLD/WMLY/WICK BS30 83 F1
Exmoor Rd BATHSE BA2 114 C5
Exmoor St BMSTR BS3 78 C2
Exmouth Rd BRSG/KWL/STAPK BS4 79 G5
Exton Cl HGRV/WHIT BS14 92 A4
Eyer's La CBRISNE BS2 5 J2

F

Faber Gv BMSTRD/HC/WWD BS13 90 D5
Fabian Dr BRSTK/PCHW BS34 27 G5
Factory Rd FRCTL/WBN BS36 29 F3
Failand Crs HNLZ/SM/SNYPK/WT BS9 49 H3
Failand Wk HNLZ/SM/SNYPK/WT BS9 49 H2
Fairacre Cl HORF/LLZ BS7 52 C3
OMX/HUT/LCK BS24 141 E2
Fairacres Cl KEYN BS31 94 B5
Fairfax St CBRIS/FH BS1 5 G3
Fairfield Av CBATH/BATHN BA1 108 D2
Fairfield Cl MTN/WRL BS22 135 G2
NAIL BS48 86 C2
Fairfield Md NAIL BS48 86 B2
Fairfield Pk CBATH/BATHN BA1 * 108 D2
Fairfield Park Rd CBATH/BATHN BA1 108 D2
Fairfield Pl BMSTR BS3 78 C2
Fairfield Rd BMSTR BS3 78 D2
CBATH/BATHN BA1 108 D3
RDLND/MONT BS6 62 A1
Fairfield Ter CBATH/BATHN BA1 * 108 D2
Fairfield Vw CBATH/BATHN BA1 * 108 D2
Fairfield Wy NAIL BS48 86 B3
Fairfoot Rd BRSG/KWL/STAPK BS4 79 H3
Fairford Cl KGWD/HNM BS15 65 E1
Fairford Crs BRSTK/PCHW BS34 26 D2
Fairford Rd AVONM BS11 48 B1
Fair Furlong BMSTRD/HC/WWD BS13 90 B5
Fairhaven YATE/CS BS37 32 B1
Fairhaven Rd RDLND/MONT BS6 51 F4
Fair Lawn OLD/WMLY/WICK BS30 82 D2
Fairlawn Rd RDLND/MONT BS6 62 A1
Fairlyn Dr KGWD/HNM BS15 55 E5
Fairoaks OLD/WMLY/WICK BS30 82 D3
Fairview MTN/WRL BS22 131 G4
Fair View Dr RDLND/MONT BS6 61 F1
Fairview Rd KGWD/HNM BS15 65 E3
Fairway BRSG/KWL/STAPK BS4 80 C5
Fairway Cl MTN/WRL BS22 135 G1
OLD/WMLY/WICK BS30 83 E2
Fairways KEYN BS31 105 F2
Fairwood Cl TRWBR BA14 121 H4
Falcon Cl BRSTK/PCHW BS34 26 A2
HNLZ/SM/SNYPK/WT BS9 37 E5
PTSHD/EG BS20 45 G4
Falcon Crs MTN/WRL BS22 136 B3
Falcondale Rd HNLZ/SM/SNYPK/WT BS9 37 E5
Falcondale Wk HNLZ/SM/SNYPK/WT BS9 37 F5
Falcon Dr BRSTK/PCHW BS34 26 A2
Falconer Rd CBATH/BATHN BA1 107 F1
Falcon Wk BRSTK/PCHW BS34 26 A2
Falcon Wy THNB/SVB BS35 9 E2
Falfield Rd BRSG/KWL/STAPK BS4 80 B3
Falfield Wk HNBRY/STHM BS10 37 H5
Falkland Rd RDLND/MONT BS6 62 A1
Fallodon Ct HNLZ/SM/SNYPK/WT BS9 51 E3
Fallodon Wy HNLZ/SM/SNYPK/WT BS9 51 E3
Fallowfield MTN/WRL BS22 131 G4
OLD/WMLY/WICK BS30 83 F2
Falmouth Cl NAIL BS48 73 H5
Falmouth Rd HORF/LLZ BS7 51 G4
Fane Cl HNBRY/STHM BS10 37 F3
Fanshawe Rd HGRV/WHIT BS14 91 H2
Farendell Rd MANG/FISH BS16 42 A4
Far Handstones OLD/WMLY/WICK BS30 82 D2
Farington Rd HNLZ/SM/SNYPK/WT BS9 51 G1
Farlands MANG/FISH BS16 57 E2
Farleigh Av TRWBR BA14 122 B2
Farleigh Ri CBATH/BATHN BA1 111 E2
Farleigh Rd CLVDN BS21 70 A4
KEYN BS31 94 A5
NAIL BS48 86 B3
Farleigh Wk BMSTRD/HC/WWD BS13 90 B1
Farier's End NAIL BS48 85 G1
Farley Cl BRSTK/PCHW BS34 27 E3
Farm Cl MANG/FISH BS16 55 G2
TRWBR BA14 * 120 C5
Farm Ct MANG/FISH BS16 54 D1
Farmer Rd BMSTRD/HC/WWD BS13 89 H5
Farmhouse Cl NAIL BS48 73 F4
Farmhouse Ct NAIL BS48 * 73 F5
Farm Rd MANG/FISH BS16 54 D1
MTN/WRL BS22 135 G2
OMX/HUT/LCK BS24 140 B4
Farmwell Cl BMSTRD/HC/WWD BS13 90 C4
Farnaby Cl BRSG/KWL/STAPK BS4 90 D2
Farnborough Rd OMX/HUT/LCK BS24 141 F1
Farndale EVILLE/WHL BS5 63 H5
Farndale Rd MTN/WRL BS22 136 A3
Farne Cl HNLZ/SM/SNYPK/WT BS9 51 E3
Farrant Cl BRSG/KWL/STAPK BS4 91 E3
Farrs La BATHSE BA2 115 E5
CBRIS/FH BS1 4 E6
Farr St AVONM BS11 34 C5
Faulkland Rd BATHSE BA2 2 A7
Faverole Wy TRWBR BA14 121 G5
Faversham Dr OMX/HUT/LCK BS24 139 F5
Fawkes Cl KGWD/HNM BS15 65 G3
Featherstone Rd MANG/FISH BS16 53 F4
Feeder Rd CBRISNE BS2 79 H1
Felix Rd EVILLE/WHL BS5 62 C3
Felstead Rd HNBRY/STHM BS10 38 B4
Feltham Rd MANG/FISH BS16 57 F3
Felton Gv BMSTRD/HC/WWD BS13 90 A1
Felton La BLAG/CWMG/WR BS40 97 E5
Felton St BLAG/CWMG/WR BS40 96 D5
Fennel Dr ALMDB BS32 28 A3
Fennell Gv HNBRY/STHM BS10 37 F3
Fenners MTN/WRL BS22 132 A4
Fenshurst Gdns LGASH BS41 88 C1
Fenswood Md LGASH BS41 76 B5
Fenswood Rd LGASH BS41 76 B5
Fenton Cl KEYN BS31 105 E1
Fenton Rd HORF/LLZ BS7 51 G4
Fermaine Av BRSG/KWL/STAPK BS4 81 E3
Fernbank Rd RDLND/MONT BS6 61 F1
Fernbrook Cl MANG/FISH BS16 40 C4
Fern Cl HNBRY/STHM BS10 37 G2
RDSTK/MIDN BA3 124 C4
Ferndale Av OLD/WMLY/WICK BS30 82 C3
Ferndale Rd CBATH/BATHN BA1 109 F1
HORF/LLZ BS7 38 D3
PTSHD/EG BS20 45 G2
Ferndene ALMDB BS32 16 A5
Ferndown YATE/CS BS37 32 A1
Ferndown Cl AVONM BS11 49 F1
Fern Gv BRSTK/PCHW BS34 27 F3
NAIL BS48 84 D1
Fernhill La AVONM BS11 36 A4
Fernhurst Rd EVILLE/WHL BS5 63 G2

ernlea Gdns PTSHD/EG BS20 ......48 A4
ernlea Rd MTN/WRL BS22 ....135 H4
ernleaze FRCTL/WBN BS36 ....30 A4
ern Rd MANG/FISH BS16 ....54 C3
ernside NAIL BS48 ....85 H2
ernsteed Rd
BMSTRD/HC/WWD BS13 ....90 A3
ern St CBRISNE BS2 ....62 A2
ernville Est CLVDN BS21 ....70 C3
erry Ct BATHSE BA2 * 3 J5
erry La BATHSE BA2 ....3 H5
erry Rd KGWD/HNM BS15 ....82 A5
erry St CBRIS/FH BS1 ....5 G5
iddes Rd RDLND/MONT BS6 ....51 F4
he Fielders MTN/WRL BS22 ......132 A4
ield Farm Cl
BRSTK/PCHW BS34 ....40 A1
ielding's Rd BATHSE BA2 ....113 H1
ieldins BOAV BA15 ....118 B2
ield La OLD/WMLY/WICK BS30....82 B3
ield Rd KGWD/HNM BS15 ....64 B2
ield View Dr MANG/FISH BS16.....54 B2
ield Wy TRWBR BA14 ....122 A3
iennes Cl MANG/FISH BS16.........54 D4
ifth Av HORF/LLZ BS7 ....38 D4
ifth Wy AVONM BS11 ....35 F3
ilby Dr BRSTK/PCHW BS34 ....27 E2
ilton Av BRSTK/PCHW BS34 ....39 E2
HORF/LLZ BS7 ....51 H2
Filton Gv HORF/LLZ BS7 ....52 A2
Filton La BRSTK/PCHW BS34 ....39 G3
Filton Rd BRSTK/PCHW BS34.......39 G3
HORF/LLZ BS7 ....38 C5
MANG/FISH BS16 ....40 A4
Filwood Broadway
BRSG/KWL/STAPK BS4 ....91 F1
Filwood Ct MANG/FISH BS16 ....54 A5
Filwood Dr KGWD/HNM BS15 ....65 E4
Filwood Rd MANG/FISH BS16 ....53 H5
Finch Cl MTN/WRL BS22 ....136 B3
THNB/SVB BS35 ....8 D2
Finch Rd YATE/CS BS37..........32 B2
Finmere Gdns MTN/WRL BS22 ..131 H4
Fircliff Pk PTSHD/EG BS20 ....45 G1
Fire Engine La FRCTL/WBN BS36...30 B3
Firework Cl KGWD/HNM BS15.......65 G3
Firfield St
BRSG/KWL/STAPK BS4 ....79 H2
Firgrove Crs YATE/CS BS37 ....21 F5
Fir Leaze NAIL BS48..........72 C5
First Av BATHSE BA2 ....114 B3
BRSG/KWL/STAPK BS4 ....80 D1
PTSHD/EG BS20..........47 F3
RDSTK/MIDN BA3 ....124 D5
The Firs BATHSE BA2..........117 F1
First Wy AVONM BS11..........34 D4
Fir Tree Cl BRSTK/PCHW BS34 .....26 A3
Fir Tree La EVILLE/WHL BS5 ....63 H5
Fisher Av KGWD/HNM BS15..........65 F2
Fisher Rd KGWD/HNM BS15..........65 F2
Fishponds Rd EVILLE/WHL BS5 ....62 D1
Fishpool Hl HNBRY/STHM BS10....37 G1
Fitchett Wk HNBRY/STHM BS10 ..37 E2
Fitzgerald Rd BMSTR BS3 ....79 G3
Fitzharding Rd PTSHD/EG BS20 ..48 D5
Fitzmaurice Cl BOAV BA15..........119 H5
Fitzmaurice Pl BOAV BA15..........119 G4
Fitzroy Rd MANG/FISH BS16 ....64 A1
Fitzroy St
BRSG/KWL/STAPK BS4 ....79 H2
Five Acre Dr MANG/FISH BS16.......53 G1
Five Arches Cl
RDSTK/MIDN BA3 ....125 E2
Flamingo Crs MTN/WRL BS22 ....136 B3
Flax Bourton Rd CFTN/FAIL BS8 ..75 G4
Flaxman Cl HORF/LLZ BS7 ....52 C2
Flaxpits La FRCTL/WBN BS36.......28 D4
Fleur De Lys Dr TRWBR BA14.......122 B5
Florence Gv MTN/WRL BS22 ....135 G3
Florence Pk ALMDB BS32..........15 H2
RDLND/MONT BS6..........51 E4
Florence Rd MANG/FISH BS16......54 D5
Flowerdown Rd
OMX/HUT/LCK BS24 ....141 F2
Flowers Hl
BRSG/KWL/STAPK BS4 ....80 D5
Flowers Hill Cl
BRSG/KWL/STAPK BS4 ....80 D5
Flowerwell Rd
BMSTRD/HC/WWD BS13 ....90 C4
Folleigh Cl LGASH BS41 ....77 E4
Folleigh Dr LGASH BS41 ....77 E4
Folleigh La LGASH BS41 ....77 E4
Folliot Cl MANG/FISH BS16 ....40 B5
Folly Bridge Cl YATE/CS BS37 * 20 C5
Folly Brook Rd
MANG/FISH BS16..........41 H3
Follyfield BOAV BA15 ....119 G5
Folly La CBRISNE BS2 ....62 B5
WSM BS23 ....138 D5
Folly Rd YATE/CS BS37 ....18 A3
The Folly KEYN BS31 ....105 G2
MANG/FISH BS16..........55 E1
Fontana Cl
OLD/WMLY/WICK BS30..........83 E3
Fonthill Rd CBATH/BATHN BA1 ..108 B2
HNBRY/STHM BS10..........38 A3
Fontmell Ct HGRV/WHIT BS14 .....92 C2
Fontwell Dr MANG/FISH BS16 .....41 G4
Footes La FRCTL/WBN BS36..........29 H3
Footshill Cl KGWD/HNM BS15 ......64 B5
Footshill Dr KGWD/HNM BS15......64 B4
Footshill Rd KGWD/HNM BS15 ....64 B5
Forde Cl OLD/WMLY/WICK BS30 ..82 C1
Fordell Pl BRSG/KWL/STAPK BS4..79 H3
Ford La MANG/FISH BS16 ....55 G2
Ford St EVILLE/WHL BS5..........62 D5
Forefield Pl BATHSE BA2 ....3 H7
Forefield Ri BATHSE BA2 ....114 D3
Forefield Ter BATHSE BA2 ....3 H7
Forest Av MANG/FISH BS16 ....54 A5
Forest Dr HNBRY/STHM BS10 ......37 H2
WSM BS23 ....7 K1
Forest Edge KGWD/HNM BS15 ....81 H2
Forester Av BATHSE BA2 ....3 H1
Forester Ct CBATH/BATHN BA1 ....3 H1
Forester La BATHSE BA2..........3 J1
Forester Rd BATHSE BA2 ....3 J2
PTSHD/EG BS20..........45 G4
Forest Hills ALMDB BS32 ....15 H2
Fore St TRWBR BA14 ....121 E5
Forest Rd KGWD/HNM BS15 ....64 C4
MANG/FISH BS16..........54 A5
Forest Wk MANG/FISH BS16 ....64 A1
Forge End PTSHD/EG BS20 ....47 F5
Fortescue Rd
RDSTK/MIDN BA3 ....125 G2
Fortfield Rd HGRV/WHIT BS14......92 A4
Forty Acre La THNB/SVB BS35.......11 G4
Forum Buildings BATHSE BA2 * 3 F6
Fosse Barton NAIL BS48 ....73 E4
Fosse Cl NAIL BS48..........72 D4
Fossedale Av HGRV/WHIT BS14....92 A3
Fosse Gdns BATHSE BA2..........116 B2
Fosse La CBATH/BATHN BA1 ....103 F5
NAIL BS48 ....72 D4
RDSTK/MIDN BA3 ....125 E1
Fosseway CLVDN BS21..........70 D4
Fosse Wy NAIL BS48 ....72 D4
Fosseway RDSTK/MIDN BA3 ......124 D5
Fosseway Gdns
RDSTK/MIDN BA3 ....124 D3
The Fosseway CFTN/FAIL BS8 ....60 D5
Foster St EVILLE/WHL BS5 ....62 C1
Foundry La EVILLE/WHL BS5 ....63 G1
Fountain Buildings
CBATH/BATHN BA1 ....3 F2
Fountaine Ct EVILLE/WHL BS5.......62 D1
Fountains Dr
OLD/WMLY/WICK BS30..........65 E5
Four Acre Av MANG/FISH BS16 ....41 F5
Four Acre Crs MANG/FISH BS16 ..41 F4
Four Acre Rd MANG/FISH BS16 ....41 F4
Four Acres
BMSTRD/HC/WWD BS13 ....89 H5
Four Acres Cl
BMSTRD/HC/WWD BS13 ....90 A5
NAIL BS48 ....85 F1
Fourth Av HORF/LLZ BS7 ....38 D3
RDSTK/MIDN BA3 ....125 E4
Fourth Wy AVONM BS11..........35 F4
Fowey Cl NAIL BS48..........85 H1
Fowey Rd MTN/WRL BS22 ....131 H4
Fox & Hounds La KEYN BS31 ....94 C4
Fox Av YATE/CS BS37 ....20 C5
Foxborough Gdns ALMDB BS32 ..16 B5
Fox Cl BRSG/KWL/STAPK BS4.........81 E1
Foxcombe Rd
CBATH/BATHN BA1 ....107 G5
HGRV/WHIT BS14..........92 A5
Foxcote KGWD/HNM BS15..........65 E4
Foxcote Rd BMSTR BS3 ....78 B3
Fox Ct OLD/WMLY/WICK BS30......82 C3
Foxcroft Cl ALMDB BS32 ....27 H4
Foxcroft Rd EVILLE/WHL BS5 ......63 E3
Fox Den Rd BRSTK/PCHW BS34.....39 G3
Foxe Rd FRCTL/WBN BS36 ....29 G2
Foxfield Av ALMDB BS32 ....16 B4
Foxglove Cl MANG/FISH BS16 ....53 F4
MTN/WRL BS22 ....131 H3
THNB/SVB BS35..........9 E2
Foxglove Dr TRWBR BA14 ....121 F2
Fox Hl BATHSE BA2 ....114 D5
Foxholes La ALMDB BS32..........10 C4
Fox Rd EVILLE/WHL BS5 ....62 B2
Fraley Rd
HNLZ/SM/SNYPK/WT BS9 ....50 D1
Frampton Ct
OLD/WMLY/WICK BS30..........82 C2
TRWBR BA14 ....122 B3
Frampton Crs MANG/FISH BS16 ..54 B4
Frampton End Rd
FRCTL/WBN BS36 ....30 A1
Francis Fox Rd WSM BS23 ....7 F5
Francis Pl
OLD/WMLY/WICK BS30..........82 C2
Francis Rd BMSTR BS3 ....78 D4
HNBRY/STHM BS10..........37 H5
Francis St TRWBR BA14 ....120 D5
Francis Wy
OLD/WMLY/WICK BS30..........66 A5
Francombe Gv
HNBRY/STHM BS10..........51 H2
Frankland Cl
CBATH/BATHN BA1 ....107 F3
Frankley Buildings
CBATH/BATHN BA1 ....109 E3
Frankley Ter
CBATH/BATHN BA1 * 108 D3
Franklin's Wy YTN/CONG BS49 ..127 F2
Franklyn La CBRISNE BS2 ....62 A2
Franklyn St CBRISNE BS2 ....62 A2
Fraser Cl MTN/WRL BS22 ....131 G4
Fraser St BMSTR BS3..........79 E3
Frayne Rd BMSTR BS3 ....78 B2
Frederick Pl CFTN/FAIL BS8 ....4 A2
Fredrick St
BRSG/KWL/STAPK BS4 ....79 H2
Freeland Buildings
EVILLE/WHL BS5 ....62 D1
Freeland Pl CFTN/FAIL BS8..........60 C5
Freelands CLVDN BS21 ....70 C5
Freemans La NAIL BS48 ....96 C2
Freemantle Gdns
EVILLE/WHL BS5 ....52 D5
Freemantle Rd EVILLE/WHL BS5..52 D5
Freestone Rd CBRISNE BS2 ....62 B5
Free Tank CBRISNE BS2 ....5 K5
Freeview Rd BATHSE BA2 ....113 F1
Fremantle La RDLND/MONT BS6..61 G2
Fremantle Rd
RDLND/MONT BS6..........61 G2
Frenchay Campus
MANG/FISH BS16 * 39 H4
Frenchay Cl MANG/FISH BS16 ......54 A1
Frenchay Hl MANG/FISH BS16......54 A1
Frenchay Park Rd
MANG/FISH BS16..........53 G2
Frenchay Rd MANG/FISH BS16 ....54 B1
WSM BS23 ....138 D2
French Cl NAIL BS48 ....73 G3
Freshland Wy KGWD/HNM BS15 ..64 A3
Freshmoor CLVDN BS21 ....71 F2
Friar Av MTN/WRL BS22 ....131 F5
Friary CBRIS/FH BS1 ....5 J6
Friary Cl BOAV BA15 ....118 B5
CLVDN BS21 ....68 A5
Friary Grange Pk
FRCTL/WBN BS36 ....29 E4
Friary Rd HORF/LLZ BS7 ....51 G5
PTSHD/EG BS20..........45 E3
Friendly Rw PTSHD/EG BS20.......48 B3
Friendship Gv NAIL BS48 ....73 G3
Friendship Rd
BRSG/KWL/STAPK BS4 ....79 G4
NAIL BS48 ....73 G3
Friezewood Rd BMSTR BS3 ....78 B2
Fripp Cl EVILLE/WHL BS5 ....62 C5
Frobisher Av PTSHD/EG BS20 ......44 D3
Frobisher Cl MTN/WRL BS22 ......131 F4
PTSHD/EG BS20..........44 D3
Frobisher Rd BMSTR BS3 ....78 B3
Frog La BLAG/CWMG/WR BS40 ....96 D4
CBRIS/FH BS1..........4 C4
FRCTL/WBN BS36 ....30 C2
Frogmore St CBRIS/FH BS1 ....4 D4
Frome Ct THNB/SVB BS35 ....8 D4
Frome Gln FRCTL/WBN BS36 ....41 F1
Frome Old Rd
RDSTK/MIDN BA3 ....125 H2
Frome Pl MANG/FISH BS16..........53 F3
Frome Rd BATHSE BA2 ....113 H5
BOAV BA15..........119 G4
RDSTK/MIDN BA3 ....125 H2
TRWBR BA14 ....122 B4
YATE/CS BS37 ....33 E1
Frome St CBRISNE BS2 ....5 J1
Frome Ter MANG/FISH BS16 * 53 F3
Frome Valley Rd
MANG/FISH BS16..........53 G2
Frome Valley Walkway
FRCTL/WBN BS36 ....19 F5
FRCTL/WBN BS36 ....41 F2
MANG/FISH BS16..........54 B1
YATE/CS BS37 ....20 B4
Frome Valley Wy YATE/CS BS37 ..33 G2
Frome Vw FRCTL/WBN BS36 ....29 H3
Frome Wy FRCTL/WBN BS36 ....29 E5
Froomshaw Rd
MANG/FISH BS16..........53 H1
Frost Hl YTN/CONG BS49 ....126 D4
Fry's Cl MANG/FISH BS16 ....53 E4
Frys Hl BRSG/KWL/STAPK BS4 ......80 C4
KGWD/HNM BS15 ....64 D2
Fryth Wy NAIL BS48..........72 D4
Fulford Rd
BMSTRD/HC/WWD BS13 ....90 D4
TRWBR BA14 ....121 F4
Fulford Wk
BMSTRD/HC/WWD BS13 ....90 C4
Fullens Cl MTN/WRL BS22 ....136 A4
Fuller Rd CBATH/BATHN BA1 ......109 F2
Fullers Wy BATHSE BA2 ....116 B2
Fulmar Cl THNB/SVB BS35 ....9 E2
Fulmar Rd MTN/WRL BS22..........136 C2
Fulney Cl TRWBR BA14 ....121 G4
Furber Ct EVILLE/WHL BS5..........64 A5
Furber Rdg EVILLE/WHL BS5 ....64 A5
Furber Rd EVILLE/WHL BS5 ....64 A5
Furber V EVILLE/WHL BS5 ....64 A5
Furland Rd MTN/WRL BS22 ....135 H1
Furlong Cl RDSTK/MIDN BA3 ....124 A5
Furlong Gdns TRWBR BA14 ....121 F5
The Furlong
HNLZ/SM/SNYPK/WT BS9 ....51 F3
Furnwood EVILLE/WHL BS5 ....63 H5
Furze Cl MTN/WRL BS22..........135 F1
Furze Rd MANG/FISH BS16..........54 B5
MTN/WRL BS22 ....130 B5
Furzewood Rd
KGWD/HNM BS15 ....65 E3
Fylton Cft HGRV/WHIT BS14 ......101 E1

G

Gable Cl THNB/SVB BS35..........14 A5
Gable Rd EVILLE/WHL BS5 * 62 B2
Gadshill Dr BRSTK/PCHW BS34 ....27 G5
Gadshill Rd EVILLE/WHL BS5 ....52 D5
Gages Cl KGWD/HNM BS15..........65 E4
Gages Rd KGWD/HNM BS15 ....65 E4
Gainsborough Dr
MTN/WRL BS22 ....131 G5
Gainsborough Gdns
CBATH/BATHN BA1 ....107 H4
Gainsborough Ms
HNBRY/STHM BS10 * 37 G3
Gainsborough Ri
TRWBR BA14 ....122 B3
Gainsborough Rd KEYN BS31 ....94 C4
Galingale Wy PTSHD/EG BS20 ......46 A3
The Galleries CBRIS/FH BS1 * 5 G3
Gallivan Cl BRSTK/PCHW BS34.......26 D3
Galway Rd
BRSG/KWL/STAPK BS4 ....79 F5
Gander Cl
BMSTRD/HC/WWD BS13 ....90 C5
Gannet Rd MTN/WRL BS22..........136 C2
Garden Cl
HNLZ/SM/SNYPK/WT BS9 ....40 H3
MTN/WRL BS22 ....136 B1
Gardeners Wk LGASH BS41 ....77 E5
Gardens Rd CLVDN BS21..........70 C1
The Gardens MANG/FISH BS16 ....40 A4
Gardner Av
BMSTRD/HC/WWD BS13 ....90 A2
Gardner Rd PTSHD/EG BS20 ....45 G2
Garfield Rd EVILLE/WHL BS5 ....63 H3
Garnet St BMSTR BS3 ....78 C4
Garnett Pl MANG/FISH BS16..........55 E1
Garonor Wy PTSHD/EG BS20 ....47 G3
Garrett Dr BRSTK/PCHW BS34 ......27 F3
Garrick Rd BATHSE BA2 ....113 E2
Garsdale Cl MTN/WRL BS22 ....136 A3
Garsdale Rd MTN/WRL BS22 ....136 A3
Garstons Cl NAIL BS48..........85 G3
The Garstons
CBATH/BATHN BA1 ....111 E2
PTSHD/EG BS20..........45 F4
Garth Rd
BMSTRD/HC/WWD BS13 ....90 B1
Gas Ferry Rd CBRIS/FH BS1 ....4 B7
The Gaskins HORF/LLZ BS7..........52 B3
Gas La CBRISNE BS2..........62 B5
Gaston Av KEYN BS31..........94 C4
The Gastons AVONM BS11 ....35 H5
Gatcombe Dr
BRSTK/PCHW BS34 ....39 H1
Gatcombe Rd
BMSTRD/HC/WWD BS13 ....90 C4
Gatehouse Av
BMSTRD/HC/WWD BS13 ....90 B4
Gatehouse Cl
BMSTRD/HC/WWD BS13 ....90 B4
Gatehouse Ct
BMSTRD/HC/WWD BS13 ....90 C4
Gatehouse Wy
BMSTRD/HC/WWD BS13 ....90 B4
Gatesby Md BRSTK/PCHW BS34 ..27 G5
Gathorne Crs YATE/CS BS37..........20 C5
Gathorne Rd BMSTR BS3 ....78 C2
Gatton Rd CBRISNE BS2 ....62 B2
Gaunts Cl PTSHD/EG BS20 ....44 C4
Gaunt's Earthcott La
ALMDB BS32..........17 F2
Gaunt's La CBRIS/FH BS1 * 4 D4
Gaunts Rd YATE/CS BS37 ....32 D2
Gay Elms Rd
BMSTRD/HC/WWD BS13 ....90 B5
Gayner Rd HORF/LLZ BS7 ....38 D4
Gay's Hl CBATH/BATHN BA1 ....108 D4
Gays Rd KGWD/HNM BS15 ....81 G2
Gay St CBATH/BATHN BA1 ....3 F3
Gaythorne Crs YATE/CS BS37 ......20 C5
Gazelle Rd OMX/HUT/LCK BS24 ..139 G3
Gazzard Cl FRCTL/WBN BS36 ....29 E3
Gee Moors KGWD/HNM BS15..........65 E4
Gefle Cl CBRIS/FH BS1..........4 A7
Geldof Dr RDSTK/MIDN BA3..........124 B2
Geoffrey Cl
BMSTRD/HC/WWD BS13 ....89 H3
George Cl NAIL BS48 ....86 C2
George Jones Rd CBRISNE BS2 ....62 B5
Georges Pl BATHSE BA2 * 3 J4
George's Rd
CBATH/BATHN BA1 ....108 D3
Georges Sq CBRIS/FH BS1 ....5 G4
George St BATHSE BA2 ....3 K4
CBATH/BATHN BA1 ....3 F3
EVILLE/WHL BS5 ....62 D3
TRWBR BA14 ....121 E5
WSM BS23 ....7 F4
George Whitefield Ct
CBRIS/FH BS1 * 5 H2
Georgian Vw BATHSE BA2 ....113 G4
Gerald Rd BMSTR BS3..........78 B3
Gerard Rd WSM BS23 ....7 F3
Gerrard Buildings BATHSE BA2 ......3 J3
Gerrard Cl
BRSG/KWL/STAPK BS4 ....91 E2
Gerrish Av EVILLE/WHL BS5 ....62 D3
MANG/FISH BS16..........55 E3
Gibbet La HGRV/WHIT BS14 ....101 F3
Gibbsfold Rd
BMSTRD/HC/WWD BS13 ....99 H1
Gibbs Leaze TRWBR BA14..........121 H5
Gibson Rd RDLND/MONT BS6 ....61 G2
Gifford Ct BRSTK/PCHW BS34 * 39 G3
Gifford Rd HNBRY/STHM BS10 ....37 E1
Giffords Pl
BMSTRD/HC/WWD BS13 ....90 B2
Gilbeck Rd NAIL BS48 ....72 D4
Gilbert Rd EVILLE/WHL BS5 ....62 D3
KGWD/HNM BS15 ....64 C2
Gilberyn Dr MTN/WRL BS22..........131 H5
Gilda Cl HGRV/WHIT BS14 ....92 A4
Gilda Crs HGRV/WHIT BS14..........92 A3
Gilda Sq West HGRV/WHIT BS14 ..92 A4
Gillard Cl KGWD/HNM BS15 ....64 A3
Gillard Rd KGWD/HNM BS15..........64 A3
Gill Av MANG/FISH BS16 ....54 A2
Gillebank Cl HGRV/WHIT BS14 ......92 C4
Gillingham Hl EVILLE/WHL BS5 ....81 G1
Gillingham Ter
CBATH/BATHN BA1 ....109 E3
Gillingstool THNB/SVB BS35..........8 D4
Gill Ms MTN/WRL BS22 ....131 H4
Gillmore Rd MTN/WRL BS22..........136 A2
Gillray Cl HORF/LLZ BS7 ....52 C2
Gillson Cl OMX/HUT/LCK BS24 ....140 A4
Gilpin Cl KGWD/HNM BS15 ....65 E2
Gilroy Cl OLD/WMLY/WICK BS30 ..83 E3
Gilslake Av HNBRY/STHM BS10 ....37 G2
Gimblet Rd MTN/WRL BS22 ....132 A4
Gingells Gn KGWD/HNM BS15 * 63 H3
Gipsy Patch La
BRSTK/PCHW BS34 ....26 D4
The Glades EVILLE/WHL BS5..........63 F1
Gladstone Dr MANG/FISH BS16 ....54 C5
Gladstone La FRCTL/WBN BS36....30 A3
Gladstone Rd BATHSE BA2..........115 F5
HGRV/WHIT BS14..........92 A3
KGWD/HNM BS15 ....64 C2
TRWBR BA14 ....122 C2
Gladstone St BMSTR BS3 ....78 C3
EVILLE/WHL BS5 ....63 E4
MANG/FISH BS16..........54 C5
RDSTK/MIDN BA3 ....124 C1
Glaisdale Rd MANG/FISH BS16......53 H3
Glanville Gdns KGWD/HNM BS15..64 D4
Glass House La CBRISNE BS2 ......80 A1
Glastonbury Cl NAIL BS48..........74 A5
OLD/WMLY/WICK BS30 * 82 C1
Glastonbury Wy
MTN/WRL BS22 ....136 D1
Glebe Av PTSHD/EG BS20 ....45 H4
Glebe Cl LGASH BS41 ....77 E4
Glebe Fld ALMDB BS32 ....15 G2
Glebelands RDSTK/MIDN BA3 ....125 E3
Glebelands Rd
BRSTK/PCHW BS34 ....38 D2
Glebe Rd BATHSE BA2 ....113 G3
CLVDN BS21 ....70 C3
EVILLE/WHL BS5 ....63 F3
LGASH BS41 ....77 F5
PTSHD/EG BS20..........45 H4
TRWBR BA14 ....122 B2
WSM BS23 ....7 F3
The Glebe THNB/SVB BS35..........13 E2
Gledemoor Dr FRCTL/WBN BS36..30 B4
Glena Av BRSG/KWL/STAPK BS4 ..80 A4
Glenarm Rd
BRSG/KWL/STAPK BS4 ....80 D4
Glenarm Wk
BRSG/KWL/STAPK BS4 ....80 D4
Glen Av CFTN/FAIL BS8 ....59 E3
Glenavon Pk
HNLZ/SM/SNYPK/WT BS9 ....49 H4
Glen Brook
HNLZ/SM/SNYPK/WT BS9 ....50 A4
Glenburn Rd KGWD/HNM BS15 ....64 A2
Glencoyne Sq
HNBRY/STHM BS10..........37 H3
Glendale CFTN/FAIL BS8 * 60 C5
MANG/FISH BS16..........41 F5
MANG/FISH BS16..........54 B5
Glendare St EVILLE/WHL BS5 ....62 D5
Glendevon Rd
HGRV/WHIT BS14..........100 D1
Glen Dr
HNLZ/SM/SNYPK/WT BS9 ....50 A3
Gleneagles YATE/CS BS37..........32 A1
Gleneagles Cl MTN/WRL BS22 ....131 G5
NAIL BS48 ....73 H5
Gleneagles Dr
HNBRY/STHM BS10 ....36 C2
Gleneagles Rd
OLD/WMLY/WICK BS30..........65 G5
Glenfall YATE/CS BS37..........31 H3
Glenfrome Rd CBRISNE BS2 ....52 C5
Glen La BRSG/KWL/STAPK BS4......80 C4
Glen Pk EVILLE/WHL BS5..........62 D1
EVILLE/WHL BS5 ....63 H3
Glen Park Gdns EVILLE/WHL BS5..63 E1
Glenroy Av KGWD/HNM BS15 ....64 A2
Glenside Campus
MANG/FISH BS16 * 53 F3
Glenside Cl MANG/FISH BS16 ....54 B1
Glenside Pk MANG/FISH BS16 ....53 F3
The Glen KEYN BS31 ....105 G3
KGWD/HNM BS15 ....81 G2
MTN/WRL BS22 ....135 G1
RDLND/MONT BS6..........51 E5
YATE/CS BS37 ....20 D5
Glentworth Rd CFTN/FAIL BS8........4 A5
RDLND/MONT BS6..........61 F1
Glenwood MANG/FISH BS16 ....54 B5
Glenwood Dr
OLD/WMLY/WICK BS30..........83 E2
Glenwood Ri PTSHD/EG BS20 ......44 C3
Glenwood Rd
HNBRY/STHM BS10..........51 F1
Glevum Cl MANG/FISH BS16..........55 H1
Gloster Av EVILLE/WHL BS5 ....53 E5
Gloucester Cl
BRSTK/PCHW BS34 ....27 F5
Gloucester La CBRISNE BS2 ....5 K2
Gloucester Rd ALMDB BS32..........15 H3
AVONM BS11 ....34 B4
BRSTK/PCHW BS34 ....26 D1
CBATH/BATHN BA1 ....102 B4
HORF/LLZ BS7 ....61 G1
MANG/FISH BS16..........54 D5
THNB/SVB BS35 ....8 D2
THNB/SVB BS35 ....11 F5
TRWBR BA14 ....122 C2
Gloucester Rd North
HORF/LLZ BS7 ....38 C4
Gloucester Rw CFTN/FAIL BS8......60 C4
Gloucester St CBATH/BATHN BA1 ..2 E2
CBRISNE BS2 ....5 H1
CFTN/FAIL BS8 ....60 C4
EVILLE/WHL BS5 ....53 E5
WSM BS23 ....6 D4
Gloucester Ter THNB/SVB BS35 * ..8 G3
Glyn V BMSTR BS3..........79 E5
Godfrey Ct
OLD/WMLY/WICK BS30..........82 C2
Godwin Dr NAIL BS48 ....72 D4
Goffenton Dr MANG/FISH BS16......54 A2
Goldcrest Rd YATE/CS BS37 ....32 B3
Golden Hl RDLND/MONT BS6 ....51 F3
Goldfinch Wy
MANG/FISH BS16..........57 F4
Goldney Av CFTN/FAIL BS8..........60 D5
OLD/WMLY/WICK BS30..........65 H4
Goldney Rd CFTN/FAIL BS8..........60 D5
Goldsbury Wk AVONM BS11..........35 H4
Golf Club La KEYN BS31 ....105 F2
Golf Course La
BRSTK/PCHW BS34 ....38 C2
Golf Course Rd BATHSE BA2 ......115 F1
Gooch Ct
OLD/WMLY/WICK BS30..........83 F3
Gooch Wy MTN/WRL BS22 ....132 A5
Goodard Dr MTN/WRL BS22..........132 A5
Goodeve Pk
HNLZ/SM/SNYPK/WT BS9 * 50 A5
Goodeve Rd
HNLZ/SM/SNYPK/WT BS9 ....60 A1
Goodhind St EVILLE/WHL BS5 ......62 B3
Goodneston Rd
MANG/FISH BS16..........53 H5
Goodrich Cl YATE/CS BS37 ....31 E1
Goodring Hl AVONM BS11 ....35 H4

Good Shepherd Cl
HORF/LLZ BS7 * 51 F4
Goodwin Dr HGRV/WHIT BS14 ....91 G5
Goodwood Cl TRWBR BA14 ....123 F5
Goodwood Gdns
MANG/FISH BS16 ....41 G4
Goold Cl BATHSE BA2 ....105 H4
Goolden St
BRSG/KWL/STAPK BS4 ....79 H3
Goose Acre ALMDB BS32 ....27 H4
Goosegreen FRCTL/WBN BS36 ....29 H2
Goose Gn
OLD/WMLY/WICK BS30 ....65 H2
YATE/CS BS37 ....20 D4
Goose Green Wy YATE/CS BS37 ..20 B3
Gooseland Cl
HGRV/WHIT BS14 ....100 C1
Goosey La MTN/WRL BS22 ....137 F1
Gordano Gdns PTSHD/EG BS20 ....48 A4
Gordano Quay
PTSHD/EG BS20 * 47 E1
Gordano Rd PTSHD/EG BS20 ....47 E1
Gordano Wy PTSHD/EG BS20 ....47 G3
Gordon Av EVILLE/WHL BS5 ....63 F2
Gordon Cl EVILLE/WHL BS5 ....63 F2
Gordon Rd BATHSE BA2 ....3 J7
CBRISNE BS2 ....62 A2
CFTN/FAIL BS8 ....4 A3
EVILLE/WHL BS5 ....63 E2
WSM BS23 ....7 G4
Gore Rd BMSTR BS3 ....78 B3
Gore's Marsh Rd BMSTR BS3 ....78 B4
Gorham Cl AVONM BS11 ....36 B3
Gorlands Rd YATE/CS BS37 ....33 E1
Gorlangton Cl
HGRV/WHIT BS14 ....91 H2
Gorse Cover Rd THNB/SVB BS35 ..12 C3
Gorse Hl MANG/FISH BS16 ....54 B5
Gorse La CFTN/FAIL BS8 ....4 A4
Gosforth Cl HNBRY/STHM BS10 ....37 G4
Gosforth Rd
HNBRY/STHM BS10 ....37 G4
Goslet Rd HGRV/WHIT BS14 ....92 D4
Goss Barton NAIL BS48 ....73 E5
Goss Cl NAIL BS48 ....72 D5
Goss La NAIL BS48 ....72 D5
Goss Vw NAIL BS48 ....72 D5
Gotley Rd
BRSG/KWL/STAPK BS4 ....80 C4
Gott Dr BRSG/KWL/STAPK BS4 ....80 C1
Goulston Rd
BMSTRD/HC/WWD BS13 ....90 B4
Goulston Wk
BMSTRD/HC/WWD BS13 ....90 B4
Goulter St EVILLE/WHL BS5 ....62 C5
Gourney Cl AVONM BS11 ....36 A3
Gover Rd KGWD/HNM BS15 ....81 H3
Govier Wy THNB/SVB BS35 ....13 E5
Grace Cl YATE/CS BS37 ....33 E1
YTN/CONG BS49 ....126 B3
Grace Ct MANG/FISH BS16 ....54 C2
Grace Dr KGWD/HNM BS15 ....65 F2
RDSTK/MIDN BA3 ....124 B2
Grace Park Rd
BRSG/KWL/STAPK BS4 ....80 C5
Grace Rd MANG/FISH BS16 ....54 B3
MTN/WRL BS22 ....132 A4
Gradwell Cl MTN/WRL BS22 ....132 A5
Graeme Cl MANG/FISH BS16 ....53 H4
Graham Rd BMSTR BS3 * 78 D3
EVILLE/WHL BS5 ....62 C2
MANG/FISH BS16 ....55 E2
WSM BS23 ....6 E6
Grainger Ct AVONM BS11 ....48 D1
Graitney Cl YTN/CONG BS49 ....127 G3
Grampian Cl
OLD/WMLY/WICK BS30 ....83 F2
Granby Hl CFTN/FAIL BS8 ....60 C5
Grand Pde CBATH/BATHN BA1 ....3 G4
Grange Av BRSTK/PCHW BS34 ....27 E4
KGWD/HNM BS15 ....82 A1
Grange Cl ALMDB BS32 ....16 A5
BRSTK/PCHW BS34 ....40 A1
WSM BS23 ....138 D5
Grange Cl North
HNLZ/SM/SNYPK/WT BS9 ....51 E2
Grange Ct KGWD/HNM BS15 ....82 A1
Grange Court Rd
HNLZ/SM/SNYPK/WT BS9 ....50 D2
Grange Dr MANG/FISH BS16 ....54 B2
Grange End RDSTK/MIDN BA3 ....124 B5
Grange Farm Rd
YTN/CONG BS49 ....126 A2
Grange Pk
HNLZ/SM/SNYPK/WT BS9 ....51 E2
MANG/FISH BS16 ....40 D5
Grange Rd
BMSTRD/HC/WWD BS13 ....90 B4
CFTN/FAIL BS8 ....60 D4
KEYN BS31 ....104 D1
WSM BS23 ....138 D5
The Grange
HNLZ/SM/SNYPK/WT BS9 ....50 A1
Grange Vw BOAV BA15 ....119 H2
Grangeville Cl
OLD/WMLY/WICK BS30 ....83 E3
Grangewood Cl
MANG/FISH BS16 ....54 B2
Granny's La KGWD/HNM BS15 ....64 D5
Grantham La KGWD/HNM BS15 ....64 B3
Grantham Rd
KGWD/HNM BS15 ....64 B2
Grantson Cl
BRSG/KWL/STAPK BS4 ....80 D4
Granville Cl KGWD/HNM BS15 ....81 G3
Granville Rd
CBATH/BATHN BA1 ....108 B1
Granville St EVILLE/WHL BS5 ....62 D5
Grasmere TRWBR BA14 ....121 F4
Grasmere Cl HNBRY/STHM BS10 ..37 F5
Grasmere Dr WSM BS23 ....139 E2
Grassington Dr YATE/CS BS37 ....32 C1
Grass Meers Dr
HGRV/WHIT BS14 ....91 H5
Grassmere Gdns
OLD/WMLY/WICK BS30 ....66 A5
Grassmere Rd YTN/CONG BS49 ..126 B3
Gratitude Rd EVILLE/WHL BS5 ....62 D2
Gravel Hill Rd YATE/CS BS37 ....21 E3
Gravel Hill Rd North
YATE/CS BS37 ....21 F3
Gravel Wk CBATH/BATHN BA1 ....2 E2
Graveney Cl
BRSG/KWL/STAPK BS4 ....80 C5
Gray Cl HNBRY/STHM BS10 ....36 D3
Grayle Rd HNBRY/STHM BS10 ....37 E2
Great Ann St CBRISNE BS2 ....5 K2
Great Bedford St
CBATH/BATHN BA1 ....2 E1
Great Brockeridge
HNLZ/SM/SNYPK/WT BS9 ....50 C2
Great Dowles
OLD/WMLY/WICK BS30 ....82 D2
Great George St CBRIS/FH BS1 ....4 C4
CBRISNE BS2 ....5 J2
Great Hayles Rd
HGRV/WHIT BS14 ....91 H2
Great Leaze
OLD/WMLY/WICK BS30 ....82 D2
Great Meadow Rd
ALMDB BS32 ....27 H3
Great Park Rd ALMDB BS32 ....16 A4
Great Pulteney St BATHSE BA2 ....3 H3
Great Stanhope St
CBATH/BATHN BA1 ....2 D4
Great Stoke Wy
BRSTK/PCHW BS34 ....39 G3
Great Western Br WSM BS23 ....7 F5
Great Western La
EVILLE/WHL BS5 ....62 D5
Great Western Rd CLVDN BS21 ....70 D2
Greatwood Cl
BMSTRD/HC/WWD BS13 ....90 D5
Greenacre MTN/WRL BS22 ....135 G1
Greenacre Rd
HGRV/WHIT BS14 ....100 D1
Greenacres CBATH/BATHN BA1 ..107 G1
Greenbank Av East
EVILLE/WHL BS5 ....62 D4
Greenbank Av West
EVILLE/WHL BS5 ....62 C2
Greenbank Gdns
CBATH/BATHN BA1 ....107 G3
Greenbank Rd BMSTR BS3 ....78 B2
EVILLE/WHL BS5 ....62 D2
KGWD/HNM BS15 ....82 A1
Greenbank Vw EVILLE/WHL BS5 ..62 D1
Green Ct THNB/SVB BS35 ....10 A5
Green Cft EVILLE/WHL BS5 ....63 H2
Greendale Rd BMSTR BS3 ....79 F3
RDLND/MONT BS6 ....51 E4
Green Dell Cl
HNBRY/STHM BS10 * 36 C2
Greenditch Av
BMSTRD/HC/WWD BS13 ....90 D4
Greendown EVILLE/WHL BS5 ....63 H4
Greendown Pl BATHSE BA2 ....117 E1
Green Dragon Rd
FRCTL/WBN BS36 ....28 D5
Greenfield Av
HNBRY/STHM BS10 ....38 A5
Greenfield Crs NAIL BS48 ....73 F3
Greenfield Pk PTSHD/EG BS20 ....45 F5
Greenfield Pl WSM BS23 ....6 B2
Greenfield Rd
HNBRY/STHM BS10 ....38 A4
Greengage Cl MTN/WRL BS22 ....136 B3
Green Hayes YATE/CS BS37 ....33 E2
Greenhill THNB/SVB BS35 ....11 G3
Greenhill Cl MTN/WRL BS22 ....131 H5
NAIL BS48 ....73 E4
Greenhill Down THNB/SVB BS35 ..11 G3
Greenhill Gdns THNB/SVB BS35 ....11 G3
TRWBR BA14 ....121 H2
Greenhill Gv BMSTR BS3 ....78 B4
Greenhill La AVONM BS11 ....36 A4
THNB/SVB BS35 ....11 F4
Greenhill Pl RDSTK/MIDN BA3 ....124 B1
Greenhill Rd RDSTK/MIDN BA3 ..124 B1
THNB/SVB BS35 ....11 G3
Greenland Rd MTN/WRL BS22 ....136 A2
Greenlands Wy
HNBRY/STHM BS10 ....36 D1
Greenland Vw BOAV BA15 ....119 H3
Green La AVONM BS11 ....34 C5
BOAV BA15 ....118 B3
CFTN/FAIL BS8 ....75 H2
FRCTL/WBN BS36 ....28 C3
HNBRY/STHM BS10 ....24 A1
THNB/SVB BS35 ....12 D1
TRWBR BA14 ....123 G1
Greenleaze
BRSG/KWL/STAPK BS4 ....80 A5
Greenleaze Av
MANG/FISH BS16 ....41 E4
Greenmore Rd
BRSG/KWL/STAPK BS4 ....80 A4
Greenore KGWD/HNM BS15 ....64 B4
Green Pk BATHSE BA2 ....2 D5
Green Park Ms BATHSE BA2 ....2 D5
Green Park Rd BATHSE BA2 ....2 E5
Greenpark Rd
HNBRY/STHM BS10 ....38 B4
Green Pastures Rd NAIL BS48 ....74 A4
Greenridge Cl
BMSTRD/HC/WWD BS13 ....89 H5
Green Side MANG/FISH BS16 ....55 F2
Greenside Cl HNBRY/STHM BS10 ..36 C2
Greenslade Gdns NAIL BS48 ....73 E3
Greensplott Rd AVONM BS11 ....22 D3
Green St BMSTR BS3 ....79 G2
CBATH/BATHN BA1 ....3 F4
The Green BRSTK/PCHW BS34 ....39 H1
KGWD/HNM BS15 ....64 D1
NAIL BS48 ....85 G4
OMX/HUT/LCK BS24 ....140 D2
PTSHD/EG BS20 ....48 C4
THNB/SVB BS35 ....10 A5
Green Tree Rd
RDSTK/MIDN BA3 ....124 C1
Greenview
OLD/WMLY/WICK BS30 ....82 D4
Green Wk
BRSG/KWL/STAPK BS4 ....79 H5
Greenway Bush La BMSTR BS3 ....78 B2
Greenway Ct BATHSE BA2 ....114 C3
Greenway Dr
HNBRY/STHM BS10 ....38 A5
Greenway Gdns TRWBR BA14 ....121 F3
Greenway La BATHSE BA2 ....114 C4
Greenway Pk CLVDN BS21 ....71 F2
HNBRY/STHM BS10 ....38 A5
Greenway Rd
RDLND/MONT BS6 ....61 E1
Greenways KGWD/HNM BS15 ....65 F2
Greenways Rd YATE/CS BS37 ....20 C4
The Greenway MANG/FISH BS16 ..54 B5
Greenwood Cl HORF/LLZ BS7 ....51 H1
Greenwood Dr THNB/SVB BS35 ..11 F3
Greenwood Rd
BRSG/KWL/STAPK BS4 ....79 H4
MTN/WRL BS22 ....136 B1
Gregory Ct
OLD/WMLY/WICK BS30 ....65 F5
Gregory Md YTN/CONG BS49 ....126 A2
Grenville Av
OMX/HUT/LCK BS24 ....140 D2
Grenville Cl EVILLE/WHL BS5 ....63 G3
Grenville Pl CBRIS/FH BS1 * 78 A1
Grenville Rd RDLND/MONT BS6 ....51 H5
Greve Ct OLD/WMLY/WICK BS30 ..82 C2
Greville Rd BMSTR BS3 ....78 C2
Greville St BMSTR BS3 ....78 D2
Greyhound Wk CBRIS/FH BS1 * 5 G3
Greylands Rd
BMSTRD/HC/WWD BS13 ....90 A2
Greystoke Av
HNBRY/STHM BS10 ....37 F5
Greystoke Gdns
HNBRY/STHM BS10 ....37 F5
Greystones MANG/FISH BS16 ....41 F4
Griffen Rd OMX/HUT/LCK BS24 ..136 B4
Griffin Cl MTN/WRL BS22 ....137 E1
Griffin Rd CLVDN BS21 ....70 D2
Griggfield Wk HGRV/WHIT BS14 ..91 G2
Grimsbury Rd KGWD/HNM BS15 ..65 F3
Grindell Rd EVILLE/WHL BS5 ....63 E4
Grinfield Av
BMSTRD/HC/WWD BS13 ....90 D5
Grinfield Cl
BMSTRD/HC/WWD BS13 ....90 D5
Grinfield Ct
BMSTRD/HC/WWD BS13 ....90 D5
Grittleton Rd HORF/LLZ BS7 ....38 B5
Grosvenor Bridge Rd
CBATH/BATHN BA1 ....109 F3
Grosvenor Pk
CBATH/BATHN BA1 ....109 F3
Grosvenor Pl
CBATH/BATHN BA1 ....109 E3
Grosvenor Rd CBRISNE BS2 ....61 H3
Grosvenor Ter
CBATH/BATHN BA1 * 109 F2
Grosvenor Vls
CBATH/BATHN BA1 * 109 E3
Grove Av CBRIS/FH BS1 ....5 F6
HNLZ/SM/SNYPK/WT BS9 ....49 H1
Grove Bank MANG/FISH BS16 ....40 D4
Grove Dr MTN/WRL BS22 ....135 H2
Grove La WSM BS23 ....6 D2
Grove Leaze AVONM BS11 ....48 C2
BOAV BA15 ....119 E3
Grove Pk BRSG/KWL/STAPK BS4 ..80 C4
RDLND/MONT BS6 ....61 F1
Grove Park Av
BRSG/KWL/STAPK BS4 ....80 C4
Grove Park Rd
BRSG/KWL/STAPK BS4 ....80 C4
Grove Park Ter
MANG/FISH BS16 ....53 G4
Grove Rd BNWL BS29 ....141 H2
HNLZ/SM/SNYPK/WT BS9 ....36 C5
MANG/FISH BS16 ....53 G4
MTN/WRL BS22 ....135 H2
RDLND/MONT BS6 ....61 E1
WSM BS23 ....6 D2
Grovesend Rd THNB/SVB BS35 ....8 D4
The Groves
BMSTRD/HC/WWD BS13 ....91 E5
Grove St CBATH/BATHN BA1 ....3 G3
The Grove CBATH/BATHN BA1 ....107 H3
CBRIS/FH BS1 ....4 E6
NAIL BS48 ....74 B3
OLD/WMLY/WICK BS30 ....82 D2
Grove Vw MANG/FISH BS16 ....53 F2
Grove Wood Rd
RDSTK/MIDN BA3 ....125 F4
Guernsey Av
BRSG/KWL/STAPK BS4 ....81 E2
Guest Av MANG/FISH BS16 ....55 G2
Guildford Rd
BRSG/KWL/STAPK BS4 ....80 D1
Guildhall Market
CBATH/BATHN BA1 * 3 G4
Guinea La CBATH/BATHN BA1 ....3 F2
MANG/FISH BS16 ....53 H4
Guinea St CBRIS/FH BS1 ....5 F7
Gulliford's Bank CLVDN BS21 ....71 E3
Gullimores Gdns
BMSTRD/HC/WWD BS13 ....90 C5
Gullivers Pl YATE/CS BS37 ....32 C2
Gullock Tyning
RDSTK/MIDN BA3 ....124 C3
Gullons Cl
BMSTRD/HC/WWD BS13 ....90 B3
Gullon Wk
BMSTRD/HC/WWD BS13 ....90 A4
Gullybrook La
EVILLE/WHL BS5 * 62 C5
The Gully FRCTL/WBN BS36 ....29 F3
Gunning Cl KGWD/HNM BS15 ....64 C5
Gunter's Hl EVILLE/WHL BS5 ....63 H5
Guthrie Rd CFTN/FAIL BS8 ....60 D3
Gwilliam St BMSTR BS3 ....79 E3
Gwyn St CBRISNE BS2 ....61 H2
Gypsy La KEYN BS31 ....104 C4

H

Haberfield Hl PTSHD/EG BS20 ....58 C1
Hacket Hl THNB/SVB BS35 ....9 G4
Hacket La THNB/SVB BS35 ....9 F4
Hackett Pl TRWBR BA14 ....121 H5
Haden Rd TRWBR BA14 ....123 E2
Hadley Ct
OLD/WMLY/WICK BS30 ....65 G5
Hadley Rd BATHSE BA2 ....115 E5
Hadrian Cl
HNLZ/SM/SNYPK/WT BS9 ....49 H4
Hadrians Wk MANG/FISH BS16 ....55 H2
Halbrow Crs
MANG/FISH BS16 ....54 B3
Haldon Cl BMSTR BS3 ....79 E5
Hale Cl KGWD/HNM BS15 ....82 A2
Hales Horn Cl ALMDB BS32 ....27 F4
Halfacre Cl HGRV/WHIT BS14 ....100 D1
Halfacre La HGRV/WHIT BS14 ....101 E1
Halfway Cl TRWBR BA14 ....121 G4
Halifax Rd YATE/CS BS37 ....20 C3
Hallam Rd CLVDN BS21 ....70 C2
Hallards Cl AVONM BS11 ....35 G5
Hallen Cl HNBRY/STHM BS10 ....36 C2
MANG/FISH BS16 ....55 H2
Hallen Dr
HNLZ/SM/SNYPK/WT BS9 ....49 H1
Hallen Rd HNBRY/STHM BS10 ....36 B1
Halletts Wy PTSHD/EG BS20 ....45 G4
Halliwell Rd PTSHD/EG BS20 ....44 A4
Halls Gdns BRSTK/PCHW BS34 ....40 B1
Halls Rd KGWD/HNM BS15 ....64 C3
Hall St BMSTR BS3 ....78 C4
Halsbury Rd RDLND/MONT BS6 ....51 F4
Halstock Av MANG/FISH BS16 ....53 G5
Halston Dr CBRISNE BS2 ....62 A3
Halswell Gdns
BMSTRD/HC/WWD BS13 ....90 C5
Halswell Rd CLVDN BS21 ....70 D4
Halt End HGRV/WHIT BS14 ....101 F1
The Halve TRWBR BA14 ....121 E5
Halwyn Cl
HNLZ/SM/SNYPK/WT BS9 ....50 A3
Hamble Cl THNB/SVB BS35 ....8 D4
Hambledon Rd MTN/WRL BS22 ..132 B4
Hambrook La
BRSTK/PCHW BS34 ....40 A1
Ham Farm La MANG/FISH BS16 ....55 G2
Ham Gn PTSHD/EG BS20 ....48 C4
Hamilton Rd BMSTR BS3 ....78 C2
CBATH/BATHN BA1 ....108 B2
EVILLE/WHL BS5 ....62 B3
WSM BS23 ....134 B2
Ham La LGASH BS41 ....98 C1
MANG/FISH BS16 ....53 F2
NAIL BS48 ....73 H2
OLD/WMLY/WICK BS30 ....67 H2
The Hamlet NAIL BS48 ....73 H3
Hammersmith Rd
EVILLE/WHL BS5 ....63 E3
Hammond Cl
BRSG/KWL/STAPK BS4 ....80 C5
Hammond Gdns
HNLZ/SM/SNYPK/WT BS9 ....50 B1
Hammond Wy TRWBR BA14 ....121 F1
Hampden Cl YATE/CS BS37 ....20 C3
Hampden Rd
BRSG/KWL/STAPK BS4 ....80 A3
MTN/WRL BS22 ....136 A1
Hampshire Wy YATE/CS BS37 ....21 E3
Hampstead Rd
BRSG/KWL/STAPK BS4 ....80 B3
Hampton Cl
OLD/WMLY/WICK BS30 ....82 D1
Hampton Cnr AVONM BS11 * 48 D2
Hampton La RDLND/MONT BS6 ..61 E2
Hampton Pk RDLND/MONT BS6 ..61 E2
Hampton Rd RDLND/MONT BS6 ..61 E1
Hampton Rw BATHSE BA2 ....3 K1
Hampton St KGWD/HNM BS15 ....64 C2
Hampton Vw
CBATH/BATHN BA1 ....109 E3
Hams Rd KEYN BS31 ....94 C2
Ham Wood Cl
OMX/HUT/LCK BS24 ....139 G5
Hanbury Cl KGWD/HNM BS15 ....82 A1
Hanbury Rd CFTN/FAIL BS8 ....60 D3
Handel Av EVILLE/WHL BS5 ....63 E4
Handel Rd KEYN BS31 ....94 A4
Handford Wy
OLD/WMLY/WICK BS30 ....83 E2
Hanford Ct HGRV/WHIT BS14 ....92 C2
Hanham Rd KGWD/HNM BS15 ....64 C5
Hanham Wy NAIL BS48 ....72 C4
Hannah More Rd NAIL BS48 ....72 D5
Hanover Cl MTN/WRL BS22 ....131 H4
TRWBR BA14 ....121 F2
Hanover Ct CBRIS/FH BS1 * 5 H2
Hanover Pl
CBATH/BATHN BA1 * 109 E4
CBRIS/FH BS1 ....4 B7
Hanover St CBATH/BATHN BA1 ..109 E3
EVILLE/WHL BS5 ....62 D4
Hanover Ter
CBATH/BATHN BA1 * 109 E3
Hansford Cl BATHSE BA2 ....116 C1
Hansford Sq BATHSE BA2 ....116 D1
Hanson's Wy CLVDN BS21 ....70 C3
Hans Price Cl WSM BS23 ....7 F3
Hantone Hl BATHSE BA2 ....110 A4
Happerton La PTSHD/EG BS20 ....58 B1
Hapsburg Cl MTN/WRL BS22 ....131 H4
Harbour Rd PTSHD/EG BS20 ....45 H2
Harbour Wall
HNLZ/SM/SNYPK/WT BS9 ....49 G4
Harbour Wy CBRIS/FH BS1 ....4 C6
Harbury Rd
HNLZ/SM/SNYPK/WT BS9 ....51 F1
Harbutts BATHSE BA2 ....110 A3
Harcombe Hl FRCTL/WBN BS36 ....41 F1
Harcombe Rd FRCTL/WBN BS36 ..28 D5
Harcourt Av EVILLE/WHL BS5 ....63 H5
Harcourt Cl KEYN BS31 * 105 F2
Harcourt Gdns
CBATH/BATHN BA1 ....107 G2
Harcourt Hl RDLND/MONT BS6 ..51 F5
Harcourt Rd RDLND/MONT BS6 ..51 E4
Hardenhuish Rd
BRSG/KWL/STAPK BS4 ....80 C1
Harden Rd HGRV/WHIT BS14 ....92 D4
Hardings Ter EVILLE/WHL BS5 * ..63 G3
Hardington Dr KEYN BS31 ....104 B2
Hardwick Cl
BRSG/KWL/STAPK BS4 ....80 D3
OLD/WMLY/WICK BS30 ....83 G1
Hardwicke YATE/CS BS37 ....31 G3
Hardwick Rd PTSHD/EG BS20 ....48 B4
Hardy Av BMSTR BS3 ....78 B3
Hardy Ct OLD/WMLY/WICK BS30 ..82 C1
Hardy Rd BMSTR BS3 ....78 B4
Hareclive Rd
BMSTRD/HC/WWD BS13 ....90 C4
Harefield Cl KGWD/HNM BS15 ....81 H4
Hare Knapp BOAV BA15 ....119 E3
Harescombe YATE/CS BS37 ....32 A3
Harewood Rd EVILLE/WHL BS5 ....63 H2
Harford Cl
HNLZ/SM/SNYPK/WT BS9 ....49 H1
Harford Dr MANG/FISH BS16 ....40 D4
Harford St TRWBR BA14 ....121 F5
Harington Pl CBATH/BATHN BA1 ....3 F4
Harlech Wy
OLD/WMLY/WICK BS30 ....83 E4
Harleston St EVILLE/WHL BS5 ....5 K1
Harley La CLVDN BS21 ....69 G4
Harley Pl CFTN/FAIL BS8 * 60 C4
Harley St CBATH/BATHN BA1 ....2 E1
Harmer Cl HNBRY/STHM BS10 ....37 E2
Harmony Dr PTSHD/EG BS20 ....44 C4
Harmony Pl TRWBR BA14 ....123 E2
Harnhill Cl
BMSTRD/HC/WWD BS13 ....90 C5
Harolds Wy KGWD/HNM BS15 ....64 B5
Harptree Cl NAIL BS48 ....85 E1
Harptree Ct
OLD/WMLY/WICK BS30 ....82 D2
Harptree Gv BMSTR BS3 ....78 C4
Harrington Av HGRV/WHIT BS14 ..92 D3
Harrington Cl
OLD/WMLY/WICK BS30 ....95 H1
Harrington Gv HGRV/WHIT BS14 ..92 D3
Harrington Rd HGRV/WHIT BS14 ..92 D3
Harrington Wk
HGRV/WHIT BS14 ....92 D3
Harris Barton FRCTL/WBN BS36 ..29 G3
Harris Ct OLD/WMLY/WICK BS30 ..82 C2
Harris La CFTN/FAIL BS8 ....59 E3
Harrison Cl MANG/FISH BS16 ....55 G2
Harrowdene Rd
BRSG/KWL/STAPK BS4 ....80 A3
Harrow Rd
BRSG/KWL/STAPK BS4 ....80 C3
Harry Stoke Rd
BRSTK/PCHW BS34 ....39 H2
Hartcliffe Rd
BRSG/KWL/STAPK BS4 ....91 F1
Hartcliffe Wk
BRSG/KWL/STAPK BS4 ....91 G1
Hartcliffe Wy BMSTR BS3 ....78 D5
BMSTRD/HC/WWD BS13 ....91 E3
BRSG/KWL/STAPK BS4 ....90 D2
Hart Cl PTSHD/EG BS20 ....48 D4
Hartfield Av RDLND/MONT BS6 ....61 F3
Hartgill Cl
BMSTRD/HC/WWD BS13 ....99 G1
Hartington Pk
RDLND/MONT BS6 ....61 E1
Hartley Cl YATE/CS BS37 ....33 E1
Harts Cft YATE/CS BS37 ....21 E3
Harts Paddock
RDSTK/MIDN BA3 ....124 A1
Harvest Cl ALMDB BS32 ....27 F1
Harvest La OMX/HUT/LCK BS24 ..137 E3
Harvest Wy MTN/WRL BS22 ....131 H3
Harvey Cl MTN/WRL BS22 ....131 H4
Harveys La EVILLE/WHL BS5 ....63 F3
Harwood Gdns MTN/WRL BS22 ..131 F4
Haselbury Gv KEYN BS31 ....105 F2
Haskins Ct
OLD/WMLY/WICK BS30 ....82 D2
Hassell Dr CBRISNE BS2 ....62 B4
Hastings Cl BMSTR BS3 ....78 D5
Hastings Rd BMSTR BS3 ....78 D5
Hatchet La BRSTK/PCHW BS34 ....39 H1
Hatchet Rd BRSTK/PCHW BS34 ....27 F5
Hatchmere THNB/SVB BS35 ....9 E4
Hatfield Buildings BATHSE BA2 ....3 J7
Hatfield Rd BATHSE BA2 ....114 B4
WSM BS23 ....7 K3
Hatherley YATE/CS BS37 ....32 A3
Hatherley Rd HORF/LLZ BS7 ....51 H4
Hathway Wk EVILLE/WHL BS5 ....62 B3
Hatters' La YATE/CS BS37 ....33 E1
Havelock St TRWBR BA14 ....122 D2
The Haven KGWD/HNM BS15 ....64 D2
Haversham Cl MTN/WRL BS22 ..136 A2
Haverstock Rd
BRSG/KWL/STAPK BS4 ....79 H3
Haviland Gv
CBATH/BATHN BA1 ....107 F1
Haviland Pk
CBATH/BATHN BA1 ....107 G2
Havory CBATH/BATHN BA1 ....109 E3
Hawarden Ter
CBATH/BATHN BA1 ....109 E3
Hawburn Cl
BRSG/KWL/STAPK BS4 ....80 C4

aweswater Cl
OLD/WMLY/WICK BS30 66 A5
awke Rd MTN/WRL BS22 131 F4
awkesbury Rd
MANG/FISH BS16 53 F5
awkesley Dr
BRSTK/PCHW BS34 27 F4
awkfield Cl
BMSTRD/HC/WWD BS13 91 E4
awkfield Rd
BMSTRD/HC/WWD BS13 91 E4
awkfield Wy
BMSTRD/HC/WWD BS13 91 E4
awkins Cl
OLD/WMLY/WICK BS30 83 F2
awkins Crs ALMDB BS32 27 F2
awkins St CBRISNE BS2 5 J3
awkley Dr ALMDB BS32 16 B4
awkridge Dr
MANG/FISH BS16 57 F3
awksmoor Cl
HGRV/WHIT BS14 91 H3
awksmoor La
MANG/FISH BS16 39 H5
awksworth Dr
KGWD/HNM BS15 81 G2
MTN/WRL BS22 132 B5
aw La THNB/SVB BS35 10 A5
awthorn Av KGWD/HNM BS15 81 G1
awthorn Cl BRSTK/PCHW BS34 26 A3
PTSHD/EG BS20 44 C3
awthorn Crs THNB/SVB BS35 8 D2
YTN/CONG BS49 126 A2
awthorne Cl MANG/FISH BS16 57 F3
awthorne Ri
HNBRY/STHM BS10 * 37 H2
he Hawthornes
MANG/FISH BS16 55 E4
awthorne St
BRSG/KWL/STAPK BS4 79 H3
awthorn Gdns
MTN/WRL BS22 136 A1
awthorn Gv BATHSE BA2 116 D1
TRWBR BA14 122 C4
awthorn Hts MTN/WRL BS22 131 E5
awthorn Hl MTN/WRL BS22 131 F5
awthorn Pk MTN/WRL BS22 131 F5
awthorns La KEYN BS31 94 B4
awthorn Wy
BRSTK/PCHW BS34 27 G5
NAIL BS48 73 G4
aycombe HGRV/WHIT BS14 91 G3
aycombe Dr BATHSE BA2 113 F3
aycombe La BATHSE BA2 113 F4
ay Ct PTSHD/EG BS20 47 H4
ayden Cl BATHSE BA2 2 D7
aydock Cl MANG/FISH BS16 41 G4
aydon Gdns HORF/LLZ BS7 52 C3
aydon Ga RDSTK/MIDN BA3 125 G4
aydon Hl RDSTK/MIDN BA3 125 G4
ayeley Dr BRSTK/PCHW BS34 27 G4
Hayes Cl CBRISNE BS2 62 B4
TRWBR BA14 121 F3
Hayesfield Pk BATHSE BA2 2 E7
Hayes Park Rd
RDSTK/MIDN BA3 124 A2
Hayes Pl BATHSE BA2 2 E7
Hayes Rd RDSTK/MIDN BA3 124 A2
Hay Hl CBATH/BATHN BA1 3 F2
Hay Leaze YATE/CS BS37 20 C3
The Haymarket CBRIS/FH BS1 5 F2
Haymarket Wk CBRIS/FH BS1 5 F1
Haynes La MANG/FISH BS16 54 C3
Haythorn Ct MANG/FISH BS16 55 E3
Haytor Pk
HNLZ/SM/SNYPK/WT BS9 50 A2
Hayward Cl CLVDN BS21 70 C4
Hayward Rd EVILLE/WHL BS5 62 D4
MANG/FISH BS16 54 C5
Haywood Cl
OMX/HUT/LCK BS24 139 F5
Haywood Gdns
OMX/HUT/LCK BS24 139 F5
Hazel Av RDLND/MONT BS6 61 E1
Hazelbury Dr
OLD/WMLY/WICK BS30 65 H5
Hazelbury Rd HGRV/WHIT BS14 92 B1
NAIL BS48 73 E5
Hazel Cote Rd HGRV/WHIT BS14 92 A5
Hazel Crs THNB/SVB BS35 9 E3
Hazeldene Rd
BRSTK/PCHW BS34 26 C3
WSM BS23 7 J2
Hazel Gdns THNB/SVB BS35 11 F3
Hazel Gv BATHSE BA2 114 A3
HORF/LLZ BS7 38 D5
RDSTK/MIDN BA3 124 C4
TRWBR BA14 122 C4
Hazelgrove FRCTL/WBN BS36 29 E5
Hazel La ALMDB BS32 11 E4
Hazell Cl CLVDN BS21 71 E4
Hazel Ter RDSTK/MIDN BA3 124 C4
Hazelton Rd HORF/LLZ BS7 51 G5
Hazel Wy BATHSE BA2 116 B2
Hazelwood Rd
HNLZ/SM/SNYPK/WT BS9 50 A5
Head Cft NAIL BS48 87 G1
Headford Av EVILLE/WHL BS5 64 A4
Headford Rd
BRSG/KWL/STAPK BS4 79 E5
Headington Cl
KGWD/HNM BS15 82 A2
Headley Ct
BMSTRD/HC/WWD BS13 90 C3
Headley La
BMSTRD/HC/WWD BS13 90 C3
Headley Park Av
BMSTRD/HC/WWD BS13 90 C2
Headley Park Rd
BMSTRD/HC/WWD BS13 90 B2
Headley Rd
BMSTRD/HC/WWD BS13 90 B3
Headley Wk
BMSTRD/HC/WWD BS13 90 C2
Heart Meers HGRV/WHIT BS14 92 A4
Heath Cl FRCTL/WBN BS36 29 E4
Heathcote Dr FRCTL/WBN BS36 30 B3
Heathcote Rd MANG/FISH BS16 64 A1
Heathcote Wk
KGWD/HNM BS15 64 B1
Heath Ct MANG/FISH BS16 54 C3
Heather Av FRCTL/WBN BS36 29 H4
Heather Cl KGWD/HNM BS15 64 A3
Heatherdene HGRV/WHIT BS14 91 G2
Heather Dr BATHSE BA2 116 B2
Heather Shaw TRWBR BA14 123 F1
Heathfield Cl
CBATH/BATHN BA1 107 F1
KEYN BS31 93 H4
Heathfield Crs HGRV/WHIT BS14 91 H5
Heathfield Rd NAIL BS48 73 F4
Heathfields MANG/FISH BS16 41 E5
Heathfield Wy NAIL BS48 73 F3
Heath Gdns FRCTL/WBN BS36 30 A4
MANG/FISH BS16 41 E5
Heathgate YTN/CONG BS49 126 B3
Heath House La
MANG/FISH BS16 52 D4
Heath Rdg LGASH BS41 76 D4
Heath Ri OLD/WMLY/WICK BS30 83 E1
Heath Rd EVILLE/WHL BS5 52 C5
KGWD/HNM BS15 81 G2
MANG/FISH BS16 54 C1
NAIL BS48 73 G4
Heath St EVILLE/WHL BS5 62 D1
Heath Wk MANG/FISH BS16 54 C1
Heber St EVILLE/WHL BS5 62 D4
Hebron Rd BMSTR BS3 78 D3
Heddington Cl TRWBR BA14 122 D4
Hedge Cl OMX/HUT/LCK BS24 137 E3
Hedgemead Vw
MANG/FISH BS16 53 E3
Hedges Cl CLVDN BS21 70 B4
The Hedges MTN/WRL BS22 132 B5
Hedwick St EVILLE/WHL BS5 63 F4
Heggard Cl
BMSTRD/HC/WWD BS13 90 B4
Hellier Wk
BMSTRD/HC/WWD BS13 99 H1
Helmdon Rd TRWBR BA14 120 B5
Helston Rd NAIL BS48 73 H5
Helting Ct CBATH/BATHN BA1 3 F5
Hemmings Pde EVILLE/WHL BS5 62 C4
Hemming Wy
OMX/HUT/LCK BS24 140 B3
Hemplow Cl HGRV/WHIT BS14 92 C2
Hempton La ALMDB BS32 15 G5
Henacre Rd AVONM BS11 35 G5
Henbury Gdns
HNBRY/STHM BS10 * 36 D3
Henbury Rd HNBRY/STHM BS10 36 D3
HNBRY/STHM BS10 37 E3
KGWD/HNM BS15 81 G1
Henbury Road Henbury Hl
HNLZ/SM/SNYPK/WT BS9 37 E5
Hencliffe Rd HGRV/WHIT BS14 92 C3
Hencliffe Wy KGWD/HNM BS15 81 G3
Henderson Cl TRWBR BA14 122 C2
Henderson Rd
KGWD/HNM BS15 81 G1
Hendre Rd BMSTR BS3 78 B4
Henfield Crs
OLD/WMLY/WICK BS30 83 E2
Henfield Rd FRCTL/WBN BS36 30 A5
Hengaston St BMSTR BS3 78 C4
Hengrove Av HGRV/WHIT BS14 92 A1
Hengrove La HGRV/WHIT BS14 92 A1
Hengrove Rd
BRSG/KWL/STAPK BS4 79 H4
Hengrove Wy
BMSTRD/HC/WWD BS13 90 C4
BRSG/KWL/STAPK BS4 91 F3
Henleaze Av
HNLZ/SM/SNYPK/WT BS9 50 D3
Henleaze Gdns
HNLZ/SM/SNYPK/WT BS9 50 D3
Henleaze Pk
HNLZ/SM/SNYPK/WT BS9 51 F3
Henleaze Park Dr
HNLZ/SM/SNYPK/WT BS9 51 F2
Henleaze Rd
HNLZ/SM/SNYPK/WT BS9 50 D3
Henleaze Ter
HNLZ/SM/SNYPK/WT BS9 51 E1
Henley Gv
HNLZ/SM/SNYPK/WT BS9 51 E3
Henley La YTN/CONG BS49 126 D4
Henley Ldg YTN/CONG BS49 126 D4
Henley Pk YTN/CONG BS49 126 C4
Hennessy Cl HGRV/WHIT BS14 100 B1
Henrietta Gdns BATHSE BA2 3 H2
Henrietta Ms BATHSE BA2 3 H3
Henrietta Pl CBATH/BATHN BA1 3 G3
Henrietta Rd BATHSE BA2 3 H2
Henrietta St BATHSE BA2 3 H3
CBRISNE BS2 61 F3
EVILLE/WHL BS5 62 C2
Henry St BMSTR BS3 79 G2
CBATH/BATHN BA1 3 G5
Henry Williamson Ct
OLD/WMLY/WICK BS30 82 D1
Henshaw Cl KGWD/HNM BS15 64 B1
Henshaw Rd KGWD/HNM BS15 64 B1
Henshaw Wk KGWD/HNM BS15 64 B1
Hensley Gdns BATHSE BA2 114 B3
Hensley Rd BATHSE BA2 114 B4
Hensman's Hl CFTN/FAIL BS8 60 D5
Hepburn Rd CBRIS/FH BS1 61 H3
Herald Cl
HNLZ/SM/SNYPK/WT BS9 50 A3
Herapath St EVILLE/WHL BS5 62 D5
Herbert Crs EVILLE/WHL BS5 55 E5
Herbert Rd BATHSE BA2 2 A7
CLVDN BS21 70 D1
Herbert St BMSTR BS3 78 D2
EVILLE/WHL BS5 62 D3
Hercules Cl BRSTK/PCHW BS34 27 F4
Hereford Rd CBRISNE BS2 62 B1
Hereford St BMSTR BS3 79 E3
Herkomer Cl HORF/LLZ BS7 52 C1
Herluin Wy WSM BS23 135 G5
Hermes Cl KEYN BS31 104 D2
Hermitage Cl AVONM BS11 48 D1
Hermitage Rd
CBATH/BATHN BA1 108 B3
MANG/FISH BS16 54 C3
Hern La NAIL BS48 88 B4
Heron Cl MTN/WRL BS22 136 B3
Heron Gdns PTSHD/EG BS20 45 H4
Heron Rd EVILLE/WHL BS5 62 C2
Heron Wy YATE/CS BS37 32 B3
Herridge Cl
BMSTRD/HC/WWD BS13 90 C5
Herridge Rd
BMSTRD/HC/WWD BS13 90 C5
Hersey Gdns
BMSTRD/HC/WWD BS13 98 D1
Hesding Cl KGWD/HNM BS15 81 H3
Hestercombe Rd
BMSTRD/HC/WWD BS13 90 C3
Hester Wd YATE/CS BS37 21 E3
Hewitt Cl TRWBR BA14 123 F2
Hewland Ct AVONM BS11 36 B3
Hewlands Ct AVONM BS11 * 36 B3
Heyford Av EVILLE/WHL BS5 52 C5
Heyron Wk
BMSTRD/HC/WWD BS13 90 C5
Heywood Rd PTSHD/EG BS20 48 B4
Heywood Ter PTSHD/EG BS20 48 B4
Hicks Av MANG/FISH BS16 42 A5
Hicks Common Rd
FRCTL/WBN BS36 29 E4
Hicks Ct
OLD/WMLY/WICK BS30 * 82 C2
Higham St
BRSG/KWL/STAPK BS4 79 G2
High Bannerdown
CBATH/BATHN BA1 103 G5
Highbury Pde WSM BS23 * 6 B1
Highbury Pl
CBATH/BATHN BA1 108 D3
Highbury Rd BMSTR BS3 78 D5
HORF/LLZ BS7 52 A1
WSM BS23 6 B1
Highbury Ter
CBATH/BATHN BA1 108 D3
Highbury Vls
CBATH/BATHN BA1 * 108 D3
CBRISNE BS2 4 C1
Highcroft
OLD/WMLY/WICK BS30 65 H5
Highdale Av CLVDN BS21 70 D2
Highdale Cl HGRV/WHIT BS14 92 A5
Highdale Rd CLVDN BS21 70 D2
High Elm KGWD/HNM BS15 64 D5
Highett Dr EVILLE/WHL BS5 62 B2
Highfield Av KGWD/HNM BS15 82 A1
Highfield Cl BATHSE BA2 113 G2
Highfield Dr PTSHD/EG BS20 44 B5
Highfield Gdns
OLD/WMLY/WICK BS30 83 F4
Highfield Gv HORF/LLZ BS7 51 G3
Highfield Rd BOAV BA15 119 G2
KEYN BS31 104 A2
OMX/HUT/LCK BS24 139 F5
YATE/CS BS37 32 C1
Highfields RDSTK/MIDN BA3 125 E2
Highfields Cl BRSTK/PCHW BS34 40 A2
High Gv
HNLZ/SM/SNYPK/WT BS9 49 G1
Highgrove St
BRSG/KWL/STAPK BS4 79 H2
High Kingsdown CBRISNE BS2 61 F3
Highland Cl MTN/WRL BS22 135 G1
Highland Crs CFTN/FAIL BS8 60 D1
Highland Pl CFTN/FAIL BS8 60 D1
Highland Rd BATHSE BA2 113 G2
Highlands La
OMX/HUT/LCK BS24 136 D3
Highland Sq CFTN/FAIL BS8 * 60 D1
Highlands Rd LGASH BS41 76 D4
PTSHD/EG BS20 45 E3
Highland Ter BATHSE BA2 2 A5
Highleaze Rd
OLD/WMLY/WICK BS30 83 F2
Highmead Gdns
BMSTRD/HC/WWD BS13 89 H5
High Mdw RDSTK/MIDN BA3 124 A3
Highmore Gdns HORF/LLZ BS7 52 D1
Highnam Cl BRSTK/PCHW BS34 26 D1
High Pk HGRV/WHIT BS14 80 A5
Highridge Crs
BMSTRD/HC/WWD BS13 90 A4
Highridge Gn
BMSTRD/HC/WWD BS13 89 H3
Highridge Pk
BMSTRD/HC/WWD BS13 90 A3
Highridge Rd BMSTR BS3 78 C4
LGASH BS41 98 B1
Highridge Wk
BMSTRD/HC/WWD BS13 89 H2
High St AVONM BS11 48 C1
BATHSE BA2 113 G1
BLAG/CWMG/WR BS40 97 H5
CBATH/BATHN BA1 3 G4
CBATH/BATHN BA1 107 G2
CBATH/BATHN BA1 110 A1
CBATH/BATHN BA1 110 D2
CBRIS/FH BS1 5 F4
CFTN/FAIL BS8 60 D1
EVILLE/WHL BS5 62 C2
FRCTL/WBN BS36 28 D4
HNLZ/SM/SNYPK/WT BS9 37 F5
KEYN BS31 94 B3
KEYN BS31 105 F1
KGWD/HNM BS15 64 D3
KGWD/HNM BS15 65 G3
KGWD/HNM BS15 81 H1
MANG/FISH BS16 54 B4
MTN/WRL BS22 136 B1
NAIL BS48 73 G4
OLD/WMLY/WICK BS30 66 A4
OLD/WMLY/WICK BS30 67 F5
OLD/WMLY/WICK BS30 83 G2
OLD/WMLY/WICK BS30 95 H1
PTSHD/EG BS20 45 G3
PTSHD/EG BS20 47 F5
RDSTK/MIDN BA3 124 C3
THNB/SVB BS35 8 C3
WSM BS23 6 D2
YATE/CS BS37 19 E3
YATE/CS BS37 32 D1
YTN/CONG BS49 126 B3
YTN/CONG BS49 127 F2
YTN/CONG BS49 128 D2
Highview BATHSE BA2 * 2 D7
High Vw PTSHD/EG BS20 44 D4
Highview Rd KGWD/HNM BS15 64 D1
Highway YATE/CS BS37 21 E5
Highwood La
BRSTK/PCHW BS34 26 A3
HNBRY/STHM BS10 25 H3
Highwood Rd
BRSTK/PCHW BS34 26 A3
Highworth Crs YATE/CS BS37 31 H2
Highworth Rd
BRSG/KWL/STAPK BS4 80 C1
Hildesheim Br WSM BS23 7 G5
Hildesheim Cl WSM BS23 7 H6
Hildesheim Ct WSM BS23 6 E5
Hill Av BATHSE BA2 116 D1
BMSTR BS3 79 F3
Hillbrook Rd THNB/SVB BS35 9 E4
Hill Burn
HNLZ/SM/SNYPK/WT BS9 51 F2
Hillburn Rd EVILLE/WHL BS5 63 H3
Hill Cl MANG/FISH BS16 42 A5
Hill Crest BRSG/KWL/STAPK BS4 80 A5
Hillcrest THNB/SVB BS35 8 C3
Hillcrest Cl NAIL BS48 73 F5
Hillcrest Dr BATHSE BA2 113 G4
Hillcrest Rd NAIL BS48 73 F5
PTSHD/EG BS20 44 B4
Hillcroft Cl MTN/WRL BS22 135 F1
OLD/WMLY/WICK BS30 82 B2
Hilldale Rd NAIL BS48 86 A4
Hill Dr CFTN/FAIL BS8 75 H3
Hill End Dr HNBRY/STHM BS10 36 C2
Hillfields Av MANG/FISH BS16 54 B5
Hill Frost YTN/CONG BS49 126 C5
Hill Gay Cl PTSHD/EG BS20 44 C4
Hill Gv HNLZ/SM/SNYPK/WT BS9 51 F2
Hillgrove St CBRISNE BS2 61 G3
Hillgrove St North CBRISNE BS2 61 G3
Hill House Rd MANG/FISH BS16 55 E3
Hill Lawn BRSG/KWL/STAPK BS4 80 C3
Hill Moor CLVDN BS21 71 E3
Hill Pk YTN/CONG BS49 129 E1
Hill Rd CLVDN BS21 70 D1
LGASH BS41 98 C2
MTN/WRL BS22 136 B1
WSM BS23 7 G2
Hill Rd East MTN/WRL BS22 136 B1
Hills Barton
BMSTRD/HC/WWD BS13 78 B5
Hillsborough Rd
BRSG/KWL/STAPK BS4 80 B2
Hills Cl KEYN BS31 94 D4
Hillsdon Rd
HNLZ/SM/SNYPK/WT BS9 37 E5
Hillside MANG/FISH BS16 55 E3
PTSHD/EG BS20 47 E5
Hillside Av KGWD/HNM BS15 64 B3
Hillside Cl FRCTL/WBN BS36 30 A3
Hillside Gdns MTN/WRL BS22 135 G2
Hillside La FRCTL/WBN BS36 30 A3
Hillside Rd BATHSE BA2 114 A3
CLVDN BS21 70 D2
EVILLE/WHL BS5 63 H4
LGASH BS41 77 E4
NAIL BS48 85 H4
PTSHD/EG BS20 44 A4
RDSTK/MIDN BA3 124 A4
Hillside St
BRSG/KWL/STAPK BS4 79 H2
Hillside West
OMX/HUT/LCK BS24 140 C3
Hill St BMSTR BS3 79 G2
CBRIS/FH BS1 4 C4
EVILLE/WHL BS5 63 G3
KGWD/HNM BS15 65 E3
TRWBR BA14 121 H2
TRWBR BA14 122 D1
The Hill ALMDB BS32 15 H3
Hilltop Gdns EVILLE/WHL BS5 63 H4
Hilltop Rd MANG/FISH BS16 64 C1
Hilltop Vw EVILLE/WHL BS5 63 H4
Hill Vw CFTN/FAIL BS8 4 A4
HNLZ/SM/SNYPK/WT BS9 51 F2
MANG/FISH BS16 64 C1
Hillview Av CLVDN BS21 70 D3
Hill View Cl
OLD/WMLY/WICK BS30 83 F2
Hillview Gdns
BLAG/CWMG/WR BS40 96 D4
Hill View Rd
BMSTRD/HC/WWD BS13 90 B2
CBATH/BATHN BA1 109 E2
MANG/FISH BS16 57 F3
WSM BS23 7 K4
Hillyfield Rd
BMSTRD/HC/WWD BS13 90 B3
Hilperton Dr TRWBR BA14 121 H4
Hilperton Rd TRWBR BA14 121 G5
Hinckley Cl MTN/WRL BS22 132 B5
Hinton Cl KEYN BS31 105 F1
Hinton Dr
OLD/WMLY/WICK BS30 65 H5
Hinton Rd EVILLE/WHL BS5 62 D2
MANG/FISH BS16 53 H4
Hiscocks Dr BATHSE BA2 114 B3
Hither Bath Br
BRSG/KWL/STAPK BS4 80 B5
Hither Gn CLVDN BS21 71 F3
Hither Md FRCTL/WBN BS36 29 H4
Hobart Rd WSM BS23 139 E3
Hobbiton Rd MTN/WRL BS22 131 H3
Hobb's La CBRIS/FH BS1 * 4 D4
KGWD/HNM BS15 65 G2
NAIL BS48 88 B5
Hobhouse Cl BOAV BA15 119 H5
HNLZ/SM/SNYPK/WT BS9 51 F1
Hobwell La LGASH BS41 77 F4
Hockey's La MANG/FISH BS16 53 H4
Hoddon La MANG/FISH BS16 57 G3
Hodshill BATHSE BA2 116 D4
Hogarth Wk HORF/LLZ BS7 52 C1
Hogues Wk
BMSTRD/HC/WWD BS13 90 C5
Holbeach Wy HGRV/WHIT BS14 100 D1
Holbrook Crs
BMSTRD/HC/WWD BS13 91 E5
Holbrook La
OLD/WMLY/WICK BS30 66 D4
TRWBR BA14 122 D3
Holcombe Cl BATHSE BA2 110 A3
Holcombe Gn
CBATH/BATHN BA1 107 G2
Holcombe Gv KEYN BS31 94 A4
Holcombe La BATHSE BA2 110 A3
Holcombe Ter
CBATH/BATHN BA1 * 107 G2
Holcombe V BATHSE BA2 110 A3
Holdenhurst Rd
KGWD/HNM BS15 64 B2
Holders Wk LGASH BS41 76 C5
Holford Cl NAIL BS48 73 F5
Holford Ct HGRV/WHIT BS14 92 A4
Holland Rd CBATH/BATHN BA1 109 E3
CLVDN BS21 70 B4
Holland St WSM BS23 7 J3
Hollidge Gdns BMSTR BS3 79 E2
Hollies La CBATH/BATHN BA1 103 F3
The Hollies RDSTK/MIDN BA3 * 124 B3
Hollis Av PTSHD/EG BS20 45 F5
Hollis Cl LGASH BS41 88 C1
Hollis Crs PTSHD/EG BS20 45 F5
Hollister's Dr
BMSTRD/HC/WWD BS13 100 A1
Holloway BATHSE BA2 3 F7
Holloway Rd THNB/SVB BS35 13 E5
Hollow La MTN/WRL BS22 131 G5
Hollowmead Cl
YTN/CONG BS49 127 F3
Hollow Rd ALMDB BS32 15 G3
KGWD/HNM BS15 64 D3
The Hollows FRCTL/WBN BS36 42 B3
The Hollow BATHSE BA2 113 F3
Hollway Cl HGRV/WHIT BS14 92 D4
Hollway Rd HGRV/WHIT BS14 92 D4
Hollybush Cl BOAV BA15 118 B2
Hollybush La
HNLZ/SM/SNYPK/WT BS9 50 C4
Holly Cl EVILLE/WHL BS5 63 H1
MANG/FISH BS16 57 F3
MTN/WRL BS22 136 D2
NAIL BS48 73 H3
THNB/SVB BS35 11 F3
Holly Ct RDSTK/MIDN BA3 * 124 C3
Holly Crs KGWD/HNM BS15 64 D2
Holly Dr BATHSE BA2 116 B2
Holly Gn KGWD/HNM BS15 65 F2
Holly Gv MANG/FISH BS16 54 B5
Hollyguest Rd KGWD/HNM BS15 64 D5
Holly Hl YATE/CS BS37 19 F4
Holly Hill Rd KGWD/HNM BS15 65 E3
Holly La CLVDN BS21 68 D4
Hollyleigh Av
BRSTK/PCHW BS34 38 C3
Holly Lodge Cl EVILLE/WHL BS5 63 H1
Holly Lodge Rd EVILLE/WHL BS5 63 G1
Hollyman Wk CLVDN BS21 71 F2
Hollymead La
HNLZ/SM/SNYPK/WT BS9 50 B4
Holly Rdg PTSHD/EG BS20 44 D3
Holly Wk RDSTK/MIDN BA3 125 F3
Hollywood La THNB/SVB BS35 24 D2
Hollywood Rd
BRSG/KWL/STAPK BS4 80 C3
Holmdale Rd
BRSTK/PCHW BS34 39 E2
Holmesdale Rd BMSTR BS3 79 F3
Holmes Gv
HNLZ/SM/SNYPK/WT BS9 51 E3
Holmes Hill Rd EVILLE/WHL BS5 63 G3
Holmes St EVILLE/WHL BS5 62 C5
Holmoak Rd KEYN BS31 93 H5
Holm Rd OMX/HUT/LCK BS24 140 B4
Holms Rd WSM BS23 139 F1
Holmwood KGWD/HNM BS15 81 H1
Holmwood Cl FRCTL/WBN BS36 28 D4
Holmwood Gdns
HNLZ/SM/SNYPK/WT BS9 37 F5
Holsom Cl HGRV/WHIT BS14 92 D3
Holsom Rd HGRV/WHIT BS14 93 E3
Holst Gdns
BRSG/KWL/STAPK BS4 90 D2
Holton Rd HORF/LLZ BS7 52 B2
Holt Rd BOAV BA15 119 H3
Holtsdown La
CBATH/BATHN BA1 102 D1
Holyrood Cl BRSTK/PCHW BS34 39 G1
TRWBR BA14 122 C4
Holy Well Cl
BRSG/KWL/STAPK BS4 63 F5
Homeapple Hl
OLD/WMLY/WICK BS30 66 B4
Home Cl HNBRY/STHM BS10 38 B3
TRWBR BA14 123 E2
Home Farm Rd CFTN/FAIL BS8 59 F4
Home Farm Wy THNB/SVB BS35 25 E1
Homefield OMX/HUT/LCK BS24 140 C1
THNB/SVB BS35 9 E4
YATE/CS BS37 20 D4
YTN/CONG BS49 128 D3
Homefield Cl KEYN BS31 105 F1
Home Field Cl MANG/FISH BS16 55 G2
Homefield Rd KEYN BS31 105 F1
MANG/FISH BS16 57 E3
Home Gnd AVONM BS11 48 C1

Homeground CLVDN BS21 ....71 E3
Home Gnd
HNLZ/SM/SNYPK/WT BS9 ....51 E1
Homeground MANG/FISH BS16....55 G2
Homelea Pk East
CBATH/BATHN BA1 ....107 F5
Homelea Pk West
CBATH/BATHN BA1 ....107 F5
Homeleaze Rd
HNBRY/STHM BS10 ....38 A2
Home Md
BRSG/KWL/STAPK BS4 * 91 F2
OLD/WMLY/WICK BS30.............82 D2
Homemead Dr
BRSG/KWL/STAPK BS4 ....80 C5
Home Orch YATE/CS BS37 ....20 C5
Homestead PTSHD/EG BS20 ....44 B5
Homestead Cl FRCTL/WBN BS36 ..30 B3
Homestead Gdns
MANG/FISH BS16.......................40 C4
Homestead Rd
BRSTK/PCHW BS34 ....38 C2
The Homestead CLVDN BS21........70 C2
KEYN BS31 ....104 A2
TRWBR BA14 * 122 D3
Honey Garston Cl
BMSTRD/HC/WWD BS13 ....90 C5
Honey Garston Rd
BMSTRD/HC/WWD BS13 ....90 C5
Honey Hill Rd KGWD/HNM BS15 ...65 E3
Honeylands PTSHD/EG BS20........45 F5
Honeymans Cl TRWBR BA14 ....123 G1
Honeymead HGRV/WHIT BS14 .....92 B3
Honeysuckle Cl ALMDB BS32..........16 C5
TRWBR BA14 ....123 F2
Honey Suckle La
MANG/FISH BS16.......................53 F4
Honeysuckle Pl
OMX/HUT/LCK BS24 ....136 D2
Honeywick Cl BMSTR BS3 ....78 D4
Honiton Rd CLVDN BS21...............71 E4
MANG/FISH BS16.......................53 H5
Hooper Rd HGRV/WHIT BS14 ....92 C4
Hoover's La YATE/CS BS37 ....18 D4
Hopechapel Hl CFTN/FAIL BS8 ......60 C5
Hope Rd BMSTR BS3 ....78 D4
YATE/CS BS37 ....19 H5
Hope Sq CFTN/FAIL BS8 ....60 C5
Hopetoun Rd CBRISNE BS2 ....52 A5
Hopewell Gdns AVONM BS11.........49 E1
Hopkin Cl THNB/SVB BS35 ....9 E5
Hopkins St WSM BS23......................6 E3
Hopland Cl
OLD/WMLY/WICK BS30.............83 E3
Hopp's Rd KGWD/HNM BS15 ....64 C4
Horesham Gv
BMSTRD/HC/WWD BS13 ....90 D4
Horfield Common
HORF/LLZ BS7 ....51 H1
Horfield Rd CBRISNE BS2 ....4 E2
Horley Rd CBRISNE BS2 ....62 B2
Horsecastle Cl YTN/CONG BS49 ..126 A2
Horsecombe Brow
BATHSE BA2 ....117 E1
Horsecombe Gv BATHSE BA2 ......117 E1
Horsecombe V BATHSE BA2........117 E1
Horsecroft Gdns
OLD/WMLY/WICK BS30..............65 F5
The Horsefair CBRIS/FH BS1 ....5 G2
Horsepool Rd
BMSTRD/HC/WWD BS13 ....89 H5
Horse Rd TRWBR BA14 ....121 F2
Horseshoe Dr
HNLZ/SM/SNYPK/WT BS9 ....49 H4
Horseshoe La YATE/CS BS37 ....32 D1
Horseshoe Wk BATHSE BA2 ....3 K6
Horse St YATE/CS BS37 ....33 E2
Horstmann Cl
CBATH/BATHN BA1 ....107 G5
Hortham La ALMDB BS32 ....16 A1
Horton Cl BOAV BA15 ....119 H5
Horton Rd YATE/CS BS37 ....21 H5
Horton St CBRISNE BS2....................5 K4
Horwood Ct
OLD/WMLY/WICK BS30..............82 D2
Horwood Rd NAIL BS48 ....73 G5
Hosey Wk
BMSTRD/HC/WWD BS13 ....90 B4
Host St CBRIS/FH BS1 ....4 E3
Hottom Gdns HORF/LLZ BS7 ....52 B1
Hot Water La KGWD/HNM BS15 ...55 E5
Hotwell Rd CFTN/FAIL BS8 ....60 C5
Houlton St CBRISNE BS2..................5 J1
Hounds Rd YATE/CS BS37...............32 D2
Howard Av EVILLE/WHL BS5 ....63 F3
Howard Cl KEYN BS31..................104 D1
Howard Rd BMSTR BS3 ....78 C2
MANG/FISH BS16........................54 C4
RDLND/MONT BS6......................51 E4
THNB/SVB BS35............................8 D2
Howard St EVILLE/WHL BS5...........63 F2
Howard Wk
OLD/WMLY/WICK BS30..............66 A5
Howecroft Gdns
HNLZ/SM/SNYPK/WT BS9 ....50 B4
Howells Md MANG/FISH BS16 ....55 G1
Howes Cl
OLD/WMLY/WICK BS30..............65 F5
Howett Rd EVILLE/WHL BS5...........62 D4
How Hl BATHSE BA2 ....113 F1
Howsmoor La MANG/FISH BS16 ..42 B5
Hoylake Dr
OLD/WMLY/WICK BS30..............65 G5
Huckford La FRCTL/WBN BS36 ......41 H1
Huckford Rd FRCTL/WBN BS36 ....29 E5
Huckley Wy ALMDB BS32...............27 H4
Hudd's Hill Rd EVILLE/WHL BS5 ...63 G3
Hudd's Vale Rd EVILLE/WHL BS5 ..63 G3
Hudson Cl YATE/CS BS37 ....32 B2
Hughenden Rd CFTN/FAIL BS8 .....60 D1
HORF/LLZ BS7 ....51 H3
WSM BS23 ....7 K3
Hulbert Cl
BRSG/KWL/STAPK BS4 ....81 F4
Hulse Rd BRSG/KWL/STAPK BS4 ..80 C5
Humberstan Wk AVONM BS11 ....35 F5
Humber Wy AVONM BS11 ....22 D5
Humphrys Barton
BRSG/KWL/STAPK BS4 ....81 E1
Hungerford Av TRWBR BA14......122 B2
Hungerford Cl
BRSG/KWL/STAPK BS4 ....92 D1
Hungerford Crs
BRSG/KWL/STAPK BS4 ....92 D1
Hungerford Gdns
BRSG/KWL/STAPK BS4 ....92 D1
Hungerford Rd
BRSG/KWL/STAPK BS4 ....80 D5
CBATH/BATHN BA1 ....107 H5
Hungerford Wk
BRSG/KWL/STAPK BS4 ....80 D5
Hung Rd AVONM BS11 ....48 D2
Hunters Cl KGWD/HNM BS15......81 H1
Hunters Dr KGWD/HNM BS15 .....65 E2
Hunters Rd KGWD/HNM BS15 .....81 H1
Hunters Rd East
KGWD/HNM BS15 ....81 H1
Hunter's Wy BRSTK/PCHW BS34 ..39 E2
Huntingdon Pl BOAV BA15..........119 F2
Huntingdon Ri BOAV BA15..........119 F1
Huntingdon St BOAV BA15..........119 F1
Huntingham Rd
BMSTRD/HC/WWD BS13 ....89 H5
Huntley Gv NAIL BS48 ....73 H5
Hunts Ground Rd
BRSTK/PCHW BS34 ....40 A1
Hunt's La YTN/CONG BS49 ....127 E3
Hurle Crs CFTN/FAIL BS8...............60 D2
Hurle Rd CFTN/FAIL BS8 ....61 E2
Hurlingham Rd
RDLND/MONT BS6......................62 A1
Hurn La KEYN BS31 ....94 C5
Hurn Rd CLVDN BS21....................71 E3
Hursley Hl PLTN/PENS BS39.........101 G5
Hursley La HGRV/WHIT BS14 ....101 H3
Hurston Rd
BRSG/KWL/STAPK BS4 ....91 E1
Hurst Rd BRSG/KWL/STAPK BS4 ..91 G1
WSM BS23 ....7 J6
Hurst Wk BRSG/KWL/STAPK BS4 ..91 F2
Hurstwood Rd MANG/FISH BS16..54 C3
Hutton Cl
HNLZ/SM/SNYPK/WT BS9 ....50 B1
KEYN BS31 ....104 B2
Hutton Hl OMX/HUT/LCK BS24 ..140 B4
Hutton Moor La
OMX/HUT/LCK BS24 ....139 H1
WSM BS23 ....135 H5
Hutton Moor Rd
MTN/WRL BS22 ....135 G4
Hutton Pk
OMX/HUT/LCK BS24 * 135 H5
Huyton Rd EVILLE/WHL BS5...........53 F5
Hyde Av THNB/SVB BS35 ....8 C1
Hyde Rd TRWBR BA14..................120 D4
The Hyde CLVDN BS21..................70 C5
Hyland Gv
HNLZ/SM/SNYPK/WT BS9 ....37 E5

I

Ida Rd EVILLE/WHL BS5..................62 D3
Iddesleigh Rd
RDLND/MONT BS6......................51 E5
Idstone Rd MANG/FISH BS16 ....54 A4
Iford Cl KEYN BS31......................105 F1
Ilchester Crs
BMSTRD/HC/WWD BS13 ....78 C5
Ilchester Rd
BMSTRD/HC/WWD BS13 ....90 C1
Iles Cl KGWD/HNM BS15 ....82 A2
Ilex Av CLVDN BS21 ....71 E3
Ilex Cl BMSTRD/HC/WWD BS13 ....90 A3
Ilminster Av
BRSG/KWL/STAPK BS4 ....79 F5
Ilminster Cl CLVDN BS21 ....71 E4
NAIL BS48 ....85 E1
Ilsyn Gv HGRV/WHIT BS14............92 C2
Imber Court Cl
HGRV/WHIT BS14......................92 A1
Imperial Pk
BMSTRD/HC/WWD BS13 * 90 D3
Imperial Rd CFTN/FAIL BS8............61 E2
HGRV/WHIT BS14......................92 B1
Imperial Wk HGRV/WHIT BS14.......80 A5
Inglesham Cl TRWBR BA14...........123 E4
Ingleside Rd KGWD/HNM BS15 .....64 B2
Ingleton Dr MTN/WRL BS22 ....131 H4
Ingmire Rd EVILLE/WHL BS5 ....52 C5
Inkerman Cl HORF/LLZ BS7 ....51 H1
The Inner Down ALMDB BS32 ....10 D4
Innox Gdns
BMSTRD/HC/WWD BS13 ....90 B4
Innox Gv BATHSE BA2 ....113 E5
Innox La CBATH/BATHN BA1 ....102 A4
Innox Mill Cl TRWBR BA14 ....120 C5
Innox Rd BATHSE BA2...................113 G2
TRWBR BA14 ....120 C5
Inns Court Av
BRSG/KWL/STAPK BS4 ....91 E2
Inns Court Dr
BRSG/KWL/STAPK BS4 ....91 E3
Inns Court Gn
BRSG/KWL/STAPK BS4 ....91 E2
Instow Rd
BRSG/KWL/STAPK BS4 ....91 F1
Instow Wk
BRSG/KWL/STAPK BS4 ....91 F1
Inverness Rd BATHSE BA2 ....113 H1
Ipswich Dr
BRSG/KWL/STAPK BS4 ....63 F5
Irby Rd BMSTR BS3 ....78 B3
Irena Rd MANG/FISH BS16 ....53 G5
Ireton Rd BMSTR BS3 ....78 C3
Iron Acton Wy YATE/CS BS37 ......19 H4
Ironchurch Rd AVONM BS11 ....22 B5
Ironmould La
BRSG/KWL/STAPK BS4 ....81 F5
Irving Cl CLVDN BS21.....................71 F2
MANG/FISH BS16.......................54 D4
The Island RDSTK/MIDN BA3 ......124 B3
Isleys Ct
OLD/WMLY/WICK BS30.............82 C3
Islington TRWBR BA14 ....121 E5
Islington Rd BMSTR BS3.................78 C2
Ison Hill Rd
HNBRY/STHM BS10 * 36 C2
Ivo Peters Rd BATHSE BA2..............2 D5
Ivor Rd EVILLE/WHL BS5 ....62 D3
Ivor Ter PTSHD/EG BS20 * 45 F4
Ivy Av BATHSE BA2 ....113 H3
Ivy Bank Pk BATHSE BA2 ....114 C5
Ivy Ct PTSHD/EG BS20....................44 C3
Ivy Gv BATHSE BA2 ....113 H3
Ivy La MANG/FISH BS16.................53 H5
Ivy Pl BATHSE BA2 ....113 H3
Ivy Ter BOAV BA15......................119 G2
Ivy Wk RDSTK/MIDN BA3 ....124 C4
Ivywell Rd
HNLZ/SM/SNYPK/WT BS9 ....50 B5
Iwood La
BLAG/CWMG/WR BS40 ....129 G5

J

Jackson Cl THNB/SVB BS35 ....13 F2
Jacobs Meadow
PTSHD/EG BS20.........................46 A4
Jacob Pl CBRIS/FH BS1 ....5 F6
Jacob St CBRISNE BS2 ....5 J3
Jacob's Well Rd CFTN/FAIL BS8 ....4 A4
Jamaica St CBRISNE BS2.................61 G3
James Cl MANG/FISH BS16 ....54 D4
James Pl CFTN/FAIL BS8 * 60 C4
James Rd MANG/FISH BS16 ....54 D5
James St CBRISNE BS2 ....62 B1
EVILLE/WHL BS5 ....5 K1
TRWBR BA14 ....121 E4
James St West
CBATH/BATHN BA1 ....2 D4
Jane St EVILLE/WHL BS5 ....62 C4
Jarvis St EVILLE/WHL BS5 ....62 C5
Jasmine Cl MTN/WRL BS22...........136 D2
Jasmine Gv AVONM BS11 ....36 B3
Jasmine La YTN/CONG BS49.........127 F1
Jasmine Wy
OMX/HUT/LCK BS24 ....136 D2
TRWBR BA14 ....123 F2
Jasper St BMSTR BS3 ....78 C3
Jean Rd BRSG/KWL/STAPK BS4 ....80 D4
Jefferies Hill Bottom
KGWD/HNM BS15 ....81 G1
Jeffery Ct
OLD/WMLY/WICK BS30..............65 G5
Jellicoe Av MANG/FISH BS16 ....53 F1
Jellicoe Ct MTN/WRL BS22 ....131 F4
Jena Ct KEYN BS31......................105 E1
Jenkins St TRWBR BA14 ....120 D4
Jenner Cl YATE/CS BS37 ....33 F2
Jersey Av
BRSG/KWL/STAPK BS4 ....81 E3
Jesmond Rd CLVDN BS21 ....70 C2
MTN/WRL BS22 ....132 B4
Jesse Hughes Ct
CBATH/BATHN BA1 ....109 F2
Jessop U/P BMSTR BS3...................78 A2
Jews La BATHSE BA2.....................113 H1
Jocelin Dr MTN/WRL BS22 ....131 G4
Jocelyn Rd HORF/LLZ BS7 ....52 A1
Jockey La EVILLE/WHL BS5.............63 H4
John Carr's Ter
CFTN/FAIL BS8 ....4 B4
John Rennie Cl BOAV BA15 ....119 H5
Johnson Dr
OLD/WMLY/WICK BS30..............82 C1
Johnson Rd MANG/FISH BS16 ....55 H3
Johnsons La EVILLE/WHL BS5 ....63 E2
Johnsons Rd EVILLE/WHL BS5 ....63 E3
Johnstone St BATHSE BA2 ....3 H4
John St CBATH/BATHN BA1 ....3 F3
CBRIS/FH BS1..............................5 F3
CBRISNE BS2 ....62 B1
KGWD/HNM BS15 ....64 B3
John Wesley Rd
EVILLE/WHL BS5 ....64 A5
Jones Hl BOAV BA15 ....119 F4
Jordan Wk ALMDB BS32 ....27 F2
Joy Hl CFTN/FAIL BS8 * 60 C5
Jubilee Crs MANG/FISH BS16 ....55 F2
Jubilee Dr CFTN/FAIL BS8 ....75 G2
THNB/SVB BS35............................9 E4
Jubilee Gdns YATE/CS BS37 ....21 F5
Jubilee Pl CLVDN BS21 ....70 D4
Jubilee Rd
BRSG/KWL/STAPK BS4 ....80 B5
CBRISNE BS2 ....62 B2
EVILLE/WHL BS5 ....63 G4
KGWD/HNM BS15 ....54 D5
RDSTK/MIDN BA3 ....125 E3
WSM BS23 ....7 F4
Jubilee St CBRISNE BS2...................5 K4
Jubilee Wy AVONM BS11 ....34 C3
MTN/WRL BS22 ....132 B5
YATE/CS BS37 ....21 E2
Julian Cl
HNLZ/SM/SNYPK/WT BS9 ....50 A5
Julian Rd CBATH/BATHN BA1 ....2 E1
HNLZ/SM/SNYPK/WT BS9 ....50 B5
Julius Cl MANG/FISH BS16..............55 H2
Julius Rd HORF/LLZ BS7 ....51 G5
Junction Av BATHSE BA2 ....2 C7
Junction Cut AVONM BS11 * 34 B4
Junction Rd BATHSE BA2 ....2 C7
BOAV BA15 ....119 G4
BRSG/KWL/STAPK BS4 ....80 B2
Juniper Ct EVILLE/WHL BS5 ....62 D1
Juniper Pl MTN/WRL BS22 ....131 G4
Juniper Wy ALMDB BS32 ....27 H3
Jupiter Rd BRSTK/PCHW BS34 ....25 H3
Justice Av KEYN BS31 ....105 F1
Justice Rd MANG/FISH BS16..........53 G5
Jutland Rd AVONM BS11.................34 C4

K

Karen Cl NAIL BS48 ....85 H5
Karen Dr NAIL BS48 ....85 H4
Kathdene Gdns HORF/LLZ BS7 .....52 A5
Kaynton Md
CBATH/BATHN BA1 ....107 G5
Keates Cl TRWBR BA14 ....121 E5
Keats Rd RDSTK/MIDN BA3 ....124 C4
Keble Av
BMSTRD/HC/WWD BS13 ....90 A4
Keeds La LGASH BS41 ....76 C5
Keedwell Hl LGASH BS41................76 C5
Keel Cl EVILLE/WHL BS5 * 63 G5
Keene's Wy CLVDN BS21................70 B3
Keen's Gv THNB/SVB BS35 ....13 E2
The Keep MTN/WRL BS22.............131 H5
OLD/WMLY/WICK BS30.............83 G1
Keinton Wk
HNBRY/STHM BS10 ....37 F3
Kelbra Crs FRCTL/WBN BS36 ....29 H4
Kellaway Av HORF/LLZ BS7 ....51 H2
Kellaway Crs HORF/LLZ BS7...........51 G2
Kellways NAIL BS48 ....85 G5
Kelso Pl CBATH/BATHN BA1 *.........2 A3
Kelston Cl KEYN BS31 ....105 E1
YATE/CS BS37 ....31 H4
Kelston Gdns
HNBRY/STHM BS10 ....38 A5
Kelston Gv KGWD/HNM BS15.........64 D5
Kelston Rd CBATH/BATHN BA1 ..106 D3
HNBRY/STHM BS10 ....37 H5
KEYN BS31 ....94 A5
MTN/WRL BS22 ....132 A4
Kelston Vw BATHSE BA2...............113 F2
Kelston Wk MANG/FISH BS16 ......54 B4
Kelting Gv CLVDN BS21 ....71 F3
Kemble Cl KGWD/HNM BS15 ....64 D5
NAIL BS48 ....73 H5
Kemperleye Wy ALMDB BS32 ......27 F3
Kempe's Cl LGASH BS41.................76 D4
Kempton Cl THNB/SVB BS35 ....8 C1
Kencot Wk
BMSTRD/HC/WWD BS13 ....99 G1
Kendall Gdns MANG/FISH BS16 ...54 C4
Kendall Rd MANG/FISH BS16 ....54 C4
Kendal Rd HORF/LLZ BS7 ....52 B1
Kendon Dr HNBRY/STHM BS10 ....51 G1
Kendon Wy HNBRY/STHM BS10 ..38 A5
Kenilworth YATE/CS BS37 ....32 B2
Kenilworth Cl KEYN BS31 ....94 A5
Kenilworth Ct
CBATH/BATHN BA1 * 108 D4
Kenilworth Dr
OLD/WMLY/WICK BS30..............83 E5
Kenilworth Rd
RDLND/MONT BS6......................61 F2
Kenmare Rd
BRSG/KWL/STAPK BS4 ....79 F5
Kenmore Crs HORF/LLZ BS7..........38 B4
Kenmore Dr HORF/LLZ BS7 ....38 B4
Kenmore Gv HORF/LLZ BS7 ....38 B4
Kennard Ri KGWD/HNM BS15 ......64 B4
Kennard Rd KGWD/HNM BS15.......64 B3
Kennaway Rd CLVDN BS21 ....70 D3
Kenn Cl WSM BS23.......................139 F1
Kennedy Wy YATE/CS BS37 ....32 A1
Kennel Lodge Rd BMSTR BS3 ....77 H2
Kennet Gdns BOAV BA15 ....119 G4
Kenneth Rd
BRSG/KWL/STAPK BS4 ....80 C4
Kennet Pk BATHSE BA2 ....109 H3
Kennet Rd KEYN BS31....................94 C5
Kennet Wy THNB/SVB BS35.............9 E4
TRWBR BA14 ....121 E3
Kennington Av HORF/LLZ BS7........51 H4
KGWD/HNM BS15 ....64 C2
Kennington Rd
CBATH/BATHN BA1 ....107 G5
Kennion Rd EVILLE/WHL BS5 ....63 H4
Kennmoor Cl
OLD/WMLY/WICK BS30..............65 F5
Kenn Moor Dr CLVDN BS21 ....71 E4
Kenn Moor Rd YTN/CONG BS49..126 B2
Kenn Rd CLVDN BS21 ....70 D2
EVILLE/WHL BS5 ....63 H4
Kensal Av BMSTR BS3....................79 F3
Kensal Rd BMSTR BS3....................79 F3
Kensington Cl THNB/SVB BS35 ......8 C2
TRWBR BA14 ....121 E4
Kensington Ct
CBATH/BATHN BA1 * 109 E3
Kensington Flds TRWBR BA14....122 B3
Kensington Gdns
CBATH/BATHN BA1 ....109 E3
Kensington Pk EVILLE/WHL BS5 ..62 B2
Kensington Park Rd
BRSG/KWL/STAPK BS4 ....80 B4
Kensington Pl
CBATH/BATHN BA1 * 109 E3
CFTN/FAIL BS8 ....60 D4
Kensington Rd EVILLE/WHL BS5 ..63 H3
MANG/FISH BS16.......................54 C4
RDLND/MONT BS6.....................61 F2
WSM BS23 ....139 E1
Kent Av YATE/CS BS37 ....21 E4
Kent Cl BRSTK/PCHW BS34............39 G1
Kenton Dr TRWBR BA14 ....121 G5
Kenton Ms
HNLZ/SM/SNYPK/WT BS9 ....51 F
Kent Rd HORF/LLZ BS7 ....51 H
YTN/CONG BS49......................128 D
Kents Gn KGWD/HNM BS15 ....64 D
Kent St BMSTR BS3 ....78 D
Kent Wy MTN/WRL BS22 ....132 A
Kenwood Cl TRWBR BA14 ....123 G
Keppel Cl KEYN BS31...................105 E
Kerry Rd BRSG/KWL/STAPK BS4 ..79 F
Kersteman Rd
RDLND/MONT BS6.....................61 F
Kestrel Cl BRSTK/PCHW BS34........26 A
THNB/SVB BS35...........................9 E
YATE/CS BS37 ....32 B
Kestrel Dr MANG/FISH BS16..........57 F
MTN/WRL BS22 ....136 B
Keswick Wk HNBRY/STHM BS10 ..37 H
Ketch Rd BMSTR BS3 ....79 G
Ketton Cl TRWBR BA14................120 B
Kew Dr TRWBR BA14...................122 B
Kew Rd WSM BS23 ....6 E
Kewside MTN/WRL BS22 ....130 C
Kewstoke Rd BATHSE BA2...........114 D
HNLZ/SM/SNYPK/WT BS9 ....50 B
WSM BS23 ....134 C
Kew Wk BRSG/KWL/STAPK BS4 ....92 B
Keyes Pth MTN/WRL BS22 ....131 G
Keynsham By-Pass KEYN BS31 ....94 B
Keynsham Rd
OLD/WMLY/WICK BS30..............94 C
Keys Av HORF/LLZ BS7 ....52 A
Kielder Dr MTN/WRL BS22 ....131 G
Kilbirnie Rd HGRV/WHIT BS14 ....100 D
Kildare Rd
BRSG/KWL/STAPK BS4 ....79 E
Kilkenney Pl PTSHD/EG BS20........45 F
Kilkenny St CBRISNE BS2 ....5 K
Kilmersdon Rd
BMSTRD/HC/WWD BS13 ....90 C5
RDSTK/MIDN BA3 ....125 F4
Kilminster Cl BRSTK/PCHW BS34..27 F4
Kilminster Rd AVONM BS11 ....48 C
Kiln Cl KGWD/HNM BS15...............64 A2
Kilnhurst Cl
OLD/WMLY/WICK BS30..............82 C4
Kilvert Cl BRSG/KWL/STAPK BS4 ..80 C
Kimberley Av MANG/FISH BS16....54 B
Kimberley Cl MANG/FISH BS16 ....55 E1
Kimberley Crs MANG/FISH BS16 ..54 B3
Kimberley Rd CLVDN BS21 ....70 C3
KGWD/HNM BS15 ....64 C2
MANG/FISH BS16.......................54 B3
Kinber Cl CBATH/BATHN BA1 ......107 F1
King Alfred Wy BOAV BA15 ....118 A2
King Edward Cl
HGRV/WHIT BS14.......................91 H3
King Edward Rd BATHSE BA2 ....2 B7
Kingfisher Cl ALMDB BS32 ....16 C5
THNB/SVB BS35............................9 E2
Kingfisher Dr MANG/FISH BS16....53 F2
RDSTK/MIDN BA3 ....124 C4
Kingfisher Rd MTN/WRL BS22....136 C3
YATE/CS BS37 ....32 C2
King George's Rd BATHSE BA2 ..113 H1
BMSTRD/HC/WWD BS13 ....90 A4
King John's Rd
KGWD/HNM BS15 ....64 A1
King Rd BRSG/KWL/STAPK BS4 ....80 A5
King Road Av AVONM BS11 ....34 B3
Kingrove Crs YATE/CS BS37 ....33 E2
Kingrove La YATE/CS BS37.............33 E3
Kings Av KGWD/HNM BS15 ....81 G2
RDLND/MONT BS6......................51 F4
Kingscote YATE/CS BS37 ....31 H4
Kingscote Pk EVILLE/WHL BS5 ....64 A5
Kingscourt Cl HGRV/WHIT BS14 ..91 H4
Kingsdown Gv
CBATH/BATHN BA1 ....111 G2
Kingsdown Pde
RDLND/MONT BS6.......................4 E1
Kingsdown Rd TRWBR BA14 ......122 D4
Kings Dr BRSTK/PCHW BS34 ....40 B1
HORF/LLZ BS7 ....51 F3
KGWD/HNM BS15 ....81 H1
Kingsfield BATHSE BA2 ....113 H4
BOAV BA15 ....119 G2
Kingsfield Cl BOAV BA15..............119 G3
Kingsfield Grange Rd
BOAV BA15 ....119 H3
Kingsfield La
OLD/WMLY/WICK BS30..............82 B2
Kings Gdns TRWBR BA14 ....121 F2
King's Head La
BMSTRD/HC/WWD BS13 ....89 H2
Kingshill NAIL BS48 ....72 D4
Kingshill Rd
BRSG/KWL/STAPK BS4 ....80 A5
Kingsholme Rd
KGWD/HNM BS15 ....64 C2
Kingsholm Rd
HNBRY/STHM BS10....................38 A5
Kingsland Rd CBRISNE BS2 ....62 B5
Kings La CLVDN BS21....................68 B5
WSM BS23 ....6 E3
Kingsleigh Ct KGWD/HNM BS15 ..65 E4
Kingsleigh Gdns
KGWD/HNM BS15 ....65 E4
Kingsley Pl TRWBR BA14 ....120 B5
Kingsley Rd CLVDN BS21 ....70 D3
EVILLE/WHL BS5 ....62 D2
RDLND/MONT BS6.....................61 G1
RDSTK/MIDN BA3 ....124 C3
WSM BS23 ....139 E3
Kingsmead NAIL BS48....................72 D4
Kingsmead North
CBATH/BATHN BA1 ....2 E5
Kingsmead Rd EVILLE/WHL BS5 ..63 H2
Kingsmead Sq
CBATH/BATHN BA1 * 3 F4
Kingsmead St CBATH/BATHN BA1..3 F4
Kingsmead Wk EVILLE/WHL BS5 ..63 H2
Kingsmead West
CBATH/BATHN BA1 ....2 E5

ngsmill
HNLZ/SM/SNYPK/WT BS9 ....50 A3
ng's Parade Av CFTN/FAIL BS8..60 D2
ng's Parade Ms
CFTN/FAIL BS8 ....60 D2
ngs Park Av CBRISNE BS2 ....62 D5
ng Sq CBRISNE BS2.....................61 G3
ng Square Av CBRISNE BS2 ....5 F1
ng's Rd BRSG/KWL/STAPK BS4..80 B3
CFTN/FAIL BS8 ....60 D4
CLVDN BS21 ....68 B5
PTSHD/EG BS20..........................44 C4
ngs Sq OLD/WMLY/WICK BS30..95 G1
ngston Av BOAV BA15...............119 H4
CLVDN BS21 ....71 E2
KEYN BS31 ....104 D2
ngston Buildings
CBATH/BATHN BA1 * 3 G5
ngston Cl MANG/FISH BS16 ....55 F1
ngston Dr MANG/FISH BS16 ....55 F1
ngston La
BLAG/CWMG/WR BS40 ....97 F4
ngston Rd BMSTR BS3...............78 D2
BOAV BA15 ....119 G3
CBATH/BATHN BA1 ....3 G5
ngston Wy NAIL BS48 ....84 D1
ngstree St
BRSG/KWL/STAPK BS4 ....79 H2
ng St AVONM BS11 ....34 B4
CBRIS/FH BS1................................4 E5
EVILLE/WHL BS5 ....62 D2
KGWD/HNM BS15 ....64 A3
ngs Wk
BMSTRD/HC/WWD BS13 ....89 H2
ingsway BATHSE BA2 ....113 H4
BRSTK/PCHW BS34 ....27 E4
EVILLE/WHL BS5 ....64 A4
ngsway Av KGWD/HNM BS15....64 A3
ingsway Crs KGWD/HNM BS15 ..64 A3
ingswear Rd BMSTR BS3 ....79 E5
ings Weston Av AVONM BS11 .....48 C1
ings Weston La AVONM BS11 .....34 D1
AVONM BS11 ....35 G5
ings Weston Rd AVONM BS11....36 A5
ington La THNB/SVB BS35 ....8 A3
ing William Av CBRIS/FH BS1 ......5 F5
ing William St BMSTR BS3 ....78 C2
insale Rd HGRV/WHIT BS14 ....92 B2
insale Wk
BRSG/KWL/STAPK BS4 ....79 F5
invara Rd
BRSG/KWL/STAPK BS4 ....91 F1
ipling Av BATHSE BA2...............114 C3
ipling Rd HORF/LLZ BS7 ....39 E4
RDSTK/MIDN BA3 ....124 D4
WSM BS23 ....139 F3
irkby Rd AVONM BS11 ....35 H4
irtlington Rd EVILLE/WHL BS5....52 C5
ite Hay Cl MANG/FISH BS16 * 53 F4
ites Cl ALMDB BS32 ....16 A5
napp Rd THNB/SVB BS35 ....9 E3
napp Rd East
THNB/SVB BS35..............................9 F2
napps La EVILLE/WHL BS5 ....63 F1
he Knapp YATE/CS BS37 ....20 D2
he Knap TRWBR BA14................121 H3
nightcott Rd CFTN/FAIL BS8 ....59 E3
nighton Rd
HNBRY/STHM BS10......................38 B4
nightsbridge Pk
BMSTRD/HC/WWD BS13 ....91 F5
nights Cl
HNLZ/SM/SNYPK/WT BS9 ....51 E2
MTN/WRL BS22 ....131 H3
Knightstone Cswy WSM BS23..........6 A2
Knightstone Pl
KGWD/HNM BS15 * 81 G3
Knightstone Rd WSM BS23 ....6 B2
Knightstone Sq
HGRV/WHIT BS14 * 92 B4
Knightswood NAIL BS48 * 73 E3
Knightwood Rd
BRSTK/PCHW BS34 ....27 H5
Knole Cl ALMDB BS32 ....15 F3
Knole La HNBRY/STHM BS10 ....37 F2
Knole Pk ALMDB BS32...................15 F4
Knoll Hl
HNLZ/SM/SNYPK/WT BS9 ....50 A5
The Knoll PTSHD/EG BS20 ....45 G1
Knovill Cl AVONM BS11 ....36 A4
Knowle Rd
BRSG/KWL/STAPK BS4 ....79 H3
Knowles Rd CLVDN BS21 ....70 C3
Knowsley Rd MANG/FISH BS16 ....53 F5
Kyght Cl KGWD/HNM BS15...........65 F3
Kylross Av HGRV/WHIT BS14 ....92 A4
Kynges Mill Cl MANG/FISH BS16 ..53 H1

L

The Labbott KEYN BS31 ....94 B4
Laburnum Cl RDSTK/MIDN BA3..124 A4
Laburnum Ct WSM BS23.............135 G4
Laburnum Gv MANG/FISH BS16.....54 A4
RDSTK/MIDN BA3 ....124 A4
TRWBR BA14 ....122 C3
Laburnum Rd KGWD/HNM BS15 ..81 H1
WSM BS23 ....7 K4
Laburnum Ter
CBATH/BATHN BA1 ....110 A1
Lacey Rd HGRV/WHIT BS14 ....92 D3
Lacock Dr
OLD/WMLY/WICK BS30...............82 C1
Ladd Cl KGWD/HNM BS15............65 E4
Ladden Ct THNB/SVB BS35 ....9 D4
Ladies Mile
HNLZ/SM/SNYPK/WT BS9 ....60 C2
Ladman Gv HGRV/WHIT BS14 ....92 D3
Ladman Rd HGRV/WHIT BS14 ....92 D4
Ladycroft CLVDN BS21 ....70 B4
Ladye Bay CLVDN BS21.................68 B4
Ladye Wake MTN/WRL BS22 ......131 G4
Ladymead PTSHD/EG BS20 ....46 A3
Ladysmith Rd
RDLND/MONT BS6.......................51 E4
Laggan Gdns
CBATH/BATHN BA1 ....108 B3
Lakemead Gv
BMSTRD/HC/WWD BS13 ....90 A3
Lake Rd HNBRY/STHM BS10..........51 F1
PTSHD/EG BS20...........................45 F2
Lakeside MANG/FISH BS16 ....53 F5
Lake View Rd EVILLE/WHL BS5 ....63 E3
Lakewood Crs
HNBRY/STHM BS10.....................37 G5
Lakewood Rd
HNBRY/STHM BS10.....................37 G5
Lamb Ale Gn TRWBR BA14 ....123 E3
Lambert Cl
BRSG/KWL/STAPK BS4 ....91 E3
Lambert Pl
BRSG/KWL/STAPK BS4 ....91 E3
Lamb Hl EVILLE/WHL BS5 ....63 F4
Lambley Rd EVILLE/WHL BS5........63 F3
Lambourn Cl BMSTR BS3 ....79 E3
Lambourne Wy PTSHD/EG BS20..46 A4
Lambourn Rd KEYN BS31 ....94 D5
Lambridge
CBATH/BATHN BA1 * 109 F3
Lambridge Buildings
CBATH/BATHN BA1 * 109 F3
Lambridge Ms
CBATH/BATHN BA1 ....109 F3
Lambridge St
CBATH/BATHN BA1 ....109 F3
Lambrok Cl TRWBR BA14 ....122 A3
Lambrok Rd TRWBR BA14 ....122 A3
Lambrook Rd MANG/FISH BS16....53 H4
Lamb St CBRISNE BS2 ....5 K2
Lamington Cl
BMSTRD/HC/WWD BS13 ....90 A3
Lamord Ga BRSTK/PCHW BS34 ....27 G5
Lampards Buildings
CBATH/BATHN BA1 ....2 E1
Lampeter Rd
HNLZ/SM/SNYPK/WT BS9 ....50 C1
Lampton Av
BMSTRD/HC/WWD BS13 ....100 B1
Lampton Gv
BMSTRD/HC/WWD BS13 ....100 B1
Lampton Rd LGASH BS41 ....76 C5
Lanaway Rd MANG/FISH BS16......54 A2
Lancashire Rd HORF/LLZ BS7........51 H5
Lancaster Cl BRSTK/PCHW BS34 ..39 G1
Lancaster Rd CBRISNE BS2............62 B1
YATE/CS BS37 ....20 D4
Lancaster St EVILLE/WHL BS5 ......62 D4
Lancelot Rd MANG/FISH BS16 ......39 H5
Landemann Circ WSM BS23............7 F1
Landemann Pth WSM BS23 ....7 F2
Landseer Av HORF/LLZ BS7 ....52 C1
Landseer Cl MTN/WRL BS22.........131 G5
Landseer Rd BATHSE BA2............113 G1
The Land FRCTL/WBN BS36 ....30 A3
Lanercost Rd
HNBRY/STHM BS10.....................37 H3
Lanesborough Ri
HGRV/WHIT BS14........................92 C2
Lanes End
BRSG/KWL/STAPK BS4 ....80 B5
Laneys Dro
OMX/HUT/LCK BS24 ....140 B1
Langdale Rd MANG/FISH BS16......53 G4
Langdon Rd BATHSE BA2 ....113 G3
Langfield Cl HNBRY/STHM BS10 ..36 D2
Langford Rd
BMSTRD/HC/WWD BS13 ....90 A1
TRWBR BA14 ....120 D4
WSM BS23 ....7 J6
Langford Wy KGWD/HNM BS15 ..64 D4
Langham Rd
BRSG/KWL/STAPK BS4 ....80 A4
Langhill Av
BRSG/KWL/STAPK BS4 ....91 E2
Langley Crs BMSTR BS3 ....77 H5
Langley Mow MANG/FISH BS16....55 G1
Langley Rd TRWBR BA14 ....122 D4
Langport Gdns NAIL BS48.............85 F1
Langport Rd WSM BS23 ....7 F7
Langthorn Cl
FRCTL/WBN BS36 ....29 H3
Langton Court Rd
BRSG/KWL/STAPK BS4 ....80 C1
Langton Pk BMSTR BS3 ....78 D2
Langton Rd
BRSG/KWL/STAPK BS4 ....80 C1
Langton Wy
BRSG/KWL/STAPK BS4 ....63 G5
Lansdown YATE/CS BS37 ....32 A2
Lansdown Cl
KGWD/HNM BS15 ....64 C1
TRWBR BA14 ....122 C2
Lansdown Crs
CBATH/BATHN BA1 ....108 C4
Lansdown Gv
CBATH/BATHN BA1 ....108 C4
Lansdown Grove Ct
CBATH/BATHN BA1 * 108 C4
Lansdown Hts
CBATH/BATHN BA1 ....108 C3
Lansdown La
CBATH/BATHN BA1 ....107 G1
Lansdown Pk
CBATH/BATHN BA1 ....108 B1
Lansdown Pl CFTN/FAIL BS8 ....60 D4
Lansdown Pl East
CBATH/BATHN BA1 ....108 C4
Lansdown Pl West
CBATH/BATHN BA1 ....108 B3
Lansdown Rd CBATH/BATHN BA1 ..3 F1
CFTN/FAIL BS8 ....60 D4
KEYN BS31 ....105 F1
KGWD/HNM BS15 ....64 C1
MANG/FISH BS16.........................57 F2
RDLND/MONT BS6.......................61 F2
Lansdown Ter
CBATH/BATHN BA1 ....3 F1
CBATH/BATHN BA1 * 107 H3
RDLND/MONT BS6.......................51 G3
Lansdown Vw BATHSE BA2 ....113 H2
KGWD/HNM BS15 ....64 D3
Lanthony Cl
OMX/HUT/LCK BS24 ....136 D3
Laphams Ct
OLD/WMLY/WICK BS30...............82 C2
Lapwing Cl ALMDB BS32...............16 B5
Lapwing Gdns MANG/FISH BS16 ..53 F2
MTN/WRL BS22 ....136 C2
Larch Cl NAIL BS48.......................73 H4
Larch Ct RDSTK/MIDN BA3 ....125 E4
The Larches MTN/WRL BS22 ......131 H5
Larch Gv TRWBR BA14 ....122 C3
Larchgrove Crs
MTN/WRL BS22 ....136 C2
Larch Rd KGWD/HNM BS15 ....54 D5
Larch Wy BRSTK/PCHW BS34........26 A3
Lark Cl RDSTK/MIDN BA3 ....124 C4
Lark Down TRWBR BA14 ....121 F5
Larkfield FRCTL/WBN BS36 ....30 B3
Larkhall Pl CBATH/BATHN BA1....109 F2
Larkhall Ter CBATH/BATHN BA1 109 F2
Larkhill Rd OMX/HUT/LCK BS24..137 E5
Lark Pl CBATH/BATHN BA1 ....2 A2
Lark Ri YATE/CS BS37 ....20 D3
Lark Rd MTN/WRL BS22 ....136 C2
Lark's Fld MANG/FISH BS16 ....53 F3
Larksleaze Rd
OLD/WMLY/WICK BS30...............82 B4
Larkspur Cl THNB/SVB BS35...........9 E2
Lasbury Gv
BMSTRD/HC/WWD BS13 ....90 D4
Late Broads BOAV BA15 ....118 A2
Latimer Cl
BRSG/KWL/STAPK BS4 ....80 D2
Latteridge Rd YATE/CS BS37 ....19 E3
Latton Rd HORF/LLZ BS7 ....38 C5
Launceston Av
KGWD/HNM BS15 ....81 G1
Launceston Rd
KGWD/HNM BS15 ....64 A2
Laura Pl BATHSE BA2 ....3 H4
Laurel Dr NAIL BS48......................73 G4
WSM BS23 ....138 D4
Laurel Gdns YTN/CONG BS49 ......126 B2
Laurel Gv TRWBR BA14 ....122 D3
The Laurels HNBRY/STHM BS10 ..25 E4
MANG/FISH BS16.........................55 F2
Laurel St KGWD/HNM BS15 ....64 C3
Laurel Ter YTN/CONG BS49.........126 B2
Laurie Crs
HNLZ/SM/SNYPK/WT BS9 ....51 G2
Laurie Lee Ct
OLD/WMLY/WICK BS30...............82 D1
Lavender Cl THNB/SVB BS35 ....9 E3
TRWBR BA14 ....123 F2
Lavender Wy ALMDB BS32............27 H3
Lavenham Rd YATE/CS BS37 ....20 A5
Lavers Cl KGWD/HNM BS15 ....64 D5
Lavington Cl CLVDN BS21 ....70 A4
Lavington Rd EVILLE/WHL BS5 .....64 A5
Lawford Av BRSTK/PCHW BS34.....27 E2
Lawfords Ga CBRISNE BS2 ....5 K2
Lawford St CBRISNE BS2 ....5 K3
Lawn Av MANG/FISH BS16 ....54 A3
Lawn Rd MANG/FISH BS16 ....54 A3
Lawns Rd YATE/CS BS37 ....20 D5
The Lawns AVONM BS11 * 48 D1
MTN/WRL BS22 ....132 A5
YTN/CONG BS49........................126 A2
Lawrence Av EVILLE/WHL BS5......62 C2
Lawrence Cl KGWD/HNM BS15 .....65 F1
Lawrence Close Ms
MTN/WRL BS22 * 136 B1
Lawrence Dr YATE/CS BS37 ....20 A5
Lawrence Gv
HNLZ/SM/SNYPK/WT BS9 ....51 E3
Lawrence Hl EVILLE/WHL BS5 ......62 C4
Lawrence Weston Rd
AVONM BS11 ....23 E5
Lawson Cl KEYN BS31 ....104 D2
Laxey Rd HORF/LLZ BS7 ....52 A1
Laxton Cl THNB/SVB BS35 ....10 A4
Lays Dr KEYN BS31......................93 H5
Leach Cl CLVDN BS21...................70 C4
Leafield Pl TRWBR BA14.............120 A5
Leafy Wy OMX/HUT/LCK BS24....141 E2
Lea Grove Rd CLVDN BS21 ....70 C1
Leaholme Gdns
HGRV/WHIT BS14......................100 D1
Leaman Cl YATE/CS BS37 ....32 C1
Leap Ga TRWBR BA14 ....121 H5
Leap V MANG/FISH BS16...............41 H5
Leap Valley Crs
MANG/FISH BS16.........................41 G5
The Leaze RDSTK/MIDN BA3 ....125 E4
YATE/CS BS37 ....20 C5
Leda Av HGRV/WHIT BS14 ....91 H2
Ledbury Rd MANG/FISH BS16 ......54 B4
Leechpool Wy YATE/CS BS37........20 D2
Lee Cl BRSTK/PCHW BS34.............26 B2
Leedham Rd
OMX/HUT/LCK BS24 ....141 F1
Leeming Wy AVONM BS11 ....34 D5
Lees Hl KGWD/HNM BS15............64 D1
Leeside PTSHD/EG BS20...............45 F3
Lees La OLD/WMLY/WICK BS30 ....83 G1
Leewood Rd WSM BS23 ....134 D2
Leicester Sq MANG/FISH BS16 .....54 C5
Leicester St BMSTR BS3 ....79 E2
Leicester Wk
BRSG/KWL/STAPK BS4 ....81 E1
Leigh Cl CBATH/BATHN BA1 ....108 D2
Leigh La YATE/CS BS37 ....43 H4
Leigh Park Rd BOAV BA15 ....119 G1
Leigh Rd CFTN/FAIL BS8 ....61 E3
Leigh St BMSTR BS3 ....78 B2
Leighton Rd BMSTR BS3...............78 C2
BRSG/KWL/STAPK BS4 ....80 A4
CBATH/BATHN BA1 ....107 F1
Leigh View Rd PTSHD/EG BS20 ....45 G1
Leighwood Dr NAIL BS48 ....72 C5
Leinster Av
BRSG/KWL/STAPK BS4 ....91 F1
Leisure Rd KGWD/HNM BS15 ....82 B1
Lena Av EVILLE/WHL BS5 ....62 D2
Lena St EVILLE/WHL BS5 ....62 C2
Lenover Gdns
BMSTRD/HC/WWD BS13 ....90 C5
Leonard La CBRIS/FH BS1 ....4 E3
Leonard Rd EVILLE/WHL BS5 ....62 D4
Leonards Av EVILLE/WHL BS5 ......62 D2
Leopold Buildings
CBATH/BATHN BA1 * 108 D4
Leopold Rd RDLND/MONT BS6 ....61 H1
Lescren Wy AVONM BS11 ....35 E4
Lester Dr MTN/WRL BS22 ....131 H5
Lewington Rd MANG/FISH BS16 ..54 B4
Lewins Md CBRIS/FH BS1 ....4 E2
Lewin St EVILLE/WHL BS5.............63 E4
Lewis Cl MANG/FISH BS16.............55 G3
OLD/WMLY/WICK BS30...............83 G1
Lewisham Gv WSM BS23 ....7 J4
Lewis Rd
BMSTRD/HC/WWD BS13 ....90 B1
Lewis St CBRISNE BS2 ....80 A1
Lewton La FRCTL/WBN BS36 ....29 E3
Leyland Wk
BMSTRD/HC/WWD BS13 ....90 A5
The Leys CLVDN BS21 ....70 B4
Leyton Vls RDLND/MONT BS6 ....61 E1
Liberty Gdns CBRIS/FH BS1 * 4 C7
Lichfield Rd
BRSG/KWL/STAPK BS4 ....63 F5
Liddington Wy TRWBR BA14 ......122 D4
Lilac Cl HNBRY/STHM BS10..........37 H4
Lilac Gv TRWBR BA14 ....122 B4
Lilac Ter RDSTK/MIDN BA3 ....124 D2
Lilac Wy MTN/WRL BS22.............131 H3
Lillian St EVILLE/WHL BS5 ....62 D3
Lilliput Av YATE/CS BS37..............32 C2
Lilliput Ct YATE/CS BS37 ....32 C2
Lilstock Av HORF/LLZ BS7.............52 A4
Lilton Wk
BMSTRD/HC/WWD BS13 ....78 B5
Lilymead Av
BRSG/KWL/STAPK BS4 ....79 H3
Lime Breach Wd NAIL BS48 * 73 E3
Lime Cl HNBRY/STHM BS10 ....37 G2
MTN/WRL BS22 ....136 D2
OMX/HUT/LCK BS24 ....141 E2
Lime Cft YATE/CS BS37 ....21 F3
Lime Gv BATHSE BA2......................3 J5
THNB/SVB BS35..........................11 F2
Lime Grove Gdns BATHSE BA2.......3 K5
Lime Kiln Cl BRSTK/PCHW BS34....39 G3
Lime Kiln Gdns ALMDB BS32 ....16 B4
Lime Kiln La CLVDN BS21 ....70 D2
Lime Kiln Rd CFTN/FAIL BS8..........4 B5
Limekilns Cl KEYN BS31...............94 C4
Limerick Rd RDLND/MONT BS6 ....61 F1
Lime Rd BMSTR BS3 ....78 C2
KGWD/HNM BS15 ....81 F1
Limestone Link BATHSE BA2 ....110 B2
CBATH/BATHN BA1 ....103 F3
Lime Ter RDSTK/MIDN BA3..........125 E3
Lime Tree Gv PTSHD/EG BS20 .....48 C5
Limpley Stoke Rd BOAV BA15 ....118 A3
Lincoln Cl KEYN BS31...................93 H5
Lincoln St EVILLE/WHL BS5..........62 C4
Lincombe Av MANG/FISH BS16 ...54 C2
Lincombe Rd MANG/FISH BS16 ...54 B3
RDSTK/MIDN BA3 ....125 E4
Linden Av WSM BS23 ....135 G3
Linden Cl FRCTL/WBN BS36 ....29 E4
KGWD/HNM BS15 ....64 A1
RDSTK/MIDN BA3 ....125 F4
Linden Dr ALMDB BS32 ....27 F2
Linden Gdns
CBATH/BATHN BA1 ....108 A4
Linden Pl TRWBR BA14 ....120 C5
Linden Rd CLVDN BS21 ....70 D1
RDLND/MONT BS6.......................51 E4
The Lindens MTN/WRL BS22 ....131 F4
Lindrea St BMSTR BS3..................78 C3
Lindsay Rd HORF/LLZ BS7 ....52 B4
Lindsey Cl PTSHD/EG BS20...........44 C4
Linemere Cl NAIL BS48 ....86 C3
Lines Wy HGRV/WHIT BS14..........101 F1
Lingfield Pk FRCTL/WBN BS36......41 G4
Link La BOAV BA15.....................111 G4
Link Rd BRSTK/PCHW BS34 ....38 D3
NAIL BS48 ....73 G4
PTSHD/EG BS20...........................45 F3
YATE/CS BS37 ....32 B1
Linkside CLVDN BS21....................68 C4
Links Rd WSM BS23 ....138 B4
Linley Cl BATHSE BA2 ....113 F2
The Linleys CBATH/BATHN BA1 ..107 H5
Linnell Cl HORF/LLZ BS7 ....52 C2
Linnet Cl BRSTK/PCHW BS34 ....26 A2
MTN/WRL BS22 ....136 B2
Linnet Wy RDSTK/MIDN BA3 ....124 C4
Lintern Crs
OLD/WMLY/WICK BS30...............65 F5
Lintham Dr KGWD/HNM BS15 ......65 E5
Linton's Wk HGRV/WHIT BS14 ......91 H2
Lion Cl NAIL BS48 ....72 D4
Lisburn Rd
BRSG/KWL/STAPK BS4 ....79 F5
Lisle Rd MTN/WRL BS22 ....132 A4
Litfield Pl CFTN/FAIL BS8 * 60 C4
Litfield Rd CFTN/FAIL BS8............60 C3
Little Ann St CBRISNE BS2 ....5 K2
Little Birch Cft
HGRV/WHIT BS14......................100 D1
Little Bishop St CBRISNE BS2 ....61 H3
Little Caroline Pl CFTN/FAIL BS8 ..78 A1
Littledean YATE/CS BS37 ....32 A4
Little Dowles
OLD/WMLY/WICK BS30...............82 D2
Little George St CBRISNE BS2 ....5 K1
WSM BS23 ....7 F4
Little Green La THNB/SVB BS35....12 C2
Little Halt PTSHD/EG BS20 ....44 B4
Little Ham CLVDN BS21.................70 C5
Little Hayes MANG/FISH BS16 ......54 A3
Little Headley Cl
BMSTRD/HC/WWD BS13 ....90 C2
Little King St CBRIS/FH BS1 ....5 F5
Little Md AVONM BS11 ....36 A4
Little Mead Cl
OMX/HUT/LCK BS24 ....140 B3
Little Meadow ALMDB BS32..........27 H4
Little Meadow End NAIL BS48.......85 F1
Little Orch WSM BS23 ....138 C5
Little Paradise BMSTR BS3............79 E2
Little Parr Cl MANG/FISH BS16......52 D3
Little Stanhope St
CBATH/BATHN BA1 * 2 D4
Little Stoke La
BRSTK/PCHW BS34 ....27 E3
Little Stoke Rd
HNLZ/SM/SNYPK/WT BS9 ....50 B4
Littleton Rd BMSTR BS3 ....79 E4
Littleton St EVILLE/WHL BS5 ....62 D2
Little Withey Md
HNLZ/SM/SNYPK/WT BS9 ....50 C2
Littlewood Cl HGRV/WHIT BS14..101 E1
Littlewood La YTN/CONG BS49 ..127 H1
Livingstone Rd BATHSE BA2 ....2 A6
Livingstone Ter BATHSE BA2 ....2 B7
Llewellyn Wy MTN/WRL BS22 .....132 A5
Lockemor Rd
BMSTRD/HC/WWD BS13 ....91 G5
Lockeridge Cl TRWBR BA14 ....123 E4
Lock Gdns
BMSTRD/HC/WWD BS13 ....89 H2
Locking Head Dro
OMX/HUT/LCK BS24 ....140 C1
Locking Moor Rd
MTN/WRL BS22 ....135 H3
Locking Rd MTN/WRL BS22 ....136 A3
WSM BS23 ....7 G5
Lockingwell Rd KEYN BS31 ....94 A4
Lockleaze Rd HORF/LLZ BS7 ....52 B2
Locksbrook Pl
CBATH/BATHN BA1 * 107 H5
Locksbrook Rd
CBATH/BATHN BA1 ....113 G1
MTN/WRL BS22 ....132 A3
Loddon Wy BOAV BA15..............119 H4
Lodge Cswy MANG/FISH BS16......53 G5
Lodge Cl YTN/CONG BS49 ....126 B3
Lodge Ct
HNLZ/SM/SNYPK/WT BS9 * 50 B4
Lodge Dr LGASH BS41 ....77 E4
OLD/WMLY/WICK BS30...............83 F4
WSM BS23 ....135 F2
Lodge Gdns BATHSE BA2 ....116 B1
Lodge Hl KGWD/HNM BS15 ....64 B1
Lodge La NAIL BS48.....................73 H4
Lodge Rd KGWD/HNM BS15..........64 B1
OLD/WMLY/WICK BS30...............66 D3
YATE/CS BS37 ....19 H5
Lodgeside Av KGWD/HNM BS15 ..64 B2
Lodgeside Gdns
KGWD/HNM BS15 ....64 B2
Lodge St CBRIS/FH BS1..................4 D3
Lodge Wk MANG/FISH BS16 ....54 C2
Lodore Rd MANG/FISH BS16 ....53 G5
Lodway PTSHD/EG BS20...............48 A4
Lodway Cl PTSHD/EG BS20 ....48 B3
Lodway Gdns PTSHD/EG BS20.......48 B4
Lodway Rd
BRSG/KWL/STAPK BS4 ....80 B4
Logan Rd HORF/LLZ BS7 ....51 G5
Logus Ct OLD/WMLY/WICK BS30..82 C2
Lombard St BMSTR BS3 ....79 E2
Lombardy Cl MTN/WRL BS22......136 B3
Lomond Rd HORF/LLZ BS7 ....38 C4
London Rd CBATH/BATHN BA1 ......3 G1
CBRISNE BS2 ....62 A2
OLD/WMLY/WICK BS30...............65 H4
OLD/WMLY/WICK BS30...............67 H5
London Rd East
CBATH/BATHN BA1 ....110 B1
London Rd West
CBATH/BATHN BA1 ....109 G2
London St KGWD/HNM BS15 ....64 C3
Long Acre CBATH/BATHN BA1 ...108 D4
Longacre CLVDN BS21..................70 B5
Longacre Rd HGRV/WHIT BS14 ..100 D1
Long Acres Cl
HNLZ/SM/SNYPK/WT BS9 ....50 A1
Long Ashton Rd LGASH BS41........76 D5
Long Av CLVDN BS21 ....70 B3
Long Barnaby
RDSTK/MIDN BA3 ....124 B2
Long Beach Rd
OLD/WMLY/WICK BS30...............82 D4
Long Cl ALMDB BS32 ....27 G4
MANG/FISH BS16.........................54 B2
Long Cft YATE/CS BS37 ....20 C2
Long Cross AVONM BS11 ....35 G4
BLAG/CWMG/WR BS40 ....97 E5
Longden Rd MANG/FISH BS16 .....55 E2
Longdown Dr MTN/WRL BS22.....132 A4
Long Eaton Dr
HGRV/WHIT BS14........................92 A1
Longfellow Av BATHSE BA2.........114 C3
Longfellow Rd
RDSTK/MIDN BA3 ....124 D3
Longfield Rd HORF/LLZ BS7..........51 H5
TRWBR BA14 ....123 E2
Longford YATE/CS BS37 ....31 G2
Longford Av
HNBRY/STHM BS10.....................38 A5
Long Handstones
OLD/WMLY/WICK BS30.............100 D2
Long Hay Cl BATHSE BA2 ....113 G2
Longleat Cl
HNLZ/SM/SNYPK/WT BS9 ....51 F3
Longleaze Gdns
OMX/HUT/LCK BS24 ....140 C3
Long Md YATE/CS BS37 ....20 D2
Longmead Av HORF/LLZ BS7 ....51 G3
Long Meadow MANG/FISH BS16 ..53 E3

Longmeadow Rd KEYN BS31...93 H5
Longmead Rd MANG/FISH BS16...42 A4
Longmoor Ct BMSTR BS3...78 B4
Longmoor Rd BMSTR BS3...78 B4
Longney Pl BRSTK/PCHW BS34...26 B1
Longreach Gv HGRV/WHIT BS14...92 C2
Longridge Wy
OMX/HUT/LCK BS24...136 C4
Long Rd MANG/FISH BS16...55 F3
Long Rw CBRIS/FH BS1 *...5 G5
Longs Dr YATE/CS BS37...20 C5
Long Thorn NAIL BS48...85 H3
Longthorne Pl BATHSE BA2 *...114 C5
Longton Grove Rd WSM BS23...6 E2
Long Valley Rd BATHSE BA2...113 E2
Longway Av HGRV/WHIT BS14...91 G5
Longwood
BRSG/KWL/STAPK BS4...81 F4
Longwood La CFTN/FAIL BS8...76 B2
Lonsdale Av WSM BS23...139 E2
Lorain Wk HNBRY/STHM BS10...37 E3
Lorton Cl HNBRY/STHM BS10...37 G4
Lorton Rd HNBRY/STHM BS10...37 G4
Lotts' Av NAIL BS48...86 A4
Louisa St CBRISNE BS2...5 K4
Louise Av MANG/FISH BS16...55 F3
Love La YATE/CS BS37...21 F3
YATE/CS BS37...32 C2
Lovelinch Gdns LGASH BS41...76 C5
Lovell Av OLD/WMLY/WICK BS30...83 G2
Lovell's Hl KGWD/HNM BS15 *...81 G1
Loveringe Cl
HNBRY/STHM BS10...37 E1
Lowbourne HGRV/WHIT BS14...91 G3
Lower Alma St TRWBR BA14...123 F1
Lower Ashley Rd
EVILLE/WHL BS5...62 B2
Lower Borough Walls
CBATH/BATHN BA1 *...3 F5
Lower Bristol Rd BATHSE BA2...2 E6
Lower Burlington Rd
PTSHD/EG BS20...45 H2
Lower Camden Pl
CBATH/BATHN BA1 *...108 D4
Lower Castle St CBRIS/FH BS1...5 H2
Lower Chapel La
FRCTL/WBN BS36...30 A3
Lower Chapel Rd
KGWD/HNM BS15...81 H1
Lower Cheltenham Pl
RDLND/MONT BS6...62 A2
Lower Church La CBRISNE BS2...4 D3
Lower Church Rd WSM BS23...6 D2
Lower Clifton Hl CFTN/FAIL BS8...4 A4
Lower Cock Rd
KGWD/HNM BS15...65 E4
Lower College St CBRIS/FH BS1...4 C5
Lower Conham V
KGWD/HNM BS15...81 E1
Lower Ct TRWBR BA14...121 E4
Lower Court Rd ALMDB BS32...15 G2
Lower Down Rd
PTSHD/EG BS20...45 E3
Lower East Hayes
CBATH/BATHN BA1 *...109 E4
Lower Fallow Cl
HGRV/WHIT BS14...91 G5
Lower Gay St CBRISNE BS2...61 G3
Lower Grove Rd
MANG/FISH BS16 *...53 F4
Lower Guinea St CBRIS/FH BS1...5 F7
Lower Hanham Rd
KGWD/HNM BS15...64 B5
Lower Hedgemead Rd
CBATH/BATHN BA1...3 G1
Lower High St AVONM BS11...35 E5
Lower House Crs
BRSTK/PCHW BS34...39 E1
Lower Kingsdown Rd
CBATH/BATHN BA1...111 G1
Lower Knole La
HNBRY/STHM BS10...37 F2
Lower Knowles Rd CLVDN BS21...70 C3
Lower Lamb St CBRIS/FH BS1...4 C5
Lower Linden Rd CLVDN BS21...70 D2
Lower Maudlin St CBRIS/FH BS1...5 F2
Lower Moor Rd YATE/CS BS37...20 D3
Lower Northend
CBATH/BATHN BA1...103 E4
Lower Norton La
MTN/WRL BS22...130 C4
Lower Oldfield Pk BATHSE BA2...2 C6
Lower Parade Ground Rd
OMX/HUT/LCK BS24...141 E1
Lower Park Rw CBRIS/FH BS1...4 E3
Lower Queen's CLVDN BS21...70 D2
Lower Redland Rd
RDLND/MONT BS6...61 E1
Lower Sidney St BMSTR BS3...78 B2
Lower Station Approach Rd
CBRIS/FH BS1 *...5 J6
Lower Station Rd
MANG/FISH BS16...53 G4
Lower Stone Cl
FRCTL/WBN BS36...30 A2
Lowlis Cl HNBRY/STHM BS10...37 G2
Lowmead TRWBR BA14...121 F5
Lowther Rd HNBRY/STHM BS10...37 H3
Loxley Gdns BATHSE BA2...113 H3
Loxton Dr BATHSE BA2...113 G1
Loxton Rd WSM BS23...139 E3
Loxton Sq HGRV/WHIT BS14...91 H3
Lucas Cl BRSG/KWL/STAPK BS4...92 C1
Luccombe Hl RDLND/MONT BS6...61 E1
Luckington Rd HORF/LLZ BS7...38 B5
Lucklands Rd
CBATH/BATHN BA1...107 H3
Luckley Av
BMSTRD/HC/WWD BS13...90 D4
Luckwell Rd BMSTR BS3...78 C3
Lucky La BMSTR BS3...79 E2
Ludlow Cl CBRISNE BS2...62 A2
KEYN BS31...94 A4
OLD/WMLY/WICK BS30...83 E4
Ludlow Rd HORF/LLZ BS7...52 B1
Ludwell Cl FRCTL/WBN BS36...28 D5
Lukes Cl RDSTK/MIDN BA3 *...125 G1
Lullington Rd
BRSG/KWL/STAPK BS4...80 A4
Lulsgate Rd
BMSTRD/HC/WWD BS13...90 B1
Lulworth Crs MANG/FISH BS16...41 G5
Lulworth Rd KEYN BS31...94 B5
Lunty Md NAIL BS48...85 H3
Lurgan Wk
BRSG/KWL/STAPK BS4...79 E5
Lutyens Cl BRSTK/PCHW BS34...39 G5
Lux Furlong
HNLZ/SM/SNYPK/WT BS9...49 G1
Luxton St EVILLE/WHL BS5...62 C3
Lychgate Pk
OMX/HUT/LCK BS24...140 D2
Lydbrook Cl YATE/CS BS37...31 H2
Lyddington Rd HORF/LLZ BS7...38 B4
Lyddon Rd MTN/WRL BS22...132 A5
Lydford Wk BMSTR BS3...78 D4
Lydiard Cft KGWD/HNM BS15...81 H2
Lydiard Wy TRWBR BA14...123 E4
Lydney Rd HNBRY/STHM BS10...38 A5
MANG/FISH BS16...54 D4
Lydstep Ter BMSTR BS3...78 D2
Lyefield Rd MTN/WRL BS22...131 F4
The Lyes YTN/CONG BS49...128 D3
Lyme Gdns CBATH/BATHN BA1...107 F5
Lyme Rd CBATH/BATHN BA1...107 G5
Lymore Av BATHSE BA2...113 H2
Lymore Gdns BATHSE BA2...113 H2
Lymore Ter BATHSE BA2...113 H3
Lympsham Gn BATHSE BA2...116 B1
Lynbrook LGASH BS41...76 C5
Lynbrook La BATHSE BA2...114 C4
Lynch Cl MTN/WRL BS22...131 G5
Lynch Ct
OLD/WMLY/WICK BS30 *...82 C2
Lyncombe Hl BATHSE BA2...3 H7
Lyncombe V BATHSE BA2...114 D3
Lyncombe Vale Rd
BATHSE BA2...114 D4
Lyncombe Wk MANG/FISH BS16...64 A1
Lyndale Av
HNLZ/SM/SNYPK/WT BS9...49 H3
Lyndale Rd EVILLE/WHL BS5...63 E3
YATE/CS BS37...31 H1
Lynde Cl
BMSTRD/HC/WWD BS13...90 C5
Lyndhurst Rd BATHSE BA2...113 H1
HNLZ/SM/SNYPK/WT BS9...50 C1
KEYN BS31...104 A1
RDSTK/MIDN BA3...124 C4
WSM BS23...138 D2
Lyndhurst Ter
CBATH/BATHN BA1...108 D4
Lyneham Wy TRWBR BA14...123 G1
Lynfield Pk CBATH/BATHN BA1...107 G2
Lynmouth Cl MTN/WRL BS22...136 D1
Lynmouth Rd CBRISNE BS2...62 B1
Lynn Rd MANG/FISH BS16...53 E3
Lynton Cl PTSHD/EG BS20...45 H4
Lynton Pl EVILLE/WHL BS5...62 D3
Lynton Rd BMSTR BS3...79 E5
RDSTK/MIDN BA3...124 C4
Lynton Wy MANG/FISH BS16...40 C4
Lynwood Cl RDSTK/MIDN BA3...124 B5
Lynwood Rd TRWBR BA14...120 B5
Lynx Crs OMX/HUT/LCK BS24...139 G4
Lyons Ct WSM BS23...7 G4
Lyons Court Rd
HGRV/WHIT BS14...92 C2
Lyppiatt Rd EVILLE/WHL BS5...63 E3
Lyppincourt Rd
HNBRY/STHM BS10...37 F2
Lysander Rd BRSTK/PCHW BS34...25 G4
Lysander Wk
BRSTK/PCHW BS34...27 G5
Lytchet Dr MANG/FISH BS16...41 G5
Lytes Cary Rd KEYN BS31...104 B2
Lytton Gdns BATHSE BA2...113 G3
Lytton Gv HORF/LLZ BS7...38 D5
KEYN BS31...94 D4
Lyveden Gdns
BMSTRD/HC/WWD BS13...90 C4
Lyvedon Wy LGASH BS41...77 E5

M

Mabberley Cl
MANG/FISH BS16...55 H3
Macaulay Buildings
BATHSE BA2...115 F3
Macauley Rd HORF/LLZ BS7...38 D5
Macey's Rd
BMSTRD/HC/WWD BS13...100 A1
Machin Cl HNBRY/STHM BS10...37 E2
Machin Gdns
HNBRY/STHM BS10...37 F2
Machin Rd HNBRY/STHM BS10...37 E2
The Macies CBATH/BATHN BA1...107 G1
Mackie Av BRSTK/PCHW BS34...39 E3
Mackie Gv BRSTK/PCHW BS34...39 E3
Mackie Rd BRSTK/PCHW BS34...39 E3
Macleod Cl CLVDN BS21...70 A3
Macmillan Wy BOAV BA15...118 D4
Macrae Ct KGWD/HNM BS15 *...64 D3
Macrae Rd PTSHD/EG BS20...48 D4
Madam La MTN/WRL BS22...136 C1
Madeira Rd CLVDN BS21...70 D2
WSM BS23...6 A1
Madeline Rd MANG/FISH BS16...63 G1
Madison Cl YATE/CS BS37...20 C5
Maesbury KGWD/HNM BS15...64 D5
Maesbury Rd KEYN BS31...104 B2
Maesknoll La
PLTN/PENS BS39...100 D4
Maesknoll Rd
BRSG/KWL/STAPK BS4...79 H3
Magdalen Av BATHSE BA2...2 E7
Magdalene Pl CBRISNE BS2...62 A2
Magdalen Rd BATHSE BA2...2 E7
Magdalen Wy MTN/WRL BS22...131 H5
Magellan Cl MTN/WRL BS22...131 G4
Maggs Cl HNBRY/STHM BS10...37 H2
Maggs La EVILLE/WHL BS5...63 F1
HGRV/WHIT BS14...92 A5
Magnolia Av MTN/WRL BS22...136 D2
Magnolia Cl MTN/WRL BS22...136 A4
Magnolia Ri TRWBR BA14...123 F2
Magnolia Rd RDSTK/MIDN BA3...125 E3
Magnon Rd BOAV BA15...119 E2
Magpie Bottom La
EVILLE/WHL BS5...64 A5
Magpie Cl MTN/WRL BS22...136 B3
Maidenhead Rd
BMSTRD/HC/WWD BS13...100 A1
Maiden Wy AVONM BS11...48 B1
Maidstone Gv
OMX/HUT/LCK BS24...139 F5
Maidstone St BMSTR BS3...79 G3
Main Rd MANG/FISH BS16...55 H4
NAIL BS48...87 E2
OMX/HUT/LCK BS24...140 A4
YTN/CONG BS49...127 H3
Main Vw FRCTL/WBN BS36...30 B3
Maisemore YATE/CS BS37...31 H4
Maisemore Av
BRSTK/PCHW BS34...26 D1
Makin Cl OLD/WMLY/WICK BS30...83 F1
Malago Rd BMSTR BS3...79 E3
Malago Wk
BMSTRD/HC/WWD BS13...89 H5
Maldowers La EVILLE/WHL BS5...63 H2
Mallard Cl ALMDB BS32...16 B5
EVILLE/WHL BS5...63 G2
YATE/CS BS37...32 C2
Mallow Cl CLVDN BS21...71 E2
THNB/SVB BS35...9 E2
TRWBR BA14...123 E3
The Mall CBATH/BATHN BA1 *...3 G6
CFTN/FAIL BS8...60 C4
Malmains Dr MANG/FISH BS16...40 C4
Malmesbury Cl
OLD/WMLY/WICK BS30...82 C2
RDLND/MONT BS6...51 F4
The Maltings MTN/WRL BS22...136 C1
RDLND/MONT BS6 *...62 A1
Maltlands MTN/WRL BS22...136 A4
Malvern Buildings
CBATH/BATHN BA1...108 D2
Malvern Ct EVILLE/WHL BS5...63 G4
Malvern Dr
OLD/WMLY/WICK BS30...83 F1
THNB/SVB BS35...9 E4
Malvern Rd
BRSG/KWL/STAPK BS4...80 C3
EVILLE/WHL BS5...63 G4
WSM BS23...138 D1
Malvern Ter
CBATH/BATHN BA1...108 D3
Malvern Vls
CBATH/BATHN BA1...108 D3
Mancroft Av AVONM BS11...49 E1
Mandy Mdw RDSTK/MIDN BA3...124 A3
Mangotsfield Rd
MANG/FISH BS16...55 F3
Manilla Rd CFTN/FAIL BS8...60 D4
Manley Cl TRWBR BA14 *...120 D5
Manmoor La CLVDN BS21...71 G4
Manor Cl FRCTL/WBN BS36...30 A4
PTSHD/EG BS20...44 D3
PTSHD/EG BS20...47 H4
TRWBR BA14...122 B3
The Manor Cl CFTN/FAIL BS8...59 F3
Manor Ct NAIL BS48...85 H4
Manor Court Dr
HORF/LLZ BS7...51 H1
Manor Dr CBATH/BATHN BA1...110 C2
Manor Farm Crs ALMDB BS32...27 F1
OMX/HUT/LCK BS24...139 G4
Manor Gdns MTN/WRL BS22...130 C4
OMX/HUT/LCK BS24...140 D2
Manor Gv BRSTK/PCHW BS34...15 H5
MANG/FISH BS16...55 F4
Manor La CFTN/FAIL BS8...59 E3
FRCTL/WBN BS36...29 F3
Manor Pk ALMDB BS32...10 C5
CBATH/BATHN BA1...107 G4
RDLND/MONT BS6...51 E5
Manor Pl BRSTK/PCHW BS34...40 B1
MANG/FISH BS16...40 D4
Manor Rd
BMSTRD/HC/WWD BS13...90 A3
CBATH/BATHN BA1...107 H3
CFTN/FAIL BS8...59 E5
HORF/LLZ BS7...51 H4
KEYN BS31...104 B1
MANG/FISH BS16...53 G3
MANG/FISH BS16...55 F4
TRWBR BA14...122 B3
WSM BS23...7 H1
Manor Va WSM BS23...7 J1
Manor Vls
CBATH/BATHN BA1...107 H3
Manor Wk THNB/SVB BS35...8 C1
Manor Wy CFTN/FAIL BS8...75 H2
YATE/CS BS37...21 H5
Mansel Cl KEYN BS31...104 D1
Mansfield Av WSM BS23...135 G3
Mansfield St BMSTR BS3...78 C4
Manston Cl HGRV/WHIT BS14...92 B2
Manton Cl TRWBR BA14...122 D4
Manvers St CBATH/BATHN BA1...3 G5
Manworthy Rd
BRSG/KWL/STAPK BS4...80 C3
Manx Rd HORF/LLZ BS7...52 A1
Maple Av MANG/FISH BS16...54 B5
THNB/SVB BS35...8 D5
Maple Cl BRSTK/PCHW BS34...27 E3
HGRV/WHIT BS14...92 C4
OLD/WMLY/WICK BS30...83 E2
WSM BS23...7 K3
Maple Dr RDSTK/MIDN BA3...125 F2
Maple Gdns BATHSE BA2...114 B3
Maple Gv BATHSE BA2...114 B3
TRWBR BA14...122 D3
Mapleleaze
BRSG/KWL/STAPK BS4...80 C3
Maplemeade HORF/LLZ BS7...51 F4
Maple Rd BRSG/KWL/STAPK BS4...80 C1
HORF/LLZ BS7...51 G3
The Maples NAIL BS48...72 D5
Maplestone Rd
HGRV/WHIT BS14...100 D1
Maple Wk KEYN BS31...94 A5
MANG/FISH BS16...57 F3
Mapstone Cl MANG/FISH BS16...40 C2
Marbeck Rd
HNBRY/STHM BS10...37 G4
Marchfields Wy WSM BS23...7 H7
Marconi Cl WSM BS23...135 G4
Marconi Rd PTSHD/EG BS20...44 C4
Mardale Cl HNBRY/STHM BS10...37 H3
Marden Rd KEYN BS31...94 D5
Marden Wk TRWBR BA14 *...123 E3
Mardon Rd
BRSG/KWL/STAPK BS4...63 E5
Mardyke Ferry Rd
CBRIS/FH BS1...4 A6
Margarets Buildings
CBATH/BATHN BA1 *...2 E2
Margate St BMSTR BS3...79 G3
Marguerite Rd
BMSTRD/HC/WWD BS13...90 A1
Marigold Wk BMSTR BS3...78 B4
Marina Dr TRWBR BA14...121 E1
Marina Gdns
MANG/FISH BS16...53 F5
Marindin Dr MTN/WRL BS22...132 A4
Marine Hl CLVDN BS21...70 C1
Marine Pde CLVDN BS21...70 C1
PTSHD/EG BS20...48 B3
WSM BS23...6 D4
WSM BS23...138 C2
Mariner's Cl MTN/WRL BS22...136 A2
NAIL BS48...85 H3
Mariners Dr
HNLZ/SM/SNYPK/WT BS9...50 A4
NAIL BS48...85 H3
Mariners' Pth
HNLZ/SM/SNYPK/WT BS9...50 A4
Mariner's Wy PTSHD/EG BS20...48 B3
Marion Rd KGWD/HNM BS15...81 G3
Marion Wk EVILLE/WHL BS5...63 H4
Marissal Cl HNBRY/STHM BS10...36 D2
Marissal Rd HNBRY/STHM BS10...36 D2
Mariston Wy
OLD/WMLY/WICK BS30...65 H5
Marjoram Pl ALMDB BS32...27 H3
Market Av MTN/WRL BS22...132 B5
Market La WSM BS23...6 D2
Market Pl
BLAG/CWMG/WR BS40...97 G5
Market Sq MANG/FISH BS16...54 B5
Market St BOAV BA15...119 G2
TRWBR BA14...123 E1
Mark La CBRIS/FH BS1...4 D4
Marksbury Rd BMSTR BS3...78 D4
Marlborough Av
EVILLE/WHL BS5 *...53 F5
Marlborough Buildings
CBATH/BATHN BA1...2 D2
Marlborough Dr
MANG/FISH BS16...40 C4
MTN/WRL BS22...132 A5
Marlborough Hl
RDLND/MONT BS6...4 E1
Marlborough Hill Pl CBRISNE BS2...4 E1
Marlborough La
CBATH/BATHN BA1...2 C3
Marlborough St
CBATH/BATHN BA1...2 D1
CBRISNE BS2...4 E2
EVILLE/WHL BS5...53 F5
Marlepit Gv
BMSTRD/HC/WWD BS13...89 H3
Marle Pits NAIL BS48...85 H3
Marlfield Wk
BMSTRD/HC/WWD BS13...89 H2
Marling Rd EVILLE/WHL BS5...63 G3
Marlwood Dr
HNBRY/STHM BS10...37 F2
Marmaduke St BMSTR BS3...79 G3
Marmion Crs
HNBRY/STHM BS10...37 E2
Marne Cl HGRV/WHIT BS14...92 C4
Marsden Rd BATHSE BA2...113 G4
Marshacre La THNB/SVB BS35...10 A1
Marshall Wk
BRSG/KWL/STAPK BS4 *...91 E2
Marsham Wy
OLD/WMLY/WICK BS30...82 C2
Marsh Cl FRCTL/WBN BS36...41 F1
Marsh Common
THNB/SVB BS35...13 F3
Marshfield Rd MANG/FISH BS16...54 A4
Marshfield Wy
CBATH/BATHN BA1...108 D3
Marsh La BMSTR BS3...78 B4
EVILLE/WHL BS5...62 D4
PTSHD/EG BS20...47 G1
Marshmead TRWBR BA14...121 G2
Marsh Rd BMSTR BS3...78 A3
TRWBR BA14...121 F1
YTN/CONG BS49...126 B4
Marsh St AVONM BS11...34 D5
CBRIS/FH BS1...4 E4
Marshwall La ALMDB BS32...15 F1
Marson Rd CLVDN BS21...70 D2
Marston Rd
BRSG/KWL/STAPK BS4...80 A4
TRWBR BA14...122 D5
Martcombe Rd PTSHD/EG BS20...48 A5
Martin Cl BRSTK/PCHW BS34...26 A2
Martindale Ct MTN/WRL BS22...135 H
Martindale Rd MTN/WRL BS22...136 A
Martingale Rd
BRSG/KWL/STAPK BS4...80 C
Martins Cl KGWD/HNM BS15...81 H
Martins Gv MTN/WRL BS22...136 B
Martin's Rd KGWD/HNM BS15...81 H
Martin St BMSTR BS3...78 C
Martlock Crs BMSTR BS3...78 D
Martock Rd BMSTR BS3...78 D
KEYN BS31...104 B
Marwood Rd
BRSG/KWL/STAPK BS4...91 F
Marybush La CBRISNE BS2...5 H
Mary Carpenter Pl
CBRISNE BS2 *...62 A
Marygold Leaze
OLD/WMLY/WICK BS30...82 D
Mary St EVILLE/WHL BS5...63 E
Mascot Rd BMSTR BS3...79 E
Masefield Wy HORF/LLZ BS7...52 B
Maskelyne Av
HNBRY/STHM BS10...51 G
Masons La BOAV BA15...119 G
Masons Vw FRCTL/WBN BS36...29 E
Materman Rd HGRV/WHIT BS14...92 D
Matford Cl FRCTL/WBN BS36...29 E
HNBRY/STHM BS10...38 A
Matthews Cl HGRV/WHIT BS14...93 E
Matthew's Rd EVILLE/WHL BS5...62 D
Maules La MANG/FISH BS16...40 A
Maunsell Rd AVONM BS11...36 A
Maurice Rd RDLND/MONT BS6...61 H
Mautravers Cl ALMDB BS32...27 F
Maxse Rd BRSG/KWL/STAPK BS4...80 A
Maybec Gdns EVILLE/WHL BS5...63 H
Maybourne
BRSG/KWL/STAPK BS4...81 F
Maybrick Rd BATHSE BA2...2 A
Maycliffe Pk RDLND/MONT BS6...62 A
Mayfair Av NAIL BS48...73 F
Mayfield Av MANG/FISH BS16...63 H
MTN/WRL BS22 *...136 B
Mayfield Pk MANG/FISH BS16...63 H
Mayfield Pk North
MANG/FISH BS16...63 H
Mayfield Pk South
MANG/FISH BS16...63 H
Mayfield Rd BATHSE BA2...2 A
Mayfields KEYN BS31...94 B
Mayflower Gdns NAIL BS48...73 H
Maynard Cl
BMSTRD/HC/WWD BS13...90 D
CLVDN BS21...71 F
Maynard Rd
BMSTRD/HC/WWD BS13...90 D
Maypole Sq KGWD/HNM BS15 *...81 H
Maysfield Cl PTSHD/EG BS20...45 G5
Maysgreen La
OMX/HUT/LCK BS24...133 G4
May's La OMX/HUT/LCK BS24...133 H5
May St KGWD/HNM BS15...64 B2
Maytree Av
BMSTRD/HC/WWD BS13...90 C2
Maytree Cl
BMSTRD/HC/WWD BS13...90 C2
May Tree Cl NAIL BS48 *...72 D5
May Tree Rd RDSTK/MIDN BA3...125 F3
Mayville Av BRSTK/PCHW BS34...38 D2
Maywood Crs MANG/FISH BS16...54 A4
Maywood Rd MANG/FISH BS16...54 B4
Maze St EVILLE/WHL BS5...62 C5
Mc Crae Rd
OMX/HUT/LCK BS24...141 E1
McLaren Rd AVONM BS11...34 C4
Mead Cl AVONM BS11 *...48 D2
BATHSE BA2...114 B4
Meadgate MANG/FISH BS16...42 A5
Mead Lands BATHSE BA2...105 H5
Meadowbank MTN/WRL BS22...131 G5
Meadow Cl MANG/FISH BS16...55 E1
NAIL BS48...73 F3
NAIL BS48...86 A3
PTSHD/EG BS20...44 C3
Meadow Court Dr
OLD/WMLY/WICK BS30...83 F3
Meadowcroft MANG/FISH BS16...41 H5
Meadow Cft
OMX/HUT/LCK BS24...139 G4
Meadow Dr BATHSE BA2...116 B2
OMX/HUT/LCK BS24...140 D2
Meadowfield BOAV BA15...119 E3
Meadow Gdns
CBATH/BATHN BA1...107 F3
Meadow Gv AVONM BS11...48 C1
Meadowland YTN/CONG BS49...126 A2
Meadowland Rd
HNBRY/STHM BS10...36 D1
Meadowlands MTN/WRL BS22...137 F1
Meadow La BATHSE BA2...109 G3
Meadow Md FRCTL/WBN BS36...29 H2
YATE/CS BS37...20 D2
Meadow Pk
CBATH/BATHN BA1...103 G5
Meadow Rd CLVDN BS21...71 E2
YATE/CS BS37...32 C1
Meadowside THNB/SVB BS35...9 E4
Meadowside Dr
HGRV/WHIT BS14...100 D1
The Meadows KGWD/HNM BS15...82 A2
Meadow St AVONM BS11...34 B4
CBRISNE BS2...5 H2
WSM BS23...6 E4
Meadowsweet Av
BRSTK/PCHW BS34...39 E2
Meadow V EVILLE/WHL BS5...63 H2
Meadow Vw FRCTL/WBN BS36...30 A3
RDSTK/MIDN BA3...125 H3
THNB/SVB BS35 *...13 E2
Meadow Wy ALMDB BS32...27 G3
Mead Ri BMSTR BS3...79 G2
Mead Rd BRSTK/PCHW BS34...27 H4
PTSHD/EG BS20...45 F5
YATE/CS BS37...33 E2

The Meads MANG/FISH BS16 ....55 E1
Mead St BMSTR BS3 ....79 G2
The Mead BOAV BA15 ....118 B2
BRSTK/PCHW BS34 ....39 E1
LGASH BS41 ....98 C2
THNB/SVB BS35 ....11 G2
Mead V MTN/WRL BS22 ....136 B3
Mead Wy THNB/SVB BS35 ....8 C5
Meadway
HNLZ/SM/SNYPK/WT BS9 ....49 H2
TRWBR BA14 ....122 B1
Meadway Av NAIL BS48 ....73 E4
Meardon Rd HGRV/WHIT BS14 ....92 D3
Meare Rd BATHSE BA2 ....114 D5
Mede Cl CBRIS/FH BS1 ....5 G7
Medical Av CFTN/FAIL BS8 ....4 D3
Medina Cl THNB/SVB BS35 ....8 D5
Medway Cl KEYN BS31 ....104 A1
Medway Ct THNB/SVB BS35........9 E4
Medway Dr FRCTL/WBN BS36 ....29 H3
KEYN BS31 ....104 B1
Meere Bank AVONM BS11 ....36 A4
Meetinghouse La
YTN/CONG BS49........127 G2
Meg Thatchers Gn
EVILLE/WHL BS5 ....64 A4
Melbourne Dr YATE/CS BS37 ....32 D1
Melbourne Rd HORF/LLZ BS7 ....51 G4
Melbourne Ter CLVDN BS21........70 D3
Melbury Rd
BRSG/KWL/STAPK BS4 ....79 H4
Melcombe Rd BATHSE BA2 ....2 A7
Melita Rd RDLND/MONT BS6 ....51 H5
Mellent Av
BMSTRD/HC/WWD BS13 ....99 H1
Mells Cl KEYN BS31 ....104 B2
Melrose Av CFTN/FAIL BS8........61 E3
YATE/CS BS37 ....21 E5
Melrose Cl YATE/CS BS37 ....21 F5
Melrose Gv BATHSE BA2 ....113 G4
Melrose Pl CFTN/FAIL BS8........61 E3
Melrose Ter
CBATH/BATHN BA1 *........108 D2
Melton Crs HORF/LLZ BS7........52 B1
Melton Rd TRWBR BA14 ....120 D4
Melville Rd RDLND/MONT BS6........61 E2
Melville Ter BMSTR BS3 ....78 D3
Melvin Sq BRSG/KWL/STAPK BS4..79 F5
Memorial Cl KGWD/HNM BS15........81 G2
Memorial Rd KGWD/HNM BS15........81 G2
Mendip Av MTN/WRL BS22 ....136 B1
Mendip Cl KEYN BS31 ....94 A4
NAIL BS48 ....73 F5
Mendip Crs MANG/FISH BS16........55 F1
Mendip Gdns BATHSE BA2 ....116 B2
YTN/CONG BS49........126 B4
Mendip Rd BMSTR BS3 ....79 E3
OMX/HUT/LCK BS24 ....141 F2
PTSHD/EG BS20........44 D3
WSM BS23 ....7 J4
YTN/CONG BS49........126 B3
Mendip Vw
OLD/WMLY/WICK BS30........67 F4
Mendip View Av
MANG/FISH BS16 ....53 H5
Mendip Wy RDSTK/MIDN BA3 ....125 G1
Merchants Quay CBRIS/FH BS1........4 E6
Merchants Rd CFTN/FAIL BS8 ....60 D4
Merchants Rw CBRIS/FH BS1 * 4 C7
Merchant St CBRIS/FH BS1 ....5 G2
Mercia Dr CBRISNE BS2........62 B1
Mercier Cl YATE/CS BS37 ....21 E5
Merfield Rd
BRSG/KWL/STAPK BS4 ....80 A4
Meridian Pl CFTN/FAIL BS8........4 A3
Meridian Rd RDLND/MONT BS6....61 F2
Meridian Ter HORF/LLZ BS7 * 51 G5
Meridian V CFTN/FAIL BS8 ....4 A3
Meridian Wk TRWBR BA14........122 B1
Meriet Av
BMSTRD/HC/WWD BS13 ....90 C5
Merioneth St BMSTR BS3 ....79 G3
Meriton St CBRISNE BS2 ....80 A1
Merlin Cl
HNLZ/SM/SNYPK/WT BS9 ....37 E5
MTN/WRL BS22 ....136 B3
Merlin Pk PTSHD/EG BS20 ....44 C4
Merlin Rdg MANG/FISH BS16 ....57 F4
Merlin Rd BRSTK/PCHW BS34 ....25 G4
Merlin Wy YATE/CS BS37 ....32 B3
Merrimans Rd AVONM BS11........35 E5
Merryweather Cl ALMDB BS32 ....27 E2
Merrywood Cl BMSTR BS3 ....78 D2
Merrywood Rd BMSTR BS3 ....78 D2
Merstham Rd CBRISNE BS2 ....62 B1
Merton Dr OMX/HUT/LCK BS24..136 D3
Merton Rd HORF/LLZ BS7........51 H3
Mervyn Rd HORF/LLZ BS7 ....51 H4
Metford Gv RDLND/MONT BS6 ....51 E5
Metford Pl RDLND/MONT BS6 ....51 F5
Metford Rd RDLND/MONT BS6 ....51 E5
Methuen Cl BOAV BA15........119 G5
Methwyn Cl WSM BS23........135 H4
The Mews CBATH/BATHN BA1 ....107 F4
Mezellion Pl
CBATH/BATHN BA1 * 108 D3
Middle Av CBRIS/FH BS1 * 4 E5
Middle La CBATH/BATHN BA1 ....109 E3
TRWBR BA14 ....121 G4
Middlepiece La KEYN BS31........104 C5
Middle Rd KGWD/HNM BS15 ....54 D5
Middleton Rd AVONM BS11 ....35 G5
Middle Yeo Gn NAIL BS48 * 73 E3
Midford Hl BATHSE BA2 ....117 G4
Midford La BATHSE BA2 ....117 G4
Midford Rd BATHSE BA2........116 D2
Midhaven Ri MTN/WRL BS22 ....131 F4
Midland Bridge Rd BATHSE BA2 ....2 D5
Midland Rd BATHSE BA2........2 B4
CBRISNE BS2 ....5 K3
MANG/FISH BS16........54 C4
Midland St CBRISNE BS2........5 K4
Midland Ter MANG/FISH BS16 ....53 G5
Midland Wy THNB/SVB BS35 ....8 C4
Midsummer Buildings
CBATH/BATHN BA1 ....108 D3
Milburn Rd WSM BS23 ....7 G4
Milbury Gdns MTN/WRL BS22 ....135 G1
Mildred St EVILLE/WHL BS5 ....62 D4
Mile End CBATH/BATHN BA1 * 109 E3
Miles Ct BATHSE BA2 * 3 H6
OLD/WMLY/WICK BS30........82 C2
Miles Rd CFTN/FAIL BS8 ....60 D2
Miles's Buildings
CBATH/BATHN BA1 ....3 F3
Miles St BATHSE BA2 ....3 H6
Milestone Ct MTN/WRL BS22 ....137 G1
Mile Wk HGRV/WHIT BS14 ....91 H2
Milford Av
OLD/WMLY/WICK BS30........67 E4
Milford St BMSTR BS3........78 D2
Milk St CBATH/BATHN BA1 ....3 F5
Millard Cl HNBRY/STHM BS10 ....37 H3
Millard's Hl RDSTK/MIDN BA3 ....124 C1
Mill Av CBRIS/FH BS1........5 F5
Millbank Cl
BRSG/KWL/STAPK BS4 ....80 D3
Millbrook Av
BRSG/KWL/STAPK BS4 ....81 E3
Millbrook Cl
OLD/WMLY/WICK BS30........65 H5
Millbrook Pl BATHSE BA2 ....3 H7
Millbrook Rd YATE/CS BS37 ....20 A5
Mill Cl FRCTL/WBN BS36 ....30 A3
Mill Crs YATE/CS BS37 ....43 G1
Millcross CLVDN BS21 ....70 C5
Millennium Cl FRCTL/WBN BS36 ..30 B3
Miller Ct WSM BS23 ....7 G3
Millers Cl PTSHD/EG BS20........48 B4
Millers Dr
OLD/WMLY/WICK BS30........83 F1
Millers Ri MTN/WRL BS22 ....131 H4
Miller Wk BATHSE BA2 ....109 H3
Millfield RDSTK/MIDN BA3 ....124 A4
THNB/SVB BS35........8 D2
Millfield Dr
OLD/WMLY/WICK BS30........65 H5
Millground Rd
BMSTRD/HC/WWD BS13 ....89 H5
Millhand Vls TRWBR BA14 ....123 F3
Millier Rd YTN/CONG BS49 ....127 G3
Milliman Cl
BMSTRD/HC/WWD BS13 ....90 D4
Millington Dr TRWBR BA14 ....122 B2
Mill La BATHSE BA2 ....110 A2
BATHSE BA2........113 G1
BMSTR BS3........79 E2
BOAV BA15........119 G3
FRCTL/WBN BS36 ....29 H2
OLD/WMLY/WICK BS30........83 F1
OLD/WMLY/WICK BS30........95 H1
YATE/CS BS37 ....33 H4
YTN/CONG BS49........128 D2
Mill Leg YTN/CONG BS49........129 E2
Millmead Rd BATHSE BA2........113 H2
Millpill Cl
HNLZ/SM/SNYPK/WT BS9 * 50 A3
Mill Rd FRCTL/WBN BS36 ....41 E1
RDSTK/MIDN BA3 ....125 H2
Mill St TRWBR BA14........123 E1
Millward Gv MANG/FISH BS16 ....54 B4
Milner Gn
OLD/WMLY/WICK BS30........82 D1
Milner Rd HORF/LLZ BS7........52 A3
Milsom St CBATH/BATHN BA1 ....3 F3
EVILLE/WHL BS5 ....62 B3
Milton Av BATHSE BA2 ....114 C3
WSM BS23 ....7 J3
Milton Brow MTN/WRL BS22 ....135 G2
Milton Cl NAIL BS48 ....73 F3
YATE/CS BS37 ....20 C5
Milton Gn MTN/WRL BS22 ....135 H2
Milton Hl MTN/WRL BS22........135 G1
Milton Pk EVILLE/WHL BS5........62 D4
Milton Park Rd MTN/WRL BS22..135 H2
Milton Ri MTN/WRL BS22 ....135 G2
Milton Rd HORF/LLZ BS7........51 H2
RDSTK/MIDN BA3 ....124 D3
WSM BS23 ....7 G3
YATE/CS BS37 ....20 C5
Miltons Cl
BMSTRD/HC/WWD BS13 ....91 E5
Milverton Gdns
RDLND/MONT BS6........62 A1
Milward Rd KEYN BS31 ....94 B3
Mina Rd CBRISNE BS2 ....52 A5
Minehead Rd
BRSG/KWL/STAPK BS4 ....79 G5
Miners Cl LGASH BS41 ....76 C4
Minerva Gdns BATHSE BA2 ....113 H3
Minor's La HNBRY/STHM BS10........23 G2
Minsmere Rd KEYN BS31 ....104 B1
Minster Wy BATHSE BA2........109 F4
Minton Cl HGRV/WHIT BS14 ....92 A5
Minto Rd CBRISNE BS2 ....62 B1
Mission Rd YATE/CS BS37........19 H3
Mitchell Ct CBRIS/FH BS1 ....5 G5
Mitchell La CBRIS/FH BS1 ....5 G5
Mitchell Wk
OLD/WMLY/WICK BS30........66 A5
Mivart St EVILLE/WHL BS5 ....62 C1
Mizzymead Cl NAIL BS48 ....73 E5
Mizzymead Ri NAIL BS48 ....73 E5
Mizzymead Rd NAIL BS48........73 F5
Modecombe Gv
HNBRY/STHM BS10........37 E2
Mogg St CBRISNE BS2 ....62 B1
Molesworth Cl
BMSTRD/HC/WWD BS13 ....90 B5
Molesworth Dr
BMSTRD/HC/WWD BS13 ....90 B5
Monarch's Wy
BLAG/CWMG/WR BS40 ....98 A5
EVILLE/WHL BS5 ....62 D5
KGWD/HNM BS15 ....81 G4
LGASH BS41 ....76 B4
OLD/WMLY/WICK BS30........67 F5
OLD/WMLY/WICK BS30........94 C2
YATE/CS BS37 ....33 E3
Monger La RDSTK/MIDN BA3........124 A1
Monk Rd HORF/LLZ BS7 ....51 G4
Monks Av KGWD/HNM BS15 ....64 A3
Monksdale Rd BATHSE BA2 ....114 A3
Monks Hl MTN/WRL BS22........130 C5
Monk's Park Av HORF/LLZ BS7 ....38 B4
Monks Park Wy
HNBRY/STHM BS10........38 B5
Monkton Av
OMX/HUT/LCK BS24 ....139 F4
Monkton Rd KGWD/HNM BS15 ....81 G2
Monmouth Cl PTSHD/EG BS20 ....44 C4
Monmouth Hl ALMDB BS32 ....14 D3
Monmouth Pl CBATH/BATHN BA1..2 E4
Monmouth Rd HORF/LLZ BS7 ....51 G4
KEYN BS31 ....94 A4
PTSHD/EG BS20........48 B3
Monmouth St BMSTR BS3 ....79 G3
CBATH/BATHN BA1 ....2 E4
Monsdale Cl HNBRY/STHM BS10..37 F3
Monsdale Dr
HNBRY/STHM BS10........37 F2
Montague Cl
BRSTK/PCHW BS34 ....27 G5
Montague Ct TRWBR BA14 ....121 H5
Montague Hl
RDLND/MONT BS6........61 G3
Montague Hl South
CBRISNE BS2 ....5 F1
Montague Rd KEYN BS31........105 E2
Montepelier WSM BS23 ....7 G4
Montgomery St BMSTR BS3 ....79 G2
Montpelier East WSM BS23 ....7 G1
Montreal Av HORF/LLZ BS7 ....38 C5
Montrose Av RDLND/MONT BS6 ..61 F2
Montrose Dr
OLD/WMLY/WICK BS30........65 G5
Montrose Pk
BRSG/KWL/STAPK BS4 ....80 C4
Montroy Cl
HNLZ/SM/SNYPK/WT BS9 ....51 F2
Moon St CBRISNE BS2 ....5 G1
Moor Croft Dr
OLD/WMLY/WICK BS30 ....82 C2
Moor Croft Rd
OMX/HUT/LCK BS24 ....140 B3
Moordell Cl YATE/CS BS37 ....31 H1
Moorend Farm Av AVONM BS11..23 E5
Moorend Gdns AVONM BS11 ....49 E1
Moorend Rd MANG/FISH BS16........41 E2
Moor End Spout NAIL BS48 ....73 E4
Moorfield Rd NAIL BS48 ....85 G2
Moorfields Rd BATHSE BA2 ....114 A3
NAIL BS48........73 E4
Moor Gv AVONM BS11........35 G5
Moorhill St EVILLE/WHL BS5........62 C2
Moorhouse La AVONM BS11 ....23 F5
HNBRY/STHM BS10........36 A1
The Moorings PTSHD/EG BS20 ....48 B4
Moorland Rd BATHSE BA2 ....2 A6
WSM BS23 ....138 C2
YATE/CS BS37 ....31 H1
Moorlands Cl NAIL BS48 ....73 E4
Moorlands Rd MANG/FISH BS16 ..63 H1
Moor La CLVDN BS21........70 D3
MTN/WRL BS22 ....136 C2
NAIL BS48........85 G3
OMX/HUT/LCK BS24 ....136 B4
OMX/HUT/LCK BS24 ....140 A3
Moor Pk CLVDN BS21 ....71 E3
Moorpark Av YATE/CS BS37........31 G1
Moorside YTN/CONG BS49 ....126 B2
Moravian Rd KGWD/HNM BS15....64 C3
Morden Wk HGRV/WHIT BS14 ....92 C2
Moreton Cl HGRV/WHIT BS14........91 H5
Morford St CBATH/BATHN BA1 ....3 F2
Morgan Cl KEYN BS31........105 E2
Morgans Hill Cl NAIL BS48 ....85 E1
Morgan St CBRISNE BS2 ....62 A2
Morley Av MANG/FISH BS16........55 F4
Morley Cl BRSTK/PCHW BS34........26 D3
MANG/FISH BS16........54 C5
Morley Rd BMSTR BS3 ....78 D2
MANG/FISH BS16........54 C5
Morley Sq HORF/LLZ BS7 ....51 H5
Morley St CBRISNE BS2........62 A2
Morley Ter BATHSE BA2 *........113 H1
KGWD/HNM BS15 ....64 C2
RDSTK/MIDN BA3 ....125 H1
Mornington Rd CFTN/FAIL BS8 ....60 D1
Morpeth Rd
BRSG/KWL/STAPK BS4 ....91 E1
Morris La CBATH/BATHN BA1........110 C1
Morris Rd HORF/LLZ BS7........52 B3
Morse Rd EVILLE/WHL BS5........62 D4
Mortimer Cl
CBATH/BATHN BA1 ....107 G2
Mortimer Rd BRSTK/PCHW BS34..39 E4
CFTN/FAIL BS8 ....60 D4
Mortimer St TRWBR BA14 ....122 D2
Morton St EVILLE/WHL BS5 ....62 C4
Morton Wy THNB/SVB BS35........9 E1
Moseley Gv WSM BS23........138 D4
Moulton Dr BOAV BA15........119 G5
Mountain Ash
CBATH/BATHN BA1 ....108 A3
Mountain Wd
CBATH/BATHN BA1 ....110 D2
Mountbatten Cl
MTN/WRL BS22 ....131 F4
YATE/CS BS37 ....20 C4
Mount Beacon
CBATH/BATHN BA1 *........108 D3
Mount Beacon Rw
CBATH/BATHN BA1 *........108 C3
Mount Cl FRCTL/WBN BS36 ....29 F2
Mount Crs FRCTL/WBN BS36 ....29 E5
Mount Gdns KGWD/HNM BS15 ....64 C5
Mount Gv BATHSE BA2 ....113 G4
Mount Hill Rd KGWD/HNM BS15 ..64 B5
Mount Pleasant BOAV BA15 ....119 G2
PTSHD/EG BS20........48 C4
Mount Pleasant Ter BMSTR BS3..78 D2
Mount Rd BATHSE BA2 ....113 G4
CBATH/BATHN BA1 ....108 C4
The Mount TRWBR BA14 ....121 E4
Mount Vw BATHSE BA2 ....113 G3
CBATH/BATHN BA1 *........108 C3
Mow Barton
BMSTRD/HC/WWD BS13 ....89 H3
YATE/CS BS37 ....20 C5
Mowbray Rd HGRV/WHIT BS14 ....92 B2
Mowcroft Rd
BMSTRD/HC/WWD BS13 ....90 D5
Moxham Dr
BMSTRD/HC/WWD BS13 ....90 D5
Moyle Pk TRWBR BA14 ....121 H5
Mud La YTN/CONG BS49 ....127 E1
Muirfield
OLD/WMLY/WICK BS30........65 F5
Mulberry Av PTSHD/EG BS20........45 H3
Mulberry Cl KGWD/HNM BS15 ....64 D3
MTN/WRL BS22 ....136 D2
NAIL BS48 ....85 H3
PTSHD/EG BS20........45 H3
Mulberry Dr KGWD/HNM BS15 ....65 E2
Mulberry Rd YTN/CONG BS49 ....129 E3
Mulberry Wk
HNLZ/SM/SNYPK/WT BS9 ....36 B5
Muller Av HORF/LLZ BS7........52 A4
Muller Rd HORF/LLZ BS7........52 A2
Mulready Cl HORF/LLZ BS7........52 D2
Murford Av
BMSTRD/HC/WWD BS13 ....90 C4
Murford Wk
BMSTRD/HC/WWD BS13 ....90 C5
Murray Rd TRWBR BA14........121 E4
Murray St BMSTR BS3........78 D2
Musgrove Cl AVONM BS11 ....36 B3
Myrtleberry MTN/WRL BS22 ....131 H3
Myrtle Dr AVONM BS11 ....48 D3
Myrtle Gdns YTN/CONG BS49........126 B3
Myrtle Hl PTSHD/EG BS20........48 C3
Myrtle Rd CBRISNE BS2........4 D1
Myrtle St BMSTR BS3 ....78 C2
Myrtle Tree Crs
MTN/WRL BS22 ....130 B2
Mythern Meadow BOAV BA15....119 H4

N

Nags Head Hl EVILLE/WHL BS5 ....63 H5
Nailsea Cl
BMSTRD/HC/WWD BS13 ....90 B2
Nailsea Ct NAIL BS48 *........84 C4
Nailsea Moor La NAIL BS48........84 A2
Nailsea Pk NAIL BS48........73 G4
Nailsea Park Cl NAIL BS48........73 G4
Nailsea Wall CLVDN BS21 ....71 H5
Nailsworth Av YATE/CS BS37........32 A1
Naishcombe Hl
OLD/WMLY/WICK BS30........67 F4
Naish La NAIL BS48 ....97 E1
Napier Miles Rd AVONM BS11 ....35 H5
Napier Rd AVONM BS11 ....34 C4
CBATH/BATHN BA1 ....107 F1
EVILLE/WHL BS5 ....62 C1
RDLND/MONT BS6........61 E1
Napier Sq AVONM BS11........34 B4
Napier St EVILLE/WHL BS5 ....62 C5
Narroways Rd CBRISNE BS2 ....52 B5
Narrow La MANG/FISH BS16 ....54 D4
Narrow Pln CBRISNE BS2 ....5 H4
Narrow Quay CBRIS/FH BS1 ....4 E5
Naseby Wk EVILLE/WHL BS5 ....63 G2
Nash Cl KEYN BS31........94 D4
Nash Dr HORF/LLZ BS7 ....52 D1
Naunton Wy MTN/WRL BS22........135 G1
Navigator Cl TRWBR BA14 ....121 F2
Neads Dr
OLD/WMLY/WICK BS30........83 F1
Neale Wy AVONM BS11 * 34 D4
Neath Rd EVILLE/WHL BS5 ....63 E3
Nelson Ct MANG/FISH BS16 * 54 C4
MTN/WRL BS22 ....131 F4
Nelson Pde BMSTR BS3 ....79 E2
Nelson Pl East
CBATH/BATHN BA1 ....3 G1
Nelson Pl West
CBATH/BATHN BA1 ....2 D4
Nelson Rd MANG/FISH BS16........54 C4
Nelson St BMSTR BS3 ....78 B4
CBRIS/FH BS1........5 F3
Nelson Ter CBATH/BATHN BA1 ....3 G1
Nelson Vls CBATH/BATHN BA1........2 C4
Neston Wk
BRSG/KWL/STAPK BS4 ....91 G1
Netham Rd EVILLE/WHL BS5 ....63 E5
Netherton Wood La NAIL BS48 ....84 A3
Netherways CLVDN BS21 ....70 B4
Nettlestone Cl
HNBRY/STHM BS10........36 D1
Nevalan Dr EVILLE/WHL BS5 ....63 H5
Neva Rd WSM BS23 ....6 E6
Neville Rd KGWD/HNM BS15 ....64 D1
Nevil Rd HORF/LLZ BS7 ....51 H4
Newark St CBATH/BATHN BA1........3 G6
New Bond St
CBATH/BATHN BA1 ....3 G4
New Bond Street Pl
CBATH/BATHN BA1 *........3 F4
Newbourne Rd
MTN/WRL BS22 ....135 H1
Newbrick Rd
BRSTK/PCHW BS34 ....28 A5
New Br BATHSE BA2 ....107 E4
Newbridge Cl
BRSG/KWL/STAPK BS4 ....63 E5
Newbridge Gdns
CBATH/BATHN BA1 ....107 F4
Newbridge Hl
CBATH/BATHN BA1 ....107 F4
Newbridge Rd
BRSG/KWL/STAPK BS4 ....63 E5
CBATH/BATHN BA1 ....107 F5
New Bristol Rd MTN/WRL BS22..136 B2
New Brunswick Av
EVILLE/WHL BS5 ....64 A4
New Buildings MANG/FISH BS16..53 G4
Newbury Rd HORF/LLZ BS7 ....52 B1
New Charlotte St BMSTR BS3 ......79 E2
New Cheltenham Rd
KGWD/HNM BS15 ....64 D2
New Church Rd WSM BS23 ....138 C4
Newcombe Dr
HNLZ/SM/SNYPK/WT BS9 ....49 H4
Newcombe Rd
HNLZ/SM/SNYPK/WT BS9 ....50 C1
Newditch La
BLAG/CWMG/WR BS40 ....96 D3
Newent Av KGWD/HNM BS15 ....64 A4
New Fosseway Rd
HGRV/WHIT BS14........92 A3
Newfoundland Rd CBRISNE BS2....5 J1
Newfoundland St CBRISNE BS2 ....5 H1
Newfoundland Wy CBRISNE BS2 ..5 K1
Newgate CBRIS/FH BS1 ....5 G3
Newhaven Pl PTSHD/EG BS20........44 B4
Newhaven Rd PTSHD/EG BS20 ....44 A5
Newhurst Pk TRWBR BA14 ....121 H4
New John St BMSTR BS3 * 78 D3
New Kingsley Rd CBRISNE BS2 *....5 J4
New King St CBATH/BATHN BA1 ....2 E4
Newland Dr
BMSTRD/HC/WWD BS13 ....90 B5
Newland Rd
BMSTRD/HC/WWD BS13 ....90 B5
WSM BS23 ....7 G7
Newlands Av FRCTL/WBN BS36....30 A3
Newlands Gn CLVDN BS21 ....70 D4
Newlands Hl PTSHD/EG BS20 ....45 F4
Newlands Rd KEYN BS31 ....94 A5
The Newlands MANG/FISH BS16 ..54 A1
Newland Wk
BMSTRD/HC/WWD BS13 ....99 F1
New Leaze ALMDB BS32........16 A4
Newleaze TRWBR BA14 ....121 G2
Newlyn Av
HNLZ/SM/SNYPK/WT BS9 ....50 A3
Newlyn Wk
BRSG/KWL/STAPK BS4 ....80 A5
Newlyn Wy YATE/CS BS37........21 E5
Newman Cl YATE/CS BS37 ....43 G1
Newmarket Av TRWBR BA14........123 F5
New Mdw HGRV/WHIT BS14 ....91 H3
Newnham Cl HGRV/WHIT BS14 ....92 C2
Newnham Pl
BRSTK/PCHW BS34 ....26 B1
New Orchard St
CBATH/BATHN BA1 ....3 G5
Newport Cl CLVDN BS21........70 C3
PTSHD/EG BS20........44 C4
Newport Rd PTSHD/EG BS20........48 B3
Newport St BMSTR BS3 ....79 F3
Newquay Rd
BRSG/KWL/STAPK BS4 ....79 G5
New Queen St BMSTR BS3........79 F2
KGWD/HNM BS15........64 A2
New Rd BNWL BS29........141 H2
BOAV BA15........119 H2
BRSTK/PCHW BS34 ....38 C2
BRSTK/PCHW BS34 ....39 G2
CBATH/BATHN BA1 ....110 D2
CLVDN BS21 ....70 D3
PTSHD/EG BS20........48 B4
THNB/SVB BS35........10 A5
TRWBR BA14 ....122 D2
Newry Wk
BRSG/KWL/STAPK BS4 ....79 F5
Newsome Av PTSHD/EG BS20........48 B4
New Stadium Rd
EVILLE/WHL BS5 ....62 C1
New Station Rd
MANG/FISH BS16........53 H4
New Station Wy
MANG/FISH BS16........53 H4
New St CBATH/BATHN BA1........2 E4
CBRISNE BS2 ....5 J2
New Ter TRWBR BA14........121 E1
New Thomas St CBRISNE BS2 ....5 J3
Newton Cl KGWD/HNM BS15........65 F2
Newton Gn NAIL BS48........84 D1
Newton Rd BATHSE BA2........113 E1
OLD/WMLY/WICK BS30........82 D1
WSM BS23 ....138 D1
Newton's Rd MTN/WRL BS22 ....131 F4
Newton St EVILLE/WHL BS5........62 B3
Newtown BOAV BA15 ....119 F3
TRWBR BA14 ....122 D1
New Wk KGWD/HNM BS15........81 G1
New Walls
BRSG/KWL/STAPK BS4 ....79 G2
Niblett Cl KGWD/HNM BS15 ....65 E5
Niblett's Hl EVILLE/WHL BS5 ....63 H5
Nibley La YATE/CS BS37 ....19 G4
Nibley Rd AVONM BS11........48 D3
Nicholas La EVILLE/WHL BS5 ....63 H5
Nicholas Rd EVILLE/WHL BS5........62 C2
Nicholas St BMSTR BS3........79 F2
Nicholettes
OLD/WMLY/WICK BS30........83 G1
Nicholls La FRCTL/WBN BS36........29 E3
Nichol's Rd PTSHD/EG BS20........44 C2
Nigel Pk AVONM BS11 ....48 D1
Nightingale Cl
BRSG/KWL/STAPK BS4 ....63 F5
FRCTL/WBN BS36 ....29 G4
MTN/WRL BS22 ....136 B2
THNB/SVB BS35........9 E2
Nightingale Gdns NAIL BS48 ....72 D4
Nightingale La
FRCTL/WBN BS36 ....29 F2
Nightingale Ri PTSHD/EG BS20 ....44 C5
Nightingale Rd TRWBR BA14........122 B1
Nightingale Wy
RDSTK/MIDN BA3 ....124 C4

Nile St CBATH/BATHN BA1 ....2 D4
Nine Tree Hl CBRIS/FH BS1 ....61 G2
Ninth Av HORF/LLZ BS7 ....39 E4
Nithsdale Rd WSM BS23 ....138 D2
Noble Av OLD/WMLY/WICK BS30 ..83 F2
Nomis Pk YTN/CONG BS49 ....129 E4
Nore Gdns PTSHD/EG BS20 ....45 F2
Nore Park Dr PTSHD/EG BS20 ....44 C3
Nore Rd PTSHD/EG BS20 ....44 B4
Norfolk Av CBRISNE BS2 ....5 H1
RDLND/MONT BS6 ....61 H1
Norfolk Buildings
CBATH/BATHN BA1 ....2 D4
Norfolk Crs CBATH/BATHN BA1 ....2 D4
Norfolk Gv KEYN BS31 ....93 H5
Norfolk Pl BMSTR BS3 ....78 D3
Norfolk Rd PTSHD/EG BS20 ....45 H4
WSM BS23 ....139 E1
Norland Rd CFTN/FAIL BS8 ....60 C3
Norley Rd HORF/LLZ BS7 ....52 A1
Normanby Rd EVILLE/WHL BS5 ....62 C2
Norman Gv KGWD/HNM BS15 ....64 C1
Norman Rd CBRISNE BS2 ....62 B1
KEYN BS31 ....105 E1
OLD/WMLY/WICK BS30 ....65 G3
The Normans BATHSE BA2 ....110 A3
Normanton Rd CFTN/FAIL BS8 ....60 D1
Norrisville Rd
RDLND/MONT BS6 ....61 H2
Northampton St
CBATH/BATHN BA1 ....2 E1
Northcote Rd CFTN/FAIL BS8 ....60 C2
EVILLE/WHL BS5 ....63 F3
MANG/FISH BS16 ....55 E2
Northcote St EVILLE/WHL BS5 ....62 C2
North Cft
OLD/WMLY/WICK BS30 ....83 G2
North Devon Rd
MANG/FISH BS16 ....53 H3
North Dro CLVDN BS21 ....72 B4
North East Rd THNB/SVB BS35 ....8 D2
North End YTN/CONG BS49 ....126 A1
Northend Av KGWD/HNM BS15 ....64 C1
Northend Rd KGWD/HNM BS15 ....64 D1
Northern Wy CLVDN BS21 ....71 F2
Northfield BOAV BA15 ....118 C2
YATE/CS BS37 ....31 H2
Northfield Av KGWD/HNM BS15 ..82 A1
Northfield Rd EVILLE/WHL BS5 ....64 A4
PTSHD/EG BS20 ....44 A5
Northfields CBATH/BATHN BA1 ..108 C3
Northfields Cl
CBATH/BATHN BA1 ....108 C3
Northgate St CBATH/BATHN BA1 ..3 G4
North Green St CFTN/FAIL BS8 ....60 C5
North Gv PTSHD/EG BS20 ....48 B4
North Hills Cl
OMX/HUT/LCK BS24 ....139 G4
North La BATHSE BA2 ....115 G2
NAIL BS48 ....72 C5
Northleach Wk AVONM BS11 ....49 E5
North Leaze LGASH BS41 ....77 E4
Northleigh Av MTN/WRL BS22 ..135 H2
Northmead Av
RDSTK/MIDN BA3 ....124 A2
Northmead Cl
RDSTK/MIDN BA3 ....124 A2
Northmead La YATE/CS BS37 ....19 E1
Northmead Rd
RDSTK/MIDN BA3 ....124 A2
Northover Rd
HNLZ/SM/SNYPK/WT BS9 ....37 E4
North Parade Buildings
CBATH/BATHN BA1 * 3 G5
North Parade Pas
CBATH/BATHN BA1 ....3 G5
North Parade Rd
CBATH/BATHN BA1 ....3 H5
North Pk KGWD/HNM BS15 ....64 D2
North Rd BATHSE BA2 ....109 F5
BATHSE BA2 ....117 F1
BMSTR BS3 ....78 B2
BRSTK/PCHW BS34 ....39 H1
CFTN/FAIL BS8 ....60 A5
FRCTL/WBN BS36 ....29 F3
RDLND/MONT BS6 ....61 G1
RDSTK/MIDN BA3 ....124 B3
THNB/SVB BS35 ....8 D2
YATE/CS BS37 ....20 A1
YATE/CS BS37 ....20 B5
North Side Rd NAIL BS48 ....96 A4
North St BMSTR BS3 ....78 C2
CBRIS/FH BS1 ....5 G1
MANG/FISH BS16 ....54 C3
NAIL BS48 ....72 C5
OLD/WMLY/WICK BS30 ....83 F2
WSM BS23 ....6 D3
Northumberland Buildings
CBATH/BATHN BA1 * 3 F4
Northumberland Pl
CBATH/BATHN BA1 ....3 G4
Northumberland Rd
RDLND/MONT BS6 ....61 F1
Northumbria Dr
HNLZ/SM/SNYPK/WT BS9 ....51 E3
North Vw MANG/FISH BS16 ....54 D3
RDLND/MONT BS6 ....50 D4
North View Cl BATHSE BA2 ....113 G2
Northville Rd HORF/LLZ BS7 ....38 D4
North Wy BATHSE BA2 ....113 F2
RDSTK/MIDN BA3 ....124 B3
TRWBR BA14 ....122 A2
Northway BRSTK/PCHW BS34 ....39 E1
Northwick Rd HORF/LLZ BS7 ....38 C5
LGASH BS41 ....100 A5
THNB/SVB BS35 ....13 F1
Northwoods Wk
HNBRY/STHM BS10 ....38 A2
Norton Cl KGWD/HNM BS15 ....65 E4
Norton La HGRV/WHIT BS14 ....101 F3
MTN/WRL BS22 ....130 D4
PLTN/PENS BS39 ....100 B5
Norton Rd
BRSG/KWL/STAPK BS4 ....79 H4
Nortons Wood La CLVDN BS21 ....69 F5
Norwich Dr
BRSG/KWL/STAPK BS4 ....63 F5
Norwood Av BATHSE BA2 ....115 H3
Norwood Gv PTSHD/EG BS20 ....44 C3
Notgrove Cl MTN/WRL BS22 ....135 G1
Nottingham Rd HORF/LLZ BS7 ....51 H5
Nottingham St BMSTR BS3 ....79 F3
Nova Scotia Pl CBRIS/FH BS1 * 78 B1
Novers Crs
BRSG/KWL/STAPK BS4 ....90 D1
Novers Hl
BRSG/KWL/STAPK BS4 ....90 D1
Novers La
BRSG/KWL/STAPK BS4 ....90 D2
Novers Park Cl
BRSG/KWL/STAPK BS4 ....79 E5
Novers Park Dr
BRSG/KWL/STAPK BS4 ....90 D1
Novers Park Rd
BRSG/KWL/STAPK BS4 ....91 E1
Novers Rd
BRSG/KWL/STAPK BS4 ....90 D1
Nowhere La NAIL BS48 * 73 H5
Nugent Hl RDLND/MONT BS6 ....61 G2
Nunney Cl KEYN BS31 ....104 B2
Nursery Cl TRWBR BA14 ....121 H3
Nursery Gdns
HNBRY/STHM BS10 ....37 F2
The Nursery BMSTR BS3 ....78 C3
Nutfield Gv BRSTK/PCHW BS34 ....39 E3
Nutgrove Av BMSTR BS3 ....79 F3
Nuthatch Dr MANG/FISH BS16 ....53 G2
Nuthatch Gdns
MANG/FISH BS16 ....53 H2
Nutwell Rd MTN/WRL BS22 ....136 B1
Nutwell Sq MTN/WRL BS22 ....136 B1
Nympsfield KGWD/HNM BS15 ....64 D1

O

Oak Av BATHSE BA2 ....113 H4
Oak Cl BRSTK/PCHW BS34 ....27 F3
YATE/CS BS37 ....20 C4
Oak Ct MTN/WRL BS22 ....132 B5
Oakdale Av MANG/FISH BS16 ....41 E5
Oakdale Cl MANG/FISH BS16 ....41 F5
Oakdale Ct MANG/FISH BS16 ....54 C1
Oakdale Gdns MTN/WRL BS22 ....136 C1
Oakdale Rd HGRV/WHIT BS14 ....91 H1
MANG/FISH BS16 ....41 F5
Oakdene Av EVILLE/WHL BS5 ....53 E5
Oak Dr PTSHD/EG BS20 ....45 E4
Oakenhill Rd
BRSG/KWL/STAPK BS4 ....80 D4
Oakenhill Wk
BRSG/KWL/STAPK BS4 ....80 D4
Oakfield Cl CBATH/BATHN BA1 ....2 A1
Oakfield Ct CFTN/FAIL BS8 * 61 E3
Oakfield Gv CFTN/FAIL BS8 ....4 A1
Oakfield Pl CFTN/FAIL BS8 ....4 A1
PTSHD/EG BS20 * 45 G5
Oakfield Rd CFTN/FAIL BS8 ....60 D3
KEYN BS31 ....104 A1
KGWD/HNM BS15 ....64 C4
Oakford Av WSM BS23 ....7 H3
Oakford La
CBATH/BATHN BA1 ....103 F1
Oak Gv PTSHD/EG BS20 ....48 B4
Oakhanger Dr AVONM BS11 ....36 A4
Oakhill HNBRY/STHM BS10 ....36 B1
Oakhill Av
OLD/WMLY/WICK BS30 ....83 F4
Oakhill Cl NAIL BS48 ....74 A5
Oakhill Rd BATHSE BA2 ....114 C5
Oakhurst Rd
HNLZ/SM/SNYPK/WT BS9 ....50 C3
Oakland Dr
OMX/HUT/LCK BS24 ....140 B3
Oakland Rd CFTN/FAIL BS8 ....61 E2
EVILLE/WHL BS5 ....63 F3
Oaklands Cl MANG/FISH BS16 ....55 G3
Oaklands Dr ALMDB BS32 ....15 G3
MANG/FISH BS16 ....40 B5
OLD/WMLY/WICK BS30 ....83 F4
Oaklands Rd MANG/FISH BS16 ....55 F3
Oak La EVILLE/WHL BS5 ....63 G1
Oakleaze Rd THNB/SVB BS35 ....8 D3
Oakleigh Av EVILLE/WHL BS5 ....63 E3
Oakleigh Cl NAIL BS48 ....86 A4
Oakleigh Gdns
OLD/WMLY/WICK BS30 ....83 F4
Oakley BATHSE BA2 ....115 H2
CLVDN BS21 ....70 B5
Oakley Rd HORF/LLZ BS7 ....52 A1
Oakmeade Pk
BRSG/KWL/STAPK BS4 ....80 A4
Oakridge Cl KGWD/HNM BS15 ....65 F4
Oak Rd HORF/LLZ BS7 ....51 H3
Oaksey Gv NAIL BS48 ....73 H4
The Oaks
BLAG/CWMG/WR BS40 ....97 G5
NAIL BS48 ....73 H4
Oak St BATHSE BA2 ....2 E6
Oak Ter RDSTK/MIDN BA3 ....125 E3
Oak Tree Av MANG/FISH BS16 ....57 F4
Oak Tree Cl KGWD/HNM BS15 ....81 H4
TRWBR BA14 ....120 C5
Oaktree Ct AVONM BS11 ....48 D1
Oaktree Crs ALMDB BS32 ....15 H5
Oaktree Gdns
BMSTRD/HC/WWD BS13 ....89 H4
Oaktree Pl MTN/WRL BS22 ....132 B5
Oakwood Av
HNLZ/SM/SNYPK/WT BS9 ....51 E2
Oakwood Gdns
FRCTL/WBN BS36 ....30 C3
Oakwood Rd
HNLZ/SM/SNYPK/WT BS9 ....51 E2
Oatfield NAIL BS48 ....96 A3
Oatlands Av HGRV/WHIT BS14 ....91 H3
Oberon Av EVILLE/WHL BS5 ....63 F1
Odins Rd BATHSE BA2 ....116 B1
Okebourne Cl
HNBRY/STHM BS10 ....37 G1
Okebourne Rd
HNBRY/STHM BS10 ....37 G2
Oldacre Rd HGRV/WHIT BS14 ....100 D2
Old Ashley Hl RDLND/MONT BS6 ..62 A1
Old Aust Rd ALMDB BS32 ....16 A1
Old Banwell Rd
OMX/HUT/LCK BS24 ....141 E2
Old Barrow Hl AVONM BS11 ....48 C1
The Old Batch BOAV BA15 ....119 E1
Old Bond St CBATH/BATHN BA1 ....3 F4
Old Bread St CBRISNE BS2 ....5 J4
Oldbridge Rd HGRV/WHIT BS14 ..101 F1
Old Bristol Rd MTN/WRL BS22 ....136 D1
Oldbury Cha
OLD/WMLY/WICK BS30 ....82 D4
Oldbury Court Dr
MANG/FISH BS16 ....53 H2
Oldbury Court Rd
MANG/FISH BS16 ....53 H3
Old Church Rd CLVDN BS21 ....70 C2
NAIL BS48 ....85 E1
WSM BS23 ....138 C4
Old Down Hl ALMDB BS32 ....10 C5
Old Farm La EVILLE/WHL BS5 ....64 A5
Old Ferry Rd BATHSE BA2 ....113 G1
Oldfield La BATHSE BA2 ....114 B3
Oldfield Pl CFTN/FAIL BS8 ....78 A1
Oldfield Rd BATHSE BA2 ....2 C7
CFTN/FAIL BS8 ....78 B1
Old Fosse Rd BATHSE BA2 ....116 A1
Old Frome Rd BATHSE BA2 ....116 C2
Old Gloucester Rd
FRCTL/WBN BS36 ....28 B3
MANG/FISH BS16 ....40 C1
THNB/SVB BS35 ....11 H2
Old Hl BLAG/CWMG/WR BS40 ....97 E5
Old Junction Rd WSM BS23 ....139 G1
Old King St CBATH/BATHN BA1 ....3 F3
Old King Street Ct
CBRIS/FH BS1 * 5 G2
Oldlands Av FRCTL/WBN BS36 ....30 A4
Old La CLVDN BS21 ....72 D2
Old Market St CBRISNE BS2 ....5 J3
Oldmead Wk
BMSTRD/HC/WWD BS13 ....89 H2
Old Midford Rd BATHSE BA2 ....117 E3
Old Millard's Hl
RDSTK/MIDN BA3 ....124 C1
Old Mill Cl YATE/CS BS37 ....43 G1
Old Mill Rd PTSHD/EG BS20 ....45 G3
Old Mill Wy
OMX/HUT/LCK BS24 ....136 C3
Oldmixon Crs
OMX/HUT/LCK BS24 ....139 F3
Oldmixon Rd
OMX/HUT/LCK BS24 ....139 F5
Old Mixon Rd
OMX/HUT/LCK BS24 ....139 H4
Old Newbridge Hl
CBATH/BATHN BA1 ....107 F4
Old Orch CBATH/BATHN BA1 ....3 G2
Old Orchard St
CBATH/BATHN BA1 ....3 G5
Old Pk CBRISNE BS2 ....4 D3
Old Park Hl CBRISNE BS2 ....4 D3
Old Park Rd AVONM BS11 ....48 C1
CLVDN BS21 ....68 B5
Old Pit Rd RDSTK/MIDN BA3 ....124 C4
Old Post Office La WSM BS23 * 6 D2
Old Priory Rd PTSHD/EG BS20 ....48 A4
Old Quarry BATHSE BA2 ....114 A5
Old Quarry Ri AVONM BS11 ....48 D1
Old Quarry Rd AVONM BS11 ....48 C1
Old Sneed Av
HNLZ/SM/SNYPK/WT BS9 ....50 A4
Old Sneed Pk
HNLZ/SM/SNYPK/WT BS9 ....50 A4
Old Sneed Rd
HNLZ/SM/SNYPK/WT BS9 ....50 A4
Old St CLVDN BS21 ....71 E2
Old Vicarage Pl CFTN/FAIL BS8 * ..60 D2
Oldville Av CLVDN BS21 ....70 D3
Old Wells Rd BATHSE BA2 ....114 C4
Old Weston Rd NAIL BS48 ....87 G2
YTN/CONG BS49 ....128 A1
Olive Gdns THNB/SVB BS35 ....11 F3
Olveston Rd HORF/LLZ BS7 ....51 H3
Olympus Cl BRSTK/PCHW BS34 ....27 F4
Olympus Rd BRSTK/PCHW BS34 ..25 H3
Onega Ter BATHSE BA2 ....2 C3
Oolite Gv BATHSE BA2 ....116 B1
Oolite Rd BATHSE BA2 ....116 B1
Oram Ct OLD/WMLY/WICK BS30 ..82 C2
Orange Gv CBATH/BATHN BA1 ....3 G4
Orange St CBRISNE BS2 ....5 J1
Orchard Av CBRIS/FH BS1 * 4 D4
RDSTK/MIDN BA3 ....124 A3
THNB/SVB BS35 ....8 D3
Orchard Bvd
OLD/WMLY/WICK BS30 ....83 E2
Orchard Cl
BLAG/CWMG/WR BS40 ....96 D4
FRCTL/WBN BS36 ....29 E4
HNLZ/SM/SNYPK/WT BS9 ....50 C3
KEYN BS31 ....93 H3
KGWD/HNM BS15 ....64 D3
MTN/WRL BS22 ....130 C5
MTN/WRL BS22 ....136 C1
NAIL BS48 ....87 F1
PTSHD/EG BS20 ....45 G3
YATE/CS BS37 ....21 E5
YTN/CONG BS49 ....128 D2
Orchard Ct YTN/CONG BS49 ....127 F2
Orchard Crs AVONM BS11 ....48 C1
Orchard Gdns KGWD/HNM BS15 ..65 E3
Orchard Gra THNB/SVB BS35 ....8 C2
Orchard La CBRIS/FH BS1 ....4 D4
Orchard Lea PTSHD/EG BS20 ....48 C4
THNB/SVB BS35 ....11 G2
Orchard Pl WSM BS23 ....6 E4
Orchard Ri THNB/SVB BS35 ....10 A5
Orchard Rd CLVDN BS21 ....70 D4
EVILLE/WHL BS5 ....63 G3
FRCTL/WBN BS36 ....30 B3
HORF/LLZ BS7 ....51 H4
KGWD/HNM BS15 ....64 D3
LGASH BS41 ....76 C4
MANG/FISH BS16 ....57 E3
NAIL BS48 ....72 D5
NAIL BS48 ....85 H3
OMX/HUT/LCK BS24 ....140 A4
TRWBR BA14 ....123 E2
Orchard Sq EVILLE/WHL BS5 ....63 E4
The Orchards
KGWD/HNM BS15 ....65 E3
PTSHD/EG BS20 * 48 B4
Orchard St CBRIS/FH BS1 ....4 D4
WSM BS23 ....6 E4
Orchard Ter BATHSE BA2 ....113 G1
The Orchard BRSTK/PCHW BS34 ..27 H5
OMX/HUT/LCK BS24 ....140 C1
PTSHD/EG BS20 ....48 B4
Orchard V KGWD/HNM BS15 ....65 E4
RDSTK/MIDN BA3 ....124 A3
Oriel Gdns CBATH/BATHN BA1 ....109 F2
Oriel Gv BATHSE BA2 ....113 G3
Orion Dr BRSTK/PCHW BS34 ....27 F4
Orland Wy
OLD/WMLY/WICK BS30 ....82 D3
Orlebar Gdns AVONM BS11 ....36 A3
Orme Dr CLVDN BS21 ....68 B5
Ormerod Rd
HNLZ/SM/SNYPK/WT BS9 ....50 B4
Ormonds Cl ALMDB BS32 ....16 C5
Ormsley Cl BRSTK/PCHW BS34 ....27 E2
Orpen Gdns HORF/LLZ BS7 ....52 C3
Orpheus Av BRSTK/PCHW BS34 ....27 F4
Orpington Wy TRWBR BA14 ....121 H5
Orwell Dr KEYN BS31 ....94 C5
Orwell St BMSTR BS3 ....79 F3
Osborne Av HORF/LLZ BS7 ....52 A5
WSM BS23 ....7 H4
Osborne Cl BRSTK/PCHW BS34 ....39 G1
Osborne Rd BMSTR BS3 ....78 D2
CBATH/BATHN BA1 ....113 G1
CFTN/FAIL BS8 ....60 D2
THNB/SVB BS35 ....12 B2
TRWBR BA14 ....121 F3
WSM BS23 ....7 H4
Osborne Ter BMSTR BS3 ....78 C4
Osborne Vls CBRISNE BS2 ....4 C1
Osprey Gdns MTN/WRL BS22 ....136 C2
Osprey Pk THNB/SVB BS35 ....9 E1
Osprey Rd EVILLE/WHL BS5 ....62 D4
Ostlings La CBATH/BATHN BA1 ..110 C2
Otterford Cl HGRV/WHIT BS14 ....92 A4
Otter Rd CLVDN BS21 ....70 D4
Ottery Cl AVONM BS11 ....35 H4
Ottrells Md ALMDB BS32 ....16 A4
The Oval BATHSE BA2 ....113 H4
Overhill PTSHD/EG BS20 ....48 B5
Over La ALMDB BS32 ....15 G3
ALMDB BS32 ....25 G1
Overndale Rd MANG/FISH BS16 ..54 B3
Overnhill Ct MANG/FISH BS16 ....54 B3
Overnhill Rd MANG/FISH BS16 ....54 B3
Overton Rd HORF/LLZ BS7 ....61 G1
Owen Dr CFTN/FAIL BS8 ....75 G2
Owen Gv
HNLZ/SM/SNYPK/WT BS9 ....51 E3
Owen St EVILLE/WHL BS5 ....62 D3
Owls Head Rd KGWD/HNM BS15 ..64 B5
Oxbarton BRSTK/PCHW BS34 ....27 H5
Oxen Leaze ALMDB BS32 ....16 B5
Oxford Pl CFTN/FAIL BS8 ....60 C5
EVILLE/WHL BS5 ....62 C2
WSM BS23 * 6 D4
Oxford Rw CBATH/BATHN BA1 ....3 F2
Oxford Sq OMX/HUT/LCK BS24 ..137 E5
Oxford St BMSTR BS3 ....79 G2
CBRISNE BS2 ....62 B5
RDLND/MONT BS6 ....61 F3
WSM BS23 ....6 D5
Oxhouse La CFTN/FAIL BS8 ....75 G1
Oxleaze
BMSTRD/HC/WWD BS13 ....91 E5
Oxleaze La LGASH BS41 ....98 D2
Ozleworth KGWD/HNM BS15 ....65 F3

P

Pack Horse La BATHSE BA2 ....116 D3
Paddock Cl ALMDB BS32 ....16 B5
MANG/FISH BS16 ....55 G2
Paddock Gdns HGRV/WHIT BS14 ..91 H5
THNB/SVB BS35 ....11 G2
The Paddocks BATHSE BA2 ....117 F1
THNB/SVB BS35 ....9 E3
WSM BS23 ....138 C4
The Paddock CLVDN BS21 ....70 D4
PTSHD/EG BS20 ....45 G4
Paddock Woods BATHSE BA2 ....115 G5
Padfield Cl BATHSE BA2 ....113 G2
Padleigh Hl BATHSE BA2 ....113 F5
Padstow Rd
BRSG/KWL/STAPK BS4 ....91 F1
Page Rd MANG/FISH BS16 ....54 C4
Pages Md AVONM BS11 ....34 D5
Painswick Av
BRSTK/PCHW BS34 ....26 D2
Painswick Dr YATE/CS BS37 ....32 A1
Painters Md TRWBR BA14 ....121 H4
Palace Yard Ms
CBATH/BATHN BA1 ....2 E4
Palairet Cl BOAV BA15 ....119 G4
Palmdale Cl
OLD/WMLY/WICK BS30 ....82 D3
Palmer Dr BOAV BA15 ....119 G1
Palmer Rd TRWBR BA14 ....121 E4
Palmer Rw WSM BS23 ....6 E3
Palmers Cl
OLD/WMLY/WICK BS30 ....65 F5
Palmers Leaze ALMDB BS32 ....28 A3
Palmerston Rd
RDLND/MONT BS6 ....51 E4
Palmerston St BMSTR BS3 ....78 C3
Palmer St WSM BS23 ....6 E3
Palmyra Rd BMSTR BS3 ....78 C4
Parade Ct EVILLE/WHL BS5 ....63 G2
The Parade AVONM BS11 ....48 D2
BMSTRD/HC/WWD BS13 * 90 B3
BRSTK/PCHW BS34 * 26 A3
HGRV/WHIT BS14 * 91 H1
YATE/CS BS37 ....32 C1
Paragon Blds CBATH/BATHN BA1 ..3 G2
Paragon Rd WSM BS23 ....6 A1
The Paragon CBATH/BATHN BA1 ..3 G2
CFTN/FAIL BS8 ....60 C5
Parish Brook Rd NAIL BS48 ....72 C5
Park Av ALMDB BS32 ....15 G5
BATHSE BA2 ....2 E7
BMSTR BS3 ....79 F3
EVILLE/WHL BS5 ....53 E5
EVILLE/WHL BS5 ....63 F3
FRCTL/WBN BS36 ....29 E4
FRCTL/WBN BS36 ....29 H3
YTN/CONG BS49 ....126 B2
Park Cl KEYN BS31 ....94 A4
KGWD/HNM BS15 ....64 D4
OLD/WMLY/WICK BS30 ....83 E1
Park Crs EVILLE/WHL BS5 ....63 E3
MANG/FISH BS16 ....40 D4
OLD/WMLY/WICK BS30 ....83 E1
Park End BNWL BS29 ....141 H2
Parkers Av
OLD/WMLY/WICK BS30 ....67 F4
Parkers Barton EVILLE/WHL BS5 ..62 C5
Parkers Cl HNBRY/STHM BS10 ....38 B1
Parker St BMSTR BS3 ....78 C3
Parkes Rd
OMX/HUT/LCK BS24 ....141 F1
Park Farm Ct
OLD/WMLY/WICK BS30 * 82 C2
Parkfield Av EVILLE/WHL BS5 ....63 E4
Parkfield Rd MANG/FISH BS16 ....56 D1
Park Gdns CBATH/BATHN BA1 ....2 A1
Park Gv RDLND/MONT BS6 ....51 F3
Park Hl AVONM BS11 ....48 D2
Parkhurst Av MANG/FISH BS16 ....54 A4
Parkhurst Rd WSM BS23 ....7 K4
Parklands KGWD/HNM BS15 ....64 D3
TRWBR BA14 ....121 E4
Parklands Av MTN/WRL BS22 ....131 G4
Parklands Rd BMSTR BS3 ....77 H2
Parkland Wy THNB/SVB BS35 ....8 C1
Park La CBATH/BATHN BA1 ....2 B2
FRCTL/WBN BS36 ....41 H1
Park Leaze BRSTK/PCHW BS34 ....26 A1
Park Pl CBATH/BATHN BA1 ....2 D1
CFTN/FAIL BS8 ....4 B3
EVILLE/WHL BS5 ....53 F5
WSM BS23 ....6 C2
Park Rd AVONM BS11 ....48 D2
BMSTR BS3 ....78 C2
CBATH/BATHN BA1 ....107 G5
CLVDN BS21 ....70 D1
HORF/LLZ BS7 ....38 C4
KEYN BS31 ....94 B4
KGWD/HNM BS15 ....64 C2
MANG/FISH BS16 ....53 E3
MANG/FISH BS16 ....54 D3
OLD/WMLY/WICK BS30 ....83 E1
THNB/SVB BS35 ....8 C2
YTN/CONG BS49 ....129 E3
Park Rw CBRIS/FH BS1 ....4 C3
FRCTL/WBN BS36 ....29 G2
Parkside Av FRCTL/WBN BS36 ....29 E4
Parkside Gdns EVILLE/WHL BS5 ..52 C4
Parkstone Av HORF/LLZ BS7 ....52 A2
Park St BRSG/KWL/STAPK BS4 ....79 H2
CBATH/BATHN BA1 ....108 B4
CBRIS/FH BS1 ....4 C3
EVILLE/WHL BS5 ....63 G3
TRWBR BA14 ....122 D2
YATE/CS BS37 ....19 E3
Park Street Av CBRIS/FH BS1 * 4 C3
Park Street Ms
CBATH/BATHN BA1 ....2 D1
The Park ALMDB BS32 ....16 A4
KEYN BS31 ....94 B3
KGWD/HNM BS15 ....64 D3
MANG/FISH BS16 ....40 C4
OLD/WMLY/WICK BS30 ....83 E5
YTN/CONG BS49 ....126 B2
Park Vw KGWD/HNM BS15 ....64 D4
THNB/SVB BS35 * 8 D1
Park View Av THNB/SVB BS35 ....8 D2
Parkwall Crs
OLD/WMLY/WICK BS30 ....82 C2
Parkwall Rd
OLD/WMLY/WICK BS30 ....82 D2
Parkway BRSTK/PCHW BS34 ....40 B1
Park Wy MTN/WRL BS22 ....137 E2
OLD/WMLY/WICK BS30 ....83 E1
RDSTK/MIDN BA3 ....124 B4
Park Wood Cl HGRV/WHIT BS14 ..91 G5
Parnall Crs YATE/CS BS37 ....20 B5
Parnall Rd MANG/FISH BS16 ....53 H5
Parnell Rd CLVDN BS21 ....71 E2
MANG/FISH BS16 ....53 F1
Parry Cl BATHSE BA2 ....113 G3
Parry's Cl
HNLZ/SM/SNYPK/WT BS9 ....50 B3
Parrys Gv
HNLZ/SM/SNYPK/WT BS9 ....50 B3
Parry's La
HNLZ/SM/SNYPK/WT BS9 ....50 C3
Parslow Barton
EVILLE/WHL BS5 ....63 H4
Parsonage La CBATH/BATHN BA1 ..3 F4
Parsonage Rd LGASH BS41 ....77 F5

Parsons Av BRSTK/PCHW BS34 ....27 H5
Parsons Gn CLVDN BS21 ....70 C5
MTN/WRL BS22 ....131 H5
Parsons Md NAIL BS48 ....87 E2
Parsons Paddock
HGRV/WHIT BS14 ....91 H2
Parson St BMSTR BS3 ....78 D5
Parsons Wk
OLD/WMLY/WICK BS30 ....66 A4
Partis Wy CBATH/BATHN BA1 ....107 F4
Partition St CBRIS/FH BS1 * 4 C5
Partridge Cl MTN/WRL BS22 ....136 C2
Partridge Rd MANG/FISH BS16 ....57 F4
Passage Leaze AVONM BS11 ....48 C2
Passage Rd
HNLZ/SM/SNYPK/WT BS9 ....37 F5
Passage Road Brentry Hl
HNBRY/STHM BS10 ....37 F2
Passage St CBRIS/FH BS1 ....5 H4
Pastures Av MTN/WRL BS22 ....132 B5
Patch Ct MANG/FISH BS16 ....41 H5
Patch Cft CLVDN BS21 ....70 C5
Paulman Gdns LGASH BS41 ....88 C1
Paul's Cswy YTN/CONG BS49 ....128 D2
Paul St CBRISNE BS2 ....4 D1
Paulton Dr HORF/LLZ BS7 ....51 F4
Paulton Rd RDSTK/MIDN BA3 ....124 A4
Paultow Av BMSTR BS3 ....79 F3
Paultow Rd BMSTR BS3 ....79 F3
Pavely Gdns TRWBR BA14 ....121 H5
Pavey Cl
BMSTRD/HC/WWD BS13 ....90 D5
Pavey Rd
BMSTRD/HC/WWD BS13 ....90 D5
The Pavilions
BRSG/KWL/STAPK BS4 ....80 B5
Pawlett Rd B
MSTRD/HC/WWD BS13 ....99 H1
Pawlett Wk
BMSTRD/HC/WWD BS13 ....99 H1
Paxcroft Wy TRWBR BA14 ....123 G1
Paxton MANG/FISH BS16 ....39 H5
Paybridge Rd
BMSTRD/HC/WWD BS13 ....90 A5
Payne Dr EVILLE/WHL BS5 ....62 C4
Payne Rd OMX/HUT/LCK BS24 ....140 A4
Peache Rd MANG/FISH BS16 ....54 D2
Peacocks La KGWD/HNM BS15 ....64 B3
Pearces Hl MANG/FISH BS16 ....54 A1
Pearl St BMSTR BS3 ....78 C3
Pearsall Rd
OLD/WMLY/WICK BS30 ....82 B4
Pearse Cl MTN/WRL BS22 ....132 A3
Peart Cl
BMSTRD/HC/WWD BS13 ....89 H4
Peart Dr
BMSTRD/HC/WWD BS13 ....89 H5
Peartree Cl
BMSTRD/HC/WWD BS13 ....90 C5
Peartree Fld PTSHD/EG BS20 ....46 A3
Pear Tree Hey YATE/CS BS37 ....20 D2
Peartree La EVILLE/WHL BS5 ....64 A5
KGWD/HNM BS15 ....65 E1
Pear Tree Rd ALMDB BS32 ....16 A5
Pedder Rd CLVDN BS21 ....70 D4
Peel St CBRISNE BS2 ....62 A3
Pegasus Rd BRSTK/PCHW BS34 ....25 H3
Peg Hl YATE/CS BS37 ....21 E3
Pelican Cl MTN/WRL BS22 ....136 B3
Pemberton Ct MANG/FISH BS16 ....54 A3
Pembery Rd BMSTR BS3 ....78 C3
Pembroke Av AVONM BS11 ....48 D2
Pembroke Cl TRWBR BA14 ....123 E3
Pembroke Gv CFTN/FAIL BS8 ....60 D4
Pembroke Pl CFTN/FAIL BS8 ....78 B1
Pembroke Rd AVONM BS11 ....48 D2
BMSTR BS3 ....78 D2
CFTN/FAIL BS8 ....60 D2
KGWD/HNM BS15 ....64 D1
PTSHD/EG BS20 ....44 A5
Pembroke St CBRISNE BS2 ....5 F1
Pembroke V CFTN/FAIL BS8 ....60 D3
Penard Wy KGWD/HNM BS15 ....65 E4
Penarth Dr
OMX/HUT/LCK BS24 ....139 F5
Pendennis Av MANG/FISH BS16 ....54 C4
Pendennis Pk
BRSG/KWL/STAPK BS4 ....80 C4
Pendennis Rd MANG/FISH BS16 ....54 C3
Pendlesham Gdns WSM BS23 ....135 F2
Pendock Cl
OLD/WMLY/WICK BS30 * 83 F5
Pendock Ct MANG/FISH BS16 ....55 G1
Pendock Rd FRCTL/WBN BS36 ....29 E5
MANG/FISH BS16 ....54 A2
Penfield Rd CBRISNE BS2 ....62 B1
Penlea Ct AVONM BS11 ....48 C1
Pennard Ct HGRV/WHIT BS14 ....92 A4
Pennard Gn BATHSE BA2 ....113 F1
Penn Dr MANG/FISH BS16 ....40 D4
Penn Gdns CBATH/BATHN BA1 ....107 F4
Penngrove
OLD/WMLY/WICK BS30 ....82 D3
Penn Hill Rd
CBATH/BATHN BA1 ....107 F3
Pennine Gdns WSM BS23 ....7 J1
Pennine Rd
OLD/WMLY/WICK BS30 ....83 F2
Pennlea
BMSTRD/HC/WWD BS13 ....90 C2
Penn Lea Rd
CBATH/BATHN BA1 ....107 G4
The Penns CLVDN BS21 ....71 E3
Penn St CBRIS/FH BS1 ....5 H2
Pennycress MTN/WRL BS22 ....136 A4
Pennyquick BATHSE BA2 ....112 B1
Pennyroyal Gv
MANG/FISH BS16 ....53 F3
Pennywell Rd EVILLE/WHL BS5 ....62 B3
Pen Park Rd HNBRY/STHM BS10 ....37 H2
Penpole Av AVONM BS11 ....48 D2
Penpole Cl AVONM BS11 ....48 C1
Penpole La AVONM BS11 ....48 D1
Penpole Pk AVONM BS11 ....48 D1
Penpole Pl AVONM BS11 ....48 D2
Penrice Cl MTN/WRL BS22 ....135 H1
Penrose HGRV/WHIT BS14 ....91 G3
Penrose Dr BRSTK/PCHW BS34 ....27 F3
Pensfield Pk
HNBRY/STHM BS10 ....38 A1
Pensford Ct HGRV/WHIT BS14 ....92 C4
Pentire Av
BMSTRD/HC/WWD BS13 ....90 B2
Pentland Av THNB/SVB BS35 ....9 F4
Pepperacre La TRWBR BA14 ....121 G5
Pepys Cl KEYN BS31 ....105 E2
Pera Pl CBATH/BATHN BA1 ....108 D4
Percival Rd CFTN/FAIL BS8 ....60 C4
Percy Pl CBATH/BATHN BA1 ....109 E3
Peregrine Cl MTN/WRL BS22 ....136 C2
Perfect Vw CBATH/BATHN BA1 ....108 D3
The Perrings NAIL BS48 ....73 F5
Perrinpit Rd FRCTL/WBN BS36 ....17 H4
Perrott Rd KGWD/HNM BS15 ....65 F2
Perry Cl FRCTL/WBN BS36 ....41 E1
Perrycroft Av
BMSTRD/HC/WWD BS13 ....90 B3
Perrycroft Rd
BMSTRD/HC/WWD BS13 ....90 B3
Perrymans Cl MANG/FISH BS16 ....53 H2
Perrymead BATHSE BA2 ....115 F4
MTN/WRL BS22 ....132 A3
Perry Rd CBRIS/FH BS1 ....4 E3
Perrys Lea ALMDB BS32 ....16 B5
Perry St EVILLE/WHL BS5 ....62 B3
Pesley Cl
BMSTRD/HC/WWD BS13 ....90 A5
Petercole Dr
BMSTRD/HC/WWD BS13 ....90 B3
Peterson Sq
BMSTRD/HC/WWD BS13 ....99 H1
Peter's Ter EVILLE/WHL BS5 ....62 C4
Petersway Gdns
EVILLE/WHL BS5 ....63 H5
Petherbridge Wy HORF/LLZ BS7 ....52 B3
Petherton Cl KGWD/HNM BS15 ....64 D4
Petherton Gdns
HGRV/WHIT BS14 ....92 A2
Petherton Rd HGRV/WHIT BS14 ....92 A1
Pettigrove Gdns
KGWD/HNM BS15 ....64 D4
Pettigrove Rd KGWD/HNM BS15 ....64 D5
Pevensey Wk
BRSG/KWL/STAPK BS4 ....91 E2
Peverell Cl HNBRY/STHM BS10 ....37 E2
Peverell Dr HNBRY/STHM BS10 ....37 E2
Philadelphia Ct CBRIS/FH BS1 * 5 H2
Philippa Cl HGRV/WHIT BS14 ....91 H2
Philip St BMSTR BS3 ....79 E2
CBRISNE BS2 ....80 A1
Phillips Rd WSM BS23 ....7 K7
Phippen St CBRIS/FH BS1 ....5 G6
Phipps Barton
KGWD/HNM BS15 ....64 A3
Phipps St BMSTR BS3 ....78 C2
Phoenix Gv RDLND/MONT BS6 ....51 F3
Piccadilly Pl
CBATH/BATHN BA1 ....109 E3
Pickwick Rd
CBATH/BATHN BA1 ....108 D2
Picton La RDLND/MONT BS6 ....61 H2
Picton Ms RDLND/MONT BS6 ....61 H2
Picton St RDLND/MONT BS6 ....61 H2
Pier Cl PTSHD/EG BS20 ....45 H1
Pierrepont Pl CBATH/BATHN BA1 ....3 G5
Pierrepont St CBATH/BATHN BA1 ....3 G4
Pier Rd PTSHD/EG BS20 ....45 G1
Pigeon House Dr
BMSTRD/HC/WWD BS13 ....91 E5
Pigott Av
BMSTRD/HC/WWD BS13 ....90 B5
Pile Marsh EVILLE/WHL BS5 ....63 E4
Pilgrims Wy AVONM BS11 * 48 B1
MANG/FISH BS16 ....41 E5
MTN/WRL BS22 ....136 B1
Pilgrims Whf
BRSG/KWL/STAPK BS4 ....63 F4
Pilkington Cl BRSTK/PCHW BS34 ....39 F3
Pillingers Gdns
RDLND/MONT BS6 ....61 E1
Pillingers Rd KGWD/HNM BS15 ....64 B4
Pill Rd CFTN/FAIL BS8 ....59 E2
PTSHD/EG BS20 ....48 C5
Pill Wy CLVDN BS21 ....70 B3
Pimms La MTN/WRL BS22 ....130 C5
Pimpernel Md ALMDB BS32 ....27 G3
Pine Cl MTN/WRL BS22 ....136 A1
THNB/SVB BS35 ....8 D3
Pine Ct RDSTK/MIDN BA3 ....125 H2
Pinecroft HGRV/WHIT BS14 ....91 G2
Pine Gv HORF/LLZ BS7 ....38 C4
Pine Grove Pl HORF/LLZ BS7 ....61 G1
Pine Hl MTN/WRL BS22 ....136 A1
Pine Ridge Cl
HNLZ/SM/SNYPK/WT BS9 * 49 H4
Pine Rd HNBRY/STHM BS10 ....37 G2
Pines Rd OLD/WMLY/WICK BS30 ....83 F5
Pines Wy RDSTK/MIDN BA3 ....125 H2
Pinetree Rd
OMX/HUT/LCK BS24 ....141 F2
Pine Wk RDSTK/MIDN BA3 ....125 F2
Pinewood KGWD/HNM BS15 ....65 E2
Pinewood Av
RDSTK/MIDN BA3 ....124 A3
Pinewood Cl
HNLZ/SM/SNYPK/WT BS9 ....51 E1
Pinewood Gv
RDSTK/MIDN BA3 ....124 A3
Pinewood Rd
RDSTK/MIDN BA3 ....124 A3
Pinhay Rd
BMSTRD/HC/WWD BS13 ....90 C3
Pinkers Md MANG/FISH BS16 ....55 H2
Pioneer Av BATHSE BA2 ....116 D1
Pioneer Pk
BRSG/KWL/STAPK BS4 ....80 B1
Pipe La CBRIS/FH BS1 ....4 D4
Piper Rd YATE/CS BS37 ....20 D4
Piplar Gnd BOAV BA15 ....119 G5
Pippin Ct
OLD/WMLY/WICK BS30 ....82 C2
Pitch & Pay La
HNLZ/SM/SNYPK/WT BS9 ....50 B5
Pitch & Pay Pk
HNLZ/SM/SNYPK/WT BS9 ....50 B5
Pitchcombe YATE/CS BS37 ....31 G3
Pitchcombe Gdns
HNLZ/SM/SNYPK/WT BS9 ....50 A1
Pitch La RDLND/MONT BS6 ....61 G2
Pithay Ct CBRIS/FH BS1 * 5 F3
The Pithay CBRIS/FH BS1 ....5 F3
Pitlochry Cl HORF/LLZ BS7 ....38 C4
Pitman Av TRWBR BA14 ....122 C2
Pitman Ct CBATH/BATHN BA1 * 109 F2
Pitman Rd WSM BS23 ....6 E7
Pit Rd RDSTK/MIDN BA3 ....124 C3
Pitt Rd HORF/LLZ BS7 ....51 H3
Pittville Cl THNB/SVB BS35 ....8 D1
Pitville Pl RDLND/MONT BS6 * 61 E2
Pixash La KEYN BS31 ....95 E4
Pizey Av CLVDN BS21 ....70 B3
Pizey Cl CLVDN BS21 ....70 B3
Players Cl MANG/FISH BS16 ....40 C1
Playford Gdns AVONM BS11 ....35 F5
Pleasant Rd MANG/FISH BS16 ....54 C3
Pleshey Cl MTN/WRL BS22 ....136 A1
Ploughed Paddock NAIL BS48 ....73 E5
Plover Cl MTN/WRL BS22 ....136 C2
YATE/CS BS37 ....20 B5
Plovers Ri RDSTK/MIDN BA3 ....125 H1
Plumers Cl CLVDN BS21 ....71 E4
Plummer's Hl EVILLE/WHL BS5 ....63 F3
Plumpton Ct MANG/FISH BS16 ....41 G4
Plumtree Rd MTN/WRL BS22 ....136 B3
Plunder St YTN/CONG BS49 ....127 H4
Podgers Dr CBATH/BATHN BA1 ....107 G2
The Podium
CBATH/BATHN BA1 * 3 G4
Poets' Cl EVILLE/WHL BS5 ....63 E3
Polden Cl NAIL BS48 ....73 F5
Polden Rd PTSHD/EG BS20 ....44 D3
WSM BS23 ....7 H2
Polebarn Gdns TRWBR BA14 * 121 E5
Polebarn Rd TRWBR BA14 ....121 E5
Pollard Rd OMX/HUT/LCK BS24 ....136 C3
Polly Barnes Cl
KGWD/HNM BS15 ....81 G1
Polly Barnes Hl
KGWD/HNM BS15 ....81 G1
Polygon Rd CFTN/FAIL BS8 ....60 D5
The Polygon CFTN/FAIL BS8 ....60 C5
Pomfrett Gdns
HGRV/WHIT BS14 ....92 D4
Pomphrey Hl MANG/FISH BS16 ....55 H4
Ponsford Rd
BRSG/KWL/STAPK BS4 ....80 A5
Ponting Cl EVILLE/WHL BS5 ....63 H2
Pool Cnr ALMDB BS32 ....10 B5
Poole Court Dr YATE/CS BS37 ....20 D5
Poolemead Rd BATHSE BA2 ....113 E2
Poole St AVONM BS11 ....34 C5
Pooles Whf CFTN/FAIL BS8 ....78 B1
Pooles Wharf Ct CFTN/FAIL BS8 ....78 B1
Pool Rd KGWD/HNM BS15 ....54 D5
Pope's Wk BATHSE BA2 ....115 E3
Poplar Av
HNLZ/SM/SNYPK/WT BS9 ....50 A2
Poplar Cl BATHSE BA2 ....114 A3
OLD/WMLY/WICK BS30 ....65 H5
Poplar Dr MANG/FISH BS16 ....57 E3
Poplar Pl MANG/FISH BS16 ....53 H5
Poplar Rd BATHSE BA2 ....116 B2
BMSTRD/HC/WWD BS13 ....90 A2
EVILLE/WHL BS5 ....63 G2
KGWD/HNM BS15 ....81 F1
OLD/WMLY/WICK BS30 ....66 A5
The Poplars MTN/WRL BS22 ....136 C2
PTSHD/EG BS20 ....48 A4
Poplar Ter KGWD/HNM BS15 ....65 E3
Poplar Wk OMX/HUT/LCK BS24 ....140 B1
Poplar Wy East AVONM BS11 ....23 E5
Poplar Wy West AVONM BS11 ....22 D4
Poppy Cl MTN/WRL BS22 ....131 H3
Poppy Md ALMDB BS32 ....27 G3
Porlock Cl CLVDN BS21 ....71 E4
WSM BS23 ....139 E4
Porlock Gdns NAIL BS48 ....73 F5
Porlock Rd BATHSE BA2 ....114 D5
BMSTR BS3 ....79 E3
Portal Rd OMX/HUT/LCK BS24 ....141 G2
Portbury Common
PTSHD/EG BS20 ....45 H4
Portbury Gv AVONM BS11 ....48 C2
The Portbury Hundred
PTSHD/EG BS20 ....46 B5
Portbury Wk AVONM BS11 ....48 C2
Portbury Wy PTSHD/EG BS20 ....47 E3
Portishead Rd MTN/WRL BS22 ....132 A4
Portland Cl NAIL BS48 ....73 E5
Portland Dr PTSHD/EG BS20 ....45 H4
Portland Pl CBATH/BATHN BA1 ....2 E1
CBRISNE BS2 * 5 H1
MANG/FISH BS16 ....54 C5
Portland Sq CBRISNE BS2 ....5 H1
Portland St CBRISNE BS2 ....61 F3
CFTN/FAIL BS8 ....60 C4
MANG/FISH BS16 ....54 C5
Portland Ter CBATH/BATHN BA1 ....2 E1
Portmeirion Cl
HGRV/WHIT BS14 ....91 H4
Port Vw PTSHD/EG BS20 ....48 B3
Portview Rd AVONM BS11 ....34 C5
Portwall La CBRIS/FH BS1 ....5 G6
Portwall La East CBRIS/FH BS1 * 5 H6
Portway AVONM BS11 ....34 D5
HNLZ/SM/SNYPK/WT BS9 ....49 G3
Portway La YATE/CS BS37 ....21 H5
Post Office La NAIL BS48 ....87 E2
Post Office Rd
OMX/HUT/LCK BS24 ....141 E1
Poston Wy BOAV BA15 ....118 A2
Pottery Cl WSM BS23 ....7 J7
Poulton BOAV BA15 ....119 G4
Poulton La BOAV BA15 ....119 H5
Pound Dr MANG/FISH BS16 ....53 G3
Pound La BOAV BA15 ....119 F3
MANG/FISH BS16 ....53 G4
NAIL BS48 ....73 E3
Pound Md
BLAG/CWMG/WR BS40 ....96 D4
Pound Rd KGWD/HNM BS15 ....65 E1
The Pound ALMDB BS32 ....15 G2
Pountney Dr EVILLE/WHL BS5 ....62 C3
Powis Cl MTN/WRL BS22 ....135 H1
Powlett Ct BATHSE BA2 ....3 J2
Powlett Rd BATHSE BA2 ....3 J1
Pow's Orch RDSTK/MIDN BA3 ....124 B3
Pow's Rd KGWD/HNM BS15 ....64 C4
Poyntz Ct
OLD/WMLY/WICK BS30 ....82 C3
Poyntz Rd
BRSG/KWL/STAPK BS4 ....91 G1
Preanes Gn MTN/WRL BS22 ....136 C1
Preddy's La EVILLE/WHL BS5 ....63 H5
Prescot Cl MTN/WRL BS22 ....135 G2
Prescott YATE/CS BS37 ....31 H2
Press Moor Dr
OLD/WMLY/WICK BS30 ....82 C2
Prestbury YATE/CS BS37 ....31 H2
Preston Wk
BRSG/KWL/STAPK BS4 ....79 H5
Prestwick Cl
BRSG/KWL/STAPK BS4 ....80 C5
Pretoria Rd BRSTK/PCHW BS34 ....26 B2
Prewett St CBRIS/FH BS1 ....5 G7
Priddy Cl BATHSE BA2 ....113 G2
Priddy Ct HGRV/WHIT BS14 ....92 A4
Priddy Dr HGRV/WHIT BS14 ....92 A4
Priests Wy MTN/WRL BS22 ....136 A1
Priestwood Cl
HNBRY/STHM BS10 * 37 F2
Primrose Cl ALMDB BS32 ....16 B5
KGWD/HNM BS15 ....64 A2
Primrose Dr THNB/SVB BS35 ....9 E2
Primrose Hl
CBATH/BATHN BA1 ....108 A3
Primrose La KGWD/HNM BS15 ....64 B3
RDSTK/MIDN BA3 ....124 C3
Princes Buildings
CBATH/BATHN BA1 * 3 F3
CFTN/FAIL BS8 ....60 C5
Princes Ct
OLD/WMLY/WICK BS30 ....82 C2
Princes' La CFTN/FAIL BS8 ....60 C5
Princes' Pl HORF/LLZ BS7 ....51 H5
Prince's Rd CLVDN BS21 ....70 D2
Princess Cl KEYN BS31 ....94 B4
Princess Gdns MANG/FISH BS16 ....53 E2
TRWBR BA14 ....121 F2
Princess Rw CBRISNE BS2 ....5 F1
Princess Royal Gdns
EVILLE/WHL BS5 * 62 D3
Princess St BMSTR BS3 ....79 F2
CBRISNE BS2 ....62 B5
Princes St CBATH/BATHN BA1 ....3 F4
CBRISNE BS2 ....62 A3
Princess Victoria St
CFTN/FAIL BS8 ....60 C5
Prince St CBRIS/FH BS1 ....4 E6
Prince Street Rbt CBRIS/FH BS1 ....4 E5
Prior Park Buildings BATHSE BA2 ....3 J7
Prior Park Gdns BATHSE BA2 ....3 J7
Prior Park Rd BATHSE BA2 ....3 J7
Priors Lea YATE/CS BS37 ....32 A1
Priory Av
HNLZ/SM/SNYPK/WT BS9 ....50 D1
Priory Cl BATHSE BA2 ....115 E4
BOAV BA15 ....119 F2
RDSTK/MIDN BA3 ....124 B3
Priory Court Rd
HNLZ/SM/SNYPK/WT BS9 ....50 D1
Priory Dene
HNLZ/SM/SNYPK/WT BS9 ....50 D1
Priory Gdns HORF/LLZ BS7 ....38 C5
PTSHD/EG BS20 ....48 A4
Priory Ms WSM BS23 ....7 K4
Priory Pk BOAV BA15 ....119 G2
Priory Rd AVONM BS11 ....48 C2
BRSG/KWL/STAPK BS4 ....80 A4
CFTN/FAIL BS8 ....4 B1
KEYN BS31 ....94 B2
PTSHD/EG BS20 ....47 E5
PTSHD/EG BS20 ....48 A4
WSM BS23 ....7 K4
Priston Cl MTN/WRL BS22 ....132 A3
Pritchard St CBRISNE BS2 ....5 H1
Probyn Cl MANG/FISH BS16 ....53 H1
Proby Pl TRWBR BA14 ....121 H5
Pro-Cathedral La CFTN/FAIL BS8 ....4 B3
Proctor Cl
BRSG/KWL/STAPK BS4 * 80 C5
The Promenade
HORF/LLZ BS7 * 61 G1
Prospect Av KGWD/HNM BS15 ....64 A1
Prospect Cl FRCTL/WBN BS36 ....29 F2
FRCTL/WBN BS36 ....41 F1
Prospect Crs KGWD/HNM BS15 ....65 E1
Prospect Gdns
CBATH/BATHN BA1 ....103 E4
Prospect La FRCTL/WBN BS36 ....29 F2
Prospect Pl BATHSE BA2 * 2 E7
EVILLE/WHL BS5 ....62 D5
TRWBR BA14 ....121 E5
WSM BS23 ....6 E3
Prospect Rd BATHSE BA2 ....115 F3
THNB/SVB BS35 ....12 C3
Prospect Ter BMSTR BS3 ....78 D3
The Prospect TRWBR BA14 * 121 F5
Providence La LGASH BS41 ....76 C4
Providence Pl CBRISNE BS2 * 5 J4
Providence Vw LGASH BS41 ....76 C5
Prowse Cl THNB/SVB BS35 ....8 D3
Prudham St EVILLE/WHL BS5 ....62 D2
Puffin Cl MTN/WRL BS22 ....136 C3
Pullin Ct OLD/WMLY/WICK BS30 ....83 G1
Pulteney Av BATHSE BA2 ....3 J5
Pulteney Br BATHSE BA2 ....3 H4
Pulteney Gdns BATHSE BA2 ....3 J5
Pulteney Gv BATHSE BA2 ....3 J6
Pulteney Ms BATHSE BA2 ....3 H3
Pulteney Rd BATHSE BA2 ....3 J4
Pulteney Ter BATHSE BA2 ....3 J5
Pump La ALMDB BS32 ....10 D3
CBATH/BATHN BA1 ....110 C3
CBRIS/FH BS1 ....5 G7
Pump Sq PTSHD/EG BS20 ....48 C3
Purcell Wk
BRSG/KWL/STAPK BS4 ....91 E2
Purdown Rd HORF/LLZ BS7 ....52 A3
Purdue Cl MTN/WRL BS22 ....132 A5
Purlewent Dr
CBATH/BATHN BA1 ....107 H3
Pursey Dr ALMDB BS32 ....27 G4
Purton Cl KGWD/HNM BS15 ....64 D5
Purton Rd HORF/LLZ BS7 ....61 G1
Puttingthorpe Dr WSM BS23 ....135 H4
Puxley Cl HGRV/WHIT BS14 ....92 D3
Puxton Rd OMX/HUT/LCK BS24 ....133 H5
Pye Cft ALMDB BS32 ....16 C4
Pyecroft Av
HNLZ/SM/SNYPK/WT BS9 ....51 E1
Pylle Hill Crs BMSTR BS3 ....79 G2
Pyne Point CLVDN BS21 ....70 C2
Pynne Cl HGRV/WHIT BS14 ....92 D3
Pynne Rd HGRV/WHIT BS14 ....93 E4
Pyracantha Wk
HGRV/WHIT BS14 ....91 H3

Q

The Quadrangle YATE/CS BS37 ....43 H1
Quadrant East MANG/FISH BS16 ....54 B5
The Quadrant
RDLND/MONT BS6 ....51 E5
Quadrant West
MANG/FISH BS16 ....54 B5
The Quadrilles
THNB/SVB BS35 * 12 C3
Quaker La THNB/SVB BS35 ....8 C3
Quaker's Cl MANG/FISH BS16 ....41 E5
Quakers' Friars CBRIS/FH BS1 ....5 G2
Quaker's Rd MANG/FISH BS16 ....41 E5
Quantock Cl
OLD/WMLY/WICK BS30 ....83 F1
Quantock Rd BMSTR BS3 ....79 E3
PTSHD/EG BS20 ....45 E3
WSM BS23 ....138 C2
Quantocks BATHSE BA2 ....114 D5
The Quarries ALMDB BS32 ....15 H2
Quarrington Rd HORF/LLZ BS7 ....51 H3
Quarry Barton MANG/FISH BS16 ....40 D1
Quarry Cl BATHSE BA2 ....116 D1
BATHSE BA2 ....118 A3
Quarry La AVONM BS11 ....36 B4
FRCTL/WBN BS36 ....41 F1
Quarrymans Ct BATHSE BA2 ....117 F1
Quarry Md THNB/SVB BS35 ....11 F2
Quarry Rd BATHSE BA2 ....115 G1
KGWD/HNM BS15 ....64 C5
MANG/FISH BS16 ....54 B1
THNB/SVB BS35 ....11 F2
YATE/CS BS37 ....32 C1
Quarry Rock Gdns
BATHSE BA2 ....115 G3
Quarry Steps CFTN/FAIL BS8 ....60 D1
Quarry Wy MANG/FISH BS16 ....41 H4
MANG/FISH BS16 ....53 F3
NAIL BS48 ....73 E4
Quarterway La TRWBR BA14 ....121 F5
Quay Head CBRIS/FH BS1 * 4 E3
Quays Av PTSHD/EG BS20 ....45 H3
Quay Side CBRIS/FH BS1 * 5 H4
Quayside La EVILLE/WHL BS5 ....63 G5
Quay St CBRIS/FH BS1 ....5 F3
Quedgeley YATE/CS BS37 ....31 G2
Queen Ann Rd EVILLE/WHL BS5 ....62 C5
Queen Charlotte St
CBRIS/FH BS1 ....5 F4
Queen Charlton La
HGRV/WHIT BS14 ....101 G1
Queen Quay CBRIS/FH BS1 * 5 F5
Queen's Av CFTN/FAIL BS8 ....4 B2
PTSHD/EG BS20 ....45 F3
Queens Club Gdns
TRWBR BA14 ....122 B1
Queenscote PTSHD/EG BS20 ....46 A3
Queensdale Crs
BRSG/KWL/STAPK BS4 ....79 H5
Queens Down Gdns
BRSG/KWL/STAPK BS4 ....80 A3
Queen's Dr BATHSE BA2 ....114 D5
HORF/LLZ BS7 ....51 F4
KGWD/HNM BS15 ....81 G2
Queens Gdns TRWBR BA14 ....121 F2
Queens Ga
HNLZ/SM/SNYPK/WT BS9 ....50 A3
Queenshill Rd
BRSG/KWL/STAPK BS4 ....79 H5
Queensholm Av
MANG/FISH BS16 ....41 F4
Queensholm Cl
MANG/FISH BS16 ....41 F4
Queensholm Crs
MANG/FISH BS16 ....41 E4
Queensholm Dr
MANG/FISH BS16 ....41 F5
Queen's Pde CBATH/BATHN BA1 ....2 E3
CBRIS/FH BS1 ....4 B5
Queen's Parade Pl
CBATH/BATHN BA1 ....2 E3
Queens Pl BATHSE BA2 ....3 J6
Queen Sq CBRIS/FH BS1 ....4 E6
KEYN BS31 ....105 G1
Queen Square Av CBRIS/FH BS1 * 5 F5
Queen's Rd
BMSTRD/HC/WWD BS13 ....90 A5
BRSG/KWL/STAPK BS4 ....80 B5

CFTN/FAIL BS8 4 B3
CLVDN BS21 70 D2
EVILLE/WHL BS5 63 G4
HORF/LLZ BS7 52 A4
KEYN BS31 94 A5
LGASH BS41 99 E1
MANG/FISH BS16 57 E3
NAIL BS48 72 D5
NAIL BS48 85 F1
OLD/WMLY/WICK BS30 82 D2
PTSHD/EG BS20 44 B4
TRWBR BA14 120 D4
WSM BS23 6 D1
Queens Sq CBATH/BATHN BA1 3 F4
Queen St AVONM BS11 34 B4
CBATH/BATHN BA1 3 F4
CBRISNE BS2 5 H3
EVILLE/WHL BS5 63 E1
KGWD/HNM BS15 64 A4
Queens Wk THNB/SVB BS35 8 C1
Queensway BRSTK/PCHW BS34 27 E4
Queen's Wy MTN/WRL BS22 131 F4
Queen Victoria Rd
RDLND/MONT BS6 50 D4
Queen Victoria St CBRISNE BS2 62 B5
Queenwood Av
CBATH/BATHN BA1 108 D3
Quickthorn Cl HGRV/WHIT BS14 91 H3
Quiet St CBATH/BATHN BA1 3 F4
Quilling Cl TRWBR BA14 123 F2
Quilter Gv
BRSG/KWL/STAPK BS4 * 91 E2

R

Raby Ms BATHSE BA2 3 J3
Raby Pl BATHSE BA2 3 J3
Rackfield Pl BATHSE BA2 113 G1
Rackham Cl HORF/LLZ BS7 52 C2
Rackhay CBRIS/FH BS1 * 5 F4
Rackvernal Rd
RDSTK/MIDN BA3 124 C3
Radley Rd MANG/FISH BS16 54 A4
Radnor Rd
HNLZ/SM/SNYPK/WT BS9 51 E3
Radstock Rd
RDSTK/MIDN BA3 124 D2
Raeburn Rd EVILLE/WHL BS5 64 A4
Ragland La CBATH/BATHN BA1 108 D3
Ragland St CBATH/BATHN BA1 108 D2
Raglan La
BLAG/CWMG/WR BS40 97 F5
CBATH/BATHN BA1 * 108 D2
Raglan Pl HORF/LLZ BS7 51 G5
THNB/SVB BS35 8 C4
Raglan Rd HORF/LLZ BS7 51 G5
Raglan St CBATH/BATHN BA1 * 108 D2
Raglan Ter
CBATH/BATHN BA1 * 108 D2
Raglan Vls
CBATH/BATHN BA1 * 108 D2
Ragleth Gv TRWBR BA14 121 F4
Railton Jones Cl
BRSTK/PCHW BS34 39 H2
Railway Pl CBATH/BATHN BA1 3 H6
Railway St CBATH/BATHN BA1 3 G6
Railway Ter MANG/FISH BS16 54 B4
Railway Vw MANG/FISH BS16 * 41 E2
Railway View Pl
RDSTK/MIDN BA3 124 C2
Raleigh Cl KEYN BS31 104 D2
Raleigh Ri PTSHD/EG BS20 45 E2
Raleigh Rd BMSTR BS3 78 C2
Ralph Allen Dr BATHSE BA2 115 E3
Ralph Rd HORF/LLZ BS7 52 A4
Rambler Cl TRWBR BA14 122 B1
Ram Hl FRCTL/WBN BS36 30 B5
Ramsay Cl MTN/WRL BS22 131 F4
Ramsbury Wk TRWBR BA14 123 E3
Ramscombe La
CBATH/BATHN BA1 103 E3
Ramsey Rd HORF/LLZ BS7 52 A1
Ranchways PTSHD/EG BS20 44 C4
Randall Cl KGWD/HNM BS15 65 E1
Randall Rd CFTN/FAIL BS8 60 D5
Randolph Av
BMSTRD/HC/WWD BS13 90 C4
YATE/CS BS37 20 C3
Randolph Cl
BMSTRD/HC/WWD BS13 90 C4
Rangers Wk KGWD/HNM BS15 81 H2
Rannoch Rd BRSTK/PCHW BS34 38 C3
Ranscombe Av MTN/WRL BS22 136 A1
Ransford CLVDN BS21 70 B4
Ratcliffe Dr BRSTK/PCHW BS34 27 G5
Rathbone Cl FRCTL/WBN BS36 30 A5
Raven Cl MTN/WRL BS22 136 B2
Ravendale Dr
OLD/WMLY/WICK BS30 83 E3
Ravenglass Crs
HNBRY/STHM BS10 37 H3
Ravenhead Dr HGRV/WHIT BS14 92 A1
Ravenhill Av BMSTR BS3 79 G4
Ravenhill Rd BMSTR BS3 79 G3
Ravenscroft Gdns
TRWBR BA14 121 G5
Ravenswood Rd
RDLND/MONT BS6 61 F2
Rawens Wd
OLD/WMLY/WICK BS30 83 E3
Rawlins Av MTN/WRL BS22 131 H3
Rayens Cross Rd LGASH BS41 76 C5
Rayleigh Rd
HNLZ/SM/SNYPK/WT BS9 50 A1
Raymend Rd BMSTR BS3 79 F3
Raymend Wk BMSTR BS3 79 F4
Raymill BRSG/KWL/STAPK BS4 81 F4
Raymore Ri LGASH BS41 88 C1
Raynes Rd BMSTR BS3 78 B3
Rector's Wy WSM BS23 7 G7
Rectory Cl NAIL BS48 73 H4
YATE/CS BS37 21 E4
Rectory Dr YTN/CONG BS49 126 C4
Rectory La BRSTK/PCHW BS34 38 D2
Rectory Rd FRCTL/WBN BS36 29 H2
PTSHD/EG BS20 48 A5
Rectory Wy YTN/CONG BS49 126 C4
Redcar Ct FRCTL/WBN BS36 41 G3
Redcatch Rd BMSTR BS3 79 G4
Redcliff Backs CBRIS/FH BS1 5 G5
Redcliffe Cl PTSHD/EG BS20 44 B5
Redcliffe Pde East CBRIS/FH BS1 5 F6
Redcliffe Pde West
CBRIS/FH BS1 5 F6
Redcliffe Wy CBRIS/FH BS1 5 G6
Redcliffe Whf CBRIS/FH BS1 * 5 F6
Redcliff Hl CBRIS/FH BS1 5 G7
Redcliff Mead La CBRIS/FH BS1 5 H7
Redcliff St CBRIS/FH BS1 5 G4
Redcross Ms CBRISNE BS2 * 5 J3
Redcross St CBRISNE BS2 5 J3
The Reddings KGWD/HNM BS15 65 E1
Redfield Gv RDSTK/MIDN BA3 124 B4
Redfield Hl
OLD/WMLY/WICK BS30 83 G2
Redfield Rd BRSTK/PCHW BS34 26 D3
RDSTK/MIDN BA3 124 A4
Redford Crs
BMSTRD/HC/WWD BS13 98 D1
Redford La MANG/FISH BS16 57 G4
Redford Wk
BMSTRD/HC/WWD BS13 99 E1
Redhill Cl MANG/FISH BS16 53 F5
Redhill Dr MANG/FISH BS16 53 F5
Red House La ALMDB BS32 15 H3
HNLZ/SM/SNYPK/WT BS9 50 B2
Redland Court Rd
RDLND/MONT BS6 51 F5
Redland Green Rd
RDLND/MONT BS6 61 E1
Redland Gv RDLND/MONT BS6 61 F1
Redland Hl RDLND/MONT BS6 60 D1
Redland Pk BATHSE BA2 113 E1
RDLND/MONT BS6 61 E2
Redland Rd PTSHD/EG BS20 47 G2
RDLND/MONT BS6 50 D5
Redland Ter CFTN/FAIL BS8 60 D1
Redshelf Wk
HNBRY/STHM BS10 37 H2
Redwick Cl AVONM BS11 36 B3
Redwick Gdns THNB/SVB BS35 13 E2
Redwick Rd THNB/SVB BS35 12 D1
Redwing Dr MTN/WRL BS22 136 B2
Redwing Gdns MANG/FISH BS16 53 F2
Redwood Cl NAIL BS48 73 H4
OLD/WMLY/WICK BS30 82 D3
RDSTK/MIDN BA3 125 F4
Redwood La NAIL BS48 87 H2
Reed Cl HNBRY/STHM BS10 51 G2
Reed Ct OLD/WMLY/WICK BS30 * 82 C3
Reedley Rd
HNLZ/SM/SNYPK/WT BS9 50 C3
Reedling Cl MANG/FISH BS16 * 53 F2
Reed Wy MTN/WRL BS22 132 B5
Regency Dr
BRSG/KWL/STAPK BS4 81 F4
Regent Rd BMSTR BS3 79 E2
Regents Cl THNB/SVB BS35 8 C1
Regents Pl BOAV BA15 119 G4
Regents St CFTN/FAIL BS8 60 D5
Regent St KGWD/HNM BS15 64 B3
WSM BS23 6 E4
The Regina CBATH/BATHN BA1 * 3 F2
Remenham Dr
HNLZ/SM/SNYPK/WT BS9 51 E3
Remenham Pk
HNLZ/SM/SNYPK/WT BS9 51 E3
Rendcomb Cl MTN/WRL BS22 135 G1
Repton Rd
BRSG/KWL/STAPK BS4 80 B3
Reubens Ct MTN/WRL BS22 131 G5
Reynolds Cl KEYN BS31 94 D4
Reynold's Wk HORF/LLZ BS7 52 B1
Rhode Cl KEYN BS31 104 B2
Rhodyate Hl YTN/CONG BS49 127 F5
Rhodyate La YTN/CONG BS49 127 G4
Rhyne Ter WSM BS23 138 C4
Rhyne Vw NAIL BS48 72 C5
Ribblesdale THNB/SVB BS35 8 D4
Richards Cl MTN/WRL BS22 132 A4
Richeson Cl HNBRY/STHM BS10 37 E3
Richeson Wk
HNBRY/STHM BS10 37 E3
Richmond Av
BRSTK/PCHW BS34 27 G5
RDLND/MONT BS6 62 A1
Richmond Cl KEYN BS31 94 A5
PTSHD/EG BS20 45 H3
TRWBR BA14 122 B2
Richmond Dl CFTN/FAIL BS8 60 D1
Richmond Gn NAIL BS48 73 G5
Richmond Hts
CBATH/BATHN BA1 108 C3
Richmond Hl
CBATH/BATHN BA1 108 C3
CFTN/FAIL BS8 4 A2
Richmond Hill Av CFTN/FAIL BS8 4 A3
Richmond La
CBATH/BATHN BA1 108 C3
CFTN/FAIL BS8 60 D4
Richmond Ms CFTN/FAIL BS8 60 D4
Richmond Park Rd
CFTN/FAIL BS8 60 D4
Richmond Pl
CBATH/BATHN BA1 108 D3
Richmond Rd
CBATH/BATHN BA1 108 C2
EVILLE/WHL BS5 63 F3
MANG/FISH BS16 55 F3
RDLND/MONT BS6 61 H2
Richmond St BMSTR BS3 79 G2
WSM BS23 6 D4
Richmond Ter AVONM BS11 34 B4
CFTN/FAIL BS8 60 D4
Ricketts La MTN/WRL BS22 136 D1
Rickfield BOAV BA15 119 E3
Rickford Rd NAIL BS48 73 G5
The Ride KGWD/HNM BS15 65 F1
Ridge Cl PTSHD/EG BS20 44 D4
Ridge Green Cl BATHSE BA2 116 B2
Ridgehill
HNLZ/SM/SNYPK/WT BS9 51 F3
The Ridge AVONM BS11 48 D1
FRCTL/WBN BS36 30 A3
YTN/CONG BS49 126 B3
Ridgeview LGASH BS41 77 E4
Ridgeway FRCTL/WBN BS36 30 A3
NAIL BS48 72 D5
YATE/CS BS37 21 F5
Ridgeway Av WSM BS23 7 F7
Ridgeway Ct
HNBRY/STHM BS10 37 E4
Ridgeway Gdns
HGRV/WHIT BS14 92 B4
Ridgeway La HGRV/WHIT BS14 92 A5
Ridgeway Pde EVILLE/WHL BS5 53 F5
Ridgeway Rd LGASH BS41 76 D5
MANG/FISH BS16 53 F5
The Ridgeway
HNBRY/STHM BS10 37 F4
MTN/WRL BS22 135 G1
Riding Barn Hl
OLD/WMLY/WICK BS30 66 D5
Ridingleaze AVONM BS11 35 H4
Ridings Cl YATE/CS BS37 33 E1
Ridings Rd FRCTL/WBN BS36 30 A4
The Ridings
BMSTRD/HC/WWD BS13 89 H5
FRCTL/WBN BS36 30 A4
Ringspit La PLTN/PENS BS39 101 H4
Ringswell Gdns
CBATH/BATHN BA1 109 F3
Ringwood Crs
HNBRY/STHM BS10 38 A4
Ringwood Gv WSM BS23 135 F2
Ringwood Rd BATHSE BA2 113 H1
Ripley Rd EVILLE/WHL BS5 63 H2
Ripon Ct MANG/FISH BS16 41 G4
Ripon Rd BRSG/KWL/STAPK BS4 63 F5
Rippleside PTSHD/EG BS20 45 F3
Rippleside Rd CLVDN BS21 68 C5
The Ripple CLVDN BS21 73 E2
Risdale Rd BMSTR BS3 78 A5
Rivendell MTN/WRL BS22 131 H4
Riverland Dr
BMSTRD/HC/WWD BS13 90 A5
Riverleaze
HNLZ/SM/SNYPK/WT BS9 49 G3
PTSHD/EG BS20 44 C2
River Md CLVDN BS21 70 D5
River Rd YATE/CS BS37 32 C1
Riverside Cl AVONM BS11 49 E3
CLVDN BS21 70 B4
RDSTK/MIDN BA3 124 A5
Riverside Ct BATHSE BA2 2 E5
BRSG/KWL/STAPK BS4 * 63 G5
Riverside Gdns BATHSE BA2 2 E5
Riverside Ms
BRSG/KWL/STAPK BS4 63 G5
Riverside Pk THNB/SVB BS35 12 B3
Riverside Rd BATHSE BA2 2 E5
RDSTK/MIDN BA3 124 A5
Riverside Steps
BRSG/KWL/STAPK BS4 63 F4
Riverside Wk EVILLE/WHL BS5 63 G5
RDSTK/MIDN BA3 124 A5
Riverside Wy KGWD/HNM BS15 81 H3
Rivers Rd CBATH/BATHN BA1 108 C4
Rivers St CBATH/BATHN BA1 2 E2
Rivers Street Ms
CBATH/BATHN BA1 * 2 E2
Rivers Street Pl
CBATH/BATHN BA1 * 3 F2
River St CBRISNE BS2 5 J2
River Ter KEYN BS31 * 94 C4
River Vw MANG/FISH BS16 53 F3
Riverway NAIL BS48 73 G3
River Wy TRWBR BA14 120 D5
Riverwood Rd MANG/FISH BS16 40 D4
Riviera Crs MANG/FISH BS16 54 D4
Roath Rd PTSHD/EG BS20 45 G3
Robbins Cl ALMDB BS32 27 H4
Robbins Ct MANG/FISH BS16 55 G2
Robel Av FRCTL/WBN BS36 29 G2
Robert Ct MANG/FISH BS16 55 G1
Robertson Dr
BRSG/KWL/STAPK BS4 63 G5
Robertson Rd EVILLE/WHL BS5 62 D1
Robert St EVILLE/WHL BS5 62 C1
Robin Cl HNBRY/STHM BS10 37 G3
MTN/WRL BS22 136 B3
RDSTK/MIDN BA3 124 C4
Robin Dr OMX/HUT/LCK BS24 140 B4
Robinia Wk HGRV/WHIT BS14 91 H2
Robin La CLVDN BS21 68 B5
Robinson Cl NAIL BS48 85 H4
Robinson Dr EVILLE/WHL BS5 62 B3
Robinson Wy NAIL BS48 85 H4
Robin Wy YATE/CS BS37 32 B3
Rochester Cl
OMX/HUT/LCK BS24 139 F5
Rochester Rd
BRSG/KWL/STAPK BS4 80 D1
Rochfort Pl BATHSE BA2 3 H1
Rock Av NAIL BS48 72 D4
Rock Cl BRSG/KWL/STAPK BS4 80 D4
Rock Hall La BATHSE BA2 117 F1
Rockingham Gdns AVONM BS11 35 H5
Rockingham Gv WSM BS23 135 F2
Rockland Gv MANG/FISH BS16 53 E2
Rockland Rd MANG/FISH BS16 54 B1
Rock La BATHSE BA2 117 F1
BRSTK/PCHW BS34 27 H5
Rockleaze
HNLZ/SM/SNYPK/WT BS9 60 B1
Rockleaze Av
HNLZ/SM/SNYPK/WT BS9 50 B5
Rockleaze Rd
HNLZ/SM/SNYPK/WT BS9 60 B1
Rockliffe Av BATHSE BA2 3 K1
Rockliffe Rd BATHSE BA2 3 J1
Rock Rd KEYN BS31 94 B4
OLD/WMLY/WICK BS30 67 G3
RDSTK/MIDN BA3 124 C2
TRWBR BA14 122 C2
YTN/CONG BS49 126 C4
Rockside Av
MANG/FISH BS16 41 G5
Rockside Dr
HNLZ/SM/SNYPK/WT BS9 51 E2
Rockside Gdns
FRCTL/WBN BS36 30 A2
MANG/FISH BS16 41 G5
Rocks La BLAG/CWMG/WR BS40 97 E3
Rockstowes Wy
HNBRY/STHM BS10 38 A2
Rock St THNB/SVB BS35 8 C4
The Rock
BRSG/KWL/STAPK BS4 80 D3
Rockwell Av AVONM BS11 36 A4
Rodborough YATE/CS BS37 31 G3
Rodbourne Rd
HNBRY/STHM BS10 51 G1
Rodfords Md HGRV/WHIT BS14 91 H2
Rodford Wy YATE/CS BS37 31 G3
Rodmead Wk
BMSTRD/HC/WWD BS13 90 B5
Rodmoor Rd PTSHD/EG BS20 45 G2
Rodney Av KGWD/HNM BS15 63 H3
Rodney Crs BRSTK/PCHW BS34 38 D1
Rodney Rd KEYN BS31 105 F2
KGWD/HNM BS15 63 H2
NAIL BS48 85 H3
Rodney Wk KGWD/HNM BS15 63 H2
Rodsleigh TRWBR BA14 122 A3
Rodway Hl MANG/FISH BS16 55 F4
Rodway Rd BRSTK/PCHW BS34 26 C2
MANG/FISH BS16 55 F3
Rodway Vw KGWD/HNM BS15 55 E5
Rodwell Pk TRWBR BA14 121 F4
Roebuck Cl MTN/WRL BS22 131 H4
Roegate Dr
BRSG/KWL/STAPK BS4 63 F5
Rogers Cl
OLD/WMLY/WICK BS30 83 E1
Rogers Ct YATE/CS BS37 33 E1
Rogers Wk
OLD/WMLY/WICK BS30 66 A4
Rokeby Av RDLND/MONT BS6 61 F2
Roman Farm
Ct AVONM BS11 * 36 B3
Roman Farm Rd
BRSG/KWL/STAPK BS4 91 F2
Roman Wk
BRSG/KWL/STAPK BS4 80 B3
BRSTK/PCHW BS34 27 G5
Roman Wy
HNLZ/SM/SNYPK/WT BS9 49 H4
Romney Av HORF/LLZ BS7 52 C3
Ronald Rd MANG/FISH BS16 53 G2
Ronayne Wk MANG/FISH BS16 54 B2
Rookery Cl MTN/WRL BS22 131 F5
Rookery La THNB/SVB BS35 14 A1
Rookery Rd
BRSG/KWL/STAPK BS4 79 H3
Rookery Wy HGRV/WHIT BS14 91 G5
Rooksbridge Wk BATHSE BA2 * 113 G2
Rose Acre HNBRY/STHM BS10 37 F2
Rosebay Md MANG/FISH BS16 53 F4
Roseberry Pk EVILLE/WHL BS5 63 E3
Roseberry Pl BATHSE BA2 * 2 A4
Roseberry Rd BATHSE BA2 113 H1
EVILLE/WHL BS5 62 D4
Rosebery Av CBRISNE BS2 62 B2
Rosebery Ter CFTN/FAIL BS8 4 A4
Rose Cl FRCTL/WBN BS36 41 F1
Rosedale Av WSM BS23 7 J5
Rosedale Gdns TRWBR BA14 120 B5
Rosedale Rd MANG/FISH BS16 54 A5
Rose Gdns MTN/WRL BS22 132 A4
Rose Green Rd EVILLE/WHL BS5 63 E1
Rose Hl CBATH/BATHN BA1 109 F2
Rose La FRCTL/WBN BS36 30 B3
Roselarge Gdns
HNBRY/STHM BS10 37 F3
Rosemary Cl ALMDB BS32 27 H3
Rosemary La EVILLE/WHL BS5 62 D1
Rose Md HORF/LLZ BS7 52 B1
Rosemount La BATHSE BA2 114 D3
Rosemount Rd NAIL BS48 87 G1
Rose Oak Dr FRCTL/WBN BS36 30 B3
Rose Oak Gdns
FRCTL/WBN BS36 30 B3
Rose Oak La FRCTL/WBN BS36 30 B3
Rose Rd EVILLE/WHL BS5 63 F4
Rosery Cl
HNLZ/SM/SNYPK/WT BS9 37 F5
The Rosery MANG/FISH BS16 54 B5
Roseville Av
OLD/WMLY/WICK BS30 82 D4
Rose Wk MANG/FISH BS16 54 B5
Rosewarn Cl BATHSE BA2 113 F3
Rosewell Ct CBATH/BATHN BA1 2 E4
Rosewood Av THNB/SVB BS35 11 F2
Rosling Rd HORF/LLZ BS7 51 H2
Roslyn Av MTN/WRL BS22 135 H2
Roslyn Rd RDLND/MONT BS6 61 F1
Rossall Av BRSTK/PCHW BS34 27 E4
Rossall Rd
BRSG/KWL/STAPK BS4 80 C3
Ross Cl YATE/CS BS37 21 G5
Rossendale Cl MTN/WRL BS22 131 G5
Rossett Gdns TRWBR BA14 122 B1
Rossiter Rd BATHSE BA2 3 H7
Rossiter's La EVILLE/WHL BS5 63 H5
Rosslyn Rd
CBATH/BATHN BA1 107 G5
Rosslyn Wy THNB/SVB BS35 8 D1
Roundhill Gv BATHSE BA2 113 G4
Roundhill Pk BATHSE BA2 113 F3
Roundmoor Cl KEYN BS31 105 E1
Roundmoor Gdns
HGRV/WHIT BS14 92 C2
Roundstone St TRWBR BA14 121 E5
Roundways FRCTL/WBN BS36 30 A4
Rousham Rd EVILLE/WHL BS5 52 B5
Rowacres BATHSE BA2 113 G4
HGRV/WHIT BS14 91 G3
Rowan Cl MANG/FISH BS16 63 H1
NAIL BS48 73 H4
Rowan Ct RDSTK/MIDN BA3 125 E3
Rowan Pl OMX/HUT/LCK BS24 137 E2
The Rowans PTSHD/EG BS20 45 E4
Rowan Wy KGWD/HNM BS15 81 G3
Rowberrow HGRV/WHIT BS14 91 G2
Rowberrow Wy NAIL BS48 73 F5
Rowden La BOAV BA15 119 G5
Rowland Av MANG/FISH BS16 52 D4
Rowlands Cl
CBATH/BATHN BA1 110 C2
Rowlandson Gdns
HORF/LLZ BS7 52 C2
Rowley St BMSTR BS3 78 D3
Rownham Cl BMSTR BS3 77 H2
Rownham Hl CFTN/FAIL BS8 60 B5
Rownham Md CFTN/FAIL BS8 78 B1
The Rows MTN/WRL BS22 136 B1
Royal Albert Rd
RDLND/MONT BS6 50 D4
Royal Av CBATH/BATHN BA1 2 D3
Royal Cl HNBRY/STHM BS10 36 C2
Royal Crs CBATH/BATHN BA1 2 D2
WSM BS23 6 C2
Royal Fort Rd CFTN/FAIL BS8 4 D2
Royal Pde WSM BS23 6 C3
Royal Pk CFTN/FAIL BS8 60 D4
Royal Portbury Dock Rd
PTSHD/EG BS20 47 G3
Royal Rd MANG/FISH BS16 55 F2
Royal York Crs CFTN/FAIL BS8 60 C5
Royal York Ms
CBATH/BATHN BA1 * 3 F3
Royal York Vls CFTN/FAIL BS8 60 D5
Royate Hl EVILLE/WHL BS5 63 E1
Roycroft Rd BRSTK/PCHW BS34 39 E3
Roy King Gdns
OLD/WMLY/WICK BS30 83 F1
Royston Wk HNBRY/STHM BS10 38 A3
Rozel Rd HORF/LLZ BS7 51 H2
Rubens Cl KEYN BS31 94 D4
Ruby St BMSTR BS3 78 C3
Ruddymead CLVDN BS21 70 D3
Rudford Cl BRSTK/PCHW BS34 26 D1
Rudge Cl KGWD/HNM BS15 65 E1
Rudgewood Cl
BMSTRD/HC/WWD BS13 91 E5
Rudgleigh Av PTSHD/EG BS20 48 B4
Rudgleigh Rd PTSHD/EG BS20 48 B4
Rudhall Gv HNBRY/STHM BS10 51 H1
Rudmore Pk
CBATH/BATHN BA1 107 F5
Rudthorpe Rd HORF/LLZ BS7 51 H3
Ruffet Rd FRCTL/WBN BS36 42 A1
Rugby Rd
BRSG/KWL/STAPK BS4 80 C3
Runnymead Av
BRSG/KWL/STAPK BS4 80 C5
Runnymede KGWD/HNM BS15 64 D2
Runswick Rd
BRSG/KWL/STAPK BS4 80 B3
Rupert St CBRIS/FH BS1 5 F3
EVILLE/WHL BS5 62 D4
Rush Cl ALMDB BS32 16 B5
Rush Hl BATHSE BA2 113 G5
Rushmoor CLVDN BS21 70 A4
Rushmoor Gv NAIL BS48 85 G4
Rushmoor La NAIL BS48 85 H4
Rushton Dr FRCTL/WBN BS36 30 B3
Rushy OLD/WMLY/WICK BS30 82 D2
Rushy Wy MANG/FISH BS16 41 H4
Ruskin Gv HORF/LLZ BS7 38 D5
Ruskin Rd RDSTK/MIDN BA3 124 D3
Russell Av KGWD/HNM BS15 64 C4
Russell Gv RDLND/MONT BS6 51 F3
Russell Rd CLVDN BS21 70 C2
MANG/FISH BS16 64 A1
OMX/HUT/LCK BS24 137 F5
RDLND/MONT BS6 51 E4
Russell St CBATH/BATHN BA1 3 F2
Russell Town Av
EVILLE/WHL BS5 62 C3
Russet Cl THNB/SVB BS35 10 A4
The Russets PTSHD/EG BS20 46 A4
Russett Cl NAIL BS48 86 A3
Russett Gv NAIL BS48 84 D1
Russ St CBRISNE BS2 5 J4
Rutherford Cl
OLD/WMLY/WICK BS30 82 D3
Ruthven Rd
BRSG/KWL/STAPK BS4 91 F1
Rutland Av
OLD/WMLY/WICK BS30 82 D4
Rutland Cl MTN/WRL BS22 135 H3
Rutland Crs TRWBR BA14 122 D3
Rutland Rd HORF/LLZ BS7 51 H5
Rydal Av OMX/HUT/LCK BS24 140 C2
Rydal Rd WSM BS23 139 E2
Ryde Rd
BRSG/KWL/STAPK BS4 80 A4
Rye Cl
BMSTRD/HC/WWD BS13 89 H3
Ryecroft Av MTN/WRL BS22 136 B2
Ryecroft Ri LGASH BS41 77 E5
Ryecroft Rd FRCTL/WBN BS36 30 A2
Ryedown La
OLD/WMLY/WICK BS30 83 F5
Ryeland Wy TRWBR BA14 123 F2
Ryland Pl CBRISNE BS2 * 62 B1
Rylestone Cl FRCTL/WBN BS36 29 F2
Rylestone Gv
HNLZ/SM/SNYPK/WT BS9 50 C3
Rysdale Rd
HNLZ/SM/SNYPK/WT BS9 50 C2

S

Sabrina Wy
HNLZ/SM/SNYPK/WT BS9 49 H4
Sadbury Cl MTN/WRL BS22 132 A4
Sadlier Cl AVONM BS11 35 G5
Saffron Cl EVILLE/WHL BS5 * 62 D3
The Saffrons MTN/WRL BS22 132 A4
Sage Cl PTSHD/EG BS20 44 B4
Sages Md ALMDB BS32 27 G2
St Agnes Av
BRSG/KWL/STAPK BS4 79 G4
St Agnes Cl
BRSG/KWL/STAPK BS4 79 G4
NAIL BS48 73 H5
St Agnes Gdns
BRSG/KWL/STAPK BS4 * 79 G4
St Agnes Wk
BRSG/KWL/STAPK BS4 79 G4
St Aidan's Cl EVILLE/WHL BS5 * 64 A5
St Aidan's Rd EVILLE/WHL BS5 63 H5
St Alban's Rd RDLND/MONT BS6 51 E4
St Aldams Dr MANG/FISH BS16 57 E3
St Aldhelm Rd BOAV BA15 119 H4
St Aldwyn's Cl HORF/LLZ BS7 38 C5
St Andrews
OLD/WMLY/WICK BS30 65 G5
YATE/CS BS37 32 B1
St Andrews Cl
MTN/WRL BS22 * 131 G5
NAIL BS48 * 73 H5
YTN/CONG BS49 * 128 D2
St Andrew's Dr CLVDN BS21 70 A3
St Andrew's Rd AVONM BS11 22 C5
AVONM BS11 34 C4
NAIL BS48 86 A4
RDLND/MONT BS6 61 H2
St Andrews Ter
CBATH/BATHN BA1 * 3 F3
St Anne's Av KEYN BS31 94 A3
St Annes Cl EVILLE/WHL BS5 * 63 G5
OLD/WMLY/WICK BS30 83 E2
St Anne's Dr FRCTL/WBN BS36 30 A5
OLD/WMLY/WICK BS30 67 E4
OLD/WMLY/WICK BS30 83 F4
St Anne's Park Rd
BRSG/KWL/STAPK BS4 80 D1
St Anne's Rd
BRSG/KWL/STAPK BS4 63 E5
EVILLE/WHL BS5 64 A5
St Anne's Ter
BRSG/KWL/STAPK BS4 80 D1
St Anns Pl CBATH/BATHN BA1 2 D4
St Ann's Wy BATHSE BA2 3 K4
St Anthony's Cl
RDSTK/MIDN BA3 * 124 B2
St Aubin's Av
BRSG/KWL/STAPK BS4 81 E3
St Aubyn's Av WSM BS23 138 C4
St Augustine's Pde
CBRIS/FH BS1 4 E4
St Augustine's Pl CBRIS/FH BS1 * 4 E4
St Augustine's Rd
TRWBR BA14 122 C1
St Augustines Yd CBRIS/FH BS1 * 4 D4
St Austell Cl NAIL BS48 85 H1
St Austell Rd MTN/WRL BS22 135 G3
St Barnabas Cl
OLD/WMLY/WICK BS30 65 H4
RDSTK/MIDN BA3 124 C1
St Bartholomew's Rd
HORF/LLZ BS7 52 A5
St Bede's Rd KGWD/HNM BS15 64 B1
St Bernard's Rd AVONM BS11 48 D2
St Brelades Gv
BRSG/KWL/STAPK BS4 80 D1
St Brendan's Wy AVONM BS11 34 C4
St Briavels Dr YATE/CS BS37 31 H2
St Bridges Cl MTN/WRL BS22 130 B2
St Catherine's Cl BATHSE BA2 115 F1
St Catherines Ct BMSTR BS3 * 79 E3
St Catherine's Md
PTSHD/EG BS20 48 C5
St Catherines Pl BMSTR BS3 79 E2
St Chad's Av RDSTK/MIDN BA3 124 B3
St Chad's Gn RDSTK/MIDN BA3 124 B4
St Charles Cl RDSTK/MIDN BA3 * 124 B2
St Christophers
Cl BATHSE BA2 109 F5
St Clements Ct KEYN BS31 94 B5
St Clements Rd KEYN BS31 94 B4
St David Ms CBRIS/FH BS1 4 C5
St David's Av
OLD/WMLY/WICK BS30 83 E1
St David's Cl MTN/WRL BS22 135 G1
St David's Crs
BRSG/KWL/STAPK BS4 80 D1
St David's Rd THNB/SVB BS35 8 D3
St Dunstans Cl KEYN BS31 94 B3
St Dunstan's Rd BMSTR BS3 78 D4
St Edward's Rd CFTN/FAIL BS8 * 4 A5
St Edyth's Rd
HNLZ/SM/SNYPK/WT BS9 49 G2
St Fagans Ct
OLD/WMLY/WICK BS30 83 E4
St Francis Dr FRCTL/WBN BS36 29 F4
OLD/WMLY/WICK BS30 67 E4
St Francis Rd BMSTR BS3 78 B2
KEYN BS31 93 H3
St Gabriel's Rd EVILLE/WHL BS5 62 B2
St Georges Av
EVILLE/WHL BS5 * 63 G5
St Georges Buildings
CBATH/BATHN BA1 2 C3
St George's Hl BATHSE BA2 109 G4
PTSHD/EG BS20 47 H5
St Georges House
EVILLE/WHL BS5 * 63 F3
St Georges Pl CBATH/BATHN BA1 2 D3
St George's Rd CBRIS/FH BS1 4 C5
KEYN BS31 94 A4
PTSHD/EG BS20 47 F1
St Georges Ter TRWBR BA14 * 122 D1
St Gregory's Rd HORF/LLZ BS7 38 C5
St Gregory's Wk HORF/LLZ BS7 38 D5
St Helena Rd RDLND/MONT BS6 51 E4
St Helens Dr
OLD/WMLY/WICK BS30 67 F4
OLD/WMLY/WICK BS30 83 F4
St Helen's Wk EVILLE/WHL BS5 63 H2
St Helier Av
BRSG/KWL/STAPK BS4 * 81 E3
St Hilary Cl
HNLZ/SM/SNYPK/WT BS9 50 A3
St Ivel Wy
OLD/WMLY/WICK BS30 65 H5
St Ives Cl NAIL BS48 * 73 H5
St Ives Rd WSM BS23 139 F1
St James's Pde
CBATH/BATHN BA1 3 F5
St James's Pl
CBATH/BATHN BA1 * 2 D1
St James's Sq
CBATH/BATHN BA1 2 D1
St James's St
CBATH/BATHN BA1 * 2 E1
MANG/FISH BS16 55 F3
St James St WSM BS23 6 D4
St John's Av CLVDN BS21 70 D2
St John's Br CBRIS/FH BS1 * 4 E3
St John's Cl WSM BS23 6 C1
St Johns Ct KEYN BS31 94 B3
St John's Crs BMSTR BS3 79 F4
RDSTK/MIDN BA3 124 B2
TRWBR BA14 122 A3
St John's La BMSTR BS3 78 D3
St Johns Ms CFTN/FAIL BS8 * 61 E3
St John's Pl CBATH/BATHN BA1 3 F4
St John's Rd BATHSE BA2 3 G2
BMSTR BS3 78 D3
CBATH/BATHN BA1 107 H5
CFTN/FAIL BS8 60 D2
CLVDN BS21 70 C2
NAIL BS48 86 A4
St John's St BMSTR BS3 78 D3
St John St THNB/SVB BS35 8 C3
St Johns Wy YATE/CS BS37 21 H5
St Joseph's Rd
HNBRY/STHM BS10 37 G2
St Jude's Ter MTN/WRL BS22 135 H2
St Keyna Rd KEYN BS31 94 B4
St Kilda's Rd BATHSE BA2 2 A7
St Ladoc Rd KEYN BS31 94 A3
St Laud Cl
HNLZ/SM/SNYPK/WT BS9 49 H3
St Laurence Rd BOAV BA15 119 H4
St Leonard's Rd
EVILLE/WHL BS5 62 D1
HORF/LLZ BS7 51 H2
St Lucia Cl HORF/LLZ BS7 38 B5
St Lucia Crs HORF/LLZ BS7 51 H1
St Lukes Cl MANG/FISH BS16 55 G1
St Luke's Crs BMSTR BS3 79 G2
St Luke's Gdns
BRSG/KWL/STAPK BS4 80 D4
St Luke's Ms
BRSG/KWL/STAPK BS4 80 D4
St Luke's Rd BATHSE BA2 114 C4
BMSTR BS3 79 F2
RDSTK/MIDN BA3 124 A2
St Luke St EVILLE/WHL BS5 * 62 C4
St Margaret's Cl KEYN BS31 94 A3
NAIL BS48 85 H4
St Margaret's Dr
HNLZ/SM/SNYPK/WT BS9 51 F3
St Margaret's Hl BOAV BA15 119 G3
St Margaret's La NAIL BS48 85 H4
St Margaret's St BOAV BA15 119 G3
St Margaret's Ter WSM BS23 6 C3
St Marks Cl KEYN BS31 94 B3
St Marks Gdns BATHSE BA2 3 G6
St Mark's Rd BATHSE BA2 3 G7
EVILLE/WHL BS5 62 C2
MTN/WRL BS22 131 H5
RDSTK/MIDN BA3 124 B2
St Mark's Ter EVILLE/WHL BS5 * 62 C2
St Martins Cl
BRSG/KWL/STAPK BS4 * 80 A5
St Martins Ct MTN/WRL BS22 * 131 F5
St Martin's Gdns
BRSG/KWL/STAPK BS4 80 A5
St Martin's Rd
BRSG/KWL/STAPK BS4 80 A4
St Martin's Wk
BRSG/KWL/STAPK BS4 * 80 A5
St Marys Buildings BATHSE BA2 2 E6
St Mary's Cl BATHSE BA2 3 K4
TRWBR BA14 121 F2
St Mary's Ct
OMX/HUT/LCK BS24 139 F5
St Mary's Gdns TRWBR BA14 121 F2
St Mary's Gv NAIL BS48 84 D1
St Mary's Pk NAIL BS48 84 D1
St Mary's Rd AVONM BS11 48 C1
CFTN/FAIL BS8 60 A5
OMX/HUT/LCK BS24 140 A4
PTSHD/EG BS20 45 F4
St Mary St THNB/SVB BS35 8 C4
St Mary's Wk AVONM BS11 48 C2
St Mary's Wy YATE/CS BS37 21 E5
St Matthew's Av
RDLND/MONT BS6 61 G2
St Matthew's Cl WSM BS23 134 C2
St Matthews Pl BATHSE BA2 * 3 J6
St Matthew's Rd
RDLND/MONT BS6 61 G3
St Matthias Pk CBRISNE BS2 5 J2
St Michael's Av CLVDN BS21 70 D4
MTN/WRL BS22 131 H5
St Michael's Cl
FRCTL/WBN BS36 29 E3
HORF/LLZ BS7 51 G4
TRWBR BA14 121 H3
St Michaels Ct KGWD/HNM BS15 64 A3
St Michael's Hl CBRISNE BS2 61 F3
St Michael's Pk CFTN/FAIL BS8 4 C1
St Michael's Pl
CBATH/BATHN BA1 3 F4
St Michaels Rd BATHSE BA2 113 F2
CBATH/BATHN BA1 2 A2
St Nicholas Cl BOAV BA15 118 A2
St Nicholas Market
CBRIS/FH BS1 * 5 F4
St Nicholas Pk
EVILLE/WHL BS5 * 62 C2
St Nicholas' Rd CBRISNE BS2 62 A2
HGRV/WHIT BS14 92 B5
WSM BS23 138 C4
St Nicholas St CBRIS/FH BS1 5 F4
St Oswald's Rd
RDLND/MONT BS6 51 E5
St Patricks Ct BATHSE BA2 3 K4
St Pauls Pl RDSTK/MIDN BA3 124 B2
St Paul's Rd BMSTR BS3 79 E2
CFTN/FAIL BS8 4 A2
WSM BS23 138 D1
St Paul St CBRISNE BS2 5 H1
St Peter's Av WSM BS23 6 C1
St Peter's Crs FRCTL/WBN BS36 29 H3
St Peter's Ri
BMSTRD/HC/WWD BS13 90 B2
St Peters Rd PTSHD/EG BS20 45 G4
RDSTK/MIDN BA3 124 D4
St Peters Ter BATHSE BA2 2 B4
St Peter's Wk
HNLZ/SM/SNYPK/WT BS9 51 E3
St Philips Cswy
BRSG/KWL/STAPK BS4 80 B2
CBRISNE BS2 62 C5
St Philips Rd CBRISNE BS2 5 K3
St Philips Trade Pk
CBRISNE BS2 * 80 A2
St Phillips Rd CBRISNE BS2 62 B4
St Pierre Dr
OLD/WMLY/WICK BS30 * 65 G5
St Ronan's Av
RDLND/MONT BS6 61 F2
St Saviours Ri FRCTL/WBN BS36 29 H4
St Saviour's Rd
CBATH/BATHN BA1 109 F3
St Saviours Ter
CBATH/BATHN BA1 109 E3
St Saviours Wy
CBATH/BATHN BA1 109 F3
St Silas St CBRISNE BS2 79 H1
St Stephen's Av CBRIS/FH BS1 4 E4
St Stephen's Cl
CBATH/BATHN BA1 108 C4
HNBRY/STHM BS10 * 37 H3
KGWD/HNM BS15 * 54 D5
St Stephens Ct
CBATH/BATHN BA1 * 108 C4
St Stephens Pl
CBATH/BATHN BA1 * 108 C4
TRWBR BA14 123 E1
St Stephen's Rd
CBATH/BATHN BA1 108 C4
MANG/FISH BS16 54 C5
St Stephen's St CBRIS/FH BS1 4 E3
St Thomas Pl CBRIS/FH BS1 * 5 G5
St Thomas Rd
RDSTK/MIDN BA3 124 C2
TRWBR BA14 121 F5
St Thomas St CBRIS/FH BS1 5 G5
St Vincent's Hl
RDLND/MONT BS6 60 D1
St Vincent's Rd CFTN/FAIL BS8 60 D5
Saint Wy BRSTK/PCHW BS34 40 B1
St Werburgh's Pk CBRISNE BS2 62 B1
St Werburgh's Rd CBRISNE BS2 62 A1
St Whytes Rd
BRSG/KWL/STAPK BS4 91 E1
St Winifreds Dr BATHSE BA2 115 G5
Salcombe Gdns
MTN/WRL BS22 136 D1
Salcombe Rd
BRSG/KWL/STAPK BS4 91 H1
Salem Rd FRCTL/WBN BS36 29 F3
Salisbury Av KGWD/HNM BS15 64 A3
Salisbury Gdns
MANG/FISH BS16 54 D3
Salisbury Rd
BRSG/KWL/STAPK BS4 80 C1
CBATH/BATHN BA1 109 E2
MANG/FISH BS16 54 D2
MTN/WRL BS22 135 H2
RDLND/MONT BS6 61 G1
Salisbury St EVILLE/WHL BS5 62 C5
EVILLE/WHL BS5 63 F3
Salisbury Ter WSM BS23 6 D3
Sallybarn Cl
OLD/WMLY/WICK BS30 82 B4
Sally Hl PTSHD/EG BS20 45 H1
Sallysmead Cl
BMSTRD/HC/WWD BS13 90 C5
Sallys Wy FRCTL/WBN BS36 29 F3
Salmon Cl THNB/SVB BS35 12 C3
Salmons Wy MANG/FISH BS16 41 H5
Salter Cl TRWBR BA14 123 F3
Salthouse Rd CLVDN BS21 70 B3
Salthrop Rd HORF/LLZ BS7 51 H5
Saltings Cl CLVDN BS21 70 B3
Saltmarsh Dr AVONM BS11 35 H4
Saltwell Av HGRV/WHIT BS14 92 B4
Sambourne La PTSHD/EG BS20 48 B3
Samian Wy BRSTK/PCHW BS34 27 G5
Sampsons Rd
BMSTRD/HC/WWD BS13 90 D5
Samuel St EVILLE/WHL BS5 62 D3
Samuel White Rd
KGWD/HNM BS15 81 H3
Samuel Wright Cl
OLD/WMLY/WICK BS30 83 G1
Sandbach Rd
BRSG/KWL/STAPK BS4 80 C2
Sandbed Rd CBRISNE BS2 62 B1
Sandburrows Wk
BMSTRD/HC/WWD BS13 90 A3
Sandcroft HGRV/WHIT BS14 91 G3
Sandcroft Av WSM BS23 138 C4
Sanders Rd TRWBR BA14 120 D4
Sand Farm La MTN/WRL BS22 130 B2
Sandford Cl CLVDN BS21 70 B4
Sandford Rd CFTN/FAIL BS8 78 B1
WSM BS23 7 H4
Sandgate Rd
BRSG/KWL/STAPK BS4 80 C3
Sand Hl BRSG/KWL/STAPK BS4 80 B2
Sandholme Cl MANG/FISH BS16 41 F5
Sandholme Rd
BRSG/KWL/STAPK BS4 80 B2
Sandhurst YATE/CS BS37 31 H2
Sandhurst Cl
BRSTK/PCHW BS34 26 D1
Sandhurst Rd
BRSG/KWL/STAPK BS4 80 B3
Sandling Av HORF/LLZ BS7 52 B1
Sandown Centre TRWBR BA14 123 F5
Sandown Cl MANG/FISH BS16 41 G4
Sandown Rd
BRSG/KWL/STAPK BS4 80 C2
BRSTK/PCHW BS34 39 F2
Sandpiper Dr MTN/WRL BS22 136 C2
Sandringham Av
MANG/FISH BS16 41 F5
Sandringham Pk
MANG/FISH BS16 41 F5
Sandringham Rd
BRSG/KWL/STAPK BS4 80 C3
BRSTK/PCHW BS34 39 G1
TRWBR BA14 122 C4
WSM BS23 139 E1
Sand Rd MTN/WRL BS22 130 C3
Sandstone Ri FRCTL/WBN BS36 41 E1
Sandwich Rd
BRSG/KWL/STAPK BS4 80 C2
Sandy Cl ALMDB BS32 27 G4
Sandy La EVILLE/WHL BS5 52 D5
Sandy Leaze BOAV BA15 119 F3
Sandyleaze
HNLZ/SM/SNYPK/WT BS9 50 B1
Sandy Ldg YATE/CS BS37 32 A2
Sandy Park Rd
BRSG/KWL/STAPK BS4 80 B2
Saracen St CBATH/BATHN BA1 3 G3
Sarah St EVILLE/WHL BS5 62 C4
Sargent St BMSTR BS3 79 F2
Sarum Cl MANG/FISH BS16 55 H2
Sarum Crs HNBRY/STHM BS10 37 H4
Sassoon Ct
OLD/WMLY/WICK BS30 82 C1
Satchfield Cl
HNBRY/STHM BS10 37 E3
Satchfield Crs
HNBRY/STHM BS10 37 E3
Sates Wy
HNLZ/SM/SNYPK/WT BS9 51 F2
Saunders Rd MANG/FISH BS16 54 D4
Saunton Wk
BRSG/KWL/STAPK BS4 91 F1
Savages Wood Rd ALMDB BS32 27 F2
Savernake Rd MTN/WRL BS22 131 G5
Saville Crs MTN/WRL BS22 135 H3
Saville Gate Cl
HNLZ/SM/SNYPK/WT BS9 50 C4
Saville Ms RDLND/MONT BS6 * 61 G3
Saville Pl CFTN/FAIL BS8 60 D5
Saville Rd
HNLZ/SM/SNYPK/WT BS9 50 C5
MTN/WRL BS22 135 H3
Saville Rw CBATH/BATHN BA1 3 F2
Savoy Rd BRSG/KWL/STAPK BS4 80 C2
Saw Cl CBATH/BATHN BA1 3 F4
Saw Mill La THNB/SVB BS35 8 C3
Sawyers Cl NAIL BS48 73 H4
Sawyers Ct CLVDN BS21 71 E2
Saxby Cl CLVDN BS21 70 B4
MTN/WRL BS22 132 A4
Saxon Ct MTN/WRL BS22 132 C5
Saxon Dr TRWBR BA14 121 F2
Saxon Rd CBRISNE BS2 62 B1
MTN/WRL BS22 135 H3
Saxon Wy ALMDB BS32 27 E1
BOAV BA15 118 C2
Say Wk OLD/WMLY/WICK BS30 66 A4
Scafell Cl WSM BS23 7 K1
Scandrett Cl HNBRY/STHM BS10 36 D2
Scantleberry Cl
MANG/FISH BS16 41 E5
The Scaurs MTN/WRL BS22 136 C1
School Cl BRSTK/PCHW BS34 27 E2
EVILLE/WHL BS5 63 E1
HGRV/WHIT BS14 91 G5
School Ct BRSTK/PCHW BS34 40 B1
School La CBATH/BATHN BA1 103 E5
NAIL BS48 88 A4
TRWBR BA14 121 E1
School Rd
BRSG/KWL/STAPK BS4 79 H3
BRSG/KWL/STAPK BS4 80 D4
FRCTL/WBN BS36 29 F2
KGWD/HNM BS15 64 B3
OLD/WMLY/WICK BS30 82 D2
School Vw NAIL BS48 74 A5
School Wk YATE/CS BS37 20 D5
School Wy THNB/SVB BS35 12 C3
The Scop ALMDB BS32 15 G2
Scotch Horn Cl NAIL BS48 73 G4
Scotch Horn Wy NAIL BS48 73 G4
Scot Elm Dr
OMX/HUT/LCK BS24 137 F2
Scots Pine Av NAIL BS48 * 73 G4
Scott Ct OLD/WMLY/WICK BS30 82 C1
Scott Lawrence Cl
MANG/FISH BS16 33 H1
Scott Rd WSM BS23 139 F2
Scott Wk
OLD/WMLY/WICK BS30 66 A4
Scott Wy YATE/CS BS37 32 B2
Seabrook Rd MTN/WRL BS22 136 A2
Seagry Cl HNBRY/STHM BS10 38 B4
Sea Mills La
HNLZ/SM/SNYPK/WT BS9 49 H4
Searle Court Av
BRSG/KWL/STAPK BS4 80 D1
Searle Crs WSM BS23 7 K7
Seaton Rd EVILLE/WHL BS5 62 D2
Seavale Rd CLVDN BS21 70 C1
Seaview Rd PTSHD/EG BS20 44 B4
Seawalls Rd
HNLZ/SM/SNYPK/WT BS9 60 A1
Second Av BATHSE BA2 114 A3
RDSTK/MIDN BA3 124 D5
Second Wy AVONM BS11 35 E4
Seddon Rd CBRISNE BS2 62 B1
Sedgefield Gdns
MANG/FISH BS16 41 G4
Sedgemoor Cl NAIL BS48 85 F1
Sedgemoor Rd BATHSE BA2 116 D1
WSM BS23 7 H1
Sedgemoor Ter BATHSE BA2 * 114 D5
Sefton Park Rd HORF/LLZ BS7 52 A5
Sefton Sq OMX/HUT/LCK BS24 136 D3
Selborne Rd HORF/LLZ BS7 52 A3
Selbourne Cl
CBATH/BATHN BA1 107 F4
Selbourne Rd WSM BS23 138 D2
Selbrooke Crs MANG/FISH BS16 54 B2
Selby Rd EVILLE/WHL BS5 63 G2
Selden Rd HGRV/WHIT BS14 92 D4
Selkirk Rd KGWD/HNM BS15 64 B1
Selley Wk
BMSTRD/HC/WWD BS13 90 B4
Selwood Cl WSM BS23 135 H4
Selworthy KGWD/HNM BS15 64 D4
Selworthy Cl KEYN BS31 94 A4
Selworthy Rd
BRSG/KWL/STAPK BS4 80 A4
WSM BS23 139 E2
Selworthy Ter BATHSE BA2 * 114 D5
Seneca Pl EVILLE/WHL BS5 63 E4
Seneca St EVILLE/WHL BS5 63 E4
Serbert Rd PTSHD/EG BS20 45 H3
Serbert Wy PTSHD/EG BS20 45 H3
Sercombe Pk CLVDN BS21 71 E4
Seven Acres La
CBATH/BATHN BA1 103 E4
The Seven Acres
OMX/HUT/LCK BS24 136 C4
Seven Dials CBATH/BATHN BA1 * 3 F4
Seventh Av HORF/LLZ BS7 39 E4
Seven View Rd THNB/SVB BS35 8 D2
Severn Av WSM BS23 138 D1
Severn Dr THNB/SVB BS35 8 C2
Severnmeade PTSHD/EG BS20 44 C3
Severn Rd AVONM BS11 23 F2
PTSHD/EG BS20 45 F3
PTSHD/EG BS20 48 B3
THNB/SVB BS35 12 D4
WSM BS23 138 D1
Severn Wy BRSTK/PCHW BS34 26 B1
KEYN BS31 94 C5
THNB/SVB BS35 12 B3
Severnwood Gdns
THNB/SVB BS35 12 C4
Sevier St CBRISNE BS2 62 B1
Seville Ct PTSHD/EG BS20 45 H1
Seville Rd PTSHD/EG BS20 45 H1
Seymour Av HORF/LLZ BS7 51 H4
Seymour Cl CLVDN BS21 71 E2
MTN/WRL BS22 131 G4
Seymour Ct TRWBR BA14 120 D5
Seymour Rd
CBATH/BATHN BA1 108 D4
EVILLE/WHL BS5 62 B2
HORF/LLZ BS7 51 H4
KGWD/HNM BS15 64 B2
MANG/FISH BS16 54 C4
TRWBR BA14 121 E4
Seyton Wk BRSTK/PCHW BS34 27 G5
Shackel Hendy Ms
MANG/FISH BS16 55 G3
Shackleton Av YATE/CS BS37 32 B2
Shadow Wk
OMX/HUT/LCK BS24 141 F3
Shadwell Rd HORF/LLZ BS7 51 G5
Shaftesbury Av
CBATH/BATHN BA1 107 H5
RDLND/MONT BS6 61 H2
Shaftesbury Cl NAIL BS48 85 E1
Shaftesbury Rd BATHSE BA2 2 B7
WSM BS23 135 G3
Shaft Rd BATHSE BA2 117 H1
THNB/SVB BS35 12 C1
Shails La TRWBR BA14 120 D5
Shakespeare Av BATHSE BA2 114 C3
HORF/LLZ BS7 38 D5
Shakespeare Rd
RDSTK/MIDN BA3 124 D3
Shaldon Rd HORF/LLZ BS7 52 B4
The Shallows KEYN BS31 105 G1
Sham Castle La BATHSE BA2 3 K3
Shamrock Rd EVILLE/WHL BS5 53 E5
Shanklin Dr BRSTK/PCHW BS34 39 E2
Shannon Ct CBRIS/FH BS1 * 5 F4
THNB/SVB BS35 9 E4
Shapcott Cl
BRSG/KWL/STAPK BS4 80 A5
Shaplands
HNLZ/SM/SNYPK/WT BS9 50 C4
Shaw Cl EVILLE/WHL BS5 62 C3
MANG/FISH BS16 55 G5
Shaw Gdns HGRV/WHIT BS14 91 H1
Shaws Wy BATHSE BA2 113 E2
Shaymoor La THNB/SVB BS35 13 H5
Shearman St TRWBR BA14 123 E2
Shearmore Cl HORF/LLZ BS7 52 B1
Sheene La BMSTR BS3 78 D3
Sheene Rd BMSTR BS3 78 D3
Sheene Wy BMSTR BS3 78 D3
Sheepcote Barton
TRWBR BA14 123 E2
Sheeps Cft
BMSTRD/HC/WWD BS13 90 B5
Sheepway PTSHD/EG BS20 46 B4
Sheepwood Cl
HNBRY/STHM BS10 37 E[illegible]

Sheepwood Rd HNBRY/STHM BS10 37 F3
Sheldare Barton EVILLE/WHL BS5 64 A4
Sheldon Cl CLVDN BS21 71 F3
Sheldrake Dr MANG/FISH BS16 53 G2
Shellard Rd BRSTK/PCHW BS34 38 D2
Shellards Rd OLD/WMLY/WICK BS30 82 C3
Shelley Av CLVDN BS21 70 D3
Shelley Cl EVILLE/WHL BS5 63 G3
Shelley Rd BATHSE BA2 114 C3
RDSTK/MIDN BA3 124 D3
WSM BS23 139 F2
Shelley Wy HORF/LLZ BS7 38 D5
Shellmor Av BRSTK/PCHW BS34 26 D1
Shellmor Cl BRSTK/PCHW BS34 27 E1
Shepherds Cl MANG/FISH BS16 54 D3
Sheppard Rd MANG/FISH BS16 54 B2
Sheppy's Ml YTN/CONG BS49 128 D1
Shepton Wk BMSTR BS3 78 D4
Sherborne Rd TRWBR BA14 120 A5
Sherbourne Av ALMDB BS32 27 G4
Sherbourne Cl KGWD/HNM BS15 65 E1
Sherbourne St EVILLE/WHL BS5 63 F3
Sheridan Rd BATHSE BA2 113 E2
HORF/LLZ BS7 38 D4
Sheridan Wy OLD/WMLY/WICK BS30 82 D4
Sherrin Wy BMSTRD/HC/WWD BS13 98 D1
Sherston Cl MANG/FISH BS16 54 A3
NAIL BS48 73 H5
Sherston Rd HORF/LLZ BS7 38 B5
Sherwell Rd BRSG/KWL/STAPK BS4 80 D3
Sherwood Cl KEYN BS31 94 B4
Sherwood Crs MTN/WRL BS22 131 G5
Sherwood Rd KEYN BS31 94 B4
KGWD/HNM BS15 63 H2
Shetland Rd HNBRY/STHM BS10 38 A4
Shetland Wy NAIL BS48 73 H5
Shickle Gv BATHSE BA2 116 A1
Shields Av HORF/LLZ BS7 38 D3
Shiels Dr ALMDB BS32 27 F3
Shilton Cl KGWD/HNM BS15 65 E4
Shimsey Cl MANG/FISH BS16 54 B2
Shiners Elms YTN/CONG BS49 126 A3
Shipham Cl HGRV/WHIT BS14 92 A4
NAIL BS48 85 G1
Ship La CBRIS/FH BS1 5 G7
Shipley Mow MANG/FISH BS16 55 G2
Shipley Rd HNLZ/SM/SNYPK/WT BS9 37 F5
Shipman Ct MANG/FISH BS16 54 D4
Shire Gdns AVONM BS11 35 E5
Shirehampton Rd AVONM BS11 49 E1
Shires Yd CBATH/BATHN BA1 3 F3
Shire Wy YATE/CS BS37 31 G4
Shockerwick La CBATH/BATHN BA1 103 G5
Shophouse Rd BATHSE BA2 113 G2
Shore Pl TRWBR BA14 120 A5
Shorthill Rd YATE/CS BS37 43 H1
Shortlands Rd AVONM BS11 35 H4
Short La LGASH BS41 76 C4
Short St CBRISNE BS2 79 H1
Short Wy CFTN/FAIL BS8 75 G3
THNB/SVB BS35 8 C5
Shortwood Hl MANG/FISH BS16 56 A3
Shortwood Rd BMSTRD/HC/WWD BS13 100 B1
MANG/FISH BS16 56 D4
Shortwood Vw KGWD/HNM BS15 65 E3
Shortwood Wk BMSTRD/HC/WWD BS13 100 B1
Showering Cl HGRV/WHIT BS14 92 C4
Showering Rd HGRV/WHIT BS14 92 C4
Shrewsbury Bow OMX/HUT/LCK BS24 136 D3
Shrewton Cl TRWBR BA14 123 E3
Shrubbery Av WSM BS23 134 B2
Shrubbery Cottages RDLND/MONT BS6 61 E1
Shrubbery Rd MANG/FISH BS16 54 C3
WSM BS23 6 B1
Shrubbery Ter WSM BS23 6 B1
Shrubbery Wk WSM BS23 6 B1
Shrubbery Wk West WSM BS23 * 6 C1
Shuter Rd BMSTRD/HC/WWD BS13 89 H4
Sibland THNB/SVB BS35 9 E4
Sibland Cl THNB/SVB BS35 9 E4
Sibland Rd THNB/SVB BS35 9 E3
Sibland Wy THNB/SVB BS35 9 E4
Sidcot BRSG/KWL/STAPK BS4 81 F4
Sideland Cl HGRV/WHIT BS14 92 D3
Sidelands Rd MANG/FISH BS16 54 B2
The Sidings BRSTK/PCHW BS34 39 F3
Sidmouth Gdns BMSTR BS3 79 E4
Sidmouth Rd BMSTR BS3 79 E4
Signal Rd MANG/FISH BS16 54 D4
Silbury Ri KEYN BS31 104 B2
Silbury Rd BMSTR BS3 77 H4
Silcox Rd BMSTRD/HC/WWD BS13 90 D5
Silklands Gv HNLZ/SM/SNYPK/WT BS9 * 49 H2
Silverberry Rd MTN/WRL BS22 136 D2
Silver Birch Cl BRSTK/PCHW BS34 27 F3
Silver Birch Rd TRWBR BA14 122 C4
Silvercourt NAIL BS48 * 72 D4
Silverhill Rd HNBRY/STHM BS10 36 D2
Silverlow Rd NAIL BS48 73 E4
…lver Md YTN/CONG BS49 128 D4
… Mdw TRWBR BA14 122 B4
… Wy
…S49 128 D3
… 119 G3

CBRIS/FH BS1 5 F2
NAIL BS48 73 E4
TRWBR BA14 123 E1
YTN/CONG BS49 128 D4
Silver Street La TRWBR BA14 122 D4
Silverthorne La CBRISNE BS2 62 B5
Silverton Ct BRSG/KWL/STAPK BS4 * 79 G5
Simmonds Vw BRSTK/PCHW BS34 27 H5
Simons Cl MTN/WRL BS22 136 D1
Singapore Rd WSM BS23 138 D3
Sion Hl CBATH/BATHN BA1 108 B4
CFTN/FAIL BS8 60 C5
Sion Hill Pl CBATH/BATHN BA1 108 B3
Sion Hill Rd CBATH/BATHN BA1 108 B3
Sion La CFTN/FAIL BS8 60 C4
Sion Pl BATHSE BA2 3 K4
CFTN/FAIL BS8 60 C4
Sion Rd BMSTR BS3 78 D3
CBATH/BATHN BA1 108 B3
The Sion NAIL BS48 * 73 F4
Sir John's La EVILLE/WHL BS5 52 C4
Sir Johns Wd NAIL BS48 * 73 E3
Siston Cl KGWD/HNM BS15 65 F1
Siston Common OLD/WMLY/WICK BS30 65 G2
Siston La OLD/WMLY/WICK BS30 66 B2
Siston Pk KGWD/HNM BS15 65 F1
Sixth Av HORF/LLZ BS7 38 D4
Sixty Acres Cl CFTN/FAIL BS8 75 G3
Skippon Ct KGWD/HNM BS15 82 B1
Sladebrook Av BATHSE BA2 113 H4
Sladebrook Rd BATHSE BA2 113 G3
Slade La NAIL BS48 87 G5
Slade Rd PTSHD/EG BS20 45 G3
Sladesbrook BOAV BA15 119 H1
Sladesbrook Cl BOAV BA15 119 G1
Slades Ct NAIL BS48 85 H3
Sleep La HGRV/WHIT BS14 101 G1
Slimbridge Cl YATE/CS BS37 32 B3
The Slipway TRWBR BA14 121 E2
Sloan St EVILLE/WHL BS5 63 E3
Sloe Cl MTN/WRL BS22 136 A4
Slowgrove Cl TRWBR BA14 123 G1
Slymbridge Av HNBRY/STHM BS10 37 F1
Smallbrook Gdns TRWBR BA14 121 E1
Small La MANG/FISH BS16 53 F3
Small St CBRIS/FH BS1 4 E3
CBRISNE BS2 79 H1
Smallway YTN/CONG BS49 126 D5
Smarts Gn YATE/CS BS37 33 E2
Smeaton Rd CBRIS/FH BS1 78 A1
Smithcourt Dr BRSTK/PCHW BS34 27 E4
Smithmead BMSTRD/HC/WWD BS13 90 C4
Smithywell Cl TRWBR BA14 123 G1
Smoke La AVONM BS11 22 D4
Smythe Cft HGRV/WHIT BS14 100 D1
Smyth Rd BMSTR BS3 78 B3
Smyths Cl AVONM BS11 34 C4
Sneyd Park Ms HNLZ/SM/SNYPK/WT BS9 * 50 A5
Snowberry Cl MTN/WRL BS22 136 D2
Snowberry Wk EVILLE/WHL BS5 63 F3
Snowdon Cl MANG/FISH BS16 53 G4
Snowdon Rd MANG/FISH BS16 53 G3
Snowdon V WSM BS23 7 J1
Snow Hl CBATH/BATHN BA1 108 D3
Solent Wy THNB/SVB BS35 9 E5
Solsbury La CBATH/BATHN BA1 102 D5
Solsbury Wy CBATH/BATHN BA1 108 D2
Somer Av RDSTK/MIDN BA3 124 A2
Somerby Cl ALMDB BS32 27 F3
Somerdale Av BATHSE BA2 114 A5
BRSG/KWL/STAPK BS4 91 G1
MTN/WRL BS22 135 H3
Somerdale Cl MTN/WRL BS22 135 H3
Somerdale Rd KEYN BS31 94 C2
Somerdale Rd North KEYN BS31 94 C2
Somerdale Vw BATHSE BA2 113 H5
Somermead BMSTR BS3 78 D5
Somer Rd RDSTK/MIDN BA3 124 A2
Somerset Av OMX/HUT/LCK BS24 136 C4
YATE/CS BS37 21 E4
Somerset Crs BRSTK/PCHW BS34 27 H5
Somerset La CBATH/BATHN BA1 108 B3
Somerset Pl CBATH/BATHN BA1 108 B3
Somerset Rd CLVDN BS21 71 E2
PTSHD/EG BS20 44 C3
Somerset Sq CBRIS/FH BS1 5 G7
Somerset St BATHSE BA2 3 F6
CBRIS/FH BS1 5 H7
CBRISNE BS2 61 G3
Somerset Ter BMSTR BS3 79 F3
Somerton Cl KGWD/HNM BS15 64 D4
Somerton Rd CLVDN BS21 71 E4
HORF/LLZ BS7 51 H2
Somervale Rd RDSTK/MIDN BA3 125 F2
Somerville Cl KEYN BS31 105 F2
Sommerville Rd RDLND/MONT BS6 51 H5
Sommerville Rd South RDLND/MONT BS6 62 A1
Soper Gdns BRSG/KWL/STAPK BS4 90 D2
Sophia Gdns MTN/WRL BS22 132 A4
Sorrel Cl THNB/SVB BS35 9 E2
TRWBR BA14 123 E4
Soundwell Rd KGWD/HNM BS15 64 C1
Southampton Gdns HORF/LLZ BS7 * 52 A3
Southampton Ms HORF/LLZ BS7 * 52 A3
South Av BATHSE BA2 2 A6
PTSHD/EG BS20 45 G2

YATE/CS BS37 31 F1
Southbourne Gdns CBATH/BATHN BA1 109 E3
Southcot Pl BATHSE BA2 3 H7
South Cft HNLZ/SM/SNYPK/WT BS9 51 F1
South Dene HNLZ/SM/SNYPK/WT BS9 50 B2
Southdown MTN/WRL BS22 131 G4
Southdown Av BATHSE BA2 113 G4
Southdown Rd BATHSE BA2 113 G3
HNLZ/SM/SNYPK/WT BS9 37 E5
Southend Rd WSM BS23 138 D2
Southernhay CFTN/FAIL BS8 * 4 A5
MANG/FISH BS16 54 B4
Southernhay Av CFTN/FAIL BS8 4 A5
Southernhay Crs CFTN/FAIL BS8 4 A5
Southern Wy CLVDN BS21 70 C4
Southey Av KGWD/HNM BS15 64 C2
Southey Rd CLVDN BS21 70 D3
Southey St CBRISNE BS2 62 A2
Southfield Av KGWD/HNM BS15 64 D2
Southfield Cl NAIL BS48 73 F3
WSM BS23 138 C5
Southfield Ct HNLZ/SM/SNYPK/WT BS9 50 D1
Southfield Rd HNLZ/SM/SNYPK/WT BS9 50 D1
NAIL BS48 73 F3
RDLND/MONT BS6 61 G2
Southfield Wy YATE/CS BS37 21 F3
Southgate CBATH/BATHN BA1 3 G5
South Green St CFTN/FAIL BS8 60 C5
South Gv PTSHD/EG BS20 48 B4
RDLND/MONT BS6 51 F3
South Hayes EVILLE/WHL BS5 52 C4
Southlands CBATH/BATHN BA1 107 G2
Southlands Wy YTN/CONG BS49 128 D1
South Lawn OMX/HUT/LCK BS24 140 C2
South Lawn Cl OMX/HUT/LCK BS24 140 C2
South Lea Rd CBATH/BATHN BA1 107 F4
Southleigh BOAV BA15 119 F4
Southleigh Rd CFTN/FAIL BS8 4 A1
South Liberty La BMSTR BS3 77 H5
Southmead Rd BRSTK/PCHW BS34 38 B4
HNBRY/STHM BS10 37 H5
HNLZ/SM/SNYPK/WT BS9 51 E1
MTN/WRL BS22 135 G4
Southmead Wy HNBRY/STHM BS10 38 A5
Southover Cl HNLZ/SM/SNYPK/WT BS9 37 F5
South Pde CBATH/BATHN BA1 3 H5
WSM BS23 6 D3
South Rd ALMDB BS32 16 B1
BMSTR BS3 * 78 D3
KGWD/HNM BS15 64 C3
PTSHD/EG BS20 45 G2
RDLND/MONT BS6 61 F1
RDSTK/MIDN BA3 124 C3
WSM BS23 134 B2
Southsea Rd BRSTK/PCHW BS34 26 C3
Southside WSM BS23 6 E2
South Side YTN/CONG BS49 129 E1
Southside Cl AVONM BS11 49 G1
Southside Crs MTN/WRL BS22 130 B4
Southstoke La BATHSE BA2 116 D3
Southstoke Rd BATHSE BA2 116 D1
South St BMSTR BS3 78 C3
South Ter RDLND/MONT BS6 60 D1
WSM BS23 6 C2
South Vw FRCTL/WBN BS36 29 H3
MANG/FISH BS16 54 D3
PTSHD/EG BS20 45 G1
Southview Cl OMX/HUT/LCK BS24 140 B4
South View Crs FRCTL/WBN BS36 30 B4
South View Pl RDSTK/MIDN BA3 124 C2
South View Ri FRCTL/WBN BS36 30 B4
South View Rd BATHSE BA2 2 A5
Southview Rd TRWBR BA14 123 E3
South View Ter YTN/CONG BS49 126 B2
Southville Pl BMSTR BS3 79 E2
Southville Rd BMSTR BS3 78 D2
BOAV BA15 119 H4
WSM BS23 138 D2
Southville Ter BATHSE BA2 114 D3
South Wy TRWBR BA14 123 E2
Southway Dr OLD/WMLY/WICK BS30 83 G1
Southway Rd BOAV BA15 119 G5
Southwell St CBRISNE BS2 4 D1
Southwood Av HNLZ/SM/SNYPK/WT BS9 36 B5
Southwood Dr HNLZ/SM/SNYPK/WT BS9 36 A5
Southwood Dr East HNLZ/SM/SNYPK/WT BS9 36 B5
Southwood Rd TRWBR BA14 123 G1
Spalding Cl CBRISNE BS2 52 B5
Spar Rd YATE/CS BS37 20 C5
Spartley Dr BMSTRD/HC/WWD BS13 90 A3
Spartley Wk BMSTRD/HC/WWD BS13 90 A3
Speedwell Av EVILLE/WHL BS5 63 E4
Speedwell Cl THNB/SVB BS35 9 E2
TRWBR BA14 123 E3
Speedwell Rd EVILLE/WHL BS5 63 G2
KGWD/HNM BS15 64 A2
Spencer Dr MTN/WRL BS22 132 A5
RDSTK/MIDN BA3 124 B2
Spencers Belle Vue CBATH/BATHN BA1 2 E1
Spencer's Ct THNB/SVB BS35 11 H1

Spencers Orch BOAV BA15 119 G4
Sperring Ct RDSTK/MIDN BA3 124 A4
Spey Cl THNB/SVB BS35 8 D4
Spindleberry Gv NAIL BS48 73 H4
Spinners Cft TRWBR BA14 123 E2
Spinners End MTN/WRL BS22 132 A4
Spinney Rd OMX/HUT/LCK BS24 141 G2
The Spinney ALMDB BS32 27 G3
FRCTL/WBN BS36 29 H3
WSM BS23 139 E5
Spires Vw MANG/FISH BS16 * 53 F3
Spring Crs BATHSE BA2 3 H6
Springfield BOAV BA15 119 H3
THNB/SVB BS35 9 E4
Springfield Av AVONM BS11 48 C2
HORF/LLZ BS7 52 A3
MANG/FISH BS16 55 F2
MTN/WRL BS22 136 A2
Springfield Buildings RDSTK/MIDN BA3 125 H1
Springfield Cl BATHSE BA2 113 G2
MANG/FISH BS16 55 F1
TRWBR BA14 121 F4
Springfield Ct RDSTK/MIDN BA3 125 H1
Springfield Gv HNLZ/SM/SNYPK/WT BS9 51 E3
Springfield Pk TRWBR BA14 121 F5
Springfield Pl CBATH/BATHN BA1 108 C3
Springfield Rd MANG/FISH BS16 55 F2
PTSHD/EG BS20 45 E3
PTSHD/EG BS20 48 B4
RDLND/MONT BS6 61 G2
Springfields BRSTK/PCHW BS34 38 D3
Spring Gdns BRSG/KWL/STAPK BS4 79 H5
Spring Gardens Rd CBATH/BATHN BA1 3 G3
Spring Hl CBRISNE BS2 61 G3
KGWD/HNM BS15 64 D1
MTN/WRL BS22 135 H1
Spring Hill Dr MTN/WRL BS22 136 A2
Spring La CBATH/BATHN BA1 109 E2
LGASH BS41 99 F3
Springleaze BRSG/KWL/STAPK BS4 79 H5
MANG/FISH BS16 55 F1
Springly Ct KGWD/HNM BS15 * 65 F3
Spring Mdw TRWBR BA14 122 C4
Spring Ri PTSHD/EG BS20 45 F5
Spring St BMSTR BS3 79 F2
Spring Street Pl BMSTR BS3 79 F2
Spring Ter MTN/WRL BS22 135 H1
Spring V CBATH/BATHN BA1 109 E2
Spring Va MTN/WRL BS22 135 H1
Springville Cl OLD/WMLY/WICK BS30 82 D3
Springwood Dr HNBRY/STHM BS10 36 C2
Spring Wood Gdns OMX/HUT/LCK BS24 140 B3
Spruce Wy BRSTK/PCHW BS34 26 A3
MTN/WRL BS22 136 B3
The Square BATHSE BA2 2 E6
BRSG/KWL/STAPK BS4 79 H5
CBRIS/FH BS1 5 J5
MANG/FISH BS16 * 54 D4
Squires Ct OLD/WMLY/WICK BS30 82 C2
Squires Leaze THNB/SVB BS35 9 E2
Stabbins Cl MTN/WRL BS22 132 A3
Stable Yd BATHSE BA2 * 2 A3
Stackpool Rd BMSTR BS3 78 D2
Staddlestones RDSTK/MIDN BA3 124 A5
Stadium Rd RDLND/MONT BS6 51 F3
Stafford Crs THNB/SVB BS35 8 C3
Stafford Pl WSM BS23 7 F2
Stafford Rd CBRISNE BS2 62 B1
PTSHD/EG BS20 45 H4
WSM BS23 7 G3
Staffords Ct OLD/WMLY/WICK BS30 65 F5
Stafford St BMSTR BS3 79 E2
Stainer Cl BRSG/KWL/STAPK BS4 91 E3
Stallard St TRWBR BA14 122 D1
Stall St CBATH/BATHN BA1 3 G5
Stanbridge Cl MANG/FISH BS16 55 E2
Stanbridge Rd MANG/FISH BS16 55 E2
Stanbury Av MANG/FISH BS16 54 A3
Stanbury Rd BMSTR BS3 79 F3
Stancomb Av TRWBR BA14 121 F5
Stancombe La NAIL BS48 86 D2
Standfast Rd HNBRY/STHM BS10 37 E2
Standish Av BRSTK/PCHW BS34 26 D1
Standish Cl HNBRY/STHM BS10 37 E4
Standon Wy HNBRY/STHM BS10 37 H3
Stane Wy AVONM BS11 48 B1
Stanfield Cl HORF/LLZ BS7 52 C2
Stanford Cl FRCTL/WBN BS36 29 F2
Stanford Pl BRSG/KWL/STAPK BS4 * 91 E2
Stanhope Pl CBATH/BATHN BA1 * 2 D4
Stanhope Rd OLD/WMLY/WICK BS30 82 C4
WSM BS23 138 D3
Stanhope St CBRISNE BS2 79 H1
Stanley Av BRSTK/PCHW BS34 39 E3
HORF/LLZ BS7 51 H5
Stanley Cha EVILLE/WHL BS5 63 E1
Stanley Ct RDSTK/MIDN BA3 124 C2
Stanley Crs BRSTK/PCHW BS34 39 E3
Stanley Gdns

OLD/WMLY/WICK BS30 83 E2
Stanley Gv WSM BS23 7 G4
Stanley Hl BRSG/KWL/STAPK BS4 79 H2
Stanley Md ALMDB BS32 16 C5
Stanley Pk EVILLE/WHL BS5 62 C2
Stanley Park Rd MANG/FISH BS16 54 D5
Stanley Rd RDLND/MONT BS6 61 F1
WSM BS23 7 H4
Stanley Rd West BATHSE BA2 2 B6
Stanley St BMSTR BS3 78 D3
Stanley St North BMSTR BS3 78 C3
Stanley St South BMSTR BS3 78 D3
Stanley Ter BMSTR BS3 78 D4
Stanshalls Cl BLAG/CWMG/WR BS40 96 D4
Stanshalls Dr BLAG/CWMG/WR BS40 96 D4
Stanshalls La BLAG/CWMG/WR BS40 96 D4
Stanshawe Crs YATE/CS BS37 32 A1
Stanshawes Dr YATE/CS BS37 31 H1
Stanshaw Rd MANG/FISH BS16 53 H1
Stanshaws Cl BRSTK/PCHW BS34 15 H5
Stanton Cl KGWD/HNM BS15 65 E2
TRWBR BA14 123 E4
Stanton Rd HNBRY/STHM BS10 38 B4
Stanway OLD/WMLY/WICK BS30 83 E5
Stanway Cl BATHSE BA2 116 B1
Staple Gv KEYN BS31 94 A4
Staple Grove Crs EVILLE/WHL BS5 63 H4
Staplehill Rd MANG/FISH BS16 54 A4
Staples Cl CLVDN BS21 71 E4
Staples Gn MTN/WRL BS22 132 A5
Staples Rd YATE/CS BS37 20 C5
Stapleton Cl MANG/FISH BS16 53 E3
Stapleton Rd EVILLE/WHL BS5 62 C1
Star Av BRSTK/PCHW BS34 40 B1
Star Barn Rd FRCTL/WBN BS36 29 E3
Starcross Rd MTN/WRL BS22 136 D1
Star La MANG/FISH BS16 53 G5
PTSHD/EG BS20 48 B4
Starling Cl MTN/WRL BS22 136 B3
Station Ap CBRIS/FH BS1 5 J6
WSM BS23 7 F5
Station Av MANG/FISH BS16 53 H4
Station Cl NAIL BS48 85 G2
OLD/WMLY/WICK BS30 65 H3
YATE/CS BS37 33 F2
YTN/CONG BS49 128 C2
Station La HORF/LLZ BS7 52 B4
Station Rd AVONM BS11 48 D2
BRSG/KWL/STAPK BS4 80 C4
BRSTK/PCHW BS34 27 E4
BRSTK/PCHW BS34 38 D2
BRSTK/PCHW BS34 39 F3
CBATH/BATHN BA1 107 H5
CLVDN BS21 70 D2
FRCTL/WBN BS36 30 A5
FRCTL/WBN BS36 41 F1
HNBRY/STHM BS10 36 D2
HORF/LLZ BS7 52 B4
KEYN BS31 94 B3
KGWD/HNM BS15 55 E5
MANG/FISH BS16 53 H4
MTN/WRL BS22 136 C1
MTN/WRL BS22 137 F1
NAIL BS48 73 G5
NAIL BS48 87 F1
OLD/WMLY/WICK BS30 65 H4
PTSHD/EG BS20 45 G2
PTSHD/EG BS20 46 D4
PTSHD/EG BS20 48 B4
RDLND/MONT BS6 61 G1
RDSTK/MIDN BA3 124 C2
THNB/SVB BS35 12 B3
THNB/SVB BS35 13 H5
WSM BS23 6 E5
YATE/CS BS37 19 E4
YATE/CS BS37 20 B5
YTN/CONG BS49 126 A2
YTN/CONG BS49 128 C2
Station Road Link KGWD/HNM BS15 65 F1
Station Wy MANG/FISH BS16 53 H4
TRWBR BA14 122 D1
Staunton Flds HGRV/WHIT BS14 101 F1
Staunton La HGRV/WHIT BS14 92 B5
Staunton Wy HGRV/WHIT BS14 92 C5
Staveley Crs HNBRY/STHM BS10 37 H3
Stavordale Gv HGRV/WHIT BS14 92 A3
Staynes Crs KGWD/HNM BS15 64 D3
Steam Mills RDSTK/MIDN BA3 124 A4
Stean Bridge Rd ALMDB BS32 27 G4
Steel Ct OLD/WMLY/WICK BS30 82 C3
Steel Mills KEYN BS31 94 C5
Stella Gv BMSTR BS3 78 B4
Stephens Dr OLD/WMLY/WICK BS30 82 C1
Stephen St EVILLE/WHL BS5 62 D3
Stepney Rd EVILLE/WHL BS5 62 D2
Stepney Wk EVILLE/WHL BS5 62 D2
Sterncourt Rd MANG/FISH BS16 53 H1
Stevens Crs BMSTR BS3 79 G2
Stevens Wk ALMDB BS32 27 F2
Steway La CBATH/BATHN BA1 103 F4
Stibbs Ct OLD/WMLY/WICK BS30 82 C2
Stibbs Hl EVILLE/WHL BS5 63 H4
Stickland CLVDN BS21 70 C4
Stile Acres AVONM BS11 35 H4
Stillhouse La BMSTR BS3 79 E2
Stillingfleet Rd BMSTRD/HC/WWD BS13 90 D4
Stillman Cl BMSTRD/HC/WWD BS13 89 H5
Stinchcombe YATE/CS BS37 32 A1
Stirling Cl YATE/CS BS37 20 C3
Stirling Rd BRSG/KWL/STAPK BS4 80 B2

Stirling Wy KEYN BS31 94 B5
Stirtingale Av BATHSE BA2 113 H4
Stirtingale Rd BATHSE BA2 113 H4
Stock La YTN/CONG BS49 129 F5
Stockton Cl HGRV/WHIT BS14 91 G5
OLD/WMLY/WICK BS30 83 E3
Stock Wy North NAIL BS48 73 F4
Stock Wy South NAIL BS48 73 F4
Stockwell Av MANG/FISH BS16 55 F2
Stockwell Cl MANG/FISH BS16 55 E1
Stockwell Dr MANG/FISH BS16 55 F2
Stockwood Crs
BRSG/KWL/STAPK BS4 79 G4
Stockwood Hl KEYN BS31 93 H2
Stockwood La HGRV/WHIT BS14 92 D4
Stockwood Ms
BRSG/KWL/STAPK BS4 81 E1
Stockwood Rd
BRSG/KWL/STAPK BS4 81 E5
HGRV/WHIT BS14 92 D4
Stodeleigh Cl MTN/WRL BS22 132 A5
Stoke Bridge Av
BRSTK/PCHW BS34 27 F4
Stokefield Cl THNB/SVB BS35 8 C3
Stoke Gv
HNLZ/SM/SNYPK/WT BS9 50 B2
Stoke Hamlet
HNLZ/SM/SNYPK/WT BS9 50 C2
Stoke Hl
HNLZ/SM/SNYPK/WT BS9 50 B4
Stokehill TRWBR BA14 123 H1
Stoke La BRSTK/PCHW BS34 27 E2
HNLZ/SM/SNYPK/WT BS9 50 D1
MANG/FISH BS16 53 F1
Stokeleigh Wk
HNLZ/SM/SNYPK/WT BS9 49 H3
Stokemead BRSTK/PCHW BS34 27 E2
Stoke Mdw ALMDB BS32 27 F1
Stoke Paddock Rd
HNLZ/SM/SNYPK/WT BS9 50 A2
Stoke Park Rd
HNLZ/SM/SNYPK/WT BS9 50 B4
Stoke Park Rd South
HNLZ/SM/SNYPK/WT BS9 50 B5
Stoke Rd
HNLZ/SM/SNYPK/WT BS9 50 C5
PTSHD/EG BS20 45 G3
Stokes Ct
OLD/WMLY/WICK BS30 82 D2
Stoke View Rd MANG/FISH BS16 53 G5
Stoneable Rd
RDSTK/MIDN BA3 125 H1
Stoneberry Rd
HGRV/WHIT BS14 100 D1
Stonebridge CLVDN BS21 70 D4
Stonebridge Pk
EVILLE/WHL BS5 63 E1
Stonebridge Rd WSM BS23 139 E2
Stonechat Gdns
MANG/FISH BS16 53 F2
Stonehenge La CLVDN BS21 73 F2
Stonehill OLD/WMLY/WICK BS30 82 B2
Stonehouse Cl BATHSE BA2 117 F1
Stonehouse La BATHSE BA2 115 E5
Stone La FRCTL/WBN BS36 41 F1
Stoneleigh Crs
BRSG/KWL/STAPK BS4 79 H4
Stoneleigh Dr
OLD/WMLY/WICK BS30 82 C1
Stoneleigh Rd
BRSG/KWL/STAPK BS4 79 H4
Stoneleigh Wk
BRSG/KWL/STAPK BS4 79 H4
Stone Mills TRWBR BA14 * 122 D1
Stonewell Dr YTN/CONG BS49 128 D3
Stonewell Gv YTN/CONG BS49 128 D3
Stonewell La YTN/CONG BS49 128 D3
Stonewell Park Rd
YTN/CONG BS49 128 D3
Stoneyfield Cl PTSHD/EG BS20 48 A4
Stoneyfields PTSHD/EG BS20 48 A4
Stoney Steep NAIL BS48 73 H1
Stoney Stile Rd THNB/SVB BS35 11 G2
Stormont Cl WSM BS23 139 E3
Stothard Rd HORF/LLZ BS7 52 C1
Stottbury Rd HORF/LLZ BS7 52 B5
Stoulton Gv HNBRY/STHM BS10 37 F2
Stourden Cl MANG/FISH BS16 53 H1
Stourton Dr
OLD/WMLY/WICK BS30 82 C2
Stowey Pk YTN/CONG BS49 126 D4
Stowey Rd YTN/CONG BS49 126 B3
Stowick Crs AVONM BS11 36 B4
Stradbrook Av EVILLE/WHL BS5 64 A4
Stradling Av WSM BS23 139 E1
Stradling Rd AVONM BS11 36 B3
Stradling Ter WSM BS23 * 139 E1
Straight St CBRISNE BS2 5 K4
Stratford Cl HGRV/WHIT BS14 100 C1
Strathearn Dr
HNBRY/STHM BS10 37 G3
Strathmore Rd HORF/LLZ BS7 51 H2
Stratton Rd KEYN BS31 105 F1
Stratton St CBRISNE BS2 5 H2
Strawberry Cl NAIL BS48 73 E5
Strawberry Hl CLVDN BS21 71 E1
Strawberry La LGASH BS41 98 D1
Strawbridge Rd
EVILLE/WHL BS5 62 C4
Stream Cl HNBRY/STHM BS10 38 A2
Streamcross YTN/CONG BS49 127 E1
Streamleaze THNB/SVB BS35 8 D4
Streamside CLVDN BS21 71 F2
Stream Side MANG/FISH BS16 55 E2
Streamside Rd YATE/CS BS37 32 C1
The Stream MANG/FISH BS16 40 C3
The Street RDSTK/MIDN BA3 125 G2
THNB/SVB BS35 10 A4
THNB/SVB BS35 11 H2
Stretford Av EVILLE/WHL BS5 63 E3
Stretford Rd EVILLE/WHL BS5 63 E3
Stride Cl THNB/SVB BS35 12 C3
Strode Common
THNB/SVB BS35 11 F2
Strode Gdns THNB/SVB BS35 11 F2
Strode Rd CLVDN BS21 70 C4
Strode Wy CLVDN BS21 70 B4
Stroud Rd AVONM BS11 48 D3
BRSTK/PCHW BS34 26 A2
Stroud Wy
OMX/HUT/LCK BS24 136 B4
Stuart Cl TRWBR BA14 121 F2
Stuart Pl BATHSE BA2 2 A5
Stuart Rd WSM BS23 139 F1
Stuart St EVILLE/WHL BS5 62 D4
Studley Ri TRWBR BA14 123 E3
Sturden La MANG/FISH BS16 40 D2
Sturdon Rd BMSTR BS3 78 B3
Sturmer Cl YATE/CS BS37 20 D3
Sturmey Wy PTSHD/EG BS20 48 D5
Sturminster Cl HGRV/WHIT BS14 92 C3
Sturminster Rd
HGRV/WHIT BS14 92 B4
Sulis Manor Rd BATHSE BA2 116 B2
Sullivan Cl
BRSG/KWL/STAPK BS4 91 E3
Sumerlin Dr CLVDN BS21 71 F2
Summer Down Wk
TRWBR BA14 122 D5
Summerfield MTN/WRL BS22 132 A5
Summerfield Rd
CBATH/BATHN BA1 108 D3
Summerfield Ter
CBATH/BATHN BA1 * 108 D3
Summerhayes
OLD/WMLY/WICK BS30 83 G1
Summer Hl
BRSG/KWL/STAPK BS4 79 H2
Summerhill Rd
CBATH/BATHN BA1 108 A3
EVILLE/WHL BS5 63 G3
Summerhill Ter EVILLE/WHL BS5 63 G4
Summerhouse CLVDN BS21 73 E2
Summer House Wy
OLD/WMLY/WICK BS30 65 G4
Summerlands NAIL BS48 86 A4
Summerlands Rd WSM BS23 7 K3
Summer La BATHSE BA2 117 F1
BNWL BS29 141 H2
MTN/WRL BS22 137 E2
Summer La North
MTN/WRL BS22 136 D1
Summerlays Ct BATHSE BA2 3 J5
Summerleaze KEYN BS31 94 B2
MANG/FISH BS16 54 B5
TRWBR BA14 122 B3
Summers Md YATE/CS BS37 20 D2
Summers Rd CBRISNE BS2 62 B2
Summer St BMSTR BS3 78 D2
Sundays Hl ALMDB BS32 15 G3
Sunderland Pl CFTN/FAIL BS8 4 B1
Sunderland St BATHSE BA2 3 H3
Sundridge Pk YATE/CS BS37 32 A2
Sunfield Rd
OMX/HUT/LCK BS24 140 B3
Sunningdale CFTN/FAIL BS8 61 E3
YATE/CS BS37 32 A2
Sunningdale Cl NAIL BS48 73 H5
Sunningdale Dr
OLD/WMLY/WICK BS30 65 G5
Sunningdale Rd
MTN/WRL BS22 131 G5
Sunnybank BATHSE BA2 115 E3
Sunny Bank KGWD/HNM BS15 64 A2
MANG/FISH BS16 * 54 D2
Sunnybank Ct
OMX/HUT/LCK BS24 137 E2
Sunny Bank Wy
OMX/HUT/LCK BS24 137 E2
Sunnydene
BRSG/KWL/STAPK BS4 80 C2
Sunny Hl
HNLZ/SM/SNYPK/WT BS9 49 H1
Sunnyhill Dr AVONM BS11 48 D2
Sunnymead KEYN BS31 104 A1
RDSTK/MIDN BA3 124 A2
Sunnymede Rd NAIL BS48 73 E4
Sunny Mt RDSTK/MIDN BA3 124 C2
Sunnyside FRCTL/WBN BS36 29 H3
HNLZ/SM/SNYPK/WT BS9 50 B3
Sunnyside Crs CLVDN BS21 70 D2
Sunnyside La MANG/FISH BS16 40 C3
YATE/CS BS37 31 G1
Sunnyside Rd CLVDN BS21 70 D2
WSM BS23 7 F7
Sunnyside Rd North WSM BS23 7 F7
Sunnyvale CLVDN BS21 70 A4
Sunnyvale Dr
OLD/WMLY/WICK BS30 83 E3
Sunny Wk KGWD/HNM BS15 64 A2
Sunridge MANG/FISH BS16 54 C2
Sunridge Cl RDSTK/MIDN BA3 124 A4
Sunridge Pk RDSTK/MIDN BA3 124 A4
Sunrise Gv
BRSG/KWL/STAPK BS4 80 C2
Surrey Rd HORF/LLZ BS7 51 H5
Surrey St CBRISNE BS2 5 H1
Suspension Br CFTN/FAIL BS8 60 B4
Sussex Pl BATHSE BA2 * 3 H7
Sussex St CBRISNE BS2 62 B5
Sutherland Av MANG/FISH BS16 54 D1
YATE/CS BS37 20 C3
Sutherland Dr
OMX/HUT/LCK BS24 140 A4
Sutherland Pl CFTN/FAIL BS8 60 D1
Sutton Av
BRSG/KWL/STAPK BS4 80 C2
Sutton Cl MTN/WRL BS22 136 B3
Sutton St BATHSE BA2 3 J3
Swainswick HGRV/WHIT BS14 91 G3
Swainswick Gdns
CBATH/BATHN BA1 109 F2
Swainswick La
CBATH/BATHN BA1 109 G1
Swaish Dr
OLD/WMLY/WICK BS30 82 C2
Swallow Cl RDSTK/MIDN BA3 * 124 C4
Swallow Dr BRSTK/PCHW BS34 26 A2
TRWBR BA14 122 C1
Swallow Gdns MTN/WRL BS22 136 A3
Swallow Pk THNB/SVB BS35 8 D1
Swallows Ct BRSTK/PCHW BS34 39 H1
The Swallows MTN/WRL BS22 136 A4
Swallow St CBATH/BATHN BA1 3 G5
Swan Cl MTN/WRL BS22 136 B3
Swan Dr TRWBR BA14 121 E1
Swane Rd HGRV/WHIT BS14 93 E3
Swan La FRCTL/WBN BS36 28 C2
Swanmoor Crs
HNBRY/STHM BS10 37 F1
Sweetgrass Rd
OMX/HUT/LCK BS24 136 C3
Sweets Cl KGWD/HNM BS15 64 D1
Sweets Rd KGWD/HNM BS15 64 C1
Swift Cl MTN/WRL BS22 136 C3
Swiss Rd BMSTR BS3 78 A4
WSM BS23 7 G4
Sycamore Cl EVILLE/WHL BS5 63 F2
KGWD/HNM BS15 81 G3
NAIL BS48 73 F4
WSM BS23 7 J3
Sycamore Dr
BRSTK/PCHW BS34 26 A3
THNB/SVB BS35 8 D3
Sycamore Gv TRWBR BA14 122 D4
Sydenham Buildings
BATHSE BA2 2 C6
Sydenham Hl
RDLND/MONT BS6 61 G2
Sydenham La
RDLND/MONT BS6 61 G2
Sydenham Rd BATHSE BA2 2 D5
BRSG/KWL/STAPK BS4 79 H3
RDLND/MONT BS6 61 G2
Sydenham Wy
KGWD/HNM BS15 81 H3
Sydney Buildings BATHSE BA2 3 K5
Sydney Ms BATHSE BA2 3 J3
Sydney Pl BATHSE BA2 3 J3
Sydney Rd BATHSE BA2 3 K3
Sydney Rw CBRIS/FH BS1 4 A7
Sydney Whf BATHSE BA2 3 K4
Sylvan Wy
HNLZ/SM/SNYPK/WT BS9 49 G2
Sylvia Av BMSTR BS3 79 G3
Symes Av
BMSTRD/HC/WWD BS13 99 H1
Symes Pk CBATH/BATHN BA1 107 F2
Symington Rd MANG/FISH BS16 54 A3
Syston Wy KGWD/HNM BS15 64 C2

T

Tabernacle Rd
KGWD/HNM BS15 64 B5
Tackley Rd EVILLE/WHL BS5 52 C5
Tadwick La CBATH/BATHN BA1 102 A4
Tailors Ct CBRIS/FH BS1 5 F3
Talbot Av KGWD/HNM BS15 64 A2
Talbot Rd BRSG/KWL/STAPK BS4 80 B4
TRWBR BA14 122 B3
Talgarth Rd HORF/LLZ BS7 52 A4
Tallis Gv BRSG/KWL/STAPK BS4 91 E3
Tamar Cl THNB/SVB BS35 9 E5
Tamar Dr KEYN BS31 94 D5
Tamar Rd CBRISNE BS2 62 D5
MTN/WRL BS22 136 D1
Tamblyn Cl RDSTK/MIDN BA3 125 H1
Tamworth Rd KEYN BS31 94 B5
Tankard's Cl CFTN/FAIL BS8 4 D2
Tanner Cl
OLD/WMLY/WICK BS30 82 C1
Tanners Wk BATHSE BA2 113 E2
Tanorth Cl HGRV/WHIT BS14 100 D1
Tanorth Rd HGRV/WHIT BS14 100 C1
The Tanyard
OLD/WMLY/WICK BS30 83 E4
Tapsters
OLD/WMLY/WICK BS30 * 82 D2
Tarnock Av HGRV/WHIT BS14 91 H2
Tarragon Pl ALMDB BS32 27 H3
Taunton Rd MTN/WRL BS22 132 A4
Taunton Wk HORF/LLZ BS7 52 B1
Taveners Wk NAIL BS48 * 73 G3
Taverner Cl
BRSG/KWL/STAPK BS4 91 E2
Tavistock Rd
BRSG/KWL/STAPK BS4 79 G5
MTN/WRL BS22 136 D1
Tavistock Wk
BRSG/KWL/STAPK BS4 79 G5
Tawny Wy MTN/WRL BS22 136 C3
Taylor Cl KGWD/HNM BS15 65 E3
Taylor Ct MTN/WRL BS22 132 A4
Taylor Gdns
BMSTRD/HC/WWD BS13 90 A5
Taylors Rw BOAV BA15 * 119 G3
Taylors Vw TRWBR BA14 121 E5
Tayman Cl
HNBRY/STHM BS10 51 H2
Tayman Rdg
OLD/WMLY/WICK BS30 95 G1
Taynton Cl
OLD/WMLY/WICK BS30 83 E4
Teal Cl ALMDB BS32 16 B5
MTN/WRL BS22 136 C2
Teasel Md ALMDB BS32 27 G3
Teasel Wk MTN/WRL BS22 136 A4
Teddington Cl BATHSE BA2 113 H3
Teesdale Cl MTN/WRL BS22 136 A3
Teewell Av MANG/FISH BS16 54 D4
Teewell Cl MANG/FISH BS16 * 54 D4
Teewell Hl MANG/FISH BS16 54 D4
Teignmouth Rd
BRSG/KWL/STAPK BS4 79 H5
CLVDN BS21 71 E2
Telephone Av CBRIS/FH BS1 4 E4
Telford Wk EVILLE/WHL BS5 63 H2
Templar Rd YATE/CS BS37 20 D4
Temple Back CBRIS/FH BS1 5 H4
Temple Back East CBRIS/FH BS1 5 J5
Temple Ga CBRIS/FH BS1 5 H6
Templeland Rd
BMSTRD/HC/WWD BS13 90 A4
Temple Rose St CBRIS/FH BS1 5 H5
Temple St BMSTR BS3 78 C4
CBRIS/FH BS1 5 H5
KEYN BS31 94 B4
Temple Wy CBRIS/FH BS1 5 H5
Temple Wy U/P CBRISNE BS2 5 J3
Tenby Rd KEYN BS31 94 A5
Tenby St EVILLE/WHL BS5 62 C4
Tennessee Gv
RDLND/MONT BS6 51 F3
Tenniscourt Rd
KGWD/HNM BS15 65 F2
Tennis Rd
BRSG/KWL/STAPK BS4 79 H4
Tennyson Av CLVDN BS21 70 B3
Tennyson Cl KEYN BS31 94 C3
Tennyson Rd CBATH/BATHN BA1 2 A2
HORF/LLZ BS7 51 H3
WSM BS23 139 E3
Tenth Av HORF/LLZ BS7 39 E4
Tereslake Gn
HNBRY/STHM BS10 38 A1
Terrace Wk
CBATH/BATHN BA1 * 3 G5
Terrell Gdns EVILLE/WHL BS5 63 E4
Terrell St CBRISNE BS2 4 E2
Tetbury Cl BRSTK/PCHW BS34 27 E2
Tetbury Gdns NAIL BS48 73 H5
Tetbury Rd KGWD/HNM BS15 64 A3
Teviot Rd KEYN BS31 94 D5
Tewkesbury Rd CBRISNE BS2 62 B1
Tewther Rd
BMSTRD/HC/WWD BS13 99 H1
Teyfant Rd
BMSTRD/HC/WWD BS13 100 B1
Teyfant Wk
BMSTRD/HC/WWD BS13 91 F5
Thackeray Av CLVDN BS21 70 D1
Thackeray Rd CLVDN BS21 71 E1
Thackeray Wk HORF/LLZ BS7 38 D5
Thanet Rd BMSTR BS3 78 C4
Thatcher Cl PTSHD/EG BS20 45 G4
Thatchers Cl EVILLE/WHL BS5 64 A4
There-and-back-again La
CFTN/FAIL BS8 * 4 C3
Theresa Av HORF/LLZ BS7 51 H4
Thestfield Dr TRWBR BA14 121 E2
Theynes Cft LGASH BS41 77 E5
Thicket Av MANG/FISH BS16 54 B5
Thicket Rd MANG/FISH BS16 54 B4
Thicket Wk THNB/SVB BS35 8 D3
Thiery Rd
BRSG/KWL/STAPK BS4 80 B4
Thingwall Pk
MANG/FISH BS16 53 F5
Third Av BATHSE BA2 2 B7
HORF/LLZ BS7 38 D4
RDSTK/MIDN BA3 125 E5
Third Wy AVONM BS11 34 D3
Thirlmere Ct
OLD/WMLY/WICK BS30 66 A5
Thirlmere Rd
BRSTK/PCHW BS34 26 C2
WSM BS23 139 F2
Thistle St BMSTR BS3 78 C3
Thomas Av MANG/FISH BS16 42 A5
Thomas La CBRIS/FH BS1 5 G5
Thomas Pring Wk
EVILLE/WHL BS5 63 H2
Thomas St CBATH/BATHN BA1 108 D4
CBRIS/FH BS1 61 H3
CBRISNE BS2 62 A3
Thomas St North
RDLND/MONT BS6 61 G2
Thomas Wy MANG/FISH BS16 53 F1
Thompson Rd
HGRV/WHIT BS14 92 D3
Thomson Rd EVILLE/WHL BS5 62 C3
Thornbank Pl BATHSE BA2 2 D6
Thornbury Dr WSM BS23 138 B4
Thornbury Rd THNB/SVB BS35 11 G2
WSM BS23 138 B4
Thorn Cl MTN/WRL BS22 137 E1
YATE/CS BS37 31 H1
Thorndale Cl MTN/WRL BS22 136 A3
Thorndale Ms CFTN/FAIL BS8 60 D3
Thornhayes Cl FRCTL/WBN BS36 29 G2
The Thornhills MANG/FISH BS16 54 A2
Thornleigh Rd HORF/LLZ BS7 51 H3
Thornmead Gv
HNBRY/STHM BS10 37 F3
Thorns Farm YATE/CS BS37 * 32 A1
Thornycroft Cl HORF/LLZ BS7 52 C1
Three Oaks Cl MANG/FISH BS16 54 B4
Three Queens' La CBRIS/FH BS1 5 G5
Three Wells Rd
BMSTRD/HC/WWD BS13 90 A5
Thrissell St EVILLE/WHL BS5 62 B3
Throgmorton Rd
BRSG/KWL/STAPK BS4 91 G2
Thrush Cl MTN/WRL BS22 136 B3
Thurlestone HGRV/WHIT BS14 91 G4
Thurlow Rd EVILLE/WHL BS5 62 D1
Thurstons Barton
EVILLE/WHL BS5 63 F2
Tibberton KGWD/HNM BS15 65 F3
Tibbott Rd HGRV/WHIT BS14 92 B4
Tibbott Wk HGRV/WHIT BS14 92 B4
Tichborne Rd EVILLE/WHL BS5 62 D4
WSM BS23 6 E1
Tickenham Hl CLVDN BS21 73 E2
Tickenham Rd CLVDN BS21 71 H1
Tide Gv AVONM BS11 35 H5
Tidenham Wy
BRSTK/PCHW BS34 26 B1
Tilley Cl KEYN BS31 104 B2
Tilling Rd HNBRY/STHM BS10 51 H1
Tilling Wk HNBRY/STHM BS10 51 H1
Tilting Rd THNB/SVB BS35 8 C2
Timber Dene MANG/FISH BS16 53 E4
Timberscombe Wk
HGRV/WHIT BS14 92 A4
The Timbers
RDSTK/MIDN BA3 124 C5
Timbrell St TRWBR BA14 121 E5
Timsbury Rd BMSTR BS3 79 F4
Tindell Ct
OLD/WMLY/WICK BS30 82 C2
Tintern Av EVILLE/WHL BS5 63 E3
Tintern Cl
OLD/WMLY/WICK BS30 65 E5
Tippetts Rd KGWD/HNM BS15 64 C5
Tirley Wy MTN/WRL BS22 135 G1
Titan Barrow
CBATH/BATHN BA1 110 D2
Tiverton Gdns MTN/WRL BS22 136 D1
Tiverton Rd CLVDN BS21 71 E4
Tiverton Wk MANG/FISH BS16 63 H1
Tivoli La WSM BS23 6 E2
Tockington La ALMDB BS32 15 G1
Toll Bridge Rd
CBATH/BATHN BA1 109 H1
Tone Rd CLVDN BS21 70 D4
Tor Cl MTN/WRL BS22 136 D1
Tormarton Crs
HNBRY/STHM BS10 37 E1
Tormynton Rd MTN/WRL BS22 136 B1
Toronto Rd HORF/LLZ BS7 38 D5
Torpoint Rd BMSTR BS3 79 E5
Torrance Cl
OLD/WMLY/WICK BS30 66 A5
Torridge Rd KEYN BS31 94 D5
Torrington Av
BRSG/KWL/STAPK BS4 91 G1
Torrington Crs MTN/WRL BS22 131 H5
Tortworth Rd HORF/LLZ BS7 51 H3
Totnes Cl MTN/WRL BS22 136 D1
Totshill Dr
BMSTRD/HC/WWD BS13 91 F5
Totshill Gv
BMSTRD/HC/WWD BS13 91 F5
Tottenham Pl CFTN/FAIL BS8 4 A3
Totterdown La
OMX/HUT/LCK BS24 139 F5
Totterdown Rd WSM BS23 139 E3
Touchstone Av
BRSTK/PCHW BS34 27 G5
Tovey Cl MTN/WRL BS22 131 F4
Towcester Rd TRWBR BA14 123 E5
Tower Cl TRWBR BA14 122 B2
Tower Hl CBRISNE BS2 5 H4
OMX/HUT/LCK BS24 141 G2
Tower House La NAIL BS48 73 G2
Tower La CBRIS/FH BS1 5 F3
OLD/WMLY/WICK BS30 65 G5
Tower Rd KGWD/HNM BS15 64 B2
PTSHD/EG BS20 44 D4
Tower Rd North
KGWD/HNM BS15 65 G3
Tower Rd South
OLD/WMLY/WICK BS30 65 G5
Tower St CBRIS/FH BS1 5 H5
Tower Wk WSM BS23 134 C2
Townsend ALMDB BS32 15 F3
Townsend Cl HGRV/WHIT BS14 93 E4
Townsend Rd HGRV/WHIT BS14 93 E4
Townshend Rd
MTN/WRL BS22 131 H3
Towpath Rd TRWBR BA14 121 E2
Tozers Hl BRSG/KWL/STAPK BS4 80 B4
Tracey Vw
OLD/WMLY/WICK BS30 * 67 H5
Tracy Cl HGRV/WHIT BS14 91 G2
Trafalgar Rd
CBATH/BATHN BA1 107 G3
Trafalgar Ter BMSTR BS3 78 C5
Tralee Wk
BRSG/KWL/STAPK BS4 79 E5
Tramway Rd
BRSG/KWL/STAPK BS4 80 B3
Tranmere Av
HNBRY/STHM BS10 37 F1
Tranmere Gv
HNBRY/STHM BS10 37 F2
Tratman Wk HNBRY/STHM BS10 37 E2
Travers Cl
BRSG/KWL/STAPK BS4 91 E3
Travers Wk BRSTK/PCHW BS34 27 G5
Trawden Cl WSM BS23 135 F2
Tredegar Rd MANG/FISH BS16 54 A5
Treefield Pl CBRISNE BS2 62 B1
Treefield Rd CLVDN BS21 70 D3
Tree Leaze YATE/CS BS37 21 E5
Tregarth Rd BMSTR BS3 78 A5
Trelawn Cl MTN/WRL BS22 137 G1
Trelawney Av EVILLE/WHL BS5 63 E3
Trelawney Pk
BRSG/KWL/STAPK BS4 80 C3
Trelawney Rd
RDLND/MONT BS6 61 F2
Trellick Wk MANG/FISH BS16 39 H5
Tremlett Ms MTN/WRL BS22 132 A4
Trenchard Rd KEYN BS31 105 E2
OMX/HUT/LCK BS24 141 G2
Trenchard St CBRIS/FH BS1 4 D4
Trench La ALMDB BS32 16 B4
Trendlewood Pk
MANG/FISH BS16 53 F4
Trendlewood Wy NAIL BS48 85 G1
Trenleigh Dr MTN/WRL BS22 136 D1
Trent Dr THNB/SVB BS35 9 E5
Trent Gv KEYN BS31 94 D5
Trentham Cl CBRISNE BS2 62 B1
Tresham Cl ALMDB BS32 16 B5
Trevanna Rd BMSTR BS3 78 A5
Trevelyan Rd WSM BS23 7 G5
Trevelyan Wk
BRSTK/PCHW BS34 28 A5
HNBRY/STHM BS10 37 E2
Treverdowe Wk
HNBRY/STHM BS10 36 C2

Trevethin Cl KGWD/HNM BS15 64 B4
Trevisa Gv HNBRY/STHM BS10 37 H1
Trewartha Cl WSM BS23 7 G2
Trewartha Pk WSM BS23 7 G2
Trewint Gdns
BRSG/KWL/STAPK BS4 91 G1
Triangle East BATHSE BA2 2 A6
Triangle North BATHSE BA2 2 A6
Triangle South CFTN/FAIL BS8 4 B3
Triangle Vls BATHSE BA2 2 A6
Triangle West BATHSE BA2 2 A6
CFTN/FAIL BS8 4 B3
Trident Cl MANG/FISH BS16 41 H4
Trim Br CBATH/BATHN BA1 * 3 F4
Trim St CBATH/BATHN BA1 3 F4
Trinder Rd PTSHD/EG BS20 48 A4
Trinity Cl CBATH/BATHN BA1 2 E5
Trinity Ms CBRISNE BS2 * 5 K3
Trinity Rd BATHSE BA2 115 E5
CBRISNE BS2 62 B4
NAIL BS48 73 E5
WSM BS23 134 B2
Trinity St CBATH/BATHN BA1 3 F5
CBRIS/FH BS1 * 4 D5
CBRISNE BS2 62 B4
Trinity Wk CBRISNE BS2 5 K2
Trin Mills CBRIS/FH BS1 5 F6
Tripps Cnr YTN/CONG BS49 126 D4
Tripps Rw LGASH BS41 76 D5
Troon YATE/CS BS37 32 A2
Troon Dr OLD/WMLY/WICK BS30 65 G5
Troopers' Hill Rd
BRSG/KWL/STAPK BS4 63 G5
Trossachs Dr BATHSE BA2 109 G4
Trowbridge Rd BOAV BA15 119 H4
HNBRY/STHM BS10 37 H4
TRWBR BA14 121 H4
Trowbridge Wk
HNBRY/STHM BS10 37 H4
Trowle TRWBR BA14 120 B4
Truro Rd BMSTR BS3 78 C3
NAIL BS48 73 H5
Trym Cross Rd
HNLZ/SM/SNYPK/WT BS9 49 H3
Trym Leaze
HNLZ/SM/SNYPK/WT BS9 49 H3
Trym Rd
HNLZ/SM/SNYPK/WT BS9 50 D1
Trym Side
HNLZ/SM/SNYPK/WT BS9 49 H3
Trymwood Cl
HNBRY/STHM BS10 37 E3
Trymwood Pde
HNLZ/SM/SNYPK/WT BS9 * 50 A2
Tucker St CBRISNE BS2 5 J2
Tuckett La MANG/FISH BS16 54 B1
Tuckmill CLVDN BS21 70 B4
Tudor Cl OLD/WMLY/WICK BS30 83 F3
Tudor Dr TRWBR BA14 121 F2
Tudor Rd CBRISNE BS2 62 A2
KGWD/HNM BS15 81 H1
MTN/WRL BS22 131 H4
PTSHD/EG BS20 45 G4
Tuffley Rd HNBRY/STHM BS10 37 H5
Tufton Av AVONM BS11 35 H5
Tugela Rd
BMSTRD/HC/WWD BS13 90 A2
Tunbridge Wy MANG/FISH BS16 41 H5
Tunstall Cl
HNLZ/SM/SNYPK/WT BS9 50 B4
Turley Rd EVILLE/WHL BS5 63 E2
Turnberry
OLD/WMLY/WICK BS30 65 G5
YATE/CS BS37 32 A2
Turnberry Wk
BRSG/KWL/STAPK BS4 * 80 C5
Turnbridge Cl
HNBRY/STHM BS10 * 38 A1
Turnbridge Rd
HNBRY/STHM BS10 37 H1
Turnbury Av NAIL BS48 73 H5
Turnbury Cl MTN/WRL BS22 131 G5
Turner Cl KEYN BS31 94 D4
Turner Ct MTN/WRL BS22 131 G5
Turner Dr YATE/CS BS37 31 F1
Turner Gdns HORF/LLZ BS7 52 C2
Turners Ct
OLD/WMLY/WICK BS30 82 C2
Turner Wk
OLD/WMLY/WICK BS30 66 A4
Turner Wy CLVDN BS21 70 B4
Turnpike Cl YATE/CS BS37 20 D5
Turtlegate Av
BMSTRD/HC/WWD BS13 89 H5
Turtlegate Wk
BMSTRD/HC/WWD BS13 89 H5
Turville Dr HORF/LLZ BS7 52 B2
Tutton Wy CLVDN BS21 70 D5
Tweed Cl THNB/SVB BS35 8 D4
Tweed Rd CLVDN BS21 70 C4
Tweeny La
OLD/WMLY/WICK BS30 66 A5
Twenty Acres Rd
HNBRY/STHM BS10 37 H3
Twerton Farm Cl BATHSE BA2 113 G1
Twickenham Rd
RDLND/MONT BS6 51 F3
Two Acres Rd HGRV/WHIT BS14 91 H2
Two Mile Ct
KGWD/HNM BS15 * 64 B3
Twomile Hill Rd
KGWD/HNM BS15 64 A3
Two Rivers Wy
YTN/CONG BS49 129 E2
The Twynings KGWD/HNM BS15 64 D1
Tybalt Wy BRSTK/PCHW BS34 27 G5
Tydeman Rd PTSHD/EG BS20 46 A3
Tyler Cl KGWD/HNM BS15 64 D5
Tylers Farm YATE/CS BS37 21 E3
Tyler's La MANG/FISH BS16 54 C3
Tylers Wy YATE/CS BS37 21 E2
Tyndale Av MANG/FISH BS16 53 H4
YATE/CS BS37 20 C4
Tyndale Rd KGWD/HNM BS15 64 D1
Tyndale Vw THNB/SVB BS35 8 C4
Tyndall Av CFTN/FAIL BS8 4 C2
Tyndall Rd EVILLE/WHL BS5 62 C3
Tyndalls Park Ms CFTN/FAIL BS8 4 C1
Tyndall's Park Rd CFTN/FAIL BS8 4 B1
Tyndalls Wy HNBRY/STHM BS10 38 B5
Tyne Rd HORF/LLZ BS7 51 G5
Tyne St CBRISNE BS2 62 B1
Tyning Cl HGRV/WHIT BS14 91 H2
TRWBR BA14 122 B2
YATE/CS BS37 20 D5
Tyning End BATHSE BA2 3 K7
Tyning La CBATH/BATHN BA1 109 E3
Tyning Rd BATHSE BA2 110 A3
BATHSE BA2 115 F5
BMSTR BS3 79 G3
BOAV BA15 118 B2
KEYN BS31 105 F2
Tynings Ms WSM BS23 138 D2
The Tynings CLVDN BS21 70 A4
Tyning Ter CBATH/BATHN BA1 108 D3
The Tyning BATHSE BA2 3 K7
Tynte Av
BMSTRD/HC/WWD BS13 100 A1
Tyntesfield Rd
BMSTRD/HC/WWD BS13 90 B2
Tyrone Wk
BRSG/KWL/STAPK BS4 91 F1
Tyrrel Wy BRSTK/PCHW BS34 27 G4

U

Ullswater Cl
OLD/WMLY/WICK BS30 66 A5
WSM BS23 139 F2
YATE/CS BS37 20 D4
Ullswater Dr
CBATH/BATHN BA1 108 D2
Ullswater Rd
HNBRY/STHM BS10 37 G4
Uncombe Cl NAIL BS48 86 C3
Underbanks PTSHD/EG BS20 48 C4
Underhill Av RDSTK/MIDN BA3 124 A2
Underhill Dr WSM BS23 138 C4
Underwood Av
MTN/WRL BS22 135 G2
Underwood Cl THNB/SVB BS35 11 G3
Underwood Rd
PTSHD/EG BS20 45 F5
Union Gallery CBRIS/FH BS1 * 5 G3
Union Pas CBATH/BATHN BA1 * 3 G4
Union Pl WSM BS23 * 6 D4
Union Rd CBRISNE BS2 5 K4
Union St CBATH/BATHN BA1 3 F4
CBRIS/FH BS1 5 F2
NAIL BS48 72 D5
TRWBR BA14 121 E5
WSM BS23 6 D5
Unity Rd KEYN BS31 94 D4
Unity St CBRIS/FH BS1 4 D4
CBRISNE BS2 5 J4
KGWD/HNM BS15 64 B3
University Hall
HNLZ/SM/SNYPK/WT BS9 50 C4
University Rd CFTN/FAIL BS8 4 C3
University Wk CFTN/FAIL BS8 4 C2
Uphill Dr CBATH/BATHN BA1 109 E2
Uphill Rd HORF/LLZ BS7 52 A3
Uphill Rd North WSM BS23 138 C2
Uphill Rd South WSM BS23 138 D5
Uphill Wy WSM BS23 138 C5
Upjohn Crs
BMSTRD/HC/WWD BS13 100 A1
Uplands Dr KEYN BS31 105 G2
Uplands Rd KEYN BS31 105 F2
MANG/FISH BS16 54 B5
The Uplands NAIL BS48 84 D2
Upper Bath Rd
THNB/SVB BS35 8 C4
Upper Belgrave Rd
CFTN/FAIL BS8 60 D1
Upper Belmont Rd
HORF/LLZ BS7 51 H5
Upper Bloomfield Rd
BATHSE BA2 116 B1
Upper Borough Walls
CBATH/BATHN BA1 3 F4
Upper Bristol Rd
CBATH/BATHN BA1 2 C3
WSM BS23 7 K1
Upper Broad St TRWBR BA14 120 D5
Upper Byron Pl CFTN/FAIL BS8 4 B3
Upper Camden Pl
CBATH/BATHN BA1 * 108 D4
Upper Chapel La
FRCTL/WBN BS36 30 A3
Upper Cheltenham Pl
RDLND/MONT BS6 61 H2
Upper Church Rd WSM BS23 6 C1
Upper Church St
CBATH/BATHN BA1 2 E2
Upper Conham V
KGWD/HNM BS15 81 G1
Upper Cranbrook Rd
RDLND/MONT BS6 51 E4
Upper East Hayes
CBATH/BATHN BA1 109 E3
Upper Hedgemead Rd
CBATH/BATHN BA1 3 F1
Upper Lambridge St
CBATH/BATHN BA1 109 F2
Upper Lansdown Ms
CBATH/BATHN BA1 108 C3
Upper Maudlin St CBRISNE BS2 4 E2
Upper Oldfield Pk BATHSE BA2 2 C6
Upper Perry Hl BMSTR BS3 78 D2
Upper Regents Pk BOAV BA15 119 G3
Upper Sandhurst Rd
BRSG/KWL/STAPK BS4 80 C2
Upper Station Rd
MANG/FISH BS16 54 B4
Upper Stone Cl
FRCTL/WBN BS36 30 A3
Upper St BRSG/KWL/STAPK BS4 79 H2
Upper Sydney St BMSTR BS3 78 C2
Upper Ter AVONM BS11 * 36 A3
Upper Tockington Rd
THNB/SVB BS35 10 A5
Upper Town La
BLAG/CWMG/WR BS40 96 D4
Upper Wells St CBRIS/FH BS1 * 4 D4
Upton La LGASH BS41 99 E3
Upton Rd BMSTR BS3 78 C2
Urchinwood La
YTN/CONG BS49 129 F3
Urfords Dr MANG/FISH BS16 54 B2

V

Valda Rd MTN/WRL BS22 135 H1
Vale Crs MTN/WRL BS22 137 F1
Vale End NAIL BS48 73 E5
Vale La BMSTRD/HC/WWD BS13 90 D1
Vale Mill Wy
OMX/HUT/LCK BS24 136 C3
Valentine Cl HGRV/WHIT BS14 92 A4
Valerian Cl AVONM BS11 49 E2
Vale St BRSG/KWL/STAPK BS4 79 H3
The Vale MANG/FISH BS16 56 C1
Valetta Cl WSM BS23 139 E3
Vale Vw RDSTK/MIDN BA3 125 H2
Vale View Pl
CBATH/BATHN BA1 109 E3
Vale View Ter
CBATH/BATHN BA1 110 A1
Valley Cl NAIL BS48 73 F4
Valley Gdns MANG/FISH BS16 41 G5
NAIL BS48 73 F4
Valley Rd
BMSTRD/HC/WWD BS13 90 B1
CFTN/FAIL BS8 59 H4
CLVDN BS21 68 D5
MANG/FISH BS16 55 F3
OLD/WMLY/WICK BS30 66 A5
PTSHD/EG BS20 44 D5
Valley View Cl
CBATH/BATHN BA1 109 E2
Valley View Rd
CBATH/BATHN BA1 109 F1
Valley Wk RDSTK/MIDN BA3 124 C2
Valley Way Rd NAIL BS48 73 F3
The Valls ALMDB BS32 27 H4
Valma Rocks EVILLE/WHL BS5 63 G5
Van Diemen's La
CBATH/BATHN BA1 108 B2
Vandyck Av KEYN BS31 94 C3
Vane St BATHSE BA2 3 J3
Varsity Wy
OMX/HUT/LCK BS24 137 E5
Vassall Ct MANG/FISH BS16 54 A3
Vassall Rd MANG/FISH BS16 54 A3
Vattingstone La
THNB/SVB BS35 11 E2
Vaughan Cl HNBRY/STHM BS10 37 E2
Vauxhall Ter BMSTR BS3 * 78 B2
Vayre Cl YATE/CS BS37 33 E1
Vee La BLAG/CWMG/WR BS40 97 E4
Vellore La BATHSE BA2 3 K3
Ventnor Rd BRSTK/PCHW BS34 39 E2
EVILLE/WHL BS5 63 G2
Venus St YTN/CONG BS49 129 E4
Vera Rd MANG/FISH BS16 63 G1
Verbena Wy MTN/WRL BS22 136 D2
Vereland Rd
OMX/HUT/LCK BS24 140 B4
Verlands YTN/CONG BS49 129 E1
Vernham Gv BATHSE BA2 116 A1
Vernon Cl KEYN BS31 105 E1
Vernon Pk BATHSE BA2 113 H1
Vernon St
BRSG/KWL/STAPK BS4 79 G2
Vernon Ter BATHSE BA2 * 113 H1
Vernslade CBATH/BATHN BA1 107 F2
Verrier Rd EVILLE/WHL BS5 62 D4
Verwood Dr
OLD/WMLY/WICK BS30 83 F5
Vian End MTN/WRL BS22 131 G4
Vicarage Cl MTN/WRL BS22 131 G5
Vicarage Ct KGWD/HNM BS15 81 G1
Vicarage La NAIL BS48 87 H3
THNB/SVB BS35 10 A4
Vicarage Rd BMSTR BS3 78 C2
BMSTRD/HC/WWD BS13 90 A3
CFTN/FAIL BS8 60 A5
EVILLE/WHL BS5 62 D3
FRCTL/WBN BS36 30 A5
KGWD/HNM BS15 81 G1
THNB/SVB BS35 13 E2
Vicars Cl MANG/FISH BS16 54 A4
Victoria Av EVILLE/WHL BS5 62 D4
Victoria Bridge Rd BATHSE BA2 2 C4
Victoria Buildings BATHSE BA2 2 B4
Victoria Cl BATHSE BA2 113 H2
PTSHD/EG BS20 45 G3
THNB/SVB BS35 8 C1
Victoria Crs THNB/SVB BS35 12 C3
Victoria Gdns
CBATH/BATHN BA1 110 A1
RDLND/MONT BS6 61 G2
TRWBR BA14 121 F4
Victoria Gv BMSTR BS3 79 F2
Victoria Ms BMSTR BS3 * 78 D3
Victoria Pde EVILLE/WHL BS5 62 D3
Victoria Pk KGWD/HNM BS15 64 C3
MANG/FISH BS16 53 H3
WSM BS23 6 C1
Victoria Pl BMSTR BS3 78 D3
CBATH/BATHN BA1 * 109 F3
WSM BS23 6 C2
Victoria Qd WSM BS23 6 E2
Victoria Rd AVONM BS11 34 C5
CBRISNE BS2 79 H1
CLVDN BS21 70 C2
KEYN BS31 105 E1
KGWD/HNM BS15 81 H1
OLD/WMLY/WICK BS30 83 G1
TRWBR BA14 121 G4
Victoria Sq CFTN/FAIL BS8 60 D4
PTSHD/EG BS20 45 G3
WSM BS23 6 C4
Victoria St CBRIS/FH BS1 5 G4
MANG/FISH BS16 54 C4
Victoria Ter BATHSE BA2 2 B5
CBRISNE BS2 80 A1
CFTN/FAIL BS8 60 C5
Victoria Wk RDLND/MONT BS6 61 G2
Victor Rd BMSTR BS3 78 D3
Victor St CBRISNE BS2 79 G2
EVILLE/WHL BS5 62 C5
View Ct OLD/WMLY/WICK BS30 67 F5
Vigor Rd
BMSTRD/HC/WWD BS13 90 C4
Village Cl YATE/CS BS37 31 H1
The Village MANG/FISH BS16 * 55 H1
Villiers Rd EVILLE/WHL BS5 62 C2
The Villings BMSTR BS3 * 77 H5
Vilner La THNB/SVB BS35 8 C5
Vimpany Cl HNBRY/STHM BS10 37 E2
Vimpennys La THNB/SVB BS35 24 B1
Vincent Cl AVONM BS11 36 B3
Vine Gdns MTN/WRL BS22 136 D1
Vineyards CBATH/BATHN BA1 3 F2
Vining Wk EVILLE/WHL BS5 62 C3
Vinny Av MANG/FISH BS16 55 F1
Vintery Leys
HNLZ/SM/SNYPK/WT BS9 51 E1
Virginia Cl YATE/CS BS37 32 C1
Vivian St BMSTR BS3 79 E3
Vivien Av RDSTK/MIDN BA3 124 B2
Vowell Cl
BMSTRD/HC/WWD BS13 90 C5
Vowles Cl NAIL BS48 73 H3
Vynes Cl NAIL BS48 73 H5
Vynes Wy NAIL BS48 74 A5
Vyvyan Rd CFTN/FAIL BS8 60 D4
Vyvyan Ter CFTN/FAIL BS8 60 D4

W

Wade Rd YATE/CS BS37 19 H4
Wades Rd BRSTK/PCHW BS34 39 E2
Wade St CBRISNE BS2 5 J1
Wadham Dr MANG/FISH BS16 40 C4
Wadham Gv MANG/FISH BS16 55 H3
Wadham St WSM BS23 6 D2
Wagtail Gdns MTN/WRL BS22 136 B3
Wainbridge Crs
THNB/SVB BS35 13 E2
Wainbrook Dr EVILLE/WHL BS5 63 E1
Wains Cl CLVDN BS21 70 C3
Wainwright Cl MTN/WRL BS22 132 A4
Wakedean Gdns
YTN/CONG BS49 126 A2
Wakeford Rd MANG/FISH BS16 41 H5
Walcot Buildings
CBATH/BATHN BA1 * 108 D4
Walcot Ga CBATH/BATHN BA1 3 G1
Walcot Pde
CBATH/BATHN BA1 * 108 D4
Walcot St CBATH/BATHN BA1 3 G3
Walcot Ter
CBATH/BATHN BA1 * 108 D4
Waldegrave Rd
CBATH/BATHN BA1 108 B3
Waldegrave Ter
RDSTK/MIDN BA3 125 H2
Walden Rd KEYN BS31 94 D5
Walford Av MTN/WRL BS22 132 B5
Walker Cl EVILLE/WHL BS5 62 C4
MANG/FISH BS16 55 F1
Walker St CBRISNE BS2 4 D1
Walker Wy THNB/SVB BS35 8 C5
Wallace Rd CBATH/BATHN BA1 109 E3
Wallingford Rd
BRSG/KWL/STAPK BS4 91 E2
Walliscote Av
HNLZ/SM/SNYPK/WT BS9 51 F2
Walliscote Rd
HNLZ/SM/SNYPK/WT BS9 51 F2
WSM BS23 6 E5
Walliscote Rd South
WSM BS23 138 C2
Wallscourt Rd
BRSTK/PCHW BS34 39 E3
Wallscourt Rd South
BRSTK/PCHW BS34 39 E4
Walmesley Cha TRWBR BA14 121 H5
Walmesley Ter
CBATH/BATHN BA1 * 108 D3
Walnut Av YATE/CS BS37 21 F5
Walnut Cl KEYN BS31 93 H5
NAIL BS48 85 F1
OMX/HUT/LCK BS24 139 F4
PTSHD/EG BS20 47 H5
THNB/SVB BS35 9 E3
Walnut Crs KGWD/HNM BS15 65 E3
Walnut Dr BATHSE BA2 114 B3
Walnut Gv TRWBR BA14 122 C3
Walnut La KGWD/HNM BS15 65 F3
Walnut Tree Cl ALMDB BS32 15 G2
Walnut Wk
BMSTRD/HC/WWD BS13 90 B3
Walsh Av HGRV/WHIT BS14 91 H2
Walsh Cl OMX/HUT/LCK BS24 139 G4
Walshe Av YATE/CS BS37 33 E1
Walsingham Rd
RDLND/MONT BS6 61 H1
Walter St BMSTR BS3 78 B2
Waltham End
OMX/HUT/LCK BS24 136 D3
Walton Av
BRSG/KWL/STAPK BS4 80 C1
Walton Cl KEYN BS31 94 A5
OLD/WMLY/WICK BS30 83 F5
Walton Dro CLVDN BS21 69 F3
Walton Heath YATE/CS BS37 32 B1
Walton Ri
HNLZ/SM/SNYPK/WT BS9 37 F5
Walton Rd AVONM BS11 48 C2
CLVDN BS21 68 D5
CLVDN BS21 69 G2
Walton St EVILLE/WHL BS5 62 C2
Walwyn Cl BATHSE BA2 113 F1
Wansbeck Rd KEYN BS31 94 D5
Wansbrough Rd
MTN/WRL BS22 132 A4
Wanscow Wk
HNLZ/SM/SNYPK/WT BS9 51 E2
Wansdyke Rd BATHSE BA2 116 A1
Wapping Rd CBRIS/FH BS1 4 E6
Warbler Cl TRWBR BA14 122 C1
Warden Rd BMSTR BS3 78 D2
Wardour Rd
BRSG/KWL/STAPK BS4 91 E1
Wareham Cl NAIL BS48 73 E5
Warleigh Dr
CBATH/BATHN BA1 110 B1
Warleigh La
CBATH/BATHN BA1 110 C4
Warleys La
OMX/HUT/LCK BS24 137 F2
Warman Cl HGRV/WHIT BS14 93 E3
Warman Rd
HGRV/WHIT BS14 93 E3
Warmington Rd
HGRV/WHIT BS14 92 B1
Warminster Rd BATHSE BA2 109 G4
CBRISNE BS2 62 B1
Warner Cl KGWD/HNM BS15 65 E5
YTN/CONG BS49 127 G4
Warne Rd WSM BS23 7 K6
The Warns
OLD/WMLY/WICK BS30 82 D2
Warren Cl ALMDB BS32 16 B4
OMX/HUT/LCK BS24 140 A4
Warren Gdns
HGRV/WHIT BS14 93 E4
Warren La LGASH BS41 76 B5
Warren Rd
BRSTK/PCHW BS34 39 E2
Warren Wy YATE/CS BS37 20 D4
Warrilow Cl MTN/WRL BS22 132 A3
Warrington Rd
BRSG/KWL/STAPK BS4 80 C4
Warry Cl NAIL BS48 74 A4
Warwick Av EVILLE/WHL BS5 62 C2
Warwick Cl MTN/WRL BS22 135 H3
OLD/WMLY/WICK BS30 83 E4
THNB/SVB BS35 8 B3
Warwick Rd
CBATH/BATHN BA1 107 G5
EVILLE/WHL BS5 62 C2
KEYN BS31 94 A5
RDLND/MONT BS6 61 E2
Washingpool Hill Rd
ALMDB BS32 10 C5
Washing Pound La CLVDN BS21 72 C2
HGRV/WHIT BS14 92 A5
Washington Av
EVILLE/WHL BS5 62 D2
Washpool La BATHSE BA2 113 E4
Watch Elm Cl ALMDB BS32 27 G4
Watchhouse Rd PTSHD/EG BS20 48 C4
Watchill Av
BMSTRD/HC/WWD BS13 90 A3
Watchill Cl
BMSTRD/HC/WWD BS13 90 A3
Waterbridge Rd
BMSTRD/HC/WWD BS13 90 A4
Watercress Cl NAIL BS48 74 A4
Watercress Rd CBRISNE BS2 52 A5
Waterdale Cl
HNLZ/SM/SNYPK/WT BS9 51 F1
Waterdale Gdns
HNLZ/SM/SNYPK/WT BS9 51 F1
Waterford Beck TRWBR BA14 122 A3
Waterford Cl THNB/SVB BS35 9 E4
Waterford Pk
RDSTK/MIDN BA3 125 F4
Waterford Rd
HNLZ/SM/SNYPK/WT BS9 51 E2
Water La BMSTR BS3 79 G3
BRSG/KWL/STAPK BS4 80 C5
CBRIS/FH BS1 5 H4
KGWD/HNM BS15 81 G4
PTSHD/EG BS20 48 B4
Waterloo Bldgs BATHSE BA2 113 G1
Waterloo Pl CBRISNE BS2 5 K3
Waterloo Rd CBRISNE BS2 5 K3
RDSTK/MIDN BA3 125 H2
Waterloo St CBRISNE BS2 5 K3
CFTN/FAIL BS8 60 C4
WSM BS23 6 D3
Watermore Cl FRCTL/WBN BS36 30 A3
Waterside Crs
RDSTK/MIDN BA3 125 E3
Waterside Dr ALMDB BS32 26 C1
Waterside Pk PTSHD/EG BS20 44 A4
Waterside Rd
RDSTK/MIDN BA3 124 D3
Waterside Wy
RDSTK/MIDN BA3 125 E3
Water's La
HNLZ/SM/SNYPK/WT BS9 50 D1
Waters Rd KGWD/HNM BS15 64 B3
Waterworks Rd TRWBR BA14 122 C2
Watery La BATHSE BA2 113 F1
NAIL BS48 72 C4
Wathen Rd RDLND/MONT BS6 52 A5
Watkins Yd
HNLZ/SM/SNYPK/WT BS9 37 F5

Watley's End Rd
FRCTL/WBN BS36 ....29 E3
Watling Wy *AVONM* BS11 ....48 C1
Watson Av
BRSG/KWL/STAPK BS4 ....80 C2
Watson's Rd
OLD/WMLY/WICK BS30 ....82 C3
Watters Cl *FRCTL/WBN* BS36 ....30 B4
Wavell Cl *YATE/CS* BS37 ....20 C3
Waveney Rd *KEYN* BS31 ....104 B1
Waverley Rd *AVONM* BS11 ....48 D2
NAIL BS48 ....85 H2
RDLND/MONT BS6 ....61 F2
WSM BS23 ....139 E2
YATE/CS BS37 ....20 A5
Waverley St *EVILLE/WHL* BS5 ....62 B2
Wayfield Gdns
CBATH/BATHN BA1 ....103 E5
Wayford Cl *KEYN* BS31 ....104 B1
Wayland Rd *MTN/WRL* BS22 ....131 F5
Wayleaze *FRCTL/WBN* BS36 ....30 B3
Wayside *MTN/WRL* BS22 ....136 A1
Wayside Cl *FRCTL/WBN* BS36 ....29 H3
Wayside Dr *CLVDN* BS21 ....68 C5
Weal Ter *CBATH/BATHN* BA1 * 107 G2
The Weal *CBATH/BATHN* BA1 ....107 G2
Weatherley Dr *PTSHD/EG* BS20 ....44 C5
Weatherly Av *BATHSE* BA2 ....114 A5
Weavers Dr *TRWBR* BA14 ....123 E2
Webbers Ct *TRWBR* BA14 ....122 B3
Webbs Heath
OLD/WMLY/WICK BS30 ....66 A4
Webb St *EVILLE/WHL* BS5 ....62 B3
Webbs Wood Rd *ALMDB* BS32 ....27 H4
Wedgewood Rd
MANG/FISH BS16 ....41 E4
Wedgwood Cl *HGRV/WHIT* BS14 ....92 A4
Wedgwood Rd *BATHSE* BA2 ....113 E2
Wedmore Cl *KGWD/HNM* BS15 ....65 E4
WSM BS23 ....139 E4
Wedmore Pk *BATHSE* BA2 ....113 F4
Wedmore Rd *CLVDN* BS21 ....70 B4
KEYN BS31 ....95 G5
NAIL BS48 ....85 F1
Wedmore V *BMSTR* BS3 ....79 F4
Weedon Cl *CBRISNE* BS2 ....62 B1
Weetwood Rd *YTN/CONG* BS49 ....129 E1
Weight Rd *EVILLE/WHL* BS5 ....62 D4
The Weind *MTN/WRL* BS22 ....136 A1
Weir La *CFTN/FAIL* BS8 ....76 B1
Weir Rd *YTN/CONG* BS49 ....129 E3
Welland Rd *KEYN* BS31 ....94 C5
Wellard Cl *MTN/WRL* BS22 * 132 A4
Well Cl *LGASH* BS41 ....77 E5
OMX/HUT/LCK BS24 ....139 G4
Wellgarth Rd
BRSG/KWL/STAPK BS4 ....79 H4
Wellgarth Wk
BRSG/KWL/STAPK BS4 ....79 H5
Well House Cl
HNLZ/SM/SNYPK/WT BS9 ....60 B1
Wellington Av
RDLND/MONT BS6 ....61 H2
Wellington Buildings
CBATH/BATHN BA1 ....107 G2
Wellington Crs *HORF/LLZ* BS7 ....51 H2
Wellington Dr
HNLZ/SM/SNYPK/WT BS9 ....51 G2
YATE/CS BS37 ....20 A5
Wellington Hl *HORF/LLZ* BS7 ....51 H2
Wellington Hl West
HNLZ/SM/SNYPK/WT BS9 ....51 F1
Wellington La
RDLND/MONT BS6 ....61 H2
Wellington Ms *AVONM* BS11 ....48 C3
Wellington Pk *CFTN/FAIL* BS8 ....60 D2
Wellington Pl *WSM* BS23 * 6 D4
Wellington Rd *CBRISNE* BS2 ....5 J2
KGWD/HNM BS15 ....64 C1
YATE/CS BS37 ....20 D3
Wellington Ter *CFTN/FAIL* BS8 ....60 C5
CLVDN BS21 ....68 A5
Wellington Wk
HNBRY/STHM BS10 ....51 F1
Well La *BNWL* BS29 ....141 H3
YTN/CONG BS49 ....126 C3
Wellow Brook Meadow
RDSTK/MIDN BA3 ....124 C2
Well Pk *YTN/CONG* BS49 ....129 E2
Wells Cl *HGRV/WHIT* BS14 ....92 B4
NAIL BS48 ....74 A5
Wellsea Gv *WSM* BS23 ....135 G4
Wells Rd *BATHSE* BA2 ....2 E7
BRSG/KWL/STAPK BS4 ....79 G2
BRSG/KWL/STAPK BS4 ....80 A5
HGRV/WHIT BS14 ....92 A1
LGASH BS41 ....98 D3
RDSTK/MIDN BA3 ....125 E3
Wells St *BMSTR* BS3 ....78 B2
Wellstead Av *YATE/CS* BS37 ....31 H1
Wellsway *BATHSE* BA2 ....114 C5
BATHSE BA2 ....116 B2
KEYN BS31 ....94 C5
Wellsway Pk *BATHSE* BA2 ....116 B2
Welsford Av *MANG/FISH* BS16 ....53 E4
Welsford Rd *MANG/FISH* BS16 ....52 D4
Welsh Back *CBRIS/FH* BS1 ....5 F6
Welton Gv *RDSTK/MIDN* BA3 ....124 B1
Welton Rd *RDSTK/MIDN* BA3 ....125 F2
Welton V *RDSTK/MIDN* BA3 ....124 C2
Welton Wk *KGWD/HNM* BS15 ....64 B1
Wemberham Crs
YTN/CONG BS49 ....126 A2
Wenmore Cl *MANG/FISH* BS16 ....41 E4
Wentforth Dr *KGWD/HNM* BS15 ....64 B1
Wentwood Dr
OMX/HUT/LCK BS24 ....139 F5
Wentworth
OLD/WMLY/WICK BS30 ....65 F5
YATE/CS BS37 ....32 A1
Wentworth Cl *MTN/WRL* BS22 ....131 G5
Wentworth Rd *HORF/LLZ* BS7 ....51 G5
Wescott Gv *AVONM* BS11 * 36 B3
Wesley Av *KGWD/HNM* BS15 ....82 A1
RDSTK/MIDN BA3 ....124 D3
Wesley Cl *EVILLE/WHL* BS5 ....63 E2
MANG/FISH BS16 * 54 C5
Wesley Dr *MTN/WRL* BS22 ....131 H5
Wesley Hl *KGWD/HNM* BS15 ....64 C2
Wesley La
OLD/WMLY/WICK BS30 ....83 E1
Wesley Pl *CFTN/FAIL* BS8 ....60 D1
Wesley Rd *HORF/LLZ* BS7 ....51 H4
RDSTK/MIDN BA3 ....124 D3
TRWBR BA14 ....122 D2
Wesley St *BMSTR* BS3 ....78 D3
Wessex Av *HORF/LLZ* BS7 ....52 A1
Wessex Ct *HORF/LLZ* BS7 * 52 A1
Wessex Rd
OMX/HUT/LCK BS24 ....139 G4
Westacre Cl *HNBRY/STHM* BS10 ....37 F3
West Ar *CBRIS/FH* BS1 * 5 F4
West Ashton Rd *TRWBR* BA14 ....123 G2
West Av *BATHSE* BA2 ....113 H2
Westaway Cl *YTN/CONG* BS49 ....126 C4
Westaway Pk *YTN/CONG* BS49 ....126 D4
Westbourne Av *CLVDN* BS21 ....70 C3
KEYN BS31 ....94 B4
Westbourne Cl
MANG/FISH BS16 ....55 E1
Westbourne Crs *CLVDN* BS21 ....70 C3
Westbourne Gdns
TRWBR BA14 ....122 C1
Westbourne Pl *CFTN/FAIL* BS8 ....4 A2
Westbourne Rd
EVILLE/WHL BS5 ....62 C3
MANG/FISH BS16 ....41 G5
TRWBR BA14 ....122 C1
West Broadway
HNLZ/SM/SNYPK/WT BS9 ....51 G2
Westbrooke Ct *CBRIS/FH* BS1 * 78 B1
Westbrook Pk
CBATH/BATHN BA1 ....107 F2
Westbrook Rd
BRSG/KWL/STAPK BS4 ....92 C1
MTN/WRL BS22 ....136 A2
Westbury Court Rd
HNLZ/SM/SNYPK/WT BS9 ....50 C1
Westbury Crs *WSM* BS23 ....139 E4
Westbury Hl
HNLZ/SM/SNYPK/WT BS9 ....50 D1
Westbury La
HNLZ/SM/SNYPK/WT BS9 ....49 H1
Westbury Ms
HNLZ/SM/SNYPK/WT BS9 ....50 D1
Westbury Pk
RDLND/MONT BS6 ....50 D4
Westbury Rd
HNLZ/SM/SNYPK/WT BS9 ....50 D2
West Cl *BATHSE* BA2 ....113 F2
West Coombe
HNLZ/SM/SNYPK/WT BS9 ....50 A2
Westcourt Dr
OLD/WMLY/WICK BS30 ....83 E2
West Cft *CLVDN* BS21 ....70 B3
HNLZ/SM/SNYPK/WT BS9 ....51 F1
Westcroft St *TRWBR* BA14 ....120 D5
West Dene
HNLZ/SM/SNYPK/WT BS9 ....50 B2
West Dundry La *LGASH* BS41 ....98 D2
West End *BMSTR* BS3 ....78 D2
CBRISNE BS2 ....4 E1
West End La *NAIL* BS48 ....84 A2
Westering Cl *MANG/FISH* BS16 ....55 F3
Westerleigh Cl
MANG/FISH BS16 ....55 E1
Westerleigh Rd *BATHSE* BA2 ....117 F1
CLVDN BS21 ....70 B3
MANG/FISH BS16 ....54 D2
MANG/FISH BS16 ....57 E2
YATE/CS BS37 ....43 G1
Western Av *FRCTL/WBN* BS36 ....29 G2
Western Dr *HGRV/WHIT* BS14 ....91 F2
Western Rd *HORF/LLZ* BS7 ....51 H2
Westfield *BOAV* BA15 ....119 E2
CLVDN BS21 ....70 D5
Westfield Cl *BATHSE* BA2 ....114 B4
KEYN BS31 ....93 H4
KGWD/HNM BS15 ....82 A1
NAIL BS48 ....85 H3
TRWBR BA14 ....122 B2
WSM BS23 ....138 C4
Westfield Dr *NAIL* BS48 ....85 H3
Westfield La
BRSTK/PCHW BS34 ....39 H2
Westfield Pk
CBATH/BATHN BA1 ....107 F5
RDLND/MONT BS6 ....61 E2
Westfield Pl *CFTN/FAIL* BS8 ....60 C4
Westfield Rd
HNLZ/SM/SNYPK/WT BS9 ....37 F5
NAIL BS48 ....85 H3
TRWBR BA14 ....122 B2
Westfield Wy *ALMDB* BS32 ....16 B5
Westgate *CBRIS/FH* BS1 * 4 B6
Westgate Buildings
CBATH/BATHN BA1 ....3 F4
Westgate St *CBATH/BATHN* BA1 ....3 F4
West Gv *RDLND/MONT* BS6 ....62 A2
Westhall Rd *CBATH/BATHN* BA1 ....2 A2
West Hl *PTSHD/EG* BS20 ....45 F3
West Hill Gdns *PTSHD/EG* BS20 ....45 F3
West Hill Rd *RDSTK/MIDN* BA3 ....125 E3
Westland Av
OLD/WMLY/WICK BS30 ....83 F2
West La *BLAG/CWMG/WR* BS40 ....96 C4
West Lea Rd
CBATH/BATHN BA1 ....107 F4
West Leaze Pl *ALMDB* BS32 ....27 G4
Westleigh Cl *HNBRY/STHM* BS10 ....38 A4
YATE/CS BS37 ....31 G1
Westleigh Pk *HGRV/WHIT* BS14 ....91 H1
Westleigh Rd
HNBRY/STHM BS10 ....37 H4
West Links Cl *MTN/WRL* BS22 ....130 C5
West Ml *CFTN/FAIL* BS8 ....60 C4
Westmarch Wy *MTN/WRL* BS22 ....131 H4
Westmead Crs *TRWBR* BA14 ....122 C4
Westmead Gdns
CBATH/BATHN BA1 ....107 F2
Westmead Rd *EVILLE/WHL* BS5 ....64 A4
Westminster Cl
HNLZ/SM/SNYPK/WT BS9 * 50 D1
Westminster Rd
EVILLE/WHL BS5 ....63 E3
Westmoreland Dr *BATHSE* BA2 ....2 D5
Westmoreland Rd *BATHSE* BA2 ....2 D6
RDLND/MONT BS6 ....50 D5
Westmoreland Station Rd
BATHSE BA2 ....2 C6
Westmoreland St *BATHSE* BA2 ....2 D6
Weston Av *EVILLE/WHL* BS5 ....63 E4
Weston Cl
HNLZ/SM/SNYPK/WT BS9 ....49 H1
Weston Crs *HORF/LLZ* BS7 ....51 H2
Weston Farm La
CBATH/BATHN BA1 ....107 G2
Weston La *CBATH/BATHN* BA1 ....107 H3
Weston Ldg *WSM* BS23 * 6 D2
Weston Pk *CBATH/BATHN* BA1 ....107 H3
Weston Pk East
CBATH/BATHN BA1 ....108 A4
Weston Pk West
CBATH/BATHN BA1 ....107 H3
Weston Rd *CBATH/BATHN* BA1 ....2 A1
CFTN/FAIL BS8 ....75 H3
LGASH BS41 ....76 C5
NAIL BS48 ....88 A1
YTN/CONG BS49 ....128 A1
Westons Brake
MANG/FISH BS16 ....41 H4
Westons Hill Dr
MANG/FISH BS16 ....41 H5
Westons Wy *KGWD/HNM* BS15 ....65 E4
Weston Wy
OMX/HUT/LCK BS24 ....140 B4
Weston Wood Rd
PTSHD/EG BS20 ....45 F5
Westover Cl
HNLZ/SM/SNYPK/WT BS9 ....37 E4
Westover Dr
HNLZ/SM/SNYPK/WT BS9 ....37 F5
Westover Gdns
HNLZ/SM/SNYPK/WT BS9 ....37 E5
Westover Ri
HNLZ/SM/SNYPK/WT BS9 ....37 F4
Westover Rd
HNLZ/SM/SNYPK/WT BS9 ....37 F5
West Pde
HNLZ/SM/SNYPK/WT BS9 ....49 H1
West Pk *CFTN/FAIL* BS8 ....61 E3
West Park Rd *MANG/FISH* BS16 ....54 D3
West Priory Cl
HNLZ/SM/SNYPK/WT BS9 ....50 D1
West Rdg *FRCTL/WBN* BS36 ....29 H3
West Rd *RDSTK/MIDN* BA3 ....124 B2
YTN/CONG BS49 ....126 B4
West Rocke Av
HNLZ/SM/SNYPK/WT BS9 ....50 A1
West Shrubbery
RDLND/MONT BS6 ....61 E1
West St *BMSTR* BS3 ....78 C4
CBRISNE BS2 ....5 K3
KGWD/HNM BS15 ....64 C3
OLD/WMLY/WICK BS30 ....83 F2
TRWBR BA14 ....122 C1
WSM BS23 ....6 D3
West Town Dr
BRSG/KWL/STAPK BS4 ....92 C1
West Town Gv
BRSG/KWL/STAPK BS4 ....92 C1
West Town La
BRSG/KWL/STAPK BS4 ....80 C5
HGRV/WHIT BS14 ....92 A1
West Town Pk
BRSG/KWL/STAPK BS4 ....80 C5
West Town Rd *AVONM* BS11 ....48 B1
NAIL BS48 ....85 H4
West Vw *THNB/SVB* BS35 ....11 F3
West View Rd *BMSTR* BS3 ....78 C3
CBATH/BATHN BA1 ....110 B1
KEYN BS31 ....94 B4
Westward Dr *PTSHD/EG* BS20 ....48 B4
Westward Gdns *LGASH* BS41 ....77 E4
Westward Rd
BMSTRD/HC/WWD BS13 ....90 A2
West Wy *CLVDN* BS21 ....70 C2
Westway *NAIL* BS48 ....73 E4
West Wick *OMX/HUT/LCK* BS24 ....137 F3
Westwood Cl *MTN/WRL* BS22 ....136 C1
Westwood Crs
BRSG/KWL/STAPK BS4 ....80 C1
Westwood Rd
BRSG/KWL/STAPK BS4 ....92 C1
Westwoods
CBATH/BATHN BA1 ....110 C1
Wetherby Ct *FRCTL/WBN* BS36 ....41 G4
Wetherell Pl *CFTN/FAIL* BS8 ....4 A3
Wetlands La *PTSHD/EG* BS20 ....45 F5
Wexford Rd
BRSG/KWL/STAPK BS4 ....91 E1
Weymouth Rd *BMSTR* BS3 ....79 E4
Weymouth St
CBATH/BATHN BA1 ....109 E4
Whaddon La *TRWBR* BA14 ....121 H3
Wharfedale *THNB/SVB* BS35 ....9 E4
Wharf La *PTSHD/EG* BS20 ....46 C3
Wharf Rd *MANG/FISH* BS16 ....53 G4
Wharnecliffe Cl
HGRV/WHIT BS14 ....92 A4
Wharnecliffe Gdns
HGRV/WHIT BS14 ....92 A4
Whatley Rd *CFTN/FAIL* BS8 ....60 D2
Wheatfield Dr *ALMDB* BS32 ....27 F1
MTN/WRL BS22 ....131 H3
Wheathill Cl *KEYN* BS31 ....93 H4
Wheelers Cl *RDSTK/MIDN* BA3 ....125 E2
Wheelers Dr *RDSTK/MIDN* BA3 ....124 D2
Wheelers Patch
MANG/FISH BS16 ....55 G3
Wheelers Rd *RDSTK/MIDN*
BA3 ....124 D2
Whinchat Gdns
MANG/FISH BS16 ....53 G2
Whippington Ct *CBRIS/FH* BS1 * 5 G2
Whitby Rd
BRSG/KWL/STAPK BS4 ....80 B2
Whitchurch La
BMSTRD/HC/WWD BS13 ....90 B4
HGRV/WHIT BS14 ....91 F4
LGASH BS41 ....99 G3
Whitecross Av *HGRV/WHIT* BS14 ....92 B3
Whitecross Rd *WSM* BS23 ....138 D1
Whitefield Av *EVILLE/WHL* BS5 ....63 H2
KGWD/HNM BS15 ....82 A1
Whitefield Cl
CBATH/BATHN BA1 ....103 G5
Whitefield Rd *EVILLE/WHL* BS5 ....63 H1
Whitefields *YATE/CS* BS37 ....33 E1
Whitehall Av *EVILLE/WHL* BS5 ....63 F2
Whitehall Gdns
EVILLE/WHL BS5 ....63 E2
Whitehall Rd *EVILLE/WHL* BS5 ....62 D3
Whiteheads La *BOAV* BA15 ....119 G2
Whitehill *BOAV* BA15 ....119 G2
White Horse Cl *TRWBR* BA14 ....123 E3
White Horse Rd *BOAV* BA15 ....118 B2
Whitehouse La *BMSTR* BS3 ....79 E3
Whitehouse Pl *BMSTR* BS3 ....79 F2
Whitehouse Rd
THNB/SVB BS35 ....13 E2
White House Rd
YTN/CONG BS49 ....127 F3
Whitehouse St *BMSTR* BS3 ....79 F2
Whiteladies Ga *CFTN/FAIL* BS8 * 61 E2
Whiteladies Rd *CFTN/FAIL* BS8 ....4 B1
Whiteleaze *HNBRY/STHM* BS10 ....37 H5
White Lodge Rd
MANG/FISH BS16 ....55 E4
Whiteoak Wy *NAIL* BS48 ....85 E1
White Park Ldg
PTSHD/EG BS20 ....45 G2
White Row Hl *TRWBR* BA14 ....122 B5
Whiterow Pk *TRWBR* BA14 ....122 B3
Whitesfield Rd *NAIL* BS48 ....73 E5
Whites Hl *EVILLE/WHL* BS5 ....63 H5
Whiteshill *MANG/FISH* BS16 ....41 E2
White St *EVILLE/WHL* BS5 ....5 K1
White Tree Rd
HNLZ/SM/SNYPK/WT BS9 ....51 E4
Whitewall La *THNB/SVB* BS35 ....9 G2
Whiteway Av *BATHSE* BA2 ....113 F4
Whiteway Cl
BRSG/KWL/STAPK BS4 ....63 F5
EVILLE/WHL BS5 ....63 H3
Whiteway Ct *EVILLE/WHL* BS5 ....63 H3
Whiteway Ms *EVILLE/WHL* BS5 ....63 H3
Whiteway Rd *BATHSE* BA2 ....113 E2
EVILLE/WHL BS5 ....63 H2
Whitewells Rd
CBATH/BATHN BA1 ....108 D2
Whitewood Rd *EVILLE/WHL* BS5 ....63 G2
Whitfield Cl *MANG/FISH* BS16 ....54 C5
Whitfield Rd *THNB/SVB* BS35 ....8 D2
Whiting Rd
BMSTRD/HC/WWD BS13 ....90 B5
Whitland Av
BMSTRD/HC/WWD BS13 ....90 C4
Whitland Rd
BMSTRD/HC/WWD BS13 ....90 C4
Whitley Cl *YATE/CS* BS37 ....20 D4
Whitley Md *BRSTK/PCHW* BS34 ....39 H2
Whitmead Gdns
BMSTRD/HC/WWD BS13 ....90 D5
Whitmore Av
BRSG/KWL/STAPK BS4 ....81 F3
Whitson St *CBRIS/FH* BS1 ....5 F1
Whitting Rd *WSM* BS23 ....138 D2
Whittington Dr
MTN/WRL BS22 ....136 A1
Whittington Rd
MANG/FISH BS16 ....54 B2
Whittock Rd *HGRV/WHIT* BS14 ....92 C4
Whittock Sq *HGRV/WHIT* BS14 ....92 C2
Whittucks Cl *KGWD/HNM* BS15 ....82 A2
Whittucks Rd *KGWD/HNM* BS15 ....81 H2
Whitwell Rd *HGRV/WHIT* BS14 ....92 A1
Whytes Cl
HNLZ/SM/SNYPK/WT BS9 ....37 F5
Wick Crs *BRSG/KWL/STAPK* BS4 ....80 C3
Wicker Hl *TRWBR* BA14 ....120 D5
The Wickets *HORF/LLZ* BS7 ....38 C4
KGWD/HNM BS15 ....64 C1
Wickfield *CLVDN* BS21 ....70 C4
Wickham Cl *YATE/CS* BS37 ....33 F2
Wickham Ct *MANG/FISH* BS16 ....53 E3
Wickham Gln *MANG/FISH* BS16 ....53 E3
Wickham Hl *MANG/FISH* BS16 ....53 E3
Wickham Vw
MANG/FISH BS16 ....53 E4
Wick House Cl *KEYN* BS31 ....105 E1
Wicklow Rd
BRSG/KWL/STAPK BS4 ....91 F1
Wick Rd *BRSG/KWL/STAPK* BS4 ....80 C3
MTN/WRL BS22 ....131 H1
OMX/HUT/LCK BS24 ....133 E3
THNB/SVB BS35 ....13 E2
Wicks Rd *MTN/WRL* BS22 ....132 A1
Widbrook Meadow
TRWBR BA14 ....122 B1
Widbrook Vw *BOAV* BA15 ....119 H4
Widcombe *HGRV/WHIT* BS14 ....91 H4
Widcombe Cl *EVILLE/WHL* BS5 ....63 H4
Widcombe Crs *BATHSE* BA2 ....3 J7
Widcombe Hl *BATHSE* BA2 ....3 J7
Widcombe Pde *BATHSE* BA2 * 3 H7
Widcombe Ter *BATHSE* BA2 ....3 K7
Widmore Gv
BMSTRD/HC/WWD BS13 * 90 C4
Wigmore Gdns *MTN/WRL* BS22 ....135 H1
Wigton Crs *HNBRY/STHM* BS10 ....37 H3
Wilbye Gv
BRSG/KWL/STAPK BS4 ....91 E3
Wilcot Cl *TRWBR* BA14 ....122 D3
Wilcox Cl *KGWD/HNM* BS15 ....64 B4
Wildcountry La *NAIL* BS48 ....88 B4
Wildcroft Rd
HNLZ/SM/SNYPK/WT BS9 ....51 E3
The Wilderness *BOAV* BA15 ....119 F2
Willada Cl *BMSTR* BS3 ....78 C4
William Mason Cl
EVILLE/WHL BS5 ....62 C4
Williams Cl
OLD/WMLY/WICK BS30 ....82 C4
Williamson Rd *HORF/LLZ* BS7 ....52 A5
William St *BATHSE* BA2 ....3 H3
BMSTR BS3 ....79 G2
CBRISNE BS2 ....62 A2
EVILLE/WHL BS5 ....62 D3
MANG/FISH BS16 ....54 A5
Willinton Rd
BRSG/KWL/STAPK BS4 ....91 G2
Willis Rd *KGWD/HNM* BS15 ....65 E1
Williton Crs *WSM* BS23 ....139 E4
Willment Wy *AVONM* BS11 ....35 E4
Willmott Cl *HGRV/WHIT* BS14 ....100 C1
Willoughby Cl
BMSTRD/HC/WWD BS13 ....90 B2
THNB/SVB BS35 ....11 G3
Willoughby Rd *HORF/LLZ* BS7 ....51 H3
Willow Bed Cl *MANG/FISH* BS16 ....54 A2
Willow Cl *BATHSE* BA2 ....116 B2
BRSTK/PCHW BS34 ....26 A3
CLVDN BS21 ....71 E2
LGASH BS41 ....76 C5
MTN/WRL BS22 ....137 G1
OLD/WMLY/WICK BS30 ....66 A5
OLD/WMLY/WICK BS30 ....67 E5
PTSHD/EG BS20 ....45 F4
RDSTK/MIDN BA3 ....125 F2
WSM BS23 ....138 D4
Willowdown *MTN/WRL* BS22 ....131 F4
Willow Dr *OMX/HUT/LCK* BS24 ....140 B1
The Willowfalls
CBATH/BATHN BA1 ....109 H1
Willow Gdns *MTN/WRL* BS22 ....137 G1
Willow Gn *BATHSE* BA2 ....114 B3
Willow Gv *MANG/FISH* BS16 ....64 B1
TRWBR BA14 ....122 C4
Willow Rd *KGWD/HNM* BS15 ....81 H2
Willowside Pk *TRWBR* BA14 * 121 E2
The Willows *ALMDB* BS32 ....27 F2
NAIL BS48 ....73 G3
YATE/CS BS37 ....20 C5
Willow Wk *HNBRY/STHM* BS10 ....37 G2
KEYN BS31 ....94 A5
Willow Wy *FRCTL/WBN* BS36 ....30 A4
Willsbridge Hl
OLD/WMLY/WICK BS30 ....82 D4
Wills Dr *EVILLE/WHL* BS5 ....62 B3
Wills Wy
BMSTRD/HC/WWD BS13 ....91 E3
Willway St *BMSTR* BS3 ....79 F2
CBRISNE BS2 ....5 K3
Wilmot Ct
OLD/WMLY/WICK BS30 ....65 F5
Wilmots Wy *PTSHD/EG* BS20 ....48 C4
Wilshire Av *KGWD/HNM* BS15 ....82 A1
Wilson Pl *CBRISNE* BS2 ....5 J1
Wilson St *CBRISNE* BS2 ....5 J1
Wilton Cl *HNBRY/STHM* BS10 ....37 H5
Wilton Dr *TRWBR* BA14 ....123 E3
Wilton Gdns *WSM* BS23 ....6 E6
Wiltshire Av *YATE/CS* BS37 ....21 F4
Wiltshire Dr *TRWBR* BA14 ....122 D4
Wiltshire Pl *KGWD/HNM* BS15 ....54 D5
Wiltshire Wy
CBATH/BATHN BA1 ....108 D2
Wimbledon Rd
RDLND/MONT BS6 ....51 F3
Wimborne Rd *BMSTR* BS3 ....78 D5
Winash Cl *HGRV/WHIT* BS14 ....92 C1
Wincanton Cl *FRCTL/WBN* BS36 ....41 G4
NAIL BS48 ....74 A5
Winchcombe Cl *NAIL* BS48 ....85 H1
Winchcombe Rd
FRCTL/WBN BS36 ....29 H2
Winchester Av
BRSG/KWL/STAPK BS4 ....80 C3
Winchester Rd *BATHSE* BA2 ....2 B6
BRSG/KWL/STAPK BS4 ....80 C3
Wincroft *OLD/WMLY/WICK* BS30 ....83 F2
Windcliff Crs *AVONM* BS11 ....35 F5
Windermere
HNBRY/STHM BS10 * 38 A3
Windermere Av *WSM* BS23 ....139 E2
Windermere Rd
BRSTK/PCHW BS34 ....26 C2
TRWBR BA14 ....121 F4
Windermere Wy
OLD/WMLY/WICK BS30 ....66 A5
Windmill Cl *BMSTR* BS3 ....79 F2
Windmill Hl *BMSTR* BS3 ....79 E3
OMX/HUT/LCK BS24 ....140 D4
Windmill La *HNBRY/STHM* BS10 ....36 C2
Windmill Rd *CLVDN* BS21 ....71 E5
Windrush Cl *BATHSE* BA2 ....113 E3
Windrush Ct *THNB/SVB* BS35 ....8 D4
Windrush Rd *KEYN* BS31 ....94 D5
Windsor Av *EVILLE/WHL* BS5 ....64 A5
KEYN BS31 ....94 B5
Windsor Bridge Rd
CBATH/BATHN BA1 ....2 A3
Windsor Cl *BRSTK/PCHW* BS34 ....39 H1
CLVDN BS21 ....70 C3
Windsor Ct *MANG/FISH* BS16 ....54 D1
Windsor Crs *HNBRY/STHM* BS10 ....36 B1
Windsor Dr *TRWBR* BA14 ....122 C4
Windsor Gv *EVILLE/WHL* BS5 ....62 C3
Windsor Pl
CBATH/BATHN BA1 * 107 H5
CFTN/FAIL BS8 ....60 C5
MANG/FISH BS16 ....55 F3
Windsor Rd *MTN/WRL* BS22 ....135 H1
OLD/WMLY/WICK BS30 ....82 C4
RDLND/MONT BS6 ....61 H1
TRWBR BA14 ....123 F5
Windsor Ter *BMSTR* BS3 ....79 G2
CFTN/FAIL BS8 ....60 C5

Windsor Vls BATHSE BA2 ....107 H5
Windwhistle Cir WSM BS23 ....139 E2
Windwhistle La WSM BS23 ....138 D3
Windwhistle Rd WSM BS23 ....138 C3
Wineberry Cl EVILLE/WHL BS5 ....63 E2
Wine St BOAV BA15 ....119 F3
CBRIS/FH BS1 ....5 G3
Winfield Rd
OLD/WMLY/WICK BS30 ....65 H4
Winford Cl PTSHD/EG BS20 ....45 H4
Winford Gv
BMSTRD/HC/WWD BS13 ....90 B1
Winford La
BLAG/CWMG/WR BS40 ....98 A4
Wingard Cl WSM BS23 ....138 C4
Wingfield Rd BMSTR BS3 ....79 F4
TRWBR BA14 ....122 B2
Winifred's La
CBATH/BATHN BA1 ....108 B3
Winkworth Pl CBRISNE BS2 ....62 A2
Winsbury Wy ALMDB BS32 ....27 E2
Winscombe Cl KEYN BS31 ....94 A3
Winscombe Rd WSM BS23 ....7 J5
Winsford St EVILLE/WHL BS5 * 62 B3
Winsham Cl HGRV/WHIT BS14 ....92 A4
Winsley Rd BOAV BA15 ....118 C2
RDLND/MONT BS6 ....61 G2
Winterbourne Hl
FRCTL/WBN BS36 ....28 D5
Winterbourne Rd
BRSTK/PCHW BS34 ....27 H4
Winterslow Rd TRWBR BA14 ....122 C4
Winterstoke Cl BMSTR BS3 ....78 C4
Winterstoke Rd BMSTR BS3 ....78 B4
WSM BS23 ....7 J7
Winton St
BRSG/KWL/STAPK BS4 ....79 G2
Wistaria Av YATE/CS BS37 ....32 C1
Wisteria Av
OMX/HUT/LCK BS24 ....140 A4
Witchell Rd EVILLE/WHL BS5 ....62 D4
Witch Hazel Rd
BMSTRD/HC/WWD BS13 ....100 B1
Witcombe YATE/CS BS37 ....31 G3
Witcombe Cl KGWD/HNM BS15 ....64 D2
Witham Rd KEYN BS31 ....104 B1
Witherlies Rd MANG/FISH BS16 ....53 G2
Withey Cl West
HNLZ/SM/SNYPK/WT BS9 ....50 B3
The Witheys HGRV/WHIT BS14 ....92 B5
Withies La RDSTK/MIDN BA3 ....124 A5
Withies Pk RDSTK/MIDN BA3 ....124 A4
Withington Cl
OLD/WMLY/WICK BS30 ....83 F4
Withleigh Rd
BRSG/KWL/STAPK BS4 ....80 A4
Withy Cl NAIL BS48 ....73 G3
TRWBR BA14 ....121 F3
Withy Cl East
HNLZ/SM/SNYPK/WT BS9 ....50 C3
Withypool Gdns
HGRV/WHIT BS14 ....92 A4
Withywood Gdns
BMSTRD/HC/WWD BS13 * 90 A5
Withywood Rd
BMSTRD/HC/WWD BS13 ....90 A5
Witney Cl KEYN BS31 ....105 E1
Woburn Cl
OLD/WMLY/WICK BS30 ....82 C1
TRWBR BA14 ....122 B1
Woburn Rd EVILLE/WHL BS5 ....52 C5
Wolferton Rd
RDLND/MONT BS6 ....62 A1
Wolfridge Gdns
HNBRY/STHM BS10 ....37 F1
Wolfridge La THNB/SVB BS35 ....11 F3
Wolfridge Ride THNB/SVB BS35 ..11 F3
Wolseley Rd HORF/LLZ BS7 ....51 G5
Wolvers Hill Rd
OMX/HUT/LCK BS24 ....137 F3
Woodbine Rd EVILLE/WHL BS5 ....62 D3
Woodborough Cl
TRWBR BA14 ....123 E4
Woodborough La
RDSTK/MIDN BA3 ....125 H1
Woodborough Rd
RDSTK/MIDN BA3 ....125 H1
Woodborough St
EVILLE/WHL BS5 ....62 C2
Woodbridge Rd
BRSG/KWL/STAPK BS4 ....79 H4
Woodchester KGWD/HNM BS15 ..54 D5
YATE/CS BS37 ....32 A4
Woodchester Rd
HNBRY/STHM BS10 ....51 F1
Woodcliff Rd MTN/WRL BS22 ....135 H2
Woodcote KGWD/HNM BS15 ....64 C5
Woodcote Rd MANG/FISH BS16 ..64 A1
Woodcote Wk MANG/FISH BS16 ..64 A1
Woodcroft Av EVILLE/WHL BS5 ....63 E3
Woodcroft Cl
BRSG/KWL/STAPK BS4 ....80 D2
Woodcroft Rd
BRSG/KWL/STAPK BS4 ....80 D2
Woodend KGWD/HNM BS15 ....64 C5
Woodend Rd FRCTL/WBN BS36 ....29 H3
Wood End Wk
HNLZ/SM/SNYPK/WT BS9 ....49 H2
Woodfield Rd
RDLND/MONT BS6 ....61 E2
Woodford Cl NAIL BS48 ....73 H5
Woodgrove Rd
HNBRY/STHM BS10 ....36 C3
Woodhall Cl MANG/FISH BS16 ....55 E2
Wood Hl YTN/CONG BS49 ....126 D5
Woodhill Av PTSHD/EG BS20 ....45 G2
Wood Hill Pk PTSHD/EG BS20 ....45 G1
Woodhill Rd PTSHD/EG BS20 ....45 G2
Woodhill Views NAIL BS48 ....73 G3
Woodhouse Gdns
TRWBR BA14 ....121 H4
Woodhouse Gv HORF/LLZ BS7 ....51 H2
Woodhouse Rd BATHSE BA2 ....113 F1
Woodhurst Rd WSM BS23 ....7 J3
Woodington Ct
OLD/WMLY/WICK BS30 ....82 C2
Woodington Rd CLVDN BS21 ....70 C4
The Wood Kilns
YTN/CONG BS49 ....126 A2
Woodland Av KGWD/HNM BS15 ..64 C1
Woodland Cl CFTN/FAIL BS8 ....75 G2
MANG/FISH BS16 ....64 B1
Woodland Ct MANG/FISH BS16 * ..54 B2
Woodland Gld CLVDN BS21 ....68 C5
Woodland Gv BATHSE BA2 ....115 H2
HNLZ/SM/SNYPK/WT BS9 ....50 A2
Woodland Pl BATHSE BA2 ....115 G2
Woodland Rd CFTN/FAIL BS8 ....4 C2
NAIL BS48 ....73 F3
WSM BS23 ....138 C2
Woodlands ALMDB BS32 ....16 B4
CLVDN BS21 ....70 C1
MANG/FISH BS16 ....54 D2
Woodlands Edge
TRWBR BA14 * 123 G2
Woodlands La ALMDB BS32 ....15 H5
ALMDB BS32 ....16 C2
Woodlands Pk
CBATH/BATHN BA1 ....109 F2
Woodlands Ri MANG/FISH BS16 ..54 C2
Woodland Ter
KGWD/HNM BS15 ....64 C4
RDLND/MONT BS6 ....61 E1
Woodland Wy CFTN/FAIL BS8 ....75 G2
KGWD/HNM BS15 ....64 B1
Wood La WSM BS23 ....7 H1
Woodleaze
HNLZ/SM/SNYPK/WT BS9 ....49 G2
Woodleigh THNB/SVB BS35 ....8 D3
Woodleigh Gdns
HGRV/WHIT BS14 ....92 B3
Woodmancote YATE/CS BS37 ....31 H2
Woodmancote Rd
RDLND/MONT BS6 ....61 H2
Woodmans Cl YATE/CS BS37 ....32 D2
Woodmans Rd YATE/CS BS37 ....32 D2
Woodmans V YATE/CS BS37 ....33 E2
Woodmarsh TRWBR BA14 ....123 E5
Woodmarsh Cl
HGRV/WHIT BS14 ....91 H5
Woodmead Gdns
BMSTRD/HC/WWD BS13 ....90 D5
Woodmill YTN/CONG BS49 ....126 A2
Woodpecker Av
RDSTK/MIDN BA3 ....124 C4
Woodpecker Crs
MANG/FISH BS16 ....57 F4
Woodpecker Dr
MTN/WRL BS22 ....136 B3
Wood Rd KGWD/HNM BS15 ....64 C3
Woodside
HNLZ/SM/SNYPK/WT BS9 * 50 A5
Woodside Av
OMX/HUT/LCK BS24 ....139 G4
Woodside Gdns PTSHD/EG BS20 ..44 B3
Woodside Gv
HNBRY/STHM BS10 ....36 C2
Woodside Rd
BRSG/KWL/STAPK BS4 ....63 F5
CLVDN BS21 ....68 C5
FRCTL/WBN BS36 ....30 B3
KGWD/HNM BS15 ....64 B3
MANG/FISH BS16 ....54 B1
Woodspring Av
MTN/WRL BS22 ....130 B5
Woodspring Crs
MTN/WRL BS22 ....130 B5
Woodstock Av
RDLND/MONT BS6 ....61 F2
Woodstock Cl
KGWD/HNM BS15 ....65 E3
Woodstock Rd
KGWD/HNM BS15 ....65 E4
MTN/WRL BS22 ....135 G3
RDLND/MONT BS6 ....61 E1
Wood St BATHSE BA2 ....2 E6
CBATH/BATHN BA1 ....3 F4
EVILLE/WHL BS5 ....62 C1
Woodview CLVDN BS21 ....71 F2
Woodview Cl AVONM BS11 ....48 D1
Woodview Dr YTN/CONG BS49 ..127 G3
Woodview Ter NAIL BS48 ....73 G4
WSM BS23 ....7 H6
Woodward Av YATE/CS BS37 ....31 F1
Woodward Dr
OLD/WMLY/WICK BS30 ....82 C2
Woodwell Rd AVONM BS11 ....48 D2
Woodyleaze Dr
KGWD/HNM BS15 ....64 B5
Wookey Cl NAIL BS48 ....85 G1
Woolcot St
RDLND/MONT BS6 ....61 E1
Wooler Rd WSM BS23 ....7 F3
Woollard La HGRV/WHIT BS14 ....101 G2
Woolley Cl BOAV BA15 ....119 H2
Woolley Dr BOAV BA15 ....119 H2
Woolley Rd HGRV/WHIT BS14 ....92 D4
Woolley St BOAV BA15 ....119 H3
Woolley Ter BOAV BA15 ....119 H2
Woolpack Mdw TRWBR BA14 ....123 F2
Woolvers Hill Rd BNWL BS29 ....141 H1
Woolvers Wy
OMX/HUT/LCK BS24 ....137 E5
Wootton Crs
BRSG/KWL/STAPK BS4 ....63 F5
Wootton Pk HGRV/WHIT BS14 ....80 A5
Wootton Rd
BRSG/KWL/STAPK BS4 ....63 F5
Worcester Buildings
CBATH/BATHN BA1 ....109 E2
Worcester Cl MANG/FISH BS16 ....64 A1
Worcester Crs CFTN/FAIL BS8 ....60 C3
Worcester Gdns NAIL BS48 ....84 C1
Worcester Pk
CBATH/BATHN BA1 ....109 E3
Worcester Pl
CBATH/BATHN BA1 * 109 E2
Worcester Rd CFTN/FAIL BS8 ....60 D3
KGWD/HNM BS15 ....64 C2
Worcester Ter
CBATH/BATHN BA1 ....109 E3
CFTN/FAIL BS8 ....60 D3
Worcester Vls
CBATH/BATHN BA1 * 109 E2
Wordsworth Rd CLVDN BS21 ....70 C3
HORF/LLZ BS7 ....52 B1
WSM BS23 ....139 F3
World's End La KEYN BS31 ....95 F4
Worlebury Cl MTN/WRL BS22 ....130 C5
Worlebury Hill Rd
MTN/WRL BS22 ....130 D5
WSM BS23 ....135 F1
Worlebury Park Rd
MTN/WRL BS22 ....130 B5
Worle Ct MTN/WRL BS22 ....131 G5
Worle Moor Rd
OMX/HUT/LCK BS24 ....136 C3
Worrall Ms CFTN/FAIL BS8 ....60 D1
Worrall Rd CFTN/FAIL BS8 ....60 D1
Worrel's La MANG/FISH BS16 ....41 E2
Worsley St EVILLE/WHL BS5 ....63 E4
Worsted Cl TRWBR BA14 ....123 F2
Worth Cl KGWD/HNM BS15 ....65 E5
Worthing Rd
BRSTK/PCHW BS34 ....26 B2
Worthy La WSM BS23 ....6 E3
Worthy Pl WSM BS23 ....6 D3
Worthy Rd AVONM BS11 ....22 D3
The Worthys ALMDB BS32 ....28 A4
Wotton Rd YATE/CS BS37 ....19 G2
Wrangle Farm Gn CLVDN BS21 ....71 E3
The Wrangle
OMX/HUT/LCK BS24 ....136 C4
Wraxall Gv
BMSTRD/HC/WWD BS13 ....90 A1
Wraxall Hl NAIL BS48 ....74 B1
Wraxall Rd KGWD/HNM BS15 ....65 F5
Wrenbert Rd MANG/FISH BS16 ....54 C3
Wren Cl MANG/FISH BS16 ....53 F1
MTN/WRL BS22 ....136 A3
Wren Ct TRWBR BA14 ....122 C1
Wren Dr MANG/FISH BS16 ....53 G2
Wright Wy MANG/FISH BS16 ....39 H5
Wrington Cl BRSTK/PCHW BS34 ..27 E3
Wrington Crs
BMSTRD/HC/WWD BS13 ....90 B2
Wrington La YTN/CONG BS49 ....129 E1
Wrington Md YTN/CONG BS49 ....129 E1
Wrington Rd YTN/CONG BS49 ....129 F2
Wroughton Dr
BMSTRD/HC/WWD BS13 ....91 E5
Wroughton Gdns
BMSTRD/HC/WWD BS13 ....91 E5
Wroxham Dr
BRSTK/PCHW BS34 ....27 E2
Wyatt Av
BMSTRD/HC/WWD BS13 ....90 A4
Wyatt Cl
BMSTRD/HC/WWD BS13 ....90 A4
Wyatt's Cl NAIL BS48 ....73 E4
Wyatts Vw
BRSG/KWL/STAPK BS4 ....63 F4
Wychwood KGWD/HNM BS15 ....64 C5
Wyck Beck Rd
HNBRY/STHM BS10 ....37 F1
Wycliffe Rd
HNLZ/SM/SNYPK/WT BS9 ....51 E1
Wycliffe Rw BMSTR BS3 * 79 G2
Wycombe Gv
BRSG/KWL/STAPK BS4 ....80 C4
Wye Ct THNB/SVB BS35 ....8 D4
Wye Croft Cl
HNBRY/STHM BS10 ....38 A2
Wyedale Av
HNLZ/SM/SNYPK/WT BS9 ....49 G1
Wyke Rd TRWBR BA14 ....121 F1
Wykis Ct KGWD/HNM BS15 * 82 B1
Wyllie Ct MTN/WRL BS22 ....131 H3
Wymbush Crs
BMSTRD/HC/WWD BS13 ....90 D4
Wymbush Gdns
BMSTRD/HC/WWD BS13 ....90 D4
Wyndham Crs
BRSG/KWL/STAPK BS4 ....81 E3
PTSHD/EG BS20 ....48 A4
Wyndham Wy PTSHD/EG BS20 ....45 H3
The Wynstones
KGWD/HNM BS15 ....64 B4
Wynter Cl MTN/WRL BS22 ....131 H5
Wytherlies Dr
MANG/FISH BS16 ....53 G2
Wyvern Cl WSM BS23 ....7 H5
Wyvern Ms WSM BS23 * 7 J5

Y

Yanleigh Cl
BMSTRD/HC/WWD BS13 ....89 F3
Yanleigh Est LGASH BS41 * 89 E1
Yanley La LGASH BS41 ....77 E5
Yarbury Wy
OMX/HUT/LCK BS24 ....137 E2
Yate Rd YATE/CS BS37 ....19 E3
Yeo Cl WSM BS23 ....139 F1
Yeolands Dr CLVDN BS21 ....70 B4
Yeomans Cl
HNLZ/SM/SNYPK/WT BS9 ....50 A3
Yeomanside Cl
HGRV/WHIT BS14 ....92 B4
Yeoman Wy TRWBR BA14 ....122 D2
Yeomead NAIL BS48 ....73 G3
Yeomeads LGASH BS41 ....76 C5
Yeo Moor CLVDN BS21 ....71 E3
Yeo Valley Wy NAIL BS48 ....74 A4
Yeoward Rd CLVDN BS21 ....71 E4
Yeo Wy CLVDN BS21 ....70 B3
Yerbury St TRWBR BA14 ....121 E5
Yewcroft Cl HGRV/WHIT BS14 ....91 H5
Yew Tree Cl NAIL BS48 * 72 D5
Yew Tree Dr KGWD/HNM BS15 ....55 E5
OMX/HUT/LCK BS24 ....137 E3
Yew Tree Gdns NAIL BS48 ....72 D5
PTSHD/EG BS20 * 48 B4
Yew Tree Pk YTN/CONG BS49 ....128 D3
Yomede Pk CBATH/BATHN BA1 ..107 F5
York Av HORF/LLZ BS7 ....52 A4
York Buildings TRWBR BA14 ....121 E5
York Cl BRSTK/PCHW BS34 ....39 G1
FRCTL/WBN BS36 ....41 G4
MTN/WRL BS22 ....131 H4
YATE/CS BS37 ....20 D3
York Ct CBRISNE BS2 * 61 H3
York Gdns CFTN/FAIL BS8 ....60 C5
FRCTL/WBN BS36 ....29 F2
York Pl CBATH/BATHN BA1 * 109 E4
CBRIS/FH BS1 ....4 C5
CFTN/FAIL BS8 ....4 A4
York Rd BMSTR BS3 ....79 F2
EVILLE/WHL BS5 ....62 D2
MANG/FISH BS16 ....54 D4
RDLND/MONT BS6 ....61 H2
York St CBATH/BATHN BA1 ....3 G5
CBRISNE BS2 ....5 G1
CBRISNE BS2 ....62 B1
CFTN/FAIL BS8 ....60 D1
WSM BS23 ....6 D4
Youngs Ct MANG/FISH BS16 ....42 A5
Youngwood La NAIL BS48 ....84 D3

Z

Zetland Rd RDLND/MONT BS6 ....61 G1
Zig Zag CLVDN BS21 ....70 D1

Index - featured places

The Abbey Hotel
CBATH/BATHN BA1 ....3 G5
Abbey Wood Business Park
BRSTK/PCHW BS34 ....39 E3
Abbotswood Primary School
YATE/CS BS37 ....31 H3
Acton Court
YATE/CS BS37 ....19 E2
Air Balloon Hill J & I School
EVILLE/WHL BS5 ....63 H4
Allen School House
OLD/WMLY/WICK BS30 ....82 D1
All Saints East Clevedon CE
Primary School
CLVDN BS21 ....71 F1
All Saints Exhibition Centre
CBRIS/FH BS1 ....5 F3
Almondsbury Business Centre
ALMDB BS32 ....16 B4
Almondsbury CE Primary
School
ALMDB BS32 ....15 G2
Almondsbury Town FC
ALMDB BS32 ....15 G3
Alveston House Hotel
THNB/SVB BS35 ....11 H2
Amelia Nutt Clinic
BMSTRD/HC/WWD BS13 ....90 A5
Amphitheatre
CBRIS/FH BS1 ....4 D6
Anchor Business Centre
CFTN/FAIL BS8 ....61 E2
Anchor Head Hotel
WSM BS23 ....6 A1
Arc Theatre
TRWBR BA14 ....122 C3
Aretians RFC
BRSTK/PCHW BS34 ....26 D3
Army Training Corps
CLVDN BS21 ....70 C1
Arnolfini
(re-opens summer 2005)
CBRIS/FH BS1 ....4 E6
Arno's Manor Hotel
BRSG/KWL/STAPK BS4 ....80 B3
Arno's Vale Cemetery
BRSG/KWL/STAPK BS4 ....80 A3
Arts Centre Cinema
CBRISNE BS2 ....61 G3
Ashbrook House School
WSM BS23 ....6 D6
Ashcombe Primary School
WSM BS23 ....7 K4
Ashley Down J & I School
HORF/LLZ BS7 ....51 H3
Ashley Down
Old Boys RFC
HORF/LLZ BS7 ....39 E5
Ashley Trading Estate
RDLND/MONT BS6 ....62 A1
Ashmead Industrial Estate
KEYN BS31 ....95 E4
Ashton Court Estate
LGASH BS41 ....77 F2
Ashton Gate Primary School
BMSTR BS3 ....78 B2
Ashton Gate Trading Estate
BMSTR BS3 ....77 H3
Ashton Park School
BMSTR BS3 ....77 H3
Ashton Vale Primary School
BMSTR BS3 ....78 A4
Atlantic Business Park
WSM BS23 ....6 B1
Avonbank Industrial Centre
AVONM BS11 ....48 A1
Avonbridge Trading Estate
AVONM BS11 ....34 D5
Avon Business Park
MANG/FISH BS16 ....53 G5
Avondale Business Centre
MANG/FISH BS16 ....64 B1
Avondale Hotel & Waterside
Restaurant BATHSE BA2 ....110 B1
The Avon Gorge Hotel
CFTN/FAIL BS8 ....60 C5
Avon Gorge Industrial Estate
AVONM BS11 ....48 B1
Avon Gorge Nature Reserve
CFTN/FAIL BS8 ....60 A4
Avonmouth CE Primary
School AVONM BS11 ....34 D5
Avonmouth Medical Centre
AVONM BS11 ....34 C5
Avon Primary School
AVONM BS11 ....35 E5
Avon Riverside Estate
AVONM BS11 ....48 A1
Avonside Industrial Park
CBRISNE BS2 ....62 D5
Avon Trading Estate
CBRISNE BS2 ....79 H1
Avon Valley Country Park
KEYN BS31 ....95 G3
Avon Valley Railway
OLD/WMLY/WICK BS30 ....83 F3
Avon View Cemetery
EVILLE/WHL BS5 ....63 F4
Aztec Hotel
ALMDB BS32 ....15 H5
B6 Sixth Form Centre
KEYN BS31 ....94 A3
Backwell Junior School
NAIL BS48 ....86 B4
Backwell Leisure Centre
NAIL BS48 ....86 A3
Backwell Medical Centre
NAIL BS48 ....86 A3
Backwell RFC
NAIL BS48 ....85 H3
Backwell School
NAIL BS48 ....86 A3
Badminton Junior School
HNLZ/SM/SNYPK/WT BS9 ....50 D3
Badminton Road Trading
Estate
YATE/CS BS37 ....31 F1
Badocks Wood Primary School
HNBRY/STHM BS10 ....37 G5
Baileys Court Primary School
ALMDB BS32 ....27 H4
Balaclava Industrial Estate
MANG/FISH BS16 ....53 G5
Bank Leaze Primary School
AVONM BS11 ....36 A2
Bannerman Road Primary
School
EVILLE/WHL BS5 ....62 C2
Barley Close Primary
MANG/FISH BS16 ....55 F2
Barnack Trading Centre
BMSTR BS3 ....78 D5
Barrow Hospital
NAIL BS48 ....88 D3
Barrs Court Primary School
OLD/WMLY/WICK BS30 ....82 C1
Barton Farm Country Park
BOAV BA15 ....118 D4
Barton Hill Infant School
CBRISNE BS2 ....62 C5

Barton Hill Primary School *EVILLE/WHL* BS5 62 C5
Barton Hill Trading Estate *EVILLE/WHL* BS5 62 C5
Bath Abbey *CBATH/BATHN* BA1 3 G4
Bathampton Primary School *BATHSE* BA2 110 A2
Bath Boating Station *BATHSE* BA2 109 E4
Bath CC *BATHSE* BA2 3 J5
Bath City FC *BATHSE* BA2 113 G1
The Bath Clinic *BATHSE* BA2 115 H5
Bath College of Higher Education *CBATH/BATHN* BA1 108 B3
Bath County Court *CBATH/BATHN* BA1 3 G5
Batheaston CE Primary School *CBATH/BATHN* BA1 103 E5
Batheaston Medical Centre *CBATH/BATHN* BA1 103 E5
Bathford Primary School *CBATH/BATHN* BA1 110 D2
Bath Golf Club *BATHSE* BA2 115 G1
Bath Marina & Caravan Park *BATHSE* BA2 107 E4
Bath Media College *CBATH/BATHN* BA1 3 F3
Bath Natural Health Clinic *CBATH/BATHN* BA1 2 D4
Bath Postal Museum *CBATH/BATHN* BA1 3 F3
The Bath Priory Hotel *CBATH/BATHN* BA1 107 H4
Bath Riverside Business Park *BATHSE* BA2 2 D5
Bath Rugby (Recreation Ground) *BATHSE* BA2 3 H4
The Bath Spa Hotel *BATHSE* BA2 109 F5
Bath Spa University College *BATHSE* BA2 112 A2
Bath Sports & Leisure Centre *BATHSE* BA2 3 H4
Bathwick Cemetery *BATHSE* BA2 115 F2
Bathwick St Mary CE Primary School *BATHSE* BA2 109 F4
Baytree School *MTN/WRL* BS22 135 H3
Beachlands Hotel *WSM* BS23 138 C2
Beacon Rise Primary School *KGWD/HNM* BS15 64 C5
Beazer Garden Maze *CBATH/BATHN* BA1 3 H4
Becket Primary School *MTN/WRL* BS22 136 D1
Becks Business Park *WSM* BS23 7 K5
Bedminster Down School *BMSTRD/HC/WWD* BS13 90 A2
Beechen Cliff School *BATHSE* BA2 114 D3
Beeches Trading Estate *YATE/CS* BS37 19 H5
Beehive Trading Estate *EVILLE/WHL* BS5 63 F4
Begbrook Primary School *MANG/FISH* BS16 53 G2
Berkeley Square Hotel *CFTN/FAIL* BS8 4 B3
Best Western Victoria Square Hotel *CFTN/FAIL* BS8 60 D4
Birdwell Primary School *LGASH* BS41 88 D1
Bishop Road Primary School *HORF/LLZ* BS7 51 G4
Bishopston House Clinic *HORF/LLZ* BS7 51 H4
Bishopsworth CE Junior School *BMSTRD/HC/WWD* BS13 90 A3
Bishopsworth Swimming Pool *BMSTRD/HC/WWD* BS13 90 B3
Bitton Station *OLD/WMLY/WICK* BS30 83 E5
Blackberry Hill Hospital *MANG/FISH* BS16 53 G3
Blackhorse Primary School *MANG/FISH* BS16 41 H5
Blaise Castle House Museum *HNBRY/STHM* BS10 36 D3
Blaise Hamlet (NT) *HNBRY/STHM* BS10 36 C3
Blaise Primary School *HNBRY/STHM* BS10 37 E3
Bonville Business Centre *BRSG/KWL/STAPK* BS4 81 E4
Bonville Trading Estate *BRSG/KWL/STAPK* BS4 81 F4
Book Museum *CBATH/BATHN* BA1 3 H6
Bournville Community Infant School *WSM* BS23 139 E1
Bournville Junior School *WSM* BS23 139 E1
Bowling Alley *CBRISNE* BS2 80 B1
WSM BS23 6 D5
Bowling Hill Business Park *YATE/CS* BS37 32 C1
The Bowl Inn Hotel *ALMDB* BS32 15 G2
Bowsland Green Primary School *ALMDB* BS32 16 B5
Bradford-on-Avon Community Hospital *BOAV* BA15 119 G1
Bradford-on-Avon Swimming Pool *BOAV* BA15 119 F3
Brassmill Lane Trading Estate *BATHSE* BA2 107 F5
Brentry Hospital *HNBRY/STHM* BS10 37 G3
Brentry Primary School *HNBRY/STHM* BS10 37 G2
Briarwood Special School *MANG/FISH* BS16 54 A5
Bridge Farm J & I School *HGRV/WHIT* BS14 91 H5
Bridge Road Business Park *WSM* BS23 7 H6
The Brigstow Hotel *CBRIS/FH* BS1 5 F4
Brimsham Green School *YATE/CS* BS37 20 C3
Brislington Retail Park *BRSG/KWL/STAPK* BS4 80 D5
Brislington School *BRSG/KWL/STAPK* BS4 93 E1
Brislington Trading Estate *BRSG/KWL/STAPK* BS4 80 D4
Bristol & Clifton Golf Club *CFTN/FAIL* BS8 76 B1
Bristol Arena (area under development) *BRSG/KWL/STAPK* BS4 5 K7
Bristol Business Park *MANG/FISH* BS16 39 H4
Bristol Cathedral *CBRIS/FH* BS1 4 D5
Bristol Cathedral School *CBRIS/FH* BS1 4 C5
Bristol City FC (Ashton Gate) *BMSTR* BS3 78 A3
Bristol City Museum & Art Gallery *CFTN/FAIL* BS8 4 C3
Bristol Civil Service Sports Club *HORF/LLZ* BS7 52 A2
Bristol County Court *CBRISNE* BS2 4 E2
Bristol County Sports Club *CBRIS/FH* BS1 4 D3
Bristol Crown Court *CBRIS/FH* BS1 4 E3
Bristol Dental Hospital *CBRIS/FH* BS1 5 F2
Bristol Gateway School *CBRISNE* BS2 62 B1
Bristol General Hospital *CBRIS/FH* BS1 5 F7
Bristol Golf Club *THNB/SVB* BS35 25 F2
Bristol Grammar Lower School *CFTN/FAIL* BS8 4 B2
Bristol Grammar School *CFTN/FAIL* BS8 4 C2
Bristol Harlequins RFC *BRSG/KWL/STAPK* BS4 81 F4
Bristol Ice Rink *CBRIS/FH* BS1 4 D4
Bristol Industrial Museum *CBRIS/FH* BS1 4 D7
Bristol International Airport *NAIL* BS48 96 B5
Bristol Marriott *CBRISNE* BS2 5 H3
Bristol Marriott Royal Hotel *CBRIS/FH* BS1 4 D5
Bristol North Baths *HORF/LLZ* BS7 51 G5
Bristol & North Somerset Sports Club *CFTN/FAIL* BS8 76 A3
Bristol Old Vic (New Vic Theatre & Theatre Royal) *CBRIS/FH* BS1 4 E4
Bristol Old Vic Theatre School *CFTN/FAIL* BS8 60 D2
Bristol Rovers FC & Bristol RFC (Memorial Stadium) *HORF/LLZ* BS7 52 A2
Bristol Rovers FC *BRSG/KWL/STAPK* BS4 81 E5
Bristol Royal Hospital for Sick Children *CBRISNE* BS2 4 D2
Bristol Royal Infirmary *CBRISNE* BS2 4 E1
Bristol South Swimming Pool *BMSTR* BS3 78 D2
Bristol Steiner School *RDLND/MONT* BS6 61 E1
Bristol Vale Trading Estate *BMSTR* BS3 78 C5
Bristol Zoo Gardens *CFTN/FAIL* BS8 60 C2
British Empire & Commonwealth Museum *CBRIS/FH* BS1 5 H6
Broadlands School *KEYN* BS31 94 A3
Broadmead Lane Industrial Estate *KEYN* BS31 94 D2
Broadoak Community School *WSM* BS23 138 C3
Broadwalk Shopping Centre *BRSG/KWL/STAPK* BS4 80 A4
Broadway Infant School *YATE/CS* BS37 21 F5
Brockeridge Infant School *FRCTL/WBN* BS36 30 A3
Brock Street Clinic *CBATH/BATHN* BA1 2 E2
Brockway Medical Centre *NAIL* BS48 73 G4
Bromley Heath J & I School *MANG/FISH* BS16 41 F5
Brooklea Clinic *BRSG/KWL/STAPK* BS4 80 D1
Broomhill J & I School *BRSG/KWL/STAPK* BS4 81 E3
Bryer Ash Business Park *TRWBR* BA14 120 D5
The Building of Bath Museum *CBATH/BATHN* BA1 3 F2
Burnbush Primary School *HGRV/WHIT* BS14 92 C4
Burnett Business Park *KEYN* BS31 104 D3
Bush Industrial Estate *EVILLE/WHL* BS5 63 E3
Butcombe Pre-Prep School *CFTN/FAIL* BS8 60 D3
BW Estates *OMX/HUT/LCK* BS24 139 F3
Cabot Primary School *CBRISNE* BS2 62 A3
Cabot Tower *CFTN/FAIL* BS8 4 B4
Cadbury Camp *CLVDN* BS21 72 B1
Cadbury Heath Health Centre *OLD/WMLY/WICK* BS30 82 D1
Cadbury Heath Primary School *OLD/WMLY/WICK* BS30 65 G5
Callicroft Infant School *BRSTK/PCHW* BS34 26 B2
Callicroft Junior School *BRSTK/PCHW* BS34 26 A2
Canford Crematorium *HNLZ/SM/SNYPK/WT* BS9 50 B1
Canons House *CBRIS/FH* BS1 4 D6
Carla Trading Estate *BMSTR* BS3 78 A3
Carlyle Business Centre *CBRISNE* BS2 62 B5
Carmel Christian Centre & School *BRSG/KWL/STAPK* BS4 81 E5
Carrick Business Park *BRSG/KWL/STAPK* BS4 81 E5
Castle Batch Primary School *MTN/WRL* BS22 131 H3
Castlemead Shopping Centre *MTN/WRL* BS22 131 H3
Castle Place Leisure Centre *TRWBR* BA14 123 E1
Castle Place Shopping Centre *TRWBR* BA14 123 E1
The Castle School *THNB/SVB* BS35 8 C2
Central Trading Estate *BRSG/KWL/STAPK* BS4 80 A2
Centurion Hotel *RDSTK/MIDN* BA3 124 D5
Chandag J & I School *KEYN* BS31 94 D5
Chandos Trading Estate *CBRISNE* BS2 79 H1
Charborough Road Primary School *BRSTK/PCHW* BS34 38 C3
Charlotte Keel Health Clinic *EVILLE/WHL* BS5 62 B2
Chatterton House *CBRIS/FH* BS1 5 G6
Cheddar Grove Primary School *BMSTRD/HC/WWD* BS13 90 B1
Cherry Garden Primary School *OLD/WMLY/WICK* BS30 83 E4
Chesterfield Hospital *CFTN/FAIL* BS8 60 D5
Chester Park J & I School *MANG/FISH* BS16 53 H5
Chipping Edge Estate *YATE/CS* BS37 32 D1
Chipping Sodbury Golf Club *YATE/CS* BS37 21 H4
Chipping Sodbury School *YATE/CS* BS37 32 D2
Chittening Industrial Estate *AVONM* BS11 22 D3
Christchurch CE Junior School *MANG/FISH* BS16 54 C3
Christ Church CE Primary School *BOAV* BA15 119 G2
Christchurch CE Primary School *KGWD/HNM* BS15 81 G2
Christ Church CE VC Infant School *MANG/FISH* BS16 54 C3
Christ Church Primary School *WSM* BS23 7 F3
Christ the King RC Primary School *THNB/SVB* BS35 8 D3
Church Farm Business Park *BATHSE* BA2 105 H5
Churchill Business Park *WSM* BS23 7 J5
Cineworld *BRSG/KWL/STAPK* BS4 91 F3
The City Academy-Bristol *EVILLE/WHL* BS5 62 D3
City Business Park *CBRIS/FH* BS1 5 F3
City Inn Hotel *CBRIS/FH* BS1 5 H5
City of Bath College *CBATH/BATHN* BA1 3 F5
City of Bristol College (Bedminster Centre) *BMSTR* BS3 79 F4
City of Bristol College (Brunel Centre) *HORF/LLZ* BS7 52 A4
City of Bristol College (College Green Centre) *CFTN/FAIL* BS8 4 B5
City of Bristol College (Downend Centre) *MANG/FISH* BS16 41 H5
City of Bristol College (Folly Lane Centre) *CBRISNE* BS2 62 B5
City of Bristol College (Hartcliffe Centre) *BMSTRD/HC/WWD* BS13 91 E5
City of Bristol College (Kingswood Centre) *KGWD/HNM* BS15 64 D3
City of Bristol College (Lawrence Weston Centre) *AVONM* BS11 36 A4
City of Bristol College (Parkway Transport Technology Centre) *BRSTK/PCHW* BS34 39 G2
City of Bristol College (Soundwell Centre) *MANG/FISH* BS16 64 D1
City & Port of Bristol Social & Sports Club *AVONM* BS11 48 D3
Civil Service Sports Club *BATHSE* BA2 115 H5
Claremont Special School *RDLND/MONT* BS6 51 F3
The Clarendon School *TRWBR* BA14 122 C3
Claverham CC *YTN/CONG* BS49 126 D4
Clevedon Community School *CLVDN* BS21 68 D5
Clevedon Court (NT) *CLVDN* BS21 71 G1
Clevedon Craft Centre *CLVDN* BS21 71 G3
Clevedon Fruit Market *CLVDN* BS21 70 D2
Clevedon Golf Club *CLVDN* BS21 68 D3
Clevedon Health Centre *CLVDN* BS21 71 E2
Clevedon Hospital *CLVDN* BS21 71 E2
Clevedon Pier *CLVDN* BS21 68 A5
Cleve House School *BRSG/KWL/STAPK* BS4 80 A3
Clifton Cathedral Church *CFTN/FAIL* BS8 60 D3
Clifton Clinic *CFTN/FAIL* BS8 60 D4
Clifton College *CFTN/FAIL* BS8 60 C3
Clifton College Preparatory School *CFTN/FAIL* BS8 60 C2
Clifton College Sports Club *CFTN/FAIL* BS8 59 G4
Clifton Down Shopping Centre *CFTN/FAIL* BS8 61 E2
Clifton High School & Lower School *CFTN/FAIL* BS8 60 C4
Clifton Hotel *CFTN/FAIL* BS8 4 A2
Clifton RC *HNBRY/STHM* BS10 24 D5
Coates Industrial Estate *NAIL* BS48 73 G3
College House *MANG/FISH* BS16 53 H3
Colston Hall *CBRIS/FH* BS1 4 E3
Colstons Collegiate School *MANG/FISH* BS16 52 D4
Colstons Girls School *RDLND/MONT* BS6 61 H2
Colstons Primary School *RDLND/MONT* BS6 61 F2
Combe Down CE Primary School *BATHSE* BA2 117 F1
Combe Down RFC *BATHSE* BA2 115 E5
Commodore Hotel *MTN/WRL* BS22 130 A5
Community Mental Health Centre *CLVDN* BS21 70 C1
The Compton Clinic *RDLND/MONT* BS6 50 D4
Coniston Primary School *BRSTK/PCHW* BS34 26 B1
Connaught Primary School *BRSG/KWL/STAPK* BS4 91 F1
Conygre Medical Centre *BRSTK/PCHW* BS34 38 D2
Corbett House Clinic *EVILLE/WHL* BS5 62 C4
Corpus Christi RC Primary School *WSM* BS23 6 D7
Cossham Memorial Hospital *KGWD/HNM* BS15 64 B1
Cotham Park RFC *CFTN/FAIL* BS8 59 F5
Cotham School *RDLND/MONT* BS6 61 F2
Court De Wyck Primary School *YTN/CONG* BS49 127 F2
Courtney Primary School *KGWD/HNM* BS15 65 E4
Craft Centre *CLVDN* BS21 71 G3
Cranleigh Court Infant School *YATE/CS* BS37 20 C4
Cribbs Causeway Regional Shopping Centre *BRSTK/PCHW* BS34 25 H4
Cribbs Causeway Retail Park *BRSTK/PCHW* BS34 25 G4
Crockerne CE Primary School *PTSHD/EG* BS20 48 B5
Crofts End Industrial Estate *EVILLE/WHL* BS5 63 F2
The Cross Bath (Thermae Bath Spa) *CBATH/BATHN* BA1 3 F5
Crossways J & I School *THNB/SVB* BS35 9 E3
Crown Industrial Estate *OLD/WMLY/WICK* BS30 65 G5
Culverhay School *BATHSE* BA2 113 G5
Culverhay Sports Centre *BATHSE* BA2 113 G5
Culverhill School *YATE/CS* BS37 31 H3
Curzon Cinema *CLVDN* BS21 70 C2
Custom House *CBRIS/FH* BS1 5 F5
Days Inn Hotel *PTSHD/EG* BS20 47 G4
Deers Wood Primary School *KGWD/HNM* BS15 65 F1
Devon Road Trading Estate *EVILLE/WHL* BS5 62 D2
Dixon Business Centre *BRSG/KWL/STAPK* BS4 81 E4
Docks Industrial Estate *AVONM* BS11 23 E2
Dolphin Square Shopping Centre *WSM* BS23 6 C5
Douglas Road Industrial Park *KGWD/HNM* BS15 64 C3
Downend CC *MANG/FISH* BS16 54 C2
Downend Lower School *MANG/FISH* BS16 54 D3
Downend School *MANG/FISH* BS16 55 E1
Downs Fitness & Health Centre *RDLND/MONT* BS6 60 D1
Drove Road Hospital *WSM* BS23 139 E1
Duckmoor Road Industrial Estate *BMSTR* BS3 78 B2
Dundry CE Primary School *LGASH* BS41 98 C2
Dunmail Primary School *HNBRY/STHM* BS10 37 H3
Eagles Wood Business Park *ALMDB* BS32 16 A4
Easton Business Centre *EVILLE/WHL* BS5 62 C3
Easton CE Primary School *EVILLE/WHL* BS5 62 B3
Easton Leisure Centre *EVILLE/WHL* BS5 62 B3
Eastpark Trading Estate *EVILLE/WHL* BS5 63 E2
Eastville Health Centre *EVILLE/WHL* BS5 62 C1
Eldonwall Trading Estate *CBRISNE* BS2 80 B1
Elmcross Business Park *BOAV* BA15 119 G5
Elmfield Special School *HNBRY/STHM* BS10 37 G5
Elmlea J & I School *HNLZ/SM/SNYPK/WT* BS9 50 C3
Elm Park Primary School *FRCTL/WBN* BS36 29 E4
Embleton Primary School *HNBRY/STHM* BS10 37 G4
Emmaus School *TRWBR* BA14 120 D1
Exhibition Centre *CBRIS/FH* BS1 4 D6
Explore-at-Bristol *CBRIS/FH* BS1 4 D5
Express by Holiday Inn *BATHSE* BA2 2 C5
Express by Holiday Inn *BRSTK/PCHW* BS34 39 F2
Express by Holiday Inn *CBRIS/FH* BS1 5 H6
The Eye Clinic *CBRIS/FH* BS1 5 G2
Fairfield High School *RDLND/MONT* BS6 62 A1
Fairfield Park Health Centre *CBATH/BATHN* BA1 109 E3
Fairfield PNEU School *NAIL* BS48 86 B3
Fair Furlong Primary School *BMSTRD/HC/WWD* BS13 90 B5
Fairway Industrial Centre *BRSTK/PCHW* BS34 38 C2
Falconride Primary School *KGWD/HNM* BS15 64 D2
Ferry Steps Industrial Estate *BRSG/KWL/STAPK* BS4 79 H2
Fieldways Hotel & Health Club *TRWBR* BA14 121 G4
Filton Airfield *HNBRY/STHM* BS10 25 H5
Filton Avenue J & I School *HORF/LLZ* BS7 52 B1
Filton Clinic *HORF/LLZ* BS7 38 D3
Filton College *BRSTK/PCHW* BS34 38 D1
Filton Golf Club *BRSTK/PCHW* BS34 38 B1
Filton High School *BRSTK/PCHW* BS34 39 G2
Filton Hill Primary School *BRSTK/PCHW* BS34 39 E1
Filton Recreation Centre *BRSTK/PCHW* BS34 38 D3
Filwood Swimming Baths *BRSG/KWL/STAPK* BS4 91 F1
Fishponds Health Centre *MANG/FISH* BS16 54 A4
Fishponds Trading Estate *EVILLE/WHL* BS5 63 G1
Fitzmaurice Primary School *BOAV* BA15 119 G4
Five C Business Centre *CLVDN* BS21 70 B4
Flax Bourton Magistrates Court *NAIL* BS48 87 G1
Florence Brown Community School *BRSG/KWL/STAPK* BS4 91 E1
Folk House *CBRIS/FH* BS1 4 D3
Fonthill Primary School *HNBRY/STHM* BS10 38 B3
Fosseway Golf Course *RDSTK/MIDN* BA3 124 D5
Fosse Way Special School *RDSTK/MIDN* BA3 124 D4
Foster Almshouses *CBRIS/FH* BS1 4 E3
Four Acres Primary School *BMSTRD/HC/WWD* BS13 89 H5
Frampton Cotterell CE Prmary School *FRCTL/WBN* BS36 29 G2
The Francis Hotel *CBATH/BATHN* BA1 3 F4
Frenchay CE Primary School *MANG/FISH* BS16 54 A1
Frenchay Hospital *MANG/FISH* BS16 40 C5
Frenchay Village Museum *MANG/FISH* BS16 40 B5

Frome Bank Junior School YATE/CS BS37 20 C4
Fromeside Clinic MANG/FISH BS16 53 G3
Fulford Centre BMSTRD/HC/WWD BS13 90 D5
Gay Elms Primary School BMSTRD/HC/WWD BS13 90 A5
Georgian House No 1 CBATH/BATHN BA1 2 D2
The Georgian House CBRIS/FH BS1 4 C4
Gillingstool Primary School THNB/SVB BS35 8 C4
The Glebe Infant School YTN/CONG BS49 128 C2
Glencoe Business Park WSM BS23 7 K5
Glenfrome Primary School EVILLE/WHL BS5 52 C4
Gloucestershire CCC (County Ground) HORF/LLZ BS7 51 H4
Glynne Wickham Studio Theatre CFTN/FAIL BS8 4 D3
Golden Valley Primary School NAIL BS48 73 G4
Gordano RFC PTSHD/EG BS20 46 D5
Gordano School PTSHD/EG BS20 45 G5
Gracefield Preparatory School MANG/FISH BS16 54 A3
Granby House Clinic BMSTR BS3 78 D3
Grand Pier WSM BS23 6 C4
The Grange School & Sports College OLD/WMLY/WICK BS30 65 G4
Great Western Business Park YATE/CS BS37 20 B4
Greenbank Cemetery EVILLE/WHL BS5 63 E1
Green Park Station CBATH/BATHN BA1 2 D4
Greystoke Business Centre PTSHD/EG BS20 45 G4
Grove Industrial Estate BRSTK/PCHW BS34 26 D3
Grove Junior School NAIL BS48 85 E1
Grove Primary School TRWBR BA14 122 C4
Grove Road Day Hospital CFTN/FAIL BS8 60 D1
Grove Sports Centre NAIL BS48 85 E1
Hambrook Primary School MANG/FISH BS16 41 E2
Hambrook Sports Club MANG/FISH BS16 41 E2
Hampset Cricket Club BATHSE BA2 114 A5
Hanham Abbots Junior School KGWD/HNM BS15 81 H2
Hanham Business Park KGWD/HNM BS15 81 G1
Hanham High School KGWD/HNM BS15 81 H2
Hannah More Infant School NAIL BS48 85 E1
Hannah More Primary School CBRISNE BS2 5 K4
Harbour Road Trading Estate PTSHD/EG BS20 45 H2
Hareclive Primary School BMSTRD/HC/WWD BS13 90 D5
Haringtons Hotel CBATH/BATHN BA1 3 F4
Hartcliffe Health Centre BMSTRD/HC/WWD BS13 90 D5
Hartcliffe School BMSTRD/HC/WWD BS13 91 F5
Harveys Wine Museum CBRIS/FH BS1 4 D4
Haslemere Industrial Estate AVONM BS11 34 D2
Hawkfield Business Park BMSTRD/HC/WWD BS13 91 F4
Hawkins Clinic CBATH/BATHN BA1 3 F4
Hawthorne Industrial Estate RDSTK/MIDN BA3 124 D4
Haycombe Cemetery BATHSE BA2 113 E3
Haydon Industrial Estate RDSTK/MIDN BA3 125 G4
Hayesfield School (Lower) BATHSE BA2 2 C5
Hayesfield School Technology College BATHSE BA2 2 C6
Hayward Road Industrial Estate MANG/FISH BS16 54 C5
Headley Park Primary School BMSTRD/HC/WWD BS13 90 C3
Heath House Priory Hospital HORF/LLZ BS7 52 C4
The Helicopter Museum OMX/HUT/LCK BS24 140 B1
Henbury Court Primary School HNBRY/STHM BS10 36 D2
Henbury Golf Club HNBRY/STHM BS10 36 D4
Henbury Lodge Hotel HNBRY/STHM BS10 36 D3
Henbury Old Boys AFC HNBRY/STHM BS10 37 E3
Henbury School HNBRY/STHM BS10 36 D2
Henbury Swimming Pool HNBRY/STHM BS10 37 E2
Henfield Business Park FRCTL/WBN BS36 42 C3
Hengrove Community College/Post 16 Centre HGRV/WHIT BS14 92 A2
Hengrove Leisure Park BRSG/KWL/STAPK BS4 91 F3
Henleaze J & I School RDLND/MONT BS6 51 F3
Heritage Centre WSM BS23 6 D3
Heron's Moor Primary School OMX/HUT/LCK BS24 136 D3
Herschel House Museum CBATH/BATHN BA1 2 E4
Hetling Pump Room (Thermae Bath Spa) CBATH/BATHN BA1 3 F5
Heywood Health Centre PTSHD/EG BS20 48 B4
Highcroft Junior School FRCTL/WBN BS36 30 A2
High Down Junior School PTSHD/EG BS20 44 D4
Highridge Infant School BMSTRD/HC/WWD BS13 90 A3
Hillcrest Primary School BRSG/KWL/STAPK BS4 79 H3
Hillfield Primary School MANG/FISH BS16 54 B5
Hill Fort CBATH/BATHN BA1 102 C5
Hillside First School MTN/WRL BS22 136 B1
Hilperton CE Primary School TRWBR BA14 121 H3
Hippodrome Theatre CBRIS/FH BS1 4 E4
Hither Green Industrial Estate CLVDN BS21 71 F2
HM Prison HORF/LLZ BS7 51 G3
Holbrook Primary School TRWBR BA14 123 E3
Holburne Museum of Art BATHSE BA2 3 J2
Holiday Inn MANG/FISH BS16 40 A3
Holloway Dental Health Centre HGRV/WHIT BS14 92 D4
Holy Cross Primary School BMSTR BS3 78 D2
Holy Family RC Primary School BRSTK/PCHW BS34 26 D2
Holymead Infant School BRSG/KWL/STAPK BS4 80 C4
Holymead Junior School BRSG/KWL/STAPK BS4 80 C3
Holy Trinity Primary School ALMDB BS32 16 A4
Homefield Industrial Estate OMX/HUT/LCK BS24 140 D1
Homeopathic Hospital CFTN/FAIL BS8 61 F3
Horfield Health Centre HORF/LLZ BS7 52 B2
Horfield Primary School HNBRY/STHM BS10 51 G1
Horfield Sports Centre HORF/LLZ BS7 52 A1
Hornets RFC WSM BS23 135 H4
Hotbath Gallery CBATH/BATHN BA1 3 F5
Hot Bath (Thermae Bath Spa) CBATH/BATHN BA1 3 F5
Hotel du Vin & Bistro CBRIS/FH BS1 4 E3
Hotspots Indoor Sports Centre BRSG/KWL/STAPK BS4 81 E4
Hotwells Primary School CFTN/FAIL BS8 60 C5
Hutton Moor Leisure Centre WSM BS23 135 G4
Hutton Primary School OMX/HUT/LCK BS24 140 B4
Hydro Estate AVONM BS11 34 C2
Ilminster Avenue Primary School BRSG/KWL/STAPK BS4 91 H1
IKEA Bristol EVILLE/WHL BS5 52 C5
IMAX Theatre-at-Bristol CBRIS/FH BS1 4 D5
Industrial Camwal Estate CBRISNE BS2 79 H1
Iron Acton CE Primary School YATE/CS BS37 19 F3
Jane Austen Museum CBATH/BATHN BA1 3 F3
John Cabot City Technology College KGWD/HNM BS15 64 B4
The John Milton Health Clinic HNBRY/STHM BS10 37 F2
The John of Gaunt School TRWBR BA14 122 C2
John Wesley's Chapel (The New Room) CBRIS/FH BS1 5 G2
Jorrocks Estate YATE/CS BS37 43 H1
Jubilee Public Baths BRSG/KWL/STAPK BS4 80 A4
Jurys Bristol Hotel CBRIS/FH BS1 4 E5
The Kendleshire Golf Club FRCTL/WBN BS36 42 B1
Kenn Business Park CLVDN BS21 71 E5
Kewstoke Primary School MTN/WRL BS22 130 C5
Keynsham Hospital KEYN BS31 94 C5
Keynsham Leisure Centre KEYN BS31 94 C4
Keynsham Primary School KEYN BS31 94 A4
Keynsham RFC KEYN BS31 94 A2
Keynsham Town FC KEYN BS31 94 A2
Kilmersdon Magistrates Court RDSTK/MIDN BA3 125 F2
King Edmund Community School YATE/CS BS37 31 H1
King Edward Pre Prep School CBATH/BATHN BA1 107 H4
King Edwards Junior School BATHSE BA2 109 F5
King Edwards School BATHSE BA2 109 F5
Kings Business Park CBRISNE BS2 62 D5
Kings Chase Shopping Centre KGWD/HNM BS15 64 C3
Kings Court Primary School YATE/CS BS37 32 A2
Kingsdown Sports Centre RDLND/MONT BS6 61 F2
Kingsfield School KGWD/HNM BS15 65 F3
Kingshill CE Primary School NAIL BS48 73 E3
Kingsland Trading Estate CBRISNE BS2 5 K4
Kingsweston Special School AVONM BS11 35 H5
Kingswood Borough Council MANG/FISH BS16 54 C4
Kingswood Health Centre KGWD/HNM BS15 64 D3
Kingswood Leisure Centre MANG/FISH BS16 54 C5
Kingswood Preparatory School CBATH/BATHN BA1 108 B3
Kingswood School CBATH/BATHN BA1 108 B2
Kingswood Trading Estate KGWD/HNM BS15 64 C2
Knightcott Industrial Estate OMX/HUT/LCK BS24 141 G4
Knowle Golf Club BRSG/KWL/STAPK BS4 92 C1
Knowle Park J & I School BRSG/KWL/STAPK BS4 79 H5
Lambretta Scooter Museum WSM BS23 7 F3
Lancaster House School WSM BS23 7 G2
Lansdown Cemetery CBATH/BATHN BA1 108 A1
Lansdown Cricket Club CBATH/BATHN BA1 107 G4
The Lansdown Grove Hotel CBATH/BATHN BA1 108 C4
Larkhall FC CBATH/BATHN BA1 109 E1
Larkrise School TRWBR BA14 121 F5
Lauriston Hotel WSM BS23 6 C2
Lawnwood Road Industrial Estate EVILLE/WHL BS5 62 C3
Lawrence Hill Health Centre CBRISNE BS2 62 B4
Lawrence Hill Industrial Estate EVILLE/WHL BS5 62 D3
Lawrence Hill Industrial Park EVILLE/WHL BS5 62 C3
Leigh Court Business Centre CFTN/FAIL BS8 59 F1
Leigh Park Hotel BOAV BA15 119 G1
Leisure Pavilion WSM BS23 6 B4
Liberty Industrial Park BMSTR BS3 78 A5
Life Boat Station WSM BS23 134 A1
Lime Grove Special School BATHSE BA2 3 J5
Little Stoke Primary School BRSTK/PCHW BS34 27 F4
Little Theatre Cinema CBATH/BATHN BA1 3 F5
Locking Farm Industrial Estate OMX/HUT/LCK BS24 140 D1
Locking Primary School OMX/HUT/LCK BS24 141 E2
Locking Road Business Park WSM BS23 7 J5
Lockleaze School HORF/LLZ BS7 39 F5
Locksbrook Cemetery CBATH/BATHN BA1 107 H5
Locksbrook Road Trading Estate CBATH/BATHN BA1 113 H1
Lodge Causeway Trading Estate MANG/FISH BS16 53 G5
Long Ashton Business Park LGASH BS41 77 E5
Long Ashton Golf Club CFTN/FAIL BS8 76 B3
Longbrook Trading Estate BMSTR BS3 77 H3
Longmeadow Primary School TRWBR BA14 123 E2
Longton Industrial Estate WSM BS23 7 J6
Longvernal Primary School RDSTK/MIDN BA3 124 A3
Longwell Green CP School OLD/WMLY/WICK BS30 82 C3
Lonsdale Business Centre KGWD/HNM BS15 64 B1
Lord Chancellors Department CBRIS/FH BS1 5 F3
Luckwell Primary School BMSTR BS3 78 B3
Madeira Cove Hotel WSM BS23 6 A1
Maes Knoll Fort HGRV/WHIT BS14 100 D3
Malago Vale Trading Estate BMSTR BS3 79 E3
The Mall Galleries CBRIS/FH BS1 5 G2
The Maltings Industrial Estate CBATH/BATHN BA1 107 F5
Mangotsfield CE Primary School MANG/FISH BS16 55 G2
Mangotsfield Golf Club MANG/FISH BS16 55 H5
Mangotsfield School MANG/FISH BS16 55 G4
Mangotsfield United FC MANG/FISH BS16 55 G3
Manor Brook Primary School THNB/SVB BS35 8 C1
Manor Farm AFC HNLZ/SM/SNYPK/WT BS9 49 G3
The Manor CE Primary School FRCTL/WBN BS36 30 A4
Margaret Coates Special School BATHSE BA2 116 C2
Margaret Stancomb Infants School TRWBR BA14 120 D5
Maritime Heritage Centre CBRIS/FH BS1 4 B6
Market Industrial Estate YTN/CONG BS49 126 B2
Marlwood School THNB/SVB BS35 11 F2
Mary Elton Primary School CLVDN BS21 70 B4
May Park Primary School EVILLE/WHL BS5 62 D1
Meadowbrook Primary School ALMDB BS32 27 G2
Meadow School OLD/WMLY/WICK BS30 95 G1
Mead Vale Primary School MTN/WRL BS22 136 B2
Mendip Green First School MTN/WRL BS22 136 B2
Mendip Leisure Centre PTSHD/EG BS20 45 G4
Menzies Waterside Hotel BATHSE BA2 3 H6
Midland Way Business Park THNB/SVB BS35 8 C4
Midsomer Norton Primary School RDSTK/MIDN BA3 124 B3
Millennium Square CBRIS/FH BS1 4 D6
Millpond Primary School EVILLE/WHL BS5 62 B2
Milsom Street Clinic CBATH/BATHN BA1 3 F3
Milton CP Infant School MTN/WRL BS22 135 G2
Milton Junior School MTN/WRL BS22 135 H2
Minto Road Industrial Centre RDLND/MONT BS6 62 A1
Mizzymead Recreation Centre NAIL BS48 73 F5
Model Yacht Pond WSM BS23 6 C3
Monks Park School HORF/LLZ BS7 38 C4
Monkton Combe Junior School BATHSE BA2 117 H1
Monkton Combe Pre-Prep School BATHSE BA2 117 G1
Monkton Farleigh & South Wraxall CE VC Primary School BOAV BA15 111 F5
Montpelier Health Centre RDLND/MONT BS6 61 H2
Moorlands J & I School BATHSE BA2 114 A4
The Mount CBATH/BATHN BA1 103 H4
Mount Zion School RDLND/MONT BS6 61 G2
Museum of Asian Art CBATH/BATHN BA1 2 E2
Museum of Bath at Work CBATH/BATHN BA1 3 F1
Museum of Costume CBATH/BATHN BA1 3 F2
Museum of Costume & Fashion Research Centre CBATH/BATHN BA1 2 E3
Nailsea Health Centre NAIL BS48 73 F4
Nailsea School NAIL BS48 73 G5
Natural Health Clinic RDLND/MONT BS6 61 E3
Nature Reserve CBATH/BATHN BA1 110 D3
Netham Industrial Estate EVILLE/WHL BS5 63 E4
Netham Industrial Park EVILLE/WHL BS5 63 E4
Netham Park Industrial Estate EVILLE/WHL BS5 63 E5
Newbridge Junior School CBATH/BATHN BA1 107 G5
Newbridge St Johns CE Infant School CBATH/BATHN BA1 107 G5
Newbridge Trading Estate BRSG/KWL/STAPK BS4 63 E5
New Fosseway Special School HGRV/WHIT BS14 92 A2
New Ocean Hotel WSM BS23 6 A1
New Royal Bath (Thermae Bath Spa) CBATH/BATHN BA1 3 F5
New Siblands Special School THNB/SVB BS35 9 E3
Newton Mill Caravan & Camping Park BATHSE BA2 113 E1
Newton Park College BATHSE BA2 112 A2
Newtown Community Primary School TRWBR BA14 122 D1
Norland College CBATH/BATHN BA1 109 E4
Northavon Business Centre YATE/CS BS37 20 B4
North Avon Magistrates Court YATE/CS BS37 31 H1
North Bristol RFC ALMDB BS32 15 G4
Northleaze Primary School LGASH BS41 77 E4
Northridge Business Centre YATE/CS BS37 20 B5
North Road Primary School YATE/CS BS37 20 A3
North Worle Shopping Centre MTN/WRL BS22 132 A5
Norton Hill School RDSTK/MIDN BA3 124 B4
Norton Radstock College RDSTK/MIDN BA3 125 G2
Novers Hill Trading Estate BMSTR BS3 78 D5
Novers Lane J & I School BRSG/KWL/STAPK BS4 90 D2
Oakfield Business Park KGWD/HNM BS15 64 C4
The Oaklands Business Park YATE/CS BS37 19 H4
Oatley Trading Estate KGWD/HNM BS15 64 C2
Odd Down FC BATHSE BA2 116 A2
Odeon Cinema CBATH/BATHN BA1 2 E5
CBRIS/FH BS1 5 G3
WSM BS23 6 E4
Old Bristolians Sports Club CFTN/FAIL BS8 76 C2
Oldbury Court Primary School MANG/FISH BS16 54 B1
Old Culverhaysians RFC BATHSE BA2 116 A1
Oldfield Old Boys RFC BATHSE BA2 2 D6
Oldfield Park Infant School BATHSE BA2 2 B5
Oldfield Park Junior School BATHSE BA2 113 H3
Oldfield School CBATH/BATHN BA1 107 E3
Old Knightstone Theatre WSM BS23 6 A2
Oldmixon Primary School OMX/HUT/LCK BS24 139 F4
Oldown Country Park ALMDB BS32 10 C3
Olveston CE Primary School THNB/SVB BS35 10 A4
Open University CBRIS/FH BS1 5 G6
Optimax Laser Eye Clinic CBRIS/FH BS1 4 E4
Oral Health Centre CBATH/BATHN BA1 3 F3
The Orchard Medical Centre KGWD/HNM BS15 64 C3
Orchard View (Ham Green Hospital) PTSHD/EG BS20 48 D4
Our Lady of Lourdes RC Primary School KGWD/HNM BS15 64 D4
Our Lady of the Rosary RC Primary School AVONM BS11 35 H4
Paragon School BATHSE BA2 114 D4
Parish Wharf Leisure Centre PTSHD/EG BS20 45 H2
Park House Clinic RDSTK/MIDN BA3 124 B4
The Park School KGWD/HNM BS15 64 D3
Parkside Infant School CBATH/BATHN BA1 2 E3
Parkwall Primary School OLD/WMLY/WICK BS30 82 D1
Parkway Trading Estate CBRISNE BS2 62 A1
Parnall Road Industrial Estate MANG/FISH BS16 53 H5
Parson Street Primary School BMSTR BS3 78 D4
Patchway CE Primary School BRSTK/PCHW BS34 27 E1
Patchway Health Clinic BRSTK/PCHW BS34 26 C2

atchway High School ALMDB BS32 26 D1
atchway Trading Estate BRSTK/PCHW BS34 25 H2
axcroft Primary School TRWBR BA14 121 G5
embroke Road Surgery CFTN/FAIL BS8 60 D2
erry Court Junior School HGRV/WHIT BS14 91 H3
etherton Road Infant School HGRV/WHIT BS14 91 H2
hoenix Business Park BMSTR BS3 78 B4
icturedrome Cinema RDLND/MONT BS6 50 D4
he Picture House CBRIS/FH BS1 5 G1
ilning CP School THNB/SVB BS35 13 G3
ines Way Industrial Estate BATHSE BA2 2 D5
izey Avenue Industrial Estate CLVDN BS21 70 B3
layhouse Theatre WSM BS23 6 D2
The Podium Shopping Centre & Library CBATH/BATHN BA1 3 G3
Portbury Sawmills Industrial Estate PTSHD/EG BS20 47 G1
Portishead Business Park PTSHD/EG BS20 45 G2
Portishead Health Centre PTSHD/EG BS20 45 G3
Portishead Primary School PTSHD/EG BS20 45 H2
Portview Trading Estate AVONM BS11 34 C5
Portway Community School AVONM BS11 48 D1
Portway Trading Estate AVONM BS11 48 B1
Pratt's Hotel CBATH/BATHN BA1 3 H5
Premier Lodge BRSTK/PCHW BS34 38 D2
Premier Lodge THNB/SVB BS35 11 H2
Premier Lodge (Bristol North West) HNBRY/STHM BS10 25 E4
Prior Park College BATHSE BA2 115 F5
Prior Park (NT) BATHSE BA2 115 F4
Priory Community School MTN/WRL BS22 132 A5
Priory Farm Trading Estate PTSHD/EG BS20 47 E5
Pucklechurch CE Primary School MANG/FISH BS16 57 F2
Pucklechurch Trading Estate MANG/FISH BS16 57 E4
QEH Sports Club CFTN/FAIL BS8 76 A3
QEH Theatre CFTN/FAIL BS8 4 A3
Quakers Friars CBRIS/FH BS1 5 H2
Queen Elizabeth Hospital CFTN/FAIL BS8 4 B4
Queen Elizabeths Hospital School CFTN/FAIL BS8 4 A3
The Queensberry Hotel CBATH/BATHN BA1 2 E2
Radnor Business Centre HORF/LLZ BS7 51 H3
Radstock Infant School RDSTK/MIDN BA3 125 G1
Radstock Museum RDSTK/MIDN BA3 125 G1
Radstock Town FC RDSTK/MIDN BA3 125 H2
Ralph Allen School BATHSE BA2 115 H5
Ravenswood Special School NAIL BS48 73 E3
Raysfield J & I School YATE/CS BS37 32 B2
Redfield Edge Primary School OLD/WMLY/WICK BS30 83 G2
Redfield Leisure Centre EVILLE/WHL BS5 62 D4
Redgrave Theatre CFTN/FAIL BS8 60 C3
Redland High Junior School RDLND/MONT BS6 61 F1
Redland High School for Girls RDLND/MONT BS6 61 F1
Red Lodge CBRIS/FH BS1 4 D3
The Red Maids Junior School HNLZ/SM/SNYPK/WT BS9 50 D2
The Red Maids School HNLZ/SM/SNYPK/WT BS9 50 D1
Redwood Lodge Hotel & Country Club CFTN/FAIL BS8 76 C2
Ridge Junior School YATE/CS BS37 21 E5
Ridgeway Industrial Centre EVILLE/WHL BS5 63 F1
Ridgeway Park Cemetery EVILLE/WHL BS5 53 E5
The Ridings High School FRCTL/WBN BS36 28 D4
Riverbank Medical Centre MTN/WRL BS22 132 A5
Riverside Business Park BATHSE BA2 2 E5
Riverside Business Park EVILLE/WHL BS5 63 E5
Riverside Leisure Centre CBRISNE BS2 62 A3
Robin Cousins Sports Centre AVONM BS11 34 D5
Rodford Primary School YATE/CS BS37 31 G3
Rodney Hotel CFTN/FAIL BS8 60 C4
Roman Baths & Pump Room CBATH/BATHN BA1 3 G5
Romney Avenue J & I School HORF/LLZ BS7 52 C2
Roundstone Prep School TRWBR BA14 123 E1
The Royal Crescent Hotel CBATH/BATHN BA1 2 D2
The Royal High School (Junior Dept) CBATH/BATHN BA1 108 C4
The Royal High School (Senior Dept) CBATH/BATHN BA1 108 C2
Royal Hotel WSM BS23 6 C3
Royal National Hospital for Rheumatic Diseases CBATH/BATHN BA1 3 F4
Royal Navy & Royal Marines CBRIS/FH BS1 4 E3
Royal United Hospital CBATH/BATHN BA1 107 G4
Royce Clinic TRWBR BA14 121 F4
RSPCA & Dogs Home CBRISNE BS2 79 H2
Russell Town Industrial Park EVILLE/WHL BS5 62 D4
St Andrews CE Primary School CBATH/BATHN BA1 2 E1
St Andrews Junior School YTN/CONG BS49 128 C2
St Annes CE Primary School OLD/WMLY/WICK BS30 83 F3
St Annes CE Primary School OMX/HUT/LCK BS24 133 G3
St Annes J & I School BRSG/KWL/STAPK BS4 80 C1
St Annes Park Primary School BRSG/KWL/STAPK BS4 80 D1
St Augustine of Canterbury RC Primary School MANG/FISH BS16 55 E1
St Augustines Catholic School & Technical College TRWBR BA14 122 C1
St Barnabas CE Primary School RDLND/MONT BS6 62 A2
St Bedes RC School AVONM BS11 35 H3
St Benedicts RC Primary School RDSTK/MIDN BA3 124 C5
St Bernadettes Catholic Secondary School HGRV/WHIT BS14 92 A3
St Bernadettes RC Primary School HGRV/WHIT BS14 92 A3
St Bernards RC Primary School AVONM BS11 48 D2
St Bonaventures RC Primary School RDLND/MONT BS6 51 F4
St Brandons School CLVDN BS21 70 C2
St Brendans RC Sixth Form College BRSG/KWL/STAPK BS4 81 E5
St Brendans Trading Estate AVONM BS11 34 C3
St Catherines Industrial Estate BMSTR BS3 79 E2
St Christophers School HNLZ/SM/SNYPK/WT BS9 50 D5
St Francis Catholic Primary School NAIL BS48 73 G5
St Gabriel's Business Park EVILLE/WHL BS5 62 C3
St George Health Centre KGWD/HNM BS15 63 H3
St Georges CE Primary School CFTN/FAIL BS8 4 B5
St Georges Industrial Estate AVONM BS11 34 C2
St Gregorys Catholic College BATHSE BA2 116 B2
St Helens Primary School THNB/SVB BS35 11 G3
St Johns Catholic Primary School BATHSE BA2 114 A3
St Johns CE Primary School CFTN/FAIL BS8 60 D1
St Johns Church & Old City Gate CBRIS/FH BS1 5 F3
St Johns Hospital TRWBR BA14 122 D3
St Johns Lane Health Centre BMSTR BS3 79 F4
St Johns Mead CE Primary School YATE/CS BS37 32 D2
St Johns Primary School KEYN BS31 94 B4
St Johns RC Primary School BATHSE BA2 3 J4
St Johns RC Primary School TRWBR BA14 122 C1
St John the Evangelist CE Primary School CLVDN BS21 70 C4
St Joseph's Catholic Primary School PTSHD/EG BS20 45 G5
St Joseph's RC Primary School MANG/FISH BS16 54 A5
St Katharine's Primary School BLAG/CWMG/WR BS40 96 B5
St Katherines School PTSHD/EG BS20 48 D5
St Laurence School BOAV BA15 119 F2
St Mark's Community Centre BATHSE BA2 3 G7
St Marks School CBATH/BATHN BA1 109 E2
St Marks VA Primary School MTN/WRL BS22 131 G4
St Martins CE Junior School MTN/WRL BS22 136 A2
St Martins Garden Primary School BATHSE BA2 116 C1
St Martins Hospital BATHSE BA2 116 C1
St Mary Redcliffe Cemetery BRSG/KWL/STAPK BS4 80 A2
St Mary Redcliffe CE VC Primary School BMSTR BS3 79 F2
St Mary Redcliffe & Temple School CBRIS/FH BS1 5 H7
St Marys Catholic School ALMDB BS32 27 H4
St Mary's Catholic Primary School ALMDB BS32 28 A3
St Marys CE VA Primary School PTSHD/EG BS20 47 F5
St Marys Hospital CFTN/FAIL BS8 4 B3
St Marys RC ALMDB BS32 16 D5
St Marys RC Primary School CBATH/BATHN BA1 107 G3
St Mary's Redcliffe CBRIS/FH BS1 5 G6
St Matth's & Dr Bells CE Primary School MANG/FISH BS16 53 H4
St Michael on the Mount Primary School CFTN/FAIL BS8 4 D3
St Michaels CE Junior School BATHSE BA2 113 E1
St Michael's Cemetery CBATH/BATHN BA1 107 H5
St Michaels CE Primary School BRSTK/PCHW BS34 27 G5
St Michaels CE VC Primary School FRCTL/WBN BS36 28 D4
St Michaels Hill Clinic CBRISNE BS2 4 E2
St Michaels Hospital CBRISNE BS2 4 D2
St Nicholas CE Infant School RDSTK/MIDN BA3 125 G2
St Nicholas CE Junior School RDSTK/MIDN BA3 125 H2
St Nicholas Chantry Primary School CLVDN BS21 71 E1
St Nicholas Market CBRIS/FH BS1 5 F4
St Nicholas of Tolentine RC Primary School EVILLE/WHL BS5 5 K1
St Patricks RC Primary School EVILLE/WHL BS5 63 E4
St Pauls Catholic Primary School YATE/CS BS37 32 A2
St Peter & Paul RC Primary School RDLND/MONT BS6 61 F3
St Peters CE Primary School PTSHD/EG BS20 45 G3
St Philips CE Primary School BATHSE BA2 114 A5
St Pius X RC Primary School BMSTRD/HC/WWD BS13 90 B4
St Saviours Infant School CBATH/BATHN BA1 109 E2
St Saviours Junior School CBATH/BATHN BA1 109 E2
St Stephens Business Centre OLD/WMLY/WICK BS30 83 F1
St Stephens CE Primary School CBATH/BATHN BA1 108 C3
St Stephens J & I School KGWD/HNM BS15 64 C1
St Swithuns Infant School CBATH/BATHN BA1 108 D4
St Teresa's Catholic Primary School HORF/LLZ BS7 38 B4
St Teresas Private Hospital BATHSE BA2 106 A4
St Thomas More Catholic School HORF/LLZ BS7 52 B5
St Ursulas High School HNLZ/SM/SNYPK/WT BS9 50 D2
St Vincents Trading Estate CBRISNE BS2 62 D5
St Werburgh's Primary School CBRISNE BS2 62 B1
Sally Lunn's Refreshment House & Museum CBATH/BATHN BA1 3 G5
Saltford CE Primary School KEYN BS31 105 E2
Saltford Golf Club KEYN BS31 105 F3
Sampson House Business Park HNBRY/STHM BS10 24 B3
Samuel Whites Infant School KGWD/HNM BS15 81 H1
Saracens RC HNBRY/STHM BS10 24 D5
Satellite Business Park EVILLE/WHL BS5 63 E4
Saville Court Business Centre CFTN/FAIL BS8 60 D4
Sawclose Health Clinic CBATH/BATHN BA1 3 F4
School of Christ the King RC BRSG/KWL/STAPK BS4 91 F2
Scotch Horn Community & Sports Centre NAIL BS48 73 G4
Sea Life Aquarium WSM BS23 6 C6
Sea Mills Infant School HNLZ/SM/SNYPK/WT BS9 49 H1
Sea Mills Junior School HNLZ/SM/SNYPK/WT BS9 49 G3
Seeley's Hotel CFTN/FAIL BS8 4 A2
Sefton Park J & I School HORF/LLZ BS7 52 A5
Severn Beach CP School THNB/SVB BS35 12 C3
Severnside Trading Estate AVONM BS11 34 D1
Severnside Trading Estate AVONM BS11 34 D4
Shails Lane Industrial Estate TRWBR BA14 120 D5
Sham Castle BATHSE BA2 115 G1
Sheene Court Industrial Estate BMSTR BS3 78 D3
The Sheiling School THNB/SVB BS35 8 B3
The Shield Retail Centre BRSTK/PCHW BS34 38 D2
Shield Road Primary School HORF/LLZ BS7 38 D4
Shirehampton Cricket Club AVONM BS11 49 E1
Shirehampton Health Centre AVONM BS11 48 D2
Shirehampton Park Golf Club AVONM BS11 49 E2
Shirehampton Primary School AVONM BS11 48 C2
Shirehampton Swimming Pool AVONM BS11 48 D2
Shires Shopping Centre TRWBR BA14 122 D1
Showcase Cinema CBRISNE BS2 80 B1
Silverhill School FRCTL/WBN BS36 29 E3
Simplex Trading Estate OLD/WMLY/WICK BS30 83 G2
The Sir Bernard Lovell School OLD/WMLY/WICK BS30 83 F2
Soaphouse Industrial Estate EVILLE/WHL BS5 63 F3
Somervale School RDSTK/MIDN BA3 124 B4
South Bristol Business Park BRSG/KWL/STAPK BS4 91 E2
South Bristol Crematorium BMSTRD/HC/WWD BS13 90 A1
South Bristol Retail Park BMSTR BS3 78 A3
Southdown J & I School BATHSE BA2 113 G4
Southfield Road Trading Estate NAIL BS48 73 G3
Southgate Shopping Centre CBATH/BATHN BA1 3 G6
Southmead Health Centre HNBRY/STHM BS10 37 H3
Southmead Health Services NHS Trust HNBRY/STHM BS10 51 G1
South Street Primary School BMSTR BS3 78 C3
South View Business Centre MANG/FISH BS16 54 D3
South View Business Park MANG/FISH BS16 54 D3
Southville Primary School BMSTR BS3 78 D2
South Wansdyke Sports Centre RDSTK/MIDN BA3 124 C3
Southwick Country Park TRWBR BA14 122 A5
Sovereign Shopping Centre WSM BS23 6 D3
Speedwell Industrial Estate CLVDN BS21 70 C3
Speedwell Swimming Baths EVILLE/WHL BS5 63 G2
Speedwell Technology College EVILLE/WHL BS5 63 H2
The Spitfire Retail Park TRWBR BA14 123 E4
Springfield School RDLND/MONT BS6 61 H1
Springwater Park Trading Estate EVILLE/WHL BS5 63 F4
SS Great Britain CBRIS/FH BS1 4 B6
Stafford Business Centre WSM BS23 7 G4
Stanbridge Primary School MANG/FISH BS16 55 E2
Staple Hill Primary School MANG/FISH BS16 54 C4
Staverton CE Primary School TRWBR BA14 121 E1
Sterling College International CBATH/BATHN BA1 3 G2
Stockwood Green Primary School HGRV/WHIT BS14 92 D5
Stockwood Vale Golf Club KEYN BS31 93 F3
Stoke Bishop CE Primary School HNLZ/SM/SNYPK/WT BS9 50 A3
Stoke Gifford Medical Centre BRSTK/PCHW BS34 39 H1
Stoke Lodge J & I School BRSTK/PCHW BS34 27 E2
Stokes Medical Centre BRSTK/PCHW BS34 27 E3
Stoke View Business Park MANG/FISH BS16 53 G4
Stone Hill Business Centre OLD/WMLY/WICK BS30 82 B2
Storybox Theatre YTN/CONG BS49 127 G3
Stover Trading Estate YATE/CS BS37 20 A5
Studley Green Primary School TRWBR BA14 122 B3
Summerfield Special School CBATH/BATHN BA1 108 A3
Summerhill J & I School EVILLE/WHL BS5 63 F3
Sun Life Sports Club HNBRY/STHM BS10 37 E1
Sunnyside Farm Trading Estate PTSHD/EG BS20 58 B1
Swainswick Primary School CBATH/BATHN BA1 102 A4
Temple Primary School KEYN BS31 94 C3
Temple Trading Estate CBRISNE BS2 80 A1
Teyfant Community School BMSTRD/HC/WWD BS13 91 E5
Theatre Royal CBATH/BATHN BA1 2 E4
Thornbury Castle Hotel THNB/SVB BS35 8 B2
Thermae Bath Spa CBATH/BATHN BA1 3 F5
Thornbury Golf Lodge Hotel & Golf Centre THNB/SVB BS35 8 A5
Thornbury Health Centre THNB/SVB BS35 8 D3
Thornbury Hospital THNB/SVB BS35 8 D3
Thornbury Leisure Centre THNB/SVB BS35 8 C5
Tickenham Primary School CLVDN BS21 72 A2
Timbertop Aparthotel WSM BS23 6 C1
Time Machine Museum WSM BS23 6 E3
Tithe Barn BOAV BA15 119 F4
Tockington Manor School ALMDB BS32 10 C5
Toll House Clinic YATE/CS BS37 33 E1
Torwood House School RDLND/MONT BS6 50 D5
Totterdown Bridge Industrial Estate CBRISNE BS2 79 H2
Travel Inn
CBRIS/FH BS1 5 F1
CBRIS/FH BS1 5 F5
HGRV/WHIT BS14 91 F3
MANG/FISH BS16 42 A5
PTSHD/EG BS20 45 H3
WSM BS23 135 G5
Travelodge CBATH/BATHN BA1 3 F3
HNBRY/STHM BS10 25 E4
Treenwood Industrial Estate BOAV BA15 119 F5
Trinity Theological College HNLZ/SM/SNYPK/WT BS9 50 B4
Tropicana Leisure Complex WSM BS23 6 C7
Trowbridge Civic Hall TRWBR BA14 123 E1
Trowbridge & District Hospital TRWBR BA14 120 D4
Trowbridge Parochial Junior School TRWBR BA14 121 F4
Trowbridge RFC TRWBR BA14 123 H1
Trowbridge Sports Centre TRWBR BA14 122 C3
TT Trading Estate YATE/CS BS37 33 E1
Tudor Lodge Health Centre WSM BS23 138 D2
Twerton Cemetery BATHSE BA2 113 H1
Twerton Infant School BATHSE BA2 113 E2
Two Mile Hill J & I School KGWD/HNM BS15 64 B3
Twyford House CC AVONM BS11 49 E1
Tyning Hengrove Junior School HGRV/WHIT BS14 91 H2
The Tynings Primary School MANG/FISH BS16 55 E4
Tyntesfield House (NT) NAIL BS48 74 D2
Unicorn Business Park CBRISNE BS2 80 B1
University of Bath BATHSE BA2 115 H2
University of Bath Sports Training Village BATHSE BA2 115 H

University of Bristol
CFTN/FAIL BS8 ....4 C1
University of Bristol Childrens Hospital
CFTN/FAIL BS8 ....4 C2
University of the West of England (Bower Ashton Campus)
BMSTR BS3 ....77 H2
University of the West of England (Frenchay Campus)
BRSTK/PCHW BS34 ....39 G4
University of the West of England
CBRIS/FH BS1 ....5 F4
University of the West of England (Glenside Campus)
MANG/FISH BS16 ....53 F3
University of the West of England (St Matthais Campus)
MANG/FISH BS16 ....53 H3
Uphill Primary School
WSM BS23 ....138 C4
Upper Horfield Primary School
HORF/LLZ BS7 ....38 D5
Victoria Art Gallery
CBATH/BATHN BA1 ....3 G4
Victoria Monument
CBATH/BATHN BA1 ....2 C2
Victoria Park Business Centre
CBATH/BATHN BA1 ....2 A3
Victoria Park J & I School
BMSTR BS3 ....79 F3
Vines Industrial Estate
NAIL BS48 ....73 H3
VUE Cinema
BRSTK/PCHW BS34 ....25 G4
Wadehurst Industrial Park
CBRISNE BS2 ....62 B4
Walliscote Primary School
WSM BS23 ....6 E5
Wallis Estate
CBRISNE BS2 ....52 A5
Walton Park Hotel
CLVDN BS21 ....68 B4
Walwayne Court Primary School *TRWBR* BA14 ....120 B5
Wansdyke Business Centre
BATHSE BA2 ....114 A3
Wansdyke Primary School
HGRV/WHIT BS14 ....91 G5
Wansdyke School
BATHSE BA2 ....116 C2
Warmley CE School
OLD/WMLY/WICK BS30 ....65 H5
Warmley Park School
OLD/WMLY/WICK BS30 ....65 G4
Water Park
ALMDB BS32 ....16 D5
Watershed Arts Complex
CBRIS/FH BS1 ....4 E5
Watershed Cinema
CBRIS/FH BS1 ....4 E5
Waycroft Primary School
HGRV/WHIT BS14 ....92 D4
Wellesley Primary School
YATE/CS BS37 ....31 H4
Wellsway School
KEYN BS31 ....94 D4
Welton Primary School
RDSTK/MIDN BA3 ....124 D2
Welton Rovers FC
RDSTK/MIDN BA3 ....124 C2
Wentworth House Hotel
BATHSE BA2 ....114 B3
Westbourne Hotel
CFTN/FAIL BS8 ....4 A1
Westbury on Trym CE Primary School
HNLZ/SM/SNYPK/WT BS9 ....37 F5
Westbury Park Primary School
RDLND/MONT BS6 ....50 D4
Westcliff College of Further Education
WSM BS23 ....134 A2
Westerleigh Crematorium
YATE/CS BS37 ....43 H4
Westfield Industrial & Trading Estate
RDSTK/MIDN BA3 ....124 D5
Westfield Primary School
RDSTK/MIDN BA3 ....124 D4
West Haven Special School
WSM BS23 ....138 B4
Westland Business Centre
OMX/HUT/LCK BS24 ....139 G3
Westlands Sports Club
OMX/HUT/LCK BS24 ....139 F2
West Leigh Infant School
NAIL BS48 ....85 G3
Weston All Saints Primary School
CBATH/BATHN BA1 ....107 F2
Weston Business Park
BNWL BS29 ....141 G3
Weston Business Park
OMX/HUT/LCK BS24 ....140 B1
Weston College *WSM* BS23 ....6 C2
Weston Express Business Park
WSM BS23 ....135 H5
Weston Gateway Caravan Site
OMX/HUT/LCK BS24 ....137 F2
Weston Park Primary School
AVONM BS11 ....35 G5
Weston Retail Park
WSM BS23 ....7 J7
Weston St Johns AFC
WSM BS23 ....139 E3
Weston Sixth Form College
WSM BS23 ....138 D4
Weston-super-Mare AFC
WSM BS23 ....139 F1
Weston-super-Mare Borough Employees Sports Club
WSM BS23 ....7 G5
Weston-super-Mare CC
WSM BS23 ....138 D3
Weston-super-Mare County Court
WSM BS23 ....6 D4
Weston-super-Mare Crematorium
MTN/WRL BS22 ....131 F4
Weston-super-Mare General Hospital *WSM* BS23 ....138 D4
Weston-super-Mare Golf Club
WSM BS23 ....138 B2
Weston-Super-Mare Health & Fitness Club *WSM* BS23 ....7 F6
Weston-super-Mare RFC
WSM BS23 ....7 F6
Westpoint Trading Estate
KGWD/HNM BS15 ....64 C4
West Town Lane Junior School
BRSG/KWL/STAPK BS4 ....80 B5
Wheatfield Primary School
ALMDB BS32 ....27 F1
Whitchuch Health Centre
HGRV/WHIT BS14 ....91 H4
Whitchurch Primary School
HGRV/WHIT BS14 ....92 B5
Whitchurch Sports Centre
HGRV/WHIT BS14 ....91 G4
Whitefield Fishponds Community School
MANG/FISH BS16 ....53 G4
Whitehall Primary School
EVILLE/WHL BS5 ....63 E2
Whitehall Trading Estate
EVILLE/WHL BS5 ....62 D3
Wick CE Primary School
OLD/WMLY/WICK BS30 ....67 E5
Widcombe CE Junior School
BATHSE BA2 ....3 J6
Widcombe Infant School
CBATH/BATHN BA1 ....3 H6
Wildwalk-at-Bristol
CBRIS/FH BS1 ....4 D5
William Budd Health Centre
BRSG/KWL/STAPK BS4 ....91 E1
Willsbridge Mill Museum & Nature Reserve
OLD/WMLY/WICK BS30 ....83 E4
Wiltshire College Trowbridge
TRWBR BA14 ....122 C3
Wilverley Trading Estate
BRSG/KWL/STAPK BS4 ....80 D5
Wincombe Trading Estate
CBRISNE BS2 ....79 H2
Windmill Farm Business Centre
BMSTR BS3 ....79 E2
Windmill Hill City Farm
BMSTR BS3 ....79 E2
Window Arts Centre
CBATH/BATHN BA1 ....3 F5
The Windsor Hotel
BATHSE BA2 ....3 H3
Windwhistle Primary School
WSM BS23 ....139 E3
Winford CE Primary School
BLAG/CWMG/WR BS40 ....97 G5
Winsley CE Primary School
BOAV BA15 ....118 B
Winter Gardens & Pavilion
WSM BS23 ....6 C
Withywood Community School
BMSTRD/HC/WWD BS13 ....90 B
Woodlands Golf & Country Club
ALMDB BS32 ....16 D
Wood Road Industrial Centre
KGWD/HNM BS15 ....64 C
Woodspring Golf & Country Club
LGASH BS41 ....89 F
Woodstock Special School
HNBRY/STHM BS10 ....36 D3
Worlebury CE VA First School
MTN/WRL BS22 ....135 G1
Worlebury Golf Club
MTN/WRL BS22 ....130 C5
Worle Community School
MTN/WRL BS22 ....136 B2
Worle Health Centre
MTN/WRL BS22 ....136 B1
Wraxall CE Primary School
NAIL BS48 ....74 A2
Wyncroft School
WSM BS23 ....138 C2
Wyvern Community School
WSM BS23 ....139 E1
Wyvern Sports Centre
WSM BS23 ....139 E1
Yate Leisure Centre
YATE/CS BS37 ....20 D5
Yate Outdoor Sports Complex
YATE/CS BS37 ....20 C2
Yate Town FC
YATE/CS BS37 ....20 A4
Yatton J & I School
YTN/CONG BS49 ....126 C3
Yeo Moor J & I School
CLVDN BS21 ....71 E3

Acknowledgements

The Post Office is a registered trademark of Post Office Ltd. in the UK and other countries.

Schools address data provided by Education Direct.

Petrol station information supplied by Johnsons

One-way street data provided by © Tele Atlas N.V. Tele Atlas

Garden centre information provided by

Garden Centre Association Britains best garden centres

Wyevale Garden Centres

The statement on the front cover of this atlas is sourced, selected and quoted from a reader comment and feedback form received in 2004